The I-Series

Microsoft® Office Excel 2003

Complete

Stephen Haag
University of Denver

James Perry
University of San Diego

Technology Education

Boston   Burr Ridge, IL   Dubuque, IA   Madison, WI   New York   San Francisco   St. Louis
Bangkok   Bogotá   Caracas   Kuala Lumpur   Lisbon   London   Madrid   Mexico City
Milan   Montreal   New Delhi   Santiago   Seoul   Singapore   Sydney   Taipei   Toronto

Technology Education

THE I-SERIES: MICROSOFT OFFICE EXCEL 2003, COMPLETE

Published by McGraw-Hill/Technology Education, a business unit of The McGraw-Hill Companies, Inc., 1221 Avenue of the Americas, New York, NY, 10020. Copyright © 2004 by The McGraw-Hill Companies, Inc. All rights reserved. No part of this publication may be reproduced or distributed in any form or by any means, or stored in a database or retrieval system, without the prior written consent of The McGraw-Hill Companies, Inc., including, but not limited to, in any network or other electronic storage or transmission, or broadcast for distance learning.

Some ancillaries, including electronic and print components, may not be available to customers outside the United States.

This book is printed on acid-free paper.

1 2 3 4 5 6 7 8 9 0 WEB/WEB 0 9 8 7 6 5 4 3

ISBN 0-07-283078-6

Editor-in-chief: *Bob Woodbury*
Publisher: *Brandon Nordin*
Senior sponsoring editor: *Donald J. Hull*
Associate sponsoring editor: *Craig S. Leonard*
Editorial assistant: *Veronica Vergoth*
Marketing manager: *Andy Bernier*
Senior producer, Media technology: *David Barrick*
Lead project manager: *Mary Conzachi*
Senior production supervisor: *Rose Hepburn*
Lead designer: *Pam Verros*
Senior supplement producer: *Rose M. Range*
Senior digital content specialist: *Brian Nacik*
Cover design: *Asylum Studios*
Interior design: *Mary Christianson*
Typeface: *10.5/12 Minion*
Compositor: *GAC Indianapolis*
Printer: *Webcrafters, Inc.*

Library of Congress Cataloging-in-Publication Data
Haag, Stephen.
    Microsoft Office Excel 2003 : complete / Stephen Haag, James Perry.
        p. cm.—(The I-series)
    Includes Index
    ISBN 0-07-283078-6 (alk. paper)
    1. Microsoft Excel (Computer file) 2. Business—Computer programs. 3. Electronic spreadsheets. I. Perry, James T. II. Title. III. Series
    HF5548.4.M523H314 2004
    005.36—dc22   2003060257

www.mhhe.com

MCGRAW-HILL TECHNOLOGY EDUCATION

At McGraw-Hill Technology Education, we publish instructional materials for the technology education market, in particular computer instruction in post-secondary education—from introductory courses in traditional 4-year universities to continuing education and proprietary schools. McGraw-Hill Technology Education presents a broad range of innovative products—texts, lab manuals, study guides, testing materials, and technology-based training and assessment tools.

We realize that technology has created and will continue to create new mediums for professors and students to use in managing resources and communicating information to one another. McGraw-Hill Technology Education provides the most flexible and complete teaching and learning tools available, and offers solutions to the changing world of teaching and learning. McGraw-Hill Technology Education is dedicated to providing the tools for today's instructors and students that will enable them to successfully navigate the world of Information Technology.

- McGraw-Hill/Osborne—This division of The McGraw-Hill Companies is known for its best-selling Internet titles, Harley Hahn's *Internet & Web Yellow Pages*, and the *Internet Complete Reference*. For more information, visit Osborne at www.osborne.com.

- Digital Solutions—Whether you want to teach a class online or just post your "bricks-n-mortar" class syllabus, McGraw-Hill Technology Education is committed to publishing digital solutions. Taking your course online doesn't have to be a solitary adventure, nor does it have to be a difficult one. We offer several solutions that will allow you to enjoy all the benefits of having your course material online.

- Packaging Options—For more information about our discount options, contact your McGraw-Hill sales representative at 1-800-338-3987 or visit our Web site at www.mhhe.com/it.

McGraw-Hill Technology Education is dedicated to providing the tools for today's instructors and students

THE I-SERIES PAGE

By using the I-Series, students will be able to learn and master applications skills by being actively engaged—by *doing*. The "I" in I-Series demonstrates Insightful tasks that will not only Inform students, but also Involve them while learning the applications.

How Will the I-Series Accomplish This for You?

Through relevant, real-world chapter opening cases.

Tasks throughout each chapter incorporating steps and tips for easy reference.

Alternative methods and styles of learning to keep the student involved.

Rich, end-of-chapter materials that support what the student has learned.

I-Series Titles Include:

Computer Concepts

Computing Concepts, 2e, Introductory

Computing Concepts, 2e, Complete

Microsoft Office Applications

Microsoft Office 2003, Volume I

Microsoft Office 2003, Volume II

Microsoft Office Word 2003 (Brief, Introductory, Complete Versions) 11 Total Chapters

Microsoft Office Excel 2003 (Brief, Introductory, Complete Versions) 12 Total Chapters

Microsoft Office Access 2003 (Brief, Introductory, Complete Versions) 12 Total Chapters

Microsoft Office PowerPoint 2003 (Brief, Introductory Versions) 8 Total Chapters

Microsoft Office Outlook 2003 (Brief, Introductory Versions) 8 Total Chapters

Microsoft Office FrontPage 2003 (Brief Version) 4 Total Chapters

Microsoft Office XP, Volume I

Microsoft Office XP, Volume I Expanded (with Internet Essentials bonus chapters)

Microsoft Office XP, Volume II

Microsoft Word 2002 (Brief, Introductory, Complete Versions) 12 Total Chapters

Microsoft Excel 2002 (Brief, Introductory, Complete Versions) 12 Total Chapters

Microsoft Access 2002 (Brief, Introductory, Complete Versions) 12 Total Chapters

Microsoft PowerPoint 2002 (Brief, Introductory Versions) 8 Total Chapters

Microsoft Internet Explorer 6.0 (Brief Version) 5 Total Chapters

Microsoft Windows

Microsoft Windows 2000 (Brief, Introductory, Complete Versions) 12 Total Chapters

Microsoft Windows XP (Brief, Introductory, Complete Versions) 12 Total Chapters

For additional resources, visit The I-Series Online Learning Center at www.mhhe.com/i-series

GOALS/PHILOSOPHY

The I-Series applications textbooks strongly emphasize that students learn and master applications skills by being actively engaged—by *doing*. We made the decision that teaching how to accomplish tasks is not enough for complete understanding and mastery. Students must understand the importance of each of the tasks that lead to a finished product at the end of each chapter.

Approach

The I-Series chapters are subdivided into sessions that contain related groups of tasks with active, hands-on components. The session tasks containing numbered steps collectively result in a completed project at the end of each session. Prior to introducing numbered steps that show how to accomplish a particular task, we discuss why the steps are important. We discuss the role that the collective steps play in the overall plan for creating or modifying a document or object, answering students' often-heard questions, "Why are we doing these steps? Why are these steps important?" Without an explanation of why an activity is important and what it accomplishes, students can easily find themselves following the steps but not registering the big picture of what the steps accomplish and why they are executing them.

I-Series Applications for 2003

The I-Series offers three levels of instruction. Each level builds upon knowledge from the previous level. With the exception of the running project that is the last exercise of every chapter, chapter cases and end-of-chapter exercises are independent from one chapter to the next, with the exception of Access. The three levels available are

Brief Covers the basics of the Microsoft application and contains Chapters 1 through 4. The Brief textbooks are typically 200 pages long.

Introductory Includes chapters in the Brief textbook plus Chapters 5 through 8. Introductory textbooks typically are 400 pages long and prepare students for the Microsoft Office Specialist (MOS) Core Exam.

Complete Includes the Introductory textbook plus Chapters 9 through 12. The four additional chapters cover advanced-level content and the textbooks are typically 600 pages long. Complete textbooks prepare students for the Microsoft Office Specialist (MOS) Expert Exam. The Microsoft Office User Specialist program is recognized around the world as the standard for demonstrating proficiency using Microsoft Office applications.

In addition, there are two compilation volumes available.

Office I Includes introductory chapters on Windows and Computing Concepts followed by Chapters 1 through 4 (Brief textbook) of Word, Excel, Access, and PowerPoint. In addition, material from the companion Computing Concepts book is integrated into the first few chapters to provide students with an understanding of the relationship between Microsoft Office applications and computer information systems.

Office II Includes introductory chapters on Windows and Computing Concepts followed by Chapters 5 through 8 from each of the Introductory-level textbooks including Word, Excel, Access, and PowerPoint. In addition, material from the companion Computing Concepts book is integrated into the introductory chapters to provide students with a deeper understanding of the relationship between Microsoft Office applications and computer information systems. An introduction to Visual Basic for Applications (VBA) completes the Office II textbook.

STEPHEN HAAG

Stephen Haag is a professor and Chair of Information Technology and Electronic Commerce and the Director of Technology in the University of Denver's Daniels College of Business. Stephen holds a B.B.A. and M.B.A. from West Texas State University and a Ph.D. from the University of Texas at Arlington. He has published numerous articles appearing in such journals as *Communications of the ACM, The International Journal of Systems Science, Applied Economics, Managerial and Decision Economics, Socio-Economic Planning Sciences,* and the *Australian Journal of Management.*

Stephen is also the author of 20 other books including *Interactions: Teaching English as a Second Language* (with his mother and father), *Case Studies in Information Technology, Information Technology: Tomorrow's Advantage Today* (with Peter Keen), and *Excelling in Finance.* He is also the lead author of the accompanying I-Series *Computing Concepts* text, released in both an Introductory and a Complete version. Stephen lives with his wife, Pam, and their four sons—Indiana, Darian, Trevor, and Elvis—in Highlands Ranch, Colorado.

JAMES PERRY

James Perry is a professor of Management Information Systems in the University of San Diego's School of Business. He holds a B.S. in mathematics from Purdue University and a Ph.D. in computer science from The Pennsylvania State University. Jim has published several journal and conference papers. He is the co-author of 60 other textbooks and trade books including *Using Access with Accounting Systems, Building Accounting Systems, Understanding Oracle, The Internet,* and *Electronic Commerce.* His books have been translated into Chinese, Dutch, French, and Korean. Jim teaches both undergraduate and graduate courses at the University of San Diego and has worked as a computer security consultant to various private and governmental organizations including the Jet Propulsion Laboratory. He was a consultant on the Strategic Defense Initiative ("Star Wars") project and served as a member of the computer security oversight committee. Jim lives with his wife, Nancy, in San Diego, California. He has three grown children: Jessica, Stirling, and Kelly.

PAIGE BALTZAN

Paige Baltzan is a professor of Information Technology and Electronic Commerce in the University of Denver's Daniels College of Business. Paige holds a B.S.B.A. from Bowling Green State University and an M.B.A. from the University of Denver. Paige's primary concentration focuses on object-oriented technologies and systems development methodologies. She has been teaching Systems Analysis and Design, Telecommunications and Networking, Software Engineering, and The Global Information Economy at the University of Denver for the past three years. Paige has contributed materials for several McGraw-Hill publications including *Using Information Technology* and *Management Information Systems for the Information Age.*

Prior to joining the University of Denver Paige spent three years working at Level(3) Communications as a Technical Architect and four years working at Andersen Consulting as a Technology Consultant in the telecommunications industry. Paige lives in Lakewood, Colorado, with her husband, Tony, and her daughter, Hannah.

AMY PHILLIPS

Amy Phillips is a professor of Information Technology and Electronic Commerce in the University of Denver's Daniels College of Business. She holds a B.S. degree in environmental biology and an M.S. degree in education from Plymouth State College. Amy has been teaching for more than 18 years: 5 years in public secondary education and 13 years in higher education. She has also been an integral part of both the academic and administrative functions within the higher educational system.

Amy's main concentration revolves around database driven Web sites focusing on dynamic Web content, specifically ASP and XML technologies. Some of the main core course selections that Amy teaches at the University of Denver include Analysis and Design, Database Management Systems, Using Technology to Communicate, and Using Technology to Manage Information. Her first book, *Internet Explorer 6.0,* written with Stephen Haag and James Perry, was published in September 2002.

MERRILL WELLS

Merrill Wells is a professor of Information Technology and Electronic Commerce in the University of Denver's Daniels College of Business. Merrill holds a B.A. and M.B.A. from Indiana University. Although her goal was to teach and write, she followed the advice of her professors and set out to gain business experience before becoming a professor herself.

Merrill began her nonacademic career as a business systems programmer developing manufacturing, accounting, and payroll software using relational databases. Throughout her first career Merrill worked in the aerospace, manufacturing, construction, and oil and gas industries. After years of writing technical manuals and training end users, Merrill honored her original goal and returned to academia to become an active instructor of both graduate and undergraduate technology courses.

Merrill is the author of several online books including *An Introduction to Computers, Introduction to Visual Basic,* and *Programming Logic and Design.* Merrill lives with her husband, Rick, in Denver, Colorado. They have four children—Daniel, Dusty, Victoria (Tori), and Evan— and foster twins Connor and Gage.

Each textbook features the following:

Did You Know   Each chapter has six or seven interesting facts—about both high-tech and other topics.

Sessions   Each chapter is divided into two or three sessions.

Chapter Outline   Provides students with a quick map of the major headings in the chapter.

Chapter and Microsoft Office Specialist Objectives At the beginning of each chapter is a list of 5 to 10 action-oriented objectives. Any chapter objectives that are also Microsoft Office Specialist objectives indicate the Microsoft Office Specialist objective number.

Chapter Opening Case   Each chapter begins with a case. Cases describe a mixture of fictitious and real people and companies and the needs of the people and companies. Throughout the chapter, the student gains the skills and knowledge to solve the problem stated in the case.

Introduction   The chapter introduction establishes the overview of the chapter's activities in the context of the case problem.

Another Way and Another Word   Another Way is a highlighted feature providing a bulleted list of steps to accomplish a task, or best practices—that is, a better or faster way to accomplish a task such as pasting a format onto an Excel cell. Another Word, another highlighted box, briefly explains more about a topic or highlights a potential pitfall.

Step-by-Step Instructions   Numbered step-by-step instructions for all hands-on activities appear in a distinctive color. Keyboard characters and menu selections appear in a **special format** to emphasize what the user should press or type. Steps make clear to the student the exact sequence of keystrokes and mouse clicks needed to complete a task such as formatting a Word paragraph.

Tips   Tips appear within a numbered sequence of steps and warn the student of possible missteps or provide alternatives to the step that precedes the tip.

Task Reference and Task Reference Summary   Task References appear throughout the textbook. Set in a distinctive design, each Task Reference contains a bulleted list of steps showing a generic way to accomplish activities that are especially important or significant. A Task Reference Summary at the end of each chapter summarizes a chapter's Task References.

Microsoft Office Specialist Objectives Summary   A list of Microsoft Office Specialist objectives covered in a chapter appears in the chapter objectives and the chapter summary.

Making the Grade   Short answer questions appear at the end of each chapter's sessions. They test a student's grasp of each session's contents, and Making the Grade answers appear at the end of each chapter so students can check their answers.

Rich End-of-Chapter Materials   End-of-chapter materials incorporating a three-level approach reinforce learning and help students take ownership of the chapter. Level One, Review of Terminology, contains fill in the blank, true/false, and multiple choice questions that enforce review of a chapter's key terms. Level Two, Review of Concepts, contains review questions and a Jeopardy-style create-a-question exercise. Level Three contains Hands-On Projects (see the paragraph following this one). Level Four, Analysis, contains short questions that require students to step back from the details of what they learned and think about higher level concepts covered in the chapter.

Hands-On Projects   Extensive hands-on projects engage the student in a problem-solving exercise from start to finish. There are seven clearly labeled categories that each contain one or two questions. Categories are Practice, Challenge!, E-Business, On the Web, Around the World, and a Running Project that carries throughout all the chapters.

We understand that, in today's teaching environment, offering a textbook alone is not sufficient to meet the needs of the many instructors who use our books. To teach effectively, instructors must have a full complement of supplemental resources to assist them in every facet of teaching, from preparing for class to conducting a lecture to assessing students' comprehension. The **I-Series** offers a complete supplements package and Web site that is briefly described below.

INSTRUCTOR'S RESOURCE KIT

The Instructor's Resource Kit is a CD-ROM containing the Instructor's Manual in both MS Word and .pdf formats, PowerPoint Slides with Presentation Software, Brownstone test-generating software, and accompanying test item files in both MS Word and .pdf formats for each chapter. The CD also contains figure files from the text, student data files, and solutions files. The features of each of the three main components of the Instructor's Resource Kit are highlighted below.

Instructor's Manual Featuring:

- Chapter learning objectives
- Chapter key terms
- Chapter outline and lecture notes
  - Teaching suggestions
  - Classroom tips, tricks, and traps
  - Page number references
- Additional end-of-chapter practice projects
- Answers to all Making the Grade and end-of-chapter questions
- Text figures

PowerPoint Presentation

The PowerPoint presentation is designed to provide instructors with comprehensive lecture and teaching resources that will include

- Chapter learning objectives followed by source content that illustrates key terms and key facts per chapter
- FAQ (frequently asked questions) to show key concepts throughout the chapter; also lecture notes, to illustrate these key concepts and ideas

- End-of-chapter exercises and activities per chapter, as taken from the end-of-chapter materials in the text
- Speaker's Notes, to be incorporated throughout the slides per chapter
- Figures/screen shots, to be incorporated throughout the slides per chapter

Test Bank

The I-Series Test Bank, using Diploma Network Testing Software by Brownstone, contains over 3,000 questions (both objective and interactive) categorized by topic, page reference to the text, and difficulty level of learning. Each question is assigned a learning category:

- Level 1: Key Terms and Facts
- Level 2: Key Concepts
- Level 3: Application and Problem-Solving

The types of questions consist of 20 percent Multiple Choice, 50 percent True/False, and 30 percent Fill-in-the-Blank Questions.

ONLINE LEARNING CENTER/ WEB SITE

To locate the I-Series OLC/Web site directly, go to www.mhhe.com/i-series. The site is divided into three key areas:

- **Information Center**   Contains core information about the text, the authors, and a guide to our additional features and benefits of the series, including the supplements.
- **Instructor Center**   Offers instructional materials, downloads, additional activities and answers to additional projects, answers to chapter troubleshooting exercises, answers to chapter preparation/post exercises posed to students, relevant links for professors, and more.
- **Student Center**   Contains chapter objectives and outlines, self-quizzes, chapter troubleshooting exercises, chapter preparation/post exercises, additional projects, simulations, student data files and solutions files, Web links, and more.

RESOURCES FOR STUDENTS

SimNet

SimNet is a simulated assessment and learning tool for either Microsoft® Office XP or Microsoft® Office 2003. SimNet allows students to study MS Office skills and computer concepts, and professors to test and evaluate students' proficiency, within MS Office applications and concepts. Students can practice and study their skills at home or in the school lab using SimNet, which does not require the purchase or installation of Office software. SimNet includes:

Structured Computer-Based Learning SimNet offers a complete computer-based learning side that presents each skill or topic in several different modes. *Teach Me* presents the skill or topic using text, graphics, and interactivity. *Show Me* presents the skill using an animation with audio narration to show how the skill is used or implemented. *Let Me Try* allows you to practice the skill in SimNet's robust simulated interface.

Computer Concepts Coverage! SimNet includes coverage of 60 computer concepts in both the Learning and the Assessment side.

The Basics and More! SimNet includes modules of content on:

Word	Windows 2000
Excel	Computer Concepts
Access	Windows XP Professional
PowerPoint	Internet Explorer 6
Office XP Integration	FrontPage
Outlook	

More Assessment Questions! SimNet includes over *1,400* assessment questions.

Practice or Pre-Tests Questions! SimNet has a separate pool of over *600* questions for Practice Tests or Pre-Tests.

Comprehensive Exercises! SimNet offers comprehensive exercises for each application. These exercises require the student to use multiple skills to solve one exercise in the simulated environment.

Simulated Interface! The simulated environment in SimNet has been substantially deepened to more realistically simulate the real applications. Now students are not graded incorrect just because they chose the wrong submenu or dialog box. The student is not graded until he or she does something that immediately invokes an action—just like the real applications!

DIGITAL SOLUTIONS FOR INSTRUCTORS AND STUDENTS

PageOut PageOut is our Course Web Site Development Center that offers a syllabus page, URL, McGraw-Hill Online Learning Center content, online exercises and quizzes, gradebook, discussion board, and an area for student Web pages. For more information, visit the PageOut Web site at www.pageout.net.

Online Courses Available OLCs are your perfect solutions for Internet-based content. Simply put, these Centers are "digital cartridges" that contain a book's pedagogy and supplements. As students read the book, they can go online and take self-grading quizzes or work through interactive exercises.

Online Learning Centers can be delivered through any of these platforms:

McGraw-Hill Learning Architecture (TopClass)

Blackboard.com

College.com (formerly Real Education)

WebCT (a product of Universal Learning Technology)

CHAPTER

one

1

Creating Worksheets for Decision Makers

did you
know?

one-third *of online shoppers abandon their electronic shopping carts before completing the checkout process.*

goldfish *lose their color if they are kept in a dim light or if they are placed in a body of running water such as a stream.*

electric *eels are not really eels but a type of fish.*

in *1963, baseball pitcher Gaylord Perry said, "They'll put a man on the moon before I hit a home run." Only a few hours after Neil Armstrong set foot on the moon on July 20, 1969, Perry hit the first and only home run of his career.*

Chapter Objectives

- Start Excel and open a workbook
- Move around a worksheet using the mouse and arrow keys
- Locate supporting information (help)—MOS XL03S-1-3
- Select a block of cells
- Type into worksheet cells text, values, formulas, and functions—MOS XL03S-2-3
- Edit and clear cell entries—MOS XL03S-1-1
- Save a workbook
- Add a header and a footer—MOS XL03S-5-7
- Preview output—MOS XL03S-5-5
- Print a worksheet and print a worksheet's formulas—MOS XL03S-5-8
- Exit Excel

task reference   Opening an Excel Workbook

- Click **File** and then click **Open**
- Ensure that the Look in list box displays the name of the folder containing your workbook
- Click the workbook's name
- Click the **Open** button

SESSION 1.1

making the grade

1. A popular program used to analyze numeric information and help make meaningful business decisions is called a _____ program.

2. _____ analysis is observing changes to spreadsheets and reviewing their effect on other values in the spreadsheet.

3. An Excel spreadsheet is called a(n) _____ and consists of individual pages called _____.

4. Beneath Excel's menu bar is the _____ toolbar, which contains button shortcuts for commands such as Print, and the _____ toolbar containing button shortcuts to alter the appearance of worksheets and their cells.

5. The _____ cell is the cell in which you are currently entering data.

Modifying the left and right margins:

1. With the Print Preview window still open, click the **Setup** button. The Page Setup dialog box opens

2. Click the **Margins** tab and double-click the **Left spin control box** to highlight the current left margin number

3. Type **0.5** to set the left margin to one-half inch

4. Double-click the **Right spin control box** to highlight the current right margin number

5. Type **0.5** to set the right margin to one-half inch

6. Click **OK** to close the Page Setup dialog box

tip: *If you still cannot see the entire worksheet on one page, you can force the worksheet to fit by clicking the **Page** tab in the Page Setup dialog box and then click the **Fit to** option button in the Scaling section of t... it fits on a single page*

7. ...lick the **Close** butto... ...nd return to the wo...

Step-by-Step Instruction

Numbered steps guide you through the exact sequence of keystrokes to accomplish the task.

Tips

Tips appear within steps and either indicate possible missteps or provide alternatives to a step.

---

hands-on projects

practice

LEVEL THREE | CHAPTER ONE

1. Creating an Income Statement

Carroll's Fabricating, a machine shop providing custom metal fabricating, is preparing an income statement for its shareholders. Betty Carroll, the company's president, wants to know exactly how much net income the company has earned this year. Although Betty has prepared a preliminary worksheet with labels in place, she wants you to enter the values and a few formulas to compute cost of goods sold, gross profit, selling and advertising expenses, and net income. Figure 1.26 shows an example of a completed worksheet.

1. Open the workbook **ex01Income.xls** in your student disk in the folder Ch01

2. Click **File** and then click **Save As** to save the workbook as **Income2.xls** in the folder Ch01

3. Scan the Income Statement worksheet and type the following values in the listed cells: Cell C5, **987453;** cell B8, **64677;** cell B9, **564778;** cell B10, **-43500;** cell B15, **53223;** cell B16, **23500;** cell B17, **12560;** cell B18, **123466;** cell B19, **87672**

4. In cell C10, write the formula **=SUM(B8:B10)** to sum cost of goods sold

5. In cell C12, type the formula for Gross Profit: **=C5-C10**

6. In cell C19, type the formula to sum selling and advertising expenses: **=SUM(B15:B19)**

7. In cell C21, type the formula **=C122C19** to compute net income (gross profit minus total selling and advertising expenses)

8. In cell A4, type **Prepared by** <your name>

9. Click the Save button on the Standard toolbar to save your modified worksheet

10. Print the worksheet and print the worksheet formulas

FIGURE 1.26
Income statement

www.mhhe.com/i-series

EX 1.41

EXCEL

End-of-Chapter Hands-On Projects

A rich variety of projects introduced by a case lets you put into practice what you have learned. Categories include Practice, Challenge, On the Web, E-Business, Around the World, and a running case project.

Screen Shots

Screen shots show you what to expect at critical points.

---

anotherword . . . on Cell Ranges

A SUM function can contain more than one cell range. For example, the function =SUM(A1:A5,B42:B51) totals two cell ranges. Place commas between distinct cell ranges within the SUM function. The collection of cells, cell ranges, and values in the comma-separated list between a function's parentheses is its *argument list*

Another Way/ Another Word

Another Way highlights an alternative way to accomplish a task; Another Word explains more about a topic.

---

task reference summary

Task	Location	Preferred Method
Opening an Excel workbook	EX 1.00	• Click **File**, click **Open**, click workbook's name, click the **Open** button
...ng a formula	EX 1.00	• Select cell, type **=**, type formula, press **Enter**
Entering the SUM function	EX 1.00	• Select cell, type **=SUM(**, type cell range, type **)**, and press **Enter**
Editing a cell	EX 1.00	• Select cell, click formula bar, make changes, press **Enter**
Saving a workbook with a new name	EX 1.00	• Click **File**, click **Save As**, type filename, click **Save** button
Obtaining help	EX 1.00	Obtaining help

Task Reference Summary

Provides a quick reference and summary of a chapter's task references.

What does this logo mean?

It means this courseware has been approved by the Microsoft® Office Specialist Program to be among the finest available for learning *Microsoft Word 2003, Microsoft Excel 2003, Microsoft PowerPoint, 2003, Microsoft Access 2003, Microsoft Outlook, 2003*. It also means that upon completion of this courseware, you may be prepared to take an exam for Microsoft Office Specialist qualification. The I-Series Microsoft Office 2003 books are available in three levels of coverage: Brief, Introductory, and Complete. The I-Series Introductory books are approved courseware to prepare you for the Microsoft Office specialist exam. The I-Series Complete books will prepare you for the expert exam.

What is a Microsoft Office Specialist?

A Microsoft Office Specialist is an individual who has passed exams for certifying his or her skills in one or more of the Microsoft Office desktop applications such as Microsoft Word, Microsoft Excel, Microsoft PowerPoint, Microsoft Outlook, Microsoft Access, or Microsoft Project. The Microsoft Office Specialist Program typically offers certification exams at the "Core" and "Expert" skill levels.* The Microsoft Office Specialist Program is the only program in the world approved by Microsoft for testing proficiency in Microsoft Office desktop applications and Microsoft Project. This testing program can be a valuable asset in any job search or career advancement.

More Information:

To learn more about becoming a Microsoft Office Specialist, visit www.microsoft.com/officespecialist.

To learn about other Microsoft Office Specialist approved courseware from McGraw-Hill Technology Education, visit www.mhhe.com/i-series/mos.

*The availability of Microsoft Office Specialist certification exams varies by application, application version, and language. Visit www.microsoft.com/officespecialist for exam availability.

acknowledgments

The authors want to acknowledge the work and support of the seasoned professionals at McGraw-Hill. Thank you to Bob Woodbury, editor in chief, for his leadership and a management style that fosters creativity and innovation. Thank you to Craig Leonard, associate sponsoring editor. Craig took on the very difficult task of both developmental editor and then sponsoring editor with eagerness and did a splendid job of bringing all the pieces together.

Thank you to Louise Stapleton, a University of San Diego graduate student, who wrote end-of-chapter exercises. Stirling Perry, a graduate student in the English Department at the University of Pittsburgh, wrote end-of-chapter problems and helped with screen captures. Thanks to Jessica Perry for creating photographs that appear in the textbook and in several end-of-chapter exercise data files. We wish to thank our schools, the University of Denver and the University of San Diego, for providing support including time off to dedicate to writing.

If you would like to contact us about any of the books in the I-Series, we would enjoy hearing from you. We welcome comments and suggestions. You can e-mail book-related messages to us at i-series@McGraw-Hill.com. For the latest information about the I-Series textbooks and related resources, please visit our Web site at www.mhhe.com/i-series.

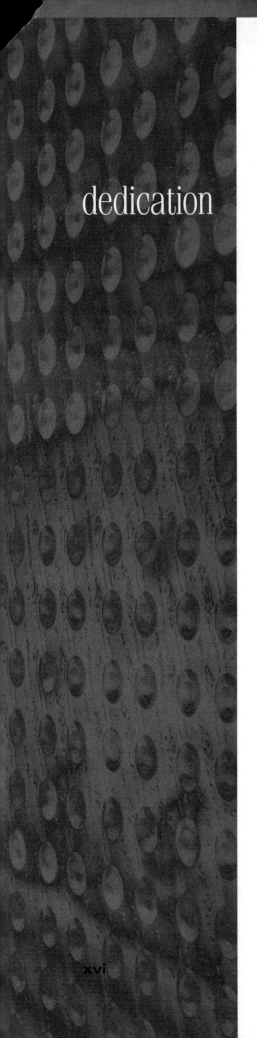

dedication

To my daughter, Kelly Allison Perry

You say "I will do that," and then you do! What an amazing, bright, and lovely young woman you are. You have taught me more than you realize.

JAMES PERRY

brief contents

table of contents

CHAPTER

one

Creating Worksheets for Decision Makers

did you know?

one-third *of online shoppers abandon their electronic shopping carts before completing the checkout process.*

goldfish *lose their color if they are kept in a dim light or if they are placed in a body of running water such as a stream.*

electric *eels are not really eels but a type of fish.*

in *1963, baseball pitcher Gaylord Perry said, "They'll put a man on the moon before I hit a home run." Only a few hours after Neil Armstrong set foot on the moon on July 20, 1969, Perry hit the first and only home run of his career.*

Chapter Objectives

- Start Excel and open a workbook
- Move around a worksheet using the mouse and arrow keys
- Locate supporting information (help)—MOS XL03S-1-3
- Select a block of cells
- Type into worksheet cells text, values, formulas, and functions—MOS XL03S-2-3
- Edit and clear cell entries—MOS XL03S-1-1
- Save a workbook
- Add a header and a footer—MOS XL03S-5-7
- Preview output—MOS XL03S-5-5
- Print a worksheet and print a worksheet's formulas—MOS XL03S-5-8
- Exit Excel

chapter case

Western University Rugby Team

Rugby is a popular sport around the world and is played at many universities in the United States. The sport has a loyal group of people who attend most of the games in the region. Often, U.S. collegiate rugby teams play on open fields that are not fenced. Occasionally, they play in soccer stadiums or on football fields where they can control access of fans and charge a nominal fee—a donation—to view a rugby game.

Western University is a small private school with a rugby team composed of 21 varsity players and 15 freshman and novice players. Stirling Leonard is a senior on the team and one of its co-captains. He is responsible for ensuring that everyone is available for each week's game and for overseeing the athletes' pregame warm-up regimen. He has also taken a lead role in organizing the annual fund-raising campaign for the team.

Unlike football or soccer, which are varsity sports at Western University, rugby is a club sport and not eligible to receive financial support from the university. The team's annual costs include transportation to games, replacement of some game uniforms each year, and sundry supplies such as tape and bandages. These costs at Western amount to over $24,000 per year—a small amount compared to the cost of a varsity sport, but a daunting cost for rugby team members to provide. Each team member must pay a fee to offset the projected cost of running the team. Some

of Western's rugby team members pay their fees directly, whereas others help with the team's annual fund-raising and use the funds they raise to pay their fees.

Past fund-raising activities included monthly car washes, club T-shirt sales, and the annual rugby alum game. This year, Stirling has devised a new and innovative way to raise money for the team: selling scrip issued by local specialty and fast-food stores near the college. Scrip is special paper issued by various merchants that are evidence of payment for a good or service from that merchant. Similar to a gift certificate, a store's own brand of scrip is the same as cash at the issuing merchant's store. Teams make money on the difference between the wholesale price at which they purchase scrip and the retail price at which they sell the scrip to customers.

Using Office Excel 2003, Stirling has created a worksheet that he and the team can use to calculate the total scrip sold each month as well as the team's profit. He has to complete the worksheet by entering the scrip sales quantities and some formulas to compute the donation value and retail value of the sales this month.

In this chapter, you will learn how to complete the Scrip Report to determine how well the team is doing toward its goal of raising the money it needs to support the team. Figure 1.1 shows the completed Scrip Sales Projection worksheet.

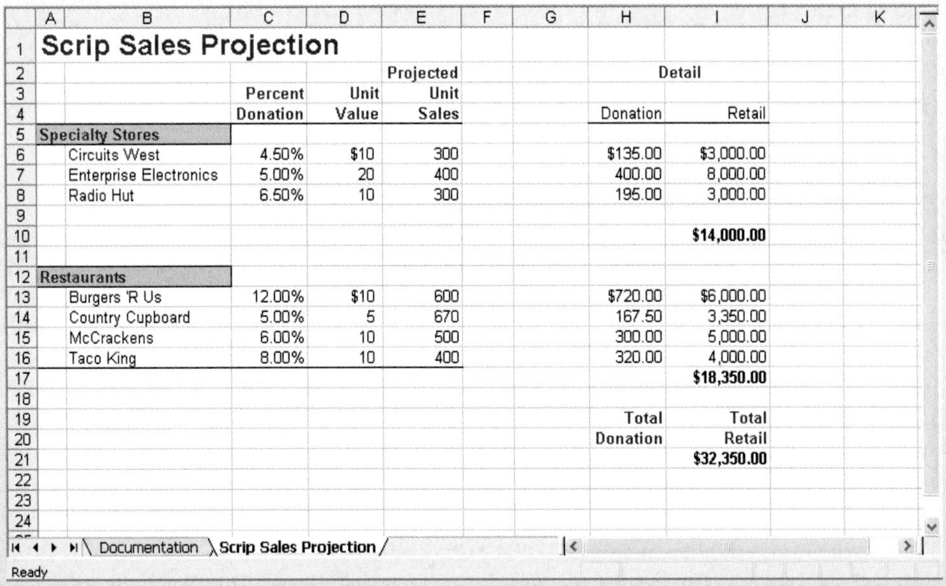

FIGURE 1.1
Scrip Sales Projection worksheet

	A	B	C	D	E	F	G	H	I	J	K
1	**Scrip Sales Projection**										
2					Projected			Detail			
3			Percent	Unit	Unit						
4			Donation	Value	Sales			Donation	Retail		
5	Specialty Stores										
6		Circuits West	4.50%	$10	300			$135.00	$3,000.00		
7		Enterprise Electronics	5.00%	20	400			400.00	8,000.00		
8		Radio Hut	6.50%	10	300			195.00	3,000.00		
9											
10									$14,000.00		
11											
12	Restaurants										
13		Burgers 'R Us	12.00%	$10	600			$720.00	$6,000.00		
14		Country Cupboard	5.00%	5	670			167.50	3,350.00		
15		McCrackens	6.00%	10	500			300.00	5,000.00		
16		Taco King	8.00%	10	400			320.00	4,000.00		
17									$18,350.00		
18											
19								Total	Total		
20								Donation	Retail		
21									$32,350.00		
22											
23											
24											

Documentation \ Scrip Sales Projection /

Ready

INTRODUCTION

Chapter 1 introduces you to Office Excel 2003. You start Office Excel 2003 and examine the Standard toolbar, Formatting toolbar, task pane, and other features of a new Excel's window. You learn several ways to move around a worksheet, including using arrow keys and the mouse. Select worksheet cells by clicking a cell and then dragging the mouse across a contiguous group of cells.

Excel worksheet cells can contain text, values (constants), formulas, functions, and a combination of these. You enter text into a cell by clicking it and then typing. You enter values, which are numbers, by typing the number preceded by an optional plus or minus sign. Formulas always begin with an equals sign (=). Following the equals sign you can type an arbitrarily complex expression involving values, mathematical operators, and Excel functions. Excel functions are built-in or prerecorded formulas that provide a shortcut for complex calculations. Writing Excel functions saves time and trouble. For example, it is far easier to write a SUM function to total several worksheet cell values than it is to write a long formula containing the plus operator and individual cell references to be summed.

Edit a cell that contains an error and then press Enter to complete the work. Alternatively, you can completely replace a cell's contents by typing a new formula. Clear a cell to empty its contents with the Clear command on the Edit menu. Attempting to clear a cell by typing a space usually leads to problems as you develop a worksheet. Specify a worksheet's print area consisting of any rectangular group of cells. When you print the worksheet, Excel remembers each worksheet's print area and prints only cells within the print area.

CHAPTER OUTLINE

SESSION 1.1 GETTING STARTED

In this section, you will learn how to start Excel, open a workbook, and observe the anatomy of an Excel worksheet and its window. You will investigate several ways to move around an Excel workbook using the mouse, arrow keys, and combinations of keyboard keys that employ shortcuts to move the worksheet cursor quickly to a particular worksheet cell. Finally, you will learn how to select a block of cells.

Introduction to Office Excel 2003

Office Excel 2003 is a computerized spreadsheet—an automated version of an accountant's ledger. A *spreadsheet* is a popular program used to analyze numeric information and help make meaningful business decisions based on the analysis. Spreadsheets are used for a variety of applications ranging from financial analysis of stock portfolios, manufacturing and production quantity assessment, inventory turnover and cost estimation, budgeting, and simple household record keeping.

Dan Bricklin and Bob Frankston invented the electronic spreadsheet in 1979. Bob Frankston joined Dan Bricklin, a Harvard MBA student, to cooperatively write the program for the new electronic spreadsheet. They formed a new company called Software Arts, Inc., and called their spreadsheet product VisiCalc. Bricklin and Frankston later sold VisiCalc to Lotus Development Corporation, where it developed into the PC spreadsheet Lotus 1-2-3. VisiCalc was the first of several spreadsheet programs to develop over the next two decades.

Spreadsheet software has been one of the most popular pieces of software of all time. Why is it so popular? Consider the way people performed a typical spreadsheet task before the advent of the electronic version. A typical application of a hard copy, paper and pencil method of creating and maintaining a spreadsheet is projecting net profit. Prior to the advent of electronic spreadsheets, accountants used paper ledgers and wrote entries in pencil so that they could easily modify various entries in the spreadsheet and then recalculate, using a calculator, the new values. Bricklin once said, "VisiCalc took 20 hours of work per week for some people and turned it out in 15 minutes and let them become much more creative."

Figure 1.2 shows a facsimile of a manual accounting spreadsheet showing projected net profit of a product whose unit price is $200. Expenses for marketing, manufacturing, and overhead are but a few of the expenses needed to advertise the product and bring it to market. People who worked with ledger spreadsheets like the one shown in

FIGURE 1.2

Hard copy accounting spreadsheet

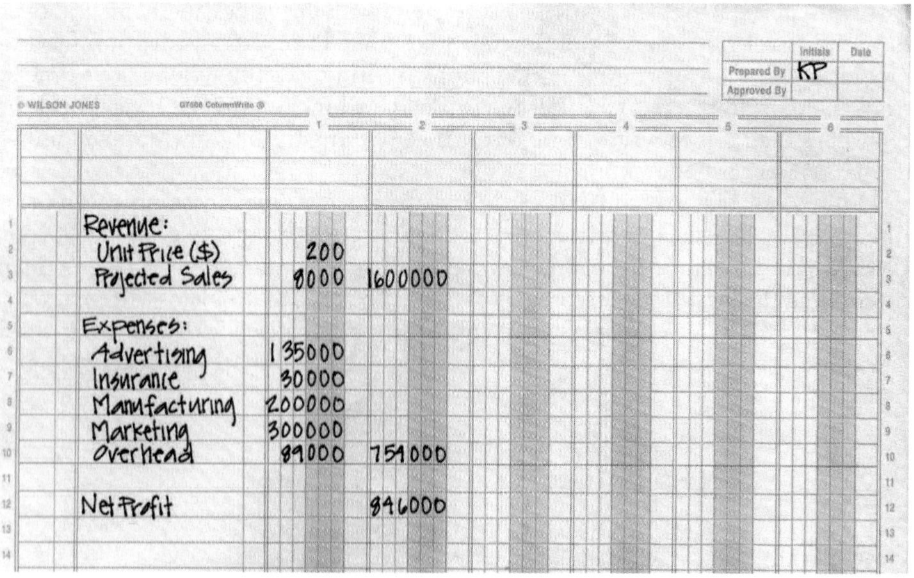

Figure 1.2 often had to modify projected sales numbers, unit sale prices, and other values and then recalculate values such as net profit. Any change to a hard copy worksheet can take a lot of time for even the simplest alteration because many values that are dependent on the change must be recalculated. Making changes to spreadsheets and reviewing their effect on other values is a classic use of spreadsheets and is called **what-if analysis**—one of the popular uses for today's electronic spreadsheets. With electronic spreadsheets, any changes you make to a spreadsheet automatically recalculate to quickly reveal new values. Formulas give Excel its power.

People refer to spreadsheet programs as electronic spreadsheets or simply spreadsheets. Using Office Excel 2003 (Excel), you create a document called a **workbook**, which is a collection of one or more individual **worksheets**. Worksheets are so named because they resemble pages in a spiral-bound workbook like the ones you purchase and use to take class notes. You will probably hear the terms *spreadsheets, workbooks,* and *worksheets* used interchangeably.

Starting Excel and Opening a Worksheet

Stirling's alarm clock wakes him at 6:30 A.M. He's an early riser and wants to get started on the worksheet so that he can show it to his rugby coach, Rod Harrington, for his comments. Stirling has discovered which of the nearby merchants and restaurants offer scrip, and he has learned that he must purchase the scrip through a broker whose warehouse contains scrip from hundreds of stores in the region. After talking to the scrip distribution center manager, Stirling was able to get a special deal: He can request and receive up to $10,000 worth of scrip to be delivered to the university's athletic office and he will have up to 45 days to pay for it.

Start Excel to design the worksheet to calculate the scrip profits and project how many units to order next time.

Starting Microsoft Excel:

1. Make sure Windows is running on your computer and the Windows desktop appears on your computer screen

2. Click the taskbar **Start** button to display the Start menu, then point to **Programs** to display the Programs menu

3. Point to **Microsoft Excel** on the Programs menu and then click **Microsoft Excel**. Within a few seconds, the Microsoft Excel copyright information page appears. Then the Excel window containing an empty worksheet appears. When both Excel and its worksheet are maximized, your screen should look like Figure 1.3

4. Microsoft Excel should fill the screen and show an empty worksheet. If it does not, then click the **Maximize** button found in the upper-right corner of the Excel window

5. If the empty worksheet is not maximized, then click the worksheet **Maximize** button

Anatomy of the Excel Window

The Excel program window shown in Figure 1.3 is typical of many Microsoft Windows applications. The Excel application is divided into several important areas. These will become very familiar to you as you gain experience with Excel.

EXCEL

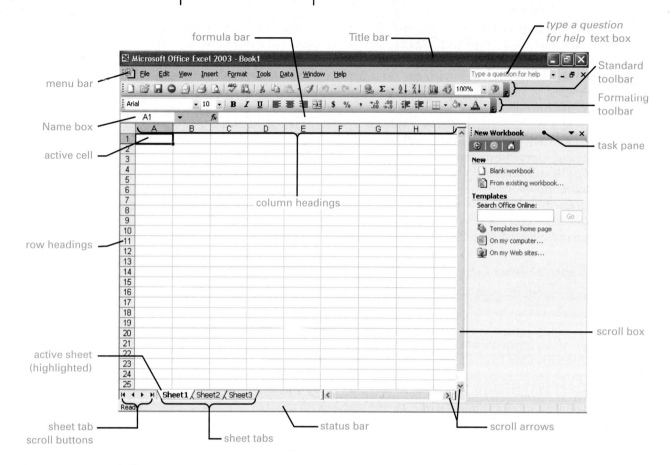

FIGURE 1.3

Excel program window containing an empty worksheet

Task Pane

A **task pane** is a dockable dialog window that provides a convenient way to use commands, gather information, and modify Excel documents. An Excel task pane can contain one or more pages, and each page is broken up into sections. The Excel task pane in Figure 1.3 contains sections for opening a workbook, creating a new workbook, and creating a workbook from a template. The task pane puts relevant features one click away.

Menu Bar

The **menu bar**, which is visible no matter which Excel activity is taking place, contains the Excel menus. Clicking a command on the menu bar reveals the menu's associated commands. Menus are arranged in a familiar way beginning on the left with the File, Edit, and View menus. Clicking the File menu, for example, reveals the New, Open, Close, and Save commands, among others, that are typical of all Windows File menu commands. Normally the menu bar appears just below the Title bar, but you can click the menu handle at the left end of the menu bar and drag the menu bar to any location on the screen, or you can dock it on any of the other three sides of the screen.

Toolbars

Toolbars allow you to execute commands with a single click. Most of the frequently used commands appear in one of the several Excel toolbars. The **Standard toolbar**, which normally appears below the menu bar, contains buttons that execute popular menu bar commands such as Print, Cut, and Insert Table. The **Formatting toolbar** contains buttons that change the appearance of a worksheet. For example, you can set the typeface or underline entries by pressing Formatting toolbar buttons.

help yourself *Press **F1**, type **toolbars** in the Search text box of the Microsoft Excel Help task pane, press **Enter**, and click the **Move a toolbar** hyperlink to display Help on moving a toolbar to another location on your screen. When you are finished reading, close the Microsoft Excel Help dialog box and close the task pane*

Formula Bar

The formula bar appears below the menu bar and toolbars just above the workbook window. The *formula bar* displays the active cell's contents, appearing at the top of the screen, in which you can enter cell contents or edit existing contents. *Cell contents* are the text, formulas, or numbers you type into a cell. A cell's contents can look different from the value it calculates and displays in a cell. A discussion of these differences appears later in this chapter. The *Name box*, appearing on the left of the formula bar, displays either the active cell's address (A1 in Figure 1.3) or its assigned name. (More information about cell addresses and names appears later in this chapter.)

Workbook Window

The document window is called the *workbook window* or *worksheet window*. It contains the workbook on which you are working. A workbook can contain up to 255 worksheets, and each worksheet contains columns and rows that are labeled with letters and numbers, respectively. A worksheet can contain up to 256 columns with labels A through IV to uniquely identify each column. A worksheet contains 65,536 rows with numeric labels from 1 to 65536. A *cell* is located at the intersection of a row and a column and identified by a cell reference, such as A1. The *cell reference*, or cell address, is a cell's identification consisting of its column letter(s) followed by its row number. The cell located at the intersection of column D and row 42 is identified as D42, for example. A worksheet cell contains data that you enter such as text, numbers, or formulas. Each cell is like a small calculator, capable of computing the value of any arbitrarily complex formulas you type. The *active cell* is the cell in which you are currently working. Its name or cell reference appears in the name box, its contents appear in the formula bar, and a dark rectangle surrounds the active cell (see Figure 1.3).

Sheet Tabs

Each of a workbook's sheets has a unique name. That name appears in its *sheet tab*. When you create a new workbook, the number of sheets varies. By default, new sheets are named Sheet1, Sheet2, and so on. You can change the name of any sheet to something more meaningful. Clicking a sheet tab makes the clicked sheet active. The sheet tab of the active sheet—the one into which you are entering data—is bright white whereas inactive sheet tabs are dark gray. If your workbook contains many worksheets, only a few sheet tabs appear just above the status bar. To move to another worksheet whose tab is not shown, click the *sheet tab scroll buttons* to scroll through the sheet tabs until you find the sheet you want. Then click the sheet tab to make the sheet active.

Status Bar

The *status bar* is located at the very bottom of the window—below the sheet tabs and above the Windows Taskbar. This shows general information about the worksheet and selected keyboard keys. Status indicators on the right side tell you about the current state of selected keys. For instance, one indicator displays NUM whenever the NumLock key is active. Another status indicator displays CAPS when the Caps Lock key is active.

Mouse Pointer

The *mouse pointer* indicates the current position of the mouse as you move it around the screen. It changes shape to indicate what duties you can perform at the location over which the mouse pointer is positioned. When the mouse is over a worksheet, it appears as a white plus sign. Move the mouse to a menu and it changes to an arrow, which

FIGURE 1.4

Keys to move around a
worksheet

Keystroke	Action
Up arrow	Moves up one cell
Down arrow	Moves down one cell
Left arrow	Moves left one cell
Right arrow	Moves right one cell
PgUp	Moves active cell up one screen
PgDn	Moves active cell down one screen
Home	Moves active cell to column A of current row
Ctrl+Home	Moves active cell to cell A1
Ctrl+End	Moves to the lower, rightmost active corner of the worksheet
F5 (function key)	Opens the Go To dialog box in which you can enter any cell address

indicates that you can select an item by clicking the mouse. When you move the mouse to the formula bar, it changes into an I-beam shape, which indicates that you can click and then type data.

Moving around a Worksheet

In order to enter information into a worksheet, you must first select the cell to make it the active cell. There are a number of ways to select a cell.

Using the Keyboard

Excel provides several ways to move to different cells in your worksheet. Pressing Ctrl+Home always makes cell A1 the active cell. Pressing the right arrow key moves the active cell one cell to the right. Other arrow keys move the active cell corresponding to the arrow's direction (right, left, up, and down). Figure 1.4 shows keys that select different worksheet cells.

Using the Mouse

The mouse is a quick and convenient way to select a cell. Simply click the cell you want to make the active cell by placing the pointer over the cell and clicking the left mouse button. Moving to cells not yet visible on the screen is simple too. Use the vertical and horizontal worksheet scroll bars or arrow keys to scroll to the area of the worksheet containing the cell to which you want to move. Then click the cell to select it.

Try moving to different parts of the worksheet. Prepare for this short exercise by ensuring that an empty Excel worksheet is open. Then do the following:

Making a cell the active cell:

1. Close the task pane by clicking the **Task Pane Close** button in the New Workbook Title bar. Position the mouse pointer over cell C4, then click the **left mouse** button to make cell C4 the active cell

2. Click cell **G7** to make it the active cell

3. Click cell **N53**. (You will have to use the horizontal and vertical scroll bars to bring cell N53 into view on your screen prior to selecting it)

4. Press the **Home** key to move to column A and make cell A53 the active cell

5. Finally, press **Ctrl+Home** to move to cell A1

6. Press the **PgDn** key to scroll the screen down one screen. The active cell is column A and a row below row 20. The exact row that becomes the active cell depends on the size and resolution of your screen. A new, previously hidden set of rows is revealed in any case

7. Press **F5** to open the Go To dialog box

tip: *Ignore any contents in your Go To panel and the Reference text box. If there is already an entry in your Reference text box, simply type over it*

8. Type **CD451** in the Reference text box and click **OK**. Cell CD451 becomes the active cell

9. Press **F5** to open the Go To dialog box again

10. Type **IV65536** and click **OK**. Cell IV65536 becomes the active cell

11. Click the **vertical scroll bar down arrow** three times to move the display up three rows, and then click the **horizontal scroll bar right arrow** two times. Notice that cell IV65536 is located at the highest row and right-most column in the worksheet (see Figure 1.5)

*another***way**
. . . to Move to a Worksheet Cell

Press **Ctrl+G** to display the Go To dialog box

Type in the Reference text box the cell reference to which you want to move

Click the **OK** button

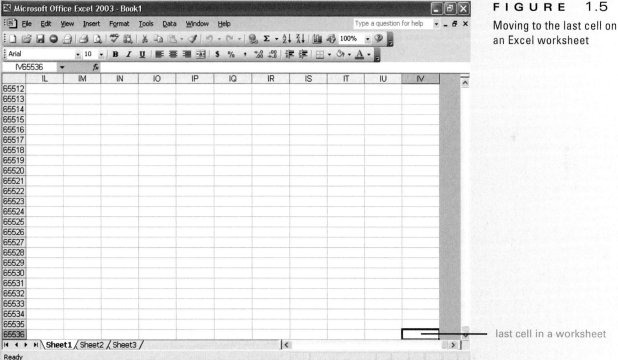

FIGURE 1.5

Moving to the last cell on an Excel worksheet

last cell in a worksheet

12. Press **Ctrl+Home** to move to cell A1

Moving from Sheet to Sheet

Workbooks can contain more than one worksheet, because worksheets are a convenient way to organize collections of related sheets. An inventory manager might keep each month's raw materials purchases on separate worksheets by month. Similarly, stock-brokers can keep records about their clients' purchases in one Excel workbook, assigning one page per client. You can move from one worksheet to another within one workbook by clicking its sheet tab. The new sheet becomes active. You can use the sheet tab scroll buttons to reveal hidden sheet tabs when necessary.

Opening an Existing Workbook

When you want to examine, modify, or work with a workbook you or someone else created previously, you must open it first. When you open a workbook, Excel locates the file on your disk, reads it from the disk, and transfers the entire file into your computer's main memory, called Random Access Memory (RAM). The disk-to-memory loading process is complete when the worksheet appears on your computer's monitor. Loading a worksheet from a removable disk takes more time than loading the same worksheet from a hard disk—a time difference you will notice. Once loaded into memory, a worksheet resides both in memory and on disk. Any changes you may make to the worksheet should be saved back to the removable disk. If you maintain your worksheets on a removable disk, remember to first save any worksheet changes before you remove the disk. Otherwise, the worksheet stored on your removable disk may be out of synchronization with the one stored in memory.

Stirling has created a workbook called **ex01Scrip.xls** to help you and the team estimate how much scrip they must sell to raise money for the team.

---

task reference   **Opening an Excel Workbook**

- Click **File** and then click **Open**
- Ensure that the Look in list box displays the name of the folder containing your workbook
- Click the workbook's name
- Click the **Open** button

Opening an existing Excel workbook:

1. Place your data disk in the appropriate drive

2. Click **File** on the menu bar and then click **Open**

3. Click the **Look in** list arrow to display a list of available disk drives. Locate the drive containing your data disk and click the drive containing your data disk. The window displays a list of folders and Excel workbook filenames

4. Locate and then click the Excel file **ex01Scrip.xls** to select it

5. Click the **Open** button located on the Standard toolbar. The first page of the Scrip workbook opens and displays the documentation worksheet. See Figure 1.6

Scrip Worksheet Design

The Scrip workbook created by Stirling consists of two worksheets, which Stirling named "Documentation" and "Scrip Sales Projection." The first worksheet is labeled Documentation. This sheet name appears on its tab (see Figure 1.6) and contains information about the workbook's designer, its use, when the workbook was created, a list of dates when the workbook was changed, and brief comments. Stirling explains that the Documentation worksheet conveys important information about the Scrip workbook to anyone who works with it. The instructions description is particularly helpful because it provides a reminder of how to use the workbook. That's especially helpful, he explains, when you work with several workbooks and want a quick reminder of how to use this particular workbook. The Documentation worksheet is not typical of most Excel worksheets as it contains no grid lines and no column or row headings. Excel provides options to remove those features. Because the Documentation worksheet is unlike others, removing the gridlines reduces confusion.

After you review the Documentation worksheet with Stirling, he opens the Scrip Sales Projection worksheet by clicking the Scrip Sales Projection worksheet tab. Figure 1.7 shows the Scrip Sales Projection worksheet. Stirling describes the two major parts of the Scrip Sales Projection worksheet. The left half of the sheet contains merchants grouped into the two categories: Specialty Stores and Restaurants. Under each category heading are lists of merchants offering scrip—one row for each merchant. Cells E6 through E16 are a critical part of the worksheet because they contain the assumptions you will be exploring. A change in the projected sales for one or more merchants' scrip causes changes in other worksheet locations.

Under the Donation and Retail columns are the projected values of the revenue that the club keeps—its profit—and the total retail value of the scrip, respectively. You can see that the projected total value of all projected scrip retail sales is $32,350.00, but the club's total profit (Total Donation) on those sales for both specialty stores and restaurants is not yet displayed (under the heading Total Donation).

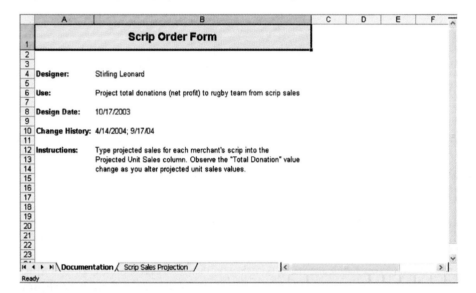

FIGURE 1.6

Scrip workbook documentation worksheet

FIGURE 1.7

Partially complete Scrip Sales Projection worksheet

The single variable in the Scrip Sales Projection worksheet that most determines the success of the scrip sales effort is the column into which Stirling will type in different numbers to see the effect—the projected unit sales. These are called the worksheet's *assumption cells*, which are cells upon which other formulas depend and whose values can be changed to observe their effect on a worksheet's entries. A change in some or all of these values directly affects the total sales and therefore the profit that the rugby team generates.

Overall, the Scrip Sales Projection worksheet provides Stirling with an estimate of how much scrip the team must sell in order to make a real dent in their team expenses. If the total donation value were very small, then the team might consider alternative fund-raising activities. The Scrip Sales Projection worksheet is a valuable decision-making tool because it provides a clear picture of the how scrip sales can translate into team profits.

SESSION 1.1

making *the grade*

1. A popular program used to analyze numeric information and help make meaningful business decisions is called a _____ program.

2. _____ analysis is observing changes to spreadsheets and reviewing their effect on other values in the spreadsheet.

3. An Excel spreadsheet is called a(n) _____ and consists of individual pages called _____.

4. Beneath Excel's menu bar is the _____ toolbar, which contains button shortcuts for commands such as Print, and the _____ toolbar containing button shortcuts to alter the appearance of worksheets and their cells.

5. The _____ cell is the cell in which you are currently entering data.

SESSION 1.2 ENTERING DATA, SAVING WORKBOOKS, AND PRINTING WORKSHEETS

In this session, you will learn how to enter data into worksheet cells, enter formulas into worksheet cells, save a workbook, and print a worksheet. Stirling wants you to modify the Scrip Sales Projection worksheet by adding another store and modifying projected scrip sales. In particular, you will learn how to enter text entries, values, formulas, and functions. You will learn how to remove information from one or more worksheet cells. You will save your workbook and print the worksheet and its formulas. When you have completed your work on the Scrip Sales Projection worksheet, you will close it and exit Excel.

Excel Data Types

You can enter three types of data into Excel worksheet cells: text, formulas, and values. You will learn the difference between these three data types in this session. Each type has a slightly different purpose. First you will learn about text entries, because they are straightforward and yet fundamental to good worksheet design.

Entering Text, Values, Formulas, and Functions

Worksheet cells can contain text, value, formula, and function entries. Text entries document and identify important elements in a worksheet. Important worksheet input numbers, such as the Scrip Sales Projection worksheet's projected unit sales, are values. More complicated entries are formulas consisting of mathematical operators, cell references, and Excel functions. Formulas compute and display numeric or text entries

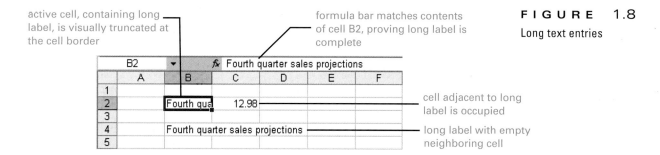

FIGURE 1.8

Long text entries

that usually change when you alter values upon which the formulas depend. Functions are prerecorded formulas that make calculations easier for you. Each of these types of cell entries has an important role to play, and each one is introduced next.

Text

Text entries are any combination of characters that you can type on the keyboard including symbols ($, #, @, and so on), numbers, letters, and spaces. While text can be used as data, it almost always identifies and documents important worksheet columns, rows, and cells. (Sometimes text entries are called labels.) The Scrip workbook contains many text entries. Text appears in the Documentation sheet shown in Figure 1.6. All the entries in column A are text. Column B contains almost all text, with the exception of cell B8. (Cell B10 contains dates separated by a semicolon and is text.) A payroll worksheet, for example, contains employee names in several rows under a particular column. Expense reports contain the days of the week as column labels.

To enter text into a worksheet cell, first select the cell by clicking it and then type the text. As you type the text, it appears in both the formula bar and the selected cell. Excel aligns text entries on the left. Whenever text is longer than the cell containing it, the text visually spills over into the adjacent cell—if the adjacent cell is empty. If the adjacent cell already contains an entry, then the long text appears to be cut off at the boundary between the two cells. In either case, the text is completely contained within the cell you select, whether you can see all of it or not. Figure 1.8 shows the same long text entered into cells B2 and B4. Cell C2, which is adjacent to cell B2, already has an entry, so the long text in B2 appears cut off. Cell C4 is empty, so the long text in Cell B4 is completely visible.

Just today, Stirling has convinced another merchant that selling their scrip will benefit the merchant and the team. Happily, the new merchant is the university bookstore. Stirling wants you to add the newly recruited merchant's name to the Specialty Stores listed in the Scrip Sales Projection worksheet. Enter the new store in the list.

Entering text labels:

1. If you closed the Scrip workbook (**ex01Scrip.xls**) following the end of the previous session, make sure Excel is running and that the Scrip Sales Projection worksheet is showing. (Click the Scrip Sales Projection worksheet tab to open it)

2. Click cell **B9** to make it the active cell

3. Type **University Bookstore** and then press **Enter**. The text appears in cell B9, and cell B10 becomes the active cell

tip: *If you press a keyboard arrow key instead of pressing the Enter key, you complete entering text into the current cell and control which cell becomes the active cell*

4. Click cell **G10** to make it the active cell, type **Subtotal**, and then press **Enter**

tip: *You may notice the text in G10 is right aligned—contrary to what you read earlier about text entries. This is because the cell has been formatted to align text on the right. You will learn about formatting in Chapter 2*

5. Click cell **G17** to make it the active cell, type **Subtotal**, and press **Enter**. Excel completes the entry because a similar entry already exists in the column. Figure 1.9 shows the worksheet after you have entered the three text values, also called labels

FIGURE 1.9

Worksheet after entering text

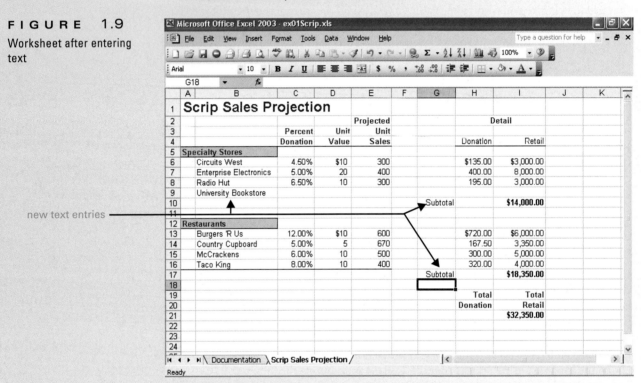

new text entries

Next, you need to enter the percent donation, scrip unit value, and the projected unit sales.

Values

Values are numbers that represent a quantity, date, or time. A value can be the number of students in a class, the quantity ordered of some vehicle part, the height in meters of a building, and so on. Examples are 15456, −35.8954, and 17. Values can be times and dates, too. For example, if you were to type 10/17/2001, Excel recognizes that value as a date. Similarly, if you were to type 15:32:30, Excel would interpret your entry as a time value. In other words, Excel can determine automatically whether you are entering text or a value based on what you type. For instance, if you were to type −9435, Excel would recognize the entry as a value and, by default, would place it right justified in the cell. Similarly, if you typed *28 ways to win*, Excel would recognize the entry as text. A number enclosed in parentheses such as (9876) is also a value—a negative value.

Common entries that appear to be values sometimes are not. For example, Excel considers a social security number such as 123-45-6789 to be text, not the value of 123 minus 45 minus 6789. Telephone numbers, with or without area codes or country codes, are text also. The key difference between text and values is that cells containing text cannot be used in a meaningful way in mathematical calculations.

Next, you will enter the values for the University Bookstore's percent donation, and scrip unit values. In addition, Stirling talked to you this morning and asked you to enter 900 for the projected unit sales. While this may be an optimistic figure, Stirling thinks that students will like the idea of spending their scrip on campus.

Entering values:

1. Click cell **C9** to make it the active cell. Type **10%** and press the **right arrow** key. The value 10.00% appears in cell C9 and cell D9 becomes the active cell

2. Type **5** into cell D9 and then press the **right arrow** key. The value 5 appears in cell D9 and E9 becomes the active cell

3. Type **900** into cell E9 and press **Enter**. See Figure 1.10

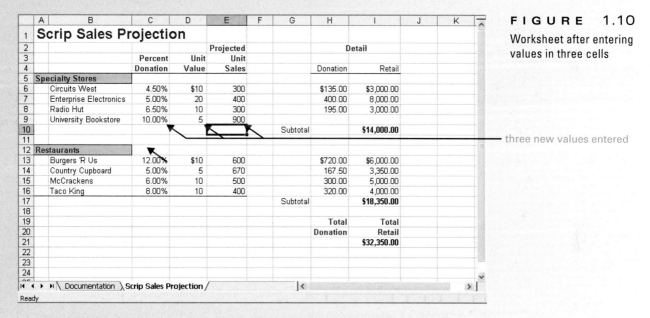

FIGURE 1.10
Worksheet after entering values in three cells

three new values entered

Next, you will enter formulas that will calculate the total donation value and total retail value for the newly added University Bookstore row. This row will contribute to the subtotal and grand totals, as you will see after you complete the following steps.

Formulas

A *formula* is an expression that begins with an equals sign and can contain cell references, arithmetic operators, values, and Excel built-in functions that result in a calculated result. Without formulas, Excel would be little more than a word processing program, incapable of producing what-if analysis and not even as capable as an inexpensive calculator. Formulas give Excel its power. Formulas that contain a reference to another cell automatically recompute whenever you change *any* cell in the worksheet. A formula can be as simple as the sum of two numbers or cells, or it can be as complex as the calculation of the present value of a lottery prize that is paid once a year for 22 years. Formulas contain arithmetic operators such as addition, subtraction, multiplication, and division. Figure 1.11 lists the arithmetic operators available in Excel.

FIGURE 1.11
Arithmetic operators

Arithmetic Operator	Operator Name	Example Formula	Description
( )	Parentheses	=(1+B4)/B52	Alters the way in which the expression is evaluated: Add 1 to the contents of cell B4 and divide the result by the value in cell B52
^	Exponentiation	=E4^6	Raises the value stored in cell E4 to the 6th power
		=17.4^B2	Raises 17.4 to the value stored in cell B2
*	Multiplication	=B4*D4	Multiplies the value in cell B4 by the value in D4
		=A21*B44*C55	Multiples the values of cells A21, B44, and C55
/	Division	=D1/C42	Divides the value in cell D1 by the value in cell C42
		=A53/365.24	Divides the value in cell A53 by the constant 365.24
		=10/17/46	Divides 10 by 17 and then divides that result by 46
+	Addition	=A4+B29	Adds the contents of cell A4 and the contents of cell B29
−	Subtraction	=A2−A1	Subtracts the value of cell A1 from the value of cell A2
		=100−A2	Subtracts the value of cell A2 from the constant, 100

Formulas begin with an equals sign, which informs Excel that you are entering a formula, not a label. A formula can contain values, arithmetic operators, and cell addresses. For example, the formula =(C5−C7)/(D43+D28)*54.987 references cells and contains a constant. The formula mathematically combines the values in cells and the constant using parentheses, division, addition, subtraction, and multiplication.

---

task reference   **Entering a Formula**

- Select the cell in which you want to type a formula

- Type = followed by the remainder of the formula

- Type cell references in either uppercase or lowercase, or use the mouse or the arrow keys to select cells as you type the formula

- Press **Enter** to complete the formula

Stirling explains that you must enter a formula to compute the donation and retail values for the University Bookstore row. The subtotal and grand totals automatically include the new calculated values you are about to add because the subtotal and grand total formulas have been written to do so. Stirling asks you to complete the University Bookstore row.

Entering formulas to calculate donation and retail amounts:

1. With the Scrip Sales Projection worksheet displayed, click cell **H9** to select it, type the formula **=C9*D9*E9** (remember to type the equals sign first), and then press **Enter** to complete the formula. The formula

multiplies the percent donation (C9), unit value (D9), and unit sales value (E9) for the University Bookstore. In this example, the formula calculates 10 percent of 900 units at 5 dollars per unit sold. The value 450.00, the result, appears in cell H9

tip: *If you make a mistake while typing a formula but __before__ you press Enter or an arrow key, simply press the* **Backspace** *key to erase the mistake and then type the correction. If you make a mistake __after__ you press Enter or an arrow key, simply select the cell again and retype the formula*

2. Click cell **H9** again to observe the formula, which appears in the formula bar. See Figure 1.12

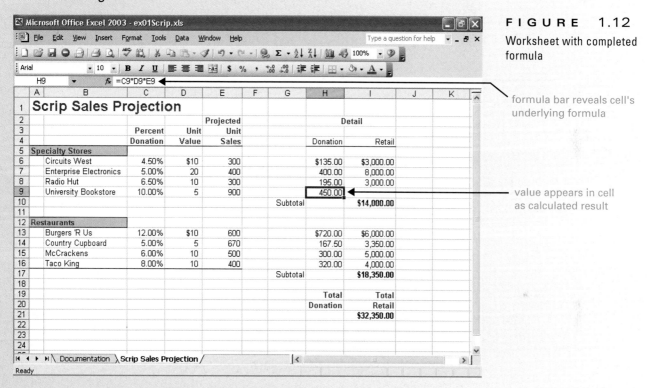

FIGURE 1.12
Worksheet with completed formula

formula bar reveals cell's underlying formula

value appears in cell as calculated result

3. Click cell **I9**, type **=E9*D9**, and then press **Enter**. The value 4,500.00 appears in cell I9, indicating the calculated value of the formula you just entered. This value is the total value of the scrip that Stirling projects will be sold for use at the University Bookstore. Of this value, the club stands to make a profit of $450, the value in cell H9. Notice that cell I10 displays $18,500.00, the updated retail subtotal. Excel automatically recalculates worksheet cells whenever you type something new in the worksheet

Functions

A *function* is a built-in or prerecorded formula that provides a shortcut for complex calculations. Excel has hundreds of functions available for your use. One example is the Excel statistical function SUM. The SUM function is a handy shortcut for summing the contents of any collection of worksheet cells. Instead of writing a long formula such as =A1+A2+A3+A4+A5+A6+A7 to sum the values stored in cells A1 through A7, you can write a shorter equivalent formula =SUM(A1:A7). The SUM function, like all

FIGURE 1.13

Cell range examples

cell range
C2:J2

cell range
B4:B4

cell range
B6:B17

cell range
D6:G12

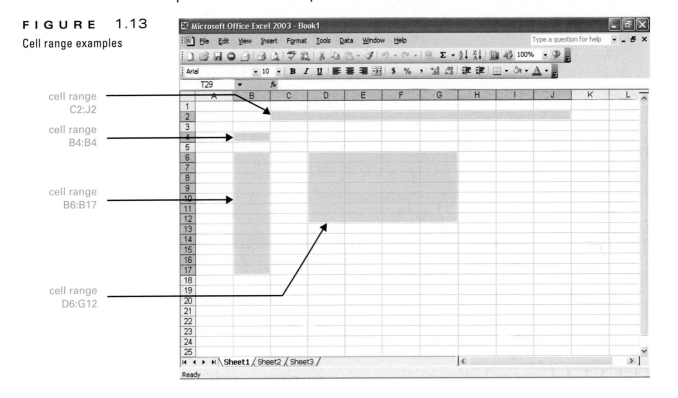

Excel functions, starts with the function's name followed by opening and closing parentheses that optionally contain a list of cells or other expressions upon which the named function operates. In the preceding example, the SUM function adds the values in the cell range A1 through A7. The function calculates and displays the sum in the cell in which the function is written. A ***cell range*** consists of one or more cells that form a rectangular group. You specify a cell range by typing the name of the upper-left cell, a colon, and the name of the lower-right cell. For example, the cell range B4:C6 consists of the six cells B4, B5, B6, C4, C5, and C6. Because Excel imposes a limit on the size of a formula you can write, the Excel function SUM solves the problem of writing an extremely long formula that contains a potentially large number of cell addresses. Figure 1.13 shows several examples of cell ranges.

---

*another*word   . . . on **Cell Ranges**

A SUM function can contain more than one cell range. For example, the function =SUM(A1:A5,B42:B51) totals two cell ranges. Place commas between distinct cell ranges within the SUM function. The collection of cells, cell ranges, and values in the comma-separated list between a function's parentheses is its ***argument list***

Stirling points out that there are three cells into which you will place the SUM function. Two of those SUM functions will calculate the subtotal of the donations for each of the two categories of merchants. The third SUM function will add the two donation subtotals to calculate and display the grand total donation value—the projected dollar value that the team can use to underwrite some of its costs.

---

task reference   **Entering the SUM Function**

- Select the cell in which you want to type a formula

- Type **=**

- Type **SUM** in either uppercase, lowercase, or a mixture of both, followed by a left parenthesis. Do not place a space between "SUM" and the left parenthesis

- Type the cell range to be summed followed by a right parenthesis

- Press **Enter** to complete the SUM function

Entering SUM functions:

1. With the Scrip Sales Projection worksheet displayed, click cell **H10** to select it, type the formula **=SUM(H6:H9)**, and press **Enter** to complete the formula

2. Click cell **H17** to select it. This time, you will type part of the formula and use the mouse to indicate the cell range to sum. Using the mouse to select a cell range while writing a formula is called *pointing*

3. With cell **H17** the active cell, type **=SUM(**

4. Next, click cell **H13**, drag the mouse pointer down to cell **H16**, and release the mouse. Notice that Excel writes the cell range into the function for you as you drag the mouse. A moving dashed line surrounds the selected cell range. See Figure 1.14

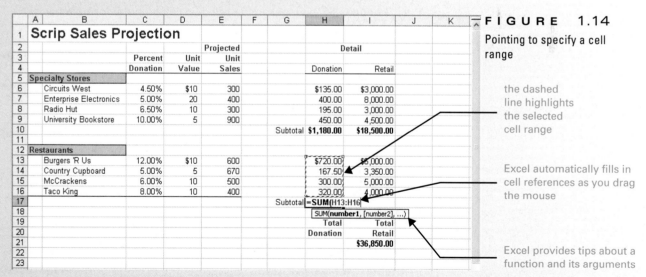

FIGURE   1.14

Pointing to specify a cell range

the dashed line highlights the selected cell range

Excel automatically fills in cell references as you drag the mouse

Excel provides tips about a function and its arguments

5. Press **Enter** to complete the function. Excel automatically supplies the right parenthesis

tip: *You can click the Enter button (a green checkmark button appearing on the left end of the formula bar) whenever you enter data into a cell instead of pressing the Enter keyboard key. The difference between the two methods is that pressing the keyboard Enter key makes another cell active, whereas clicking the Enter button on the formula bar does not make another cell active*

6. Click cell **H21**, type **=SUM(H10,H17)**, and press **Enter** to complete
   the function

tip: *Notice that you typed a comma between the two cell references in the SUM function, not a colon. In this formula, SUM is adding two single-cell ranges, not the cell range H10 through H17. SUM can have a large number of cell ranges separated by commas in one function, indicating that all the cells in the several cell ranges are summed*

You show your nearly complete worksheet to Stirling. He likes the work you have done, but points out that the entry Country Cupboard is incorrect. The merchant's name is Country Kitchen. Stirling asks you to make that correction.

Editing Cell Entries

Periodically, you may want to make changes to text, values, formulas, or functions. The change may be small and subtle, or you may want to completely replace the contents of a cell. When you modify the contents of a cell, that process is called *editing*.

---

task reference   **Editing a Cell**

- Select the cell that you want to edit
- Click in the formula bar and type any changes
- Press **Enter** to finalize the changes

or

- Select the cell that you want to edit
- Press **F2** and make changes in the selected cell or in the formula bar
- Press **Enter** to finalize the changes

or

- Double-click the cell and make changes to it
- Press **Enter** to finalize the changes

Editing a text entry by using the F2 edit key:

1. Select cell **B14** and press the **F2** function key

2. Press the **Backspace** key eight times to erase *Cupboard*

3. Type **Kitchen** and press **Enter** to complete the change and move to cell B15

You notice that *McCrackens* is misspelled. The correct spelling contains an apostrophe before the letter *s*: McCracken's.

Editing a text entry by typing in the formula bar:

1. Make sure that B15 is the active cell and then click in the formula bar

2. Press the **left arrow** key to move the insertion point between the letters *n* and *s*

3. Type **'** (apostrophe) and press **Enter** to complete the change

Stirling learned that the University Bookstore misquoted its donation percentage. Instead of 10 percent, the correct value is 7.5 percent. Also, he thinks that 900 units is a bit optimistic and asks you to reduce the projection for University Books scrip to 650 units. Stirling asks you to make those changes.

When changes to a cell are extensive, you can save time by simply typing a completely new formula, which replaces the original formula when you press Enter or select another cell. Next, you make the changes that Stirling requests.

Replacing worksheet cells with new contents:

1. Click cell **C9**, type **7.5%**, and press **Enter** to replace the University Bookstore percentage donation value with 7.5%

2. Click cell **E9** and type **650**

3. Press **Enter** to complete the change to cell E9. Notice that the values in cells H9, H10, I9, I10, H21, and I21 all change automatically. See Figure 1.15

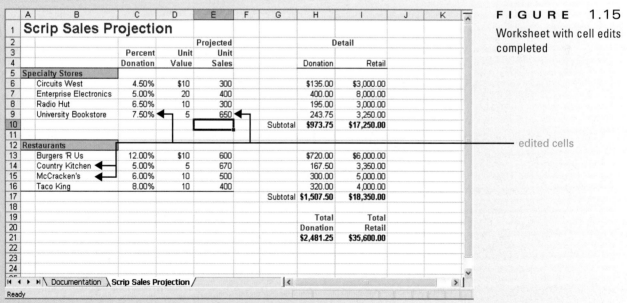

FIGURE 1.15

Worksheet with cell edits completed

edited cells

Saving a Workbook

Whenever you first create a workbook or make extensive changes to a workbook, you should save your work frequently. By storing a workbook as a file on a disk, you can later recall it, make changes to it, and print it without retyping all the cell entries. You can save a workbook under a new filename by selecting Save As in the File menu or, for existing workbooks, you can click Save to replace the workbook with the newer version. If you save a file under a new name (Save As), the original workbook file remains on disk unchanged. Choose the Save As command when you want to preserve the original workbook. Use the Save command when you want to replace the original workbook stored on disk with the new one using the same name. The Standard toolbar has a Save button for your convenience, because Excel users save their workbooks frequently.

---

another**word**   . . . on Saving Workbooks

You can never save your workbook too frequently. If your computer should fail, your current work in memory is lost. Saving your work frequently avoids having to reenter large amounts of information that was lost as a result of the computer failure

---

task reference   Saving a Workbook with a New Name

- Click the **File** menu and then click **Save As**

- Make sure the Save in list box contains the name of the disk and folder in which you want to save your workbook. If not, use the mouse to navigate to the correct disk and folder

- Change the filename in the File name list box

- Click the **Save** button

You have made a number of changes to the Scrip Sales Projection workbook and it is time to preserve those changes.

Saving an altered workbook under a new filename:

1. Click **File** on the menu bar and then click **Save As**. The Save As dialog box opens and displays the current workbook name in the File name text box

2. If necessary, click the **Save in** list box arrow and then select the disk and folder in which you want to save your workbook

3. Click in the **File name** list box, drag across the filename to select the entire name, and type **Scrip2.xls**

4. Ensure that the Save as type list box specifies "Microsoft Excel Workbook (*.xls)" (see Figure 1.16)

5. Click the **Save** button to save your Excel workbook under its new filename. After you save a workbook, you will notice that the new workbook name appears in the Excel Title bar

Stirling tells you that the workbook is designed so that anyone using it can change the values in the Projected Unit Sales column and observe the changes to the worksheet. He wants to save the workbook without any assumptions about the values in the Projected Unit Sales column. That way, a new user can load the Scrip Sales Projection workbook and type in a new set of unit sales assumptions without first deleting the

FIGURE 1.16
Saving a workbook under
a new filename

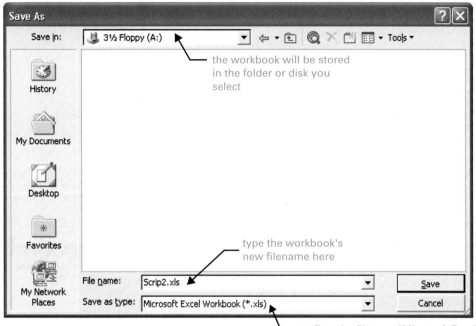

previous assumptions. You are not sure how to empty or delete a cell's contents, and you wonder if simply selecting the cell and pressing Spacebar or typing a zero will clear out the cells. You remember Stirling telling you that whenever you have questions and no one is available for help, you can go to online help. You decide to investigate Excel's online help to answer your question.

Getting Help

Excel provides online help to answer many of your questions. If you don't know how a function is written, or if you have a question about how to complete an Excel task, use Excel's extensive Help feature. Help in Excel is similar to Help in the other Office products. You can obtain help from the Office Assistant, from the Excel Help menu, or from Microsoft's Web site.

---

task reference   Obtaining Help

- Click the **Microsoft Excel Help** command from the **Help** menu (or click the Microsoft Excel **Help** button on the Standard toolbar)

- Type an English-language question on the topic with which you need help and click the **Start Searching** icon to the right of the Search text box

---

Using Help, you can locate an answer to your question about deleting cells' contents.

Obtaining help:

1. Click **Help** on the menu bar and then click **Microsoft Excel Help**. The Microsoft Excel Help dialog box appears

2. If necessary, click the **Search** text box

EXCEL

3. Type **how do I delete cells** in the Search text box, and then click the **Start Searching** icon to display help alternatives

tip: *You can also press the Enter key instead of clicking the Search key*

4. Click **Clear cell formats or contents** in the *Select topic to display* list to display information about removing cells' contents. See Figure 1.17

FIGURE 1.17

Obtaining help

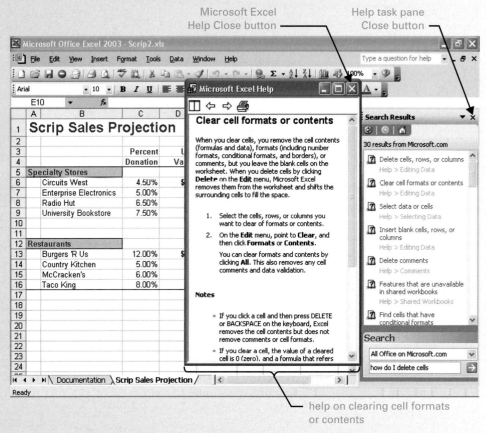

help on clearing cell formats or contents

5. Read the information and print it out if you wish (click the printer icon on the Help toolbar). Click the **Close** button on the Microsoft Excel Help Title bar to close the Help dialog box and click the Close button on the task pane

Now you know how to empty cells' contents. Deleting cells is not quite what Stirling wants. He wants the cells to remain but their contents to be emptied. Now that you have obtained help, you know just what to do.

Clearing Cells

Periodically you may want to delete the contents of a cell containing text, a value, a formula, or a function. You have a couple of choices. You can empty a cell by selecting it with the mouse and then pressing the Delete key or by clicking Edit on the menu bar, then clicking Clear, and finally clicking Contents from the command list. Either way, Excel erases the cell's contents. You might be tempted to simply select the cell and press the Spacebar in order to clear the cell. While the cell *appears* to be empty, it is not—it contains a space. This is the "colorless, odorless, tasteless gas" that later can harm your worksheet. Cells containing one or more spaces (blanks) are treated differently from those that are empty and they are very difficult to locate.

---

task reference — Clearing Cells' Contents

- Click the cell or cells you want to empty
- Press the **Delete** keyboard key

or

- Click **Edit** on the menu bar, click **Clear**, and then click **Contents** to empty the contents of the cell or cells you selected

---

Clearing several cells' contents:

1. Click cell **E6**, drag the mouse down through cell **E9**, and release the mouse

tip: *If you select the wrong cells, simply repeat the click-and-drag sequence in step 1*

2. Press the **Delete** keyboard key to clear the contents of the selected cells

tip: *If you delete the wrong cells, click **Edit** in the menu bar and then click **Undo Clear**. Alternatively, you can press the **Undo** button on the Standard toolbar*

3. Click cell **E13**, drag the mouse down through cell **E16**, and release the mouse

4. Right-click anywhere *within* the selected range of cells. A pop-up command list appears (see Figure 1.18)

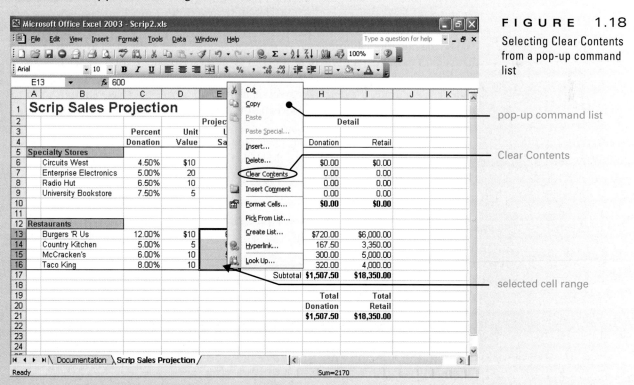

FIGURE 1.18

Selecting Clear Contents from a pop-up command list

5. Click **Clear Contents** from the pop-up command list to clear the contents of the selected cell range

6. Click on any cell to deselect the range

7. To save the workbook under a new name, click **File** and then click **Save As**

8. Select the **Save in** list box and select the disk and folder into which you will save your workbook

9. Type **Scrip3.xls** in the File name list box and click the **Save** button. Excel saves the Scrip workbook

You may notice that the subtotal values and the total values are all zero. Cells that reference empty cell ranges often display zero because empty cells are treated mathematically as if they contained zero. The moment anyone types a value into any cell in the Projected Unit Sales column adjacent to one of the merchant rows, all the subtotals and totals will recalculate nonzero values. Looking at the calculated values for different sets of input information is performing what-if analysis. Doing so can reveal how many units a factory needs to produce in order to be profitable, or how many scrip units a rugby team must sell to produce $3,000 in profits. You will do that next.

Conducting What-If Analysis

The power of a workbook lies in its ability to recalculate the entire workbook quickly whenever you enter new values to see the overall effect of the changes you propose. Using your knowledge of students' preferences and how many students are likely to purchase scrip, you can change the values for some or all of the Projected Unit Sales values for each merchant and observe how much profit each combination of values generates. Cell H21 displays the total donations, or club profit. That value is recalculated whenever you enter new data.

Trying different combinations of scrip sales units in the worksheet produces results that help the team decide where it wants to focus its scrip sales efforts. What-if analysis like this may reveal whether or not selling scrip generates enough profit to be worthwhile. For example, if everyone agrees that students won't purchase enough scrip to make a significant dent in the club's expenses, they may choose to pursue other fundraising opportunities.

Stirling wants to see the profit generated if the team could sell 400 units of each merchant's scrip, except for Burgers 'R Us. "Let's plug in 850 units for Burgers 'R Us and see what happens," an e-mail sent by Stirling concludes.

Conducting what-if analysis by changing all unit sales values:

1. With the Scrip Sales Projection worksheet open, click cell **E6** and drag the mouse down through cell **E9** to select the cell range E6:E9.
   After selecting a range of cells, you can enter data into the range by typing each cell's contents and pressing Enter to move to the next cell. Excel proceeds through the entire list of selected cells, eventually returning to the first cell after you have pressed Enter a sufficient number of times. Using this technique can save time

2. With the cell range E6:E9 highlighted, type **400** and press **Enter**

3. Type **400** in cell E7 and press **Enter**. Repeat this step two more times to fill each of the four selected cells with the value 400

4. Click cell **E13** and drag the mouse down through cell **E16**

5. Type **850** and press **Enter**

6. Type **400** and press **Enter**

7. Repeat step 6 two more times

8. Click any cell to deselect the block of cells. Your worksheet should resemble the worksheet in Figure 1.19

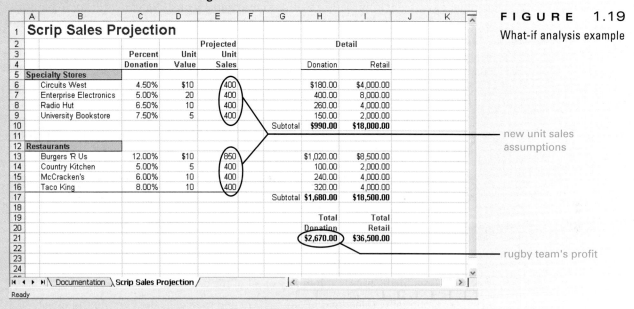

FIGURE 1.19
What-if analysis example

new unit sales assumptions

rugby team's profit

With the new projected sales units, or sales assumptions, the team will produce a total donation of $2,670. That will help a lot to reduce their projected team expenses this season. Naturally, their profit will be more or less if they sell more or fewer units of scrip than shown in the worksheet.

You are ready to show Stirling your work, but you must first print the worksheet so that you can give it to Stirling for review.

Printing a Worksheet

Printing a worksheet provides you and others with a portable copy that you can peruse, review, and modify with a pen or pencil. You can print an Excel workbook or worksheet using the Print command in the File menu or by clicking the Print button on the Standard toolbar. The toolbar Print button is handy because it is a one-click way to produce output. However, the Print button doesn't offer any printing options. On the other hand, the File menu Print command displays the Print Dialog box allowing you to select a number of values and settings to customize your output. You can adjust a number of important settings such as the number of output copies, which pages to print, whether to print all worksheets in the workbook or just the active sheet or a selected range of cells, and which printer to select. Most importantly, you can click the Print dialog box Preview button to preview your output before you print it—an important way to ensure you don't waste paper when you print the workbook.

First, there are a few preliminary tasks to perform before producing a printed worksheet. One of these important tasks is creating a worksheet header and footer. A **header** contains text that appears automatically at the top of each printed page in the header margin, which is located directly above the worksheet print area on a page. A **footer** contains text that appears automatically at the bottom of each printed page in the footer margin, which is located below the worksheet print area on a page. Though worksheet headers and footers are optional, you will find a well-labeled worksheet is a good way to document and identify your printed worksheets.

Labeling an Output with a Header or Footer

If you are printing your worksheet on a shared printer located in a computer laboratory, several people may be producing the same or similar outputs. The best way to label your output is to place either your first and last names on the header or footer or other identifying information such as your company or student identification number.

There is more than one way to identify your output. You can type your name into one of the worksheet cells, perhaps adding it to a documentation worksheet similar to the Scrip workbook's Documentation worksheet, or you can type your name into the worksheet's header or footer. The advantage of a header or footer is that your identification will appear automatically on *each* output page, not just on the first output page. Having your identification appear on every page, with each page numbered, unequivocally identifies the work as yours. Of course, you want to follow the guidelines your instructor provides for output. Here, you will learn how to create a header and footer prior to printing your worksheet.

---

task reference   Creating a Header or Footer

- Click **View** on the menu bar and then click the **Header and Footer** tab
- Click **Custom Header** or **Custom Footer**
- Select the Left section, Center section, or Right section
- Type the header text into any or all of the sections
- Optionally, select text in any section and then click the **Font** button to set font characteristics
- Click **OK** to confirm your header or footer choices
- Click **OK** to close the Page Setup dialog box

An Excel header can appear in three sections: left, center, or right. If you type text in the header's Left section, the text will appear on the top left portion of each page. Text typed into the Center section of the Header dialog box appears in the top center of each page. Text typed into the Right section of the Header dialog box appears in the top right of each page. You decide to place your name on the right side of each page top.

Creating a worksheet header:

1. Ensure that the Scrip Sales Projection worksheet is displayed. Click **View** and then click **Header and Footer**. The Header/Footer tab of the Page Setup dialog box appears

2. Click the **Custom Header** button, click in the **Right section** text box, type **Modified by**, and then type your first and last names following "Modified by"

3. Drag the mouse over the text in the Right section, click the **Font** button, click **Bold** under the Font style list, and then click **OK**. The Header dialog box reappears

4. Click the Header dialog box **OK** button to complete the header. The Page Setup dialog box reappears

Next, you will ensure that your printed worksheet pages contain numbers by placing a page number in the page footer.

Placing a page number in the worksheet footer:

1. With the Page Setup dialog box open, click the **Custom Footer** button, click in the **Center section** text box, and click the **Page Number** button. The characters *&[Page]* appear in the Center section. The symbol represents a page number variable that automatically numbers pages in sequence beginning with 1

2. Click the Footer dialog box **OK** button. The Page Setup dialog box reappears. Figure 1.20 shows the Page Setup dialog box. Of course, your page header will be slightly different because you have typed your own name where *Stirling Leonard* appears in the header preview text box

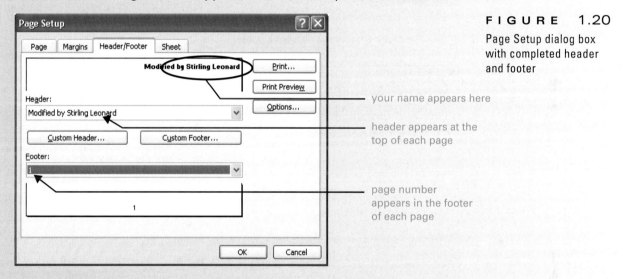

FIGURE 1.20

Page Setup dialog box with completed header and footer

your name appears here

header appears at the top of each page

page number appears in the footer of each page

3. Click the **OK** button in the Page Setup dialog box to complete the footer. The dialog box closes

Previewing Output

Before you print any worksheet, you should preview it. Previewing output lets you catch any small errors that might cause more pages to print than you expected. Page margins, font size, and header and footer margins all can affect how many pages you print. Previewing your output gives you a chance to make adjustments so that the worksheet prints correctly and on as few pages as possible.

Previewing output:

1. Click **File** on the menu bar

2. Click **Print Preview** command in the File menu. The first page of output appears on the screen. Although the header and footer are unreadable at the standard magnification, you can zoom in to inspect them

EXCEL

tip: *Preview output quickly by clicking the **Print Preview** button found on the Standard toolbar*

3. Click the **Margins** button, and then move the mouse to the top right portion of the preview page—near the header. The mouse pointer becomes a magnifying glass. Click the mouse to increase the magnification. The dashed lines indicate the page margins. See Figure 1.21

FIGURE   1.21

Magnified page preview

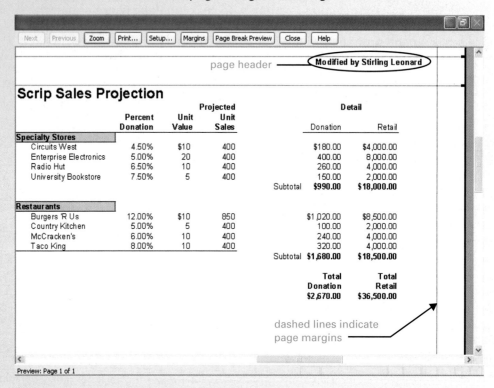

4. Click the **Zoom** button on the Print Preview toolbar. The preview zooms back to a smaller magnification and displays the entire page on the screen

tip: *The Margins button on the Print Preview toolbar is a toggle. Click it to display page margins and click it again to remove the dashed lines indicating the page margins*

5. Click the **Close** button on the Print Preview toolbar to the worksheet

Printing

The output appears to be fine, and the header and footer are where you expected them to be. You are ready to print the worksheet.

---

task reference   **Printing a Worksheet**

- Click **File** and then click **Print**
- Make any needed changes in the Print dialog box
- Click **OK**

or

- Click the **Print** button on the Standard toolbar

You are ready to print your worksheet. The print preview revealed that the entire worksheet would fit on one page. You decide that you want to check the print settings before printing, so you select the Print command from the File menu rather than risk using the Print button—at least until you become more comfortable with printing.

One of the important settings you will want to check in the Print dialog box is in the *Print what* section of the Print dialog box. Which of the three option buttons you choose determines how much and which portions of the workbook or worksheet print. You can choose one of *Selection, Active sheet(s),* or *Entire workbook.* Click *Selection* if you have highlighted a block of cells and want to print only that section of a worksheet. Click *Active sheet(s)* if you want to print the active worksheet or if you have selected more than one worksheet and want to print the selected worksheets from one workbook. Select *Entire workbook* if you want to print all of a workbook's worksheets. You will see where these choices appear in the steps that follow.

Checking the print settings and printing the worksheet:

1. Click **File** on the menu bar and then click **Print**. The Print dialog box opens (see Figure 1.22)

FIGURE 1.22

Print dialog box

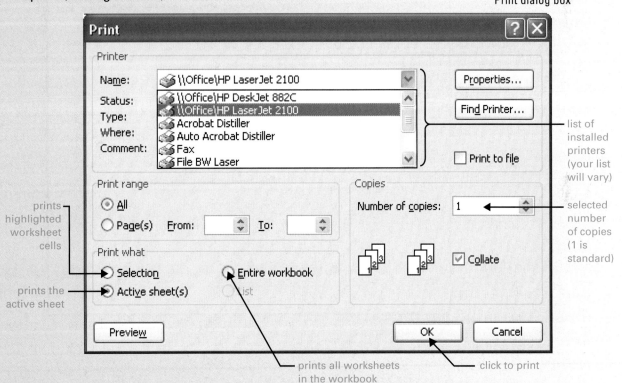

prints highlighted worksheet cells

prints the active sheet

list of installed printers (your list will vary)

selected number of copies (1 is standard)

prints all worksheets in the workbook

click to print

2. To select a different printer than the one listed in the Name list box, click the **Name** list box arrow to reveal a list of installed printers (see Figure 1.22). Then select the printer you want by clicking it. Your Print dialog box will probably have a different number and types of printers listed

3. If necessary, select the **Active sheet(s)** option button in the *Print what* panel of the Print dialog box so that only the Scrip Sales Projection worksheet prints. You do not need to print the Documentation worksheet

4. Click **All** in the Print range section, if necessary

EXCEL

5. Ensure that the Number of copies box displays 1. You need only one copy of the worksheet

6. Click the **OK** button to print the worksheet. Figure 1.23 shows the printed worksheet. Of course, your worksheet will contain your name in the header instead of Stirling Leonard

FIGURE   1.23

Printed Scrip Sales
Projection worksheet

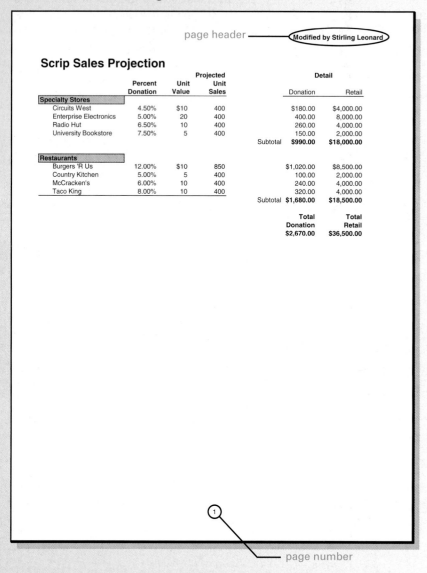

Printing Worksheet Formulas

Part of documenting a worksheet and learning how Excel works is printing the worksheet's formulas. Typically, businesses do not require that reports showing Excel worksheet results also show the formulas. However, you may want to refer to both the worksheet output and the formulas that produced that output. Additionally, your instructor may want to view the worksheet formulas so that she or he can see exactly what formulas and functions you used to produce the results. In any case, it is helpful to know exactly how to print worksheet formulas in case Stirling wants to study them and give you suggestions.

task reference   Printing Worksheet Formulas

- Click **Tools** and then click **Options**
- Click the **View** tab
- Click the **Formulas** check box in the Window options panel to place a checkmark in it
- Click **OK**
- Click **File** and then click **Print**
- Click **OK** to print the worksheet formulas

You ask Stirling if he wants worksheet formulas for documentation. Stirling thinks that is a great idea and thanks you for thinking of it.

help yourself *Press **F1**, type **printing formulas** in the Search text box of the Microsoft Excel Help task pane, press **Enter**, and click the **Print a worksheet with formulas displayed** hyperlink to display help on that topic. When you are finished reading, close the Microsoft Excel Help dialog box and close the task pane*

Printing worksheet formulas:

1. Click **Tools** on the menu bar and then click **Options**. The Options dialog box opens

2. Click the **View** tab on the Options dialog box

3. Click the **Formulas** check box to check it. The Formulas check box is located in the Window options section of the dialog box. See Figure 1.24

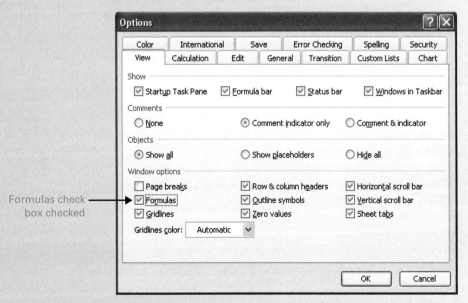

Formulas check box checked

FIGURE 1.24

Selecting the Formulas check box

4. Click **OK** to close the Options dialog box

5. Click the Formula Auditing toolbar **close** button, if necessary, to close the toolbar. The Excel worksheet displays its formulas on screen

6. Drag the **horizontal scroll arrow** until columns H and I come into view. See Figure 1.25. With the Formulas option selected, you can print formulas for the entire worksheet or for a selection of cells

FIGURE   1.25

Excel formulas on screen

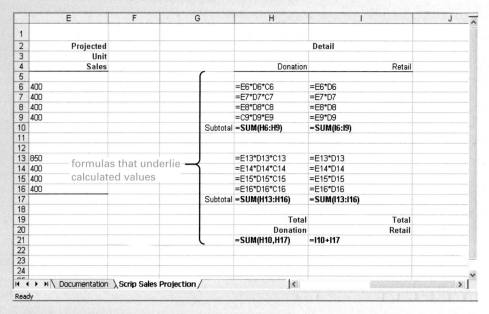

	E	F	G	H	I	J
1						
2	Projected			Detail		
3	Unit					
4	Sales			Donation	Retail	
5						
6	400			=E6*D6*C6	=E6*D6	
7	400			=E7*D7*C7	=E7*D7	
8	400			=E8*D8*C8	=E8*D8	
9	400			=C9*D9*E9	=E9*D9	
10			Subtotal	=SUM(H6:H9)	=SUM(I6:I9)	
11						
12						
13	850			=E13*D13*C13	=E13*D13	
14	400			=E14*D14*C14	=E14*D14	
15	400			=E15*D15*C15	=E15*D15	
16	400			=E16*D16*C16	=E16*D16	
17			Subtotal	=SUM(H13:H16)	=SUM(I13:I16)	
18						
19				Total	Total	
20				Donation	Retail	
21				=SUM(H10,H17)	=I10+I17	
22						
23						
24						

formulas that underlie calculated values

Documentation \ Scrip Sales Projection /

Ready

anotherway
. . . to Display Formulas

Press **Ctrl+`** (hold Ctrl and press accent grave) to display formulas. Press **Ctrl+`** again to toggle back to normal display

7. Click **File** and then click **Print**

8. Click **OK** in the Print dialog box to print the worksheet formulas. Excel prints your worksheet's formulas

tip: *Excel remembers the settings you choose in the Options dialog box. It is best to return those settings to their original values. Once the worksheet starts printing its formulas, revisit the Options dialog box and clear the Formulas check box before continuing work*

9. Click **Tools**, click **Options**, and then click the **View** tab

10. Click **Formulas** check box to clear it and then click **OK**. Excel redisplays values in place of formulas

Closing a Workbook

When you finish a worksheet and the workbook containing it and want to move on to another activity, you close the workbook. If you have made changes to the worksheet that you have not saved, Excel will display a dialog box asking if you want to save the altered workbook before closing it. Normally you should affirm saving a changed workbook, even if you cannot remember making any changes to it. That way, the most current version is saved on disk.

task *reference*	Closing a Workbook
• Click **File**	
• Click **Close**	
• Click **Yes** to save changes	

Your work is finished for now and you are ready to close the Scrip workbook.

Closing an Excel workbook:

1. Click **File** on the menu bar and then click **Close**. A dialog box opens and displays the message "Do you want to save the changes you made to 'Scrip3.xls'?"

tip: *You can close the active workbook by clicking the workbook's **Close Window** button. If the workbook window is maximized, the workbook's Close Window button appears on the right side of the Excel menu bar. Always be careful to not click the Close Application button, which is located on the Excel Title bar. That will cause Excel to close all loaded workbooks, not just the active workbook*

2. Click **Yes** to save the changes you made since you last saved the workbook before closing it. (If you click No, Excel does not save the changes before closing the workbook. If you click Cancel, Excel cancels the close operation and redisplays the active worksheet)

Excel remains available, allowing you to create new workbooks or open existing ones. You can exit Excel because you have finished your work.

Exiting Excel

Exiting Excel unloads it from memory and closes any open workbooks. When you are finished using Excel, it is wise to close it so that the internal memory it occupies becomes available to other programs. Follow these steps to close Excel.

Exiting Excel:

1. Click **File** on the menu bar and then click **Exit**

tip: *You can close Excel by clicking the **Close** button on Excel's Title bar*

Stirling has reviewed your work on the Scrip Sales Projection worksheet and is pleased with your work. He's also enthusiastic about the projected sales and is holding a team meeting next Saturday to discuss the details about obtaining and selling scrip to Western University students.

---

*another*word   . . . on Exiting Excel

Wait to remove your floppy disk containing your Excel worksheets until after you have exited Excel. Sometimes Excel does a final bit of housekeeping on the workbook you stored on your floppy disk, such as writing the last little piece of the workbook to the file just before exiting Excel

---

---

making the grade

1. An Excel worksheet cell can contain text, values, formula, and _____ entries.

2. Indicate which of the following cell entries are text, values, or formulas.
   a. =A1+B2
   b. 11/12/02
   c. 42,350
   d. Sum(A1:B2)
   e. 1st Quarter Sales
   f. 401-555-1212
   g. =11/12/19

3. You could write the formula **=B4+B5+B6+C4+C5+C6** to sum values in the six cells, but the SUM function is a better solution. The SUM function to sum the preceding six cells is _____.

4. You can store an Excel workbook on disk by executing the **File** menu _____ or _____ _____.

5. To empty the contents of a worksheet cell, right-click the cell and then click _____ _____ on the pop-up menu.

SESSION 1.3 SUMMARY

Excel is a spreadsheet program in which you can type text, values, formulas, and functions and conduct what-if analysis by changing worksheet assumptions and viewing the changes. You can edit worksheet entries by selecting a cell, pressing F2, and typing the changes. Completely replace cell contents by selecting a cell and typing the new contents. Save a workbook periodically to preserve its contents on disk. Click File and then click Save to save an existing workbook or Save As to save a workbook under a new filename or for the first time.

Clear cell contents by selecting the cell or cells and then pressing the Delete key. Clearing cells empties their contents; pressing the spacebar does not clear a cell—it places a blank in a cell. Click F1 or click Help on the menu bar to search for help on any Excel topic. Preview a worksheet before printing it to ensure that the correct cells and pages will print. Print a worksheet for review or documentation purposes by clicking File, Print, and selecting print parameters.

When you have completed your Excel work, close the workbook and then close Excel. Excel will prompt you to save any workbooks whose contents have changed since they were last saved. You can choose to save the workbook, not save it, or cancel the Excel exit operation. Be sure to visit the series Web site at www.mhhe.com/i-series for more information.

MICROSOFT OFFICE SPECIALIST OBJECTIVES SUMMARY

- Edit and clear cell entries—MOS XL03S-1-1
- Locate supporting information (help)—MOS XL03S-1-3
- Type into worksheet cells text, values, formulas, and functions— MOS XL03S-2-3
- Preview output—MOS XL03S-5-5
- Add a header and a footer—MOS XL03S-5-7
- Print a worksheet and print a worksheet's formulas—MOS XL03S-5-8

making the grade *answers*

SESSION 1.1

1. spreadsheet

2. What-if

3. workbook, worksheets

4. Standard, Formatting

5. active

SESSION 1.2

1. function

2. a. Formula

   b. Value

   c. Text

   d. Text

   e. Value

   f. Text

   g. Formula

3. =Sum(B4:C6)

4. Save, Save As

5. Clear Contents

task reference *summary*

Task	Location	Preferred Method
Opening an Excel workbook	EX 1.10	• Click **File**, click **Open**, click workbook's name, click the **Open** button
Entering a formula	EX 1.16	• Select cell, type **=**, type formula, press **Enter**
Entering the SUM function	EX 1.19	• Select cell, type **=SUM(**, type cell range, type **)**, and press **Enter**
Editing a cell	EX 1.20	• Select cell, click formula bar, make changes, press **Enter**
Saving a workbook with a new name	EX 1.22	• Click **File**, click **Save As**, type filename, click **Save** button
Obtaining help	EX 1.23	• Click the **Microsoft Excel Help** command from the **Help** menu (or click the Microsoft Excel **Help** button on the Standard toolbar) • Click the **Answer Wizard** tab • In the What would you like to do text box, type an English-language question (replacing the words displayed and highlighted in blue) on the topic with which you need help and click the **Search** button
Clearing cells' contents	EX 1.25	• Click cell, press **Delete** keyboard key
Creating a header or footer	EX 1.28	• Click **View**, click **Header and Footer**, click **Custom Header** or **Custom Footer**, select section, type header/footer text, click the **OK** button
Printing a worksheet	EX 1.30	• Click **File**, click **Print**, click the **OK** button
Printing worksheet formulas	EX 1.33	• Click **Ctrl+`**, click **File**, click **Print**, and click **OK**
Closing a workbook	EX 1.34	• Click **File**, click **Close**, click **Yes** to save

EXCEL

TRUE OR FALSE

1. Only two types of data can be entered into Excel worksheet cells: text and formulas.

2. A cell range consists of one or more cells that form a rectangular group.

3. A cell's contents can be cleared by simply selecting the cell and pressing the Spacebar key.

4. A formula does not always have to begin with an equals sign.

5. Assumption cells are cells upon which other formulas depend and whose values can be changed to observe their effect on a worksheet's entries.

6. You don't have to worry about saving your workbook while you are editing. Excel does this automatically.

FILL-IN

1. A(n) _____ is the name of the entity that holds a text entry, value, or formula.

2. The first spreadsheet program, called _____, was introduced in 1979.

3. To the left of the formula bar is the _____, which contains the name of the active worksheet cell.

4. Click the _____ to make another worksheet of a workbook active.

5. Suppose you type 333-56-8866 in a cell. Excel interprets the entry as a(n) _____ entry.

6. The address of a cell at the intersection of row 43 and column F is _____.

MULTIPLE CHOICE

1. The task pane
   a. is another name for the menu bar.
   b. is a dockable dialog window.
   c. contains the Excel menus.
   d. is also referred to as the workbook window.

2. Clicking a worksheet tab will do what?
   a. erase its contents
   b. print its contents
   c. activate the worksheet whose worksheet tab you clicked
   d. inactivate the worksheet whose worksheet tab you clicked

3. Which of the following is not a valid formula in Excel?
   a. =SUM(A5:A14)
   b. =B4*C4
   c. =10/20/19
   d. 1000–A23

4. An active cell's contents is displayed in the
   a. menu bar.
   b. formula bar.
   c. sheet tab.
   d. scroll box.

5. Which of the following changes the appearance of a worksheet?
   a. menu bar
   b. Standard toolbar
   c. Formatting toolbar
   d. formula bar

6. A header contains text that appears automatically on each printed page. To find the Header dialog box, start by clicking
   a. Format on the menu bar.
   b. Tools on the menu bar.
   c. Insert on the menu bar.
   d. View on the menu bar.

review of concepts

REVIEW QUESTIONS

1. Suppose cells A3 through A5 contained the values 5, 10, and 15, respectively. Discuss what would happen if you typed **SUM(A3:A5)** in cell B15 and pressed **Enter**. *Hint:* You type only the 10 characters shown. Do not assume anything.

2. What is the most important feature of electronic spreadsheet software that makes them especially attractive when compared to the way people created spreadsheets with pencil and paper? In other words, electronic spreadsheets save time. However, which general feature of electronic spreadsheets do you think saves time?

3. Discuss what happens if a text label is wider than the cell in which you enter it and the adjacent cell contains information.

4. Why should you save a workbook to disk?

CREATE THE QUESTION

For each of the following answers, create an appropriate short question.

ANSWER	QUESTION
1. A built-in formula that is a shortcut for complex calculations	_____
2. It is shorter than writing =A1+A2+A3+A4+A5	_____
3. The F2 function key	_____
4. The Office Assistant appears	_____
5. Although the cell appears empty, it is not. It contains the blank text character, and doing this activity can cause problems later	_____
6. You should do this before printing a worksheet to ensure that you don't print more pages than you expected	_____

1. Creating an Income Statement

Carroll's Fabricating, a machine shop providing custom metal fabricating, is preparing an income statement for its shareholders. Betty Carroll, the company's president, wants to know exactly how much net income the company has earned this year. Although Betty has prepared a preliminary worksheet with labels in place, she wants you to enter the values and a few formulas to compute cost of goods sold, gross profit, selling and advertising expenses, and net income. Figure 1.26 shows an example of a completed worksheet.

1. Locate and then open the workbook **ex01Income.xls**

2. Click **File** and then click **Save As** to save the workbook as **<yourname>Income2.xls**

3. Scan the Income Statement worksheet and type the following values in the listed cells: Cell C5, **987453**; cell B8, **64677**; cell B9, **564778**; cell B10, **−43500**; cell B15, **53223**; cell B16, **23500**; cell B17, **12560**; cell B18, **123466**; cell B19, **87672**

4. In cell C10, write the formula **=SUM(B8:B10)** to sum cost of goods sold

5. In cell C12, type the formula for Gross Profit: **=C5−C10**

6. In cell C19, type the formula to sum selling and advertising expenses: **=SUM(B15:B19)**

7. In cell C21, type the formula **=C12−C19** to compute net income (gross profit minus total selling and advertising expenses)

8. In cell A4, type **Prepared by** <your name>

9. Click the **Save** button on the Standard toolbar to save your modified workbook

10. Print the worksheet and print the worksheet formulas

	A	B	C	D	E	F	G	H
1	Carroll's Fabricating							
2	Income Statement							
3	Year Ended December 31, 2004							
4	Prepared by <student's name here>							
5	Sales		987,453					
6								
7	Cost of goods sold							
8	Beginning finished goods inventory	64,677						
9	Purchases	564,778						
10	Less: Ending finished goods inventory	(43,500)	585,955					
11								
12	Gross Profit		401,498					
13								
14	Selling and advertising expenses							
15	Advertising	53,223						
16	Depreciation	23,500						
17	Insurance	12,560						
18	Salaries	123,466						
19	Rent	87,672	300,421					
20								
21	Net Income		101,077					
22								
23								
24								
25								

Income Statement / Sheet2 / Sheet3 /

Ready

FIGURE 1.26

Income statement

2. Creating a Time Card Worksheet

You have a part-time job at Harry's Chocolate Shop, an ice cream parlor near the university. You work Tuesdays, Thursdays, and Saturdays. Every Saturday, you fill out a time card indicating the hours you worked the previous week and leave it on your manager's desk. Last week, you worked Tuesday, October 15, from 9:30 A.M. to 12:00 P.M., took a one-hour lunch break, and then worked until 3:00 P.M. Thursday, you worked 8:00 A.M. to 11:00 A.M., and on Saturday, you worked from 8:00 A.M. until 5:00 P.M. with an hour break from noon until 1:00 P.M. Fill out your time card and write a formula to compute your total work hours for the week (see Figure 1.27).

1. Open the workbook **ex01Timecard.xls**. Notice that there are no worksheet gridlines. This is an option you will learn about later. Several cells, especially those containing formulas, are protected so that valuable prewritten formulas cannot be disturbed inadvertently. Save the workbook as **<yourname>Timecard.xls**.

2. Click cell **B11** and try to type **10**. An error message dialog box opens, demonstrating that some cells are protected from change

3. Click **OK** to close the dialog box, click cell **A2**, type your first and last names, and then press **Enter**

4. Click cell **A4** and type **334**; click cell D4 and type **25**; click cell F4 and type **12**; click cell G4 and type **123-45-6789**

5. Click cell **B6**, type **10/11/04**, and press the **right arrow** key to move to cell C6

6. Repeat step 5 a total of six times, typing the remaining dates, in sequence, into cells **C6** through **H6**

7. Click cell **C7** and type **9:30 am** (type a space before "am") and press **Enter**. You notice that cell C11 displays #NUM! Don't be concerned with that error message. It will go away once you enter all your times in and out that day

8. Click cell **C8**, type **12:00 pm** (remember to type a space before "pm"), click cell **C9**, type **1:00 pm**, click cell **C10**, and type **3:00 pm**. Cell C11 should display the value 4.5.

tip: *If you see the error message* #VALUE! *in cell C11, check to make sure you did not type a semicolon instead of a colon in the time entries*

9. Type in your hours (see the introductory paragraph before these steps for the hours) for Thursday and Saturday, using step 8 as a guide

10. Click cell **I11** ("eye-eleven") and type a SUM formula to total hours for the cell range B11:H11

11. Print your time card worksheet

12. Sign and date your time card on the line above the Employee signature and Date found near the bottom of the time card

13. Save your workbook: Click **File** and then click **Save**

FIGURE 1.27

Time card worksheet

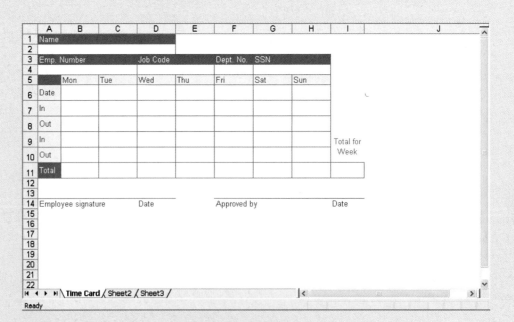

1. Creating a Purchase Order

Sheridan's Fresh Flowers is a retail flower store that produces flower arrangements from flowers that the store orders from wholesalers. Allison Sheridan, the owner, did a quick inventory check last night and found that she needed more supplies. Today is the last Friday of the month, and Allison must place her order with her wholesaler for supplies for the next month. By carefully reading her wholesaler's catalog, Allison knows the wholesale price for each of the flower supplies she needs. In addition to the charges for items Allison orders, her wholesaler charges $75 to ship any size order to Sheridan's Fresh Flowers.

Because Sheridan's purchases supplies for resale, it does not pay state sales tax to the wholesaler for its purchases. Allison needs to know how much each item will cost and the total charges, including shipping.

Open a new workbook and create a new worksheet containing the text and values shown in Figure 1.28. In addition, place the title "Sheridan's Fresh Flowers" in the first row of the worksheet. Write formulas to compute each item's total cost and place them in the Item Total Cost column. Write a formula to sum the item costs and place that formula next to the Subtotal label. In the cell to the right of Shipping (D17), place the shipping cost. Finally, write a formula to sum the Subtotal and Shipping values and place it in the cell to the right of the Total label (D18). Place your name in the worksheet header. Print the worksheet and be prepared to turn it in to your instructor. Print the worksheet formulas. Save your workbook under a new name.

	A	B	C	D
1	Sheridan's Fresh Flowers			
2				
3		Quantity	Unit	Item Total
4	Supplies	Needed	Cost ($)	Cost ($)
5				
6	Baskets	10	15.55	155.5
7	Bows	20	15.95	319
8	Candles	20	4.25	85
9	Cutter	30	7.75	232.5
10	Knife	40	7.75	310
11	Leafshine	20	5.25	105
12	Ribbons	10	30.45	304.5
13	Snapper	20	11.25	225
14	Styrofoam	20	13.56	271.2
15				
16			Subtotal:	2007.7
17			Shipping:	75
18			Total:	2082.7

FIGURE 1.28

Sheridan's flower supplies order worksheet

2. Tracking Inventory with a Worksheet

Thurgood Johnson's Hardware has been offering some new products and wants to see how they are selling. Thurgood Johnson, the store owner, has been keeping track of the number of each item sold. Figure 1.29 shows the number of items Johnson's has sold by month and item.

Open the workbook **ex01Johnsons.xls**. Save the workbook as **<yourname>Johnson.xls**. Modify the worksheet in the following ways. Title the worksheet "Thurgood Johnson's Hardware" by placing that text in cell A1. Place the label **Products** in the cell above the product names. Write formulas to sum the number of items sold each month, placing each of the six sums in their column in row 10. Type formulas to sum the number of items sold for each item for six months in column H—the column immediately to the right of June. Place the label **Totals** in cells H2 and A10. Finally, in cell H10, write a formula that is the grand total of all the items sold for all six months.

Locate the product that sold the fewest items overall for six months and type the **fewest number of items sold** to the right of its row sum. Locate the product that sold the largest number of items overall for six months and type **largest number of items sold** to the right of its row sum. Place your first and last names in one of the unoccupied worksheet cells in row one. Print the worksheet. Save the workbook.

FIGURE   1.29

Johnson's Hardware supplies worksheet

	A	B	C	D	E	F	G	H	I	J	K	L
1												
2		January	February	March	April	May	June					
3												
4	Drills	57	58	54	11	25	10					
5	Hacksaws	46	21	36	10	42	19					
6	Hammers	45	57	29	59	59	22					
7	Levels	34	16	61	10	53	60					
8	Pliers	66	13	10	45	45	65					
9	Saws	33	12	19	32	50	37					
10												
11												
12												
13												
14												
15												
16												
17												
18												
19												
20												
21												
22												
23												
24												
25												

Hardware / Sheet1 / Sheet2 /

Ready

e-business

1. Web Host Price Comparison Worksheet

All About Batteries sells batteries for hundreds of electronic devices ranging from CD players to mobile phones. The business generates most of its revenue through catalog sales. Some customers still prefer to order from the store where they can talk to a salesperson about their needs. Producing and mailing catalogs every three months to thousands of customers and potential customers is costly, and Paul DeMaine, the owner of All About Batteries, wants to open an online store and place the entire catalog online. He knows he must find an online commerce service provider to host his online business. Figure 1.30 shows a list of Web hosting services, their monthly fees for a basic Web hosting package, and the amount of disk storage they provide for their monthly service fees.

Create a workbook that contains this information. Write a formula for each Web host that calculates the cost of the first year of hosting—the setup fee plus 12 times the monthly fee—and place those formulas in the Cost for First Year column. Compute the average monthly cost per megabyte of storage for each listed host, placing that formula in the row corresponding to the Web host name. Place a label next to the Web host that provides the least costly storage per megabyte. Label your output with your name. Execute either Print or Save As, according to your instructor's direction. If you are interested in learning more about Web hosting costs and options, point your Web browser to webhosting.Yahoo.com and read through their pages. Web hosting costs change quickly.

	A	B	C	D	E	F	G	H	I	J	K	L
1	Web Hosts											
2			Monthly	Disk	One-time	Cost	Cost					
3	Company		Service	Storage	Setup	for First	Per					
4	Name		Fee	(MB)	Fee ($)	Year	Megabyte					
5	HalfPrice Hosting		16.63	100	50							
6	HostPro		14.95	40	40							
7	Interland		19.95	150	40							
8	Webhosting.com		29.95	125	50							
9	Verio.com		49.95	60	50							
10												
11												
12												
13												
14												
15												
16												
17												
18												
19												
20												
21												
22												
23												
24												
25												

Sheet1 / Sheet2 / Sheet3 /

Ready

FIGURE 1.30
Web hosts and their fees

2. Redwood Rides

Redwood Rides is one of the most popular amusement parks for roller-coaster fanatics. Boasting 16 roller coasters, 5 of which exceed 200 feet and 70 miles per hour, the park's attendance remains steady throughout its season. As a result of the coasters' popularity, park entrance lines tend to exceed a 45-minute wait during peak times. The theme park experience is what matters the most to customers. Long waits in line will not deter them from coming back again and again.

Customers can purchase Redwood Rides' season tickets, daily passes, and other ticket packages through their Web site, but any purchases must occur 7 to 10 days prior to the visit date. This allows adequate time for processing and mailing tickets to the customers.

Redwood Rides would like to move to an online purchase system for same-day use to reduce the entrance wait and to offer reduced lead time for other ticket packages as well. First, they want to project the net revenue benefit, if any, for online ticket sales over

three years. The park anticipates an overall increase in sales of 3 percent per year with online ticketing. Redwood Rides' analysts project that online purchasing costs will be approximately 7 percent of the total sales.

You are to complete a workbook that compares online sales and traditional sales by filling in formulas for Year 3, the Totals column, and the Net Benefit row. Write formulas that refer to the assumptions cells, B2 through B4, for tickets sold at the booth, tickets sold online, revenues generated by booth sales and online sales, online ticket expense, revenue with and without online sales, and the three year row totals. The cells you are to fill in with formulas are already formatted and highlighted in pale yellow.

Begin by opening the workbook **ex01RedwoodRides.xls** (see Figure 1.31). Place your name in the worksheet header, and print the worksheet, print the worksheet formulas, or save the workbook according to your instructor's directions.

FIGURE 1.31

Redwood Rides online sales analysis

	A	B	C	D	E	F
1	**Redwood Rides online purchase analysis**					
2	Average Ticket Price	$35.00				
3	Average Number Tickets Sold Annually	2,400,000				
4	Online Ticket Expense as % of Sales	7%				
5						
6						
7	**Revenue Benefit Analysis**	Year 1	Year 2	Year 3	Totals	
8	Anticipated Increase in Tickets Sold	0%	3%	3%		
9	Number of Ticket Sales	2,400,000	2,472,000	2,546,160	7,418,160	
10						
11	**Ticket Sales Adjustment**					
12	**Booth Sales**					
13	% of Total Sales	90%	80%	70%		
14	Number Tickets Sold at Booth	2,160,000	1,977,600			
15	Revenue Generated	$75,600,000	$69,216,000			
16	**Online Sales**					
17	% of Total Sales	10%	20%	30%		
18	Number Tickets Sold Online	240,000	494,400			
19	Revenue Generated	$8,400,000	$17,304,000			
20	Online Ticket Expense	$588,000	$1,211,280			
21						
22	Revenue Generated With Online Sales	$83,412,000	$85,308,720			
23	Revenue Generated Without Online Sales	$84,000,000	$84,000,000			
24	**Net Benefit**	($588,000)	$2,398,872			

Online Sales Analysis

Ready

1. Tracking Product Sales by Store Location

The Coffee and Tea Merchant has been selling coffee in the same store in the mall for almost 10 years. They have hired a consultant to build a Web site where they can advertise their store and some of their coffees. The Coffee and Tea Merchant is not ready to build an electronic commerce store, but they do want to be competitive with similar online coffee stores. They want to prepare a worksheet comparing the prices of coffee beans from several coffee regions. Go to the Web and look for three online coffee stores. Record in a worksheet the coffee prices per pound from the three online stores to serve as a comparison. The coffees are shown in Figure 1.32.

Create a new workbook whose worksheet is similar to Figure 1.32. Fill in real store names in place of *Store 1*, *Store 2*, and *Store 3*. Fill in coffee prices in the columns below the store names. Use the Web and search engines to locate prices per pound for the listed coffee types. Search for online coffee stores by going to www.hotbot.com. Hotbot has an excellent search engine. In the search box, type **coffee beans** and click the **Search** button. Then click several links that Hotbot returns in search of three representative online coffee stores.

Write formulas to compute the average price of each type of coffee by summing the prices for each and dividing by three. Place your name and other required identification information in a worksheet header. Either print the worksheet or execute Save As, according to the direction of your instructor.

2. Building a Product Feature and Price Comparison Worksheet

You want to purchase a new personal computer, but you aren't sure which manufacturer offers the best deal for the machine you want. You've drawn up a list of features that your computer should have and you want to compare machines from three manufacturers: Dell, Gateway, and IBM. First, load and print the workbook **ex01Computer.xls**. The worksheet lists features in column A and each of the three computer makers' names at the top of a column.

With the preliminary worksheet as your guide, go to the Web and shop for a Dell, Gateway, and IBM desktop computer, noting any additional price for component upgrades listed in the worksheet. Select a PC category called **Home and Home Office** for each manufacturer, and locate and click the **CUSTOMIZE** button when available. The customization process will reveal individual prices for upgraded hardware. When you have jotted down base prices and any additional component costs, load **ex01Computer.xls** and immediately save the worksheet as **<yourname>Computer2.xls**. Then, enter the values under the manufacturer's column and in the row associated with the machine or component. Write a formula, in the Total row, to compute the total price of each machine. Type your name in cell C1. Print the worksheet.

The Coffee Merchant				
Coffee Price per Pound Comparison				
				Average
	Store 1	Store 2	Store 3	Price
Ethiopia Sidamo				
Kenya AA				
Kona				
Zimbabwe				

FIGURE 1.32

Coffee price comparison

hands-on projects

around the world

1. Comparing Gross National Products of Several Countries

Your economics professor has asked you to look up statistics about the population, surface area, and gross national product (GNP) of eight countries. Furthermore, the economics professor would like you to create a worksheet showing the data and displaying the population density and GNP per capita (a measure of productivity) for each country. Start by opening the workbook called **ex01GNP.xls**, which contains the selected eight countries along with population data and GNP data, and save the worksheet as **<yourname>GNP2.xls**.

To complete the worksheet, type formulas for population density and GNP per capita for each of the eight countries listed. Population density is the number of people per square kilometer. You calculate that number by dividing the population by the surface area. Remember that the population value is in millions, so you will have to multiply the population in the formula by one million; the surface area of each country is in thousands of square kilometers, so remember to multiply that number in the formula by 1,000.

Alternatively, simply divide the population number by the surface area and multiply the entire value by 1,000. For example, the per capita GNP is $290.3*1,000,000,000/36*1,000,000. You can divide both the numerator and denominator by 1 million to reduce the value to $290.3*1,000/36, or approximately $8,000 per capita. Of course, you will use cell references in place of values in all your formulas. Place your name in the worksheet header and print the worksheet. Save the workbook.

2. Water Desalinization Cost and Usage Comparison

Water conservation programs have been active around the globe for some time now, but nowhere is the concern for an adequate water supply stronger than in the Middle East. Saudi Arabia leads the world in desalinization technology. However, Saudi Arabia will have to invest $53.9 billion over the next two decades in additional desalinization plants and water system infrastructures to meet the needs of its growing population. Although the United States has long enjoyed the luxury of readily available freshwater, future water supplies for most southwestern states are a growing concern. While some states have made progress in reducing desalinization costs, an incentive to invest in new technology is not present. Most state desalinization programs are in mothballs, and most states rely on private companies to supply inexpensive water to the public from fresh rivers and lakes.

The daily usage rates of the selected U.S. states appear in the workbook **ex01SaltyWater.xls** along with the usage rates of three prominent cities in Saudi Arabia. Begin by opening the worksheet and converting to gallons. Then, compare the average annual usage rates in Saudi Arabia to the United States. Is the United States lagging in its water conservation programs in those states as compared to Saudi Arabia?

The current average cost of desalinated water in the United States is $650/acre-foot, whereas the cost for normal water is $200/acre-foot. Calculate the average annual costs for each process and the cost differential between the two. In Saudi Arabia the price for desalinated water is 1.87 Saudi riyals per cubic meter. Calculate the average annual cost per person for desalinated water in Saudi Arabia. (The required currency conversion values are at the bottom of the worksheet.) Insert your name in the worksheet header, print the worksheet, and print the worksheet formulas, or save the worksheet according to your instructor's directions.

Pro Golf Academy

Pro Golf Academy is a golf pro shop that provides everything an amateur golfer could want. Operating in a store across the street from the Hidden Hills golf course in La Jolla, California, Pro Golf Academy has several professional golfers on staff who are available to provide golf lessons for reasonable fees. In addition, the store has a large variety of golf clubs, golf balls, bags, apparel, and miscellaneous gifts for sale in its large, modern store. The store is owned by a former touring golf pro, and it is managed by Betty Carroll, who is a former golf pro and member of the Professional Golfers' Association (PGA®). The pro shop employs both full-time sales personnel and part-timers who fill in during especially busy times. These well-trained part-time employees have varying work schedules that accommodate their other jobs' work requirements. Several of the part-timers have asked for a raise from their current rate of $10.25 per hour to $11.45 per hour. Betty Carroll wants to compute the total cost of the raise given the typical work schedule of her part-time employees.

Figure 1.33 shows a worksheet Betty has started. Create a workbook containing a worksheet that resembles Figure 1.33, and write formulas in cells D9:F14 and cell F15. In particular, fill in the Current Wage column with formulas that multiply each employee's hours per week times the current hourly rate. Be sure to write the formula to reference the *cell* containing 10.25 rather than use 10.25 in the formula directly. Write a similar formula to fill in the Proposed Wage column, but this time write the product of Hours per Week values and the proposed hourly rate cell for each employee. Finally, write formulas in the Wage Difference column to compute the difference between the proposed wage and the current wage for each employee. Sum the Wage Difference column at its foot to see the total effect of the proposed wage increase for the company. Place your name in a worksheet cell to identify it, print the worksheet, and then print the worksheet formulas. Save your workbook.

	A	B	C	D	E	F
1	Pro Golf Academy Hourly Employee Wage Analysis					
3	10.25	current hourly rate				
4	11.45	proposed hourly rate				
6	First	Last	Hours per	Current	Proposed	Wage
7	Name	Name	Week	Wage	Wage	Difference
9	Ellen	Fittswater	12			
10	Kim	Fong	8			
11	Ted	Garcia	4			
12	Randy	Hutto	14			
13	Luca	Pacioli	9			
14	Sharon	Stonely	18			

FIGURE 1.33

Employee wage analysis

1. What-If Analysis for a Manufacturer

You work for a manufacturer that builds products and ships them to distributors who, in turn, sell the products to the public. Your supervisor has asked you to create a workbook that allows him to modify a few key values such as the average cost of utilities and the average hourly labor rates and to examine the effect of changing the values. Describe how you would design a worksheet to provide what-if analysis. Differentiate between assumptions and output. Create a small worksheet illustrating your design.

2. Comparison of Two Different Workbooks

Compare and contrast the design of two workbooks called **ex01AnalysisOne.xls** and **ex01AnalysisTwo.xls**. While the results appear the same, the organization and formulas differ between them. Open each one in turn and note its layout, formulas, and visual impact. Which of the two is the better workbook? Explain fully.

did you know?

the *penny is the only coin currently minted in the United States with a profile that faces to the right. All other U.S. coins feature profiles that face to the left.*

the *world's largest wind generator is on the island of Oahu, Hawaii. The windmill has two blades 400 feet long on the top of a tower, 20 stories high.*

the *only house in England that the Queen may not enter is the House of Commons, because she is not a commoner. She is also the only person in England who does not need a license plate on her vehicle.*

former *U.S. Vice President Al Gore and Oscar-winning actor Tommy Lee Jones were roommates at Harvard.*

Chapter Objectives

- Plan and document a workbook
- Create formulas containing cell references and mathematical operators—MOS XL03S-2-3
- Write functions including SUM, AVERAGE, MAX, and MIN—MOS XL03S-2-4
- Use Excel's AutoSum feature to automatically write SUM functions
- Learn several ways to copy a formula from one cell to many other cells—MOS XL03S-5-2
- Differentiate between absolute, mixed, and relative cell reference—MOS XL03S-2-3
- Set a print area—MOS XL03S-5-7
- Move text, values, and formulas—MOS XL03S-5-2
- Insert and delete rows and columns—MOS XL03S-3-3
- Create cell comments—MOS XL03S-4-1

Intercity Recycling Contest

Each year for 12 years, a group of five California cities has held a recycling contest to see which city does the best job of recycling plastic, glass, and aluminum. Cities participating in this year's contest are Arcata, Los Gatos, Pasadena, San Diego, and Sunnyvale. Mayors of each of the competing cities elect a contest organizer from a slate of candidates. Although the recycling contest chairperson position is unpaid, it is a great honor to be chairperson. Many candidates vie for the chairperson's position. To avoid any conflict of interest, contest rules require that the chairperson not be a resident of any of the competing cities.

This year's contest chairperson is Kelly Allison. She is a member of the Los Angeles Chamber of Commerce and is well known in the Los Angeles area for her work with businesses and the Los Angeles city council.

This year, the contestants want to recycle aluminum cans. To help keep track of each city's recycling, Kelly has designated several recycling collection points in each of the five cities. Because the populations of the participating cities vary, a large city such as San Diego will probably recycle the largest number of aluminum cans as its population is over 2.8 million people. To make the contest fair for both large and small cities, the winning city will be the one that recycles the largest number of cans per capita—the number of cans recycled by a city divided by the number of residents of that city.

Each city has a recycling supervisor who monitors and records that city's recycling for every month for the contest's duration. The first of each month, the contest supervisors e-mail the recycling numbers to Kelly Allison. Kelly needs your help to compile the numbers in an Excel worksheet and create the formulas to compute the total recycling by city each month, total recycling for all cities each month, and the all-important per capita recycling value that determines the contest winner. In addition, Kelly wants to know a few statistics about the monthly recycling efforts including the minimum, average, and maximum number of cans recycled.

Figure 2.1 shows the completed Aluminum Can Recycling Contest worksheet. You will be developing the worksheet in this chapter.

FIGURE 2.1

Completed Aluminum
Can Recycling Contest
worksheet

	A	B	C	D	E	F	G	H	I	J	K	L
1	0.02	per can										
2												
3	Aluminum Can Recycling Contest											
4												
5	City	Population	Jan	Feb	Mar	Total	Per Capita					
6	Arcata	15855	10505	24556	12567	47628	3.003974					
7	Los Gatos	28951	24567	21777	26719	73063	2.523678					
8	Pasadena	142547	102376	105876	121987	330239	2.316703					
9	San Diego	2801561	2714664	2503344	1999877	7217885	2.57638					
10	Sunnyvale	1689908	1523665	1487660	1002545	4013870	2.3752					
11		Total	4375777	4143213	3163695	11682685						
12												
13		Minimum	10505	21777	12567							
14		Average	875155.4	828642.6	632739							
15		Maximum	2714664	2503344	1999877							
16												
17	Potential Revenue		87515.54	82864.26	63273.9							
18												

INTRODUCTION

Chapter 2 covers writing formulas in worksheet cells, using Excel functions, copying and moving cell contents, and formatting. In this chapter you will create a new workbook from scratch. First, you will type text to identify the worksheet's columns of numbers. You will write expressions using the Excel functions SUM, MIN, AVERAGE, and MAX. Using Excel's AutoSum feature, you will build expressions to total columns by selecting cell groups and then clicking the AutoSum to automatically build the SUM function. You will learn to write formulas and then save time by copying them to other cells in the worksheet to create a family of related formulas. Chapter 2 describes the differences between using relative, mixed, and absolute cell references in expressions and the advantages of each form. You will learn how to use spell-checking to reduce the chances of your worksheets containing misspellings and how to save your workbook. Finally, Chapter 2 describes how to adjust a worksheet page's print settings such as print margins and the print area.

CHAPTER OUTLINE

SESSION 2.1 WRITING FORMULAS, USING FUNCTIONS, AND COPYING AND MOVING CELL CONTENTS

In this section, you will learn how to build a worksheet; enter text, formulas, and use Excel functions; and copy and paste formulas to create a family of related formulas.

Planning a Workbook and Its Worksheets

Kelly brainstorms with you about the recycling contest and the structure of the worksheet that will record the recycling values reported by contest supervisors. The worksheet should show in the clearest possible way the following:

- What is the overall purpose of the worksheet?
- What are the important results to display in the worksheet?
- What types of data must the supervisors collect and report back to Kelly in order to compute the results?
- What formulas and functions create the answers? The answer to this question specifies the formulas the worksheet designer must write

FIGURE 2.2

Recycling contest worksheet planning guide

Objective:

Produce a worksheet comparing per capita recycling among cities

Input Data:

1. City names
2. City populations
3. Recycling amounts by city for each of the three months

Calculated Results (formulas):

- Per capita recycling for each city
- Total recycling per month for all cities
- Smallest recycling amount for each month
- Average recycling amount for each month
- Maximum recycling amount for each month
- Three-month recycling total for each city
- Grand total recycling for all cities for the entire contest period
- Total revenue generated for all recycled cans

With the preceding questions in mind, Kelly creates a list answering the questions. The answers will guide her in designing the worksheet or directing someone else to do so. The following is a list of specific answers to the preceding worksheet design questions. See Figure 2.2.

With the list of input data values and formulas that Kelly wants to appear in the worksheet, she draws a rough sketch. This helps her decide where totals, labels, and input values look best and allows her to visualize the worksheet's design. Figure 2.3 shows her sketch of the finished worksheet with x representing values or calculated results.

Building a Worksheet

Using Kelly's worksheet planning guide (Figure 2.2) and her rough sketch of the approximate layout (Figure 2.3), you proceed to create the worksheet.

FIGURE 2.3

Worksheet sketch

```
0.02 per can

Aluminum Can Recycling Contest
```

City	Population	Jan	Feb	Mar	Total	Per Capita
Arcata	xxxxx	xxxxx	xxxxx	xxxxx	xxxxxx	xx
Los Gatos	xxxxx	xxxxx	xxxxx	xxxxx	xxxxxx	xx
Pasadena	xxxxxx	xxxxxx	xxxxxx	xxxxxx	xxxxxx	xx
San Diego	xxxxxxx	xxxxxxx	xxxxxxx	xxxxxxx	xxxxxx	xx
Sunnyvale	xxxxxxx	xxxxxxx	xxxxxxx	xxxxxxx	xxxxxx	xx
	Total	xxxxxxxx	xxxxxxxx	xxxxxxxx	xxxxxxxx	
	Minimum	xxxxxx	xxxxxx	xxxxxx		
	Average	xxxxxx	xxxxxx	xxxxxx		
	Maximum	xxxxxx	xxxxxx	xxxxxx		
Potential Revenue		xxxxx	xxxxx	xxxxx		

Starting Microsoft Excel:

1. Start Excel by clicking **Start**, pointing to **Programs**, and clicking **Microsoft Excel**

2. Ensure that both Excel and the empty worksheet are maximized

3. If the task pane is open, then click **View**, and click **Task Pane** to close it

Entering Text

Frequently, people begin building a worksheet by entering most or all of the text (labels). With labels in place, the worksheet has a guide indicating where to place values and formulas. It is a good idea to enter row and column labels first.

Typing a worksheet title and column labels:

1. Click cell **A1**, type **Aluminum Can Recycling Contest**, and press **Enter**. Notice that the title spills over into adjacent cells B1 through C1

2. Click cell **A3** and type **City**

3. Click cell **B3** and type **Population**

4. Enter the remaining column heads as indicated below

tip: *When you are entering data in a row, press the **right arrow** key after typing a cell's entry to finalize the contents and move right one cell in the row. That saves time*

Cell C3: **Jan**

Cell D3: **Feb**

Cell E3: **Mar**

Cell F3: **Total**

Cell G3: **Per Capita**

See Figure 2.4.

FIGURE 2.4
Worksheet with title and column headings in place

tip: *If you make a mistake typing any cell's text, select that cell and simply retype it. For short labels, it is usually faster to retype the text than to edit and correct mistakes*

This year, five cities are entered in the recycling contest. Kelly wants you to enter the city names in alphabetical order in a single column. Enter the city names next.

Entering the names of participating cities:

1. Click cell **A4**, type **Arcata**, and press the **down arrow** keyboard key to move to cell A5

2. Type **Los Gatos** and press the **down arrow** keyboard key to move to cell A6

3. Enter the remaining city names as follows:

Cell A6: **Pasadena**

Cell A7: **San Diego**

Cell A8: **Sunnyvale**

Next, enter summary statistics labels. They identify the values that will appear to their right to indicate the sum, smallest, average, and largest recycling value for each month from the five cities.

Entering summary labels:

1. Click cell **A9**, and type **Total**

2. Click cell **A10** and type **Minimum**

3. Click cell **A11** and type **Average**

4. Click cell **A12**, type **Maximum**, and press **Enter**

Figure 2.5 shows the worksheet containing the labels you just typed.

FIGURE 2.5

Worksheet with all labels entered

	A	B	C	D	E	F	G	H	I	J	K	L
1	Aluminum Can Recycling Contest											
2												
3	City	Population	Jan	Feb	Mar	Total	Per Capita					
4	Arcata											
5	Los Gatos											
6	Pasadena											
7	San Diego											
8	Sunnyvale											
9	Total											
10	Minimum											
11	Average											
12	Maximum											
13												
14												

Entering Values

With a little Web research, Kelly has gotten accurate population data for each of the cities entered in the recycling contest. In addition, the recycling data arrived in Kelly's office and she wants you to enter both the population data and three months' recycling values into the worksheet. Throughout the data entry process, be sure to type the number zero and the number 1 and *not* the letter o ("oh") or the letter l ("ell").

Entering population and recycling values:

1. Click cell **B4** and type **15855**

2. Click cell **B5**, type **28951**, and press **Enter**

3. Enter the remaining population values as follows, pressing Enter after each entry:

Cell B6: **142547**

Cell B7: **2801561**

Cell B8: **1689908**

4. Click cell **C4**, type **10505**, which is the number of cans that Arcata recycled in January, and press the **down arrow** keyboard key

5. Continue entering the recycling values as follows. (Press **Enter** or the **down arrow** key to move down the column to the next cell after typing each entry)

   Cell C5: **24567**

   Cell C6: **102376**

   Cell C7: **2714664**

   Cell C8: **1523665**

6. Click cell **D4**, type **24556**, and press **Enter**

7. Continue entering the recycling values for February as follows (press **Enter** after typing each value):

   Cell D5: **21777**

   Cell D6: **105876**

   Cell D7: **2503344**

   Cell D8: **1487660**

8. Click cell **E4**, type **12567**, press **Enter**, and then continue entering the recycling values for March as follows (press Enter after typing each value):

   Cell E5: **26719**

   Cell E6: **121987**

   Cell E7: **1999877**

   Cell E8: **1002545**

   Figure 2.6 shows the worksheet with the population and three months' recycling values entered.

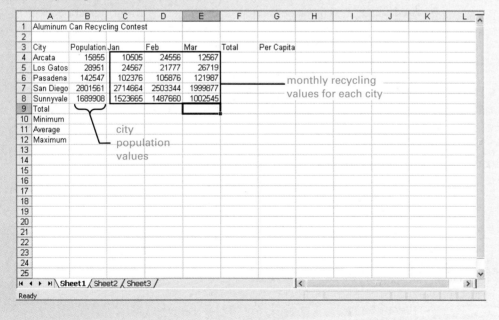

FIGURE 2.6

Worksheet with population and recycling values

Saving Your Worksheet

Once you have invested more than 30 minutes or so developing a worksheet, especially a new one, you should save it—even if you haven't completed it. More times than you can believe, nearly completed worksheets are lost due to power failures, computer glitches, or other mistakes. Because you created the worksheet from scratch, you do not have a backup copy stored safely on disk. Now is a good time to save it.

Saving your worksheet:

1. Click **File**, and then click **Save As**. The Save As dialog box appears
2. Using the Save in list box at the top of the Save As dialog box, navigate to the disk drive and folder where you want to store your workbook
3. Type **Recycle** in the File name text box to change the workbook's name
4. Click the Save As dialog box **Save** button to save the file. The new name appears in the Excel Title bar

Now you have a backup copy safely stored on your floppy disk. If something would happen to reset the computer on which you are working, then you can use the **Recycle.xls** worksheet you stored on disk as the starting point to rebuild any lost work.

Writing Formulas

Now you have the fundamental recycling data on which you can base formulas that compute the results. Among the first results that Kelly wants you to create are the formulas that display each month's minimum, average, and maximum recycling values. The first formula Kelly would like you to write is one to total each month's recycling values.

Creating Sums Automatically

The most frequently used Excel function is SUM. It totals one or more cells. Because the SUM function is so popular, Excel provides the AutoSum button on the Standard toolbar. When you click the AutoSum button, Excel creates a SUM function, complete with a proposed range of cells to be totaled. Excel makes assumptions about which group of contiguous cells you want to total and creates a SUM function based on cells adjacent to the current active cell. You accept Excel's proposed cell range by pressing Enter, or you can select a different range of cells by using arrow keys or the mouse.

***task* reference**   **Writing Formulas**

- Select the cell to contain a formula

- Type **=**

- Type the remainder of the formula

- Press **Enter** or press an arrow key to complete the entry and move to another cell

---

Next, you will use the AutoSum button to create a SUM function to total the recycling values for January.

Calculating the number of cans recycled in January:

1. Click cell **C9**, the cell to contain the total cans recycled in January

2. Click the **AutoSum** $\boxed{\Sigma \,\cdot}$ button on the Standard toolbar. Excel creates a SUM function in cell C9 and suggests a cell range to sum by placing a dashed line around the cell range C4:C8 (see Figure 2.7). That is the correct cell range

FIGURE 2.7

Using AutoSum to build a SUM formula

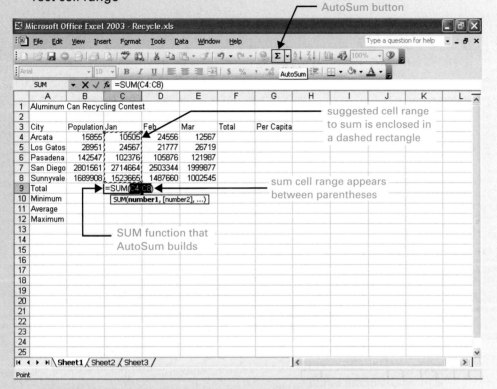

3. Press **Enter** to complete the formula. The result, 4375777, appears in cell C9

Using the same approach, create the remaining two sums. Notice that Kelly did not ask you to total population for the five cities because the total population is not a meaningful value in this application.

Entering formulas to calculate the number of cans recycled in February and March:

1. Click cell **D9**, the cell to contain the total cans recycled in February

2. Click the **AutoSum** $\boxed{\Sigma \,\cdot}$ button on the Standard toolbar. Excel creates the appropriate SUM function in cell D9

3. Press **Enter** to complete the formula. The result, 4143213, appears in cell D9

tip: *If the sum your worksheet displays for column D does not match the preceding value, be sure to check the values in cells D4 through D8 to make sure they match the values shown in Figure 2.7*

4. Click cell **E9**, the cell to contain the total cans recycled in March

5. Click the **AutoSum** button. Excel creates the appropriate SUM function in cell E9

6. Press **Enter** to complete the formula. The result, 3163695, appears in cell E9

---

*another***word**

. . . on Quickly Viewing the Sum of a Selected Cell Range

If you select a range of cells, their sum appears in the status bar located at the bottom of the worksheet. Selecting a range provides you a quick view of the sum without writing a SUM function in the worksheet

---

Modifying AutoSum-Suggested Cell Ranges

Each city's total three-month recycling number is crucial to calculating which city wins the contest. Kelly asks you to enter formulas to total each city's recycling and to create a grand total that is the number of total cans recycled by all cities for three months. Each city's total and the grand total recycling numbers will appear in column F, headed by the column label Total.

---

task reference　　　Modifying an AutoSum Cell Range by Pointing

- With the AutoSum cell range outlined, press an arrow key repeatedly to outline the leftmost or topmost cell in the range through to the desired starting cell of the range

- Press and hold the **Shift** key

- Press the **right** or **down arrow** key repeatedly to move right or down until reaching the last cell in the cell range

- Release the **Shift** key

- Press **Enter** to complete the AutoSum formula

Create the row totals for each city next.

Creating a row total for each city with AutoSum and changing the summed cell range:

1. Click cell **F4**, the cell to contain the total cans recycled by Arcata

2. Click the **AutoSum** button. Excel suggests summing the cell range B4:E4. Because cell B4 is Arcata's population, you will exclude it from the sum in the next steps

3. Press the **right arrow** key to move the outline to cell C4 (see Figure 2.8)

4. Press and hold the **Shift** key

5. Press the **right arrow** key twice to outline the cell range C4:E4

6. Release the **Shift** key

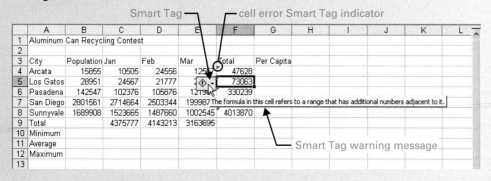

outline indicates cell selected by pointing

	A	B	C	D	E	F	G	H	I	J	K	L
1	Aluminum Can Recycling Contest											
2												
3	City	Population	Jan	Feb	Mar	Total	Per Capita					
4	Arcata	15855	10505	24556	12567	=SUM(C4						
5	Los Gatos	28951	24567	21777	26719	SUM(number1, [number2], ...)						
6	Pasadena	142547	102376	105876	121987							
7	San Diego	2801561	2714664	2503344	1999877							
8	Sunnyvale	1689908	1523665	1487660	1002545							
9	Total		4375777	4143213	3163695							
10	Minimum											
11	Average											
12	Maximum											
13												

partially complete SUM formula

FIGURE 2.8

Changing the beginning cell in an AutoSum cell range

7. Press **Enter** to finalize the formula. The value 47628 appears in cell F4, along with a cell error Smart Tag symbol that appears in the upper-left corner of the cell. The Smart Tag warns that the SUM range has omitted a value adjacent to it. That's okay

You can ask Excel to create more than one SUM function at a time by selecting rows or columns of values with an empty adjacent column or row (respectively) in the range of cells. Then you click the AutoSum button to have Excel build multiple SUM functions in one operation.

Creating multiple SUM functions at once:

1. Click cell **C5** and drag the mouse through cell **F8** to select the cell range C5:F8

2. Click the **AutoSum** button. Excel automatically creates SUM functions in the cell range F5:F8. Additional cell error Smart Tags appear in the cell range F5:F8

3. View a Smart Tag by clicking cell **F5** and then hovering the mouse over the Smart Tag icon. A warning message appears stating "The formula in this cell refers to a range that has additional numbers adjacent to it."(see Figure 2.9)

Smart Tag — — cell error Smart Tag indicator

	A	B	C	D	E	F	G	H	I	J	K	L
1	Aluminum Can Recycling Contest											
2												
3	City	Population	Jan	Feb	Mar	Total	Per Capita					
4	Arcata	15855	10505	24556	125	47628						
5	Los Gatos	28951	24567	21777	◇	73063						
6	Pasadena	142547	102376	105876	1219	330239						
7	San Diego	2801561	2714664	2503344	199987	The formula in this cell refers to a range that has additional numbers adjacent to it.						
8	Sunnyvale	1689908	1523665	1487660	1002545	4013870						
9	Total		4375777	4143213	3163695							
10	Minimum											
11	Average											
12	Maximum											
13												

— Smart Tag warning message

FIGURE 2.9

Smart Tag and warning message

---

anotherword   **. . . about Smart Tags**

Microsoft Office Smart Tags are a set of buttons that are shared across the Office applications. The buttons appear when needed, such as when Excel detects you may have made an error in an Excel formula, and gives the user appropriate options to change the given action or error

---

EXCEL

Finally, Kelly asks you to write a formula for the grand total—the total number of cans the five cities recycled during the three-month contest. You do that next.

Creating a grand total formula:

1. Select cell **F9**, and then click the **AutoSum** button. Excel suggests the SUM range F4:F8

2. Press **Enter** to accept the suggested cell range and complete the SUM formula. The grand total value 11682685 appears in cell F9. This means that the cities involved have recycled nearly 12 million cans (see Figure 2.10)

FIGURE 2.10

Worksheet with row totals and grand total

	A	B	C	D	E	F	G	H	I	J	K	L
1	Aluminum Can Recycling Contest											
2												
3	City	Population	Jan	Feb	Mar	Total	Per Capita					
4	Arcata	15855	10505	24556	12567	47628						
5	Los Gatos	28951	24567	21777	26719	73063						
6	Pasadena	142547	102376	105876	121987	330239						
7	San Diego	2801561	2714664	2503344	1999877	7217885						
8	Sunnyvale	1689908	1523665	1487660	1002545	4013870						
9	Total		4375777	4143213	3163695	11682685						
10	Minimum											
11	Average											
12	Maximum											
13												

◄————————— grand total

The cell error indicators in cells F4 through F8 are distracting to Kelly and she asks you to remove them.

Removing cell error indicators from cells:

1. Select the cell range **F4:F8**

2. Hover the mouse over the Smart Tag, then click the Smart Tag list arrow to open the list of choices

3. Click **Ignore Error** in the list of choices displayed in the Smart Tag list. Excel removes the cell error indicators from all selected cells

4. Click any cell to deselect the cell range

Using Mathematical Operators

Excel formulas begin with an equals sign (=) and are followed by a mixture of cell references, Excel functions, and values mathematically combined into a meaningful expression. When you type an equals sign, you are signaling to Excel that you are writing a formula, not a label or a value. For example, you recall that Excel recognizes 11/22/02 as a value—the date November 22, 2002. However, if you type =11/22/02, Excel knows you are entering a formula that instructs Excel to divide 11 by 22 and divide that result by 02. Excel computes and displays the result, 0.25.

The divide sign (/) is one of several mathematical operators. A **mathematical operator** is a symbol that represents an arithmetic operation. When several mathematical operators occur in a formula, Excel employs the widely recognized **precedence order** to determine the order in which to calculate each part of the formula—which mathematical operators to evaluate first, which to evaluate second, and so on. If a formula con-

FIGURE 2.11
Precedence order of
mathematical operators

Precedence	Operator	Description
1 (highest)	( )	Parentheses. Alters the order of evaluation. Expressions inside parentheses are evaluated first
2	^	Exponentiation. Raises to a power
3	/ or *	Division or multiplication
4 (lowest)	− or +	Subtraction or addition

FIGURE 2.12
Examples of expressions
and precedence rules

Formula	Result	Precedence Rule
A = 30 B = 20 C = 10		
=C+B*A	610.00	Multiplication first followed by addition
=(C+B)*A	900.00	Parentheses force addition to occur first followed by multiplication
=C*B/A	6.67	Equal precedence among the two operators; proceed left to right
=A/B+C	11.50	Division higher precedence than addition
=A/(B+C)	1.00	Parentheses force addition to occur before division
=C/B*A	15.00	Equal precedence among the two operators; proceed left to right
=A+B−C	40.00	Equal precedence among the two operators; proceed left to right

tains more than one operator, the order of precedence determines which operations to perform first. For example, Excel evaluates the formula =A1/(B1+B2)*C1^D1 following the precedence order rules. First, Excel computes the value of B1+B2, because that expression is inside parentheses and saves the result temporarily. Then, Excel computes C1^D1, which is the value in cell C1 raised to the power in cell D1 power, and temporarily saves that partial result. When the remaining operators are all of equal precedence, Excel evaluates an expression left to right. Therefore, Excel divides A1 by the value derived earlier for B1+B2. Finally, Excel multiplies the previous partial result, A1/(B1+B2), by the temporarily saved value of C1^D1.

Whenever Excel encounters an expression in which all operators are of equal precedence, it evaluates the expression left to right. Figure 2.11 shows the Excel mathematical operators in precedence order, first to last. Figure 2.12 shows other examples of formulas, precedence rules, and computed results. You will write formulas using mathematical operators throughout the book.

Writing Arcata's per capita recycling formula:

1. Select cell **G4** to make it the active cell

2. Type **=F4/B4** and then press **Enter** to complete the formula. The value 3.003974 appears in cell G4. In other words, Arcata's recycling amounted to slightly over three cans per person for every person living in the city

EXCEL

While it seems natural to write the remaining Per Capita formulas for the remaining cities, you have a feeling that there may be a better way. You've heard Kelly mention that you can copy formulas that belong to a family of similar formulas, so you wait until you have a chance to talk to her before writing the rest of the per capita recycling formulas in column G.

Using Excel Functions

Based on Kelly's recycling contest worksheet planning guide (Figure 2.2), you need to write formulas to produce statistics for each month. To enter these statistics, you will use three of the Excel functions that are in the same group of functions as the SUM function. The group, called statistical functions, contains several functions including AVERAGE, MAX, and MIN.

An Excel function, you recall from Chapter 1, is a built-in or prerecorded formula that provides a shortcut for complex calculations. Excel functions compute answers, such as the average or maximum, using software instructions that are hidden from view. Excel has hundreds of functions ranging from a function to generate a random number to a function to compute the monthly payment for a particular loan amount. Excel functions are organized in categories containing related functions. The categories are Database, Date & Time, Financial, Information, Logical, Lookup & Reference, Math & Trig, Statistical, and Text.

Functions are written in a particular way. Rules governing the way you write Excel functions are called the function's *syntax*. Syntax rules include properly spelling the function's name, whether or not the function has arguments, and the order in which you list the function's arguments. A function's *argument list* is data that a function requires to compute an answer, and individual list entries are separated by commas. The entire argument list is enclosed in parentheses and follows the function name with no intervening space.

For example, the function SUM(A1, C8:C20, 43.8) contains three arguments in the argument list: a cell reference (A1), a cell range (C8:C20), and a value (43.8). You can write the function name in uppercase, lowercase, or a mixture. Excel converts the function name to uppercase after you enter the complete formula and move to another cell. The general form of an Excel function is this:

```
Function name(argument₁, argument₂, . . . , argumentₙ)
```

A function's name describes what action the function takes. AVERAGE, for example, computes the mean of all arguments in its argument list. The function's *arguments*, which specify the values that the function uses to compute an answer, can be values, cell references, expressions, functions, or an arbitrarily complex combination of the preceding that results in a value.

MIN Function

MIN is a statistical function that determines the minimum, or smallest value, of all the cells and values in its argument list. It is useful for determining, for example, the lowest temperature from a long list of temperatures or finding the lowest golf score from 800 players' scores. The function is written this way:

```
MIN(argument₁, argument₂, . . . , argumentₙ)
```

Often workbook creators write MIN functions with only one argument—a cell range that Excel examines to determine the smallest value. You must specify multiple arguments when you cannot specify the cells in one cell range. For example, to find the smallest value of those in cells A1, A2, A3, B4, B5, C4, and C5, you must write two arguments, one for each cell range:

```
MIN(A1:A3,B4:C5)
```

Like other statistical functions, MIN ignores empty cells and cells containing text when computing its answer.

task reference	Writing a Function Using Insert Function

- Click **Insert** and then click **Function** (or click the **Insert Function** button, *f*ₓ, on the left end of the formula bar)
- Click the *Or select a category* list and then click the Function category of the function type you want
- Scroll the *Select a function* list, if necessary, to locate the function you want
- Click the function in the *Select a function* list box
- Click **OK** to open another dialog box
- Enter information in the edit boxes for each argument, and click **OK**

Kelly wants you to write the MIN function to produce the smallest recycling value for January.

Building a MIN function using the Insert Function command:

1. Ensure that Excel is running and that the Recycle workbook is loaded
2. Select cell **C10**, the cell in which you want the MIN function built
3. Click **Insert** on the menu bar, click **Function**, and then click the **Or select a category list arrow**. A list of available function categories appears
4. Click **Statistical** in the *Or select a category* list to choose the category containing the MIN function
5. Drag the *Select a function* scroll box until you locate MIN in the alphabetically sorted list of statistical functions
6. Click **MIN** in the Select a function list. Figure 2.13 shows the MIN function syntax in the Insert Function dialog box. A brief description appears there also

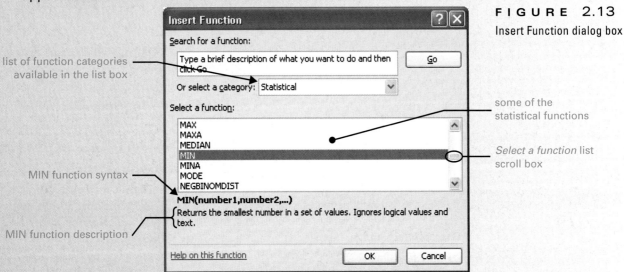

FIGURE 2.13
Insert Function dialog box

7. Click the **OK** button to open the Function Arguments dialog box. Two text boxes appear, one for each of two arguments. The dialog box also displays a description of the function, a description of the argument

list, the current values of the arguments, the current results of the function, and a model of the entire formula. Notice that Excel suggests the cell range C4:C9 for Argument1. That is not the correct cell range, so you will correct it next (see Figure 2.14)

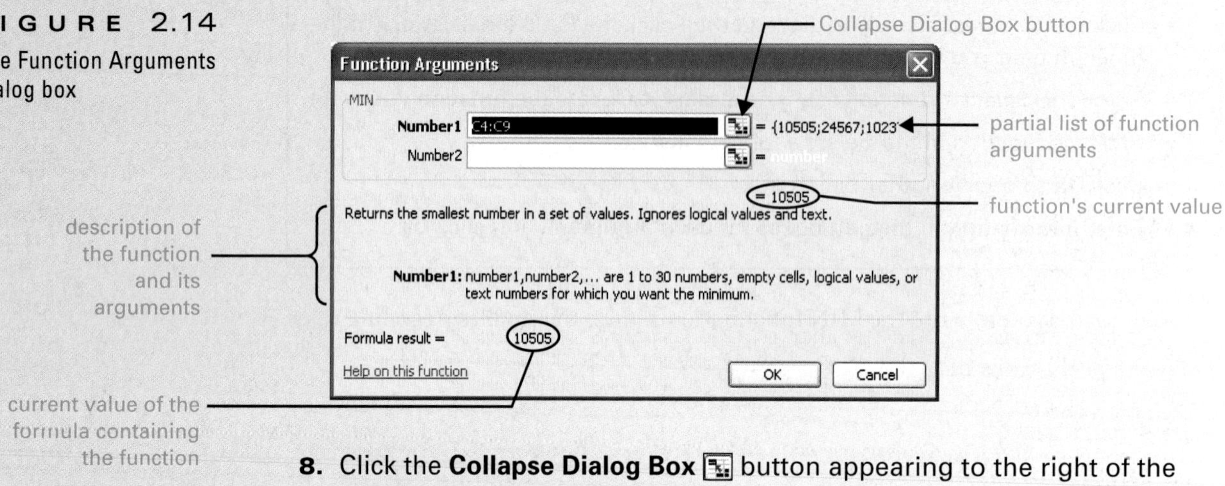

FIGURE 2.14

The Function Arguments dialog box

Collapse Dialog Box button

partial list of function arguments

function's current value

description of the function and its arguments

current value of the formula containing the function

8. Click the **Collapse Dialog Box** [icon] button appearing to the right of the Number1 text box. The Function Arguments dialog box collapses to its Title bar, making it easier for you to locate and point to the correct cell range

9. Click the Function Arguments dialog box Title bar and drag it to the right so that you can see cells C3 through C9

10. Click and drag the cell range C4:C8. Notice that as you are dragging the cell range, the ScreenTip 5R × 1C appears, indicating you have selected five rows and one column

11. Click the **Expand Dialog Box** [icon] button to restore the collapsed dialog box. Notice that the correct range, C4:C8, appears in the Number1 text box, and the minimum value 10505 appears near the bottom of the dialog box next to the text "Formula result ="

12. Click the **OK** button to accept the MIN formula that Excel built for you and return to the worksheet. The minimum value of the selected range, 10505, appears in cell C10

Based on Kelly's plan, you need to enter two more functions to complete January's statistical information. Those functions yet to be added to the worksheet are AVERAGE and MAX.

AVERAGE Function

AVERAGE is a statistical function that determines the average (arithmetic mean) of all the cells and values in its argument list. It is useful for determining, for example, the average grade of all students taking a test (empty cells or cells with labels are ignored), determining the average price of a stock from a list of weekly closing prices, or computing the average rainfall for the year. The function is written this way:

$$\text{AVERAGE}(\text{argument}_1, \text{argument}_2, \ldots, \text{argument}_{30})$$

Kelly wants you to use the AVERAGE function to compute and display the average number of cans recycled each month. You begin by writing an AVERAGE function to determine the average number of cans recycled in January.

help yourself *Press **F1**, type **average function** in the Search text box of the Microsoft Excel Help task pane, press **Enter**, and click the **AVERAGE** hyperlink to display help on the average function. To better view help, click the Help screen's **Maximize** button. If you want to print the help text, click the **Print** button on the Microsoft Excel Help toolbar. When you are finished, click the Help screen **Close** button and close the task pane*

Writing an AVERAGE function:

1. Click cell **C11**, if necessary, to make it the active cell
2. Type **=AVERAGE(C4:C8)** and then press **Enter**. Cell C11 displays 875155.4, the average number of cans recycled in January by all five cities

The last statistical value you need is the maximum number of cans recycled in January. For that formula, you will use the MAX function.

MAX Function

MAX is a statistical function that determines the largest number. MAX can seek out, for example, the highest-priced real estate from a list of sale prices, the highest examination score, or the largest stock price gain over a time period. The function is written this way:

$$\text{MAX}(\text{argument}_1,\ \text{argument}_2,\ \ldots,\ \text{argument}_{30})$$

Kelly wants you to write a MAX function to compute and display the value for the largest number of cans recycled in January.

Writing a MAX function by pointing to cell ranges:

1. Click cell **C12**, if necessary, to make it the active cell, because that cell will contain the formula displaying the maximum number of cans recycled in January
2. Type **=MAX(** to start the formula
3. Move the mouse pointer to cell **C4**, and then click and drag the mouse to select cells **C4** through **C8**. A dashed line indicates the cells you have selected as you drag the mouse
4. Release the left mouse button and press **Enter**. Figure 2.15 shows the worksheet with the three statistical functions displaying January's recycling results

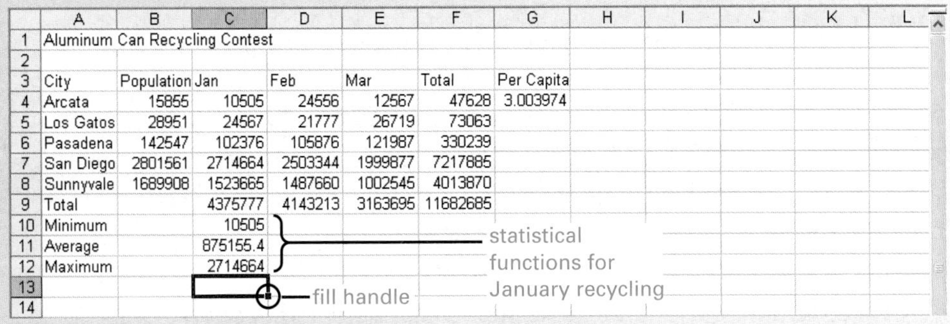

	A	B	C	D	E	F	G	H	I	J	K	L
1	Aluminum Can Recycling Contest											
2												
3	City	Population	Jan	Feb	Mar	Total	Per Capita					
4	Arcata	15855	10505	24556	12567	47628	3.003974					
5	Los Gatos	28951	24567	21777	26719	73063						
6	Pasadena	142547	102376	105876	121987	330239						
7	San Diego	2801561	2714664	2503344	1999877	7217885						
8	Sunnyvale	1689908	1523665	1487660	1002545	4013870						
9	Total		4375777	4143213	3163695	11682685						
10	Minimum		10505									
11	Average		875155.4									
12	Maximum		2714664									
13												
14												

FIGURE 2.15
January's statistical functions

Copying Formulas to Save Time

Worksheets often contain expressions that are repeated across a row, down a column, or both. Although such expressions may consist of the same mathematical operators and functions, any cell references within formulas are slightly different. Whenever you identify families of expressions—formulas that are identical with the exception of their cell references—avoid creating each expression individually. That approach is time consuming and unnecessary. Instead, take advantage of Excel's ability to create copies of formulas. Examples of functions that you can clone to save time are the MIN, AVERAGE, and MAX. While you could re-create these three formulas manually for February and March, Excel can do the same job much more quickly.

Unlike a copy operation that Word carries out, Excel copies formulas and then *adjusts* all cell references in the copied formulas. You can choose to copy one cell's contents (a formula, value, or text) to another cell, you can copy one cell's contents to many cells, or you can copy many cells' contents to an equal-sized many-cell group. The copied cell(s) are called the *source cell(s)*, and the cell or cells to which the contents are copied are known as *target cell(s)*.

There are several equally convenient ways to copy a cell's contents to other cells. You can copy a cell's contents using Excel menu commands, a cell's fill handle, or toolbar buttons. A cell's fill handle is the small black square in the lower-right corner of the active cell (see Figure 2.15).

Copying Formulas Using Copy/Paste

You can copy the contents of one or more cells by copying the cell or cell range to the Clipboard and then pasting the copy into one or more cells in the same worksheet or in a different worksheet. When you copy one or more cells, Excel surrounds the source cell or cells with a dashed line, or marquee, to indicate the Clipboard's contents. Pressing the Escape key empties the Clipboard and removes the dashed line surrounding the source cells.

---

task reference   **Copying and Pasting**

- Select the cell or cells to copy
- Click the **Edit** menu **Copy** command
- Select the target cell range into which you want to copy the source cell's contents
- Click the **Edit** menu **Paste** command

Copying a formula from one cell to many cells:

1. Click cell **G4** to make it the active cell. The cell's formula, =F4/B4, appears in the formula bar

2. Click **Edit** on the menu bar and then click **Copy** to copy the cell's contents to the Clipboard

tip: *You can press **Ctrl+C** instead of using the Copy command. Those of you who keep your hands on the keyboard may favor this keyboard shortcut*

3. Click and drag cells **G5** through **G8** to select them

4. Click **Edit** on the menu bar and then click **Paste**. Excel copies the Clipboard's contents into each of the cells in the selected range and then adjusts each cell's formula to correspond to its new location (see Figure 2.16)

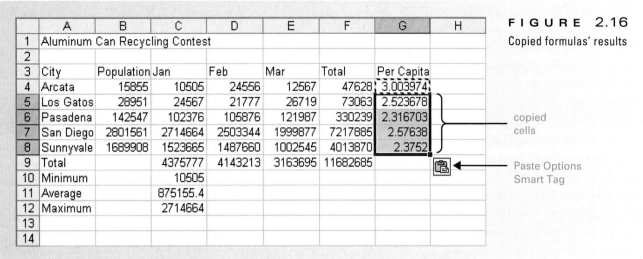

FIGURE 2.16
Copied formulas' results

tip: *You can press* **Ctrl+V** *instead of using the Edit menu Paste command to paste the Clipboard's contents. This may be a faster alternative*

5. Press **Escape** to clear the Clipboard and remove the dashed line from the source cell. Click any cell to deselect the range and view the formulas' results

If you click any cell in the range of cells you just copied, you will see that Excel has made changes to the copied formula. Cell G6 contains the formula =F6/B6. Similarly, Cell G8 contains =F8/B8. The changed cell reference reflects each copied formula's new location compared to the original source cell. For example, cell G8's formula is exactly four rows higher than the source in cell G4. Excel adds four to the row portion of each cell reference to account for its new location four rows higher than the original.

Cell references such as the preceding ones are called relative cell references. *Relative cell references* in formulas always change when Excel copies them to another location. When you copy a function or formula horizontally, Excel changes the column letters automatically while leaving the row number unchanged. When you copy a formula or function vertically, the column letters will stay the same, but Excel changes the row numbers automatically.

Copying Formulas Using the Fill Handle

Sometimes you may find it more convenient and quicker to copy a cell's contents by dragging its fill handle.

---

task reference   Copying Cell Contents
                                       Using a Cell's Fill Handle

- Select the cell whose contents—value, formula, or text—you want to copy. If you want to copy a group of cells, select the cell range you want to copy

- Create an outline of the target cells by clicking and dragging the fill handle of the source cells to the target cells where you want the copied contents to appear

- Release the mouse button

You want to make a copy of the three statistical formulas summarizing January recycling to the other two months, creating six new formulas.

Copying several formulas at once:

1. Click cell **C10** and drag through cell **C12** and release the mouse

2. Move the mouse pointer over the fill handle in the lower-right corner of cell C12 until the pointer changes to a thin plus sign

3. Click and drag the mouse to the right to outline cells **D10** through **E12**. See Figure 2.17

FIGURE 2.17

Dragging the fill handle to copy cells

	A	B	C	D	E	F	G	H
1	Aluminum Can Recycling Contest							
2								
3	City	Population	Jan	Feb	Mar	Total	Per Capita	
4	Arcata	15855	10505	24556	12567	47628	3.003974	
5	Los Gatos	28951	24567	21777	26719	73063	2.523678	
6	Pasadena	142547	102376	105876	121987	330239	2.316703	
7	San Diego	2801561	2714664	2503344	1999877	7217885	2.57638	
8	Sunnyvale	1689908	1523665	1487660	1002545	4013870	2.3752	
9	Total		4375777	4143213	3163695	11682685		
10	Minimum		10505					
11	Average		875155.4					
12	Maximum		2714664					
13								
14								

cell contents being copied

target cells receiving copy

mouse pointer is small plus sign as you drag the fill handle

4. Release the mouse button to complete the copy operation. Excel displays the AutoFill Options Smart Tag

5. Click any cell to deselect the range. Figure 2.18 shows the results after copying the statistical functions

FIGURE 2.18

Worksheet after copy operation

	A	B	C	D	E	F	G	H
1	Aluminum Can Recycling Contest							
2								
3	City	Population	Jan	Feb	Mar	Total	Per Capita	
4	Arcata	15855	10505	24556	12567	47628	3.003974	
5	Los Gatos	28951	24567	21777	26719	73063	2.523678	
6	Pasadena	142547	102376	105876	121987	330239	2.316703	
7	San Diego	2801561	2714664	2503344	1999877	7217885	2.57638	
8	Sunnyvale	1689908	1523665	1487660	1002545	4013870	2.3752	
9	Total		4375777	4143213	3163695	11682685		
10	Minimum		10505	21777	12567			
11	Average		875155.4	828642.6	632739			
12	Maximum		2714664	2503344	1999877			
13							Copy Options	
14							Smart Tag	

Creating and Copying a Revenue Formula

Kelly wants an estimate of the total value of the aluminum cans recycled during the contest. Although prices paid at recycling centers vary by city, the average is two cents per can. So, Kelly would like you to add a formula to calculate the total value of the recycled cans for each month, placing those formulas below the maximum statistic for each month.

Adding text and a value for the approximate value of each recycled can:

1. Click cell **A14**, type **Potential Revenue**, and press **Enter**

2. Click cell **H1**, type **0.02**, and press the **right arrow** key to make cell I1 the active cell. The value 0.02 (two cents) is the assumed average value per recycled can

3. In cell I1, type **per can** and then press **Enter**

Kelly wants you to write a formula for the potential revenue for January for all cans recycled by the five cities.

Writing the recycling revenue formula:

1. Click cell **C14** to make it the active cell

2. Type **=C9*H1** and press **Enter**. The expression is the product of the total number of cans recycled in January and the assumed amount per can, 2 cents

You ask Kelly why she wants the value .02 in cell H1. Instead, why not write the formula =C9*0.02 for January's potential revenue? She responds that the value per can is an *assumption* that she may want to change later to see the effect on the potential value of the recycled cans. If that assumption were written directly into each formula, what-if analysis would require editing the revenue formulas, an unnecessary activity if the assumption is stored in a separate cell.

Next, you will copy the January revenue formula to the right to fill in formulas for February and March. Then, you will copy a formula to two other cells and cause errors to occur. By performing this operation, you will learn how to avoid the problem in other worksheets.

Copying January's revenue formula using copy and paste:

1. Click cell **C14** to make it the active cell

2. Press **Ctrl+C** to copy the selected cell's contents to the Clipboard

3. Click and drag the cell range **D14:E14** and then release the mouse

4. Press **Ctrl+V** to paste the formula into the target cell range, cells D14 through E14. Figure 2.19 shows the results of the copy operation

5. Press **Escape** to empty the Clipboard and remove the outline from cell C14

That did not go as expected. Excel displays an error Smart Tag indicating it has detected an error. Cell D14 displays "#VALUE!" This is a special Excel constant called an

FIGURE 2.19

Worksheet containing errors in copied formulas

	A	B	C	D	E	F	G	H	I
1	Aluminum Can Recycling Contest							0.02	per can
2									
3	City	Population	Jan	Feb	Mar	Total	Per Capita		
4	Arcata	15855	10505	24556	12567	47628	3.003974		
5	Los Gatos	28951	24567	21777	26719	73063	2.523678		
6	Pasadena	142547	102376	105876	121987	330239	2.316703		
7	San Diego	2801561	2714664	2503344	1999877	7217885	2.57638		
8	Sunnyvale	1689908	1523665	1487660	1002545	4013870	2.3752		
9	Total		4375777	4143213	3163695	11682685			
10	Minimum		10505	21777	12567				
11	Average		875155.4	828642.6	632739				
12	Maximum		2714664	2503344	1999877				
13									
14	Potential Revenue		87515.54	#VALUE!	0				
15									
16									
17									

copied formulas containing errors

error value. The constant indicates that something is wrong with the formula or one of its components. Cell E14 displays "0," which is not correct either. Whenever you encounter unexpected results from a formula, the best action is to examine the cell's formula carefully to determine the error. You do that next.

Viewing a cell's contents:

1. Click cell **D14** to make it the active cell

2. Press the **F2** function key to display the cell's contents within the worksheet grid. F2 is called the Edit function key. Excel color-keys both the formula and the cells to which the formula refers so that you can easily see which cells depend on which other cells. Notice that cell D14 contains the formula =D9*I1. The first cell reference, D9, is correct because that is February's recycling total. The second cell reference, I1, is incorrect. It should be H1 instead

3. Click cell **E14** to examine its contents in the formula bar

4. Press the **F2** function key to observe how Excel adjusted the cell references in that formula

5. Press the **Escape** key to end the Edit operation on cell E14

The formula errors occur because Excel adjusts all cell references in copied formulas based on their new position relative to the original cell formula. Occasionally, you alter cell references to avoid the kinds of problems that have occurred here. The answer to avoiding these problems lies in understanding three types of cell references: relative, mixed, and absolute.

Relative, Mixed, and Absolute Cell References

Sometimes, you do not want Excel to adjust all the cell references in a formula that you copy. (Any cell reference you have used so far in this text is a relative cell reference.) Excel automatically adjusts relative cell references to reflect the new location of the copied formulas containing the relative cell references. That is what Excel did to the revenue formula.

When you want a cell reference to remain unchanged no matter where the formula containing it is copied, you use an *absolute cell reference*. You indicate that a cell reference is absolute by placing a dollar sign ($) before both the column and row portions of the cell reference. For example, in the formula =C14/H1, you can make the cell reference to cell H1 absolute by rewriting the formula as =C14/$H$1. No matter where you copy that formula, Excel will not adjust the $H$1 reference—it remains anchored to cell H1.

A third type of cell reference allows you to specify that one portion of a cell reference remains fixed while the other can be adjusted. A *mixed cell reference* is a cell reference in which either the column or the row is never adjusted if the formula containing it is copied to another location. For example, if you did not want the row to change in the preceding reference to cell H1, then rewrite the formula to =C14/H$1. An easy way to remember this notation is to substitute the word "freeze" for $. Then a cell reference such as H$1 reads "H freeze 1" and helps remind you that the row is unchanging when copying the formula containing the cell reference. The other form of mixed cell reference is to hold the column portion unchanged, for example, $H1.

To include a dollar sign in a cell reference as you create a formula, type a dollar sign as you type the cell reference. Alternatively, you can press the F4 function key when you edit a cell's contents to cycle through the four combinations of references for a cell. Figure 2.20 shows examples of relative, mixed, and absolute cell references.

FIGURE 2.20

Relative, mixed, and absolute cell references

Formula	Cell Reference Type
=A43	Relative
=$A43	Mixed
=A$43	Mixed
=$A$43	Absolute

---

task reference Changing Relative References to Absolute or Mixed References

- Double-click the cell containing the formula that you want to edit or click the cell and then press **F2**
- Move the insertion point, a vertical bar, to the left of the cell reference you want to alter
- Press function key **F4** repeatedly until the absolute or mixed reference you want appears
- Press **Enter** to complete the cell edit procedure

To correct the problem that showed up in the revenue formulas, the best course of action is to correct the original source cell and then recopy the cell. Then both the source cell and the target cells will have a corrected copy of the formula. You want to change the original relative-reference revenue formula in cell C14 from =C9*H1 to the formula =C9*$H1 so that Excel does not adjust the column portion of the reference to the per can recycling cell, H1.

Altering a relative cell reference to a mixed reference:

1. Click cell **C14** to make it the active cell

2. Press the **F2** function key to edit the formula in place. Notice that each cell reference in the formula is color coded to an outline surrounding the referenced cell in the worksheet. Called the *Range Finder* feature, it helps you locate cells that the formula references. A cell upon which a formula depends is called a *precedent cell*

3. Ensure that the insertion point is to the right of the multiplication operator and next to or within the cell reference H1 by clicking the mouse or
using the keyboard arrow keys (see Figure 2.21)

FIGURE 2.21

Insertion point while
editing a cell reference

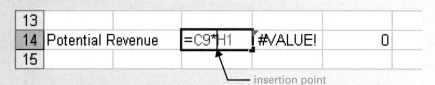

insertion point

4. Press the **F4** function key three times to change the cell reference to $H1

tip: *If you press F4 too few or too many times, continue pressing it slowly until the desired
reference, $H1, appears*

5. Press **Enter** to complete the formula alteration

Now you can recopy the corrected January recycling revenue cell to cells D14 and
E14, corresponding to February and March.

Copying January's corrected revenue formula using copy and paste:

1. Click cell **C14** to make it the active cell

2. Press **Ctrl+C** to copy the selected cell's contents to the Clipboard

3. Click and drag the cell range **D14:E14** and then release the mouse

4. Press **Ctrl+V** to paste the formula into the target cell range, cells D14
through E14

5. Press **Escape** to empty the Clipboard and remove the outline from
cell C14

6. Click any cell to deselect the cell range. Figure 2.22 displays the corrected revenue results

FIGURE 2.22

Worksheet with corrected
revenue formulas

	A	B	C	D	E	F	G	H	I
1	Aluminum Can Recycling Contest							0.02	per can
2									
3	City	Population	Jan	Feb	Mar	Total	Per Capita		
4	Arcata	15855	10505	24556	12567	47628	3.003974		
5	Los Gatos	28951	24567	21777	26719	73063	2.523678		
6	Pasadena	142547	102376	105876	121987	330239	2.316703		
7	San Diego	2801561	2714664	2503344	1999877	7217885	2.57638		
8	Sunnyvale	1689908	1523665	1487660	1002545	4013870	2.3752		
9	Total		4375777	4143213	3163695	11682685			
10	Minimum		10505	21777	12567				
11	Average		875155.4	828642.6	632739				
12	Maximum		2714664	2503344	1999877				
13									
14	Potential Revenue		87515.54	82864.26	63273.9				
15									

corrected revenue cells

Moving Text, Values, and Formulas

When you modify a worksheet, you may want to rearrange some blocks of cells containing text, values, or formulas so that they appear in other locations. For example, you might decide that key values should be grouped together so that they appear in the top of the worksheet. Whatever the reason, you can move information from place to place with little effort. When you move one or more cells, both the contents and the formatting move to the new location. Unlike copying cells, moving cells involves taking a cell's contents and formatting away from its current location and placing them in a new location.

Formulas are not changed when they are moved. Of course, moving text or labels does not change their value either. For example, suppose you moved the formula stored in cell C14 to compute potential revenue for January, =C9*$H1, to cell C2. After the move operation, cell C14 would be empty and the formula =C9*$H1 would occupy cell C2. In other words, Excel does not adjust cell references in the formula that you move. However, all cells that referenced a *moved* formula are adjusted. For example, if you were to move cell H1 containing the value of a single can to H5, any formulas that referenced cell H1 are adjusted to reference cell H5 automatically. That is, moving a cell's contents causes all dependent cells to adjust their references to the new location of the moved formula.

---

task reference   **Moving Cells' Contents**

- Select the cell or cell range that you want to move

- Move the mouse pointer to an edge of the selected range

- When the mouse pointer changes to an arrow, click the edge of the selected cell or cell range and drag the outline to the destination location

- Release the mouse

Kelly would like you to move the four labels in cells A9 through A12 to the right so that they are closer to the values they identify.

Moving four labels:

1. Click and drag the mouse through the cell range **A9:A12**

2. Release the mouse

3. Move the mouse pointer toward an edge of the selected cell range until the mouse pointer changes from a large plus sign to a four-headed arrow.

4. Click any edge of the selected cells and drag the outline to the right so that it surrounds cells B9 through B12 (see Figure 2.23)

5. Release the mouse. Excel moves the cells to their new target location

6. Click any cell to deselect the cell range

Moving a cell's contents to another location is a cut action followed by a paste action. Cutting removes the cell's contents from its current location and places it on the

anotherway
. . . to Move Cells' Contents

Drag the mouse across the source cell or cell range you want to move

Click the **Cut** command in the Edit menu

Drag the mouse across the target cell or cell range to which the contents will move

Click the **Paste** command in the Edit menu

FIGURE 2.23

Moving cells' contents

	A	B	C	D	E	F	G	H	I
1	Aluminum Can Recycling Contest							0.02	per can
2									
3	City	Population	Jan	Feb	Mar	Total	Per Capita		
4	Arcata	15855	10505	24556	12567	47628	3.003974		
5	Los Gatos	28951	24567	21777	26719	73063	2.523678		
6	Pasadena	142547	102376	105876	121987	330239	2.316703		
7	San Diego	2801561	2714664	2503344	1999877	7217885	2.57638		
8	Sunnyvale	1689908	1523665	1487660	1002545	4013870	2.3752		
9	Total		4375777	4143213	3163695	11682685			
10	Minimum		10505	21777	12567				
11	Average		B9:B12 .4	828642.6	632739				
12	Maximum		2714664	2503344	1999877				
13									
14	Potential Revenue		87515.54	82864.26	63273.9				
15									

— indicates current destination cell range

selected cells being moved

outline indicates cell block destination

Clipboard temporarily. Pasting moves the Clipboard contents to the new location. Of course, you can move any block of cells in one operation, regardless of its size. If the destination cell or cell range already contains information, Excel issues a warning and asks you if it is okay to overwrite existing contents. Clicking OK approves overwriting cell contents, while clicking the Cancel button calls off the attempted move operation.

Renaming a Worksheet

A handy way to add documentation to a worksheet is to name the sheet in a meaningful way to reflect its contents. Examine the leftmost sheet tab in the recycling workbook you created. Notice the sheet tab is labeled *Sheet1,* which is the name Excel automatically assigns to the first sheet in a workbook. If your workbook has other worksheets, they are named Sheet2, Sheet3, and so on. (The number of worksheets Excel creates when creating a new workbook depends on how Excel is set up on *your* computer.) Because your worksheet is nearly complete, you will give it a name that reflects its contents.

Renaming a worksheet:

1. Double-click the **Sheet1** sheet tab to select it

2. Type **Recycling Contest** to replace the current name, Sheet1

3. Press **Enter** to complete the worksheet renaming operation. The sheet tab displays the name "Recycling Contest"

Spell-Checking a Worksheet

Excel contains a spell-check feature that helps you locate spelling mistakes and suggests corrections. Comparing words in Excel's dictionary to the words in your worksheet, Excel finds words that appear to be misspelled and suggests one or more corrections. You can choose to leave unchanged each word Excel locates, or you can select an alternative spelling. You should always spell-check your worksheet before presenting it to others. It is easy to overlook misspelled words in any document, and this is especially true for worksheets.

> ### *task reference* Spell-Checking a Worksheet
>
> - Click cell **A1** to begin spell-checking from the top of a worksheet
> - Click the **Spelling** command in the Tools menu or click the **Spelling** [ABC] button on the Standard toolbar
> - Choose to correct misspelled words that the spell-checker identifies
> - Click **OK** to close the dialog box

Kelly knows that a lot of people will see the recycling contest worksheet. She wants to make sure that any misspellings in the worksheet are corrected. She asks you to check the worksheet for spelling mistakes.

Checking a worksheet's spelling:

1. Click cell **A1** to begin spell-checking at the top of the worksheet
2. Click **Tools** on the menu bar and then click **Spelling** to start the spell-check operation

tip: *You can click the **Spelling** [ABC] button on the Standard toolbar to check spelling*

3. Correct any misspellings. A message box opens when all spelling is correct
4. Click **OK** to close the message box

Saving Your Modified Workbook

You have made many changes to your worksheet. It is time to save your work permanently on your disk so that you have a portable copy and to preserve it for future use.

Saving your workbook under its current name:

1. Click **File** and then click **Save**

making the grade

SESSION 2.1

1. Explain how AutoSum works and what it does.
2. Suppose you select cell A14 and type D5+F5. What is stored in cell A14: text, a value, or a formula?
3. You can drag the _____, which is a small black square in the lower-right corner of the active cell, to copy the cell's contents.
4. Evaluation of a formula such as =D4+D5*D6 is governed by order of precedence. Explain what that means in general and then indicate the order in which Excel calculates the preceding expression.
5. Suppose Excel did not provide an AVERAGE function. Show an alternative way to compute the average of cell range A1:B25 using the other Excel statistical functions.

EXCEL

SESSION 2.2 MODIFYING, DOCUMENTING, AND PRINTING A WORKSHEET

In this session, you will complete the worksheet by formatting it to apply a more professional look, increase the width of a column to accommodate longer text entries, insert rows and columns to provide visual boundaries between worksheet sections, undo worksheet changes, and format groups of cells with Excel's AutoFormat command. You will explore how to establish worksheet headers and footers, set page margins, establish a worksheet's print area, and add cell-level documentation and worksheet-wide documentation.

Modifying a Worksheet's Appearance

Kelly wants you to insert two rows above the Aluminum Can Recycling Contest title and to insert a blank row between the recycling Total row and the row containing the Minimum recycling values for each month. Finally, Kelly wants you to move the revenue per can value and its label to cells A1 and B1 so that what-if assumption value is near the top of the worksheet.

Inserting and Deleting Rows

Excel allows you to add rows or columns at any point and accommodates existing work by moving existing rows to accommodate inserted or deleted rows. Likewise, if you insert or delete columns, Excel automatically moves columns to accommodate them. Inserting rows or columns follows the same procedure: You select the number of rows or columns you want to insert and then click the Insert command. After Excel repositions existing rows or columns to accommodate the insertion operation, it adjusts all cell references in formulas to reflect the new locations of cells referenced by the formulas.

---

task reference   **Inserting Rows**

- Click any cell above which you want to insert a row or select a range of cells in several rows above which you want to insert several rows

- Click **Insert** and then click **Rows**. Excel inserts one row for each row you selected

                                                    Inserting Columns

- Click one or more cells in columns to the left of which you want to insert one or more new columns

- Click **Insert** and then click **Columns**. Excel inserts as many new columns as there are in the range you selected

---

Inserting rows into a worksheet:

1. Click cell **A1** and drag the mouse through cell **A2** to indicate the row above which you want Excel to insert two additional rows

2. Click **Insert** on the menu bar and then click **Rows**. Excel inserts two rows at the top of the worksheet and moves existing rows down

3. Click cell **A11** to prepare to insert a blank row between the Total row, containing monthly recycling totals, and the Minimum row

4. Click **Insert** and then click **Rows**. Excel inserts the new row 11 (see Figure 2.24)

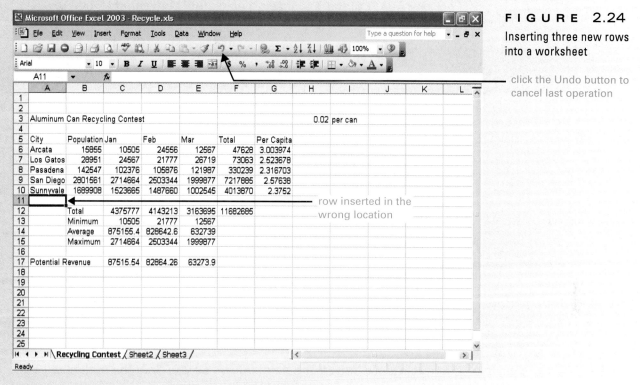

FIGURE 2.24

Inserting three new rows into a worksheet

click the Undo button to cancel last operation

row inserted in the wrong location

Correcting Mistakes with Edit Undo

The last row you inserted is not where you want it to be. To correct that error, you can delete the newly inserted row or you can click the Undo button to cancel the last operation. You can click the row label to the left of column A to select the entire row. Then, click Delete in the Edit menu to delete the row. You will find the Undo method helpful in so many other situations that you decide to use it to cancel the insert row action. Whenever possible, use the Undo method immediately after you realize that you want to reverse one or more actions.

Canceling the previous row insertion action:

1. Click the **Undo** button on the Standard toolbar (see Figure 2.24). Excel deletes the row you previously inserted

Now you are ready to insert a new row in the correct position—between the Total and Minimum rows.

help yourself *Press **F1**, type **insert row** in the Search text box of the Microsoft Excel Help task pane, and press **Enter**. When help appears, click the **Insert blank cells, rows, or columns** hyperlink to display help on inserting cells, rows, or columns. Click the help screen's **Maximize** button if needed. Close the Microsoft Excel Help dialog box and close the task pane when you are through*

EXCEL

Inserting a row into a worksheet:

1. Click cell **A12** to prepare to insert a blank row between the Total row, containing monthly recycling totals, and the Minimum row

2. Click **Insert** and then click **Rows**. Excel inserts the new row—row 12—and moves all other rows below it down one row

Because it is convenient to place cells in a convenient location when they are used in what-if analysis, you move the recycling value per can assumption and its label to cells A1 and A2. That way, anyone who wants to see the effect of changing the value per can to three cents can locate the cell quickly and change it easily.

Moving cells to another location in a worksheet:

1. Select the cell range **H3:I3**, which contains the value and label you want to move

2. Hover the mouse over cell **H3** and slowly move the mouse toward one of the selected cell range's edges until the mouse pointer changes to a four-headed arrow

3. Click the mouse button and hold it down as you drag the outline to cells **A1** through **B1** (see Figure 2.25)

FIGURE 2.25

Moving cells' contents

drop cell range address

outline indicates drop destination

cells being moved

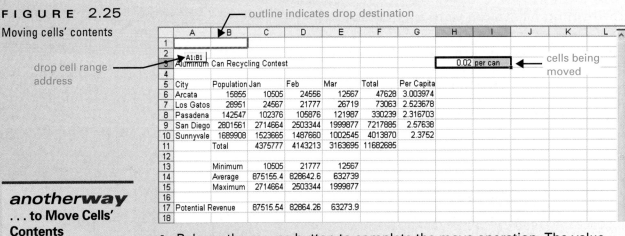

4. Release the mouse button to complete the move operation. The value *0.02* and label *per can* now occupy cells A1 and B1, respectively

5. Click any cell to deselect the cell range

anotherway

. . . to Move Cells' Contents

Select the cell range you want to move

Press **Ctrl+X** to cut the selected cells

Select the cell range to which you want to move the cells

Click **Ctrl+V** to paste the cells to their new location

Establishing Worksheet Headers and Footers

You learned in Chapter 1 how important page headers and footers are in identifying printed output. Kelly wants you to add a header with the title "Aluminum Can Recycling Contest Results" centered on the page. In addition, she wants the worksheet footer to contain your first and last names to identify its author.

Creating a worksheet header and footer:

1. Click **View** on the menu bar and then click **Header and Footer**
2. Click **Custom Header**, click in the **Center section**, type **Aluminum Can Recycling Contest Results**, and click **OK**
3. Click **Custom Footer**, click in the **Center section**, type your first and last names, and click **OK**
4. Click the **Print Preview** button in the Page Setup dialog box to preview the worksheet complete with the new header and footer
5. After you have examined the output to ensure that it looks as you expected, click the **Close** button to close the Preview window and return to the worksheet window

The output looks great. Save the worksheet and then print it so that Kelly can scan the worksheet before you make it available to the public.

Printing a worksheet:

1. Click **File** on the menu bar
2. Click **Print**
3. Click **OK** to print the worksheet

Adjusting Page Settings

You give the worksheet printout to Kelly so that she can comment on it. She is pleased with your work and suggests that you change the left margin to 1.5 inches and set the top, bottom, and right margins to one inch. She wants another printout that contains only rows 3 through 11 of the worksheet.

Setting the Print Area

Unless you specify otherwise, Excel prints the entire worksheet, including any incidental or scratch areas of the worksheet you may have used. Many times you want to print just a selected part of a worksheet. To restrict the print output to part of a worksheet, you select the area to be printed and then execute the Excel Set Print Area command to tell Excel the print range.

Setting a worksheet's print area:

1. Drag the mouse pointer through the cell range **A3:G11** to select it
2. Click **File**, point to **Print Area**, and then click **Set Print Area**
3. Click **File**, and then click **Print Preview** to examine the output prior to printing it. Notice that the statistics do not appear in the output. Neither does the value per can assumption cell in row 1 of the worksheet
4. Click **Close** to return to the worksheet, and click any cell to deselect the area

EXCEL

To print the entire worksheet after you have set the print area, you must remove the print area before printing the worksheet. A worksheet's print area is stored with the worksheet, so Excel remembers if a print area is set or not. Remove the print area by clicking File, point to Print Area, and click Clear Print Area. Once you remove the print area, the entire worksheet will print.

Setting Print Margins

Print margins define the area of a printed page in which a worksheet appears. The left, right, top, and bottom margins define the area. The *left margin* defines the size of the white space between a page's left edge and the leftmost edge of the print area. Similarly, the *right margin* defines the white space between the print area's rightmost position and the right edge of a printed page. Header information appears within the *top margin*, which is the area between the top of the page and topmost edge of the print area. The *bottom margin* is the area at the bottom of the page between the bottommost portion of the print area and the bottom edge of the page. A worksheet's page footer, if any, appears in the bottom margin.

You can set each worksheet's page margins independently using several techniques. Set the margins by executing the Page Setup command in the File menu and clicking the Margins tab. Alternatively, you can click the Margins button in the Print Preview window and move any margin by dragging the dashed line representing each margin.

Setting a worksheet's print margins:

1. Click **File** on the menu bar

2. Click the **Page Setup** command. The Page Setup dialog box opens

3. Click the **Margins** tab

4. Type **1** in the Left spin control box. This sets the left margin to 1 inch

5. Type **1** in the Top, Right, and Bottom spin control boxes (see Figure 2.26). This sets the margins to 1 inch

FIGURE 2.26

Adjusting print margins

line corresponds to the active spinner box— the one with the insertion point

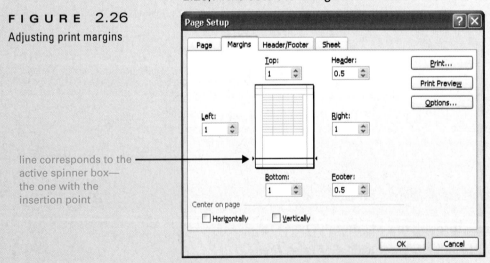

6. Click the **Print Preview** button on the Standard toolbar to preview the worksheet with its changed print margins

7. Click **Close** to close the Print Preview window

You have made a large number of changes to the Aluminum Can Recycling Contest worksheet since you last saved it. It is time to save your work so that you preserve all the changes.

Saving your worksheet:

1. Click **File** on the menu bar
2. Click **Save**

Documenting the Workbook

It is always smart to document your work so that the next person assigned to modify or extend your work can easily and quickly understand the purpose and use of your worksheet. Besides external documentation such as printouts of worksheet formulas and your own notes, you can create internal documentation. As you recall, the first page of a workbook can contain extensive documentation including the author's name, the dates of major changes to the worksheet, and instructions on how to input data and use the worksheet. Small simple worksheets such as the Recycling worksheet require simple instructions. Larger, more complex worksheets require more extensive instructions including which cells constitute the input area, which cells contain formulas whose results depend on the input area(s), and which workbook worksheets contain additional information or instructions.

One valuable but often overlooked source of documentation is the Properties dialog box found on the File menu. The **Properties dialog box** contains several text boxes that you can fill in with helpful information including the fields Title, Subject, Author, Manager, Company, Category, Keywords, and Comments. A workbook's creator can enter his or her name in the Author field. Another way to document a workbook is to include internal notes on individual worksheet cells. Called **comments**, these worksheet cell notes are particularly helpful to indicate special instructions about the contents or formatting of individual cells.

Setting File Properties

Kelly wants you to fill in the Title, Author, and Manager fields of the Property dialog box to record within the worksheet these important pieces of documentation.

FIGURE 2.27

Completed Properties dialog box

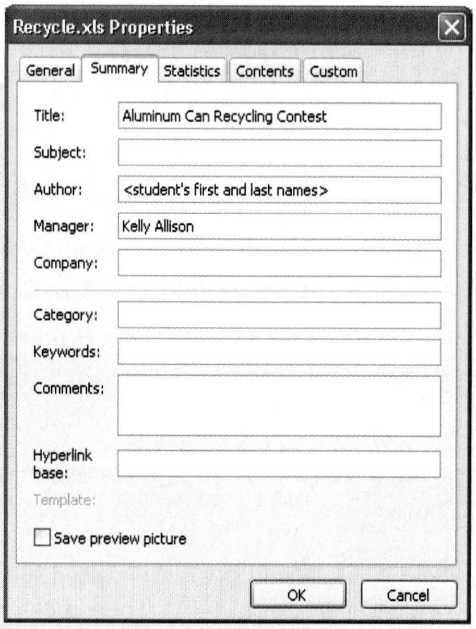

Documenting a worksheet using the Properties dialog box:

1. Click **File** on the menu bar, click **Properties**, and click the **Summary** tab, if necessary

2. In the Title text box, type **Aluminum Can Recycling Contest** and then press the **Tab** key twice to move to the Author text box

3. Type your first and last names in the Author text box and then press the **Tab** key

4. In the Manager text box, type **Kelly Allison** (see Figure 2.27)

5. Click **OK** to close the Properties dialog box

EXCEL

Adding Cell Comments

Kelly also wants you to place a note in cell A1 indicating that the two-cent per can recycling value is approximate. This will help others who use the worksheet in the future to understand that the value is a variable that anyone can change to observe changes in potential revenue from recycling. In cell B5, Kelly wants you to place a comment indicating the source of the population numbers—the World Wide Web.

Cell comments are analogous to sticky notes on which you can write reminders and attach to paper. Like sticky notes, cell comments can remind a worksheet developer or user about special conditions attached to a worksheet or cell, explain any restrictions on user input values, or provide an outline of the steps required to complete an unfinished worksheet.

---

task reference   Inserting a Comment

- Click the cell to which you want to add a comment
- Click **Insert** and then click **Comment** to display the comment text box
- Type the comment
- Click any other cell to close and store the comment

Create the cell comment that Kelly asked you to insert in cells A1 and B5.

Insert comment in cells:

1. Click cell **A1** to make it the active cell

2. Click **Insert** and then click the **Comment** command. The comment text box opens

3. If the comment text box contains text, such as a user or computer name, delete the text

4. Type **Kelly Allison:** (type a space after the colon)

5. Continue by typing the text **Per can value is an approximation. Change it for revenue what-if analysis.** (Be sure to include a period to end the comment's second sentence)

6. Click cell **B5**, click **Insert**, and click **Comment**

7. Repeat steps 3 and 4

8. Type **Population figures obtained from the Web,** and click any cell besides cell B5 to complete the comment and close the text box

9. View the hidden comment by hovering the mouse pointer over cell **A1**. The Comment text box pops up (see Figure 2.28)

10. Hover the mouse pointer over cell **B5** to view that cell's comment

11. Save your worksheet to preserve the changes you have made in this chapter

12. Close Excel

To delete a comment, select the cell containing the comment you wish to delete. Then click Edit on the menu bar, point to Clear, and click Comments to delete the selected cell's comment.

red triangle indicates cell contains a comment

	A	B	C	D	E	F	G	H	I	J	K	L
1	0.02	pe	Kelly Allison: Per can									
2			value is an									
3	Aluminum Ca		approximation.									
4			Change it for revenue									
			what-if analysis.									
5	City	Population	Jan	Feb	Mar	Total	Per Capita					
6	Arcata	15855	10505	24556	12567	47628	3.003974					
7	Los Gatos	28951	24567	21777	26719	73063	2.523678					
8	Pasadena	142547	102376	105876	121987	330239	2.316703					
9	San Diego	2801561	2714664	2503344	1999877	7217885	2.57638					
10	Sunnyvale	1689908	1523665	1487660	1002545	4013870	2.3752					
11		Total	4375777	4143213	3163695	11682685						
12							comment text box					
13		Minimum	10505	21777	12567							
14		Average	875155.4	828642.6	632739							
15		Maximum	2714664	2503344	1999877							
16												
17	Potential Revenue		87515.54	82864.26	63273.9							
18												

making the grade

1. Briefly describe how you might test a worksheet to determine whether its formulas are correct.

2. If you make a mistake in entering a formula, you can reverse the operation by executing the _____ command on the _____ menu.

3. Which of the following is the correct formula to add cells B4 and A5 and multiply the sum by cell C2?
   a. =C2*B4+A5
   b. =B4+A5*C2
   c. =(B4+A5)*C2
   d. =B4+(A5*C2)
   e. none of the above is correct

4. Suppose cell A5 contains the formula =C1+D12 and you *move* that cell's contents to cell C6. After the move, what is the formula in cell C6?
   a. =E2+F3
   b. =C1+C6
   c. =B1+D12
   d. =C1+D12

SESSION 2.3 SUMMARY

Enter a value or text into an Excel cell by selecting the cell and typing the value or text. Excel formulas such as =D3−B4 begin with an equals sign to indicate the entry is not text. Excel provides AutoSum to automatically build a SUM function whose argument is an adjacent, contiguous row or column of values or expressions resulting in values. When necessary, you can adjust the AutoSum cell range suggested by Excel.

Excel provides standard mathematical operators of exponentiation, multiply, divide, add, and subtract. The mathematical operators conform to a precedence order that dictates which parts of an expression are evaluated before other parts. When you want to alter the order in which Excel evaluates expressions in a formula, you can use parentheses to group parts of the formula. For example, you use parentheses to cause Excel to evaluate the expression A1+B2 first in the formula =B17*(A1+B2) even though addition has lower precedence than multiplication.

Three other important statistical functions Excel provides are MIN, AVERAGE, and MAX. MIN determines the smallest value of its arguments. AVERAGE calculates the average value of its argument list. MAX displays the largest value in its list of arguments. Similar to other functions, these three statistical functions ignore empty cells or text cells in argument cell ranges. You can write arguments in the argument list in any order.

Most spreadsheet projects include formulas that are similar to one another. Take advantage of Excel's ability to quickly create formulas by copying a formula to other cells. When you copy a formula such as =SUM(A1:A4) to another cell, Excel creates a copy of that formula and *adjusts* all cell references to reflect the copied formula's new position. Cell adjustment is automatic when you use *relative* cell references. When you do not want Excel to adjust selected cell references in a copied formula, then you must use either *mixed* or *absolute* cell references. Moving a cell's contents to another location has no effect on the formula—all cell references remain unaltered.

Insert additional rows or columns into a worksheet wherever needed. Select a cell above which you wish to insert additional rows or to the left of which you wish to insert additional columns and then execute the Insert Rows or Insert Columns command. Excel automatically adjusts all formulas affected by the Insert procedure to reflect the new location of referenced cells, regardless of whether the cell references are relative, mixed, or absolute. Deleting one or more rows or columns is equally simple. Select the row(s) or column(s) to delete and then execute the Edit menu Delete command. When you delete cells, Microsoft Excel removes them from the worksheet and shifts the surrounding cells to fill the space.

Before printing a worksheet, preview your output. If necessary, adjust a worksheet's print margins by executing Page Setup in the File menu and clicking the Margins tab. Set a worksheet's Print Area to specify printing less than all the nonempty worksheet cells. Document a workbook by filling in the text boxes found in the Properties dialog box that you access from the File menu. In addition, you can use comments to attach internal notes to worksheet cells to explain any unusual circumstances or remind the worksheet user or developer about the content of selected cells.

MICROSOFT OFFICE SPECIALIST OBJECTIVES SUMMARY

- Create formulas containing cell references and mathematical operators— MOS XL03S-2-3
- Differentiate between absolute, mixed, and relative cell reference— MOS XL03S-2-3
- Write functions including SUM, AVERAGE, MAX, and MIN— MOS XL03S-2-4
- Insert and delete rows and columns—MOS XL03S-3-3
- Create cell comments—MOS XL03S-4-1
- Learn several ways to copy a formula from one cell to many other cells— MOS XL03S-5-2
- Move text, values, and formulas—MOS XL03S-5-2
- Set a print area—MOS XL03S-5-7

making the grade *answers*

SESSION 2.1

1. AutoSum automatically creates a sum formula with selected cells adjacent to it in its argument list. An AutoSum on the right end of a row contains the sum of the row, whereas an AutoSum below a column includes all the contiguous cells above it in the argument list. Sometimes AutoSum guesses the range incorrectly. In that case, you have to adjust the cell range.

2. Because an equals sign (=) does not precede the formula, Excel creates a text entry that is "D5+F5."

3. Fill handle

4. Order of precedence consists of rules that govern the order in which Excel evaluates mathematical operators in an expression. Excel first evaluates D5*D6 and then adds that product to D4 to produce the result. In other words, multiplication occurs first in the expression =D4+D5*D6 because multiplication has precedence over addition, the first operator in the formula.

5. You can produce the average of a range by dividing its sum by the number of elements in the range. The equivalent of the formula =AVERAGE(A1:B25) is =SUM(A1:B25)/50

SESSION 2.2

1. Test a worksheet by entering zero to observe the computed values. Use a calculator to compare one or two worksheet formula results with the calculator's answers.

2. Undo, Edit

3. c

4. b

EXCEL

task reference *summary*

Task	Location	Preferred Method
Writing formulas	EX 2.8	• Select a cell, type =, type the formula, press **Enter**
Modifying an AutoSum cell range by pointing	EX 2.10	• Press an arrow key repeatedly to select leftmost or topmost cell in range, press and hold **Shift**, select cell range with arrow keys, release **Shift**, press **Enter**
Writing a function using Insert Function	EX 2.15	• Select a cell, click the Insert Function button, click a function category, click a function name, click **OK**, complete the Formula Palette dialog box, click **OK**
Copying and pasting	EX 2.18	• Select source cell(s), click **Edit**, click **Copy**, select target cell(s), click **Edit**, click **Paste**
Copying cell contents using a cell's fill handle	EX 2.19	• Select source cell(s), drag the fill handle to the target cell(s) range, release the mouse button
Changing relative references to absolute or mixed references	EX 2.23	• Double-click the cell, move insertion point to the cell reference, press **F4** repeatedly as needed, press **Enter**
Moving cells' contents	EX 2.25	• Select the cell(s), move the mouse pointer to an edge of the selected range, click the edge of the selected cell or cell range, drag the outline to the destination location, release the mouse
Spell-checking a worksheet	EX 2.27	• Click cell **A1**, click the **Spelling** button, correct any mistakes, click **OK**
Inserting rows	EX 2.28	• Click a cell, click **Insert**, click **Rows**
Inserting columns	EX 2.28	• Click a cell, click **Insert**, click **Columns**
Inserting a comment	EX 2.34	• Click a cell, click **Insert**, click **Comment**, type a comment, and click another cell

TRUE OR FALSE

1. Whenever Excel encounters an expression in which all operators are of equal precedence, it evaluates the expression right to left.

2. AVG represents the statistical function that determines the average of all the cells and values in its argument list.

3. Relative cell references in formulas will not change when Excel copies them to another location. You must update them accordingly.

4. Formulas are not changed when they are moved.

5. The Properties dialog box contains fields such as Title and Subject that you fill in to provide additional documentation.

6. Some formatting can change the cell's contents.

FILL-IN

1. The _____ function totals one or more cells.

2. While writing a formula, you can use a technique called _____ to select a cell range rather than using the keyboard to type the cell range.

3. The _____ order determines the sequence in which Excel evaluates expressions containing addition, subtraction, multiplication, division, or exponentiation.

4. If you copy a formula such as =B4−C9, Excel _____ the copied formula's cell references.

5. There are three types of cell references: relative, _____, and _____.

6. The menu bar _____ _____ command helps you write a function and fill in the arguments.

MULTIPLE CHOICE

1. Which is not an Excel syntax rule?
   a. properly spelling the function's name
   b. whether or not the function has arguments
   c. the order in which you list the function's arguments
   d. the case in which you write the function name

2. The general name for the cell or cells to which other cells are copied is
   a. target cell(s).
   b. source cell(s).
   c. destination cell(s).
   d. result cell(s).

3. The quickest method to copy a cell's contents to an adjacent cell is by
   a. clicking menus and commands.
   b. pressing Ctrl+X and Ctrl+V keys.
   c. using the cell handle.
   d. using the fill handle.

4. Which of the following is a cell upon which a formula depends?
   a. active cell
   b. results cell
   c. source cell
   d. precedence cell

5. A mixed cell reference is a cell reference
   a. in which Excel automatically adjusts when the formula is copied to another cell.
   b. in which either the column or the row is not adjusted when copied to another cell.
   c. in which multiple functions are used on multiple cells.
   d. that remains unchanged no matter where the formula containing it is copied.

6. This value is displayed when Excel detects an error in writing a formula.
   a. #ERROR!
   b. ?VALUE
   c. ?ERROR!
   d. #VALUE!

review of concepts

REVIEW QUESTIONS

1. Suppose cell D1 contains 0.14, the proposed salary percentage increase for next year, and cells B5 through B8 contain current salaries. Next year's increased salaries—computed from formulas—are in cells C5 through C8. All other cells are empty. You write the formula **=B5*(1+D1)** in cell C5 and then copy that formula to cells C6 through C8. Explain, briefly, what is wrong with the original formula in cell C5 and how you would correct it before recopying the formula.

2. If Excel did not have an AVERAGE function, how would you write an expression to compute the average of cells A5 through A10 using other Excel functions?

3. Describe in two or three sentences what Excel does to modify *copied* formulas.

4. Briefly describe what Excel does, if anything, to the contents of a formula that you *move* to another location. What happens, if anything, to formulas that refer to a moved cell?

5. Does formatting a cell alter its contents? Explain.

6. Experiment with Excel to answer this question. Describe what happens when you enlarge or narrow a column having an unformatted cell whose formula is $=1/7$?

CREATE THE QUESTION

For each of the following answers, create an appropriate, short question.

ANSWER	QUESTION
1. Builds a SUM function automatically	
2. Provides a variety of predefined formats	
3. Do this to view worksheet output before printing	
4. Set this to restrict the cells that Excel prints	
5. This command can reverse a mistake you made in the previous operation	
6. Dragging this object copies formulas to other cells	

1. Managing Employees' Work Hours

You are a project manager for Wexler's Tool and Die Manufacturing and manage a group of five people. Each employee in your group has a different hourly rate, and you must record on a weekly basis the number of hours each employee works, the total wages per employee, and percentage of the whole group's wages that each employee's weekly wage represents. Keeping the information on a worksheet is the most efficient way to record and report employee activity. Alan Barker, the company's chief operating officer, wants you to prepare an Excel worksheet to report your group's weekly hours and gross wages. You create a worksheet to track the hours and wages. (See Figure 2.29.)

1. Open the workbook **ex02Wages.xls** and save it as **<yourname>Wages2.xls**

2. Review the Documentation sheet and then click the **Sheet2** tab to move to that worksheet

3. Insert two new rows above row 1: Click cell **C1**, drag through cell **C2**, and release the mouse. Click **Insert** on the menu bar and then click **Rows**

4. Click cell **A1** to deselect the range and type **Employee**

5. Click cell **B1**, type **Rate**, click cell **C1**, type **Hours**, click cell **D1**, type **Wages**, click cell **E1**, and type **Percentage**

6. Type the following employee hours in the corresponding cells:

   Cell C3: **25**

   Cell C4: **40**

   Cell C5: **30**

   Cell C6: **20**

   Cell C7: **35**

7. Click cell **D3**, type **=B3*C3**, the formula to compute Bushyeager's wage, and press **Enter**

8. Copy Bushyeager's wage formula to the cell range **D4:D7**

9. Click cell **B8** and type **Totals**

10. Select cell range **C8:D8** and click the **AutoSum** $\boxed{\Sigma \cdot}$ button

11. Click cell **E3** and type the formula that represents the employee's percentage of the total wages: **=D3/D$8*100**

12. Copy the formula in cell **E3** to the cell range **E4:E7**

13. Click cell **A10** and type your first and last names

14. Set the left, right, top, and bottom margins to two inches

15. Either execute **Print** or execute **Save As**, according to your instructor's direction

	A	B	C	D	E	F	G
1	Employee	Rate	Hours	Wages	Percentage		
2							
3	Bushyeager	22.5	25	xxxx	xx.xxxx		
4	Goldberg	25	40	xxxx	xx.xxxx		
5	Haralambopoulos	20.75	30	xxxx	xx.xxxx		
6	Laskowski	14.5	20	xxxx	xx.xxxx		
7	O'Reily	27.75	35	xxxx	xx.xxxx		
8		Totals	xxx	xxxxx			
9							
10							
11							
12							
13							
14							
15							
16							

Documentation / Sheet2 /

Ready

FIGURE 2.29

Wexler's Tool and Die Manufacturing worksheet

2. Creating an Invoice

As office manager of Randy's Foreign Car, one of your duties is to produce and mail invoices to customers who have arranged to pay for their automobile repairs up to 30 days after mechanics perform the work. Randy's invoices include parts, sales tax on parts, and labor charges. State law stipulates that customers do not pay sales tax on the labor charges. Only parts are subject to state sales tax. State sales tax is 6 percent. Create and print an invoice whose details appear below. (See Figure 2.30.)

1. Open the workbook **ex02Randys.xls**, and save it as **<yourname>Randys2.xls**

2. Insert rows in which you can enter the customer's name and address: Click cell **A5**, drag the mouse down through cell **A8**, and release the mouse

3. Click **Insert** and then click **Rows**

4. Type the following in the indicated cells:

   cell A5: **Customer:**

   cell B5: **Craig Shaffer**

   cell B6: **21121 Bluff Place**

   cell B7: **Lincoln, NE**

5. Click cell **E11** and type the extended price (unit price times quantity) formula: **=A11*D11**

6. Select **E11** and drag its fill handle to copy the formula in E11 to cells **E12** through **E15**

7. Click cell **E17**, drag the mouse down to cell **E18**, release the mouse, click **Insert**, and then click **Rows**

8. Click cell **D17** and type **Subtotal**. Click cell **D18** and type **Tax**. Click Cell **D24** and type **Subtotal**, and click cell **D26** and type **Total**

9. Click cell **E17** and type **=SUM(E11:E15)**

10. Click cell **E18** and type **=E17*B1**

11. Click cell **E24** and type **=D21+D22**

12. Click Cell **E26** and type **=SUM(E17,E18,E24)**

tip: *Typing commas between the single-cell references allows you to sum cells that are not adjacent to one another*

13. Select cell range **A2:E26** and then click **File**, **Print Area**, **Set Print Area**

14. Click cell **D5**, type your first and last names, and save the worksheet

15. Either **Print** the worksheet and print the worksheet formulas or execute **Save As**, according to your instructor's direction

FIGURE 2.30

Randy's Foreign Car worksheet

	A	B	C	D	E	F	G	H	I	J	K
1	Sales tax	0.06									
2	Invoice										
3	Randy's Foreign Car										
4											
5		Part	Part	Unit	Extended						
6	Quantity	Number	Description	Price	Price						
7		4 GA433	Gasket	23.95							
8		4 SJ-009	Seal set	6.35							
9		1 4432-Wrk	Water pump	123.45							
10		3 BLT-04	Belt	14.55							
11		8 SPAU-31	Spark plug	8.78							
12											
13											
14	Labor		Activity	Flat Rate							
15			Install water pump	150							
16			Install gasket	35							
17											
18											
19											
20											
21											
22											
23											
24											
25											

Sheet1 / Sheet2 / Sheet3

Ready

1. Building a Product Comparison Worksheet

Jacob's Fine Stationers carries different lines of fine pens. You have been asked to help them figure out the profits the store generates from pen sales. The information is as follows: The store has 20 Stylo pens in stock, which sell for $27 each and cost the store $8 each. There are 15 Royal pens in stock, which sell for $45 and cost the store $12. There are 50 Hans pens in the store, which sell for $78 and cost the store $50. There are 6 Tower pens in stock, which sell for $120 and cost the store $60.

Create a spreadsheet with the following column labels: **Pen**, **Quantity**, **Cost**, and **Price**. Enter the pen names Stylo, Royal, Hans, and Tower in the column headed by the label "Pen." Write formulas below the Quantity, Cost, and Price columns that indicate the minimum, average, and maximum values for Quantity, Cost, and Price. Create a column labeled **Profit**. Create a formula and copy it to fill in these cells with the difference between price and cost. Create a column labeled **Total Profits**. Fill the cells in this column with formulas that multiply profit per pen by quantity in stock for each pen. Add a formula below the last entry in the Total Profits per Pen to compute total profits for all pens, assuming all pens in stock sell.

Insert two rows at the top of the worksheet and type your first and last names. Print the worksheet. (See Figure 2.31.)

Change a cell in the worksheet to answer this question: If the store decides not to sell any of its Royal pens, how will total profits be affected? (Type 0 in the Quantity cell for the Royal pen.) Add text to the worksheet indicating that this shows what happens to the total profits if Royal pens are not sold. Print the worksheet (once again), and print the worksheet formulas.

	A	B	C	D	E	F	G	H	I	J	K	L
1	\<your name\>											
2												
3	Pen	Quantity	Cost	Price	Profit	Total Profits						
4	Stylo	20	8	27	xxx	xxx						
5	Royal	15	12	45	xxx	xxx						
6	Hans	50	50	78	xxx	xxx						
7	Tower	6	60	120	xxx	xxx						
8												
9	Minimum	xxx	xxx	xxx								
10	Average	xxx	xxx	xxx								
11	Maximum	xxx	xxx	xxx		xxx						
12												
13												
14												
15												
16												
17												
18												
19												
20												
21												
22												
23												
24												
25												

Sheet1 / Sheet2

Ready

FIGURE 2.31

Jacob's Fine Stationers worksheet

2. Writing a Payroll Worksheet

Bateman Leisure Properties wants you to create a payroll worksheet that provides management with an overview of the hourly workers' pay and taxes. Alicia Hernandez, the human resources manager, provides you with a preliminary worksheet containing employee names—there are quite a few—column labels, and some tax rate information. She asks you to complete the worksheet and save it under a new name when you are done. She would like you to document the tax rate cell and the overtime rate cell with short comments. In preparation for this exercise, open the workbook **ex02Payroll.xls** stored on your disk (see Figure 2.32).

Start by writing a formula for Patti Stonesifer's gross pay. Compute gross pay as regular pay plus overtime pay. Regular pay is the employee's pay for up to 40 hours and is computed as hourly rate times hours worked. Overtime pay is paid for overtime hours—any hours over 40. Compute overtime pay at an hourly rate that is 1.5 times the regular rate times the overtime hours. Be sure to reference cell C2 in the gross pay formula using a mixed cell reference form, C$2 instead of using the constant 1.5. When her gross pay formula is correct, copy it down through the remaining employees' gross pay cells.

In the Federal Tax column, write one formula and copy it to the other employees' rows. Federal tax is gross pay times the federal tax rate found in cell C1. Be sure to reference cell C1 using the mixed reference, C$1. Otherwise, you will not get the correct answer. Write a formula for net pay, remembering that net pay is gross pay minus federal tax (in this example). Copy the net pay formula to other employees' cells.

Add a blank row between the column labels and the first employee row. Select the Federal Tax Rate value stored in cell C1 and type this comment: **This is a flat tax rate for experimentation**. Click the overtime rate cell and type the comment **Normal overtime rate is 1.5 times regular rate. Change this value to review overall changes to gross pay**. (If the comments remain visible after you press Enter, you can make them disappear by clicking **Tools** on the menu bar, clicking **Options**, clicking the **View** tab, and clicking the **Comment indicator only** option button in the Comments section.)

Create a header in page setup, placing your name in the worksheet header (in the Center section), and then print the worksheet. Print the Gross Pay, Federal Tax, and Net Pay formulas for all employee rows. (*Hint:* Check the Formulas option on the View tab of the Options dialog box. Set the print area to include only the three columns containing formulas.) Save the worksheet under the name <**yourname**>**Payroll2.xls**.

FIGURE 2.32
Payroll worksheet

	A	B	C	D	E	F	G	H	I
1		Fed. Tax Rate	0.25						
2		Overtime rate	1.5						
3				Hourly	Regular	Overtime	Gross	Federal	Net
4	ID	First Name	Last Name	Rate	Hours	Hours	Pay	Tax	Pay
5	1301	Patti	Stonesifer	23.10	40	13			
6	1364	Kevin	Pruski	17.00	22				
7	1528	Luca	Pacioli	19.70	40	8			
8	1695	Ted	Nagasaki	21.80	40				
9	2240	Sharon	Stonely	20.30	13				
10	2318	Helen	Hunter	19.50	40	18			
11	2754	Phillipe	Kahn	16.20	40	19			
12	3370	David	Kole	18.70	19				
13	3432	Melinda	English	24.70	40	16			
14	3436	William	Gates	22.50	14				
15	3458	Alanis	Morrison	25.00	26				
16	3609	Annie	Chang	16.40	17				
17	3692	Steve	Ballmer	18.20	40	11			
18	3700	Larry	Ellison	18.80	24				
19	3892	Brad	Shoenstein	18.60	30				
20	3943	Barbara	Watterson	24.30	40	12			
21	4012	Barbara	Minsky	23.10	40	15			
22	4029	Sharad	Manispour	16.60	32				
23	4057	Giles	Bateman	17.60	40	4			
24	4058	Whitney	Halstead	24.20	24				
25	4082	Hillary	Flintsteel	22.00	40	19			
26	4112	Ted	Goldman	23.90	13				
27									

1. Investigating E-Commerce Service Providers

Green Gardens is a one-stop gardening store located in Lincoln, Nebraska. They have been a successful brick-and-mortar store for over 22 years, but their owner, Orlando Madrigal, wants to create an online store that will complement their existing store. Because they do not have room or the expertise to buy computing equipment and software to create an online store, Orlando wants to locate a commerce service provider (CSP) to host the store and provide a complete menu of online services. The CSP provides computer hardware, commerce software, and merchant account processing (to process credit cards). There are several hosting plans available, and each one offers the same basic service. Orlando wants you to find a least-cost provider.

Your investigation reveals that most CSPs charge a one-time setup fee when you sign up for their service, monthly store rental fee to pay for disk space, and transaction fees charged when a customer submits his or her credit card to pay for a purchase. You have found four representative CSPs and want to create a worksheet to compare your costs. Orlando estimates that the online store can sell approximately 10,000 items each month for the first year. Each sale, he estimates, will average $50. Armed with those sales assumptions, you build a worksheet to compare CSP costs.

Figure 2.33 shows the partially complete worksheet. You are to complete the sheet by filling in formulas for the estimated annual cost, the minimum annual cost, and the six statistics showing the minimum, average, and maximum setup fees and monthly rental fee.

Begin by opening the E-Commerce worksheet **ex02EMerchant.xls**. Save the file under the name **<yourname>Merchant2.xls**. Annual costs consist of the sum of the one-time setup fee (for the first year), 12 times the monthly rental fee, and the transaction costs. The transaction costs consist of a fixed per-transaction charge, shown in Column D of Figure 2.33, and a percentage charge for each transaction. For example, Yoddle charges 15 cents for each transaction plus 2.1 percent of the transaction value. In other words, Yoddle charges a transaction cost for selling one $10 garden implement of $0.15 + 0.021 * 10, or a total of $0.36. The four formulas for estimated annual cost should reference the monthly transactions value in cell B1 and the average transaction value, $50, in cell B2. (*Hint:* ClickEnsure's estimated annual price is 10900.)

Print the worksheet and print the worksheet formulas. Based on Orlando's transaction volume and per-transaction value assumptions, which CSP is the least expensive? Which one is the most expensive?

	A	B	C	D	E	F
1	Monthly Transactions:	10000				
2	Average Trans. Value: ($)	50				
3						Estimated
4		One-time	Monthly	Per-Transaction Costs		Annual
5	Host	Setup Fee	Rental Fee	Fixed ($)	Variable (%)	Price
6	ClickEnsure	500	200	0	0.016	
7	HostWay	200	400	0.25	0.015	
8	ShopSmart	0	250	0.12	0.017	
9	Yoddle	125	100	0.15	0.021	
10						
11	Minimum				Minimum	
12	Average					
13	Maximum					

FIGURE 2.33

E-Commerce hosting cost comparison

write formulas for estimated annual cost

write a formula for minimum annual cost

write statistical formulas for setup and monthly rental

2. Plato's Sanctuary

Plato's Sanctuary is an exclusive rare bookstore in Los Angeles. Its reputation for authenticity is world renown. The store's owner, Hershel Smithers, has just completed his second month of weekly online auction sessions of rare books. The books chosen are mainly first editions, and most are signed by the author. Contrary to the average retail business, rare books sell slowly because they are expensive, and pricing too low would cause the books to move faster than they could be replaced. Ideally, the shelves of a bookstore selling rare books must contain many different books at any given time, and a typical book takes six months to sell.

The costs associated with online bidding of quality rare books are high. Plato's Sanctuary is currently absorbing all of those costs rather than passing them onto their customers. These costs include online fees, sales tax for out-of-state purchasers, unique packaging, special shipping carriers, and insurance to cover the market value of the book. Each cost is unique to the book being sold and its destination. To understand if Plato's Sanctuary should continue the online auctions, construct a worksheet that evaluates the results of the first two months of online operations.

Open the workbook **ex02PlatosSanctuary.xls** (see Figure 2.34), save it as **<yourname>Platos2.xls**, and complete the worksheet provided by filling in the appropriate formulas to determine each book's online costs and resulting profit margin. For reporting and evaluation purposes provide the minimum, average, and maximum gross profit percentages, average sales price, total sales price, and total online costs for the two months. Gross profit percentage is sales less costs divided by sales. Assume the following cost structure based on sales price (market value): sales tax averages 8 percent, insurance is 2 percent, packing & shipping is 9 percent, and online fees are 15 percent. Initial offering is 400 percent of book cost. Target profit margin is 50 percent. Based on your calculations, should Plato's Sanctuary continue the online auction? (*Hint:* Gross Profit Percentage column formula is Final Sales Price − (Actual Cost + Total Online Fees & Taxes))/Final Sales Price)

Type your name in the worksheet header. Print the worksheet in landscape orientation and print the worksheet formulas. Save your workbook.

FIGURE 2.34

Plato's Sanctuary worksheet

	A	B	C	D	E	F	G	H
1							Packaging	
2		Actual	Initial	Final Sales	Sales	Insurance	Shipping	Online
3	Title & Author	Cost	Offering	Price	Tax	Fee	Fee	Fee
4	Dante's Inferno, Dante Alighieri	15000	60000	78000	6240	1560	7020	1
5	Ivanhoe, Sir Walter Scott	4300		18000				
6	A Tale of Two Cities, Charles Dickens	7000		44000				
7	Gunga Din, Rudyard Kipling	200		6000				
8	Aesop's Fables Vol. 1	1200		6700				
9	Don Quixote, Miguel de Cervantes Saavedra	10000		52000				
10	The Canterbury Tales, Geoffrey Chaucer	7600		30600				
11	Atlas Shrugged, Ayn Rand	500		3300				
12	The Adventures of Huckleberry Finn, Mark Twain	500		7500				
13	Fahrenheit 451, Ray Bradbury	600		5000				
14	Das Kapital, Karl Marx	3000		22000				
15	For Whom the Bell Tolls, Ernest Hemingway	5000		40000				
16	Animal Farm, George Orwell	400		1600				
17								
18	**Gross Profit %**							
19	Minimum							
20	Average							
21	Maximum							
22								
23	Average Sales Price							
24	Total Online Costs							
25	Total Online Sales							
26								
27								

Sheet1 / Sheet2 / Sheet3

Ready

1. Selecting an Online Broker

Erik Engvall is trying to decide which online brokerage firm he should use for trading stocks. After some research, he came up with the following list of five online brokerages that are highly rated. The brokerages are Ameritrade, Charles Schwab & Co., HARRISdirect, and Fidelity. Figure 2.35 shows the Web addresses of each of these online brokers. To help Erik, you will use the Web to look up how much each service charges for stock transactions. The annual fees vary and are sometimes difficult to find. Assume that the annual charges are as follows: Ameritrade—$49, Charles Schwab—$35, HARRISdirect—$40, and Fidelity—$50. (The preceding fees are contrived costs—the listed online brokers have different annual fees or none at all.) Arrange this information in columns, with each brokerage firm in a separate row.

Label the columns the following way: **Company**, **Price per Trade**, and **Annual Fee**. In a cell, enter **4**, which is the number of brokerage transactions per month that Erik estimates he executes with a broker. (That number will be the what-if analysis value you can change to determine the overall cost differences between the brokers you have selected.) Write formulas to compute the minimum, average, and maximum charge per transaction and formulas to compute the minimum, average, and maximum annual fee. Create a column labeled **Total Cost per Month** and label another column to the right of the monthly cost column called **Total Yearly Cost**. Beneath the Total Cost per Month column, write a formula for each brokerage indicating the cost for four transactions (refer to a cell containing 4 that you created earlier). Write formulas for each brokerage row indicating the total annual cost, assuming Erik continues to execute four transactions per month for the year. Remember to add the annual fee.

You forgot to include another important brokerage, E*Trade. Insert a new row between HARRISdirect and Fidelity and enter **E*Trade** under the Company column. Complete the information in the E*Trade row including Price per Trade. Assume they do not charge an annual fee. Copy formulas from HARRISdirect to complete E*Trade's missing formulas.

Place your name in your worksheet to identify it and then print the worksheet. Save your workbook as <**yourname**>**Brokerage2.xls**. Based on this information, which online broker is the least expensive?

FIGURE 2.35

Brokerage Web addresses

Brokerage	Web Address
Ameritrade	www.ameritrade.com/
Charles Schwab	www.schwab.com/
HARRISdirect	www.harrisdirect.com/
E*Trade	www.etrade.com/
Fidelity	www.fidelity.com/

around the world

1. Comparing Living Expenses Around the World

What does it cost to live for a month in a foreign country? You've been considering living in Europe or South America for a month next summer and want to know the total cost of living abroad. Costs include an apartment locator agency fee, one month's rental charges, the cost of food, utilities, transportation to the foreign country, and transportation costs within the country for the month. Using the Web, research the cost of renting a one-bedroom apartment in Florence (Italy), Paris, Buenos Aires, and Santiago. Include cell comments for each city indicating the source—Web URL or other reference—for your rental cost information. Document the workbook by entering information in the Properties dialog box. Print the worksheet.

2. Adventure Travel

Your new job with Adventure Travel requires you to verify the weather at seven destination cities for a six-week journey around the globe. Adventure Travel customers like interesting cities and various climates. Using the Web, find the current weather for Akurnes, Iceland; Lisbon, Portugal; Siirt, Turkey; Jakarta, Indonesia; Allanton, New Zealand; Base Jubany, Antarctica; and Puerto Maldonado, Peru. Open the workbook **ex02Adventure.xls** and enter each city's expected low and high temperatures and humidity. Insert cell comments in the cells containing the city names: Use terms such as "mostly cloudy," "heavy snow," or "thunderstorms" to help customers understand what type of last-minute travel gear they might need to pack. Ensure that your worksheet summarizes all the data and provides a final minimum and maximum expected temperature. Display all temperatures in both Fahrenheit and Celsius in the indicated columns. Use the following formula to convert Fahrenheit to Celsius:

$$Celsius = (Fahrenheit - 32) * 5/9$$

Place your name in the worksheet header. Rename the worksheet tab to **Weather Summary**. (See Figure 2.36.) Print the worksheet and print the worksheet formulas.

FIGURE 2.36

Adventure Travel worksheet

	A	B	C	D	E	F	G	H
1	Destination	Low Temp F	Hi Temp F	Low Temp C	Hi Temp C	% Humidity		
2	Akurnes, Iceland							
3	Lisbon, Portugal							
4	Siirt, Turkey							
5	Jakarta, Indonesia							
6	Allanton, New Zealand							
7	Base Jubany, Antarctica							
8	Puerto Maldonado, Peru							
9								
10		Degree F	Degree C					
11	Minimum							
12	Maximum							
13								
14								
15								
16								
17								
18								
19								
20								
21								
22								
23								
24								
25								

Sheet1 / Sheet2 / Sheet3 /

Ready

Pro Golf Academy

Pro Golf Academy ("Pro Golf") has a complete line of golf products. Betty Carroll, Pro Golf's manager, wants to compare the profitability of seven golf bags that she's interested in selling. There are several costs associated with purchasing and shipping any products, and golf bags are no different. A wholesaler, from which Betty purchases the golf bags, charges a fixed order fee of $100—a one-time fee charged for each order any customer places with the wholesaler. Of course, the wholesale cost of each golf bag varies, depending on brand. Shipping costs $0.10 per pound, and the shipper charges a one-time delivery fee of $25 to deliver and unload the products at the store.

Modify a golf bag comparison worksheet showing the total cost of each product if Betty orders three of each of the seven brand-name golf bags. Begin by opening the workbook **ex02ProGolf.xls** and save it as **<yourname>ProGolf2.xls**. Compute the total profit Pro Golf will earn if the employees sell all three of the seven different golf bags. Remember to in-

clude the shipping and delivery charges in your calculations. Figure 2.37 indicates the way you can organize your worksheet. Start by entering the constant **3** in the Purchase Quantity column for each of the seven products. Then, write formulas wherever Xs occur. The Xs to the right of the label Order fee represent a formula you write referencing the order fee found among the assumptions at the top of the worksheet. Write formulas for extended cost, extended price, and shipping (sum the units sold, use the average weight of 14 pounds found in the assumptions, and then multiply it times the cost per pound). The delivery fee is a one-time fee whose value is found in the assumptions also. Form a subtotal with a formula summing the order fee, shipping, and delivery costs. The total cost is the sum of the subtotal and the summed extended cost of the equipment. The net profit is the sum of the extended price minus the total cost. Place your name in the worksheet header, print the worksheet, and print the worksheet formulas. Save your workbook.

FIGURE 2.37
Golf Bag worksheet

	A	B	C	D	E	F	G	H	I
1	Golf Bag Cost Comparison								
2	Assumptions:								
3	Order fee ($):	100	per order						
4	Shipping/lb. ($)	0.1							
5	Golf Bag Avg. Wt. (lbs.)	14							
6	Delivery ($)	25	per order						
7									
8	Purchase				Extended	Extended			
9	Quantity	Brand	Cost	Price	Cost	Price			
10		Titleist S24	182.5	280	XXXX	XXXX			
11		Ogio Monster	126.75	200	XXXX	XXXX			
12		Tommy Armour	151.35	200	XXXX	XXXX			
13		Taylor Made R500	320.45	360	XXXX	XXXX			
14		MaxFli Series 20	212.75	250	XXXX	XXXX			
15		BagBoy NCX	121.54	150	XXXX	XXXX			
16		Ram 8.5 inch	100.25	110	XXXX	XXXX			
17				Subtotal	XXXX	XXXX			
18									
19			Order fee	XXXX					
20			Shipping	XXXX					
21			Delivery	XXXX					
22			Subtotal	XXXX					
23									
24			Total Cost	XXXX					
25			Net Profit	XXXX					
26									

Cost Comparison

Ready

1. Improving a Worksheet's Readability and Why Use Ratios

Examine the final can recycling worksheet and describe, in general terms, what you would do to improve its readability. The answer may require tools you have not yet read about in the first two chapters. Carefully write a short paragraph on why the recycling campaign manager used per capita recycling as the determining factor. Clearly, San Diego is the winner in terms of overall number of cans that were recycled.

2. Analysis of a Mathematical Function

Discuss the advantages, if any, of using the AVERAGE function over writing an alternative formula that does not employ the AVERAGE function. Discuss, for instance, the differences between using a formula such as =(A1+A2+A3+A4+A5)/5 to compute the average of the values in cell range A1:A5 compared to using the formula =Average(A1:A5). What consideration, if any, does one or more empty cells in the cell range being averaged play in your answer?

Formatting a Worksheet

did you
know?

the *city in the United States that purchases the most ice cream on a per capita basis is Portland, Oregon.*

the *Great Lakes have a combined area of 94,230 square miles—larger than the states of New York, New Jersey, Connecticut, Rhode Island, Massachusetts, and Vermont combined.*

"however *fascinating it may be as scholarly achievement, there is virtually nothing that has come from molecular biology that can be of any value to human living."—Nobel Prize–winning immunologist Frank MacFarlane Burnett (1899–1985) whose work made organ transplantation possible.*

paul *Saffo, a director of the Institute for the Future, in February 1996 predicted the Web would mutate into "something else very quickly and be unrecognizable within 12 months."*

bricks *are the oldest manufactured building material still in use. Egyptians used them 7,000 years ago.*

you *can attach graphic objects to your worksheet. Read this chapter to find out how.*

Chapter Objectives

- Apply currency and accounting formats to numbers— MOS XL03S-3-1
- Left-, center-, and right-align text—MOS XL03S-3-1
- Modify the typeface and point size of text and numbers— MOS XL03S-3-1
- Apply boldface, italics, and underlines to cells—MOS XL03S-3-1
- Clear all formatting from selected cells—MOS XL03S-3-1
- Modify column widths and row heights—MOS XL03S-3-3
- Hide and reveal rows and columns—MOS XL03S-3-3
- Remove worksheet gridlines—MOS XL03S-3-1
- Modify the worksheet's print characteristics—MOS XL03S-5-7
- Print multiple, selected worksheets at once—MOS XL03S-5-8

The Exotic Fruit Company

The Exotic Fruit Company is a wholesale exotic fruits, nuts, and roots distributor headquartered in La Mesa, California. Exotic Fruit's customers include most of the large grocery store chains in the western United States. Corporate buyers for the grocery stores contract with Exotic Fruit to supply and ship exotic fruits to stores' warehouses scattered throughout the West. Exotic Fruit's chief procurement officer, Nancy Carroll, oversees the purchase and distribution operations for all divisions from her La Mesa office.

Exotic Fruit also maintains a small Web site from which it sells exotic fruit to consumers. While the online store is not a large part of its revenue stream, it is an essential and growing part of Exotic Fruit's business. Nancy has asked her financial analyst to quickly develop a sales forecast for the coming year of selected exotic fruits, using the previous year's figures as the basis of the projection. Nancy wants to investigate sales predictions based on the assumption that next year's wholesale sales will increase by approximately 10 percent for each product included in the projection.

Due to time constraints, her financial analyst, Angel Hernandez, did not have time to format the worksheet. Consequently, the worksheet looks unprofessional and, frankly, it is a little difficult to read and understand. While Nancy understands that Angel is stretched to the limit and has little time to format the projection, Nancy wants to improve the worksheet's appearance. She asks you to spend a little time formatting it so that the labels and numbers are easier to read and the entire worksheet is ready for presentation at the annual board meeting next month.

Figure 3.1 shows the completed Exotic Fruit Sales Forecast worksheet. You will be developing the worksheet in this chapter beginning with a fundamental worksheet that Nancy and Angel provide for you.

FIGURE 3.1
Exotic Fruit Sales Forecast worksheet

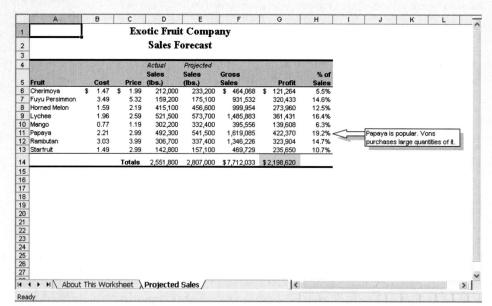

INTRODUCTION

Chapter 3 covers formatting. In this chapter you will open and use an existing worksheet —complete with formulas, text, and values—and apply various formats to its cells. Formats that you will apply include aligning numeric results in columns by their decimal places, controlling the number of decimal places that display, and displaying currency symbols for column-heading monetary values. Other formatting you will apply includes indenting a label and formatting the worksheet title and subtitle by merging several cells and centering the title in the merged cells. Drawing objects can add interest to a worksheet, and Excel has several drawing objects from which you can choose. You will add two of the available objects—an arrow and a text box—to the highlighted example used in this chapter. The chapter concludes by describing ways to customize printing a worksheet including selecting either landscape or portrait orientation, centering output on the page, and printing multiple worksheets at once.

SESSION 3.1 ALIGNING DATA AND APPLYING CHARACTER FORMATS

In this section, you will learn how to render your worksheets more professional looking by using various formatting methods. You will format text so that it wraps to a new line within a cell, indent text, format numeric cells with currency and accounting numbers, paint existing formats over other cells, and explore other numeric formatting details. You will align data on the right and left edges of cells and across several cells. This section introduces how to modify typefaces, apply boldface, apply underline, and modify a typeface point size.

Locating and Opening the Workbook

Angel has entered all the formulas, values, and text. Consequently, Nancy wants you to focus on formatting the cells to maximize their visual impact. You can accomplish this by formatting individual cells and columns so that numbers and text are formatted and by providing visual cues about data and labels that are related. Nancy wants selected areas of the worksheet to draw the reader's attention—to be formatted to attract attention without overwhelming the worksheet and without making the overall design look garish.

Starting Microsoft Excel:

1. Start Excel

2. Ensure that the Excel application window is maximized

You can open the worksheet. Angel cautioned you that she wants to preserve the original worksheet, **ex03Fruit.xls**, just in case she needs to adjust some of the formulas. She asked you to save the worksheet under a different name before beginning work on it. You will save the worksheet under the name **ExoticFruit.xls**, as a safety measure, before you get deeply involved with worksheet formatting changes.

Opening the Exotic Fruit workbook and saving it under a new name:

1. Open the workbook **ex03Fruit.xls**. The first sheet, About This Worksheet, appears (see Figure 3.2)

FIGURE 3.2

Exotic Fruit documentation worksheet

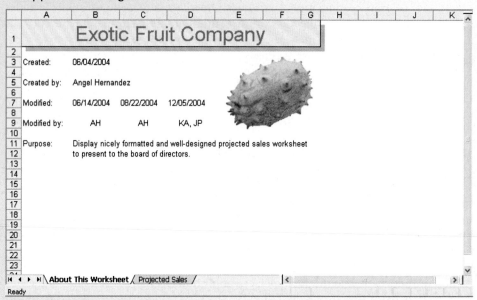

2. Click the **Projected Sales** worksheet tab to move to that worksheet (see Figure 3.3)

FIGURE 3.3

The unformatted worksheet, Projected Sales

	A	B	C	D	E	F	G	H	I	J	K	L
1	Exotic Fruit Company											
2	Sales Forecast											
3												
4				Actual	Projected							
5	Fruit	Cost	Price	Sales (lbs.	Sales (lbs.	Gross Sale	Profit	% of Sales				
6	Cherimoya	1.47	1.99	212000	233200	464068	121264	0.055155				
7	Fuyu Pers	3.49	5.32	159200	175100	931532	320433	0.145743				
8	Horned Me	1.59	2.19	415100	456600	999954	273960	0.124605				
9	Lychee	1.96	2.59	521500	573700	1485883	361431	0.16439				
10	Mango	0.77	1.19	302200	332400	395556	139608	0.063498				
11	Papaya	2.21	2.99	492300	541500	1619085	422370	0.192107				
12	Rambutan	3.03	3.99	306700	337400	1346226	323904	0.147322				
13	Starfruit	1.49	2.99	142800	157100	469729	235650	0.107181				
14			Totals	2551800	2807000	7712033	2198620					
15												
16												
17												
18												
19												
20												
21												
22												
23												
24												
25												

About This Worksheet \ **Projected Sales** /

Ready

3. Save your file as **ExoticFruit.xls**

Formatting Data

Formatting a worksheet is the process of altering the appearance of data in one or more worksheet cells. Formatting is purely cosmetic—changing only the *appearance*, not the contents—of the formulas, values, or text stored in cells. Using the appropriate formatting renders a worksheet easier to read and understand and enhances a worksheet's

FIGURE 3.4

The Formatting toolbar

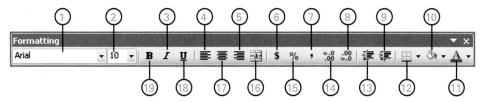

1 Font
2 Font Size
3 Italic
4 Align Left
5 Align Right
6 Currency Style
7 Comma Style
8 Decrease Decimal
9 Increase Indent
10 Fill Color
11 Font Color
12 Borders
13 Decrease Indent
14 Increase Decimal
15 Percent Style
16 Merge and Center
17 Center
18 Underline
19 Bold

overall appearance, making it more professional looking. Choosing inappropriate formatting has the opposite effect. It distracts the reader and creates a bad impression that extends beyond the worksheet to the company or activity illustrated by the worksheet.

Often, you can provide the exact appearance you desire only by executing particular formatting commands that each make small changes to the appearance of cells. For example, you can apply a currency format with zero decimal places to the value 1234.5678 so that the cell displays $1,235, but the underlying value—the value you typed into the cell—remains unchanged. Only the cell's *appearance* changes. Suppose a cell contains the formula =A1*25.89 and it displays the result 0.6789945. You can format the cell using the Percentage format with two decimal places so that the cell's appearance changes—it displays 67.90% in the cell. When you apply formatting changes to a worksheet carefully, the changes enhance the worksheet tremendously.

By default, Excel formats all worksheet cells with a standard format called General. The *General* format aligns numbers on the right side of a cell, aligns text on the left side, indicates negative numbers with a minus sign on the left side of a number, and displays as many digits in a number as a cell's width allows. When you clear a cell's format, it takes on the General format. General format and no format are synonymous.

Many of the more popular formatting operations appear as buttons on the Formatting toolbar. While many Formatting toolbar icons' graphics adequately describe the formats they apply, others may not. If you have trouble remembering what a particular Formatting toolbar button does, hover the mouse pointer over it and observe the ToolTip that appears within a few seconds. The ToolTip text tersely describes the format that a button applies. Figure 3.4 shows the Formatting toolbar.

Formatting Numeric Entries

Excel's default numeric format General is not always the best format choice. Numeric entries and formulas that display values should have commas, or thousand separators, every three digits to make the numbers easier to read. The topmost number in a column of numbers representing money should display the currency symbol. Optionally, all values representing money could display the currency symbol.

Some values in the Projected Sales worksheet represent percents and would look better if they were formatted as percentages with one or two decimal places. Excel provides these formatting choices for cells containing values and many format choices for a wide variety of situations.

Common format choices for numeric entries include General (the default format), Accounting, Currency, Date, Number, Percentage, Scientific, and formats you build yourself called Custom.

- General format displays numbers without commas or currency symbols (the dollar sign in the United States)

- Accounting provides left-aligned dollar signs, comma separators, a specified number of digits after the decimal place, and displays negative numbers inside a pair of parentheses

- Currency is similar to Accounting, except the currency symbol is just to the left of the most significant digit and negative values are enclosed in parentheses
- Date provides special formats to display month, day, and year. Number format lets you designate the number of digits following the decimal place and the option to use comma separators. Negative values display a leading minus sign
- Percentage inserts a percent sign to the right of the least significant digit and allows you to set the number of decimal places
- Scientific displays a number between 1 and 10 followed by the letter E representing 10 raised to the exponent that follows E. For example, the number 123.45 formatted with Scientific displays 1.2345E+02, which reads "1.2345 times 10 to the 2nd power." This format is not used much in nonscientific applications
- Customer allows you to create your own format when none of Excel's built-in number formats is suitable. Consisting of four sections separated by semicolons, you can specify how positive, negative, zero, and text appears with a custom format

---

task reference   Formatting Numbers

- Select the cell or cell range to which you will apply a format
- Click **Format**, click **Cells**, and click the **Number** tab
- Click the format category you want and then select options for the format choice
- Click **OK** to finalize your format choices and format the selected cell(s)

If you change your mind and decide another format is better, simply select the cell or cell range whose format you want to change, click Format, click Cells, select the new format choices, and click OK.

---

another**word**
. . . on Removing All Formatting from a Cell or Cell Range

If you decide to remove all formatting from a cell or cell range, select the cell(s) whose formatting you want to remove, click Edit on the menu bar, point to **Clear**, and click **Formats**

Applying Accounting and Currency Formats

Reviewing Nancy's Exotic Fruit worksheet, you can see several distinct groups of numeric formats that will improve the worksheet. Columns B, C, D, F, and G all contain money values and should be formatted with commas. The first entries in those columns and the Totals row entries should display currency symbols—a generally accepted format that accountants frequently prefer.

Formatting cells with the Accounting format:

1. Select cell range **D6:G14**
2. Click **Format** on the menu bar and click **Cells**. The Format Cells dialog box opens

3. Click the **Number** tab if necessary

4. Click **Accounting** in the Category list box

5. Type **0** in the Decimal places list box. The default currency symbol is the dollar sign if you installed the U.S. version of Excel

6. Click the **Symbol** list box arrow and then click **None** in the drop-down list (see Figure 3.5)

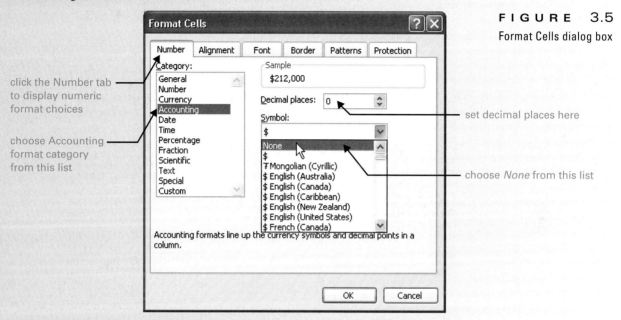

click the Number tab to display numeric format choices

choose Accounting format category from this list

set decimal places here

choose *None* from this list

F I G U R E   3.5
Format Cells dialog box

7. Click the **OK** button to affirm your formatting choices. The values in the formatted cell range display comma separators and are offset from the right cell wall by one character (see Figure 3.6)

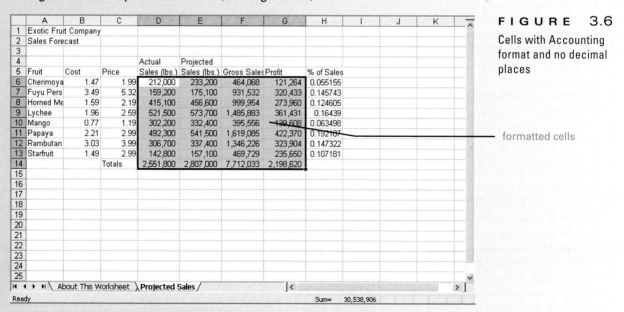

formatted cells

F I G U R E   3.6
Cells with Accounting format and no decimal places

8. Click any cell to deselect the cell range

A cell displaying a series of pound signs ("#######") indicates that the column is too narrow to display the values in the cells as formatted. If your display shows a series of pound signs, you must widen the column to see the full formatted number. It is best to wait to widen the columns until you have formatted the remaining numeric values in a column that requires widening. Subtotals and totals, for example, usually are wider than other values because they are the sum of a possible large list of numbers.

Accountants, financial analysts, and others often format the top cell in a column of currency values with the currency symbol. The same is true for cells containing subtotals or totals. Displaying currency symbols on every value in a column creates visual clutter and is distracting.

Formatting selected cells with the Accounting format and currency symbol:

1. Select cell range **F6:G6**

2. Click **Format** on the menu bar and then click **Cells**

3. Click the **Number** tab if necessary

4. Click the **Symbol** list box and click **$** appearing just below *None* in the Symbol drop-down list

5. Click **OK** to finalize your formatting selections, and click any cell to deselect the range. Figure 3.7 shows the worksheet with currency symbols displayed in cells F6 and G6

FIGURE 3.7

Worksheet with some currency symbols in place

cells display the currency symbol

	A	B	C	D	E	F	G	H	I	J	K
1	Exotic Fruit Company										
2	Sales Forecast										
3											
4				Actual	Projected						
5	Fruit	Cost	Price	Sales (lbs.)	Sales (lbs.)	Gross Sales	Profit	% of Sales			
6	Cherimoya	1.47	1.99	212,000	233,200	$ 464,068	$ 121,264	0.055155			
7	Fuyu Pers	3.49	5.32	159,200	175,100	931,532	320,433	0.145743			
8	Horned Me	1.59	2.19	415,100	456,600	999,954	273,960	0.124605			
9	Lychee	1.96	2.59	521,500	573,700	1,485,883	361,431	0.16439			
10	Mango	0.77	1.19	302,200	332,400	395,556	139,608	0.063498			
11	Papaya	2.21	2.99	492,300	541,500	1,619,085	422,370	0.192107			
12	Rambutan	3.03	3.99	306,700	337,400	1,346,226	323,904	0.147322			
13	Starfruit	1.49	2.99	142,800	157,100	469,729	235,650	0.107181			
14			Totals	2,551,800	2,807,000	7,712,033	2,198,620				
15											
16											
17											
18											
19											
20											
21											
22											
23											
24											
25											

About This Worksheet \ Projected Sales /

Ready

Painting Formats onto Other Cells

Cells F14 and G14 display totals for their respective partial columns. Instead of repeating the command sequence you used above for cells F6 and G6, to save time and effort you will copy the cell format (but not the contents) by using the Format Painter button, located on the Standard toolbar. The advantage of painting a format instead of using formatting commands is that the painter duplicates *all* of a cell's formats at once.

<table>
<tr><td>task reference</td><td>Copying a Cell Format to a
Cell or Cell Range</td></tr>
</table>

- Select the cell whose format you want to copy
- Click the **Format Painter** 🖌 button
- Click the cell where you want to paint the format, or click and drag the cell range where you want to paint the format

Rather than repeat the formatting sequence to apply the currency symbol to cells F14 and G14, you will copy the format with the Format Painter.

Formatting cells with the Accounting format and currency symbol and widening columns:

1. Click cell **F6**, the cell whose format you want to copy to another cell or cells

2. Click the **Format Painter** 🖌 button on the Standard toolbar

3. Click and drag the cell range **F14:G14** (see Figure 3.8) to copy the format to those cells. The newly formatted cells probably display ########

	A	B	C	D	E	F	G	H	I	J	K
1	Exotic Fruit Company										
2	Sales Forecast										
3											
4				Actual	Projected						
5	Fruit	Cost	Price	Sales (lbs.)	Sales (lbs.)	Gross Sales	Profit	% of Sales			
6	Cherimoya	1.47	1.99	212,000	233,200	$ 464,068	$ 121,264	0.055155			
7	Fuyu Pers	3.49	5.32	159,200	175,100	931,532	320,433	0.145743			
8	Horned Me	1.59	2.19	415,100	456,600	999,954	273,960	0.124605			
9	Lychee	1.96	2.59	521,500	573,700	1,485,883	361,431	0.16439			
10	Mango	0.77	1.19	302,200	332,400	395,556	139,608	0.063498			
11	Papaya	2.21	2.99	492,300	541,500	1,619,085	422,370	0.192107			
12	Rambutan	3.03	3.99	306,700	337,400	1,346,226	323,904	0.147322			
13	Starfruit	1.49	2.99	142,800	157,100	469,729	235,650	0.107181			
14			Totals	2,551,800	2,807,000	########	########				
15											
16											
17											
18											
19											
20											
21											
22											
23											
24											
25											

About This Worksheet \ **Projected Sales** /

Ready   Sum= $ 9,910,653

FIGURE 3.8
Worksheet totals with copied format

pound signs signal that a column is too narrow to display formatted numeric value

4. With F14 and G14 still selected, click **Format** on the menu bar, point to **Column**, and click **AutoFit Selection**

Other Number Formats

You can apply other number formats by using buttons on the Formatting toolbar, shown in Figure 3.4, such as Currency Style, Percent Style, Increase Decimal, or Decrease Decimal. Many other formatting options are available in the Format Cells dialog box, shown in Figure 3.5. Number format options allow you to select whether or not to display a comma to delimit numbers every three digits, to select the number of decimal places that display, and the exact format of negative numbers.

Percent Style

Column H displays values beneath the column label "% of Sales." These values are percentages, although they are somewhat difficult to interpret because they display five or six decimal places. Nancy wants you to format these column values (such as 0.107181, the Starfruit percentage) to display 10.7% instead—a percentage displaying one decimal place.

Formatting column H with percent and one decimal place:

1. Click and drag the cell range **H6:H13**

2. Click the **Percent Style** % button to apply the Percent Style format to the selected cell range

3. With the cell range H6:H13 still selected, click the **Increase Decimal** button on the Formatting toolbar to increase, by one, the number of decimal places the selected cells display

tip: *If the Increase Decimal button is not visible on the Formatting toolbar, it is farther right on the Formatting toolbar and out of sight—probably sharing space with the Standard toolbar. If so, drag the Formatting toolbar below the Standard toolbar and to the left edge to view the entire toolbar. Then click the Increase Decimal button*

4. Click any cell to deselect the range (see Figure 3.9)

FIGURE 3.9

Worksheet cells formatted with the Percent Style

	A	B	C	D	E	F	G	H	I
1	Exotic Fruit Company								
2	Sales Forecast								
3									
4				Actual	Projected				
5	Fruit	Cost	Price	Sales (lbs.)	Sales (lbs.)	Gross Sales	Profit	% of Sales	
6	Cherimoya	1.47	1.99	212,000	233,200	$ 464,068	$ 121,264	5.5%	
7	Fuyu Pers	3.49	5.32	159,200	175,100	931,532	320,433	14.6%	
8	Horned Me	1.59	2.19	415,100	456,600	999,954	273,960	12.5%	
9	Lychee	1.96	2.59	521,500	573,700	1,485,883	361,431	16.4%	
10	Mango	0.77	1.19	302,200	332,400	395,556	139,608	6.3%	
11	Papaya	2.21	2.99	492,300	541,500	1,619,085	422,370	19.2%	
12	Rambutan	3.03	3.99	306,700	337,400	1,346,226	323,904	14.7%	
13	Starfruit	1.49	2.99	142,800	157,100	469,729	235,650	10.7%	
14			Totals	2,551,800	2,807,000	$7,712,033	$2,198,620		
15									

Percent Style applied to column H values

Nancy has reviewed your formatting work and suggests that you format the values at the top of the Cost and Price columns to display a currency symbol and two decimal places.

Formatting selected cells with the Accounting format and currency symbol:

1. Click cell **B6** and drag the mouse through cell **C6**

2. Click the **Currency Style** $ button on the Formatting toolbar

Look carefully on your screen at the cell range B6 through C13. Do you notice that cell B6 is not aligned on the right side with cell B7 or the remainder of the cells in the Cost column? Similarly, Cell C6 is no longer aligned on the right side with the other cells in the Price column. This is because the Currency Style also adds one character, a space, to the right side of all values so that there is room for a right parenthesis. Under the Accounting format, negative numbers are surrounded with parentheses.

It is sloppy to leave the values beneath the formatted cell out of alignment with the top value in the column. You can correct this by applying a comma format to the remaining cells in the Cost and Price columns.

Comma Style

Even though commas are not needed for values less than 1,000, comma formatting also aligns values the same way the Currency format does—by adding a character to the right side of each value. You will format cells B7 through C13 with the Comma format to align those values the same as the first two entries in each column.

Formatting cells with the Comma Style:

1. Click cell **B7** and drag the mouse through cell **C13**

2. Click the **Comma Style** button on the Formatting toolbar

3. Click any cell to deselect the range. Notice that all values in the Cost and Price columns are aligned (see Figure 3.10)

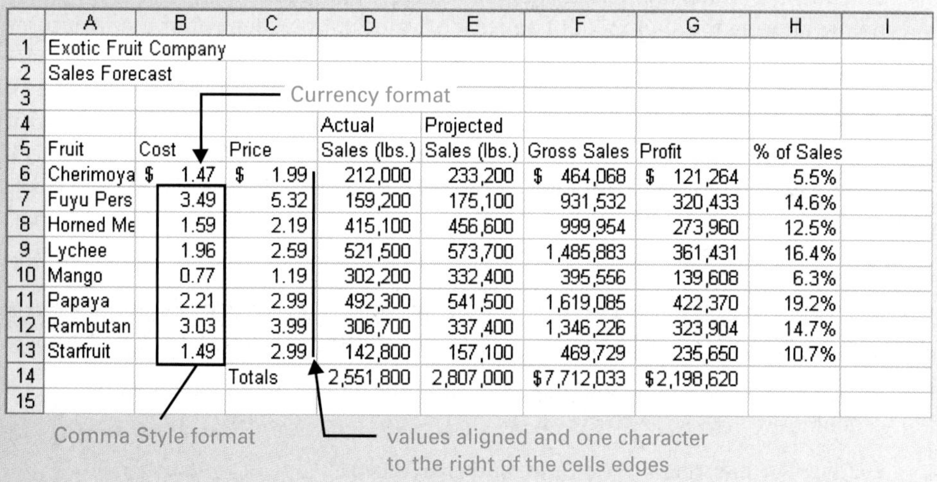

FIGURE 3.10

Applying the Comma Style to numeric values

Aligning Data

Excel allows you to align data within a cell. Data *alignment* refers to the position of the data relative to the sides of a cell. You alter a cell's alignment with formatting commands. You can align data on the left or right sides of a cell, or you can center it between the two cell walls. A special center alignment command called Merge and Center allows you to center data across several cells in a single row—to create a heading over several columns of numbers, for example. Figure 3.11 shows examples of these four alignment options.

General rules about aligning data have evolved over time. As you know, Excel automatically aligns text on the left side and aligns values or formulas that result in values on the right side. While you certainly can choose data alignment that suits your style and

EXCEL

FIGURE 3.11

Cell alignment examples

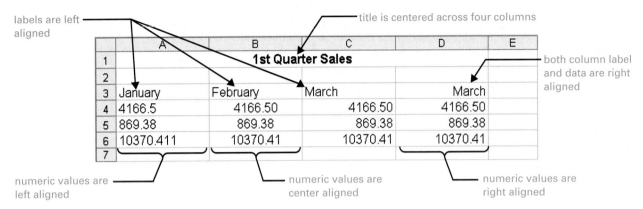

labels are left aligned

title is centered across four columns

both column label and data are right aligned

numeric values are left aligned

numeric values are center aligned

numeric values are right aligned

taste, here are some suggestions about cell alignment. Align a column of text on the left side, the default alignment provided by Excel. If you align text on the right, the result can be a disorienting ragged left edge down the column. You can center numeric values if all values have the same number of digits. Examples are employee identification numbers that are all the same number of digits long. In a column of numeric values that are not all the same size, align the values so that their decimal places are lined up vertically (column D, Figure 3.11). To do so, you may have to format values to display the same number of decimal places. Text that labels a column of values below it should be right aligned, the same way the values are. This makes the number column easy to identify.

Before altering the alignment of any text or values, you widen column A to accommodate the widest entry in the list of fruit. Notice that two labels identifying the worksheet, "Exotic Fruit Company" and "Sales Forecast," are also in column A (Figure 3.10). This is important because you want to enlarge the column enough to display the fruit names in cells C6 through C13, but the column need not be as wide as the text in cell A1. Widening the column to completely contain the text in cell A1 would make the column far too wide.

---

task reference   Modifying a Column's Width

- Select the column heading(s) of all columns whose width you want to change

- Click **Format**, point to **Column**, and click **Width**

- Enter the new column width in the **Column Width** text box and click **OK**, or click **AutoFit Selection** to make the column(s) optimal width—as wide as the widest entry in the column

or

- Double-click the right edge of the column heading line to make the column(s) optimal width(s)—as long as the longest entry in the column(s)

or

- Drag the column heading dividing line of any one of the selected columns to the left to decrease the column width or to the right to increase the column width

Widening column A to accommodate the longer fruit names:

1. Select cells **A6** through **A13**

2. Click **Format** on the menu bar, point to **Column**, and then click **AutoFit Selection**

Centering Data across Columns

Nancy wants you to center the worksheet title and subtitle found in cells A1 and A2, respectively, across columns A through H.

Centering a worksheet title and subtitle across several columns:

1. Select the cell range **A1:H2**

2. Click **Format** and then click **Cells**

3. Click the **Alignment** tab in the Format Cells dialog box

4. Click the Horizontal list box arrow to display a list of alignment choices (see Figure 3.12)

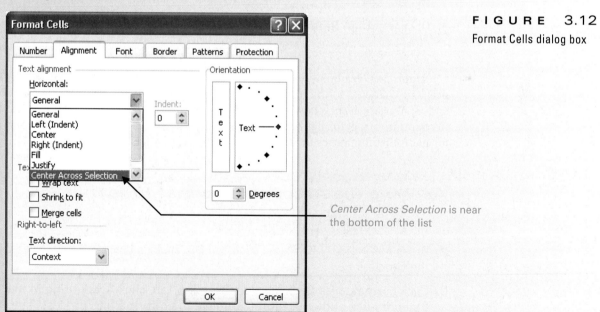

F I G U R E   3.12
Format Cells dialog box

Center Across Selection is near the bottom of the list

5. Click the entry **Center Across Selection** in the drop-down list

6. Click **OK** to complete the operation. Excel centers the two titles in cells A1 and A2 across the eight columns (see Figure 3.13)

EXCEL

FIGURE 3.13

Centering titles across
several columns

labels centered across columns A through H

	A	B	C	D	E	F	G	H	I	J
1				Exotic Fruit Company						
2				Sales Forecast						
3										
4				Actual	Projected					
5	Fruit	Cost	Price	Sales (lbs.)	Sales (lbs.)	Gross Sales	Profit	% of Sales		
6	Cherimoya	$ 1.47	$ 1.99	212,000	233,200	$ 464,068	$ 121,264	5.5%		
7	Fuyu Persimmon	3.49	5.32	159,200	175,100	931,532	320,433	14.6%		
8	Horned Melon	1.59	2.19	415,100	456,600	999,954	273,960	12.5%		
9	Lychee	1.96	2.59	521,500	573,700	1,485,883	361,431	16.4%		
10	Mango	0.77	1.19	302,200	332,400	395,556	139,608	6.3%		
11	Papaya	2.21	2.99	492,300	541,500	1,619,085	422,370	19.2%		
12	Rambutan	3.03	3.99	306,700	337,400	1,346,226	323,904	14.7%		
13	Starfruit	1.49	2.99	142,800	157,100	469,729	235,650	10.7%		
14			Totals	2,551,800	2,807,000	$7,712,033	$2,198,620			
15										

Right Aligning Data

Text labels that appear above columns containing values often look best if the text labels align the same way as the data beneath them. There are four labels in the Exotic Fruit worksheet, shown in Figure 3.13, which should be right aligned to match the data columns beneath the labels. They are the text in cells B5, C5, G5, and H5. (It is difficult to tell that the text in cell H5 is left aligned, but it is.)

Right aligning text:

1. Click and drag the cell range **B5:C5**

2. Press and hold the **Ctrl** key, click cell **G5**, click cell **H5**, and then release the Ctrl key

3. Click the **Align Right** ▤ button on the Formatting toolbar

Upon close examination, you notice that the labels Excel right-aligned actually appear one character to the right of the values beneath each text label in columns B, C, and G. You ask Nancy how to correct this, and she tells you that you can use the Accounting format to align text as well as numbers. The advantage of using Accounting format is that it matches the format you applied earlier to the numbers.

Applying the Accounting format to text:

1. Click and drag the cell range **B5:C5**

2. Press and hold the **Ctrl** key, click cell **G5**, click cell **H5**, and then release the Ctrl key

3. Click **Format**, click **Cells**, click the **Number** tab, click **Accounting** in the Category list, and click **OK** to complete the reformatting process (see Figure 3.14)

4. Click any cell to deselect the range

Wrapping Data in a Cell

Recall that text that is too long to display in a cell extends beyond the cell into the adjacent cell as long as the adjacent cell is empty. If it is not, the long label is visually truncated at the cell boundary. Labels in cells D5, E5, F5, and H5 are all longer than their

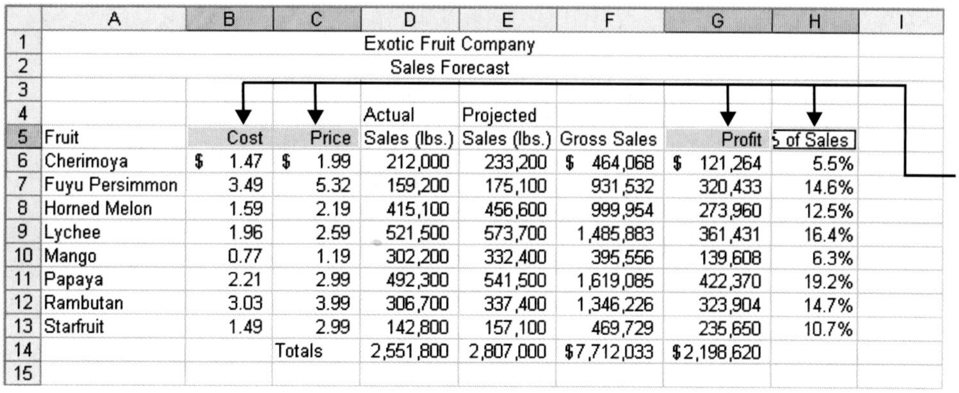

FIGURE 3.14

Applying the Accounting format to text cells

Accounting format aligns text to match formatting of numbers beneath

respective columns are wide. One solution would be to increase the width of the three columns until the labels completely fit within the cells. However, this is not always the best solution because especially long labels force their columns to become exceptionally wide, wider than is attractive. An alternative solution is to format long labels so they appear in multiple rows *within* a cell, much the same way that a text line in a word-processed document wraps around to the next line when it approaches the right margin. Excel uses the same term as Word—**wrap text**—to describe what happens to long text that continues onto the next line of the same cell.

help yourself *Press **F1**, type **format text** in the Search text box of the Microsoft Excel Help task pane, and press **Enter**. Scroll the results list box, if needed, to locate and click the hyperlink **change formatting of text** and then click the hyperlink **show multiple lines of text in a cell** (in the Microsoft Excel Help dialog box) to display help on formatting text entries. Click the Help screen **Close** button when you are finished, and then close the task pane*

***task* reference** Wrapping Long Text within a Cell

- Select the cell or cell range to which you will apply a format

- Click **Format**, click **Cells**, and click the **Alignment** tab

- Click the **Wrap text** check box

- Click **OK** to finalize your format choice

Wrapping text within a cell:

1. Click and drag the cell range **D5:F5**

2. Press the **Ctrl** key, click cell **H5**, and release the Ctrl key. This adds H5 to the list of selected cells

3. Click **Format**, click **Cells**, and then click the **Alignment** tab

4. Click the **Wrap text** check box, in the Text control panel, to place a checkmark in it

5. Click **OK** to complete the format operation and close the Format Cells dialog box

6. Click any cell to deselect the range (see Figure 3.15)

EXCEL

FIGURE 3.15

Wrap text format

Wrap text format

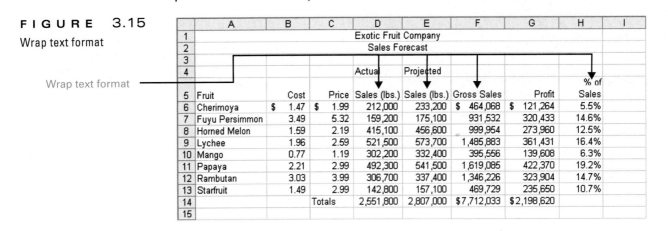

	A	B	C	D	E	F	G	H	I
1				Exotic Fruit Company					
2				Sales Forecast					
3									
4				Actual	Projected				
5	Fruit	Cost	Price	Sales (lbs.)	Sales (lbs.)	Gross Sales	Profit	% of Sales	
6	Cherimoya	$ 1.47	$ 1.99	212,000	233,200	$ 464,068	$ 121,264	5.5%	
7	Fuyu Persimmon	3.49	5.32	159,200	175,100	931,532	320,433	14.6%	
8	Horned Melon	1.59	2.19	415,100	456,600	999,954	273,960	12.5%	
9	Lychee	1.96	2.59	521,500	573,700	1,485,883	361,431	16.4%	
10	Mango	0.77	1.19	302,200	332,400	395,556	139,608	6.3%	
11	Papaya	2.21	2.99	492,300	541,500	1,619,085	422,370	19.2%	
12	Rambutan	3.03	3.99	306,700	337,400	1,346,226	323,904	14.7%	
13	Starfruit	1.49	2.99	142,800	157,100	469,729	235,650	10.7%	
14			Totals	2,551,800	2,807,000	$7,712,033	$2,198,620		
15									

Indenting Text

You can indent text within a cell by clicking the Increase Indent or Decrease Indent button on the Formatting toolbar. Indenting text allows finer control over text placement within a cell, somewhere between the extremes of left-aligning and right-aligning data. Each time you press the Increase Indent button, Excel moves the text or a value within a cell to the right a few character spaces. Pressing the Decrease Indent button does the opposite: It moves a value or text in a cell to the left a few spaces. You decide to move the label "Totals" in cell C14 right a few spaces.

Indenting text within a cell:

1. Click cell **C14**

2. Click the **Increase Indent** ⊞ button on the Formatting toolbar to indent "Totals" within cell C14

3. Since it has been a while since you saved your worksheet, click the **Save** ⊞ button to save your workbook

Changing Font and Font Characteristics

Excel allows you to select from a wide variety of typefaces, character formatting characteristics, and point sizes. A *font* is the combination of typeface and qualities including character size, character pitch, and spacing. Typefaces have names such as Garamond, Times Roman, and Helvetica. The height of characters in a typeface is measured in *points*, where a point is equal to 1/72 of an inch. Characters' widths are measured by *pitch*, which refers to the number of characters horizontally per inch. A font is *fixed pitch* (or monospace) if every character has the same width, whereas a font is called a *proportional* font if characters' pitches vary by character. Most people agree that proportional fonts are easier to read than fixed pitch fonts. (The typeface in this book is a proportional font.) Excel provides a large number of fonts from which you can format text and numbers.

Excel also provides the font styles regular, bold, and bold italic. Most fonts are available in a variety of sizes, and you can apply special effects to fonts such as strikethrough, superscript, subscript, a variety of colors, and various types of underlines. You access all of the preceding—fonts, font styles, and font special effects—through the Format Cells dialog box, which opens when you click Format and then Cells. Applying font characteristics is straightforward.

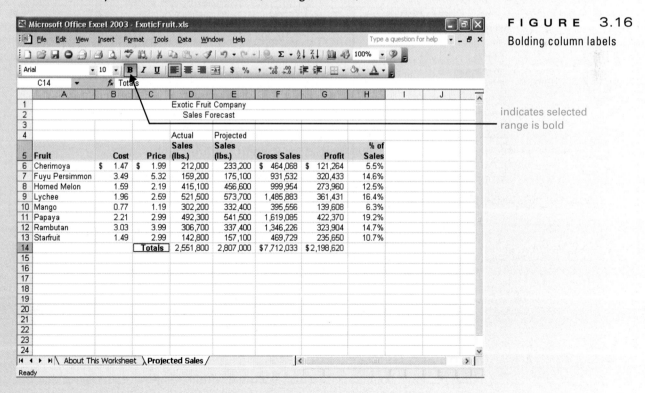

task reference

Applying Fonts and Font Characteristics

- Select the cell or cell range that you want to format
- Click **Format**, click **Cells**, and click the **Font** tab
- Select a typeface from the Font list box
- Select a font style and a font size
- Click **OK** to finalize your choices

Applying Boldface

Applying font size and characteristic changes to the worksheet title, subtitle, column headings, and selected cells in the Exotic Fruit worksheet will yield a more professional worksheet. Column labels in row 5 will look better if they stand out, and the label in cell C14 will improve too.

Applying boldface style to labels:

1. Select the cell range **A5:H5**

2. Click and hold the **Ctrl** key and then click cell **C14**

3. Release the **Ctrl** key

4. Click the **Bold** B button on the Formatting toolbar. Excel applies the boldface style to the selected labels (see Figure 3.16)

FIGURE 3.16

Bolding column labels

indicates selected range is bold

Applying Italic

Next, you will italicize the column labels in cells D4 and E4 and the numeric cells D14 through G14 for emphasis.

Applying italic to column labels and values:

1. Select the cell range **D4:E4**

2. Press and hold the **Ctrl** key and select the cell range **D14:G14**

3. Release the Ctrl key

4. Click the **Italic** ⌐I⌐ button on the Formatting toolbar

Applying Boldface and Changing Point Size and Typeface

The worksheet title and subtitle would look better bolded and with a larger point size. You also want to change the typeface from Arial to Times New Roman. You make those changes in the following steps.

Applying boldface style and modifying the point size and typeface:

FIGURE 3.17

Setting typeface and font characteristics

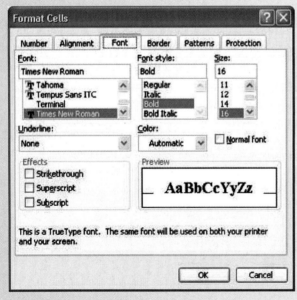

1. Select the cell range **A1:A2**. Though the worksheet title and subtitle are centered across several columns, they are actually stored in cells A1 and A2, respectively

2. Click **Format** on the menu bar, and then click **Cells**. The Format Cells dialog box opens

3. Click the **Font** tab

4. Drag the mouse across the typeface name displayed in the Font list box to select it and type **Times New Roman**

5. Click **Bold** in the Font style list box

6. In the Size list box, click the **down-pointing scroll arrow** to locate and then click **16** (see Figure 3.17)

7. Click **OK** to confirm your choices and close the Format Cells dialog box

The title and subtitle look better with the larger point size, Times New Roman typeface, and boldface applied (see Figure 3.18).

Removing Selected Formats

Nancy reviewed your worksheet and is pleased with it. However, she believes that the italic style applied to the values appearing in cells D14 through G14 is distracting. She asks you to remove that formatting entirely but to maintain the Accounting format.

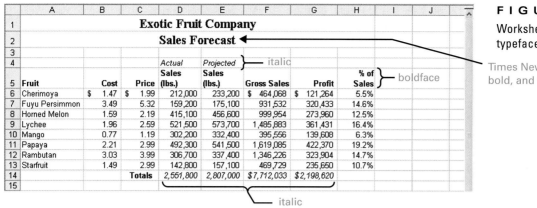

FIGURE 3.18

Worksheet with font and typeface changes

Times New Roman typeface, bold, and 16-point font

Removing one style while retaining others:

1. Select the cell range **D14:G14**. Notice that the Italic button is outlined and light tan, indicating the entire range has the Italic format

2. Click the **Italic** button to remove the Italic format from the selected cells

Clearing Formats

When you want to remove all formatting from a cell or cell range, you use the Clear Formats command. Doing so clears all formats, returning the selected cells to their default, General format.

---

task reference   **Clearing Formats from a Cell, Cell Selection, Rows, or Columns**

- Select the cell, cell range, rows, or columns whose format you want to clear

- Click **Edit**, point to **Clear**, and then click **Formats** to remove all formatting

---

Although you do not need to clear any formats, experiment with the procedure in the following steps. Then you can click Edit, Undo to restore or cancel the Format Clear operation and restore the original formatting.

Clearing one or more cells' formatting:

1. Select the cell range **A5:H5**

2. Click **Edit** on the menu bar, point to **Clear**, and click **Formats**. The cell range formats all return to the General format. Notice that the cells' contents are unaffected. Only the cells' appearances change

3. After observing the cleared formats, reverse the effects of step 2 by clicking **Edit** and then clicking **Undo Clear**. The cell range displays its bold and wrapped text formats

4. Click any cell to deselect the cell range

EXCEL

You have made several changes to your worksheet since you last saved it. Save your worksheet before continuing.

Saving your workbook under a new name:

1. Click **File** on the menu bar

2. Click **Save As**

3. Type **ExoticFruit2.xls** in the File name list box and then click the **Save** button. Excel saves your workbook under its new name

Nancy reviews your progress on the Exotic Fruit worksheet. She's pleased with the worksheet's appearance and makes some suggestions that you note. You will implement her suggested enhancements in the next section of this chapter.

SESSION 3.1

making the grade

1. What does formatting do to the contents of a cell?

2. By default, Excel worksheet cells are formatted with what format?

3. Excel aligns numbers on the _____ and aligns text on the _____ by default.

4. The Accounting format allows you to specify an optional _____ symbol, specify the number of _____ _____, and adds a space on the right side of all entries.

SESSION 3.2 ADVANCED FORMATTING

In this session, you will continue formatting a worksheet. You will alter the row height of a row, enlarging it to add emphasis. Borders delineate particular areas of a worksheet, and you will learn how to apply borders for maximum effect. In order to provide information protection, you will hide information in a column. You will use the Drawing toolbar to add text boxes and arrows to the worksheet to draw attention to especially important elements on it. Finally, you will learn how to add and remove gridlines on the screen and on the printed output and how to specify important print settings such as repeating rows and columns.

Controlling Row Heights

Earlier in this chapter, you adjusted several columns' widths. You can adjust the height of rows to provide more room for labels or values or to simply add emphasis. When you enlarged the worksheet title and subtitle, Excel compensated for the taller characters by increasing the rows' heights automatically. You can increase or decrease the height of one or more rows manually in several ways.

- Click the row heading to select the row whose height you want to modify
- Click **Format**, point to **Row**, and click **Height**
- Type the row height in the Row height text box
- Click **OK** to finalize your choices

You decide that row 14 containing totals would look better if it were taller. Increase the row's height by following these steps.

Increasing a row's height:

1. If you took a break at the end of the last session, make sure Excel is running and then open the **ExoticFruit2.xls** workbook that you saved at the end of Session 3.1

2. Click row 14's **row heading**, which is located to the left of column A in row 14. Excel selects the entire row

3. Click **Format**, point to **Row**, and click **Height**. The Row Height dialog box appears

4. Type **20** in the Row height text box (see Figure 3.19) and click **OK** to complete the row-height alteration process

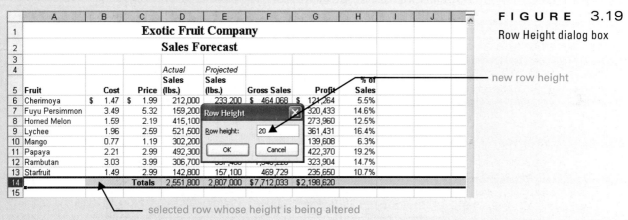

FIGURE 3.19
Row Height dialog box

new row height

selected row whose height is being altered

Employing Borders, a Text Box, an Arrow, and Shading

Like many worksheets, the Exotic Fruit Company Sales Forecast worksheet has distinct regions or zones that contain groups of related information. Using lines to delineate these groups adds impact to your worksheet and makes the groups easier to identify.

Adding Borders

A *cell border* is a format that applies lines of various types to one or more edges (left, right, top, bottom) of the selected cell(s). You create borders among or around selected cells by selecting the Borders button on the Formatting toolbar or by selecting options on the Border tab of the Format Cells dialog box. Using the Outline option, you can

anotherway
. . . to Modify a Row's Height

Drag the boundary line below the row heading until the row is the height you want

Release the mouse

place a border around one cell or the rectangle created by a selection of several cells. You can create a horizontal line by selecting cells in the same row and then formatting either the top or bottom edge with a border. Similarly, you create a vertical line by formatting a border on the left or right side of a selection of cells in a single column.

Using the Formatting dialog box, you have several border styles available, including solid lines of various thicknesses, dashed lines, and double lines. The Border button provides a few of the more popular border options. Removing borders from a cell is straightforward with the Format Cells dialog box. You select the cell(s) whose borders you want to remove, click the Border tab of the Format Cells dialog box, and click None.

---

task reference   Adding a Border to a Cell

- Click the cell to which you want to add a border
- Click **Format**, click **Cells**, and click the **Border** tab
- Click the line style in the Style list that you want to apply to the selected cell or cells
- Click one or more of the buttons indicating which cell walls you want to format with a border
- Click **OK** to apply your border formatting choices

Formatting a border below the column headings:

1. Select the cell range **A5:H5**

2. Click the Borders button list arrow on the Formatting toolbar. A series of borders appears (see Figure 3.20)

FIGURE 3.20

Border choices

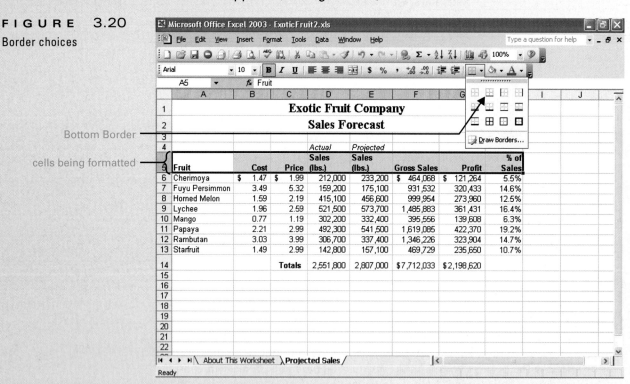

3. Click the thin **Bottom Border** button (top row, second from the left)

Formatting a border above column headings:

1. Select the cell range **A4:H4**
2. Click **Format**, click **Cells**, and click the **Border** tab on the Format Cells dialog box
3. Click the **thick line** in the Line Style box (the second line from the bottom on the right side of the Line Style box)
4. Click the **top border** button. Excel places a thick line at the top of the Border preview window indicating the relative position of the line in the selected cell range (see Figure 3.21)

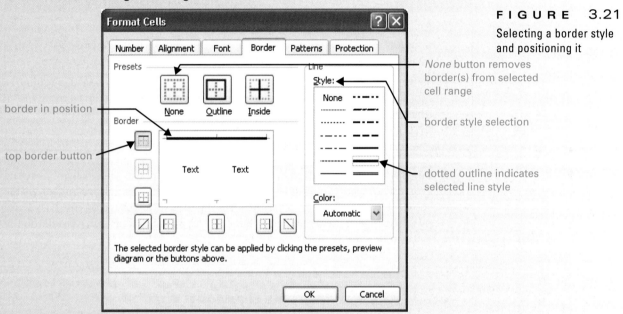

border in position

top border button

FIGURE 3.21

Selecting a border style and positioning it

None button removes border(s) from selected cell range

border style selection

dotted outline indicates selected line style

5. Click **OK** to complete the operation, and click any cell to deselect the cell range

The last pair of borders will be similar to the first two you created. A thin line will separate product information from totals in row 14. Finally, you will format the bottom edge of row 14 with a thick border to enclose the product sales information in a pair of thick lines.

Adding a thin and thick border:

1. Select the cell range **A14:H14**
2. Click **Format**, click **Cells**, and then click the **Border** tab on the Format Cells dialog box
3. Click the **thin line** in the Line Style box (the bottom line on the left side of the Line Style box)
4. Click the **top border** button
5. Click the **thick line** in the Line Style box and then click the **bottom border** button
6. Click **OK**

EXCEL

Adding and Removing Toolbars

Excel provides several useful drawing tools that allow you to create graphic elements on a special drawing layer of a worksheet. Drawing elements float over the top of a worksheet. They include arrows, text boxes, various lines and connector lines, over 30 basic shapes such as rectangles and trapezoids, WordArt, and clip art. You access these features on the Drawing toolbar.

You are already familiar with Excel's Standard toolbar and Formatting toolbar. In addition, Excel has other toolbars, including the Chart toolbar, Drawing toolbar, Forms toolbar, and Visual Basic toolbar. *Activating a toolbar* is the process of making it appear on the desktop.

---

task reference   Activating or Removing a Toolbar

- Activate a toolbar by right-clicking any toolbar or the menu bar. The toolbar shortcut menu appears. Click the name of the toolbar you want to use, which places a checkmark next to the toolbar name and makes the toolbar appear

- Remove a toolbar by right-clicking any toolbar or the menu bar. The toolbar shortcut menu appears. Click the name of the toolbar you want to remove, which removes the checkmark next to the toolbar name and makes the toolbar disappear

---

If your worksheet is obscured by too many toolbars, you can selectively remove the toolbars you do not want. You can remove all toolbars, leaving only the menu bar visible if you choose. However, in order to use the Drawing toolbar features, you must ask Excel to display the Drawing toolbar. If the Drawing toolbar is not visible, do the following

F I G U R E   3.22

Excel toolbar shortcut menu

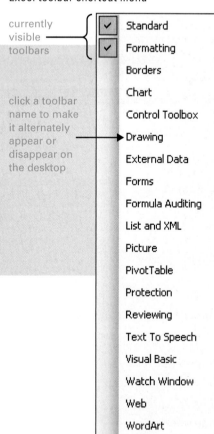

currently visible toolbars

click a toolbar name to make it alternately appear or disappear on the desktop

Displaying the Drawing toolbar:

1. Right-click the menu bar. The toolbar shortcut menu appears (see Figure 3.22)

2. Click **Drawing** in the shortcut menu. The Drawing toolbar appears

tip: *If a toolbar is **floating** on the worksheet, it can appear anywhere in the worksheet window. If so, you can dock it on any of the four edges of your display. (When you **dock** a toolbar, it clings to the edge of the window.) Simply click the toolbar's Title bar and drag it toward an edge of the worksheet window. It will dock on the edge when the mouse nears it*

Adding a Text Box

Excel's *text box* is a rectangular-shaped drawing object that contains text. It floats above a worksheet's cells and is useful to annotate an especially important point. Graphic elements provide ways to enhance your worksheet. You can move or delete an object easily. First, move the pointer over the object and click it to select it. An object displays small square *selection handles* around its perimeter or on its ends to indicate it is selected. Once you select an object, you can press the Delete key to delete it or click within the object and drag it to a new location. You can adjust the size of an object by clicking one of its selection handles and dragging until the object obtains the desired size.

---

task reference   **Adding a Text Box to a Worksheet**

- Activate the Drawing toolbar and then click the **Text Box** ⬛ button
- Click the worksheet in the location where you want the text box
- Drag an outline away from the initial point until the text box outline is the right size and shape
- Type the text you want to appear in the text box
- Click anywhere outside the text box to deselect it

Exotic Fruit's best-selling product this year and projected best-seller next year is papaya. You want to draw attention to the projected profit and overall percentage of sales for papaya. A text box is a good way to emphasize the projected sales of papaya.

Adding a text box to a worksheet:

1. With the Drawing toolbar visible, click the **Text Box** ⬛ button, and then move the mouse over any cell in the worksheet

2. Move the mouse pointer to the upper-left corner of cell **J11** and then click the mouse to establish the upper-left corner of the text box. (You may have to scroll the worksheet to the left so that columns J, K, and L are in view.) A narrow box appears with four circular selection handles—one at each corner of the box

3. Move the mouse to the lower-right text box selection handle. The mouse pointer changes to a two-headed arrow

4. Click and drag the mouse to the right until you reach the lower-right corner of cell **L11**, and then release the mouse

5. Type **Papaya is popular. Vons purchases large quantities of it.**

6. Carefully move the mouse pointer to any border of the text box until the pointer changes to a four-headed pointer and then **right-click** the border. A shortcut menu appears

7. Click **Format Text box** in the shortcut menu, click the **Colors and Lines** tab, click the **Color** list box found in the Fill section, and click **Automatic**, which appears above the color palette

8. Click the **Color** list box in the Line section of the Format Text Box dialog box, click **Automatic**, which appears above the color palette, and then click **OK** to apply the text box formatting and close the dialog box

You can see that the message is longer than the text box can display, and it appears that only part of the message is available. Therefore, you need to enlarge the text box just enough so that the entire message is visible.

EXCEL

Modifying the Size of a Text Box:

1. Click the **text box** to select it. Six circular selection handles appear around the text box indicating it is selected

2. Move the cursor until it is directly above the center handle on the bottom edge of the text box. The pointer changes to a double-headed arrow pointing up and down

3. Click and drag the selection handle so that the bottom edge of the text box is aligned with the bottom edge of row 12 so that the text box covers approximately two rows

4. Release the mouse. The text box is large enough to display the entire message (see Figure 3.23)

FIGURE   3.23

Adding a text box for emphasis

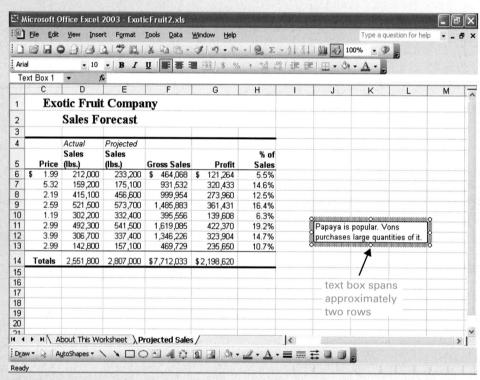

Adding an Arrow

The text box adds just the right emphasis without overpowering the worksheet. You decide to add an arrow leading from the text box to the right end of the papaya row—to cell H11—so that it is clear to which row the text box refers. There are several arrows available in the Drawing toolbar from which you can choose.

Adding an arrow graphic behind the text box:

1. Click the **AutoShapes** menu on the Drawing toolbar

2. Point to **Block Arrows** and then click the **Left Arrow** (see Figure 3.24), which is in the top row, second arrow from the left. The mouse pointer changes to a small plus sign

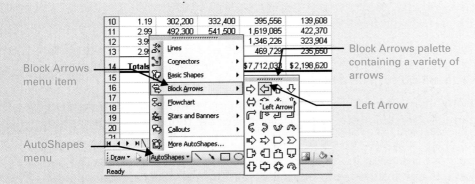

Block Arrows
menu item

AutoShapes
menu

FIGURE 3.24

Selecting an arrow from
the AutoShapes menu

Block Arrows palette
containing a variety of
arrows

Left Arrow

3. Move the mouse pointer just to the right of the word *Papaya* in the
   text box

4. Click and drag the mouse to the left and down so that the outline of the
   arrow completely fills cell **I11** and covers the word Papaya and the tip of
   the arrow just touches the right edge of cell **H11**. Release the mouse

tip: *If you are dissatisfied with the arrow for any reason (its right end does not cover
Papaya, it is too skinny, for example), then select the arrow, press the **Delete** key, and repeat
the preceding steps until you are pleased with the arrow*

5. With the arrow selected, move the mouse pointer *inside* the arrow and
   right-click the mouse. A shortcut menu appears

6. Point to **Order** on the shortcut menu and click **Send to Back**. Excel places
   the arrow in a layer beneath the text box and the word *Papaya* becomes
   visible again (see Figure 3.25)

FIGURE 3.25

Placing an arrow behind a
text box

	C	D	E	F	G	H	I	J	K	L	M
1	**Exotic Fruit Company**										
2		**Sales Forecast**									
3											
4		Actual	Projected								
5	Price	**Sales (lbs.)**	**Sales (lbs.)**	**Gross Sales**	**Profit**	**% of Sales**					
6	$ 1.99	212,000	233,200	$ 464,068	$ 121,264	5.5%					
7	5.32	159,200	175,100	931,532	320,433	14.6%					
8	2.19	415,100	456,600	999,954	273,960	12.5%					
9	2.59	521,500	573,700	1,485,883	361,431	16.4%					
10	1.19	302,200	332,400	395,556	139,608	6.3%					
11	2.99	492,300	541,500	1,619,085	422,370	19.2%		Papaya is popular. Vons			
12	3.99	306,700	337,400	1,346,226	323,904	14.7%		purchases large quantities of it.			
13	2.99	142,800	157,100	469,729	235,650	10.7%					
14	**Totals**	2,551,800	2,807,000	$7,712,033	$2,198,620						
15											

arrow is partially
behind the text box

7. Click in any cell to deselect the arrow

Grouping Drawing Objects

Joining two graphics into one object is called *grouping*. Once grouped, multiple objects
act as one and one set of selection handles surrounds the larger grouped object. You can
ungroup objects later if you want to adjust their position and then regroup them.
Grouping objects makes it easier to move them as a unit.

Grouping two graphic objects:

1. Click the text box to select it. Selection handles appear around the
   text box

2. Press and hold the **Shift** key

3. Move the mouse over the arrow graphic and click the mouse to select the arrow graphic. Release the **Shift** key. Both objects should be selected. If not, repeat steps 1 through 3

4. With the mouse within the arrow graphic (the mouse pointer displays the four-headed arrow pointer) right-click the mouse. A shortcut menu appears

5. Point to **Grouping** in the shortcut menu and then click **Group**. The two objects are grouped, and one set of selection handles surrounds the grouped graphic (see Figure 3.26)

FIGURE 3.26

Grouped objects

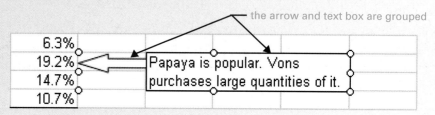
the arrow and text box are grouped

6. Click any cell to deselect the grouped objects

Adding a Drop Shadow

You can make some drawing objects look three-dimensional by adding a drop shadow. A **_drop shadow_** is the shadow that is cast by the object. Adding a drop shadow to the grouped object—the arrow and text box—enhances the object and adds a little flair.

Adding a drop shadow to a drawing object:

1. Ensure that the Drawing toolbar is visible and then click the arrow and text box grouped object to select it. Selection handles appear around the object

2. Click the **Shadow Style** ▣ button on the Drawing toolbar. A palette of drop shadow choices appears (see Figure 3.27)

3. Click **Shadow Style 6**, which is in the second row from the top and second from the left. (The Shadow Style 6 is consistent with the way Office products produce shadows for buttons and other Windows objects)

4. Click any cell to deselect the drawing object. The arrow and text box combination display an attractive drop shadow (see Figure 3.28)

Because you do not need to use the Drawing toolbar in the remainder of this chapter, you can remove it. Doing so provides a little more room for your worksheet.

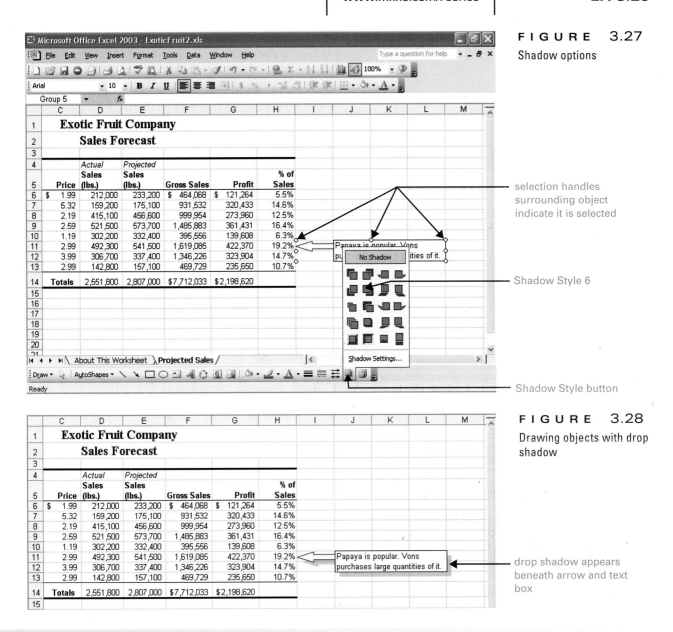

FIGURE 3.27
Shadow options

FIGURE 3.28
Drawing objects with drop shadow

Remove the Drawing toolbar from the work surface:

1. Click the **Drawing** ⊞ button on the Standard toolbar. The Drawing toolbar disappears from the work surface and the Drawing button no longer appears highlighted (selected)

2. Just to be safe, save your workbook by clicking the **Save** button on the Standard toolbar

Hiding and Unhiding Rows and Columns

The Cost column contains prices that Exotic Fruit Company pays to its suppliers and is company confidential. Nancy wants you to somehow make that column not appear in any printouts you or any of the managers produce. Naturally, you cannot *delete* the column from the worksheet because the Profit column depends on the Cost column. The

Percent of Sales column depends indirectly on the Cost column. If you deleted the Cost column, Excel would display the error message #REF! in the Profit column and the Percent of Sales column. Hiding a column is the best solution.

task reference — **Hiding Rows or Columns**

- Select the rows or columns you want to hide
- Click **Format**, point to **Row** (or **Column**), and click **Hide**

Hiding the Cost column:

1. Click the **column B header**. Excel selects the entire column
2. Click **Format**, point to **Column**, and then click **Hide**. Excel hides column B (see Figure 3.29)

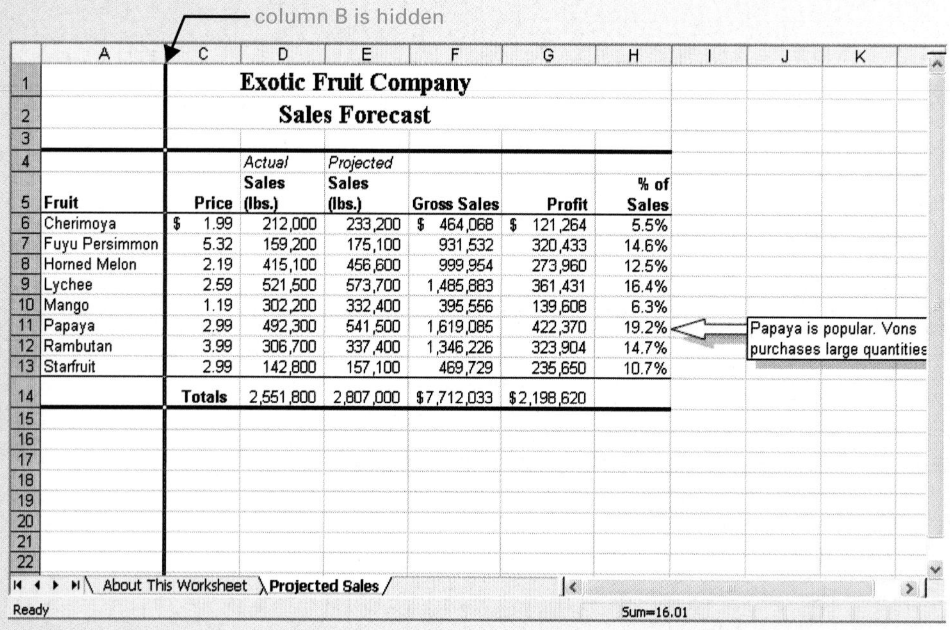

	A	C	D	E	F	G	H
1		Exotic Fruit Company					
2		Sales Forecast					
3							
4			*Actual*	*Projected*			
5	Fruit	Price	Sales (lbs.)	Sales (lbs.)	Gross Sales	Profit	% of Sales
6	Cherimoya	$ 1.99	212,000	233,200	$ 464,068	$ 121,264	5.5%
7	Fuyu Persimmon	5.32	159,200	175,100	931,532	320,433	14.6%
8	Horned Melon	2.19	415,100	456,600	999,954	273,960	12.5%
9	Lychee	2.59	521,500	573,700	1,485,883	361,431	16.4%
10	Mango	1.19	302,200	332,400	395,556	139,608	6.3%
11	Papaya	2.99	492,300	541,500	1,619,085	422,370	19.2%
12	Rambutan	3.99	306,700	337,400	1,346,226	323,904	14.7%
13	Starfruit	2.99	142,800	157,100	469,729	235,650	10.7%
14		Totals	2,551,800	2,807,000	$7,712,033	$2,198,620	

FIGURE 3.29
Hiding a worksheet column

3. Click any cell to deselect the hidden column

anotherway
. . . to Hide Rows or Columns

Select the rows or columns you want to hide

Right-click the selected rows or columns to display a shortcut menu

Click **Column Width** in the shortcut menu

Type **0** in the Column width text box and click **OK**

Column B disappears, although it is still part of the worksheet because the formulas that depend on column B entries, such as formulas in column G and H, still display correct values.

Using Color for Emphasis

Using colors and patterns carefully can emphasize areas of the worksheet, highlight input areas where users type assumption values, or provide an attractive design element to your worksheet. An important key to effective use of color is restraint. Use color sparingly. Too much color or too many colors in a worksheet can yield a garish, unattractive, or confusing overall appearance. On the other hand, the subtle use of color results in an attractive worksheet that others can easily understand and use. If you plan to make color transparencies from your worksheet output, you will need a color printer. However, you can print out color-enhanced worksheets on a noncolor printer. Be aware that black text in cells containing a colored background may not be legible.

Experiment with different text and cell background colors if you cannot print your worksheet on a color printer. Generally, lighter colors work better on noncolor printers. As an alternative, you can use patterns to emphasize areas when the output device is a noncolor printer.

Nancy's office has both color printers and noncolor printers (sometimes called monochrome printers or black-and-white printers). She wants you to add a splash of color to the worksheet that looks good on both types of printers. After consulting other people in the office, you decide to use light colors such as pale yellow and light gray for emphasis. Those colors don't obscure black text and look good on both types of printers.

---

task reference — Applying Color or Patterns to Worksheet Cells

- Select the cells to which you want to apply a color or pattern
- Click **Format**, click **Cells**, and click the **Patterns** tab in the Format Cells dialog box
- If you want to apply a pattern, click a pattern from the Pattern list box
- If you want the pattern to appear in color, click the Pattern list box again and click a color from the Pattern palette
- If you want to apply a colored background, click a color in the Cell shading color palette in the Format Cells dialog box

---

Applying a background color to column labels:

1. Click and drag the cell range **A4:H5**

2. Click **Format** on the menu bar, click **Cells**, and then click the **Patterns** tab on the Format Cells dialog box (see Figure 3.30)

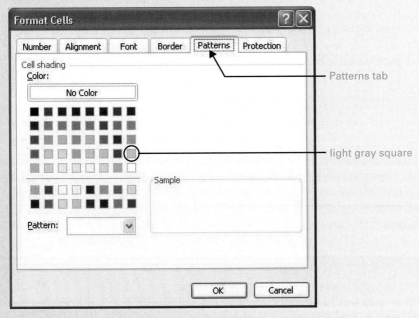

FIGURE 3.30

Patterns tab of the Format Cells dialog box

3. Click the **light gray square** (in the fourth row from the top and in the rightmost column) of the Cell shading Color palette

4. Click **OK**

Next, you will apply another background color to the total profit cell, G14, to high-light that value. Instead of using the Format menu to apply a color, you will use the Fill Color button on the Formatting toolbar, a faster alternative for this type of formatting.

Applying a background color to the total profit cell:

1. Click cell **G14** and click the **Fill Color** button list arrow to display the Cell shading Color palette

2. Click the **Yellow** color square found in the fourth row from the top and the third square from the left. The background of cell G14 changes to yellow. Figure 3.31 shows the two color formatting changes you have made

FIGURE 3.31

Applying a background color to a cell

Fill Color button

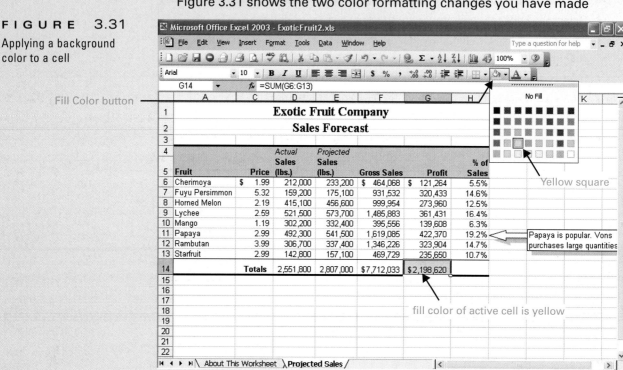

3. Press **Ctrl+Home** to make cell A1 active

You have finished applying the formatting changes to the Exotic Fruit Company worksheet. Nancy has reviewed the worksheet and is very pleased with its overall look. She wants you to make one more change to it, however. Nancy thinks that the gridlines that Excel displays onscreen by default are distracting and lessen the visual impact of the worksheet.

Controlling Gridlines

Excel normally outlines worksheet cells in gray (onscreen). The gridlines are very handy because they help you locate cells as you are building your worksheet models. When your worksheet is complete, you may wish to eliminate the onscreen gridlines.

You can also control whether Excel displays gridlines on *output* or not. Normally Excel does not display gridlines on output. However, you may want to display them for documentation or demonstration purposes.

Removing and Displaying Gridlines Onscreen

Gridline display is an option that you can set for each worksheet or for all worksheets at once. If you remove the gridlines from one worksheet, they need not be removed from other worksheets in the same workbook.

Removing gridlines from the Projected Sales worksheet:

1. Click **Tools** on the menu bar and then click **Options**. The Options dialog box opens

2. If necessary, click the **View** tab

3. Click the **Gridlines** check box in the Window options section to remove the checkmark and remove the onscreen gridlines

4. Click **OK** to complete your changes and display the worksheet without gridlines (see Figure 3.32)

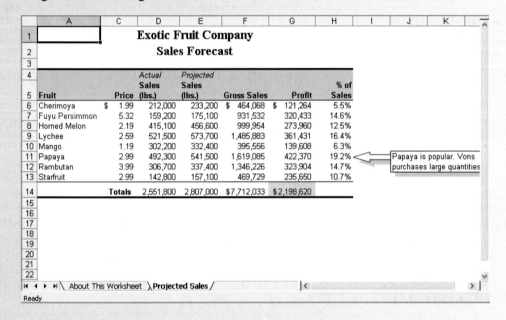

FIGURE 3.32

Worksheet without gridline display

Restoring worksheet gridlines is the reverse of the preceding steps. That is, you click Tools, click Options, click View, click the Gridlines check box to check it, and click OK.

Removing and Displaying Gridlines on Output

When you want to display worksheet gridlines in *output pages,* set that option prior to printing a page. While output worksheets containing gridlines are not as professional looking as those without gridlines, you may want to print out the worksheet with gridlines as well as the row and column headings for documentation purposes.

Adding gridlines and row and column headings to a worksheet to be printed:

1. Click **File** on the menu bar and then click **Page Setup**. The Page Setup dialog box opens

2. Click the **Sheet** tab in the Page Setup dialog box and then click the **Gridlines** check box (in the Print section) to place a checkmark in it

3. Click **Row and column headings** check box to place a checkmark in it. The Row and columns headings check box controls whether or not worksheet row and column headings appear in output (see Figure 3.33)

FIGURE 3.33

Setting print options

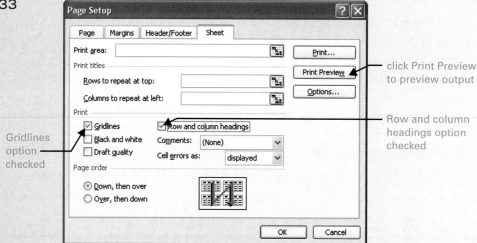

click Print Preview to preview output

Row and column headings option checked

Gridlines option checked

4. Click the **Print Preview** button (see Figure 3.33) to preview the output

5. Click the **Setup** button in the Print Preview toolbar to redisplay the Page Setup dialog box

6. Click the **Gridlines** check box to clear it and then click the **Row and column headings** check box to clear it. You don't want to print the worksheet gridlines or the row and column headings at this time

7. Click **OK** in the Page Setup dialog box

8. Click the **Close** button on the Print Preview toolbar to return to your worksheet

Printing

When you are ready to print a worksheet, you should preview the output using the Print Preview command. That way, you can check to ensure that the worksheet looks right or check to make sure the output is not several pages long. Print Preview shows margins, page breaks, headers and footers, and other elements that you do not see in the worksheet window.

Previewing output:

1. Click the **Print Preview** 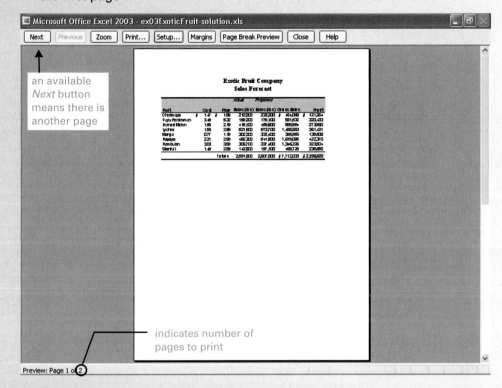 button on the Standard toolbar. The Print Preview window opens, revealing a facsimile of the first page (see Figure 3.34). You notice that the text box and arrow do not appear on the first page

FIGURE 3.34

Print Preview window

an available *Next* button means there is another page

indicates number of pages to print

Preview: Page 1 of 2

2. Click the **Next** button to view the second page. Ah ha! The text box and arrow appear on the second page

3. Click the **Previous** button to go back to the first page

Previewing the output reveals that the worksheet is slightly larger than can currently fit on one page. One remedy is to reduce the left and right margins until there is enough room to fit all the output on one page. Another possibility is to reduce the font size of the entire worksheet until it is small enough to squeeze the entire worksheet on one page. A third alternative is to reorient the worksheet printout.

Controlling Print Orientation

Excel provides two print orientations called portrait and landscape. *Portrait* orientation prints a worksheet so that the paper is taller than it is wide—the standard way books and notebook paper are written. It borrows its name from the way artists paint portraits. *Landscape* orientation prints a worksheet that is wider than it is tall. The term landscape reminds you of an artist's painting depicting a landscape, which is often wider than it is tall. The Exotic Fruit worksheet should be printed in landscape orientation to fit nicely on a printed page.

Changing an output orientation to landscape:

1. With the Print Preview window still open, click the **Setup** button, which opens the Page Setup dialog box

2. Click the **Page** tab and then click the **Landscape** option button in the Orientation section to select Landscape orientation

3. Click **OK** to return to Print Preview (see Figure 3.35). Notice that the entire worksheet fits on the page and the Next button is dimmed, which indicates there is only one output page

FIGURE 3.35

Landscape orientation

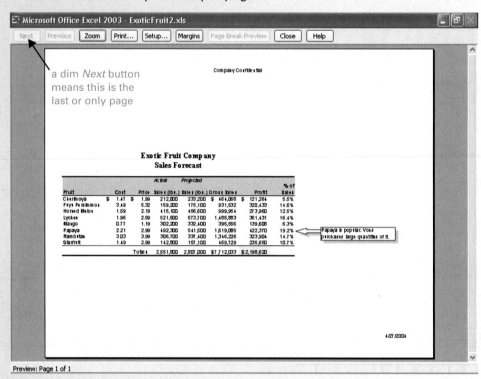

Centering Output on a Page

Before printing the worksheet, you can center the worksheet on a page and add a header and footer. First, center the worksheet.

Vertically centering worksheet output:

1. With the Print Preview window still open, click the **Setup** button

2. Click the **Margins** tab in the Page Setup dialog box

3. Click the **Vertically** check box to place a checkmark in the check box (see Figure 3.36)

4. Click **OK**

In an e-mail message she sent a week ago, Nancy requested that you print the worksheet with the header "Company Confidential" in the center and a footer containing your name and the current date. You decide to place your name on the left side of the page and the current date on the right side.

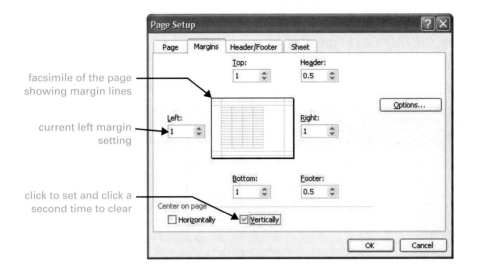

Placing information in a worksheet header and footer:

1. With the Print Preview window still open, click the **Setup** button
2. Click the **Header/Footer** tab in the Page Setup dialog box
3. Click the **Custom Header** button and click in the **Center section**
4. In the Center section, type **Company Confidential** and then click **OK**
5. Click the **Custom Footer** button, click in the **Left section**, and type your first and last names
6. Click in the **Right section** and click the **Date** 📅 button to insert the current date
7. Click **OK** to close the Footer dialog box
8. Click **OK** again to close the Page Setup dialog box
9. Click the **Close** button in the Print Preview toolbar to close the window

Unhiding a Column

Your work on the Exotic Fruit Company Sales Forecast worksheet is almost done, and you are ready to give Nancy the printed copy for her to check before her presentation next week. Before you print the worksheet, unhide column B, check the output once more in the Print Preview window, and make any necessary output adjustments. Then you can save the worksheet and exit Excel.

Unhiding column B:

1. Position the mouse pointer over the column A header
2. Click and drag the mouse through the **column C header** to select the three columns (column A, hidden column B, and column C). Notice that the two visible columns are highlighted
3. Right-click anywhere inside the selected columns. A shortcut menu appears

4. Click **Unhide** in the shortcut menu

5. Click any cell to deselect the three selected columns

6. Click the **Print Preview** button to check the output (see Figure 3.37)

FIGURE 3.37

Preview of expanded worksheet

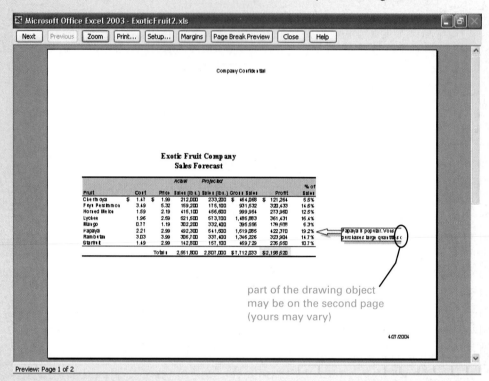

part of the drawing object may be on the second page (yours may vary)

Depending on where you positioned the drawing objects in the steps presented earlier in this chapter, your output may (still) not fit on one page. The example shown in Figure 3.37 shows a tiny part of the graphic missing from the right end of the text box. One way to handle this kind of problem is to enlarge your worksheet page by adjusting the left and right margins. Any space released by left and right margins is allocated to the worksheet printing area, just enough to print the entire worksheet and drawing object on one page.

Modifying the left and right margins:

1. With the Print Preview window still open, click the **Setup** button. The Page Setup dialog box opens

2. Click the **Margins** tab and double-click the **Left spin control box** to highlight the current left margin number

3. Type **0.5** to set the left margin to one-half inch

4. Double-click the **Right spin control box** to highlight the current right margin number

5. Type **0.5** to set the right margin to one-half inch

6. Click **OK** to close the Page Setup dialog box

tip: *If you still cannot see the entire worksheet on one page, you can force the worksheet to fit by clicking the **Page** tab in the Page Setup dialog box and then click the **Fit to** option button in the Scaling section of the Page tab settings. This shrinks the overall worksheet so that it fits on a single page*

7. Click the **Close** button on the Print Preview toolbar to close the window and return to the worksheet

Printing Several Worksheets

Your work on the Exotic Fruit Company worksheet is complete. Always save your work when you have completed a significant number of changes. That way, your work is safely stored in case you need to open the latest version of the workbook.

Saving your workbook:

1. Click the **File** on the menu bar

2. Click **Save**

Nancy asks you to print the main worksheet and the documentation sheet. You have printed single worksheets before, but not multiple worksheets in one print statement.

Printing multiple worksheets is almost the same process as printing a single worksheet. There is only one small difference in the procedure: You press and hold the Ctrl key and then click the worksheet tabs corresponding to all the worksheets you want to print. Then release the Ctrl key. Then you print as usual.

When you click multiple worksheet tabs, they turn white to indicate they are selected. You probably noticed that there are three option buttons available in the *Print what* section of the Print dialog box. The default option selected is *Active sheets*, which instructs Excel to print all selected sheets. Selected sheets are called ***active sheets***.

---

task *reference*　　　Printing Multiple Worksheets

- Press and hold the **Ctrl** key
- Click the sheet tabs of each sheet you want to print
- Release the **Ctrl** key
- Click the **Print** button on the Standard toolbar

---

help yourself *Press **F1**, type **print what** in the Search text box of the Microsoft Excel Help task pane, and press **Enter**. Click the hyperlink **print**, scroll the results list box to locate and click the hyperlink **Define what part of the worksheet to print**. Close the Help dialog box when you are done, and close the task pane*

EXCEL

Printing multiple Exotic Fruit worksheets:

1. Press and hold the **Ctrl** key
2. With the Projected Sales worksheet displayed (active), click the worksheet tab **About This Worksheet**. Both worksheet tabs turn white, indicating both worksheets are active (see Figure 3.38)

FIGURE 3.38

Selecting multiple worksheets

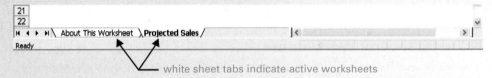

white sheet tabs indicate active worksheets

3. Release the **Ctrl** key
4. Click the **Print** 🖨 button on the Standard toolbar
5. Click the **About This Worksheet** tab to deselect the multiple active worksheets

---

*another*word   ...on Selecting and Deselecting Multiple Worksheets

Select multiple worksheets in a contiguous group by clicking the leftmost worksheet tab in the group

Then press and hold the **Shift** key and click the rightmost worksheet tab in the group (using the tab scroll buttons if necessary)

Ctrl-clicking worksheet tabs allows you to select noncontiguous worksheets

Deselect multiple worksheet tabs by clicking any worksheet tab that is *not* selected

If all worksheet tabs are selected, click any one of the worksheet tabs to deselect all the other tabs

---

SESSION 3.2

making the grade

1. Describe how to modify a row's height.

2. Click the _____ tab in the Format Cells dialog box to add borders to selected cells.

3. Activate the Drawing toolbar by right-clicking any _____ or the _____ bar and then clicking Drawing in the list.

4. When you click a drawing object such as a text box, _____ _____ appear around the object.

SESSION 3.3 SUMMARY

Formatting worksheet entries alters the appearance of labels and values but does not alter the cells' contents. Clicking Clear and then Formats from the Edit menu restores selected cells to an unformatted state.

Common formatting choices display values with leading currency symbols, allow you to select the number of decimal places to display, and provide comma separators for larger numbers.

Excel repeats the symbol # in formatted numeric cells in which the values are larger than the column can display. In that case, widen the column until the # symbols disappear. When possible, delay altering column widths until you complete all formatting. Use the Format Painter button to apply one cell's format characteristics to other cells. Doing so relieves you from executing several multistep formatting commands to apply a series of formats. Excel includes a wide variety of typeface, point size, and character formatting choices. Typeface choices range from Arial to ZaphDingbats, and you can format text or numbers in point sizes ranging from 4 points to over 96, depending on the typeface you choose. Boldface, Italic, and Underline are popular character formatting choices that you can apply to any cells.

Excel provides several toolbars whose name you can see by right-clicking in the menu or in any toolbar. You can activate a toolbar from the shortcut menu by clicking the toolbar's name. The Drawing toolbar contains graphic objects that you can place on a layer above the worksheet. Text boxes are handy for pointing out special worksheet features or simply noting important facts about the worksheet. Clicking an object selects it and selection handles appear around the object's perimeter.

Clicking the Print Preview button allows you to preview output before you print it. If the worksheet is too wide to fit on a page, try landscape orientation rather than portrait. Landscape orientation is wider than it is tall. Print multiple pages of a worksheet by ctrl-clicking multiple tabs before printing. Modify page margins when needed to provide more space for worksheet output. Hide selected columns when necessary to prevent printing confidential or proprietary information. Select the column and select Column Hide from the Format menu. Hiding a column is synonymous with making its width equal to zero.

MICROSOFT OFFICE SPECIALIST OBJECTIVES SUMMARY

- Apply currency and accounting formats to numbers—MOS XL03S-3-1
- Left-, center-, and right-align text—MOS XL03S-3-1
- Modify the typeface and point size of text and numbers—MOS XL03S-3-1
- Apply boldface, italic, and underlines to cells—MOS XL03S-3-1
- Clear all formatting from selected cells—MOS XL03S-3-1
- Remove worksheet gridlines—MOS XL03S-3-1
- Modify column widths and row heights—MOS XL03S-3-3
- Hide and reveal rows and columns—MOS XL03S-3-3
- Modify the worksheet's print characteristics—MOS XL03S-5-7
- Print multiple, selected worksheets at once—MOS XL03S-5-8

making the grade *answers*

SESSION 3.1

1. Formatting does not change the *contents* of a cell. It changes the *appearance* of a cell's displayed results.

2. The General format is the default Excel cell format

3. right; left

4. currency; decimal places

SESSION 3.2

1. Select a row by clicking its row heading. Then click Format, Row, Height, type in the height, and click OK.

2. Border (not Borders)

3. toolbar; Menu

4. selection handles

EXCEL

task reference summary

Task	Location	Preferred Method
Formatting numbers	EX 3.6	• Select cell(s) • Click **Format**, click **Cells**, click **Number** • Click format category and select options • Click **OK**
Copying a cell format to a cell or cell range	EX 3.9	• Select the cell whose format you want to copy • Click the **Format Painter** button • Click (click/drag) the target cell(s)
Modifying a column's width	EX 3.12	• Select the column heading(s) of all columns whose width you want to change • Click **Format**, point to **Column**, and click **Width** • Enter the new column width in the **Column Width** text box and click OK, or click **AutoFit Selection** to make the column(s) optimal width—as wide as the widest entry in the column
Wrapping long text within a cell	EX 3.15	• Select the cell or cell range to which you will apply a format • Click **Format**, click **Cells**, and click the **Alignment** tab • Click the **Wrap text** check box • Click **OK**
Applying fonts and font characteristics	EX 3.17	• Select the cell or cell range that you want to format • Click **Format**, click **Cells**, and click the **Font** tab • Select a typeface from the Font list box • Select a font style and a font size • Click **OK**
Clearing formats from a cell, cell selection, rows, or columns	EX 3.19	• Select the cell, cell range, rows, or columns • Click **Edit**, point to **Clear**, and click **Formats**
Modifying a row's height	EX 3.21	• Click the row heading • Click **Format**, point to **Row**, and click **Height** • Type the row height in the Row height text box • Click **OK**
Adding a border to a cell	EX 3.22	• Click the cell to which you want to add a border • Click the Formatting toolbar Borders list box arrow, and click the border you want
Activating or removing a toolbar	EX 3.24	• **Right-click** the menu bar • Click the name of the toolbar you want to activate or remove
Adding a text box to a worksheet	EX 3.25	• Activate the Drawing toolbar • Click the **Text Box** button • Click the worksheet in the location where you want the text box • Drag an outline away from the initial point until the text box outline is the right size and shape • Type the text you want to appear in the text box
Hiding rows or columns	EX 3.30	• Select the rows or columns • Click **Format**, point to **Row** (or **Column**), and click **Hide**
Applying color or patterns to worksheet cells	EX 3.31	• Select the cells to which you want to apply a color or pattern • Click **Format**, click **Cells**, and click the **Patterns** tab in the Format Cells dialog box • If you want to apply a pattern, click a pattern from the Pattern list box • If you want the pattern to appear in color, click the Pattern list box again and click a color from the Pattern palette • If you want to apply a colored background, click a color in the Cell shading Color palette in the Format Cells dialog box
Printing multiple worksheets	EX 3.39	• Ctrl-click the sheet tabs of each sheet you want to print • Click the **Print** button

TRUE OR FALSE

1. By default, Excel formats all worksheet cells with a standard format called Normal.

2. Font is the name for the combination of typeface, character size, and spacing.

3. Comma formatting adds a character to the left side of each value.

4. A drop shadow is the shadow that is cast by the object.

5. An arrow, if grouped, will be moved with the object selected.

6. Gridline display can be set for each worksheet or for all worksheets at once.

FILL-IN

1. Use the numeric format _____ when you want to format a value such as 0.3478 to display 34.78%.

2. Use the Format _____ to copy the format of one cell to another.

3. The _____ format displays a left-justified currency symbol for numeric entries.

4. Apply a cell _____ format to produce lines and to outline an area of related cells.

5. Click the _____ menu on the Drawing toolbar to display a palette of shapes such as Block Arrows and lines.

6. Select _____ orientation for wide worksheets. The default orientation, _____, is best for narrow worksheets.

MULTIPLE CHOICE

1. The General format
   a. aligns numbers on the left side of a cell.
   b. aligns text on the right side of a cell.
   c. indicates negative numbers with parentheses.
   d. displays as many digits in a number as a cell's width allows.

2. Which of the following is the process of making a toolbar appear on a desktop?
   a. floating
   b. activating
   c. formatting
   d. highlighting

3. What is the term that refers to the position of the data relative to the sides of a cell?
   a. justification
   b. location
   c. point
   d. alignment

4. Joining two graphics into one object is called
   a. grouping.
   b. selecting.
   c. attaching.
   d. embedding.

5. If the pitch of the characters varies, then this font is called a(n)
   a. conditional font.
   b. varying font.
   c. proportional font.
   d. Italic font.

6. To apply lines to one or more edges of a cell, select
   a. the Border button on the Drawing toolbar.
   b. the Border button on the Formatting toolbar.
   c. the Border button on the Standard toolbar.
   d. the Border button on the Chart toolbar.

review of concepts

CHAPTER THREE

REVIEW QUESTIONS

1. Suppose you have a column of numbers representing the wholesale cost of various quantities of produce, and suppose the label "Whole produce cost" heads the column. Discuss how you would format the numeric entries in the column and discuss which formats you might apply to the column's identifying label.

2. Discuss the impact of a worksheet in which five columns each are formatted with a different background color. Is such formatting suitable for professional presentations? What improvements, if any, would you suggest?

3. What are Excel drawing objects and how are they useful? Are drawing objects attached to particular cells, stored as part of the cells' contents, or in some other position in a worksheet? Explain.

4. Explain why you might want to hide one or more columns in a worksheet.

CREATE THE QUESTION

For each of the following answers, create an appropriate, short question.

ANSWER	QUESTION
1. So that the label and numeric values alignments match	_____
2. Selection handles appear when you do this	_____
3. Changes a cell's background color	_____
4. Proportional typeface	_____
5. Excel merges cells and centers text within the merged cells	_____
6. Excel sets the column width to zero	_____

1. Formatting a College Bookstore Book Order

Mr. Waldron Madden is an instructor in the Philosophy Department at South-Western College. Each semester for more years than he can remember, Mr. Madden has ordered his books for each semester through the college bookstore using one of its multi-part book order forms. Mr. Madden asks you to help him format the worksheet so that it resembles the paper form. Execute each of the steps that follow to create a book order form containing Mr. Madden's book request. First, ensure Excel is running and the application window is maximized.

1. Open the workbook **ex03Bookstore.xls** and then click **File**, click **Save As**, type **<yourname>Bookstore2** in the Filename text box, and click the **Save** button to save the file under a new name. Ensure that the Formatting toolbar is visible

2. Type the following in the indicated cells:

   Cell B10: **Mr. W. Madden**

   Cell B11: **1, 2, 5**

   Cell F10: **Philosophy 101**

   Cell F11: **Spring, 2004**

   Cell H10: **10/17/2003**

3. Click cell **A1**, click the Font Size list box arrow on the Formatting toolbar, and click **36** in the Font Size list box (scroll it if necessary)

4. Click cell **A2**, click the Font Size list box arrow on the Formatting toolbar, and click **24** in the Font Size list box (scroll it if necessary)

5. Select cell range **A1:I1** ("eye-one") and then click the **Merge and Center** button on the Formatting toolbar

6. Select cell range **A2:I2** and then click the **Merge and Center** button

7. Alter the column widths of columns A through I by right-clicking each column heading in turn, clicking **Column Width**, and then typing a width—listed below for each column—and then clicking **OK**. Column A: **16**, column B: **21**, column C: **12**, columns D and E: **4**, column F: **21**, columns G and H: **10**, and column I: **12**

8. Click and drag the cell range **A14:I20**, click the **Borders list box arrow**, and click the **All Borders** square to place borders around all cell walls of the selected cell range

9. Click and drag the cell range **I21:I24** and click the **Borders** button

10. Click and drag the cell range **A14:I14**, click the **Fill Color list box arrow**, and click the **Gray-25%** square. Click the **Bold** button on the Formatting toolbar

11. Click **B10**, press and hold the **Ctrl** key, click **B11**, **F10**, **F11**, and **H10**, and then release the Ctrl key

12. Click the **Borders list box arrow** and click the **Bottom Border** square to place a line on the lower edge of each selected cell

13. Click the cell range **B14:C14** and click the **Center** formatting toolbar button

14. Click **D14**, press and hold the **Ctrl** key, and click cells **E14**, **G14**, **H14**, and **I14**, release the Ctrl key, and click the **Align Right** Formatting toolbar button

15. Select the cell range **I15:I24**, click **Format**, click **Cells**, click the **Number** tab, click **Accounting** in the Category list, click the **Symbol list box arrow**, and click **None**. Click the **Decimal places spinner** so that it displays 2 and click **OK**

16. Click the **Format Painter** button and then select the cell range **H15:H20**

17. Click **I15**, press and hold the **Ctrl** key, click **I21**, click **I24**, release the Ctrl key, click the **Currency Style** button on the Formatting toolbar, and press **Ctrl+Home** to deselect the cell range

18. Click **View**, click **Header and Footer**, click the **Custom Header** button, replace the text in the Right section with your name, click **OK**, and click **OK** again

19. Click the **Print Preview** button on the Standard toolbar. Then click the **Setup** button on the Print Preview toolbar, click the **Page** tab, click the **Landscape** option under the Orientation section, click the **Margins** tab, and change the Left and Right margins to **0.75**. Finally, click the Page Setup dialog box **OK** button and then click the Print Preview toolbar **Close** button

20. Click the Save button on the Standard toolbar, print the worksheet, and close Excel

2. CREATING A BUSINESS CARD

Carmen Cervantes is the president of the Professional Students Association, which is a club that meets once a month to hear a professional speaker from the community speak about various topics in both business and society. The association has almost 40 members, and Carmen thought it would be nice if the members had cards, similar in format to business cards, that identify each of them as members of the Professional Students Association (PSA). Unfortunately, PSA's budget is very limited. Therefore there is not enough money to supply each member with a set of business cards. As an interim measure, Carmen wants to make business cards using Excel. She can print the cards on heavier stock paper to give the printed output the feel of real business cards. Follow these steps to print a business card similar to Carmen's organization. (See Figure 3.39.)

1. Start Excel and open a blank workbook

2. Click **A1** and type **Professional Students Association**

3. Click **B3** and type your first and last names

4. Click **B4** and type your school's name

5. Click **B5** and type the street address of your school

6. Click **B6** and type the city and state, separated by a comma, and the zip code where your city is located

7. Click **B7** and type your telephone number, beginning with the area code. Enclose the area code in parentheses, type a space, and type the rest of your phone number

8. Click **A1** and click the **Bold** button on the Formatting toolbar. Change the point size of the typeface to **14**. Widen column E to 10

9. Click **B3** and click the **Bold** button on the Formatting toolbar. Change the point size of the typeface to **12**

10. Select the cell range **B4:B7** and click the **Increase Indent** button twice

11. Click **B4** and click the Formatting toolbar **Italic** button

12. Select cell range **A1:E11**

13. Click the **Borders** button on the Formatting toolbar and then click the **Thick Box Border** square

14. Click **File**, click **Save As**, type **<yourname>BusinessCard** in the File name text box, and click **Save**

15. Click **File**, click **Print**, and click **OK** to print your business card

FIGURE 3.39

Business card

	A	B	C	D	E	F	G	H
1	**Professional Students Association**							
2								
3		**Elliot Schmedley**						
4		*Burr Cold College*						
5		1333 Burr Ridge Parkway						
6		Burr Ridge, IL 60527						
7		(630) 789-5400						
8								
9								
10								
11								
12								
13								
14								
15								
16								

Sheet1

Ready

1. Formatting a Class Schedule

You just received your Spring class schedule and you want to create a copy of it using Excel. Once you create the schedule, you can post it to the Web for others to view. Begin by loading the workbook **ex03Schedule.xls**. It contains an example class schedule containing a total of 17 credit hours.

Format and then print the schedule by doing the following. Set the title in A1 to bold, **18** point **Times New Roman** typeface and merge and center it over columns A through E. Set row 1's Row Height to **24**. **Bold** cell range **A2:E2**. Change the column widths of column A to **5**, columns B and C to **8**, column D to **22**, and column E to **8**. Format cell range A2:E2 with wrap text alignment. Format cells A1 through E7 with the **All Borders** selection so that borders appear around each cell in the range. Remove the gridlines from the on-screen display. Center all entries in column E, and right-align labels in cells B2 and C2. Format the times in columns B and C to display AM or PM. Adjust column widths so that they are no wider than necessary to accommodate the existing data. Finally, color the background of cells A2 through E2 with **Yellow** and the background of cells A3 through E7 with **Light Yellow**. (See Figure 3.40.) Place your name somewhere in the worksheet header or footer and then execute File, Save As, or print the worksheet according to your instructor's direction.

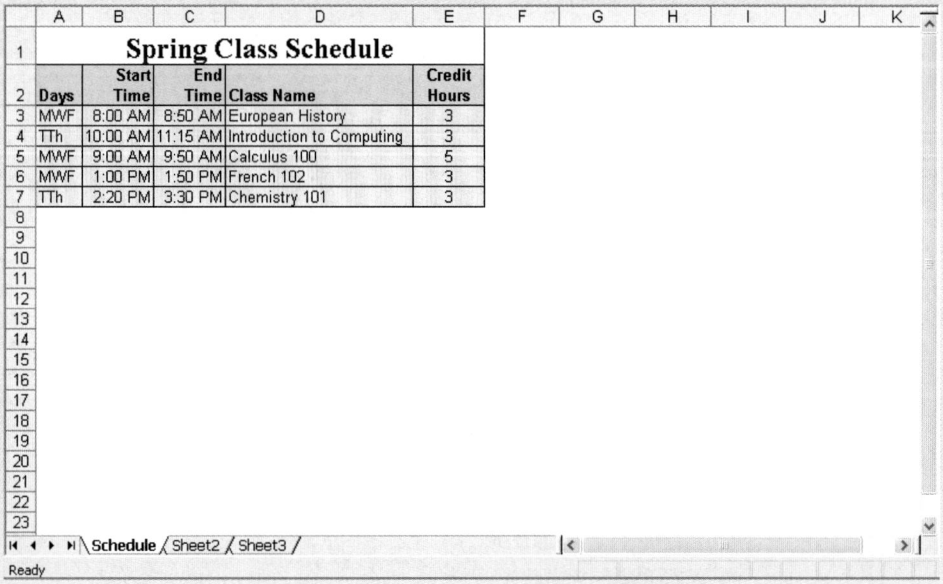

FIGURE 3.40

Class schedule

	Days	Start Time	End Time	Class Name	Credit Hours
1	Spring Class Schedule				
3	MWF	8:00 AM	8:50 AM	European History	3
4	TTh	10:00 AM	11:15 AM	Introduction to Computing	3
5	MWF	9:00 AM	9:50 AM	Calculus 100	5
6	MWF	1:00 PM	1:50 PM	French 102	3
7	TTh	2:20 PM	3:30 PM	Chemistry 101	3

2. Formatting a Payment Ledger

John Kirry purchased a new automobile last year. He received a bank loan for $10,000 for the car and paid the dealer a down payment of just over $5,000. His bank sent a statement at the end of the year detailing all of his loan payments during the year. The worksheet shows the amount of John's payment that is applied toward interest and the amount that reduces the outstanding loan balance. John, a commercial airline pilot, understands enough about spreadsheet programs to enter data and save workbooks, but he is reluctant to format the data. He calls you up and asks you to format it for him. (To return the favor, John promises to take you up in a private plane for an hour to tour the city.) You agree to help John and ask him to send you the worksheet as an e-mail attachment. He does. The file is called **ex03Payment.xls**. You detach it from the e-mail message and load it into Excel. Figure 3.41 shows you the formatted version of the payment ledger.

Reproduce the formatting shown in that figure as accurately as you can. The font is Arial 10 point. Column labels are bold, some column labels are centered, but the labels above numeric values are right aligned. Column-top numeric values contain the Accounting format. Notice the Interest Payment label. It has a superscript—a footnote. Type the word **Payment1** and then highlight the digit 1. Click **Superscript** from the Font tab of the Format Cells dialog box. Follow the same procedure for the text box at the bottom of the figure. It contains the same superscript. The text box and the callout Drawing objects both have drop shadows. Remember to place your name in the header or footer. Set all margins to 1 inch. Use borders and shading as shown in the figure. Save the workbook as **<yourname>Payment3.xls** and print the Payment worksheet.

FIGURE 3.41

Formatting a payment ledger

	Payment Number	Date	Interest Payment[1]	Principal Payment	Unpaid Balance
1					
2	1	Jan-04	$ 72.92	$ 175.08	$ 9,825
3	2	Feb-04	71.64	176.36	9,649
4	3	Mar-04	70.36	177.64	9,471
5	4	Apr-04	69.07	178.93	9,292
6	5	May-04	67.76	180.24	9,112
7	6	Jun-04	66.45	181.55	8,930
8	7	Jul-04	65.13	182.87	8,747
9	8	Aug-04	63.80	184.20	8,563
10	9	Sep-04	62.46	185.54	8,378
11	10	Oct-04	61.11	186.89	8,191
12	11	Nov-04	59.75	188.25	8,002
13	12	Dec-04	58.38	189.62	7,813
14		Total:	$ 788.83	$ 2,187.17	

Balance after first year

[1]$10,000 for 4 years at 8.75%

e-business

1. Developing a Rowing Product Worksheet

Marcia Sandoval was on the lightweight women's crew in college. She rowed for Radcliffe seven years ago and has maintained her passion for rowing ever since. Since she graduated from college, she has been rowing at an all-women's rowing club in Santa Monica. Marcia majored in journalism and she minored in business in college. She has always had an entrepreneurial spirit. Three years ago, she started a mail-order store from her garage selling rowing accessories and athletic equipment. She wants to open a rowing store on the Internet selling her rowing items that appeal to both recre-

ational and competitive rowers. She has created a fundamental worksheet that she will present to her loan officer next Monday, but she has to format it to make it more professional looking.

Open the worksheet **ex03Rowing.xls** and format it to make it more attractive and professional looking. Make at least six formatting changes to the worksheet and print it. Marcia has introduced some indenting that is incorrect. All values should be formatted to two decimal places. (See Figure 3.42.) Print the worksheet and print the worksheet formulas. Save the workbook as **<yourname>Rowing3.xls**.

FIGURE 3.42

Rowing Products worksheet

	Unit Cost	Unit Price	Projected Sales (Units)	Projected Profit ($)
Rigging Tools				
Rigger jigger	$ 6.50	$ 8.90	2,300.00	$ 5,520.00
Nut spinner	6.97	8.60	3,455.00	5,631.65
Pitch gauge	19.36	28.55	1,000.00	9,190.00
			subtotal	$ 20,341.65
Megaphones				
KV22	$ 135.00	$ 194.50	500.00	$ 29,750.00
KV45	167.00	225.00	400.00	23,200.00
			subtotal	$ 52,950.00
Oarlocks & hardware				
Grip	$ 7.50	$ 9.00	1,200.00	$ 1,800.00
Oarlock	12.35	15.00	7,800.00	20,670.00
Oarlock spacers	0.08	0.10	2,000.00	40.00
			subtotal	$ 22,510.00
Seats				
Standard Seat track	$ 31.56	$ 36.00	300.00	$ 1,332.00
Super Hard Seat Track	36.67	42.00	460.00	2,451.80
Complete seat	84.00	95.00	2,000.00	22,000.00
Custom padded seat	170.00	199.00	300.00	8,700.00
			subtotal	$ 34,483.80
			Total	$ 130,285.45

Recreational and Competitive Crew Tools and Accessories

2. Vroom Automotive Components

Vroom is one of the world's leading automotive component suppliers. They manufacture brushless DC motors for automobile sunroofs and seats. Automotive supply profits are low and customers demand price reductions each year, causing tremendous pressure on every department at Vroom to reduce costs. As a result, the Purchasing Department has established a contract with FreeMarkets (www.freemarkets.com), a business-to-business online auction company. FreeMarkets has been coordinating supplier auctions to help drive down the costs of purchased goods. Soon, Vroom will be participating in an online bidding session for a single lot of raw steel. One of Vroom's steel purchasers has supplied a raw material worksheet called **ex03Vroom.xls** (see Figure 3.43). However, it needs to be modified prior to e-mailing to FreeMarkets. Example prices have been inserted into the worksheet. FreeMarkets will set these prices to zero at the time of the auction, and the competing vendors will enter their raw steel prices when the bidding session opens.

Open the worksheet **ex03Vroom.xls** and format the worksheet so it is more attractive and professional looking. Change the worksheet's font to Times New Roman 10 point. Format product dimensions so they display three decimal places. Material weights should display one decimal place. Ensure that all dollar amounts display dollar signs and four decimal places, but the total lot price should display only two decimal places. Apply a light yellow background to the column headings and bold each heading. The cell containing the total lot price should have a tan background. The column headings should be centered and the text below them left aligned. Numeric data should be right aligned (the default). Format the first two column widths to 24.00 and the others to 12.00. Make the column headings and information below legible by wrapping the text. Merge the seven cells in the row containing **Vroom Steel Lot #1**, increase the font size to 14, and center the text. Create the look of two separate tables with borders, one for **Flat Roll Stock** and one for **Bar Stock**, using the "all border" selection. Left align and bold each table heading as well as **Specifications**. Merge the first two cells of each row for the text below **Specifications** and left align. Place your name and the date in the worksheet header, print the worksheet (ensure it prints on one page), and print the worksheet's formulas.

FIGURE 3.43

Vroom Steel worksheet

	A	B	C	D	E	F	G	H	I	J	K	L
1	Vroom Steel Lot #1											
2												
3	Flat Roll Stock											
4	Steel Desc	Type	Width in in	Gauge in i	Average W	Price per P	Total Price					
5	HSLA 4140	Chromium	60	0.525	29500	0.0528	1557.6					
6	1016	Low-carbo	54.9	0.3	30500	0.0352	1073.6					
7												
8												
9	Bar Stock											
10	Steel Desc	Type	Bar Length	Diameter	Average B	Price per P	Total Price					
11	12L14	Resulfurize	12	0.25	300.6	0.75	225.45					
12	A2	Deep hard	20	0.375	1128	0.25	282					
13	1040	Medium-ca	20	0.625	3129	0.58	1814.82					
14	1020	Low-carbo	12	0.875	3681	0.47	1730.07					
15	302	Stainless	12	0.5	469.8	0.85	399.33					
16												
17	specifications					Total Lot F	7082.87					
18	Gauge and diameter tolerance +/- .006											
19	Width and bar length tolerance -.000, +.500											
20	Bar stock is to be delivered in bundles of 150 bars.											
21												
22												
23												
24												
25												

Steel Lot

Ready

1. Building and Formatting a Product Comparison Worksheet

Ernie Kildahl wants to open an online store to carry audio equipment. The real physical store he owns sells a variety of electronic equipment but has only a limited selection of audio equipment. Ernie is particularly interested in offering a variety of brand-name stereo headphones in his online store. He wants you to research a few brands on the Web, collect a bit of information about the headphones, and report back to him. He is interested in the following brands and models: AKG, Beyerdynamic, Etymotic Research, Grado, and Sennheiser. Using Web search engines, locate three prices for each headphone and model and compare their prices on these five brands. The particular models you are to price-shop—one per brand—are in the worksheet **ex03Headphones.xls**. Load and print the worksheet for reference as you conduct your Web research.

After you have collected three prices for each brand and model, format the worksheet with currency symbols, borders, bold, and at least two typefaces—one for the title (Headphone Price Survey) and a different font for the remainder of the worksheet. Bold column titles, and use a larger point size for the column titles than the five product rows. One Web location to get you started is www.headphone.com (what else!). (Additional links are found on the Web Links worksheet—the first worksheet in the **ex03Headphones.xls** workbook.) Use one or more search engines such as www.hotbot.com and www.google.com to search for "headphone" to locate prices. If those search results are not satisfying, search for particular brand and model combinations. For example, search for "Grado SR224" and look for any vendor's prices. Identify your worksheet, save it when you are done as <**yourname**>**Headphones2.xls**, and print the results.

2. Formatting an "Audio Rippers and Encoders" Comparison Worksheet

You have an extensive collection of MP3 files that you have purchased from various reputable online MP3 distribution sites. Now you want to convert several of your MP3 sound tracks into a CD-compatible format. First, do a little feature, cost, and popularity comparisons be-fore choosing a conversion program by creating a worksheet with features across a row and different encoding and ripping program names down a particular column. Format the results into an attractive worksheet with commas where needed. Start your research by using any Web browser and going to www.download.com. Click the *Rippers* link under the heading *Audio & Video*. After the browser displays the Rippers and Encoders page, click the *Downloads* link at the top of the column displaying the number of downloads. This sorts the resulting rows into descending order by popularity. Place the following information into a worksheet.

In column A (beginning in cell A4, for example), list at least five of the most popular entries in the sorted list of encoders. In row 3, beginning in cell B3, place the following labels left to right: **Software Cost**, **Date Added to List**, **Number of Downloads**, and **File Size (KB)**. Format these long labels by clicking Format, Cells, and then clicking the Alignment tab. Format the column labels wrap text so that they completely display. Next, fill in the rows and columns with information for each of the five products and their features (software cost, date added to list, etc.). Place a zero in a cell whenever the software cost indicates "free." For "shareware" or "check latest prices" software, determine the software's price by clicking the appropriate links and then insert the price into your worksheet. (Leave it blank if the price is not readily available.) Be sure the file sizes are in thousands of kilobytes so that the units are comparable in the File Size column. List the file size for a 2.9MB file as 2,900 or a 950K file as 950. Remember that 1MB is equal to 1000K. Use cell borders in any way you choose to enhance the worksheet.

Place a worksheet title (such as "Encoder Price Comparison") in row 1 and increase the title's font size. Bold the title to make it stand out. Center the title across all information-containing columns (product name, software cost, and so on). Insert a comment in the cell containing the File Size label. The comment should contain the statement "All information obtained from Download.com." Remember to label your output with your name in the header, footer, or in the worksheet itself. Execute either Print or Save As, according to your instructor's direction.

hands-on projects

around the world

1. Investigating the Value of the U.S. Dollar

Format a table showing the exchange rate for $100 U.S. There are several exchange rate calculators on the Web. Open **ex03Currency.xls**. The first worksheet contains links to Web sites that display the value of currency. Click a link to automatically launch your browser and open the specified Web page. Determine the exchange rate of $100 U.S. in the following currencies: Australian dollar, EU (European Union) euro, British pound, Indian rupee, Japanese yen, and South African rand.

Format the worksheet to resemble Figure 3.44. Select any three consecutive months, and compute each currency's average value against the U.S. dollar. Click the **Currency Exchange Rates** worksheet tab to make it active, and enter your data on that worksheet. Color the $100 red (second row of the figure), shade the column headers, use a background color, and format values in the four columns with commas and zero decimal places. Enter your name in the worksheet header, and print the Currency Exchange Rates worksheet. Save your workbook as <**yourname**>**Currency3.xls**.

FIGURE   3.44

Formatting a foreign currency table

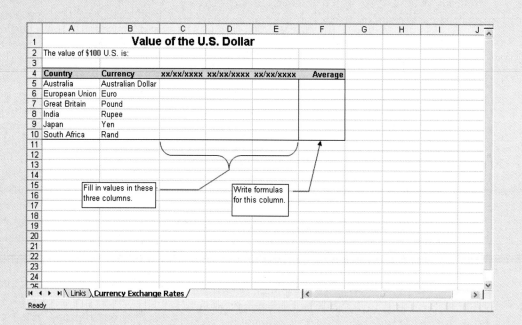

EX 3.52

2. Complex Cell Solutions

You've just been promoted to program manager for a hot new project in the Manufacturing Engineering Department of Complex Cell Solutions. Your job is to integrate the fabrication of the raw components into an existing motor manufacturing facility. To keep costs within the quoted price and potentially improve the profit margin, your supervisor asks you to locate, from anywhere in the world, a machine builder. The machine builder will supply equipment for your new flexible production cell. This will require you to travel to several different countries and evaluate potential vendors' machine building capabilities (nice!). Since you will be traveling multiple times during the vendor selection and qualification phase, you will develop a worksheet to aid in determining the trip durations.

Your first trip will be to Germany and then Switzerland, the home of more technically experienced machine builders. Begin by opening the workbook **ex03ComplexCell.xls** and then immediately save it as **<yourname>ComplexCell3.xls**. Using the workbook as the beginning point, format the worksheet to match the one shown in Figure 3.45. Use Arial 10 point as the font for most entries. The column headings are bold and the widths are 22.00 and 12.00. The background colors are a light blue. Note the different font sizes in the first three text lines. The sheet title is 14 point and the following lines are both 12 point. The text box has a drop shadow.

To obtain an estimate of the mileage, travel time between each city, and the total travel time, open your Web browser and go to uk.maps.yahoo.com and click the **Driving Directions** link. Next, plug in the starting and ending addresses and click the **Get Directions** button to obtain distances and times. Use Yahoo's mileage and time estimates for your trip evaluation. You will have to create formulas to convert the times provided by Yahoo to decimal form to determine a total travel time. Place your name and the date in the worksheet header, print the worksheet (ensure it prints on one page), and print the worksheet's formulas.

	A	B	C	D	E	F
1	**Travel Time Worksheet**					
2	**Arrival City: Frankfurt, Germany**					
3	**Departure City: Zurich, Switzerland**					
4						
5	**From City**	**To City**	**Mileage**	**Driving Time Hours**	**Driving Time Minutes**	**Total Time**
6	Frankfurt 914, Germany	Leipzig 04, Germany	XX.XX	XX	XX	X.XX
7	Leipzig 04, Germany	Bad Doberan 048, Germany	XX.XX	XX	XX	X.XX
8	Bad Doberan 048, Germany	Stuttgart 70, Germany	XX.XX	XX	XX	X.XX
9	Stuttgart 70, Germany	Bern 30, Switzerland	XX.XX	XX	XX	X.XX
10	Bern 30, Switzerland	Luzerne 600, Switzerland	XX.XX	XX	XX	X.XX
11	Luzerne 600, Switzerland	Zurich 8, Switzerland	XX.XX	XX	XX	X.XX
12						
13		**Total Miles**	**XXXX.XX**		**Total Driving Time**	**XXX.XX**

Note: Close destination cities may be coupled for same-day visits. However, a minimum of 3 hours per visit will be necessary for sound supplier evaluations.

Travel Time

Ready

FIGURE 3.45
Formatted Complex Cell worksheet

running project

Pro Golf Academy

Betty Carroll wants to assemble a worksheet showing the previous month's sales and remaining inventory of Polo shirts, sweaters, and hats. The worksheet will help her order golf apparel next month based on sales for the previous month and the amount of inventory on hand. She has created a rudimentary worksheet called **ex03ProGolf.xls**, but she wants you to format it so that it is easier to understand and use. First, write formulas for the Units Sold column (Ending Inventory minus Beginning Inventory), Inventory Value (the product of Ending Inventory and Retail Price), and Total Sales (the product of Units Sold and Retail Price). Next, format the worksheet using borders, at least one text box and arrow combination that points out the inventory item on hand with the largest value, and use some foreground and background color to highlight the product that has the highest total sales. Format the Beginning Inventory, Ending Inventory, and Units Sold columns using the Accounting numeric format with zero decimal places. Format the Inventory Value and Total Sales columns with Accounting with two decimal places. Remember to place a dollar sign on each column-top numeric value per product category. Use at least two different typefaces but no more than four in the worksheet. Use foreground and background color for the three product category names and separate the categories with one blank row. Center the worksheet both horizontally and vertically on the page. Place your name in the worksheet header and save the workbook as **<yourname>ProGolf3.xls**. Print the worksheet in landscape orientation, and print the worksheet formulas. Figure 3.46 suggests one way you could format the worksheet. Use your imagination and be creative formatting your worksheet.

FIGURE 3.46
Formatted Pro Golf Academy worksheet

	A	B	C	D	E	F	G	H	I	J
1	**Pro Golf Academy Apparel Sales and Inventory**									
2		**Beginning Inventory**	**Ending Inventory**	**Retail Price**	**Units Sold**	**Inventory Value**	**Total Sales**			
3	**Polo Shirts**									
4	Adidas Solid Mercerized	14	5	44.99	9	$ XXXXXX	$ XXXXXX			
5	Ashworth Jacquard Shirt	23	7	44.97	16	XXXXX	XXXXX			
6	Ashworth Twist Pique	6	2	59.99	4	XXXXX	XXXXX			
7	Cutter & Buck Palma	22	12	59.99	10	XXXXX	XXXXX			
8	Taylor Made Solid	20	12	49.99	8	XXXXX	399.92			
9						***Subtotal***	$ XXXXXX			
10	**Sweaters**									
11	Adidas Crew	25	15	89.99	10	$ XXXXXX	$ XXXXXX			
12	Adidas Sweater Vest	14	6	69.99	8	XXXXX	XXXXX			
13	Ashworth Basket weave	45	7	74.99	38	524.93	XXXXX			
14	Ashworth Rib	40	32	75.00	8	XXXXX	600.00	largest inventory value		
15						***Subtotal***	$ XXXXXX			
16	**Hats**									
17	Mizuno 8-panel	55	3	19.99	52	$ XXXXXX	$ XXXXXX			
18	Taylor Made Tour Visor	44	28	17.99	16	XXXXX	XXXXX			
19	Titleist Low Profile Visor	34	24	14.99	10	XXXXX	XXXXX			
20	MaxFli Structured Adjusta	56	16	14.99	40	XXXXX	599.60			
21						***Subtotal***	$ XXXXXX			
22										
23						***Total Sales***				

Sheet1

Ready

1. Formatting Has an Impact

Discuss the role of worksheet formatting in communicating, or not, information to the observer. Supply two examples of the effective use of formatting a worksheet and a very ineffective use. Describe the differences and the merits and faults of both.

2. AutoFormat

AutoFormat, not discussed in this chapter, is available on the Format menu. Experiment with it and compare using it to format a group of cells to formatting cells using the Cells command on the Format menu. Discuss advantages you observe using AutoFormat. In order to answer the question, use AutoFormat on a worksheet and note the options and number of steps required to accomplish the desired formatting—both using AutoFormat and formatting cells manually.

4

Creating Charts

did you
know?

the *"Cereal Bowl of America" is in Battle Creek, Michigan, where the most cereal in the United States is produced.*

oak *trees are struck by lightning more often than any other tree. Historians theorize that this is one reason why the ancient Greeks considered oak trees sacred to Zeus, god of thunder and lightning.*

on *a bingo card of 90 numbers, there are approximately 44 million ways to make B-I-N-G-O.*

ostriches *are such fast runners that they can outrun a horse. Male ostriches can roar like a lion.*

the *Sears Tower contains enough phone wire to wrap around the earth 1.75 times and enough electrical wiring to run a power line from Chicago to Los Angeles.*

a *radar graph is a great way to represent what type of information? Read on and find out.*

Chapter Objectives

- Define a data series and data categories—MOS XL03S-2-5
- Create an embedded chart and a chart sheet—MOS XL03S-2-5
- Modify an existing chart by revising data, altering chart text, and labeling data—MOS XL03S-2-5
- Use color and patterns to embellish a chart—MOS XL03E-2-4
- Add a new data series to a chart—MOS XL03S-2-5
- Alter a chart type and create a three-dimensional chart—MOS XL03S-2-5
- Create a pie chart with a title, exploding slice, labels, and floating text—MOS XL03S-2-5
- Add texture to a chart—MOS XL03E-2-4
- Delete embedded charts and chart sheets
- Save a chart as a Web page—MOS XL03S-5-10

Big Wave Surfboards

Keoki Lahani founded Big Wave Surfboards in 1971 in his garage in Napili, Maui, Hawaii, where he designed and built his first surfboards. Keoki ships surfboards all around the world today. Since 1971, Keoki has enlarged his shop in Napili and created two more surfboard design and manufacturing facilities and accompanying outlet stores in Malibu, California, and Melbourne, Florida. A master board builder at each of his three stores oversees the design and manufacture of Keoki's surfboards, which bear his Big Wave logo.

Each facility builds surfboards from scratch using Keoki's time-honored hand craftsmanship and quality control methods. Starting with a foam blank, a shaper uses foam planers to create the rough shape for each custom-designed board to exacting customer specifications. If a board is going to contain a color or logo, it is applied after the blank is sanded. In the second major step of the four-step manufacturing process, a skilled technician applies fiberglass (called "glassing") followed by a coating of resin to hold the fiberglass in place to supply waterproofing and to give the board strength and integrity. The third step, called sanding, follows the glassing. An experienced sander carefully sands the board to remove any irregular-

ities and ensures that the surface is smooth and even. The final step is called finishing. A finisher typically applies a gloss finish. The gloss finish supplies the final seal and gives the board a smooth, uniform, glossy look.

Big Wave offers a wide variety of surfboards ranging from smaller boards, called shortboards, that are as short as 5 feet long up to the largest surfboards, called longboards, that can be over 11 feet long. Each of the three manufacturing centers can build any surfboard from shortboards to longboards. Big Wave classifies the surfboards they sell into these groups: Shortboard, Fish, Funboard, Retro, and Longboard. Surfboard length, shape, and features classify them into the different groups.

Keoki and his chief financial officer, Stephen French, have created a worksheet summarizing sales for last year and broken out sales by sales outlet and board type. In this chapter, you will help Stephen create various charts from the raw worksheet data and enhance charts to convey sales information graphically. Charts provide the reader with a quickly understandable and simple picture of the sales patterns. Figure 4.1 shows the completed Big Wave Sales worksheet and accompanying embedded graph.

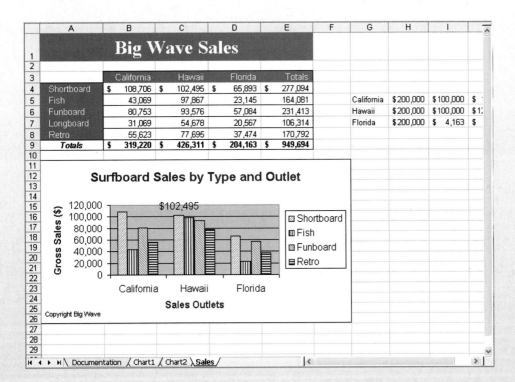

FIGURE 4.1

Completed Big Wave
surfboard sales worksheet

INTRODUCTION

Chapter 4 covers creating Excel charts. In this chapter, you will use a worksheet from Big Wave, a surfboard manufacturer and seller. Using the sales values for three separate sales locations and several different surfboard categories, you will create graphs that pictorially display sales in a chart. Using the Chart Wizard and various chart formatting features, you will create and modify both an embedded chart and a chart stored on a separate worksheet. Formatting and graph features you will explore include altering a chart's title, legend, data markers, X- and Y-axis titles, background colors, and Y-axis scaling. Color and patterns add excitement to a chart. You will learn how to apply both. Three-dimensional charts simplify understanding the values in a worksheet, and you will create a 3-D pie chart with special features such as an exploded pie slice. The chapter concludes by describing how to add various text elements to charts, adding and modifying textures, printing chart sheets, and saving and deleting charts.

SESSION 4.1 CREATING AN EXCEL CHART

In this section, you will learn how to create your first Excel chart from existing sales data supplied in the Big Wave sales worksheet. First you will learn about data series and data categories. Then you will learn about the different chart types available in Excel and which situations favor one chart type over others. Using the Excel Chart Wizard, you will create an embedded chart displaying sales of different types of surfboards for each sales outlet. After creating a graph, you will update and modify it by changing the underlying data, changing text in the chart, and adding labels to the charted data. Next you will add color and modify color to enhance the chart's appearance. Finally you will preview the worksheet and chart and then print it.

Data Series and Categories

Two important terms you should understand before you work with charts are data series and categories. A *data series* is a set of values that you want to chart. For example, if you want to chart sales of Big Wave surfboards in California, the data series is the set of sales values under the column heading California. Similarly, if you want to chart temperatures in Nebraska for the month of January, the data series is the set of temperature readings for each day of January found in contiguous cells in a row or column. Each data series in a chart can have up to 32,000 values, or *data points*, for two-dimensional charts or 4,000 values for three-dimensional charts. You can chart as many as 255 data series in a chart, although a two-dimensional chart is limited to a total of 32,000 total data points.

You use *categories* to organize the values in a data series. For example, a data series of sales for surfboards sold in Florida contains the categories Shortboard, Fish, Funboard, Retro, and so on (see Figure 4.1). Similarly, the categories for a series of sales values for the past year are January, February, March, and so on—the month names under which sales are recorded. In a chart that plots value changes over time, such as fluctuating prices of a particular stock for the last month, the categories are always the time intervals (days, months, or years). To keep this clear in your mind, simply remember that the data series is the series of values you are charting and categories are the labels or headings under (or next to) which the values are stored.

Locating and Opening the Workbook

Stephen French, an avid surfer and Big Wave's chief financial officer, sits down with you and outlines what he wants you to do to the Big Wave sales worksheet. He sets milestones for you to complete in time for the important presentation coming up this month. The results of that meeting with Stephen are these points:

- Goal: Create charts from the Big Wave sales data in an attractive form ready for printing and presentation to the board of directors this month
- Information needed to complete the work: Sales data for California, Hawaii, and Florida by surfboard model for previous year
- New formulas or values needed: None. The worksheet data are complete as is. Only charts are missing from the workbook

With Keoki's guidance, Stephen has entered all the formulas, values, and text for the Big Wave workbook. It consists of one worksheet displaying sales for five categories of surfboards broken out by sales location. For example, the worksheet sales figures indicate that shortboard-style surfboards sold far more units in California last year than in either Hawaii or Florida. Similarly, longboards are more popular in Hawaii than they are in either Florida or California based on last year's sales. However, it takes careful study of the sales values to determine the preceding facts. A graph would make that fact obvious more quickly.

You begin by opening the Big Wave workbook.

Opening the Big Wave workbook and saving it under a new name:

1. Start Excel

2. Open the workbook **ex04BigWave.xls**. The documentation sheet displays (see Figure 4.2)

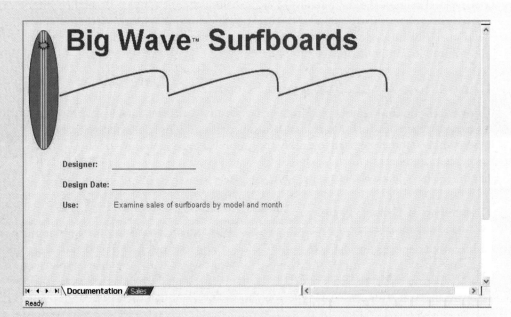

FIGURE 4.2
Big Wave documentation
worksheet

3. Type your name in the cell to the right of the label *Designer* and type the current date in the cell to the right of the label *Design Date.* Notice that the Documentation worksheet does not display column and row headers

4. Save the worksheet as **BigWave2.xls** to preserve the original workbook in case you want to revert to that version

5. Click the **Sales** tab to display that worksheet (see Figure 4.3)

	A	B	C	D	E	F	G	H	I	J
1		Big Wave Sales								
2										
3		California	Hawaii	Florida	Totals					
4	Shortboard	$ 198,706	$ 102,495	$ 65,893	$ 367,094					
5	Fish	43,069	97,867	23,145	164,081					
6	Funboard	80,753	123,575	57,084	261,412					
7	Longboard	31,069	154,678	20,567	206,314					
8	*Totals*	$ 353,597	$ 478,615	$ 166,689	$ 998,901					
9										

Documentation \ Sales
Ready

FIGURE 4.3
Big Wave sales data
worksheet

The Sales worksheet shows sales of four types of surfboards in the three states where Big Wave has outlets—California, Hawaii, and Florida. At the bottom of each state's column is the total value of sales for the year in that state's store. Details of individual models of each type of surfboard are not displayed in the worksheet because the Sales worksheet summarized sales for Keoki. Other worksheets maintained by store managers in each of the three states list each surfboard built and sold. Detailed information on each surfboard includes the exact dimensions, weight, construction, number and size of fins, sale price, and so on. Worksheet data arranged in row categories and column locations are ideal to graph.

Choosing a Chart Type and Format

Using Excel, you can create sophisticated charts from worksheet data. Excel provides 14 chart types, each of which has at least two sub-types providing alternative representations. While you may be used to calling the graphical representations of data "graphs," Excel refers to them as **charts**. Each of the 14 chart types has a unique use and purpose. Figure 4.4 lists the Excel chart types and provides a brief description of their uses.

Choosing a Chart Type

The choice of Excel chart types is almost too much. What chart is best for your application? That depends on what you want to show. Choosing the chart type that best carries your message is critical, and some data look better with one chart type than another. Before readers review, in detail, the data represented by a chart, they first will receive a message from the chart type you choose. Even though the Chart Wizard suggests a type of chart, it does not always know the best type to choose. You may want to try several different types with your data to determine which chart best conveys your message. Perhaps the best way to understand the use of various chart types is to show examples of the use of several of the 14 types. The following paragraphs will provide guidance.

BAR CHART.   It plots bars as separate data points horizontally—particularly counts of volumes. Dating back to the 1700s, the bar chart was the original way to display data. They are a terrific way to show the size of independent values against one another. For example, a bar chart is a good choice to display the total score of each student in the class. The longest bar represents the highest total score. Sorting the data before plotting them displays bars in order from longest to shortest, or vice versa.

FIGURE 4.4

Excel chart types and their uses

Chart Type	Purpose
Area	Shows size of change over time
Bar	Displays comparisons between independent data values
Bubble	A scatter chart showing relationships between sets of data
Column	Displays comparisons between independent data values
Cone, Cylinder, Pyramid	Displays and compares data represented by each cone
Doughnut	Shows the contribution of each part to a whole at the outer edge
Line	Shows a trend over time of a series of data values
Pie	Shows the relative size of the parts to a whole
Radar	Illustrates data change relative to a central point
Stock	Displays low, high, open, and close values for stock prices
Surface	Depicts relationships among large volumes of data
XY (scatter)	Shows the relationship between two sets of data points

COLUMN CHART.   A column chart is almost the same as the bar chart, except the data values are represented by vertical columns, much like skyscraper buildings. Column charts, like bar charts, show the value of independent entities compared to one another. A column chart is a good choice to show the height of a child from birth to 18 years old, taken once a year each year.

LINE CHART.   Line charts are excellent for plotting continuously over time. A classic example is a line chart showing the rise and fall of the stock market from 1940 to the present. Along the X-axis is time, and the vertical axis represents the dollar value of the Dow or some other measure of the stock market's worth. Line charts are a great way to spot trends. In contrast, a bar chart or a column chart would be poor choices to display the price of a stock over time, because the individual bars or columns transmit the subtle message that they represent different, individual elements, not the same stock over time.

PIE CHART.   A pie chart is the best way to show the contribution of several related parts to the whole—their percentage of the whole. A common example is the distribution of tax dollars to education, defense, health and human resources, and so on. Each pie slice visually depicts the size of the represented piece relative to the whole "pie." Pie charts can plot only one set of data, so a pie would be inappropriate in plotting three years' sales in five different regions. Additionally, if you have more than 10 or 11 data values to plot, a pie chart can become crowded. Switch to a bar or column chart instead. On the other hand, a pie is perfect for comparing one year's sales in five regions. Each region would be a pie slice and the whole pie represents the year's total revenue.

DOUGHNUT CHART.   Doughnut charts are similar to pie charts with two exceptions. Doughnut charts can display data from more than one series, and doughnut charts have holes in the middle of them. For example, a doughnut chart is convenient for comparing two years' sales in four regions. Figure 4.5 shows an example.

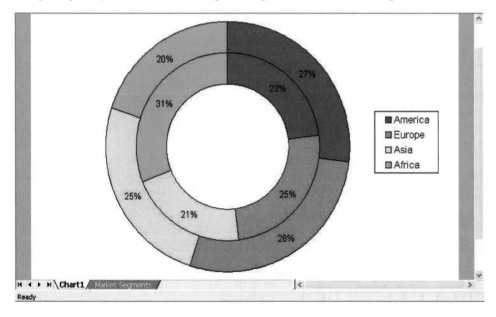

FIGURE 4.5
Doughnut chart

SCATTER CHART.   A scatter (xy) chart shows the relationship between two factors or variables. Scatter charts are most often used for scientific data to compare two factors in an experiment. For example, you could demonstrate the relationship between age and quiz scores among a group of students. The way in which the data are arranged on the worksheet is very important when creating an xy chart. The data must be arranged with the x values in one row or column, followed by one or more corresponding y values in the adjacent rows or columns. Plotting the average weight of a group of people versus their age is another example where a scatter chart is best.

EXCEL

FIGURE 4.6

Stock chart of
temperature fluctuations

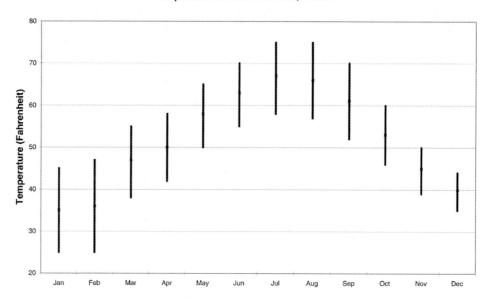

Temperature Variations in Paris, France

STOCK CHART.   Stock charts are designed for an obvious reason—plotting the highs, lows, and close prices of one or more stocks over time. Stock charts can also be useful for plotting, for instance, the high, low, and average rainfall over time or daily temperature fluctuations of a particular state or region. Figure 4.6 shows the temperature fluctuations (Fahrenheit) in Paris, France, over a typical year.

CONE, CYLINDER, AND PYRAMID CHARTS.   Cone, cylinder, and pyramid charts are just bar or column charts with 3-D shapes replacing the bars or columns. In other words, use these types to add flair where you would otherwise use a bar or column charts.

SURFACE CHART.   A surface chart is a good choice when you want to display a topographical map that is a 3-D representation of the high (mountain peaks) and low (valleys) values of two sets of data. For example, you could produce a surface chart to convey sales profits over time.

Chart Elements

Different chart types have different elements. A column chart is typical of an Excel chart. Figure 4.7 shows the elements of a column chart. All of a chart's elements reside in the **chart area**. Within the chart area is the **plot area**, which is the rectangular area bounded by the Y-axis on the left and the X-axis on the bottom. By default the plot area is gray, but you can change the color. An **axis** is a line that contains a measurement by which you compare plotted values. The **X-axis** contains markers denoting category values, and the **Y-axis** contains the value of data being plotted. Normally the Y-axis is vertical. The **Y-axis title** identifies the values being plotted on the Y-axis. Above a chart is a **chart title**, which labels the entire chart. Below the X-axis are **category names**, which correspond to worksheet text you use to label data. Below the category names is the **X-axis title**, which briefly describes the X-axis categories. **Tick marks** are small lines, similar to marks on a ruler, that are uniformly spaced along each axis and identify the position of category names or values. **Gridlines** are extensions of tick marks that help identify the value of the data markers. A **data marker** is a graphic representation of the value of a data point in a chart; a data marker can be a pie slice, a bar, a column, or other graphic depending on the graph type. The data marker in the Big Wave sales chart is a column (see Figures 4.1 and 4.7). A chart's **legend** indicates which data marker represents each series when you chart multiple series. The legend in Figure 4.7

FIGURE 4.7

Anatomy of an Excel column chart

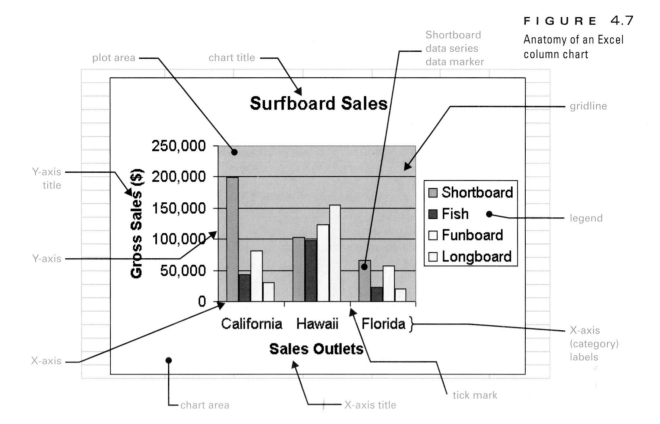

contains the series names (Shortboard, Fish, and so on) and the color-coded bar associated with that name. It is always a good idea to include a legend so that the reader can associate a particular data series with its assigned color or fill pattern.

Chart Placement Choices

You can place charts in one of two places: on a worksheet along with the data being charted or on a separate sheet. When you place a chart on a worksheet near the data you are charting, it is called an ***embedded chart***. Embedded charts have the advantage that you can see the data and the accompanying chart on the same page. Often you can print both the data and chart on a single page. When you place a chart on a separate sheet, called a ***chart sheet***, it is much larger and there are no other data on the chart sheet. In addition, a chart sheet contains no gridlines, which can distract from the chart's usefulness. Chart sheets are particularly handy when you want to print color transparencies for a presentation. In this first session, you will create an embedded chart. In the second section, you will create a chart sheet.

Developing and Planning a Chart

Keoki wants you to create a chart summarizing the sales of surfboards. He wants a chart to show the sales by sales outlet and surfboard type. Another chart he'd like to have is total sales of each of the surfboard types, regardless of sales outlet. He has sketched the basic form of the two graphs on an output worksheet page containing sales data. Figure 4.8 shows Keoki's sketch. A column graph shows sales by surfboard type for each sales outlet. The pie chart is a good way to show overall sales by surfboard type.

Creating an Embedded Column Chart

After calling Keoki and discussing the drawing he faxed, you decide you have all the information you need to create a chart. Creating an Excel chart is a simple two-step

EXCEL

FIGURE 4.8

Sketch of two surfboard
sales charts

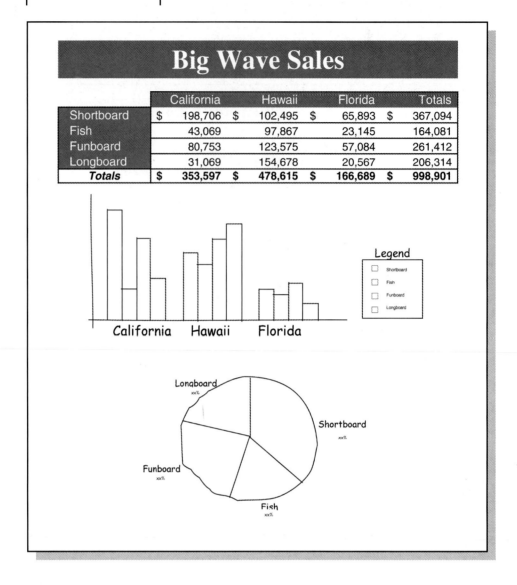

process. First, select the worksheet cells you want to chart including any text cells containing row or column headings. Second, launch the Chart Wizard by clicking the Chart Wizard button and follow the multistep Chart Wizard's prompts. The Chart Wizard consists of four steps corresponding to four dialog boxes in which you make choices and proceed to the next step. Figure 4.9 outlines the choices you can make in each step.

FIGURE 4.9

Chart Wizard steps and
dialog boxes

Dialog box	Tasks and Choices
Chart Type	Select a chart type from a palette of choices
Chart Source Data	Specify or modify the worksheet cell range containing data to be charted
Chart Options	Alter the look of a chart by selecting from a tabbed set affecting gridlines, titles, axes, and data labels
Chart Location	Choose either an embedded chart or a chart sheet style chart

---

task reference   Creating a Chart

- Select the cell range containing the data you want to chart
- Click the Standard toolbar **Chart Wizard** 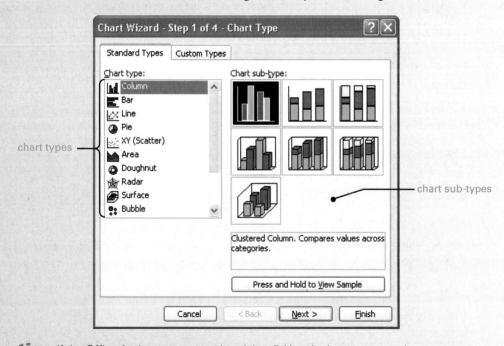 button
- Respond to the series of Chart Wizard dialog box choices, clicking the **Finish** button on the last step

---

Invoking the Chart Wizard to create a column chart:

1. With the Sales worksheet displayed, drag the mouse to select the cell range **A3:D7**, which includes labels at the top of the sales columns and labels on the left of the surfboard data rows

   tip: *Do not include row 8 in the selected cell range. It contains totals for each numeric column and would be an inappropriate row to include or compare to individual sales*

2. Click the **Chart Wizard** button located on the Standard toolbar. The first of several Chart Wizard dialog boxes opens (see Figure 4.10)

chart types

chart sub-types

FIGURE 4.10
Chart Wizard step 1 dialog box

   tip: *If the Office Assistant appears, close it by clicking the button next to the message "No, don't provide help now"*

3. Click the **Column** chart choice in the Chart type list, if needed, to select it

4. To view a sample of a sub-type, click and hold the **Press and Hold to View Sample** button. A sample displays in the Chart sub-type panel as long as you hold down the left mouse button. The default sub-type, clustered column, is a good choice

5. Click the **Next** button, located at the bottom of the dialog box, to move to the next Chart Wizard dialog box

6. Ensure that the Data range text box displays "=Sales!$A$3:$D$7." The dialog box displays a preliminary chart of your data (see Figure 4.11)

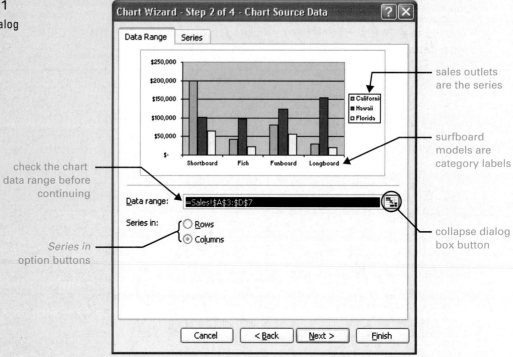

Chart Wizard Step 2 allows you to modify the data series in case you selected an incorrect range accidentally. Notice that the preview of the chart looks different from the chart Keoki wants. Looking closely, you see that the series shown by each bar represents sales outlets, and the four groups represent the four surfboard types. You want just the reverse—series representing each surfboard type and three groups representing the three sales outlets. You modify the way the data series is represented—by rows or columns—with the *Series in* option. You will change this in the steps that follow.

Altering the data series and completing the Chart Wizard steps;

1. Click the **Rows** option in the "Series in" section of the Chart Wizard dialog box

2. Click the **Next** button to move to the next Chart Wizard step

3. If necessary, click the **Titles** tab to display chart title text boxes, click the **Chart title** text box, and then type **Surfboard Sales**. After a short pause, the title appears above the chart in the chart preview area of the dialog box

4. Click the **Category (X) axis** text box and then type **Sales Outlets**. After a brief pause, the category title appears below the X-axis in the chart preview area (see Figure 4.12)

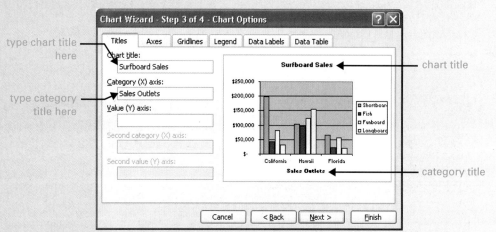

FIGURE 4.12

Chart Wizard step 3 dialog box

5. Click the **Next** button to proceed to the final Chart Wizard step (see Figure 4.13). In this step, you choose whether to create an embedded chart or a chart sheet. Because you want an embedded chart, you leave unchanged the default option, *As object in*

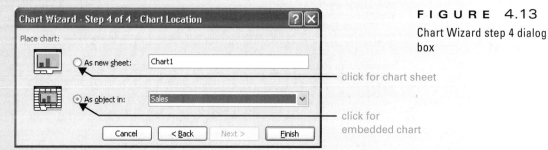

FIGURE 4.13

Chart Wizard step 4 dialog box

6. Click the **Finish** button to complete the chart specification process and prepare to place the chart in the Sales worksheet

7. Notice that the chart area displays *selection handles* (also known as *sizing handles*) around its perimeter. These indicate that the chart is selected. Normally the floating Chart toolbar appears automatically whenever you select the chart (see Figure 4.14)

8. If the Chart toolbar is not visible, click **View**, point to **Toolbars**, and then click **Chart**. The Chart toolbar appears somewhere on the screen (Figure 4.15 shows the Chart toolbar icons and lists their meanings)

9. Click anywhere outside the selected chart to deselect it. The selection handles disappear and so does the Chart toolbar

Moving and Resizing an Embedded Chart

The embedded chart you produced for Keoki is too small to distinguish sales details, and the labels are small as well. It would be nice to somehow enlarge the chart slightly. Because an embedded chart is an object, you can resize it or move it to another location. Like other Windows objects, you modify an object's size by selecting the object and then moving the mouse over one of the object's selection/resizing handles. When the mouse pointer changes to a double-headed arrow, you can drag any selection handle away from the object's center to enlarge the object or toward the object's center to shrink it.

FIGURE 4.14

Finished column chart

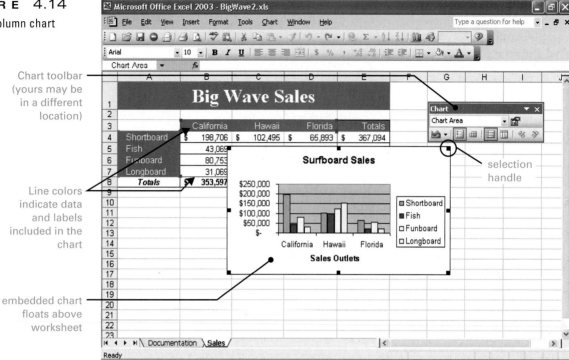

Chart toolbar (yours may be in a different location)

Line colors indicate data and labels included in the chart

selection handle

embedded chart floats above worksheet

FIGURE 4.15

Chart toolbar icons

Icon	Name	Meaning
Chart Area ▾	Chart Objects	List box contains names of all objects on the current chart
	Format	Displays Format dialog box for the selected object (plot area, chart area, and so on)
	Chart Type	List box contains list of chart types (radar, bar, etc.)
	Legend	On/off toggle that adds or removes the legend
	Data Table	On/off toggle that adds or removes a chart data table
	By Row	Displays data series using rows
	By Column	Displays data series using columns
	Angle Text Downward	On/off toggle to angle text down at a 45 degree angle
	Angle Text Upward	On/off toggle to angle text up at a 45 degree angle

Sometimes you want to move an embedded chart to a specific position on a worksheet. For example, you may want to fit a chart exactly within a particular range of cells. Or you might want to modify several embedded charts so that they are the same height and width. In all these cases, you can use a handy Excel snap-to feature to place embedded charts precisely on a worksheet. Otherwise, you can move a chart by clicking the Chart Area and dragging the chart to a new location. (Be careful to click the Chart Area and not the Plot Area or other chart element.)

task reference   Snapping an Embedded Chart into Place

- Select the chart that you want to move or resize
- Press and hold down the **Alt** key
- Drag a chart left, right, up, or down until the chart edge snaps to a cell boundary
- Still holding down the **Alt** key, move the cursor to a chart selection handle
- Click and drag a chart selection handle until the chart's selected boundary snaps to a cell border
- Release the mouse and **Alt** key

Moving an embedded chart to a cell boundary:

1. Click in any white area within the chart border, being careful not to click another chart object such as the chart title or the legend

tip: *Alternatively, you can click the* **Chart objects** *list box on the Chart toolbar and then select* **Chart Area***. Selection handles appear around the border of the embedded chart*

tip: *If the Chart toolbar is in your way, move it to another location by dragging it. You can dock the toolbar on the bottom of the window by dragging it close to the bottom of the screen until it automatically snaps into place*

2. Press and hold the **Alt** key (doing so helps you move the chart to an exact cell boundary)

3. Drag the chart down and to the left until the upper-left corner is positioned over cell A10 and the top edge of the chart aligns with the bottom edge of worksheet row 9. (The mouse pointer changes to a four-headed arrow as you drag the chart)

4. Release the mouse and then release the **Alt** key

help yourself *Press* **F1***, type* **charting** *in the Search text box of the Microsoft Excel Help task pane, and press* **Enter***. Click the hyperlink* **About charts** *and then click the* **Show All** *hyperlink near the top of the Microsoft Excel Help dialog box to reveal information on creating charts. (Maximize the dialog box.) Click the Help screen* **Close** *button when you are finished, and close the task pane*

Once you move the chart, it no longer obscures the data. However, the chart is still too small. The next task you want to accomplish is to enlarge the chart.

Resizing a chart:

1. Scroll the worksheet up on the screen so that the top of the embedded chart is near the top of the screen and row 25 is also visible

2. Click in any white area within the chart border, being careful not to click another chart object such as the chart title. Selection handles appear around the border of the chart

3. Position the mouse pointer on the bottom-right selection handle

4. When the mouse pointer changes to a two-headed arrow, drag the selection handle down and to the right until the lower-right corner of the chart covers cell F25 (see Figure 4.16) and release the mouse

FIGURE 4.16

Resized and relocated chart

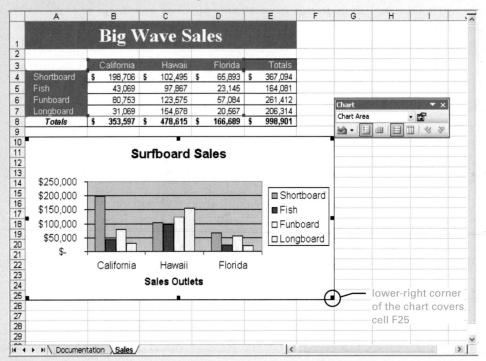

5. Click anywhere outside the chart area to deselect it

You show the Sales worksheet containing the embedded chart to Keoki. He's pleased with the chart but notices that there are three values in the worksheet that are incorrect. Luckily, Keoki catches the errors before you distribute a printed copy. The California Shortboard sales value should be $108,706. The other two incorrect values are in the Hawaii sales column. Hawaiian Funboard sales should be $93,576, not $123,575. Hawaiian Longboard sales should be $54,678, not $154,678.

Updating a Chart

Charts are automatically linked to the data from which they have been created. Consequently, when you change a worksheet value, the portion of the chart representing that data point is automatically updated to reflect the new value. The same is true of worksheet labels that are in the range of cells you selected to create a chart. Any text values in a worksheet that are also part of a chart will change automatically when you change them in the worksheet. An example of this is the text "California" found in cell B3 of the Big Wave Sales worksheet. Changing that cell's contents would also cause the chart category label "California" to change to the new value.

You are ready to make changes to the erroneous data in cells B4, C6, and C7. Any changes you make to the data will change the chart also. Before continuing, notice the leftmost bar in the California category and the rightmost two columns in the Hawaii category. Those bars will decrease in size when you make the changes in the steps below.

Notice, in particular, that the first California column almost touches the gridline marked $200,000 and that the third and fourth bars in the Hawaii category are both taller than the first two bars in the Hawaii category.

Changing worksheet data linked to a chart:

1. Scroll the worksheet so that you can see row 1 again, click cell **B4** to select it, type **108706**, and then press **Enter**

2. Click cell **C6**, type **93576**, and then press **Enter**

3. Click cell **C7**, type **54678**, and press **Enter**. Notice that the fourth bar from the left in the Hawaii group becomes shorter and the Value axis (Y-axis) values adjust (see Figure 4.17)

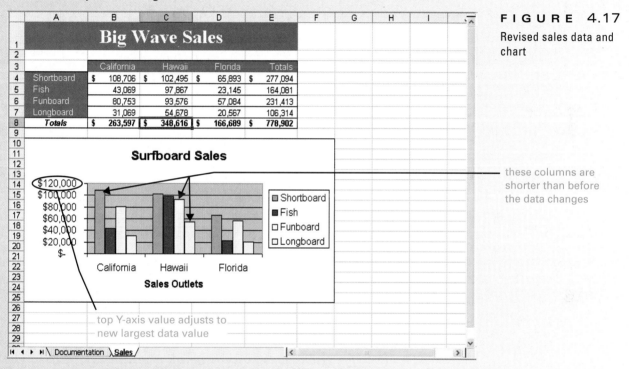

FIGURE 4.17
Revised sales data and chart

these columns are shorter than before the data changes

top Y-axis value adjusts to new largest data value

Modifying a Chart

You can modify every aspect of an Excel chart. For example, you can add a new data series to a chart, modify the foreground and background colors of text objects, alter the colors of data markers in a series, change the typeface of text, and reposition objects on a chart. One of the most dramatic changes you can make to a chart is to add, delete, or hide a series in the chart. You do that by adding, deleting, or hiding rows in the data range of the associated worksheet data. Keoki wants you to add a new line of surfboards to the sales totals so that he can compare their sales to the other types of surfboards.

Adding and Deleting Chart Data Series

Adding a new data series to an existing embedded chart is straightforward. There are several ways to add a series to a chart, but perhaps the simplest way is to add a row to the worksheet and then drag the new data and label cell range to the embedded chart.

---

task reference   Adding a New Data Series
to an Embedded Chart

- Add the new data, both labels and values or formulas that display values, to the worksheet adjacent to existing chart data

- Select the cell range, including category labels and data, of the data series you want to add to the embedded chart

- Move the mouse to any edge of the selected worksheet cell range

- When the mouse pointer changes to an arrow, click and drag the range into the chart area and release the mouse

---

Inserting a new surfboard category and sales information into the worksheet:

1. Click cell **A8**, click **Insert** and then click **Rows**

2. Type **Retro** in cell A8 and press the **Tab** key

3. Type **55623**; press the **Tab** key, type **77695**, press the **Tab** key, and type **37474**

4. Click cell **E8**. Notice that Excel automatically fills in the SUM function in cell E8. Cell A8 contains a line on its top border because its format is copied from the previous cell A8, which contained "Total." Remove that line in the steps that follow

5. Click Cell **A8**, click **Format**, click **Cells**, and click the **Border** tab

6. Click the top line in the preview panel of the Border section. The top line in the preview panel disappears

7. Click **OK** to close the Format Cells dialog box

Excel automatically adjusts the column sales totals located in row 9 to account for the new surfboard data you added in row 8. However, the new series is not added automatically to the chart. Now that you have added the new surfboard category and sales information for the three sales outlets to the worksheet, you can proceed to add a new series to the existing embedded column chart.

Adding a new series to a chart by dragging the worksheet data:

1. Drag the mouse through the cell range **A8:D8** and then release the mouse

2. Move the mouse to the edge of the cell range until it turns into a four-headed arrow

3. Click any line surrounding the cell range, drag the cell range to anywhere in the embedded chart area, and release the mouse to create a new data series (see Figure 4.18)

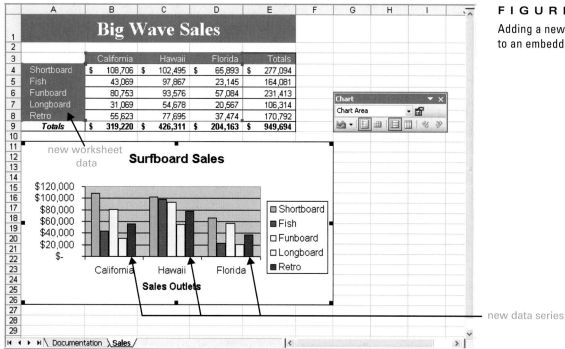

FIGURE 4.18

Adding a new data series
to an embedded chart

After examining a chart, you may discover that you have a data series that should
not be included in the chart. Similarly, you may decide that the chart should display a
different data series. In either case, you can delete a series from a chart without affect-
ing the data series in the worksheet. You can temporarily remove a data series by hiding
the data in the worksheet. A more permanent solution is to delete a data series by deleting it from the chart.

---

task reference   Deleting a Data Series
                                                      from a Chart

- Select the chart area by clicking anywhere within the chart

- Click the data marker for the series you want to delete

- Press the **Delete** key

Keoki wants to remove the Longboard from the chart but leave it in the worksheet.
He asks you to show him the modified chart after you remove the series.

anotherway
**. . . to Add a New
Data Series to a
Chart**

Click near the chart
border to select the
entire chart

Click **Chart** on the
menu bar and then
click **Add Data**

Select the data you
want to plot by
dragging the mouse
across the worksheet
cell range, including
the category text, or
by typing the cell
range in the Range
text box

Click **OK**

Deleting a data series from a chart:

1. Click the Chart Objects list box arrow in the Chart toolbar and then click
Chart Area in the list to select the Chart

tip: If the Chart floating toolbar is not visible, click inside the chart to display the Chart
toolbar

2. Click any of the Longboard data markers (the fourth column in each group). Notice that Excel outlines the corresponding data range in the worksheet—cell range B7:D7—and that a ScreenTip appears identifying the data marker whenever you hover the mouse over it (see Figure 4.19)

FIGURE 4.19

Selecting a data series prior to deleting it

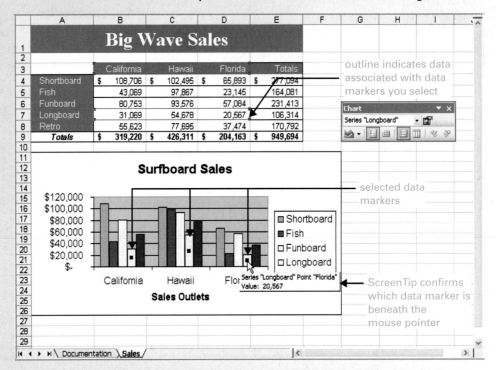

3. Press the **Delete** key. The data series disappears from the chart

tip: *If you accidentally delete the wrong series, simply click the **Undo** button on the Standard toolbar, if necessary, and then select and delete the correct data series*

Hiding Chart Data Series

An alternative to deleting a data series from a chart is hiding it. When you *hide* data (by reducing its row height to zero) in a worksheet that corresponds to a chart's data series, it is removed from the chart temporarily. Removing the data series from the chart is temporary because the data series reappears when you unhide the corresponding worksheet data row or column.

Hiding a data series by hiding the worksheet data:

1. Right-click the row 5 heading button

2. Click **Hide** on the shortcut menu that opens. Excel hides row 5 and removes the data series corresponding to that row from the chart. You show the resulting chart to Keoki

3. Because you don't want to hide the data after Keoki examines the new chart, click the Standard toolbar **Undo** button to reverse the row-hiding operation and then click any cell to deselect row 5. Row 5 reappears

Altering Chart Text

Keoki wants you to change the chart title and add a Y-axis title. Since neither title gets its value from worksheet cells, you can alter and add them directly to the chart.

Altering the chart title:

1. Click the **Chart Title** object to select it. Selection handles and an outline appear around the chart title. The Name box displays the name "Chart Title" when you select the chart title

2. Move the I-beam-shaped mouse pointer to the end of the word "Sales" and then click the mouse to remove the selection handles. The blinking vertical bar insertion point appears to the right of the word *Sales*

3. Press the **Spacebar** and type **by Type and Outlet**

4. Click anywhere within the chart area but outside the Chart Title object to deselect it

Next, you will add a Y-axis title to identify the values on that axis.

Adding a Value (Y-axis) title:

1. If necessary, select the **Chart Area**. Selection handles appear around the border of the entire chart area

2. Click **Chart** on the menu bar and then click **Chart Options** to open the Chart Options dialog box

3. Click the **Titles** tab if necessary, click the **Value (Y) axis** text box, and type **Gross Sales ($)**

4. Click **OK** to complete the process and close the Chart Options dialog box (see Figure 4.20)

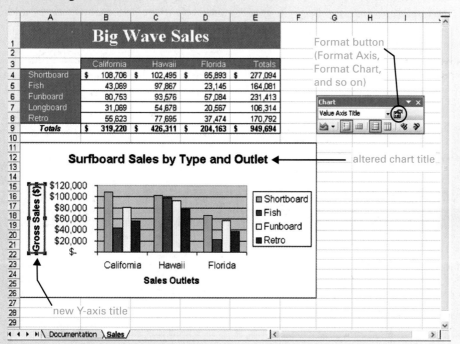

FIGURE 4.20

Chart with altered title and new Y-axis title

Modifying the Y-Axis Number Format

Excel determines the values to display on the Y-axis based on the largest and smallest values in the data series you plot. The interval between consecutive Y-axis values is uniform. Excel picks the format for Y-axis values from the formatting of the cell range represented by the data series. You can modify the Y-axis formatting using the same formats Excel provides for formatting numeric entries in a worksheet. You format the Y-axis next to remove the currency symbol, which is indicated in the Y-axis title.

Formatting the Value (Y-axis) values:

1. Click the **Value axis** (Y-axis) to select it. Notice that the Chart Objects list box in the Chart toolbar displays "Value Axis"

tip: *If the Chart toolbar is not visible, click* **View** *on the menu bar, point to* **Toolbars**, *and click* **Chart**

2. Click **Format** on the menu bar, click **Selected Axis**, and click the **Number** tab

tip: *You can also click the* **Format Axis** 🖼 *button on the Chart toolbar instead of Format/Selected Axis (see the Chart toolbar in Figure 4.18)*

3. Click **Number** in the Category list, type **0** in the Decimal places spin control, and check the **Use 1000 Separator** check box

4. Click **OK** to complete the formatting process

Labeling Data

While charts provide a handy way to represent numeric data that are easily understood, the exact values of significant data projected by charts are not always clear—especially when you use three-dimensional charts. It is helpful to anyone who reads your charts if you label some or all of the data markers with text that indicates their values. Look at the chart in Figure 4.20, for example. If that chart were made into a transparency and presented to an audience and someone in the audience asked you, "What is the value of the gross sales of Shortboards in California?" would you be able to answer them with a precise answer? The best answer you could give is that the value is between $100,000 and $120,000. To precisely answer that question using only a chart, you need to add one or more data labels to your chart. A *data label* is the value or name assigned to an individual data point. Data labels are optional.

You can choose to display a data label to all data series in the chart, to one of the data series, or to a single data marker in a data series.

task reference	Adding a Data Label to All Data Series in a Chart

- Select the chart
- Select any data series in the chart
- Click **Chart**, click **Chart Options**, click the **Data Labels** tab
- Click the **Show value** option button and then click **OK**

<table>
<tr><td>task reference</td><td>Adding a Data Label to a
Data Series</td></tr>
</table>

- Select the chart
- Select the data series
- Click **Format**, click **Selected Data Series**, click the **Data Labels** tab
- Click the **Show value** option button and then click **OK**

<table>
<tr><td>task reference</td><td>Adding a Data Label to a
Data Marker</td></tr>
</table>

- Select the chart
- Select the data series containing the data marker to label
- Click the data marker in the series
- Click **Format**, click **Selected Data Point**, and then click the **Data Labels** tab
- Click the **Show value** option button, and then click **OK**

Adding a data label to the Shortboard data marker for Hawaii:

1. Click any **Shortboard data marker**

2. Click the **Hawaii Shortboard** data marker. Eight selection handles outline the data marker

3. Click **Format** on the menu bar, click **Selected Data Point**, and click the **Data Labels** tab on the Format Data Point dialog box

4. Click the **Value** check box to place a checkmark in it (see Figure 4.21)

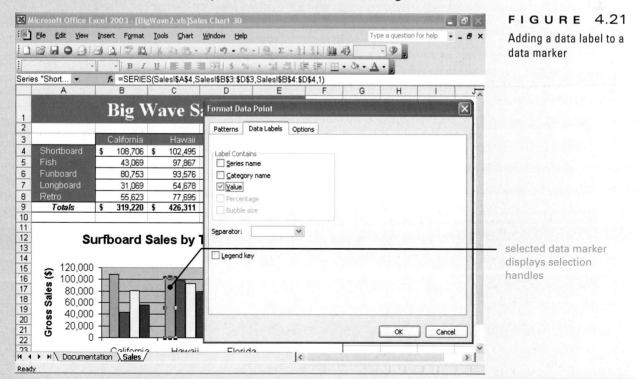

FIGURE 4.21

Adding a data label to a data marker

selected data marker displays selection handles

5. Click **OK** to complete the data label procedure, and click anywhere outside the chart to deselect the data marker (see Figure 4.22)

FIGURE 4.22

Displaying a data marker's value

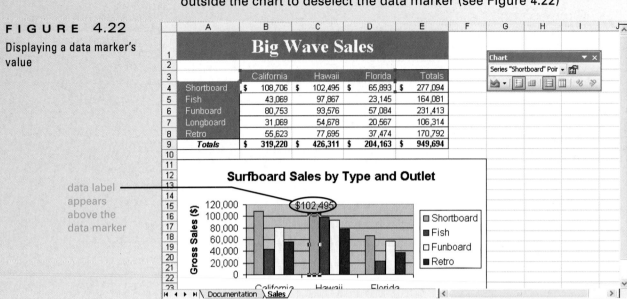

data label appears above the data marker

Keoki makes some other suggestions to you about enhancing the chart. You will apply those suggestions next.

Embellishing a Chart

There are a large number of alterations or embellishments you can make to a chart. You can apply foreground and background color to any object on a chart or to the chart background itself. There is a wide selection of patterns and textures you can add to a background also. Gradients, which are color fades that change from dark to light across an object, are available. In fact, the number of enhancements you can apply to a chart is almost endless. However, be careful to not go overboard. The resulting chart can become garish and difficult to view if you use too many colors, textures, and color blends in a single chart.

Remember that not everyone has access to a color printer. Some charts printed on laser printers may yield unreadable text due to the foreground and background color and texture combinations you choose. Data markers may blend together if you choose colors that register as very similar grayscale values on a laser printer. In other words, exercise restraint when you enhance charts with color and textures. The final result will enhance the worksheet rather than detract from it.

Adding a Text Box for Emphasis

Keoki wants you to add text to indicate that the chart belongs to the Big Wave company. The text box should contain the phrase "Copyright Big Wave" and be placed near the lower-left corner of the chart in 8-point (Arial) typeface.

Adding a text box to the embedded chart:

1. Click the **Chart Area**

2. If the Drawing toolbar is not visible, click **View** on the menu bar, point to **Toolbars**, and click **Drawing**. The Drawing toolbar appears on the screen

3. Click the **Text Box** 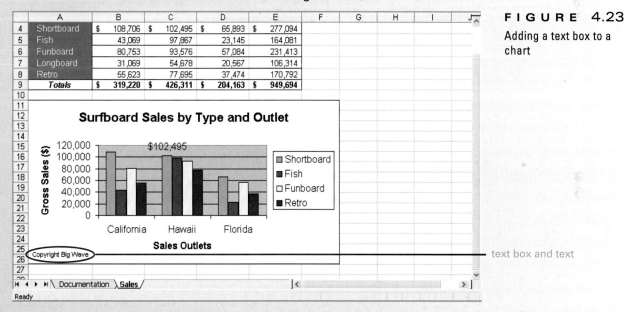 button on the Drawing toolbar

4. Move the mouse to the left side of the chart area near row 25 (scroll the worksheet if necessary), click the mouse to drop the text box onto the chart, and type **Copyright Big Wave**

5. With the mouse pointer in an I-beam shape, select the text inside the text box by dragging the mouse from right to left across the text within the text box until all the text is selected

tip: *Selecting text in a text box takes a little practice. If the mouse pointer becomes a four-headed arrow, you are near the edge of the text box itself. In that case, move back slightly until the mouse changes to an I-beam. Then drag the I-beam mouse pointer across the text until all of it is selected*

6. Click in the Font Size list box arrow on the Formatting toolbar, click **8**, and then click outside the Chart Area (see Figure 4.23)

FIGURE 4.23

Adding a text box to a chart

text box and text

7. If you need to adjust the position of the text box, move the mouse near the text box edge. When the mouse pointer changes to a four-headed arrow, click the text box edge and drag it within the Chart Area

8. Click **View**, point to **Toolbars**, and click **Drawing**, to close the Drawing toolbar

Emphasizing and Enhancing with Color

There are hundreds of combinations of ways to spruce up a chart including varying the typeface, using color in the background of objects, using color in the text or foreground of objects, and adding graphics. After examining the worksheet for a few minutes, Keoki asks you to experiment with using a dark blue color for the chart title text.

EXCEL

Changing the color of the chart, value axis, and category axis titles:

1. Click the **Chart Title** object. Selection handles surround the chart title
2. Click the **Format** 🖼 button on the Chart toolbar to open the Format Chart Title dialog box
3. Click the **Font** tab, click the Color list box arrow to reveal the palette of text colors, click the **Dark Blue** square (see Figure 4.24), and click **OK** to close the Format Chart Title dialog box

FIGURE 4.24

Changing the chart title foreground color

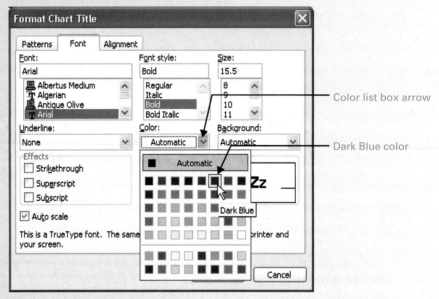

4. Select the **Value Axis Title** object and repeat steps 2 and 3 above. (The dialog box that opens is called the Format Axis Title dialog box)
5. Select the **Category Axis Title** object and repeat steps 2 and 3 above. Press the **Esc** key to deselect the category axis title. All three titles are now dark blue

Changing Patterns and Colors

Colors look great on the screen, but they may not have the same visual impact when you print a worksheet on a noncolor printer. Noncolor laser printers display colors as shades of gray, which can diminish the effectiveness of color. In the absence of color, you can use stripes or textures to differentiate elements of a chart and add impact in a noncolor printer environment. Data markers are particularly difficult to distinguish when they contain the wrong combination of colors.

Keoki wants you to use different patterns for each of the data markers to avoid confusion about which gross sales are due to each surfboard category.

Applying a data pattern to a data series and changing a data series color:

1. Click any **Shortboard data marker** in the series. Excel selects all data markers in the series
2. Click the **Format** 🖼 button on the Chart toolbar. The Format Data Series dialog box opens

3. Click the **Patterns** tab, if necessary, and click the **Fill Effects** button to open the like-named dialog box

4. Click the **Pattern** tab and then click the **Dark upward diagonal** pattern in the fourth row from the top, third column (see Figure 4.25)

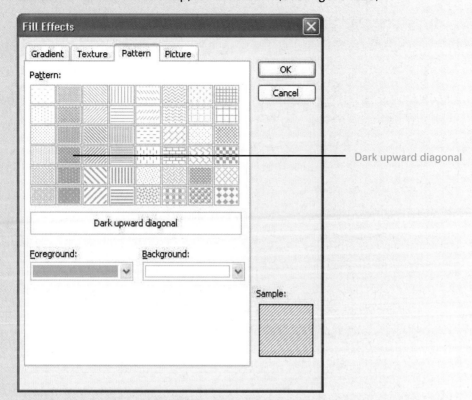

Dark upward diagonal

FIGURE 4.25
Fill Effects dialog box

5. Click **OK** to close the Fill Effects dialog box. Click **OK** to close the Format Data Series dialog box

6. Click any **Fish data marker** in the series and repeat steps 2 through 5, clicking the **Dark vertical** pattern (fifth row from the top, fourth column) in step 4

7. Click any **Funboard data marker** in the series, click the **Format** button on the Chart toolbar, click the **Patterns** tab, click the **Fill Effects** button, and click the **Pattern** tab

8. Click the Foreground list box arrow and then click the **Sea Green** square (third row from the top, fourth column) to change the series color

9. Click the **Dark downward diagonal** square (third row from the top, third column)

10. Click **OK** to close the Fill Effects dialog box and click **OK** to close the Format Data Series dialog box

11. Click any **Retro data marker** in the series and repeat steps 2 through 5, choosing **Dark horizontal** pattern (sixth row from the top, fourth column) in step 4

12. Click any worksheet cell to deselect the data marker. Each of the data series has a distinguishable pattern that will be visible even when printed on a noncolor printer

EXCEL

---

anotherword   . . . on Data Series and Fill Effects

If you decide to remove all fill effects from a data series, click any marker of the data series in the chart, click **Edit** on the menu bar, point to **Clear**, and click **Formats**

Previewing and Printing a Chart

You know by now to preview your output before you actually print it, because you can catch small mistakes before printing too many pages. Often a multipage output can be trimmed to one or two pages simply by minimizing the margins or reorienting the output to landscape.

Previewing and Printing a Worksheet and Chart

Preview the worksheet and chart prior to printing it. Check to ensure that both the chart and worksheet fit on one page.

---

task reference   Printing a Worksheet and Embedded Chart

- Ensure that the embedded chart is not selected by clicking any worksheet cell
- Click **File** and click **Print Preview**
- Click **Print** and click **OK**

Saving, previewing, and printing the worksheet and embedded chart:

1. Click **File** and then click **Save** to save the completed worksheet and chart

2. Click cell **A2** to be doubly sure that the chart is not selected

3. Click the **Print Preview** 🔍 button on the Standard toolbar to open the Print Preview window. Check to ensure that both the worksheet and chart appear on the same page

tip: *If the entire worksheet does not appear on the first page or if both the worksheet and chart do not appear on the same page, adjust the page margins. Click the **Margins** button on the Print Preview toolbar. The margin lines appear on the preview. Drag the left and right margin lines toward the edge of the paper to decrease the margins (see Figure 4.26)*

4. Click the **Setup** button on the Print Preview toolbar to open the Page Setup dialog box, click the **Header/Footer** tab, click the **Custom Header** button, and type your name in the Right section of the header

5. Click **OK** twice to close the Header and Page Setup dialog boxes

6. Click the **Print** button on the Print Preview toolbar to open the Print dialog box, then click the **OK** button to print the worksheet

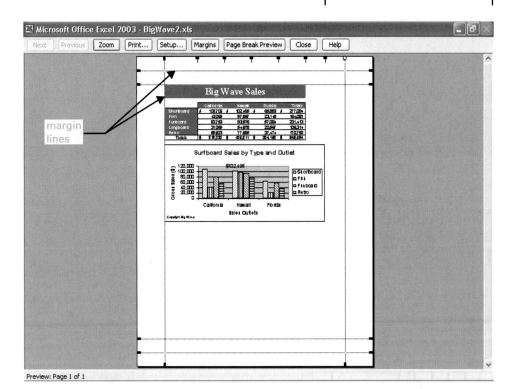

FIGURE 4.26
Preview of worksheet and chart displaying margin lines

Previewing and Printing an Embedded Chart

Printing an embedded chart without the accompanying worksheet is only slightly different from printing the worksheet and chart together. The main difference between the two procedures is that you select the chart before previewing or printing it.

task *reference*	Printing an Embedded Chart

- Click the embedded chart
- Click the **Print** button on the Standard toolbar

Because Keoki wants the embedded chart printed separately, you print it next.

Printing an embedded chart:

1. Click the **Chart Area**. Selection handles appear around it
2. Click the **Print** button on the Standard toolbar to print the chart (see Figure 4.27)
3. Click the **Documentation** worksheet tab, and then click the **Save** button on the Standard toolbar
4. Close Excel

Your work on the embedded chart is done. Keoki is very happy with the results. You can go on to learn about adding another type of graph to the output. This type will be a chart sheet containing a pie chart showing another aspect of Big Wave's surfboard sales.

FIGURE 4.27

Embedded chart output

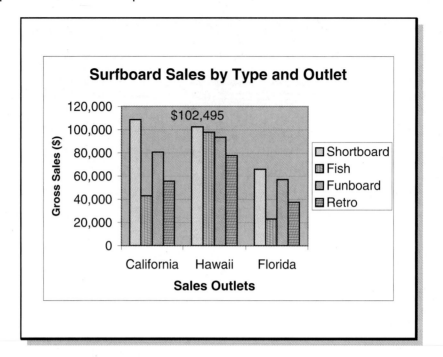

making *the grade*

1. A _____ _____ is a set of values that you want to chart.

2. In a column chart, the labels appearing along the X-axis are called _____ titles.

3. A chart on the same worksheet as the data it represents is called a(n) _____ chart. The other type of chart is called a _____ _____ and resides on its own sheet that is different from normal worksheets.

4. The _____ _____ helps you create a chart by displaying a series of dialog boxes that you fill in to complete the chart.

SESSION 4.2 MODIFYING AND IMPROVING A CHART

In this session, you will create a pie chart and learn how to select nonadjacent data ranges for charting. You will learn about three-dimensional chart types including pie charts, exploding a pie slice to emphasize it, and the use of text and titles in three-dimensional charts. You will explore how textures can add interest to charts and learn how to create a chart sheet containing a freestanding chart. Finally, you will create a stacked column chart and learn how to format its components to highlight significant data.

Creating a Chart in a Chart Sheet

Keoki wants to look at a broader picture of his surfboard sales in a chart—a chart you will create in a chart sheet. He wants you to create a chart showing total sales of each surfboard type in a pie chart, based on his sketch shown in Figure 4.8. A pie chart is a good chart choice when you want to show the contribution of parts to the whole. In the case of Big Wave, the pie chart will demonstrate visually the contribution of each surfboard type to the overall sales. In a similar way, you could create a pie chart by sales outlet and examine the sales attributable to each sales outlet compared to the sum of all sales.

Defining a Series

Creating a chart begins by first selecting the worksheet cells in the data range to be plotted. This time, the data selection process is different because you want to select two columns from a group of five columns, leaving out three columns in the middle of a range of contiguous cells. Using the sketch in Figure 4.8 as a general guideline, notice that the labels around the perimeter of the pie chart match text in worksheet cells A4 through A8 (A7, originally).

Selecting Nonadjacent Data Ranges

Prior to launching the Chart Wizard to create a chart, select the cell range(s) that are to be charted. Because the cell ranges are in columns that are not adjacent to each other, you cannot simply drag the mouse through both ranges. Doing so would result in a chart containing two distinct types of data—sales detail information and sales sum information—that should not appear in the same chart.

---

task reference   Selecting Nonadjacent
                                       Cell Ranges

- Click and drag the mouse through the first cell range you want to select

- Press and hold the **Ctrl** key

- Click additional cells or click and drag additional cell ranges

- When finished selecting all cells or cell ranges, release the **Ctrl** key

---

Selecting nonadjacent data ranges:

1. If you took a break after the last session, make sure that Excel is running and open to **BigWave2.xls**

2. Save the file as **BigWave3.xls**

3. Click the **Sales** tab to open that worksheet, and select cell range **A4:A8**

4. Press and hold the **Ctrl** key, click and drag the cell range **E4** through **E8**, and release the **Ctrl** key. The cell range E4:E8 contains the data points you want to plot on a chart and the two nonadjacent cell ranges, A4:A8 and E4:E8, are selected (see Figure 4.28)

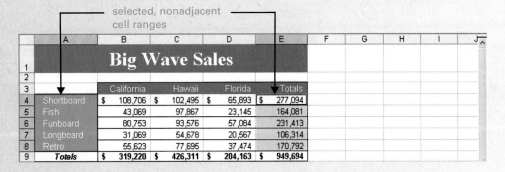

FIGURE 4.28

Selecting nonadjacent cell ranges

Creating a Three-Dimensional Pie Chart

Once you have selected the data ranges to chart, you can proceed to create the chart. Keoki wants a pie chart on a separate workbook page—a chart sheet. Charts on separate sheets are convenient to print and you can easily move chart sheets around in the workbook to reorganize their order. You can rename chart sheet tabs with meaningful names to make the charts easy to locate. If you are making a slide presentation, chart sheets are particularly convenient because you can organize the chart sheets in the same order as the slide presentation. Then you can print the chart sheets directly to a color transparency-capable printer.

Creating a Pie Chart:

1. Click the **Chart Wizard** ▥ button on the Standard toolbar

2. Click **Pie** in the Chart type list box. Several pie chart sub-types appear in the Chart sub-types panel

3. Click the **Pie with a 3-D visual effect** chart sub-type (top row, second column) and then click the **Press and Hold to View Sample** button to see an example of the chart. That sample is the chart that Keoki wants. Release the **Press and Hold to View Sample** button

4. Click the **Next** button to proceed to Chart Wizard Step 2. Make sure that the Data range text box displays the data range value =Sales!$A$4:$A$8,Sales!$E$4:$E$8, which is a special form of the cell range notation for the two nonadjacent cell ranges you selected previously

   tip: *If the Data range text box does not show the correct cell range, click the Collapse Dialog button and select the two nonadjacent data ranges A4:A8 and E4:E8 before continuing with the Chart Wizard*

5. Click the **Next** button, click the **Titles** tab, click the **Chart Title** text box, and type **Surfboard Sales by Type**

6. Click the **Legend** tab, and click the **Show legend** check box to clear it (see Figure 4.29)

FIGURE 4.29

Removing the chart's legend

clear to remove the chart's legend

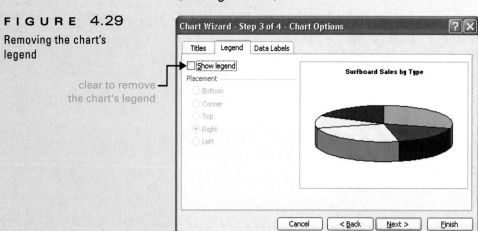

7. Click the **Data Labels** tab, click the **Category name** check box to display category names for each pie slice, and click the **Percentage** check box button to display percentages for each pie slice

8. Click the **Next** button and then click the **As new sheet** option button to create the chart as a chart sheet rather than as an embedded chart

9. Click the **Finish** button to complete the preliminary version of the three-dimensional pie chart (see Figure 4.30)

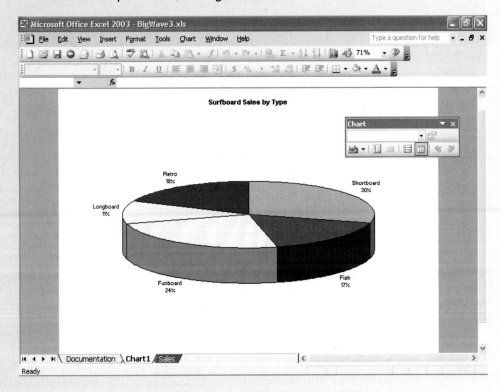

FIGURE 4.30

Preliminary 3-D pie chart

Exploding a Pie Chart Slice

Keoki gives his approval and requests that you find a way to highlight the Shortboard sales to make the data stand out to a viewer. You review several options including special colors and other methods and suggest that the best choice is to pull the Shortboard pie slice away from the rest of the chart.

Exploding a pie slice:

1. If necessary, click the chart sheet tab **Chart1** (your chart sheet tab may have a different name)

2. Click the pie chart. Selection handles appear around the pie, one on each slice, and the Chart Objects list box displays "Series 1"

3. Hover the mouse over the Shortboard pie slice. The ScreenTip "Series 1 Point "Shortboard" Value: $277,094 (30%)" appears

4. Click the **Shortboard pie slice** to select it. Selection handles disappear from all other pie slices

5. Click and drag the **Shortboard pie slice** a short distance away from the center of the pie and release the mouse (see Figure 4.31)

6. Click the **Chart Area** to deselect the pie slice

EXCEL

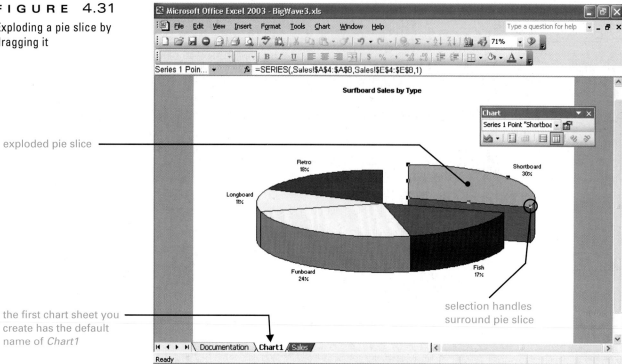

Rotating and Elevating a Three-Dimensional Chart

While the 3-D pie chart certainly is impressive and self-explanatory, Keoki thinks the
exact proportions of the pie slices are not obvious to a casual reader. He thinks that the
pie chart should be tilted up, by raising the back edge, to provide a better perspective.
Additionally, Keoki wants the Shortboard pie slice to appear on the right side of the
chart at the 3 o'clock position, considering the pie to be a clock face.

Elevating and rotating a pie chart:

1. With the Chart Area of the 3-D chart sheet selected, click **Chart** in the
   menu bar and click **3-D View**. The Elevation text box displays 15,
   indicating that the entire pie chart is tilted up 15 degrees
   (see Figure 4.32)

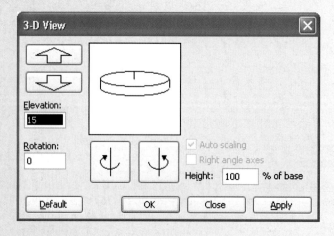

2. Double-click the **Elevation** text box, if necessary, to select its current value and then type **35**

3. Click and drag the **3-D View dialog box Title bar** so that you can see the Shortboard portion of the pie chart

4. Double-click the **Rotation** text box to highlight its current value, type **20**, and click the 3-D View dialog box **Apply** button. Excel rotates the pie chart clockwise 20 degrees, but that is not quite enough

5. Double-click the **Rotation** text box, type **30** to rotate the pie chart clockwise 30 degrees, and click the **Apply** button. That looks just right (see Figure 4.33)

FIGURE 4.33

Elevating and rotating a 3-D pie chart

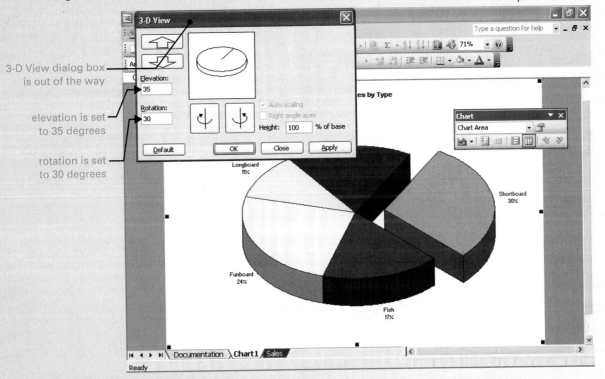

6. Click the **OK** button to complete the operation and close the 3-D View dialog box

You can see why Keoki wanted you to elevate the 3-D pie chart. It is much easier to see the pie chart and judge the size differences between the five pie slices representing total sales of the five types of surfboards.

Changing the Chart Type

Excel has several chart types from which you can choose. You can choose a type as you create a chart. You can choose to change chart types after you have created a chart sheet or an embedded chart. With the current chart selected, you can change to a different chart type by clicking the Chart Type command on the Chart menu or by clicking the Chart Type button on the Chart toolbar. Keoki is satisfied with the 3-D pie chart you created and he does not want to change chart types. It's good to know you can change chart types easily, though.

help yourself *Press **F1**, type **changing the chart type** in the Search text box of the Microsoft Excel Help task pane, and press **Enter**. Click the hyperlink **Select a different chart type** and maximize the Excel Help dialog box to more easily read the help offered. Close the Help dialog box when you are finished*

Adding Texture for Emphasis

Texture or gradient fills are applicable to the chart area, bars, and several other chart objects. When used sparingly, texture fills and gradient fills can add just the right touch to a chart to make it look professional. Because the 3-D pie chart visually represents sales of surfboards by type, Keoki wants you to add a background texture to the chart area that is related to sun, surf, or water. Doing so, he reasons, will add just the right adornment and enhance the chart's impact on all who view it.

Adding texture fill to a chart area:

1. Click the **Chart Area** object (the white area around the chart)

2. Click **Format** on the menu bar and then click **Selected Chart Area**

3. Click the **Patterns** tab, if necessary, and then click the **Fill Effects** button. The Fill Effects dialog box opens

4. Click the **Texture** tab and then click the **Texture scroll down arrow** until the Water droplets texture appears (second row from the bottom, first column)

5. Click the **Water droplets** square. The text "Water droplets" appears in the label below the Texture palette when you select the correct square (see Figure 4.34)

FIGURE 4.34

Selecting the Water droplets texture

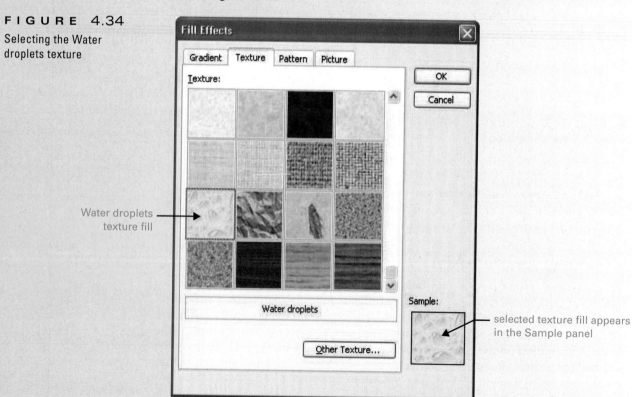

Water droplets texture fill

selected texture fill appears in the Sample panel

6. Click **OK** to close the Fill Effects dialog box and click **OK** again to close the Format Chart Area dialog box. The Water droplets texture fill appears in the chart area background (see Figure 4.35)

FIGURE 4.35
Chart with texture fill

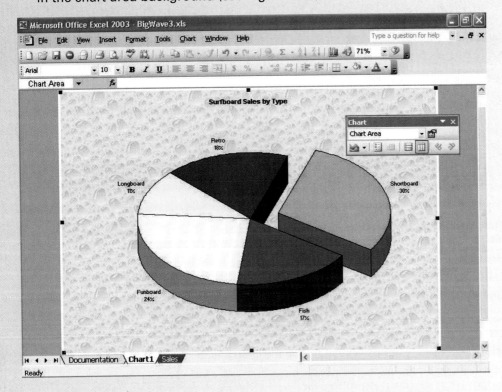

The pie chart is complete and ready to print.

Saving and Printing a Chart Sheet

Keoki reviews your work and is satisfied with the final result. He asks you to save the workbook and print the chart sheet. Printing chart sheets follows the same procedures as printing any worksheet. You either click the Standard toolbar print button or click File, then Print, and set options in the Print dialog box before you click OK to print the page.

> ### *another***word** ... on Chart Area Background Fill Effects
>
> If you decide to *remove* fill effects from a chart area background, click the chart area, click **Format** on the menu bar, click **Selected Chart Area**, click **Patterns** tab, click the **None** option button in the Area panel, and click the OK button to close the Format Chart Area dialog box and remove the background texture fill from the chart area

Saving the workbook and printing a chart sheet:

1. Click the **Save** button on the Standard toolbar to save your workbook

2. If necessary, click the **Chart1** sheet tab to select the chart sheet

tip: *If you have created other chart sheets and deleted them before creating the final chart sheet, your chart sheet tab may not be called Chart1. It may have another name such as Chart2 or Chart3*

EXCEL

3. Click **File**, click **Page Setup**, click the **Header/Footer** tab, click the **Custom Header** button, type your name in the Right section, click **OK** to close the Header dialog box, and click **OK** to close the Page Setup dialog box

4. Click the **Print** 🖨 button to print the chart sheet. After a short pause, the chart sheet prints

Deleting Charts

Although you will not delete any charts you have created, you should learn how to delete both embedded charts and chart sheets in case you later need to do so. Delete an embedded chart by selecting it and then pressing the Delete key.

task reference	Deleting an Embedded Chart
• Click the embedded chart • Press the **Delete** key	

Deleting a chart sheet is equally simple. Be careful. Unlike deleting an embedded chart, there is no way to reverse the deletion process.

task reference	Deleting a Chart Sheet
• Click the tab corresponding to the chart sheet • Click **Edit**, then click **Delete Sheet** • Click **OK**	

Saving a Chart as a Web Page

Because Keoki wants to share the worksheet with his Big Wave employees in all three locations—Hawaii, California, and Florida—he asks you to create a Web page from the Excel worksheet. For now, Keoki will post the worksheet in a protected area of the Web server that only employees can access.

You can create Web pages from Excel charts about as simply as you can save a worksheet. Once you create the Web pages, make them available to anyone by posting them on a server connected to the Internet that displays Web pages. However, you do not need access to a Web server to create Web pages. You can view your Web pages on any PC that has a Web browser regardless of whether it is connected to the Internet.

task reference	Creating Web Pages from an Excel Chart
• Click the chart sheet tab • Click **File** and click **Save as Web Page** • Select a drive and folder in the Save in text box • Click the **Selection: Chart** option • Click the **Change Title** button, type a Web page title in the title text box, and click **OK** • Type the Web page filename in the File name text box • Click the **Save** button	

You are ready to create a Web page from the pie chart on the chart sheet you created in this session.

Saving a chart sheet as a Web page:

1. Click the chart sheet tab corresponding to your chart sheet, if necessary

2. Click **File** and then click **Save As**. The Save As dialog box opens

3. Select the disk drive and folder in the Save in list box in which you want to save your Web pages

4. Click **Single File Web Page** in the Save as type list box

5. Click the **Selection: Chart** option

6. Click the **Change Title** button, type **Big Wave Surfboard Sales by Type** in the Title text box of the Set Title dialog box. The title you type appears in the browser's Title bar whenever you open the Web page

7. Click **OK** to close the Set Title dialog box

8. Drag the mouse across the text in the File name text box and type **BigWave** to replace the Excel-suggested filename (see Figure 4.36)

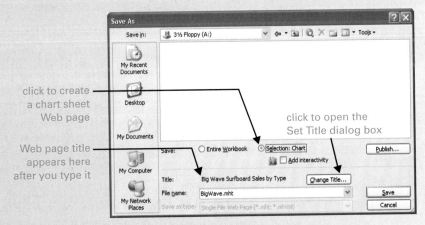

click to create a chart sheet Web page

click to open the Set Title dialog box

Web page title appears here after you type it

FIGURE 4.36

Saving a chart as a Web page

9. Click the **Save** button to save the Web page archive file

Creating a Bar Chart

Keoki has encouraged competition between his three Big Wave sales outlets by offering incentives if the sales outlet reaches or exceeds selected gross sales goals. He expects gross sales at each outlet to exceed $200,000 per year—the amount he calculates he must make just to keep the sales outlet open. Keoki is pleased when annual sales exceed $200,000 in any sales outlet. He pays a bonus to sales associates in those regions. For sales outlets selling more than $300,000 in one year, Keoki promises a double bonus for the sales associates in those regions.

Keoki thinks that a bar graph is the best way to show the progress of each sales outlet and to display the annual totals to every Big Wave salesperson. Keoki asks you to figure out a way to color-code each segment of a bar so that it colorfully indicates when the sales region reaches selected sales milestones.

A bar chart is similar to a column chart and can be used interchangeably. Bar charts can illustrate competitions slightly better than column charts because bar charts are drawn from left to right and resemble progress toward a goal or a race proceeding from left to right. Bar charts are often used to highlight values that exceed a critical level—blood pressure is too high, temperatures are reaching a critical value, or fuel reserves are below a safety point. One way to highlight critical goals or value points with a bar chart is to color-code a data marker to indicate when the data marker has surpassed one or more critical points. Figure 4.37 illustrates this concept. Each segment of a bar is color coded to indicate when campaign funds for each candidate exceed successive $3 million boundaries. Color codes help a reader quickly grasp the big picture.

The ***stacked bar chart***, a subtype of the bar chart, combines the data markers in a data series together to form one bar, placing each marker at the end of the preceding one in the same data series. A stacked bar chart is particularly well suited in situations that Figure 4.37 illustrates—when data series constitute a category and you are interested in viewing the sum of the data values in the series.

FIGURE 4.37

Bar chart with color-coded value alerts

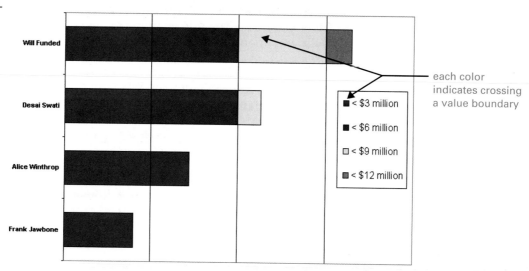

each color indicates crossing a value boundary

Creating data series for a stacked bar chart:

1. Click the **Sales** sheet tab

2. Click cell **G5** and type **California**, click cell **G6** and type **Hawaii**, click cell **G7**, and type **Florida**

3. Click cell **H5**, type =**MIN(B9,200000)**, click cell **H6**, type =**MIN(C9,200000)**, click cell **H7**, type =**MIN(D9,200000)**, and then press **Enter**. These formulas calculate values that represent the first segment—up to $200,000—of the sales for each sales outlet. Next, you will add another data marker that represents the value between $200,000 and $300,000

tip: *You may want to widen columns H, I, and J, as necessary, to view the results of the formulas*

4. Click cell **I5**, type =**MIN(B9-H5,100000)**, click cell **I6**, type =**MIN(C9-H6,100000)**, click cell **I7**, type =**MIN(D9-H7,100000)**, and then press **Enter**. These formulas calculate values that represent the second segment—from $200,000 to $300,000—of the sales for each sales outlet

5. Click cell **J5**, type **=B9-H5-I5**, click cell **J6**, type **=C9-H6-I6**, click cell **J7**, type **=D9-H7-I7**, and then press **Enter**. These formulas calculate values that represent the final segment—above $300,000—for each sales outlet (see Figure 4.38)

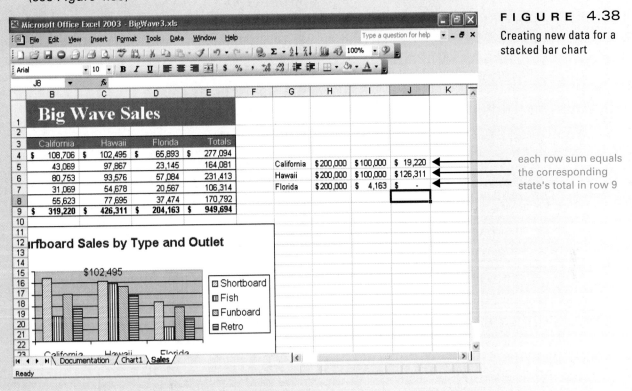

FIGURE 4.38

Creating new data for a stacked bar chart

each row sum equals the corresponding state's total in row 9

The new data show the sales for each sales outlet broken down into three segments: $0 to $200,000, $200,001 to $300,000, and greater than $300,000. Using this new data, you can create a stacked bar graph that shows how each series' segment contributes to the total sales represented by a bar in the bar chart. You create the chart next.

Creating a stacked bar chart:

1. Click and drag the cell range **G5:J7**

2. Click the **Chart Wizard** button, click **Bar** in the Chart type list box, click the **Stacked Bar** square in the Chart sub-type panel (top row, second column), and click the **Next** button

3. Click the **Columns** option button and click the **Next** button

4. Click the **Titles** tab, if necessary, and then click the **Chart title** text box and type **Critical Sales Boundaries**

5. Click the **Legend** tab, click the **Show Legend** check box to remove the checkmark, and click **Next**

6. Click the **As new sheet** option button and then click the **Finish** button. The stacked bar chart appears in its own chart sheet, Chart2, following the Chart1 chart sheet (see Figure 4.39)

FIGURE 4.39

Stacked bar sales chart

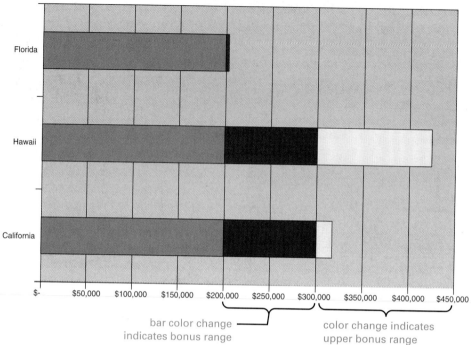

Critical Sales Boundaries

bar color change
indicates bonus range

color change indicates
upper bonus range

Keoki couldn't be happier. He's pleased with all three charts and sends you a nice e-mail expressing how much he appreciates your hard work.

Saving the workbook:

1. Type your name in the worksheet header of the stack bar chart sheet
2. Click the **Documentation** sheet tab to make it active
3. Save your workbook and then exit Excel

You have completed your work in this chapter and have created an embedded chart and two chart sheets.

SESSION 4.2

making *the grade*

1. You select nonadjacent cell ranges by selecting the first cell range, pressing the _____ key, and selecting the second cell range.
2. A(n) _____ chart resides on a worksheet page, whereas a(n) _____ is on a separate sheet.
3. A _____ chart is a good choice when you want to depict contribution of parts to a whole.
4. You can _____ a three-dimensional pie chart to get a better perspective of it.

SESSION 4.3 SUMMARY

Excel charts pictorially display values and provide a graphic way for viewers to easily understand the magnitude or change in data values. You can create either two-dimensional or three-dimensional charts including column, bar, line, pie, scatter, area, and doughnut. For each chart type, you can choose from several chart sub-types. Column sub-type charts include simple column, stacked column, and stacked column with a 3-D visual effect. Chart data are called data series—the set of values you chart. Categories organize values in the data series. The X-axis in a column chart displays category names.

Choosing the correct type of chart to display your data is important. Each chart has a different purpose. A pie chart best displays the contribution of parts to the whole—how much of your tax dollar goes to education, for example. Line charts are a good choice to show trends. The plot area contains the chart and other elements surrounding the chart include the chart title, category names, and the X- and Y-axes. Excel supports both embedded charts and chart sheets. Embedded charts appear on a worksheet along with data and float on a layer above the worksheet. A chart sheet is a separate sheet that contains a chart but does not contain worksheet data. Embedded charts and chart sheets are otherwise exactly the same—both types can display any of the Excel chart types.

Chart data—the values represented by the data series—are linked to the data markers. This dynamic relationship means that you can change the value of worksheet data and the chart will automatically adjust to reflect the changes. Category names are linked to worksheet cells too, though they typically display text.

You can modify every aspect of a chart including the overall chart type, the format (color, typeface, and size) of any text or numeric value on a chart, the background color of the plot area or chart area, the color or existence of gridlines and data labels, the format and scaling of Y-axis values, and whether a legend appears on the chart.

Delete data series from a chart by hiding the data in the worksheet (hide the row or column) or by selecting the data series and pressing the Delete key. Print an embedded chart by printing the worksheet on which it resides. Alternatively, click an embedded chart to print just the embedded chart.

MICROSOFT OFFICE SPECIALIST OBJECTIVES SUMMARY

- Define a data series and data categories—MOS XL03S-2-5
- Create an embedded chart and a chart sheet—MOS XL03S-2-5
- Modify an existing chart by revising data, altering chart text, and labeling data—MOS XL03S-2-5
- Use color and patterns to embellish a chart—MOS XL03E-2-4
- Add a new data series to a chart—MOS XL03S-2-5
- Alter a chart type and create a three-dimensional chart—MOS XL03S-2-5
- Create a pie chart with a title, exploding slice, labels, and floating text—MOS XL03S-2-5
- Add texture to a chart—MOS XL03E-2-4
- Save a chart as a Web page—MOS XL03S-5-10

making the grade answers

SESSION 4.1
1. data series
2. category
3. embedded; chart sheet
4. Chart Wizard

SESSION 4.2
1. Ctrl
2. embedded; chart sheet
3. pie
4. elevate

EXCEL

task reference *summary*

Task	Page #	Recommended Method
Creating a chart	EX 4.11	• Select data cell range, click the **Chart Wizard** 📊 button • Respond to the series of Chart Wizard dialog box choices
Snapping an embedded chart into place	EX 4.15	• Select the chart • Press and hold the **Alt** key • Drag a chart left, right, up, or down until the chart edge snaps to a cell boundary • Release the mouse and Alt key
Adding a new data series to an embedded chart	EX 4.18	• Select the cell range of the data series you want to add • Move the mouse to any edge of the selected worksheet cell range • When the mouse pointer changes to an arrow, click and drag the range into the chart area and release the mouse
Deleting a data series from a chart	EX 4.19	• Select the data marker • Press **Delete**
Adding a data label to all data series in a chart	EX 4.22	• Select a data series • Click **Chart**, click **Chart Options**, click the **Data Labels** tab • Click the **Show value** option, click **OK**
Adding a data label to a data series	EX 4.23	• Select the data series • Click **Format**, click **Selected Data Series**, click the **Data Labels** tab • Click the **Show value** option, click **OK**
Adding a data label to a data marker	EX 4.23	• Select the data series, click the data marker in the series • Click **Format**, click **Selected Data Point**, click the **Data Labels** tab • Click the **Show value** option, click **OK**
Printing a worksheet and embedded chart	EX 4.28	• Click any worksheet cell • Click the **Print** 🖨 button
Printing an embedded chart	EX 4.29	• Click the chart • Click the **Print** 🖨 button
Selecting nonadjacent cell ranges	EX 4.31	• Select the first cell range • Press and hold the **Ctrl** key • Select additional cells or cell ranges • When finished selecting cells, release the **Ctrl** key
Deleting an embedded chart	EX 4.38	• Click the embedded chart • Press the **Delete** key
Deleting a chart sheet	EX 4.38	• Click the chart sheet tab • Click **Edit**, click **Delete Sheet**, click **OK**
Creating Web pages from an Excel chart	EX 4.38	• Click the chart or chart sheet tab • Click **File**, click **Save As** • Select a drive and folder • Click **Web Archive** in the Save As type list box • Click the **Selection: Chart** option • Optionally type a page title and click **OK** • Click **Save**

TRUE OR FALSE

1. Excel refers to graphical representations of data as graphs.

2. A data marker is a graphical representation of the value of a data point.

3. Category names always appear in the legend.

4. A chart sheet deletion cannot be undone.

5. Selecting nonadjacent cell ranges is very complicated and should be avoided.

FILL-IN

1. A _____ _____ is a set of values that you chart.

2. The values in a data series are named by a _____.

3. The _____ area of a chart is bounded by the X-axis and the Y-axis.

4. The _____ identifies which data marker represents each series when you chart multiple series.

5. A _____ chart is a better choice than a pie chart to represent the daily average temperature in a city for a month.

6. The _____ box is a drawing object into which you can type text and place on a chart to highlight a feature.

MULTIPLE CHOICE

1. This text includes tick mark labels, the X-axis title, and the Y-axis title.
   a. unattached text
   b. attached text
   c. label text
   d. chart text

2. Which is not a characteristic of a chart sheet?
   a. The chart is much larger than a chart placed in the other location.
   b. There are no gridlines.
   c. It is easy to print and move.
   d. The accompanying data are conveniently located next to the chart on the same sheet.

3. A bar graph displays
   a. the size of change over time.
   b. the comparison between independent data values.
   c. the relationship between two sets of data points.
   d. trends over time of a series of data values.

4. Which step is not an appropriate step in selecting nonadjacent cell ranges?
   a. Click and drag the mouse through the first cell range.
   b. Press and hold the Ctrl key.
   c. Drag the mouse through both ranges.
   d. Click additional cells and then release the Ctrl key.

5. When you change a worksheet value, then
   a. you must create a new chart.
   b. you can use the same chart but must edit the chart with the new value.
   c. save the worksheet under a new name and create a new chart.
   d. you need not modify the chart.

REVIEW QUESTIONS

1. Suppose you create a column chart using data from the Big Wave surfboard data in which each row is a data series and row totals are in the rightmost column. You select the cells to plot, but you accidentally include the Totals column. The totals are plotted as a separate series in the chart. Explain how to remove the Totals column from the chart and still display the Totals column in the worksheet.

2. Explain briefly how to remove dollar signs from the Y-axis values in a column chart.

3. The legend Excel created is too small. Legend names are difficult to read. How do you increase the size of the legend? What do you do to make the labels inside the legend larger?

4. You click a chart sheet tab and then click Edit, Delete Sheet, and click OK. You realize you deleted the wrong chart sheet. How do you recover the accidentally deleted chart sheet?

CREATE THE QUESTION

For each of the following answers, create an appropriate, short question.

ANSWER	QUESTION
1. Click Edit and then click Delete Sheet	_____
2. One of the set of values being charted	_____
3. Extensions of tick marks that help identify the value of data markers	_____
4. Click and drag one of these to resize an embedded chart	_____
5. They display the numeric value of a data marker	_____
6. Click this button on the Chart toolbar to change a pie chart into a bar chart	_____

1. Charting Olympic Gold, Silver, and Bronze Medals

Olsen, Kramer, and Shubert (OKS) is a public relations firm that has been hired to do post-Olympic analysis of the games. They have hired Alison Najir and you to produce statistics about the competition and graph the results. In particular, OKS wants you to produce a chart of the medals that competing countries have won. They think a three-dimensional stacked bar chart showing bronze, silver, and gold medals in a single bar for each country would be a good way to chart the results. There are too many countries winning medals to conveniently represent each one, so the company asks you to produce a chart sheet showing the number of medals won by teams winning at least 10 medals total. You have done your Web research and prepared a list of medal winnings—bronze, silver, and gold—in descending order by total medals won. You proceed to produce the chart.

1. Open the workbook **ex04Olympics.xls** and use the Save As command in the File menu to save the workbook under the name **<yourname>Olympics2.xls**

2. Click the **Medal Data** tab (see Figure 4.40) and then drag the mouse to select the cell range **A3:D14** (to include in the chart all countries winning at least 10 medals and the column title row)

3. Click the **Chart Wizard** button, click **Bar** in the Chart type, click the **Stacked bar with 3-D visual effect** in the Chart sub-type panel, click **Next** to go to Step 2, and click **Next** again to go to Step 3

4. Click the **Chart title** text box and type **Top Medal Winners, 2000 Olympics**

5. Click the **Value (Z) axis** text box and type **Medals**

6. Click the **Data Labels tab**, click the **Value** check box, and then click **Next**

7. Click the **As new sheet** option button and then click the **Finish** button

8. In the Chart toolbar, click the Chart Objects list arrow, scroll the list, click any **Series "Bronze"** to select all Bronze data markers, click the **Format Data Series** button in the Chart toolbar, click the **Patterns** tab, and click the **Brown** square (top row, second column) in the Area frame, and click **OK**

tip: *Be careful when selecting a data marker not to select the data label inside a data marker. You select a data marker when the Chart toolbar Chart Object list box contains "Series . . ."*

9. Repeat Step 8 for the **Silver data marker** (second from the left in any bar), but this time select the **Gray-40%** color square on the Patterns tab (third row from the top, column eight), and then click **OK**

10. Repeat Step 8 for the **Gold data marker** (third from the left in any bar), but this time select the **Light Yellow** square (fifth row from the top, column three) and then click **OK**

11. Place your name in the chart sheet header, click the **Cover Sheet** tab and type your name next to the label "Workbook designer," and enter today's date next to the "Design date" label

12. Print the Cover Sheet and the Chart1 chart sheet, save the workbook, and exit Excel

FIGURE 4.40

Charting Olympics medal data

	A	B	C	D	E
1	2000 Summer Olympics Medal Winners				
2					
3		Bronze	Silver	Gold	Totals
4	USA	10	10	11	31
5	Australia	8	9	8	25
6	France	4	9	7	20
7	Russia	8	8	4	20
8	China	7	4	8	19
9	Italy	9	2	7	18
10	Germany	7	5	3	15
11	South Korea	5	5	3	13
12	Great Britain	3	5	2	10
13	Romania	4	2	4	10
14	Netherlands	2	2	6	10
15	Ukraine	3	4	2	9
16	Japan	1	3	4	8
17	Cuba	2	1	2	5
18	Slovakia	1	3	1	5
19	Bulgaria	1	1	3	5
20	Switzerland	1	3	1	5
21	Belarus	4	1	0	5
22	Czech Rep.	3	0	1	4
23	Sweden	1	1	2	4
24	Indonesia	2	1	1	4
25	Hungary	1	1	2	4

Cover Sheet \ Medal Data /

Ready

2. Mapping Rainfall in Hawaii

The field office of the Hawaii visitor's bureau in Kauai, Hawaii, wants you to produce a line chart of the average rainfall for the previous year—January through December. A line chart is the best way to represent these data because it shows trends for each of the five regions. Follow these steps to produce and print the chart.

1. Open **ex04Rainfall.xls**, type your name in the Designer line, type the current date in the Design Date line, and save the file as **<yourname>Rainfall2.xls** (click **File**, click **Save As**, type the new name, and click the **Save** button)

2. Click the **Rainfall Averages** tab (see Figure 4.41), click cell **A2**, and type your first and last names

3. Click and drag the mouse to select the cell range **A3:M8** and click the **Chart Wizard** button

4. Click **Line** in the Chart type list box, click the Chart sub-type **Line with markers displayed at each data value** (second row, first column), and click **Next**

5. Click **Next** again, click the **Chart title** text box, and type **Average Rainfall, Kauai, Hawaii**, click the **Value (Y) axis** and type **Inches**, click **Next**, and click **Finish**

6. Drag the embedded chart until its upper-left corner covers cell A10

7. Click the **chart selection handle** in the lower-right corner of the chart area and drag it down and to the right until the lower-right corner of the chart area just covers cell M30. (Remember, you can press the Alt key as you drag the corner to snap it to exact cell boundaries)

8. Click cell **A1** to deselect the embedded chart

9. Save the workbook again, print the Rainfall Averages worksheet, and then click the **Documentation** tab, print the Documentation worksheet, and exit Excel

FIGURE 4.41

Charting rainfall in Hawaii

	A	B	C	D	E	F	G	H	I	J	K	L	M
1		**Average Rainfall, Kauai, Hawaii**											
2													
3		Jan	Feb	Mar	Apr	May	Jun	Jul	Aug	Sep	Oct	Nov	Dec
4	West Side	6.6	5.1	5.5	5.1	3.8	2.2	2.8	3.1	2.6	4.9	6.4	6.5
5	Poipu	5.4	3.1	3.3	2.9	2.2	1.5	1.6	1.3	1.6	3.2	4.6	3.9
6	Lihue	6.4	3.2	3.4	4.1	3.3	2.2	2.8	2.4	2.7	4.8	6.4	5.8
7	Kapaa	6.6	5.1	5.5	5.1	3.8	2.2	2.8	3.2	2.6	4.9	6.4	6.5
8	Hanalei	8.3	7.4	9.6	6.8	6.3	5.1	6.2	7.3	4.8	6.3	7.9	9.2

1. Charting California's Expenditures

The director of finance for the State of California, G. Timothy Gage, has collected data about the expenditures by fund source for the State of California. The data are in a workbook called **ex04California.xls**. He wants you to help him get the data into shape. Specifically, he wants you to do two things for him. First, he wants you to format the worksheet data so that it looks better—currently it is in raw form and difficult to read. Second, he wants you to produce a two-dimensional pie chart showing the percentage contribution to the total expenditures. He wants the chart to display a legend and the chart title to be "California Expenditures (2003–2004)." While he leaves other chart formatting details to you, he insists that you emphasize the Education pie slice by exploding it out from the rest of the chart, and he wants the chart on its own chart sheet.

Figure 4.42 shows one way you can format the worksheet. (*Hint:* It is formatted using Merge and Center for the title and subtitle, colors, boldface, background color, and a shadow around the table.) Make column B wide enough to display the widest text in its column.

Start by loading **ex04California.xls** and save the worksheet as **<yourname>California2.xls**. Then type your name on the Documentation worksheet to the right of the "Designer:" text. Type the current date in cell C8. On the Expenditures worksheet, place your name in the worksheet header. Do the same for the Chart1 chart sheet page. Print all three pages. Save your workbook.

widen column · foreground color and merge/center

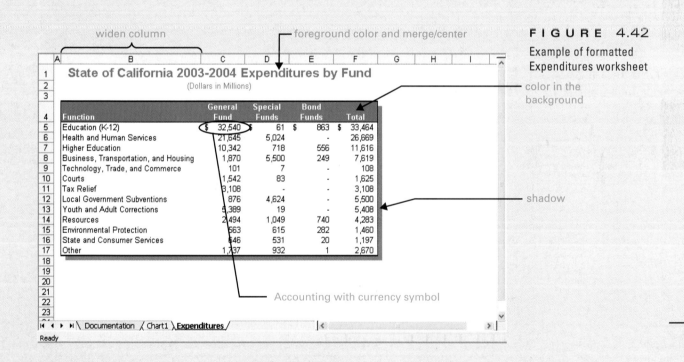

FIGURE 4.42

Example of formatted Expenditures worksheet

color in the background

shadow

Accounting with currency symbol

2. Charting the Rental Car Market

Herb Klein is researching the U.S. rental car market. He conducted part of his research on the Web and through professional magazines. One Web site, Auto Rental News, is chock full of car rental statistics (www.autorentalnews.com) that have helped Herb understand the magnitude of the rental car market. While Herb is a marketing wizard and understands Excel enough to enter data, he has difficulty understanding how to chart the data. He wants you to help him by producing two charts of the data he has collected in a worksheet called **ex04RentalCar.xls**.

Two charts interest Herb. The first one will be a chart sheet column chart showing the estimated U.S. rental revenue by each of nine top car rental companies. The second chart will be an embedded two-dimensional pie chart showing the number of cars in service of each company in comparison to the total cars in service. Start by opening **ex04RentalCar.xls** (see Figure 4.43) and immediately save it under the new name, **<yourname>RentalCar2.xls**. Here are the details of what he wants.

The chart sheet column chart, when completed, will show car rental companies in the X-axis as cate-gories. The Y-axis values should not show currency symbols and should be expressed in whole dollars. The chart title is "U.S. Rental Revenue Est. (Millions)" and is 16-point bold text. The Y-axis title is "Revenue (Millions)" with default formatting. Add data labels to two columns—the highest revenue and the lowest revenue—so those two columns display the amount at their column tops. Place your name in the chart sheet page header's left section.

Embed the second chart, a two-dimensional pie chart, on the same page as the worksheet data. The chart area should occupy cells A14 through G36. Display values only on the pie segments, display the legend on the left side of the chart area, and create a chart title "Cars in Service" formatted bold and 16-point typeface. Place your name in the page header's left section.

On the Documentation page, type your name and the current date in the underlined areas to the right of Designer and Design Date, respectively. Modify the worksheet data page, called Car Rental Statistics, any way you want or not at all. Print all three worksheets. Save your workbook again.

FIGURE 4.43

U.S. rental car chart

	A	B	C	D
1	Company	U.S. Cars in Service (Avg.)	# of U.S. Locations	U.S. Rental Revenue Est. (Millions)
2	Enterprise	399,941	3,600	$ 3,450
3	Hertz	280,500	1,220	3,600
4	Avis	210,000	1,000	2,400
5	Alamo	150,000	101	1,400
6	Budget	146,000	1,056	1,800
7	National	140,000	500	1,700
8	Dollar	70,000	250	840
9	FRCS (Ford)	48,000	3,353	363
10	Thrifty	46,000	548	511
11	(all others)	242,950	11,710	836
12	Total	1,733,391	23,338	$ 16,900

Documentation / Car Rental Statistics

Ready

1. Researching the Largest Coffee Exporting Countries

Jehad Nasser wants to open a Web store to sell coffee beans and coffee supplies. He wants to know which countries export the most coffee and then determine from which countries he will purchase raw coffee beans. To start his research, he has asked you to search the Web for information on coffee bean production and export. One of his acquaintances from Java, Indonesia, suggests Jehad investigate Web sites such as the International Coffee Organization (www.ico.org) to locate statistics on coffee production and export. Jehad has done some work and collected data from the Web including production and export values for 45 coffee-producing nations. He wants you to produce a pie chart showing the percentage of production by the top six coffee exporters. The top six exporters are those who export the largest number of bags of coffee per year. Fortunately, Jehad has gone to the trouble of sorting the list he produced in descending order by the number of bags each country exports.

To accomplish this task, Jehad wants you to complete the Documentation worksheet by doing the following. Start by opening Jehad's preliminary workbook called **ex04ExportCoffee.xls** (see Figure 4.44). Then add a label such as **Designed by:** and fill in your name. Add a label "Design date:" and fill in the current date next to it. Add a title at the top of the Documentation worksheet that describes, in three or four words, the

title of the worksheet. Finally, add a **Purpose:** label and a sentence describing what the workbook contains.

Create a two-dimensional pie chart on a chart sheet showing the export percentages of the top six countries and that of all other coffee-producing countries. The "all others" category is the *sum* of export bags for all other countries. (*Hint:* You will want to add a row after the sixth country that sums the 7th through 45th countries' exports.) In other words, the pie chart will have seven slices. The pie chart data labels should show the percent and the country names. Delete the legend. Title the chart, in 14-point bold typeface, "Top Six Coffee Exporters." Explode the pie slice of the largest exporter, Brazil. Include your name in the header of all worksheets.

The Coffee Production and Export worksheet contains the data you will chart. Place your name in the worksheet header. Next, open up a row below the entry for Mexico, place all others in cell B12, and sum up production and export values for Uganda through Benin, placing the sum of production in cell C12 and the sum of export in cell D12. Chart the export values of Brazil through "all others," including the country names as category along with the export values. Set the Coffee Production and Export print range to the first 12 rows (the title through the "all others" row). Save the completed workbook as **<yourname>ExportCoffee2.xls**. Print the entire workbook.

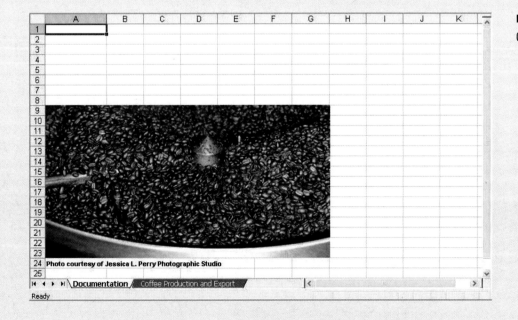

FIGURE 4.44

Charting coffee exports

Photo courtesy of Jessica L. Perry Photographic Studio

2. Healthy Skin Products

Healthy Skin is a new Internet company that offers several lines of skin care products that are sold only through dermatologists or online through direct distributors such as Healthy Skin. The CEO has asked that each divisional manager conduct an annual communication meeting to share the company's accomplishments for the previous year (their first year) and next year's targets. The CEO has scheduled a meeting to review the sales data prior to an employee presentation before the board. As the divisional manager for the southwestern states division, your presentation to the CEO must include a chart showing your division's sales performance. The chart should be a column chart that will compare projected sales to actual sales for each product line. The chart should also include next year's projected sales targets.

The director of sales has provided you with a worksheet containing your division's results. Begin by opening the worksheet called **ex04HealthySkin.xls** (see Figure 4.45). Save it immediately as **<yourname>HealthySkin2.xls**. This workbook contains the data you will be charting. You will need to add a third column of data titled *New Sales Target* and write a formula to calculate the new target for each product

brand. The new target will be an additional 5 percent of the larger value between the projected sales and actual sales. Bold font each column title prior to charting.

Create an embedded column graph with the brand names along the X-axis and the dollar values along the Y-axis. Be sure to chart all four columns—including the New Sales Target column. The chart title should be *Year One Projected Sales vs. Actual Sales, Southwestern States Division.* The X-axis should be labeled *Product Brand Name.* Include a legend. After the chart is finished, modify the Y-axis number format to display the dollar sign and decimal places. Also, adjust the Y-axis scale to have a maximum value of $315,000, a minimum value of $0, and major unit of $50,000. Position the chart directly below the data with the upper-right corner in cell F17 and resize to fit the lower-left corner in A37. Change the color of each bar to be light blue for projected sales, light yellow for actual sales, and light green for new sales targets. Change the chart background color to white. Then add a data label for the product brand whose actual value exceeded its projected sales by more than any other product brand. Position the data label so that it is legible and is a font point size of 10. Place your name in the worksheet header. Print the worksheet and the worksheet formulas. Save your workbook.

FIGURE 4.45

Healthy Skin workbook

	A	B	C
1	Southwestern States Division Year One Results		
3	Brand	Projected Sales	Actual Sales
4	M.D. Forte	250,000	285,500
5	Gly Derm	230,000	210,600
6	K-Derm	112,000	163,000
7	Sunstoppers	120,000	140,700
8	Kinerase	135,000	137,400
9	ScarFade	120,000	110,000
10	Rogaine	75,000	90,000
11	Mederma	95,000	65,300
12	Revivogen	65,000	25,400
13	Body Innovations	30,000	12,200
15	Sales values are in US dollars.		

1. Graphing Agricultural Production Values

Terry Branson is the county agent for Lancaster County, Nebraska, and is responsible for aiding citizens of the county and state of Nebraska with agricultural questions. Lately, Terry has been getting a number of inquiries about crop production in Nebraska and neighboring states. Several farmers in the region have been growing sugar beets and alfalfa with some success, but the prices in both those products have been poor in recent years. Many of the questions have been about alternative crops and their viability in Nebraska. Terry wants to include productivity rates, measured in bushels per acre, for Kansas, Oklahoma, and Texas as well as for Nebraska. Because Terry does not have these statistics at his fingertips, he asks you to use the Internet to look up statistics about corn, sorghum, and soybean production and produce a graph.

The graph will use a column chart listing the three crops along the X-axis as categories and the bushels per acre plotted along the Y-axis. The four data series will correspond to states. Include a legend listing the four states of Kansas, Nebraska, Oklahoma, and Texas. The chart title should be "Crop Production per Acre," the Y-axis title should be "Bushels/Acre," and the X-axis title should be "Crops." Change the color of all three titles to a dark green, and resize and reposition the

chart so that the embedded chart covers the cell range A10 through F30.

Begin by opening **ex04Crop.xls**. Fill in cells B5:E7 with the values for bushels per acre for the crops in the corresponding states. Graph the cell range A4:E7. Here's how you find the bushels per acre values required to complete this assignment: Launch your Web browser and go to www.fedstats.gov and locate the MapStats section of the home page (see Figure 4.46). Start with Kansas. Click the list box arrow beneath MapStats, click **Kansas** in the list, and then click the **Submit** button to the right of the list box. Click the **Browse more data sets for Kansas** link located on the right side of the page and above the table. When the next page appears, click the **Field Crops** link under the Agriculture heading near the top of the page. A *Field Crops* page opens. On this page is a table containing crops and their bushels per acre values (in a column labeled "Yield per harvested acre (bushels)"). Write down the values from that column for corn, sorghum, and soybeans. Click the **Back to Fedstats home page** link to return to the FedStats home page. Repeat this Web search procedure for Nebraska, Oklahoma, and Texas. After you gather the 12 values, close your browser, fill in the values in the worksheet, create an embedded column graph, insert your name in the worksheet header, and print the worksheet. Save your workbook.

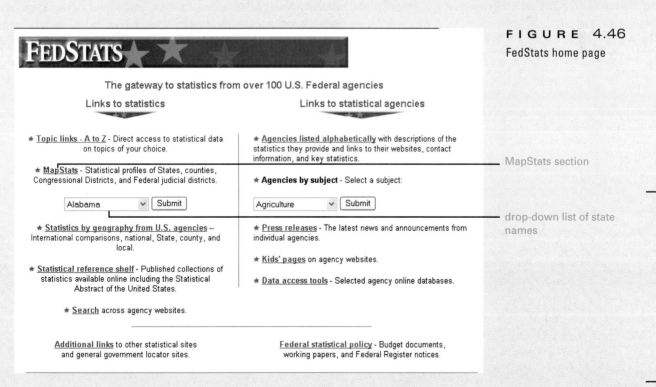

FIGURE 4.46
FedStats home page

MapStats section

drop-down list of state names

2. Longevity Energy Drink

Longevity Energy Drink (LED) is a new health product that was just launched with success in Florida and California. It is a low-cost noncarbonated energy drink packed with vitamins to give the consumer an alternative to boring vitamin tablets. Individuals 65 years and older are the largest consumers of Longevity Energy Drink. You are one week into your new position as director of distribution and marketing for LED. It is your job to keep your boss abreast of the new product launch plans. You need to provide a quick summary of the next states that have been chosen for new introduction. The previous director used a written summary in a recent presentation with population numbers from the late 1990s. Your boss has suggested that you try something different. You've decided that a better communication tool would be a pie chart with more recent data. Your predecessor left behind an incomplete worksheet that provides a good start for what you want to accomplish.

Begin by opening **ex04EnergyDrink.xls**. You will notice that the population figures and percentages for persons 65 years old and over are missing for the new targeted states. California and Florida have already been completed, as have the formulas for calculating the number of persons 65 years old and over. Launch your Web browser and go to the U.S. Census Bureau Web site at www.census.gov (see Figure 4.47) to obtain the most recent population figures and the percentages for each state. Locate *State & County Quick Facts* and type Texas in the selection box. Click **Go**. When the

next page appears, the values you need will be displayed. Under the column titled *People Quick facts*, note that the first row of data contains the most recent population estimation. You do not want an estimate. You want the most recent *Population and Persons 65 years old and over* percent. Record the required values for Texas and then go back to the home page. Repeat this process for the remaining six states. Once you have finished collecting all the data, close your browser and fill in the worksheet. After the worksheet has been completed, you are ready to create your chart. Type your name in the worksheet header and save your worksheet as **<yourname>EnergyDrink2.xls**.

Since California and Florida markets have already been established, hide these first two rows of data. Hide the last two rows that contain the states with the lowest figures. Then, create a chart in a chart sheet using the names of the states and the number (not percent) of persons 65 and over. Choose a pie chart with a 3-D visual effect. Do not use a legend. Title the chart *Number of People 65+*. Use data labels that include both category name and value. After the chart is finished, explode the largest pie slice and elevate the pie chart to 30 degrees. Add a text box in the lower-left corner that contains the text *LED Confidential Document*. Place your name in the worksheet header, place your name in the chart sheet header, save the workbook, print the worksheet, print the worksheet formulas, and print the chart sheet.

FIGURE 4.47

U.S. Census Bureau home page

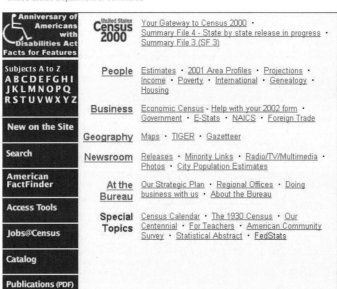

1. Charting Hourly Compensation Rates around the World

The Bureau of Labor Statistics (www.bls.gov) maintains tables comparing hourly compensation rates, in U.S. dollars, for the employees in the manufacturing sector for several countries. Melissa Franklin, your supervisor at Applied Economics, Inc., wants you to produce a chart of the data that she can present at a talk she is giving to a group of businesspersons next week in Atlanta. The raw data, shown in Figure 4.48, shows the hourly compensation values for seven countries for selected years between 1975 and 1999. Hourly compensation includes wages, bonuses, vacation, holidays, premiums, insurance, and benefit plans.

Begin by loading the worksheet, called **ex04HourlyLabor.xls**. Format the worksheet so that the column labels and the numbers are attractive and easy to read. Then create a chart in a chart sheet that is well labeled and displays, in the best form possible, the information in a chart. Which chart type is best to display the changes in the hourly compensation for a country? Use that chart type choice for all countries. Add a text box displaying your name in the lower-right corner of the chart. Save the workbook and then print the worksheet and the chart.

2. Charting Unemployment Rates around the World

The U.S. Bureau of Labor Statistics (BLS) collects all sorts of information about the U.S. labor force and provides statistical summaries. In addition to tracking the U.S. labor force, the BLS provides comparisons of U.S. labor segments with foreign countries and provides the information in various types of tables. The BLS maintains a large Web site at www.bls.gov, and you can use your browser to go to that location and view some of their reports. (Most reports are in PDF, or portable document format, that are rendered using the free software product called Acrobat Reader.)

Janet Morrison, the Sonoma County chief of labor statistics, is interested in charting unemployment rate trends between the United States and France during the 1960s as an embedded chart. She would like to compare the United States and France to see if there is a trend both for each country and between the two countries. She wants you to produce a line chart of the unemployment rates with the 1960s along the X-axis and unemployment rates along the Y-axis. Change the color of the chart title, Y-axis label, X-axis label, and X-axis category names to dark blue. Place the chart after the last data row so that it will fit along with the worksheet data on one printed page. Add the appropriate chart title and axes titles.

Start by loading the unemployment worksheet called **ex04Unemployment.xls**. Before you make any changes to the worksheet, save it under the new name **<yourname>Unemployment2.xls** to preserve the original worksheet. To identify the chart as yours, place a text box containing your first and last names somewhere on the chart. Print the chart and be sure to save the altered worksheet before leaving Excel.

FIGURE 4.48

Hourly compensation comparison

	A	B	C	D	E	F	G	H
1	Hourly compensation costs in U.S. dollars for production workers in manufacturing							
2								
3		1975	1980	1985	1990	1995	1999	
4	Canada	5.96	8.67	10.95	15.95	16.1	15.6	
5	France	4.52	8.94	7.52	15.49	20.01	17.98	
6	Italy	4.67	8.15	7.63	17.45	16.22	16.6	
7	Japan	3	5.52	6.34	12.8	23.82	20.89	
8	Spain	2.53	5.89	4.66	11.38	12.88	12.11	
9	Sweden	7.18	12.51	9.66	20.93	21.44	21.58	
10	United States	6.36	9.87	13.01	14.91	17.19	19.2	
11								

running project

Pro Golf Academy

Betty Carroll, Pro Golf Academy's manager, wants you to chart the sales of golf balls and golf gloves for January through June. She has gathered sales information about four of her most popular golf ball brands and four of the most popular golf glove brands in a workbook she has started. Betty wants you to create two chart sheets.

The first chart sheet is a stacked column chart (on its own sheet) showing sales of each of the four golf ball brands by month. Each column represents a month, and the four data markers in each column are the sales of each type of distinct ball brand. When completed, the stacked column chart sheet will display six columns, one for each sales month. Type the chart title **Golf Ball Sales**. The legend should display a different color for each ball brand. The Y-axis displays sales, and values should display the currency symbol.

The second chart sheet is a three-dimensional pie chart showing the percent of the total golf glove sales each brand contributes. Tilt the 3-D chart 45 degrees and explode the Etonic pie slice. Title the chart **Golf Glove Sales**. Display a legend, and label each slice with the percent (only) of each product's sales.

Begin by loading the worksheet **ex04ProGolf.xls** (see Figure 4.49). Then, write expressions to sum each row's sales, and place each one beneath the Total column for both ball and glove products. Format the values in the Total column to match the rest of the row, and bold the Subtotal and Grand Total values. Subtotal golf glove sales in the cell next to the label "Subtotal" and do the same for Golf Glove sales. Sum the two subtotals in the cell H16.

Reorient the worksheet containing sales data so that it prints in landscape orientation. Place your name in the center section of a page header for all three sheets. Print the two chart sheets and the worksheet. Print the worksheet formulas only for column H.

FIGURE 4.49

Pro Golf Academy worksheet

	A	B	C	D	E	F	G	H	I	J
1	**Golf Ball and Glove Sales Analysis**									
2										
3	**Golf Balls**	**January**	**February**	**March**	**April**	**May**	**June**	**Total**		
4	Maxfli	$ 5,963	$ 3,589	$ 1,633	$ 3,760	$ 3,247	$ 2,146			
5	Strata Tour	3,534	1,391	2,942	2,798	2,990	2,478			
6	Titleist	1,585	3,286	3,183	1,676	2,949	831			
7	Top-Flite	4,519	4,214	2,633	799	2,345	2,973			
8							**Subtotal**			
9										
10	**Golf Gloves**	**January**	**February**	**March**	**April**	**May**	**June**	**Total**		
11	Callaway XSPANN	$ 629	$ 2,373	$ 620	$ 1,501	$ 1,250	$ 2,436			
12	Etonic	320	2,237	959	1,678	1,750	1,055			
13	FootJoy SofJoy	2,445	1,686	1,534	1,774	1,398	807			
14	House of Kangaroo	707	1,120	551	413	982	1,012			
15							**Subtotal**			
16							**Grand Total**			
17										
18										
19										
20										
21										
22										
23										
24										

Golf ball and glove sales

Ready

1. Which Chart Is Best?

Open the workbook **ex04ChartAnalysis.xls** (see Figure 4.50). Review each of the chart sheets and discuss which one best shows sales growth. Carefully explain your reasoning and be sure to discuss why other charts are inappropriate.

2. Selecting the Data to Chart

Think about the concept of charting data. Then write a few sentences describing why charts are helpful where data and worksheet figures are not. Would your answer change if you were presenting financial news to a large audience? Explain.

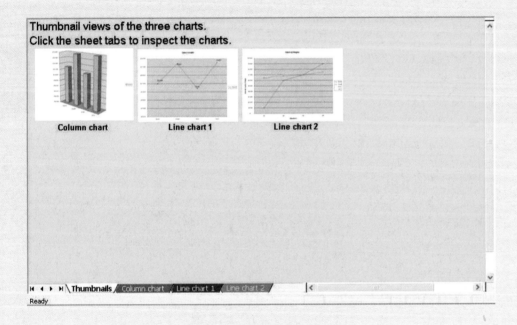

FIGURE 4.50

Chart Analysis workbook

Exploring Excel's List Features

did you know?

Microsoft *reports that there are over 250 million users of Office worldwide.*

Japan *is one of the most competitive soft drink markets in the world; approximately 1,000 new soft drinks are launched in Japan every year, of which only a small number survive.*

Thomas *Jefferson drafted the Constitution of the United States on a portable desk that carried all of his favorite tools.*

team *members at Microsoft consumed approximately 115,000 slices of pizza while developing the Microsoft XP suite.*

the *word "stewardess" is the longest word in the English language that you type with one hand.*

a *pivot table is also known as a _____ . (Find the answer in this chapter.)*

Chapter Objectives

- Create and maintain a list—MOS XL03E-1-14
- Freeze rows and columns—MOS XL03S-5-6
- Sort a list on multiple sort keys—MOS XL03S-2-2
- Enter, search for, modify, and delete records in a list with a data form—MOS XL03S-1-2
- Group and outline structured data—MOS XL03E-1-3
- Create outlines and subtotals—MOS XL03E-1-1
- Create and apply conditional formatting—MOS XL03E-2-2
- Create filters and advanced filters with AutoFilter—MOS XL03E-1-2
- Use worksheet labels and names in formulas—MOS XL03E-1-14
- Create a pivot table and pivot chart—MOS XL03E-1-8
- Create and use folders for workbook storage—MOS XL03S-5-9

Computer Security, Inc.

Computer Security, Inc. (Comsec) is a small computer security contractor that provides computer security analysis, design, and software implementation for the U.S. government and commercial clients. Comsec competes for both private and U.S. government computer security contract work by submitting detailed bids outlining the work they will perform if awarded the contracts. Because all of their work involves computer security—a highly sensitive area—almost all of Comsec's work requires access to classified material or company confidential documents. Consequently, all of the security engineers (simply known as "engineers" within the company) have U.S. government clearances of either Secret or Top Secret. Some have even higher clearances for the 2 percent of Comsec's work that involves so-called black box security work. Most of the employees also hold clearances because they must handle classified documents.

Alice Rovik is Comsec's Human Resources (HR) manager. She maintains all employee records and is responsible for semiannual review reports, payroll processing, personnel records, recruiting data, employee training, and pension option information. At the heart of an HR system are personnel records. Personnel record maintenance includes activities such as maintaining employee records, tracking cost center data, recording and maintaining pension information, and absence and sick leave record keeping—to name a few. While most of this information resides in sophisticated database systems, Alice maintains a basic employee worksheet for quick calculations and ad hoc report generation. Because Comsec is a small company, Alice can take advantage of Excel's excellent list management facilities to satisfy many of her personnel information management needs. One of the worksheets Alice keeps close at hand lists employees' names, departments, titles, and other fundamental information. Figure 5.1 shows the worksheet, which she calls simply the "employee" worksheet. During the course of reading this chapter, you will be asked to manipulate the worksheet in various ways to produce summaries, filter the list, add and delete employee records, and produce pivot tables summarizing department data.

FIGURE 5.1

Employee worksheet

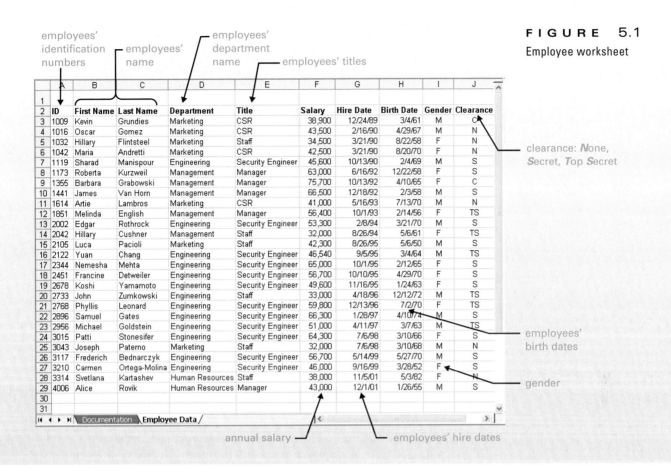

Chapter 5 covers building and maintaining Office Excel 2003 lists, which are also called databases, and creating pivot tables. In this chapter you will use a personnel worksheet from Comsec, a computer security consulting and contracting company. You will sort the data various ways so that the list is in a more useful order. Using Excel's form feature, you will add, modify, and delete values in the list through a simple and intuitive form-based interface, which also facilitates searching for particular values.

Creating a data filter allows you to hide selected rows of the list to easily locate groups of records—worksheet rows—that contain the same value. You will learn how to sort a list into related groups and then create salary subtotals and other statistics for each identified group. Creating pivot tables, the capstone feature described in this chapter, illustrates how to create summaries by pairs of variables, or values. For example, you will learn how to use the PivotTable Wizard to quickly create a table displaying the average salary by department—all with a few simple keystrokes.

SESSION 5.1 CREATING AND USING LISTS

In this section, you will learn how to use Microsoft Office Excel 2003 to manage a list, or database. One of the most common uses of worksheets is to maintain lists of information: names and addresses of business contacts and students, and symbols and purchase prices of stocks, for example. You will learn how to sort the list into a meaningful order, modify the amount of the worksheet that displays on the page, find and replace information in a list, and use a data form to add, modify, and delete data.

Building a List

A *list* is a collection of data arranged in columns and rows in which each column displays one particular type of data. A list has the following characteristics:

- Each column contains the same category of information. In the personnel list highlighted in this chapter, for example, the ID column contains employee identification numbers and no other data

- The first row in the list contains labels identifying each column and its contents

- A list does not contain any blank rows

- A list is bordered on all four sides by empty rows and columns, or a list begins in row 1 or column A, each of which serves to delimit the list on the top or the left side, respectively

Figure 5.1 shows the employee worksheet containing a small amount of employee data. It contains fewer rows and columns than a typical employee worksheet to keep the example understandable without sacrificing elegance. Each column of a list is a *field* of related information describing some characteristic of the object, person, or place. Each row is called a *record,* which contains the fields that collectively describe a single object, person, or place. A collection of these records constitutes a list. Observe the Hire Date column. It contains only date values, and the dates recorded in the column—field—are the dates when each employee was hired—his or her first day to report to work. Observe one other important attribute about the list shown in Figure 5.1: The labels at the top of the list, or names that identify each column, are unique and formatted differently (boldface) from the information in rows below the label row. This is important, because it helps Excel determine that the first row is a label row identifying each column.

Begin your work on the employee workbook by opening it and saving it under its new name.

Opening the Employee worksheet and saving it under a new name:

1. Start Excel

2. Open the workbook **ex05Employee.xls** and immediately save it as **Employee1.xls** (see Figure 5.2)

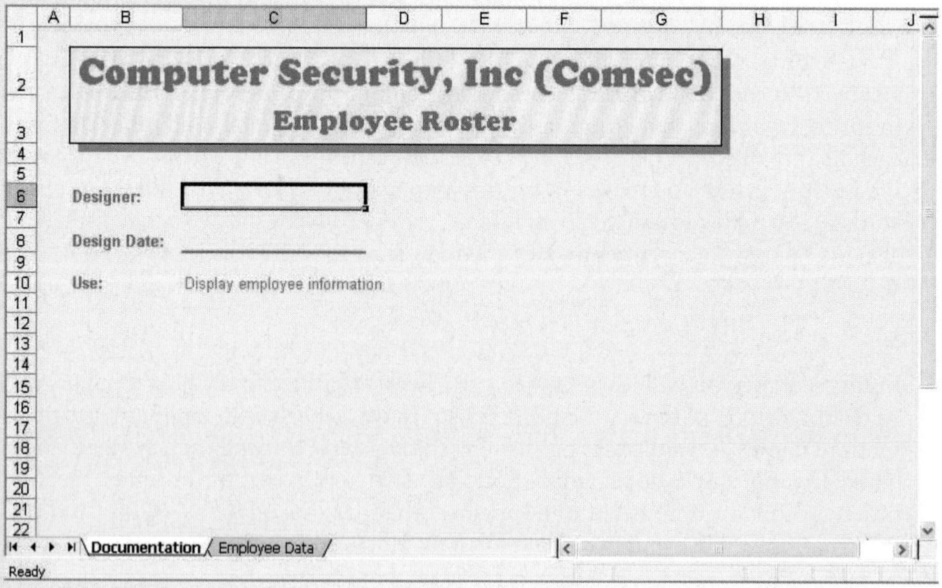

FIGURE 5.2

Documentation worksheet

Computer Security, Inc (Comsec)

Employee Roster

Designer:

Design Date:

Use: Display employee information

3. Switch to the **Employee Data** worksheet (click the yellow **Employee Data** tab) to display the employee list. Row 2 contains labels that name each column. Scroll down the worksheet to reveal other rows in the employee list. Notice that the column headings go out of view as you scroll down the worksheet

A common problem occurring when you use a long list of data is that the labels identifying the columns soon scroll out of view as you go to the bottom of the list to enter new data. Without the labels at the top of the column, it is difficult to remember what to enter in each column—particularly when two columns contain similar data such as the Hire Date and Birth Date. There is more than one way to handle this problem.

Freezing Rows and Columns

Freezing rows and columns prevents certain columns, rows, or both from scrolling off the screen when you scroll an Excel window down or to the right. When you freeze one or more rows or columns, they form a two-sided frame that remains in place—almost like a two-sided picture frame in which the picture can move up or down while the frame remains in place.

---

task reference　　　　Freezing Rows and Columns

- Select the cell below and to the right of the row(s) and column(s) you want to freeze
- Click **Window** on the menu bar and then click **Freeze Panes**

You decide to freeze rows 1 and 2 containing the column headings and freeze columns A through C containing the employees' names.

Freezing label rows and employee name columns:

1. Click cell **D3**

2. Click **Window** on the menu bar and then click **Freeze Panes**. Notice dark lines appear at the boundaries of the frozen rows and columns

3. Click the vertical scroll bar down arrow to scroll down the worksheet. Notice that the labels remain fixed at the top of the worksheet

4. Click the horizontal scroll bar right arrow to scroll a few columns to the right. Notice that the first three columns (ID, First Name, and Last Name) remain fixed. Columns appear to scroll beneath the frozen columns (see Figure 5.3)

5. Press **Ctrl+Home**. When columns or rows are frozen, pressing Ctrl+Home makes active the cell directly below and to the right of frozen rows or columns

You can unfreeze rows or columns by clicking Unfreeze Panes in the Window menu. For now, leave the panes frozen.

FIGURE 5.3

Freezing rows and
columns in place

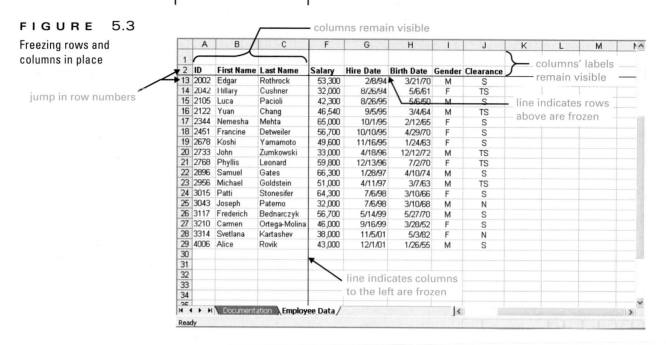

FIGURE 5.3

Freezing rows and columns in place

jump in row numbers

Using a Data Form to Maintain a List

Alice Rovik has several changes she wants to make to the Employee worksheet. You can make changes to lists using existing Excel commands to insert a row to add an employee record or delete a row to remove a record. However, you will find it easier to use Excel's Form command. A *data form* is a dialog box displaying one row of a list in text boxes in which you can add, locate, modify, or delete records. One advantage of using an Excel data form for record maintenance operations—updates, insertions, or deletions—is that it greatly reduces the chances of making data entry mistakes. Because a data form displays a single row at a time, your chance of transposing values from one row to another are smaller.

Adding a Record

task reference	Adding a Record to a List Using a Data Form

- Click any cell within the list
- Click **Data** and then click **Form**
- Click the **New** button
- Type the values for each field in the corresponding form text boxes, pressing the **Tab** key to move from one text box to another
- Press the **Enter** key
- Click the **Close** button after adding all records to the list

The first modification is to add a new employee to the list of employees on the Employee Data worksheet.

Adding a new record by using the data form:

1. Click any cell within the list (cell F4, for example)

tip: *Be sure to select only one cell in the list. Otherwise, Excel might not display the correct column headings in the form*

2. Click **Data** on the menu bar and then click **Form** to display the Employee Data form (see Figure 5.4)

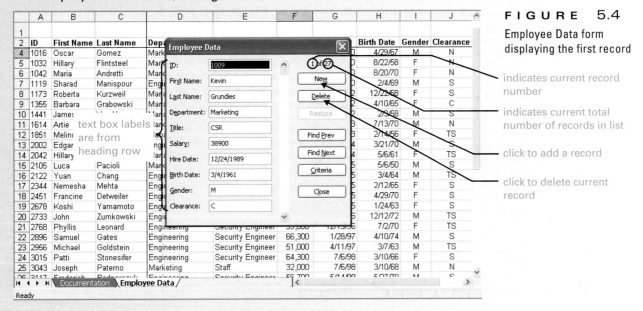

FIGURE   5.4

Employee Data form displaying the first record

indicates current record number

indicates current total number of records in list

click to add a record

click to delete current record

3. Click the data form's **New** button to clear the text boxes. Notice that "New Record" appears where the record number and total record count were previously

tip: *A form displays the current record number and the total number of records in the list*

4. Type **4123** in the ID text box and then press **Tab** to move to the next text box

tip: *If you pressed the **Enter** key instead of the **Tab** key, Excel displays a blank data form and stores the previous information. Click the **Find Prev** button to return to the record you were working on and then continue entering information*

5. Type **Steve** in the First Name text box and then press **Tab**

6. Type **Ballmer** in the Last Name text box and then press **Tab**

7. Type **Engineering** in the Department text box and then press **Tab**

8. Type **Security Engineer** in the Title text box and then press **Tab**

9. Type **42900** in the Salary text box and then press **Tab**

10. Type **5/1/2002** in the Hire Date text box and then press **Tab**

11. Type **4/14/1970** in the Birth Date text box and then press **Tab**

12. Type **M** (uppercase, please) in the Gender text box and then press **Tab**

13. Type **N** (uppercase, please) in the Clearance text box

14. Press the **Enter** key to add the record to the list. Excel automatically adds the record to the end of the current data list and displays an empty data form

15. Click the **Close** button to close the data form and return to the worksheet

16. Press and hold the **End** key, then press the **down arrow** key, and release the **End** key to move to the last record in the list. Ensure that the last record in the list is Ballmer's record

After adding the new record to the list, you can proceed to make other alterations that Alice requested to the list. Recall that she wants one record deleted and another record edited.

Searching for a Record

The employee list is short and it is easy to locate any particular record by examining the list. In larger lists containing perhaps 500 rows or more, looking for a particular employee's record or a particular customer's invoice could be much more difficult. Fortunately, Excel's data form provides search capabilities. You will use the data form search method to locate a record just as you would for a very large list.

You can search for one or more records by specifying *search criteria*, which are values that the data form should match in specified data form fields. Beginning with the first record in the list, Excel inspects each record in turn until it either finds a record matching the search criteria or reaches the end of the list without finding a match. If more than one record matches the search criteria, Excel displays the first record it encounters in the data form. When you click the Find Next button, Excel continues the search by searching for the next matching record.

To modify or delete a record from a list, you have to locate it first. The fastest way to locate a record is to use the data form search facility. Once Excel finds the requested record, you can choose to change it, delete it, or do nothing at all to the record.

Searching for a record using a data form:

1. Click any cell within the employee list

2. Click **Data** on the menu bar and then click **Form**

3. Click the **Criteria** button. Excel blanks all the form's text boxes

4. Click the **Last Name** text box and type **manispour** to specify the search criteria

   tip: *When typing character search criteria—names, street names, or other text labels—you need not worry about capitalization*

   tip: *You can type information in more than one text box to specify multiple search criteria. All specified criteria must be satisfied to match a record*

5. Click the **Find Next** button. Sharad Manispour's record appears in the data form (see Figure 5.5)

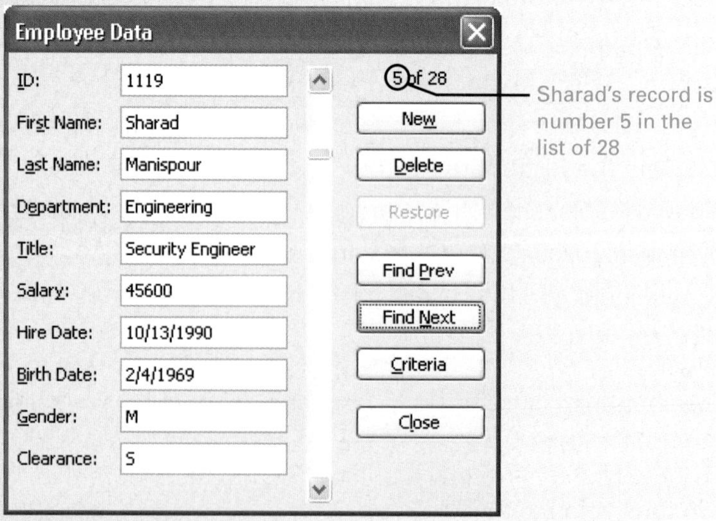

FIGURE 5.5

Employee Data form displaying Sharad Manispour's record

Sharad's record is number 5 in the list of 28

Press the Find Next button to continue the search. If no record is found matching the criteria, the first record found appears in the data form

6. Drag the mouse across the **Title** text box to select its contents and then type **Manager** to correct Sharad's title

7. Double-click the **Salary** text box and then type **54500** (without a currency symbol or a comma)

8. Click the **Close** button. Excel replaces the record with its new contents

9. Examine row 7 to verify that Excel altered the Title and Salary fields for Sharad Manispour

Deleting a Record

The procedure you follow to delete a record from a list is similar to updating a record. You display the data form for the employee list, click the Criteria button, and type in suitable search criteria. When you locate the record, then you click the data form Delete button.

Unless you specify the exact spelling of text values, the search will fail to locate a matching record. One way to reduce the chance of this happening is to specify fewer characters in the search criteria field and use a wild card character on the end of the search criteria. A *wild card character* is a character that stands for one or more characters—a "don't care" symbol. Excel has two such characters: asterisk (*) and question mark (?). Use the question mark to substitute for a single character in a search criteria character string. Use the asterisk to match any number of characters. For example, the search text "pat?rno" matches paterno, patorno, or patirno. The more powerful wild character asterisk matches any characters that appear where it does in the search criteria. For example, the search criteria "G*" in the employee Last Name field matches Grundies, Gomez, Grabowski, Gates, and Goldstein. The more characters you specify preceding the asterisk, the more specific the search criteria are because all the characters preceding an asterisk wild card must match the corresponding field in those positions exactly.

---

task *reference*   **Deleting a Record from a List with a Data Form**

- Click any cell within the list
- Click **Data** and then click **Form**
- Click the **Criteria** button and enter the search criteria in one or more text boxes
- Click the **Find Next** button repeatedly until you locate the record to be deleted
- Press the **Delete** button and then click the **OK** button to confirm the deletion

---

Searching for a record using the asterisk wild card:

1. Click any cell within the employee list, click **Data** on the menu bar, and then click **Form** to display the first employee record in the data form

2. Click the **Criteria** button to prepare to enter the search criteria

3. Click the **Last Name** text box and type **pa*** (see Figure 5.6)

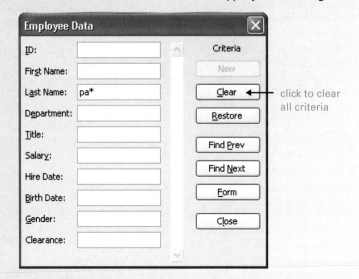

4. Click the **Find Next** button to launch the search and display the first record satisfying the criteria. The data form displays Luca Pacioli's record. That is not the one you want to remove from the list

5. Click the **Find Next** button to continue searching down the list for a record whose last name field begins with "pa." Excel locates and displays Joseph Paterno's record—the record you want to delete

6. Click the **Delete** button. A warning dialog box appears

7. Click **OK** to confirm that you want to permanently delete the selected record

8. Click the **Close** button to close the data form and redisplay the worksheet

Scroll down so you can see rows 23 through 26. Prior to the deletion operation, Paterno's record occupied row 25. Notice that Frederich Bednarczyk's record now occupies that row. In other words, when you delete a record with a data form, Excel removes the entire row and moves up rows below it to fill the void.

Locating and Modifying Data with Find and Replace

When you must make a few modifications to various fields in an Excel list, the data form method illustrated above is the best way. However, when you have to make a change to one particular field in the list involving many records, then the Excel Find and Replace command is your best choice. For example, suppose you had to change the entries in the Gender column by replacing "M" with "Male" and "F" with "Female." Modifying each entry by hand would be tedious at best because each of the 27 employee rows would have to be modified individually. Using the Find and Replace command reduces the effort.

Alice observes the computer security industry trend that engineers working in security engineering and engineering departments typically hold the title "engineer" rather than "security engineer." She wants you to change that name wherever it occurs in the Title column.

Replacing a character string in many cells:

1. Select the cell range **E3:E29**

tip: *The fastest way to select the range of cells in a single column that contains no "holes"—each cell in the column has a value—is to click the topmost cell in the range, press and hold the **Shift** key, tap the **End** key, tap the **down arrow** key, and then release the **Shift** key. Excel highlights the entire range of filled cells between the first cell you select and the bottommost cell in the range*

2. Click **Edit** on the menu bar and then click **Replace** to display the Find and Replace dialog box

3. Click the **Find what** text box and type **security engineer**

4. Click the **Replace with** text box and type **Engineer** (be sure to capitalize the first letter of the title). Figure 5.7 shows the dialog box with both the search text and the replacement text in place

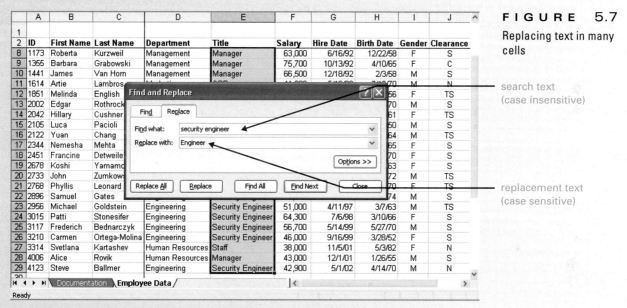

FIGURE 5.7
Replacing text in many cells

search text
(case insensitive)

replacement text
(case sensitive)

5. Click the **Replace All** button to replace all occurrences of *Security Engineer* in column E with *Engineer*. Excel displays in an information dialog box indicating it has made 12 replacements

6. Click **OK** to close the information dialog box, and then click **Close** to close the Find and Replace dialog box

Sorting Data

The employee list is kept in Hire Date order. When a new employee joins the company, his or her record is placed at the end of the list. Alice Rovik has a meeting next week with several top management people to discuss retirement benefits, and she wants to have the list in order by the Birth Date field for easy reference.

To sort rows of a list, you use one or more fields (columns) to determine the final position in the list that each row occupies. The field or fields you use to sort a list are called *sort fields* (or *sort keys*). For instance, if you wanted to rearrange the rows of the Employee list so that they are in alphabetical order by last name, Last Name is the sort field. If more than one sort field is required to reorder a list, the first sort field is called the *primary sort field*. Other sort fields used to reorder rows break any ties that occur in the primary sort field. This is common in telephone books, for example. Telephone book lists are sorted by last name, then first name, and then by middle initial. The primary sort field is last name, the secondary sort field is first name, and the third sort field (needed to break a tie between two or more with the name Joe Smith, for example) is middle initial.

Once you decide which fields are your list's sort fields, you decide whether to order the list in ascending or descending order for each sort field. ***Ascending order*** arranges text values alphabetically from A to Z, arranges numbers from smallest to largest, and arranges dates from earliest to most recent. ***Descending order*** does the opposite—it arranges text values alphabetically from Z to A, arranges numbers from largest to smallest, and arranges dates from most recent to earliest. Whether sorting in ascending order or descending order, blank fields are always placed at the bottom of the list.

While a list in employee ID order may be handy when adding employees, it is not a useful way to organize records when you want to know how many people work in the Engineering Department, for example. When you want to look up a particular employee's record, it is easier to do so if the list is in order by last name.

help yourself *Press **F1**, type **sort** in the Search text box of the Microsoft Excel Help task pane, and press **Enter**. Click the hyperlink **Sort a range** and then click the hyperlink **Sort by 4 columns** to reveal information about sorting on more than three fields. Click the Help screen **Close** button when you are finished, and then close the task pane*

Sorting a List by One Column

You can sort Excel list data on one column by using the Sort Ascending and Sort Descending buttons on the Excel Standard toolbar. Alternatively, you can use the Sort command of the Data menu. If you need to sort a list on only one field, the toolbar method is the fastest and simplest way. For more complex sort operations involving more than one column, use the Sort command.

---

task reference   Sorting a List on One Column

- Click any cell in the column in which you want to sort a list
- Click the **Sort Ascending** or the **Sort Descending** button

---

Sorting the employee list in ascending order by Birth Date:

1. Click cell **H3**, a birth date cell for the first employee row

tip: *You do not need to select the entire list or the entire column on which the list is sorted. Excel determines the list's boundaries by finding blank rows to the left and right of the list and blank columns above and below the list*

2. Click the **Sort Ascending** button on the Standard toolbar. Excel sorts the rows in order by the Birth Date column (see Figure 5.8)

Never select the entire column you want to designate as the sort field because Excel misinterprets your intentions and sorts the entries in the selected column only, rather than sorting the entire record along with the sort field. If you make this mistake, click Undo in the Edit menu to reverse the effects of the incorrect sort operation.

sort field

FIGURE 5.8

Employee list sorted by Birth Date

	A	B	C	D	E	F	G	H	I	J
1										
2	ID	First Name	Last Name	Department	Title	Salary	Hire Date	Birth Date	Gender	Clearance
3	2105	Luca	Pacioli	Marketing	Staff	42,300	8/26/95	5/6/50	M	S
4	3210	Carmen	Ortega-Molina	Engineering	Engineer	46,000	9/16/99	3/28/52	F	S
5	4006	Alice	Rovik	Human Resources	Manager	43,000	12/1/01	1/26/55	M	S
6	1851	Melinda	English	Management	Manager	56,400	10/1/93	2/14/56	F	TS
7	1441	James	Van Horn	Management	Manager	66,500	12/18/92	2/3/58	M	S
8	1032	Hillary	Flintsteel	Marketing	Staff	34,500	3/21/91	8/22/58	F	N
9	1173	Roberta	Kurzweil	Management	Manager	63,000	6/16/92	12/22/58	F	S
10	1009	Kevin	Grundies	Marketing	CSR	38,900	12/24/89	3/4/61	M	C
11	2042	Hillary	Cushner	Management	Staff	32,000	8/26/94	5/6/61	F	TS
12	2678	Koshi	Yamamoto	Engineering	Engineer	49,600	11/16/95	1/24/63	F	S
13	2956	Michael	Goldstein	Engineering	Engineer	51,000	4/11/97	3/7/63	M	TS
14	2122	Yuan	Chang	Engineering	Engineer	46,540	9/5/95	3/4/64	M	TS
15	2344	Nemesha	Mehta	Engineering	Engineer	65,000	10/1/95	2/12/65	F	S
16	1355	Barbara	Grabowski	Management	Manager	75,700	10/13/92	4/10/65	F	C
17	3015	Patti	Stonesifer	Engineering	Engineer	64,300	7/6/98	3/10/66	F	S
18	1016	Oscar	Gomez	Marketing	CSR	43,500	2/16/90	4/29/67	M	N
19	1119	Sharad	Manispour	Engineering	Manager	54,500	10/13/90	2/4/69	M	S
20	2002	Edgar	Rothrock	Engineering	Engineer	53,300	2/8/94	3/21/70	M	S
21	4123	Steve	Ballmer	Engineering	Engineer	42,900	5/1/02	4/14/70	M	N
22	2451	Francine	Detweiler	Engineering	Engineer	56,700	10/10/95	4/29/70	F	S
23	3117	Frederich	Bednarczyk	Engineering	Engineer	56,700	5/14/99	5/27/70	M	S
24	2768	Phyllis	Leonard	Engineering	Engineer	59,800	12/13/96	7/2/70	F	TS
25	1614	Artie	Lombroso	Marketing	CSR	41,000	5/16/93	7/13/70	M	N

Documentation \ **Employee Data** /

Ready

Sorting a List on Multiple Fields

Often, sorting a list on only one field is not adequate because larger lists frequently have groups of entries that are identical in a particular field. A *tie* exists when one or more records have the same value for a field. When ties occur, you must sort the groups of records that tie on a particular field by another field—the ***secondary sort field***—to break the tie. For large lists, groups of records can match on both the primary sort field and the secondary sort field. In that case, sorting a list on three sort fields is necessary. Three sort fields are almost always sufficient to sort a list into order and eliminate all ties.

Alice Rovik wants the employee list sorted in order by department and then by employee last name and first name within each department. This type of sort operation goes beyond the capabilities of a single-key sort provided by the Sort Ascending or the Sort Descending buttons on the Standard toolbar. The Data menu Sort command provides the multiple-field sorting capability Alice requires.

---

task reference

Sorting a List on More Than One Field

- Click any cell within the list to be sorted
- Click **Data** on the menu bar and click **Sort**
- Click the **Sort by** list arrow to display the list's column headings. Click the column heading corresponding to the primary sort field, and click the **Ascending** or **Descending** option button
- Click the first **Then by** list arrow to display the list's column headings. Click the column heading of the secondary sort field, and then click the **Ascending** or **Descending** option button for the second sort field
- If necessary, click the second **Then by** list arrow to display the list's column headings. Click the column heading of the third sort field, and then click the **Ascending** or **Descending** option button for the third sort field
- Click the **OK** button to sort the list

EXCEL

Sorting the employee list in order by department and name within department:

1. Click any cell in the list

2. Click **Data** on the menu bar and then click **Sort**

3. Click the **Sort by** list box arrow to display a list of column headings, click **Department**, and, if necessary, click the **Ascending** option button

4. Click the first **Then by** list box arrow to display a list of column headings, click **Last Name**, and, if necessary, click the **Ascending** option button

5. Click the second **Then by** list box arrow to display a list of column headings, click **First Name**, and, if necessary, click the **Ascending** option button. Figure 5.9 shows the Sort dialog box after specifying three sort fields

FIGURE 5.9

Sort dialog box

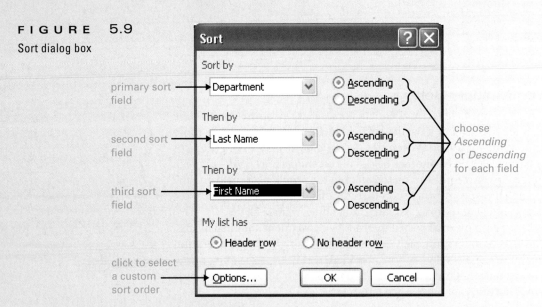

6. Click **OK** to sort the list into order on three sort fields. Excel sorts the list in order by department (first) and then last and first name within each department (see Figure 5.10)

Creating and Using Custom Sort Orders

Excel does not limit you to the standard sorting sequence. If you want to sort a series of labels in a particular order, you can define a custom sorting series. A ***custom sorting series*** or list is an ordered list you create to instruct Excel in what order to sort rows containing the list items. For example, imagine a list of student records containing a field called Year in School. The Year in School would contain "Freshman," "Sophomore," "Junior," and "Senior." Under normal circumstances, records sorted on the Year in School would rearrange rows so that they appear in this order: Freshman, Junior, Senior, and then Sophomore. However, most schools want the list sorted by year in school beginning with Freshman and ending with Senior. Creating a custom list containing Freshman, Sophomore, Junior, and then Senior—in that order—solves that particular sorting problem. (Excel already has the days of the week and the months of the year as custom sort orders, so you can sort time cards in Monday through Friday order or January through December.)

FIGURE 5.10

Sorted employee list

	A	B	C	D	E	F	G	H	I	J
1										
2	ID	First Name	Last Name	Department	Title	Salary	Hire Date	Birth Date	Gender	Clearance
3	4123	Steve	Ballmer	Engineering	Engineer	42,900	5/1/02	4/14/70	M	N
4	3117	Frederich	Bednarczyk	Engineering	Engineer	56,700	5/14/99	5/27/70	M	S
5	2122	Yuan	Chang	Engineering	Engineer	46,540	9/5/95	3/4/64	M	TS
6	2451	Francine	Detweiler	Engineering	Engineer	56,700	10/10/95	4/29/70	F	S
7	2896	Samuel	Gates	Engineering	Engineer	66,300	1/28/97	4/10/74	M	S
8	2956	Michael	Goldstein	Engineering	Engineer	51,000	4/11/97	3/7/63	M	TS
9	2768	Phyllis	Leonard	Engineering	Engineer	59,800	12/13/96	7/2/70	F	TS
10	1119	Sharad	Manispour	Engineering	Manager	54,500	10/13/90	2/4/69	M	S
11	2344	Nemesha	Mehta	Engineering	Engineer	65,000	10/1/95	2/12/65	F	S
12	3210	Carmen	Ortega-Molina	Engineering	Engineer	46,000	9/16/99	3/28/52	F	S
13	2002	Edgar	Rothrock	Engineering	Engineer	53,300	2/8/94	3/21/70	M	S
14	3015	Patti	Stonesifer	Engineering	Engineer	64,300	7/6/98	3/10/66	F	S
15	2678	Koshi	Yamamoto	Engineering	Engineer	49,600	11/16/95	1/24/63	F	S
16	2733	John	Zumkowski	Engineering	Staff	33,000	4/18/96	12/12/72	M	TS
17	3314	Svetlana	Kartashev	Human Resources	Staff	38,000	11/5/01	5/3/82	F	N
18	4006	Alice	Rovik	Human Resources	Manager	43,000	12/1/01	1/26/55	M	S
19	2042	Hillary	Cushner	Management	Staff	32,000	8/26/94	5/6/61	F	TS
20	1851	Melinda	English	Management	Manager	56,400	10/1/93	2/14/56	F	TS
21	1355	Barbara	Grabowski	Management	Manager	75,700	10/13/92	4/10/65	F	C
22	1173	Roberta	Kurzweil	Management	Manager	63,000	6/16/92	12/22/58	F	S
23	1441	James	Van Horn	Management	Manager	66,500	12/18/92	2/3/58	M	S
24	1042	Maria	Andretti	Marketing	CSR	42,500	3/21/90	8/20/70	F	N

---

task reference   Creating a Custom Sort Order

- Click **Tools** on the menu bar, click **Options**, and then click the **Custom Lists** tab
- Click **NEW LIST** in the Custom lists list box
- In the List Entries section of the dialog box, type each item and press **Enter** to place it on the list
- When the list is complete, click the **Add** button to move the proposed list to the Custom lists panel
- Click the **OK** button to close the Options dialog box

Alice would like you to sort the list in a third way so that the departments appear in this order: Marketing, Human Resources, Management, and Engineering. You begin by defining a custom sort order. Once you have defined the list, you can sort the worksheet rows in order by the custom list.

Creating a custom sort order:

1. Click **Tools** on the menu bar and then click **Options**
2. Click the **Custom Lists** tab, and then click **NEW LIST** in the Custom lists box
3. In the List entries box, type **Marketing** and press **Enter**
4. Type **Human Resources** and press **Enter**
5. Type **Management** and press **Enter**
6. Type **Engineering** and click the **Add** button to add the list you typed to the Custom lists (see Figure 5.11)
7. Click **OK** to complete the custom sort list definition

EXCEL

Defining a custom sort
order

custom sort order list
in ascending order

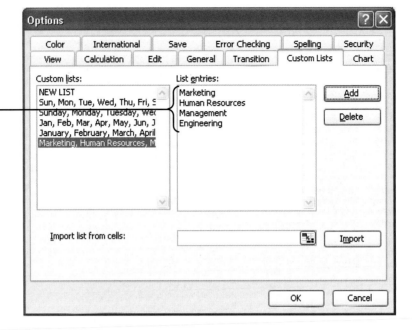

---

anotherword
. . . on Creating a Custom Sort Order

If the items in your custom list already appear in the correct order as text in your worksheet, you do not have to type them on
the Custom Lists tab of the Tools, Options dialog box. Instead,
select the list before choosing the Options command of the
Tools menu. Your highlighted text list will appear automatically
in the dialog box. Simply click the Import button to add the
new custom sort order sequence to Excel's custom lists. The
lists are remembered for all workbooks you load from Excel
on that particular computer

Now you can sort the employee list by
department names and then by employee
names within the department using a
procedure similar to the sort you performed above.

To delete a custom sort order list, select the list on the Custom Lists tab and
click the Delete button. The list is elimi-
nated. For now, leave the custom list in
place to use in the next steps to sort your
employee list by department names.

Sorting using a custom sort order:

1. Click any cell in the employee list

2. Click **Data** on the menu bar and then click **Sort**

3. Click the **Options** button to display the Sort Options dialog box

4. Click the **First key sort order** list box arrow, click the **Marketing, Human
Resources** entry to notify Excel to use that custom sort order (see Figure
5.12), and then click **OK**

Selecting a custom sort
order

Because Excel remembers the field names and sort order for the Sort by and the two *Then by* sort fields, you do not need to reinstate them. Ensure that they say Department, Last Name, and First Name, respectively

5. Click **OK** to sort the list into order. Figure 5.13 shows the list sorted with the custom department sort order

a custom sort order based on *Department*

	A	B	C	D	E	F	G	H	I	J
1										
2	ID	First Name	Last Name	Department	Title	Salary	Hire Date	Birth Date	Gender	Clearance
3	1042	Maria	Andretti	Marketing	CSR	42,500	3/21/90	8/20/70	F	N
4	1032	Hillary	Flintsteel	Marketing	Staff	34,500	3/21/90	8/22/58	F	N
5	1016	Oscar	Gomez	Marketing	CSR	43,500	2/16/90	4/29/67	M	N
6	1009	Kevin	Grundies	Marketing	CSR	38,900	12/24/89	3/4/61	M	C
7	1614	Artie	Lambros	Marketing	CSR	41,000	5/16/93	7/13/70	M	N
8	2105	Luca	Pacioli	Marketing	Staff	42,300	8/26/95	5/6/50	M	S
9	3314	Svetlana	Kartashev	Human Resources	Staff	38,000	11/5/01	5/3/82	F	N
10	4006	Alice	Rovik	Human Resources	Manager	43,000	12/1/01	1/26/55	M	S
11	2042	Hillary	Cushner	Management	Staff	32,000	8/26/94	5/6/61	F	TS
12	1851	Melinda	English	Management	Manager	56,400	10/1/93	2/14/56	F	TS
13	1355	Barbara	Grabowski	Management	Manager	75,700	10/13/92	4/10/65	F	C
14	1173	Roberta	Kurzweil	Management	Manager	63,000	6/16/92	12/22/58	F	S
15	1441	James	Van Horn	Management	Manager	66,500	12/18/92	2/3/58	M	S
16	4123	Steve	Ballmer	Engineering	Engineer	42,900	5/1/02	4/14/70	M	N
17	3117	Frederich	Bednarczyk	Engineering	Engineer	56,700	5/14/99	5/27/70	M	S
18	2122	Yuan	Chang	Engineering	Engineer	46,540	9/5/95	3/4/64	M	TS
19	2451	Francine	Detweiler	Engineering	Engineer	56,700	10/10/95	4/29/70	F	S
20	2896	Samuel	Gates	Engineering	Engineer	66,300	1/28/97	4/10/74	M	S
21	2956	Michael	Goldstein	Engineering	Engineer	51,000	4/11/97	3/7/63	M	TS
22	2768	Phyllis	Leonard	Engineering	Engineer	59,800	12/13/96	7/2/70	F	TS
23	1119	Sharad	Manispour	Engineering	Manager	54,500	10/13/90	2/4/69	M	S
24	2344	Nemesha	Mehta	Engineering	Engineer	65,000	10/1/95	2/12/65	F	S

Documentation **Employee Data**

Ready

FIGURE 5.13

Sorting with a custom sort order

---

*another*way

. . . **to Increase or Decrease a Worksheet's Zoom Percentage**

If you have a wheel button on your mouse, then you can use it in conjunction with the Ctrl key to quickly increase or decrease a worksheet's zoom percentage. Press and hold the **Ctrl** button and scroll the wheel button one direction to decrease the zoom percentage in small increments. Similarly, press and hold the **Ctrl** button and scroll the wheel button the opposite direction to increase the zoom percentage in small increments. Release the Ctrl button when you are done

---

Changing the Zoom Setting of a Worksheet

Sometimes it is handy to get a bird's eye view of a worksheet—to back up and view a larger portion of it on screen. Normally, Excel displays a worksheet at 100 percent magnification. The Zoom command of the View command (or the Zoom list box on the Standard toolbar) provides several preset viewing percentages, or you can specify an exact percentage of magnification. To view more of a worksheet—more columns and rows—you reduce the Zoom percentage. Similarly, you can zoom in and carefully examine a portion of a worksheet by increasing the Zoom percentage. Experiment with the Zoom percentage.

Decreasing the Zoom percentage:

1. Click **View** on the menu bar and then click **Zoom**

2. Click the **50%** option button to reduce the worksheet display to 50% of its normal size (see Figure 5.14)

3. Click **OK** to reduce the worksheet to 50% magnification

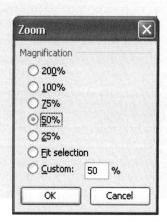

FIGURE 5.14

Zoom dialog box

When you want to zoom in for a close inspection of a few cells on the worksheet, you can do so by increasing the Zoom percentage to a value greater than 100 percent.

Increasing the Zoom percentage:

1. Click the **Zoom** control list arrow on the Standard toolbar

2. Click **200%**. Examine the worksheet

3. Return the worksheet to its normal display by clicking the **Zoom** control list arrow on the Standard toolbar and then clicking **100%**

4. Save the **Employee1.xls** workbook to preserve the work you completed in this session

SESSION 5.1

making the grade

1. A column of a data list is also called a _____.

2. A data list's row is also called what?

3. Execute the _____ _____ command of the Window menu to freeze rows and columns.

4. A _____ _____ is a dialog box displaying one row of a list in text boxes.

5. You can sort a list in order on a field containing department names by first creating a _____ list containing those names.

SESSION 5.2 CREATING FILTERS AND SUBTOTALS

In this section, you will learn how to create data filters to hide selected rows, how to apply conditional formats to draw attention to selected cells in the employee list, and how to insert subtotals beneath groups of related employee records.

Using Filters to Analyze a List

When viewing a long data list such as the employee list or lists with hundreds or thousands of rows, you may want to view just a portion of the list. For example, if you want to view records of customers who live in Michigan from your list of 3,000 customers, then you could sort the list on the State field and then scroll down to the section containing Michigan customers. Locating a group of records by sorting and scrolling is tedious and time-consuming. Filtering a list is easier.

Filtering a List with AutoFilter

Alice frequently needs to have a list of the engineers who work for Comsec. She is putting together a brochure that outlines the background and capabilities of the company and its engineers. She wants to list the names and clearance levels of the engineers. Alice thought about using a data form and specifying the search criteria "engineer" in the Title text box to locate the engineers, but that method displays only one record at a time. The best way to display the list of engineers is to ask Excel to list only records that match particular criteria, hiding the rows that do not. This method is called *filtering*.

Other Office products use filtering too. Microsoft Access uses filtering to retrieve rows that satisfy criteria through its query facility.

---

task reference — Filtering a List with AutoFilter

- Click any cell in the list

- Click **Data**, point to **Filter**, and click **AutoFilter** to turn each column into a list box with a list arrow beside each label

- Click the list arrow next to the label you want to use as a filter

- Click the criteria in the drop-down list by which you want to filter the list

---

AutoFilter is the filtering command that allows you to hide all rows in a list except those that match the criteria you specify. You will create a filter on the Title column to list the employees with the title "Engineer."

Filtering a list with the AutoFilter command:

1. Save the employee workbook as **Employee2.xls** to establish a new workbook name for this session

2. Click any cell within the employee list

3. Click **Data** on the menu bar, point to **Filter**, and click **AutoFilter**. Excel places list box arrows next to each label in the list's heading row

4. Click the **Title column** list arrow to display the filtering criteria available for that column. Excel analyzes each column, sorts it, and removes the duplicate values to form the filtering list for each column (see Figure 5.15)

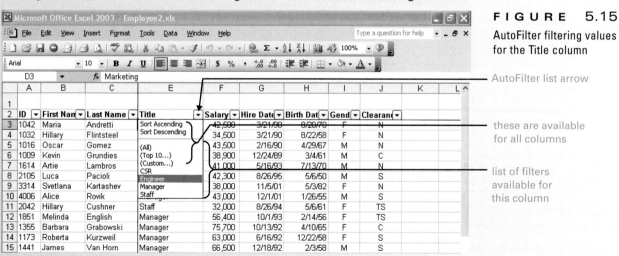

FIGURE 5.15

AutoFilter filtering values for the Title column

AutoFilter list arrow

these are available for all columns

list of filters available for this column

5. Click **Engineer** to hide all employees except those containing "Engineer" in the Title column

Excel counts the total number of records it filters and the total number of records and displays those numbers in the status bar ("12 of 27 records"). Missing rows are hidden, not deleted (see Figure 5.16).

FIGURE   5.16

Filtering records

blue row numbers indicate filtered rows satisfying the criteria

	A	B	C	E	F	G	H	I	J	K	L
1											
2	ID	First Nan	Last Name	Title	Salary	Hire Date	Birth Dat	Gend	Clearan		
16	4123	Steve	Ballmer	Engineer	42,900	5/1/02	4/14/70	M	N		
17	3117	Frederich	Bednarczyk	Engineer	56,700	5/14/99	5/27/70	M	S		
18	2122	Yuan	Chang	Engineer	46,540	9/5/95	3/4/64	M	TS		
19	2451	Francine	Detweiler	Engineer	56,700	10/10/95	4/29/70	F	S		
20	2896	Samuel	Gates	Engineer	66,300	1/28/97	4/10/74	M	S		
21	2956	Michael	Goldstein	Engineer	51,000	4/11/97	3/7/63	M	TS		
22	2768	Phyllis	Leonard	Engineer	59,800	12/13/96	7/2/70	F	TS		
24	2344	Nemesha	Mehta	Engineer	65,000	10/1/95	2/12/65	F	S		
25	3210	Carmen	Ortega-Molina	Engineer	46,000	9/16/99	3/28/52	F	S		
26	2002	Edgar	Rothrock	Engineer	53,300	2/8/94	3/21/70	M	S		
27	3015	Patti	Stonesifer	Engineer	64,300	7/6/98	3/10/66	F	S		
28	2678	Koshi	Yamamoto	Engineer	49,600	11/16/95	1/24/63	F	S		
30											

blue list arrow indicates a filter is active on the column

Documentation Employee Data

12 of 27 records found

---

anotherword   . . . on Filtering a List

Because AutoFilter hides entire rows in the active sheet that do not match the AutoFilter criteria, avoid placing other worksheet information in the same rows as the list. Though outside the list, information in the same list as a hidden row is hidden also

---

Three filter choices appear in all list columns. They are *All*, *Top 10*, and *Custom*. *All* displays all items in the list and removes filtering from the column. *Top 10* displays the top or bottom *n* items, when sorted, in the list. You can click *Custom* to specify more complex filtering criteria.

The AutoFilter list also displays the choices *(Blanks)* and *(NonBlanks)* at the bottom of the AutoFilter list for any column that contains at least one blank entry. The (Blanks) and (NonBlanks) choices are handy because they allow you to display rows whose selected field contains blanks. Blank entries are often errors, and locating them can be difficult in long lists.

With any criteria in effect, you can refine your query by using several AutoFilter drop-down filters in tandem. Doing so further restricts the rows that appear in the filtered list. For example, if you want a list of engineers who have top secret clearances, you select Engineer from the Title drop-down filter list and then select TS from the Clearance drop-down list to combine filtering criteria.

Filtering a list with multiple criteria:

1. With the Title filter criteria ("Engineer") still in effect, click the **Clearance column** list arrow

2. Click **TS** in the Clearance filter list to limit rows to engineers with a top secret clearance (see Figure 5.17)

FIGURE   5.17

Using multiple criteria to filter a list

Filter criteria: "Engineer"   Filter criteria: "TS"

	A	B	C	E	F	G	H	I	J	K	L
1											
2	ID	First Nan	Last Name	Title	Salary	Hire Date	Birth Dat	Gend	Clearan		
18	2122	Yuan	Chang	Engineer	46,540	9/5/95	3/4/64	M	TS		
21	2956	Michael	Goldstein	Engineer	51,000	4/11/97	3/7/63	M	TS		
22	2768	Phyllis	Leonard	Engineer	59,800	12/13/96	7/2/70	F	TS		
30											

3. Remove the Clearance column filter by clicking the **Clearance column** list arrow and then by clicking **(All)** at the top of the list

task reference	Clearing All AutoFilter Filtering Criteria
• Click **Data**, point to **Filter** • Click **Show All**	

Removing all AutoFilter list filters:

1. Click **Data** on the menu bar

2. Point to **Filter** and then click **Show All**. All the records reappear, but the AutoFilter list arrows remain next to each column heading

Using Custom AutoFilters

The AutoFilters you applied in the preceding examples work for ***exact match criteria***—criteria in which a row's field exactly matches a particular filter value. With custom criteria, you can specify the low and high values range that a field must satisfy instead of a single value.

Custom AutoFilters allow you to specify other relationships besides "is equal to." You specify criteria using any of the six relational operators: Less than, less than or equal to, greater than, greater than or equal to, or not equal to, or equal to. A ***relational operator*** compares two values, and the expression containing the values and the conditional operator result in either true or false. Relational operators in Excel expressions are written as the symbols $<, <=, =, >, >=, <>$. In Custom AutoFilters, relational operators appear in a list box as English phrases such as "is greater than or equal to" rather than their symbolic equivalent such as "$>=$".

Alice wants to send out mailers to all male employees who were born in the 1960s because a company policy change affects their health benefits. While she could sort the list and try to write down the affected employees' names born between 1960 and 1969 (inclusive), she knows that using a custom AutoFilter is a better solution.

Creating a more complex AutoFilter:

1. With all criteria cleared but the AutoFilter list arrows still visible, click the **Birth Date** column list arrow. The criteria filter list appears below the Birth Date column heading

2. Click **(Custom...)** to display the Custom AutoFilter dialog box (see Figure 5.18)

3. Click the top left list box and then click **is greater than or equal to**

4. Click the top right list box and then type **1/1/1960**

5. Click the **And** option button, if necessary

6. Click the bottom left list box and then click **is less than or equal to**

7. Click the bottom right list box and then type **12/31/1969** in the list box (see Figure 5.19)

8. Click **OK** to apply the custom filter and display the filtered employee list

EXCEL

FIGURE 5.18

Custom AutoFilter dialog box

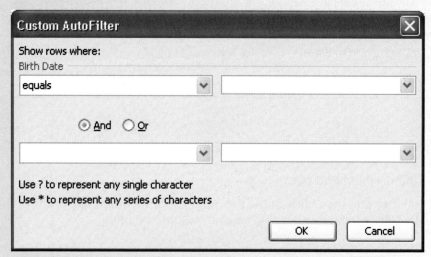

FIGURE 5.19

Custom AutoFilter dialog box with filters filled in

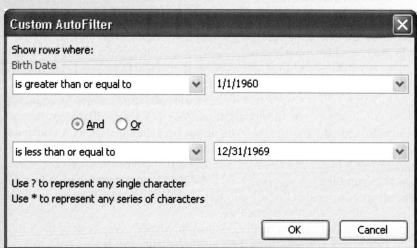

9. Click the **Gender** column list arrow. The criteria filter list appears below the Gender column heading

10. Click **M** in the Gender filter list to further restrict the list to males. Excel filters the list producing the required list of males born in the 1960s (see Figure 5.20)

FIGURE 5.20

Filtered list of males born in the 1960s

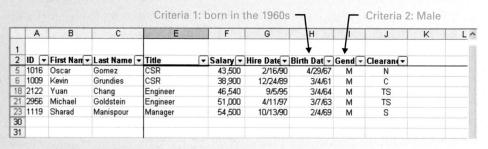

Criteria 1: born in the 1960s   Criteria 2: Male

	A	B	C	E	F	G	H	I	J	K	L
1											
2	ID	First Nam	Last Name	Title	Salary	Hire Date	Birth Dat	Gend	Clearanc		
5	1016	Oscar	Gomez	CSR	43,500	2/16/90	4/29/67	M	N		
6	1009	Kevin	Grundies	CSR	38,900	12/24/89	3/4/61	M	C		
18	2122	Yuan	Chang	Engineer	46,540	9/5/95	3/4/64	M	TS		
21	2956	Michael	Goldstein	Engineer	51,000	4/11/97	3/7/63	M	TS		
23	1119	Sharad	Manispour	Manager	54,500	10/13/90	2/4/69	M	S		
30											
31											

Alice wants to interview the employees whose records are shown in Figure 5.20 in order of their birth data—oldest to youngest. She asks you to sort the list on the Birth Date field and then show her the resulting list (still filtered). After Alice reviews the list, she wants you to remove the AutoFilter so that all the employee rows reappear.

Sorting a filtered list and then restoring hidden rows:

1. Click any cell in the **Birth Date** column—inside the list, the column label, or outside the list

2. Click the **Sort Ascending** ![sort ascending icon] button on the Standard toolbar to sort the list in ascending birth date order. The filtered list appears in ascending birth date order

3. Click **Data** on the menu bar, point to **Filter**, and click **AutoFilter** to remove all filters. (You cannot undo the result of removing an AutoFilter)

Using Subtotals to Analyze a List

Whenever you have an Excel list with data whose columns each contain one type of data—a database or list such as the employee worksheet, for example—you can produce summary information about the numeric columns. The Employee worksheet is a typical example. With data arranged in order by department, it is convenient to insert SUM functions to compute the total salary of each department. Although you could write four SUM functions to total the salaries of all employees in each department, Excel provides a more convenient solution—the Subtotals command.

help yourself *Press **F1**, type **subtotal** in the Search text box of the Microsoft Excel Help task pane, and press **Enter**. Click the hyperlink **About subtotals** and then read the help information describing how the Subtotals command works. When you are done, click the Help screen **Close** button or click the **Print** icon in the toolbar to print the Help screen. Close the task pane*

Subtotals offers several list summary features including count, sum, average, minimum, and maximum—the same features provided by the stand-alone statistical functions of COUNTA, SUM, AVERAGE, MIN, and MAX. Unlike those functions, the Subtotals command automatically creates the appropriate formula when it senses a change in the value of a specified field. For the employee list, that field could be Department. Subtotals also provides the added convenience of outlining whereby you can display the rows that constitute a group or you can collapse the list, hiding all rows except the subtotal rows. Excel handles the details of hiding and revealing list rows as needed. The only requirement for the Subtotals command to do its work properly is that the list be sorted so that it is in order by the field you specify as the grouping field before you use the subtotals command.

How Subtotals Are Built

task *reference*   Subtotaling a List's Entries
• Sort the list by the column whose groups you want to subtotal
• Click any cell inside the list
• Click **Data** and then click **Subtotals**
• In the *At each change in* list box, click the name of the group on which you want a subtotal
• From the *Use function* list box, select the aggregate function you want to use
• In the *Add subtotal to* list box, select the column(s) containing the values you want to aggregate; in the *Add subtotal to* list box, clear the column(s) containing checkmarks for any values you *do not* want to aggregate
• Click **OK**

EXCEL

Alice wants to view the total salaries by department and the total of all departments' salaries. In preparation, first sort the list into order by Department, which is the field upon which subtotals are created. Remember, the last time you sorted the list, you used a custom sort list. You have to remove that list to sort the Department field in a "normal" way. First, you will remove the custom sort order.

Canceling a custom sort order:

1. Click cell **H3**, click **Data** on the menu bar, click **Sort**, and click the **Options** button to open the Sort Options dialog box (see Figure 5.12)

2. Click the **First key sort order** list box, and then click **Normal** at the top of the list

3. Click **OK** to close the Sort Options dialog box, and then click **OK** to close the Sort dialog box

Now you can sort the list in alphabetical order by department, because you canceled the custom Department sort order.

Sorting a list prior to creating subtotals:

1. Click cell **D3**, the first data cell under the Department column label

2. Click the **Sort Ascending** ⬆↓ button on the Standard toolbar

Now that the list is sorted into department order, you can create summary information about departments. Because Alice wants a sum of salaries by department and the grand total salary value, you use the Subtotals command.

Summing salaries by departments:

1. Click **Data** on the menu bar and then click **Subtotals**. The Subtotal dialog box opens

2. Click the **At each change in** list box and then click **Department** in the drop-down list to tell Excel to create subtotals by department

3. Click the **Use function** list box and then click **Sum**. You want to sum the salary field, not count or average it

4. Scroll to the top of the *Add subtotal to* list box, then slowly scroll down the Add subtotal to list and remove any checkmarks in the column name check boxes

5. Scroll the list, if necessary, to locate and then click the **Salary** check box to place a checkmark in it. Salary is the column you want to sum (see Figure 5.21)

6. Ensure that the *Replace current subtotals* and the *Summary below data* check boxes are checked and that the *Page break between groups* check box is clear (see Figure 5.21)

tip: *By default, the* Replace current subtotals *check box is checked, meaning the subtotal you specify will replace the selected list's current subtotal. However, if you want to use more than one function, sum and average for example, you can execute the Data Subtotals a second time and specify the second subtotal function. The second time, however, deselect the* Replace current subtotals *check box to display both subtotal functions at once. You can repeat this for as many subtotal functions as you want for a group*

FIGURE 5.21

Completed Subtotal dialog box

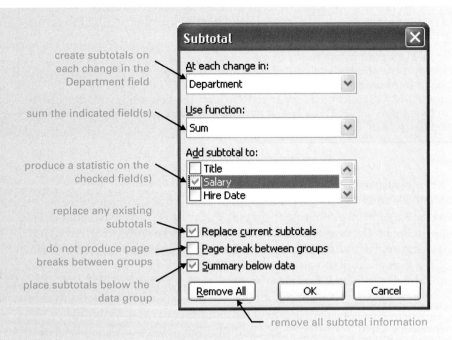

create subtotals on each change in the Department field

sum the indicated field(s)

produce a statistic on the checked field(s)

replace any existing subtotals

do not produce page breaks between groups

place subtotals below the data group

remove all subtotal information

7. Click **OK** to insert the subtotals below each department group and the grand total below the last group's subtotal (see Figure 5.22)

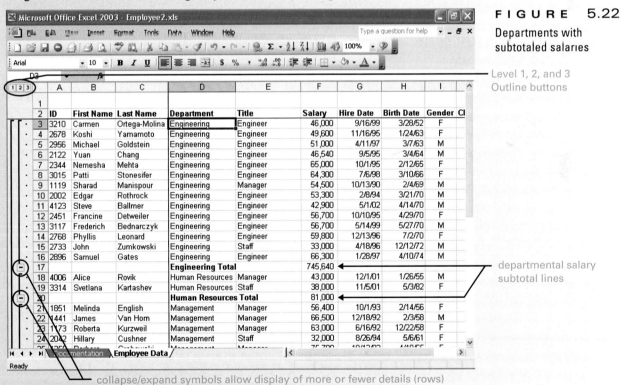

FIGURE 5.22

Departments with subtotaled salaries

Level 1, 2, and 3 Outline buttons

departmental salary subtotal lines

collapse/expand symbols allow display of more or fewer details (rows)

8. Scroll through the list to view each department's subtotal and the total salary value for all departments (the value is 1,362,940, which is in cell F34)

9. If necessary, widen column F so that the total salary displays. Click cell **F34** containing the total salary for all departments, click **Format** on the menu bar, point to **Column**, and click **AutoFit Selection**. The column enlarges enough to display the total in cell F34

---

anotherword   . . . on Using Subtotal to Sum a Column

If you want to sum a column of numbers such as employees' salaries, avoid using the SUM function when the rows are likely to be filtered. The SUM function adds both visible and invisible cells in the specified range, whereas the Subtotal function ignores any hidden cells (rows) in the range. For example, writing **=Subtotal(9,F3:F29)** tells the function to total (9 as the first argument) the *visible* cells in the range F3:F29. The value of the first argument specifies the subtotal function to use such as average, min, count, and so on

---

Using the Subtotals Outline View

The subtotals by department are very handy and easy to create. Alice also wants to see just the subtotals and not all the details about the rows that are in each department. Upper management people commonly want the "big picture" instead of all the details. Often, the higher up the corporate ladder one is, the fewer details one needs to make sweeping decisions. Fortunately, Excel makes creating summaries a snap with another feature that is part of the Subtotals command—Outlines.

The Subtotals command produces two results when you use it. Not only does it produce subtotal statistics for identified groups, but it also outlines the worksheet's list. You can choose how much detail to view in the outline by clicking one of three outline buttons located at the top left side of the worksheet (see Figure 5.22). Commonly, the highest level, 3, is active. It displays all active list members, subtotals, and the grand total. Level 2 hides the individual list-member rows but displays subtotal information. The lowest level of detail, level 1, displays only the grand total information. Try the outline buttons to see how they work by doing the next exercise.

Using the outline feature of the subtotals:

1. Make D3—the upper leftmost cell in the frozen panels—the active cell by pressing **Ctrl+Home**

2. Click the **Level 2 Outline** 2 button (see Figure 5.23). Notice that the departmental salary subtotals and grand total appear, but Excel hides the detail rows

FIGURE 5.23

Level 2 outline

outline level buttons

outline expand buttons

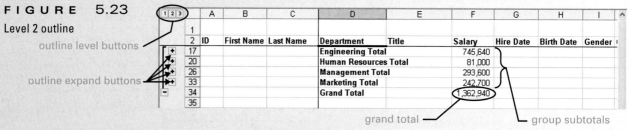

grand total —   — group subtotals

3. Click the **Expand** + button to the left of row 26 to expand the Management department details

4. Click the **Level 1 Outline** 1 button to hide all information in the list except the grand total

5. Click the **Level 3 Outline** 3 button to expose all departments' detail rows

Although the employee list is relatively short, you can see how outlining a really long list can be useful. It allows anyone to see an overview of crucial statistics without having to see the details at the same time. Removing details helps a viewer focus on the "bottom line," much the same way a chart does.

Inserting Page Breaks into a List with Subtotals

Alice wants to distribute the employee information to four department heads for their use. Because she wants to keep each department's information confidential among the departments, she wants to print each department's employee information on a separate page so that she can distribute the four one-page reports to each department head. Though the worksheet prints on one page, you can create your own page breaks easily.

Inserting page breaks into a list containing subtotals:

1. Click **Data** on the menu bar and then click **Subtotals** to display the Subtotal dialog box

2. Click the **Page break between groups** check box (see Figure 5.21) to place a checkmark in it

3. Click **OK** to close the Subtotal dialog box. Dashed lines appear on the worksheet where Excel inserts page breaks

4. Click the **Print Preview** button on the Standard toolbar

5. Click the **Next** button on the Print Preview toolbar. Look at the top of the page (zoom in if necessary). Notice that the column labels do not appear at the top of the second page, but they do appear on the top of the first page

6. Click the **Close** button on the Print Preview toolbar to close the Print Preview window

Printing Row and Column Titles on Each Page

You noticed as you reviewed the worksheet in the previous exercise that the column headings appear only on the first page. Typically, you should display column headings on every page so that a reader does not have to leaf back to the first page to see the headings. Similarly, if you have a wide output in which every other page displays columns in the right half of a worksheet, you can tell Excel to print row headings in the first column of every page.

---

task reference — **Displaying Row or Column Headings on Each Page**

- Click **File** and then click **Page Setup**

- Click the **Sheet** tab

- Click the **Collapse dialog box** button on the **Rows to repeat at top** or **Columns to repeat at left** text boxes in the Print titles section

- Select the row(s) or column(s) you want to print on each page

- Click the **Expand dialog box** button again to reveal the Page Setup dialog box

- Click **OK**

Printing selected rows on each page:

1. Click **File** on the menu bar, click **Page Setup** to open the Page Setup dialog box, and then click the **Sheet** tab

2. Click the **Collapse dialog box** 🔲 button to the right of the **Rows to repeat at top**

3. Click the row 2 header to select the entire row, and then click the **Expand dialog box** 🔲 button to restore the Page Setup dialog box (see Figure 5.24)

FIGURE 5.24

Seleting a row to repeat on every page

Collapse dialog box button

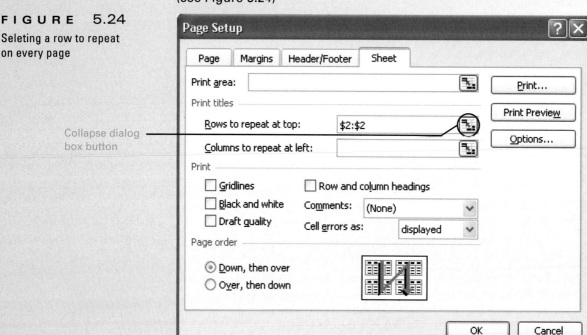

4. Click **OK**

5. Click the **Print Preview** button on the Standard toolbar and then click the **Next** button repeatedly to preview each output page and confirm that the first output line—the column labels—appears on every page

6. Click the **Close** button on the Print Preview toolbar

Clearing All Subtotal Information

You can remove subtotal information by executing the Data Subtotals command and then clicking a button that removes all totals.

Removing subtotals from a list:

1. Click any cell within the list, including a subtotal row, and then click **Data** on the menu bar

2. Click **Subtotals**. The Subtotal dialog box opens

3. Click the **Remove All** button. Excel removes all subtotal rows and closes the Subtotal dialog box

Manually Inserting and Removing Page Breaks

Excel removes all subtotal information from the employee worksheet and displays all employee rows. Excel allows you to insert manually your own page breaks without using the Subtotals command. Similar to the way you insert page breaks in Microsoft Word documents, Excel provides a Page Break command on the Insert menu.

Manually inserting page breaks into a worksheet:

1. Click the **row 17 header** button

2. Click **Insert** on the menu bar, and then click **Page Break**. Excel inserts a page break above the selected row and displays a dashed line to indicate the position of the page break

3. Repeat steps 1 and 2 two more times but substitute row headers **19** and then **24** in step 1. When you are done, Excel displays page breaks following rows 16, 18, and 23

4. Click any cell to deselect row 24

5. Click the **Print Preview** button on the Standard toolbar

6. Click repeatedly the **Next** button on the Print Preview toolbar to view each of the remaining three pages. Notice that the column heading row prints on each page because you set that option in an earlier series of steps

7. Click the **Close** button when you are finished previewing the page breaks

You can easily remove all manually inserted page breaks. Do that next.

Removing all page breaks from a worksheet:

1. Click the **Select All** button located at the intersection of the row heading and the column heading of the worksheet

tip: *You can press **Ctrl+A** to select all worksheet cells if you prefer*

2. Click **Insert** on the menu bar and then click **Reset All Page Breaks**. Excel removes all page breaks

Applying Conditional Formatting

Managers often want to highlight unusual values in a worksheet to draw attention to them. Perhaps you want to highlight exceptional sales volume, superior quality measures, or cars with unusually high repair costs. One way to highlight exceptional values is to locate a value you want to highlight, click Format on the menu bar, and then specify a series of format changes such as a background color or a change in the font color. While this is one solution, it is both laborious and error-prone.

Excel provides a better solution: *conditional formatting*. Conditional formatting automatically takes effect in a cell whenever the data in the cell satisfy criteria that you specify when you create the conditional format. Conditional formatting is an easy way to highlight significant values, because you can format a group of cells at once. Only the cells that meet the specified criteria display under the control of the conditional format. Cells containing the conditional format but not meeting the criteria display normally.

EXCEL

For example, suppose you are tracking accounts receivable and want to display groups of values in different font colors. To display accounts with a balance of more than $10,000 in blue, you can use conditional formatting. Balances less than or equal to $10,000 display in their usual black color.

---

task reference   Applying a Conditional
                                                              Format to Cells

- Click the cell range to which you want to apply a conditional format
- Click **Format** on the menu bar and then click **Conditional Formatting**
- Enter the criteria for which Excel is to apply the special formatting
- Click the **Format** button on the Conditional Formatting dialog box, select the font color, style, underlining, borders, or other formatting to apply conditionally
- Click **OK** to close the Conditional Formatting dialog box
- Click **OK** to apply the conditional formatting to the selected cell(s)

Alice would like to highlight employee salaries that are at least $55,000. This will help her quickly identify the highest-paid employees. She asks you to apply a conditional format to the Salary column so that any value equal to or greater than $55,000 displays a background color of red and a font color of white.

Applying a conditional format to the Salary column:

1. Select cell range **F3:F29**

tip: *You can select a filled partial column of cells by clicking the first cell (F3 in this case), holding the **Shift** key, tapping the **End** key, and then tapping the **Down Arrow** key*

2. Click **Format** on the menu bar and click **Conditional Formatting** to open the Conditional Formatting dialog box

3. Ensure that **Cell Value Is** appears in the first list box for Condition 1, because the Salary column contains values, not formulas that compute and display values

4. Click in the second list box for Condition 1 to display a list of choices and then click the **greater than or equal to** choice

5. Click in the third list box for Condition 1 and then type **55000**

6. Click the **Format** button in the Conditional Formatting dialog box. The Format Cells dialog box opens

7. Click the **Font** tab, if necessary, click the **Color** list box arrow, and then click the **white square** (fifth row from the top, eighth column) in the Font Color palette

8. Click the **Patterns** tab and then click the **red square** (third row from the top, first column)

9. Click **OK** to close the Format Cells dialog box (see Figure 5.25)

10. Click **OK** to apply the conditional formatting to the selected cell range

11. Click **Ctrl+Home** to make D3 the active cell. Excel displays 10 cells in the Salary column with the special conditional format (see Figure 5.26)

conditional formatting criteria

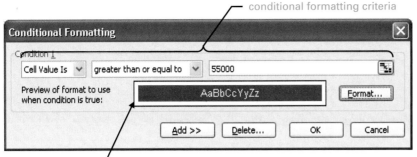

conditional formatting: red background and white characters

FIGURE 5.25

Setting conditional formatting criteria and format options

	A	B	C	D	E	F	G	H	I	J
1										
2	ID	First Name	Last Name	Department	Title	Salary	Hire Date	Birth Date	Gender	Cleara
3	3210	Carmen	Ortega-Molina	Engineering	Engineer	46,000	9/16/99	3/28/52	F	S
4	2678	Koshi	Yamamoto	Engineering	Engineer	49,600	11/16/95	1/24/63	F	S
5	2956	Michael	Goldstein	Engineering	Engineer	51,000	4/11/97	3/7/63	M	TS
6	2122	Yuan	Chang	Engineering	Engineer	46,540	9/5/95	3/4/64	M	TS
7	2344	Nemesha	Mehta	Engineering	Engineer	65,000	10/1/95	2/12/65	F	S
8	3015	Patti	Stonesifer	Engineering	Engineer	64,300	7/6/98	3/10/66	F	S
9	1119	Sharad	Manispour	Engineering	Manager	54,500	10/13/90	2/4/69	M	S
10	2002	Edgar	Rothrock	Engineering	Engineer	53,300	2/8/94	3/21/70	M	S
11	4123	Steve	Ballmer	Engineering	Engineer	42,900	5/1/02	4/14/70	M	N
12	2451	Francine	Detweiler	Engineering	Engineer	56,700	10/10/95	4/29/70	F	S
13	3117	Frederich	Bednarczyk	Engineering	Engineer	56,700	5/14/99	5/27/70	M	S
14	2768	Phyllis	Leonard	Engineering	Engineer	59,800	12/13/96	7/2/70	F	TS
15	2733	John	Zumkowski	Engineering	Staff	33,000	4/18/96	12/12/72	M	TS
16	2896	Samuel	Gates	Engineering	Engineer	66,300	1/28/97	4/10/74	M	S
17	4006	Alice	Rovik	Human Resources	Manager	43,000	12/1/01	1/26/55	M	S
18	3314	Svetlana	Kartashev	Human Resources	Staff	38,000	11/5/01	5/3/82	F	N
19	1851	Melinda	English	Management	Manager	56,400	10/1/93	2/14/56	F	TS
20	1441	James	Van Horn	Management	Manager	66,500	12/18/92	2/3/58	M	S
21	1173	Roberta	Kurzweil	Management	Manager	63,000	6/16/92	12/22/58	F	S
22	2042	Hillary	Cushner	Management	Staff	32,000	8/26/94	5/6/61	F	TS
23	1355	Barbara	Grabowski	Management	Manager	75,700	10/13/92	4/10/65	F	C
24	2105	Luca	Pacioli	Marketing	Staff	42,300	8/26/95	5/6/50	M	S
25	1032	Hillary	Flintsteel	Marketing	Staff	34,500	3/21/90	8/22/58	F	N
26	1009	Kevin	Grundies	Marketing	CSR	38,900	12/24/89	3/4/61	M	C
27	1016	Oscar	Gomez	Marketing	CSR	43,500	2/16/90	4/29/67	M	N
28	1614	Artie	Lambros	Marketing	CSR	41,000	5/16/93	7/13/70	M	N
29	1042	Maria	Andretti	Marketing	CSR	42,500	3/21/90	8/20/70	F	N
30										
31										

Documentation \ Employee Data /

FIGURE 5.26

Selected cells displaying the conditional format

If the value of any of the Salary cells changes and no longer meets the criteria for the conditional format, then Excel displays the cell in the usual way without the conditional format. The conditional format remains with the cells until you either reformat the cells or clear their formats.

Deleting a conditional format:

1. Select cell range **F3:F29**, the range of cells containing the conditional format

2. Click **Format** on the menu bar and click **Conditional Formatting** to open the Conditional Formatting dialog box

3. Click the **Delete** button on the Conditional Formatting dialog box. The Delete Conditional Format dialog box opens

4. Click the **Condition 1** check box to place a checkmark in it (see Figure 5.27), click **OK** to confirm your choice, and close the Delete Conditional Format dialog box

5. Click **OK** to close the Conditional Formatting dialog box and remove the conditional formatting from the selected cell range

EXCEL

FIGURE   5.27

Deleting a conditional format

cells with conditional format are highlighted

check *Condition 1* to delete that conditional format

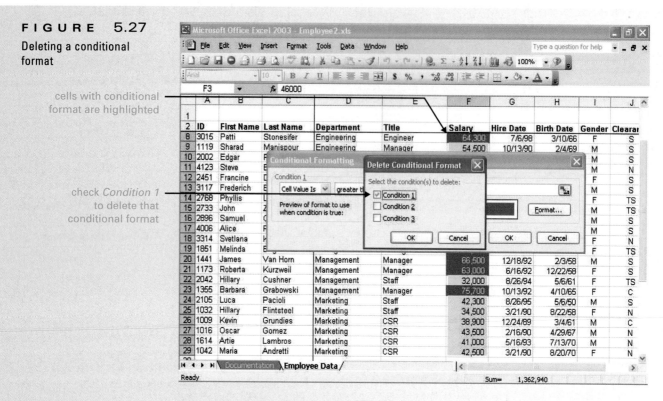

6. Press **Ctrl+Home** to make cell D3 active

7. Click the **Save** button on the Standard toolbar to save this version of the Employee worksheet **(Employee2.xls)**, close the worksheet, but leave Excel running. If you decide to take a break, close Excel. Remember to open Excel again before beginning Session 5.3

SESSION 5.2

making the grade

1. You have a list of 635 employees who work at the university and you want to print the list of employees who work in Warren Hall. You would use the _____ command from the menu bar to list the subset of employees who work in Warren Hall.

2. In order to print a list of banks in South Florida in order by City and then by bank name within each city, you would do what?

3. Suppose you want to display employees who earn $40,000 or less per year. How would you produce a list of those employees? Assume that the salary information is in a column called "Salary."

4. A list called Monthly Customer Sales contains sale dates, customer names, customer addresses, and total value of sales in three columns labeled "Sale Date," "Customer," "Address," and "Sales." Any customer may have several sales recorded in the list when he or she makes more than one purchase in the month. Describe in a sentence or two how you would produce a list, grouped by customer name, displaying each customer's list of sales followed by a total of all sales for each customer and a grand total for the month.

5. In a column containing dates, you could highlight selected dates—say dates that occur before June 14, 1980—by using the Cells command on the Format menu and applying font attributes to the selected cells directly. A better choice would be to execute a command that forces Excel to automatically highlight dates occurring before June 14, 1980. What is that command?

SESSION 5.3 CREATING AND USING PIVOT TABLES

In this section, you will learn how to summarize data in an Excel list to provide insights that are otherwise masked by the size and volume of data in a list.

Pivot Table Basics

Pivot tables provide a three-dimensional view of data that is often too complicated to understand in its raw list form. A *pivot table* is an interactive table enabling you quickly to group and summarize large amounts of data. The employee list is an example of a list that you could create a pivot table from in order to locate hidden information from the list. Pivot tables summarizing longer data lists are particularly valuable tools for revealing the information hidden in the details. A pivot table uses a two-dimensional list to create a three-dimensional table that summarizes large amounts of information in a small amount of space. Pivot tables are interactive because you can drag a field to another location and thus pivot the structure of the table. Pivot table data are linked to their underlying two-dimensional list. You can change the data in one or more parts of the list and then execute the Refresh pivot table command to recalculate the summary information.

In order to create a pivot table from data, the data must meet certain criteria. First, the data must be in tabular form. Each column must have a unique column label to identify each field. Each row must represent a unique fact or piece of data. Third, date values in the list should be formatted with a date format. Fourth, remove blank rows or columns from the list so Excel can easily identify the complete unbroken list.

Pivot tables can contain these elements: *row fields, column fields,* and *page fields.* Frequently, data such as year, gender, ID number, sales date, birth date, or hire date appear in pivot tables as row, column, or page fields. Numeric data appear in pivot tables' central position—*data fields.* The data fields contain the summary information such as average sales, average age, total sales, number of sales per month, or number of students in the sophomore class. The ability to move row fields to column fields and vice versa—to pivot the data—is the origin of the name for this analytical tool.

Pivot tables can help you simplify and understand the data in an Excel table or list. Consider the example of all the sales transactions for a large corporation, such as the worksheet shown in Figure 5.28 containing over 900 rows of transaction data. The Accounting Department creates financial statements from a series of internal financial reports that are based on the thousands of sales transactions, vendor payments, and other transactions. The highest levels of management rarely see transaction details. As you move down through levels of a company's organization, managers at successively lower rungs of the corporate ladder look at progressively more detail. In order to manage effectively, all managers depend on summary information. Pivot tables serve a function of creating summary information from a myriad of details contained in an Excel list of individual transactions. Figure 5.29 shows a pivot table that summarizes the data partially displayed in Figure 5.28 and provides a fact that the dollar volume of sales to New York customers by female sales representatives is greater than sales by male sales representatives. By clicking the list box displaying "NY," managers can compare performance of male versus female sales persons in other states.

While managers' financial and database reports are often static objects, pivot tables are dynamic and flexible, providing up-to-the-minute results and in a way that allows managers to alter their view of the summary. Instead of passively reading a report, anyone with an Excel pivot table can slice, dice, twist, and turn it until they change the summary into the information they are looking for. By altering a variable here and moving another variable there, you can make the sales per month by region suddenly jump out of the details of a list, much like viewing a hologram from a different angle.

EXCEL

FIGURE 5.28

Sales list example

SaleID	Date	State	Sales Rep	Gender	Amount
12101	7/3/2004	CA	Watterson, Barbara	F	$ 5,470
12102	7/3/2004	NM	Goldman, Ted	M	$ 9,687
12103	7/3/2004	TX	Kole, David	M	$ 7,495
12104	7/3/2004	WI	Morrison, Alanis	F	$ 5,239
12105	7/3/2004	TX	Kole, David	M	$ 5,920
12106	7/3/2004	IL	Stonesifer, Patti	F	$ 3,349
12107	7/3/2004	CA	Pacioli, Luca	M	$ 4,061
12108	7/3/2004	IN	Kahn, Phillipe	M	$ 7,658
12109	7/3/2004	GA	Halstead, Whitney	F	$ 6,172
12110	7/3/2004	NH	English, Melinda	F	$ 9,253
12111	7/3/2004	CA	Minsky, Barbara	F	$ 8,586
12112	7/3/2004	TX	Bateman, Giles	M	$ 6,666
12113	7/3/2004	IL	Halstead, Whitney	F	$ 6,714
12114	7/3/2004	OH	Stonely, Sharon	F	$ 4,574
12115	7/3/2004	CA	English, Melinda	F	$ 11,150
12116	7/3/2004	ME	Watterson, Barbara	F	$ 7,299
12117	7/3/2004	CA	Pacioli, Luca	M	$ 4,740
12118	7/3/2004	OK	English, Melinda	F	$ 6,614
12119	7/3/2004	IL	Halstead, Whitney	F	$ 3,444
12120	7/3/2004	CA	Minsky, Barbara	F	$ 5,593
12121	7/3/2004	WI	Gates, William	M	$ 4,482
12122	7/3/2004	IA	Flintsteel, Hillary	F	$ 6,464
12123	7/4/2004	NV	Kole, David	M	$ 10,064
12124	7/4/2004	MI	Pacioli, Luca	M	$ 5,480
12125	7/4/2004	IN	Goldman, Ted	M	$ 2,458
12126	7/4/2004	CA	Stonely, Sharon	F	$ 5,210
12127	7/4/2004	FL	Kahn, Phillipe	M	$ 6,390
12128	7/4/2004	TX	Manispour, Sharad	M	$ 10,225
12129	7/4/2004	NY	Chang, Annie	F	$ 3,085
12130	7/4/2004	OH	Gates, William	M	$ 9,821

FIGURE 5.29

Pivot table summarizing
sales data

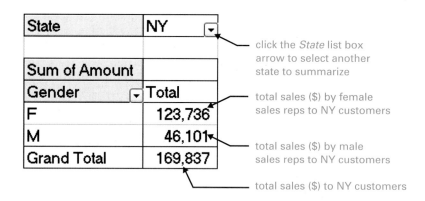

State	NY ▾
Sum of Amount	
Gender ▾	Total
F	123,736
M	46,101
Grand Total	169,837

— click the *State* list box arrow to select another state to summarize

— total sales ($) by female sales reps to NY customers

— total sales ($) by male sales reps to NY customers

— total sales ($) to NY customers

help yourself *Press **F1**, type **pivot table** in the Search text box of the Microsoft Excel Help task pane, and press **Enter**. Scroll the results panel, if necessary, and click the hyperlink **About PivotTable reports** to reveal information on creating pivot tables from data lists. You may want to click the **Print** icon on the Help toolbar to obtain a hard copy of the Help screen. Click the Help screen **Close** button when you are finished. Close the task pane*

When should you use a pivot table and when should you not? Pivot tables are useful to summarize data from a relatively long list of individual observations or transactions—hundreds or thousands of invoice lines for the year, a list of dates, times, and measurements of an experiment over time, or a long list of financial transactions. Extensive listings of observations logged into columns of characteristics provide the best material for creating revealing pivot tables. On the other hand, a pivot table is not useful to analyze data that are already in summary form. You can find many examples of already summarized data, data for which a pivot table makes little sense, maintained and available at the U.S. Census Bureau. They have collected thousands of statistical facts that summarize level of education by ethnicity, average income level by age, and so on.

Creating a Pivot Table

Alice wants you to create some pivot tables based on the raw data in the employee worksheet. Even though the list is short, there are several pieces of important information buried in the data list. For example, Alice would like a listing of the average salary by department. Then, she wants you to produce a breakdown of the employees by birth date so that she can get a better picture of the number of employees likely to retire in the next few years.

The best way to create a pivot table, especially if this is your first experience, is to use Excel's PivotTable Wizard. Like other Excel Wizards, the PivotTable Wizard guides you through a few steps to create a pivot table. You begin by opening the Employee workbook and then launching the PivotTable Wizard.

---

task reference   Creating a Pivot Table with the PivotTable Wizard

- Click **Data** on the Standard toolbar and then click **PivotTable and PivotChart Report**

- Specify the data's location (Excel worksheet, external data source, and so on)

- Select the **PivotTable** option

- Click the **Layout** button (Wizard step 3)

- Design the layout by selecting the column fields, row fields, page fields, and data fields, and click **OK**

- Designate a location for the pivot table: on its own, separate page, or embedded on an existing worksheet page, and click the **Finish** button

---

Creating a pivot table:

1. If you took a break since the last session, be sure to launch Excel, if necessary, open **Employee2.xls**, and immediately save the workbook under the name **Employee3.xls**

2. Click **Window** on the menu bar and then click **Unfreeze Panes** to remove the panes you established earlier

3. Click any cell within the list, click **Data** on the menu bar, and then click **PivotTable and PivotChart Report** to launch the Pivot Table and PivotChart Wizard (Step 1) as shown in Figure 5.30

    Specify the source of the data that you want to summarize, including all rows and header columns

FIGURE 5.30

First dialog box displayed
by the PivotTable Wizard

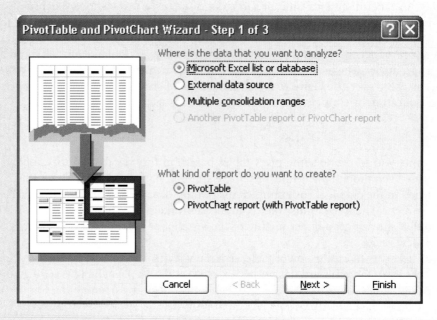

4. Click the **Microsoft Excel list or database** option button, if necessary,
click the **PivotTable** option button in the lower panel of the first pivot
table dialog box, and then click the **Next** button (see Figure 5.31)

FIGURE 5.31

PivotTable Wizard, Step 2

cell range of list
to analyze

In the second PivotTable Wizard dialog box you specify the exact cell
range containing the list (and column headers) to summarize. Because
you clicked a member of the list *before* launching the Wizard, Excel correctly identifies the boundaries of your list

5. Click the **Next** button to open the third step dialog box (see Figure 5.32)

FIGURE 5.32

PivotTable Wizard, Step 3

click to design the
layout of a pivot table

click to back up one step
and make adjustments

click to go to
the last step

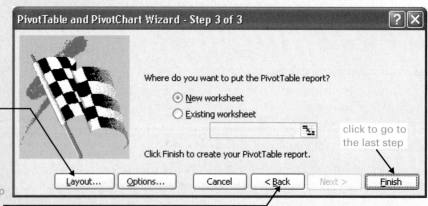

6. Ensure that the **New worksheet** option is selected to place the pivot
table on its own page and then click **Finish**. Excel creates an empty
pivot table on a new worksheet (see Figure 5.33)

FIGURE   5.33
Pivot table without data

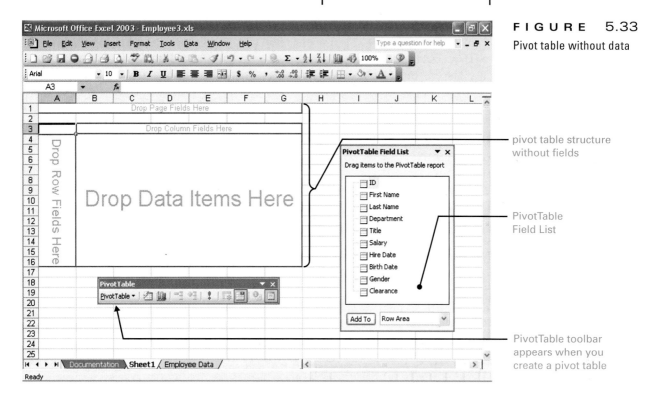

pivot table structure without fields

PivotTable Field List

PivotTable toolbar appears when you create a pivot table

Designing the Pivot Table Layout

You can define the initial layout of a pivot table within the framework of the PivotTable report. You select the fields you want to place in the row field, column field, page field, and data field whose design is outlined in the empty pivot table report framework. Into the data field of the pivot table frame, you drop the field name(s) from the data list that you want to summarize—to count, sum, average, and so forth. The PivotTable toolbar (see Figure 5.33 and Figure 5.34) contains field buttons that correspond to the list's

FIGURE   5.34

PivotTable toolbar tools

Toolbar Icon	Button Name	Description
PivotTable ▾	PivotTable	Drop-down that displays shortcut menu of pivot table commands
	Format Report	Displays a list of pivot table report styles
	Chart Wizard	Creates a chart sheet from a pivot table
	Hide Detail	Hides detail lines of a pivot table field
	Show Detail	Reveals detail lines of a pivot table field
	Refresh External Data	Updates a pivot table after you have made changes to the underlying data
	Include Hidden Items in Totals	Items you have hidden are still counted in the PivotTable totals
	Always Display Items	Controls when Excel goes to an external data source to determine a pivot table value
	Field Settings	Opens the PivotTable Field dialog box containing options you can apply to the selected pivot table field
	Hide/Show Field List	Toggles between hiding and displaying the field list

EXCEL

field names. You can drag a field name button to any of the four areas of the pivot table framework—Drop Row Fields Here, Drop Column Fields Here, Drop Page Fields Here, or Drop Data Items Here—to design the layout of the pivot table.

The first pivot table you will create is average salary by department and gender. The values of the department will appear as row labels and the gender values will be column headings. In the Data Items area will be the expression that averages the Salary column in each of the several groups defined by department/gender value pairs. Create the pivot table layout next.

---

task reference   **Selecting Pivot Table Fields**

- Click and drag each field containing the data you want to summarize to the **Drop Data Items Here** area of the pivot table framework

- Click and drag each field you want to appear in columns to the **Drop Column Fields Here** area of the pivot table framework

- Click and drag each field you want to appear in rows to the **Drop Row Fields Here** area of the pivot table framework

- Click and drag each field you want to appear in pages to the **Drop Page Fields Here** area of the pivot table framework

---

Creating the pivot table layout:

1. Click and drag **Department** from the PivotTable Field List to the **Drop Row Fields Here** area of the pivot table framework. After you release the mouse, the Department field appears with a list arrow at the top of the Drop Row Fields Here area

tip: _If you click and drag the wrong field to the pivot table frame, remove the field by clicking the field button and dragging it anywhere off the pivot table frame_

2. Scroll the PivotTable Field List, if necessary, to reveal the Gender field, and then click and drag **Gender** from the PivotTable Field List to the **Drop Column Fields Here** area of the pivot table framework

3. Click and drag **Salary** from the PivotTable Field List to the **Drop Data Items Here** area of the pivot table framework. After you release the mouse, values immediately appear in rows and columns corresponding to the salary of each department by gender (see Figure 5.35)

tip: _The Sum of Salary button at the intersection of the row and column headings indicates the type of statistic displayed in the data area of the pivot table—salary sums_

SUM is the default function Excel uses for numeric fields placed in the Drop Data Items Here area of a pivot table. You can change the function to any of several other available statistical functions including COUNT, AVERAGE, MAX, MIN, PRODUCT, and others. The default function for nonnumeric data is COUNT. To change the summary value function displayed in the pivot table data field, simply click the Field Settings button on the PivotTable toolbar and select the summary function from the list Excel displays. Next, you will modify the numeric function summarizing the data from SUM to AVERAGE so that you can display average salaries by department and gender.

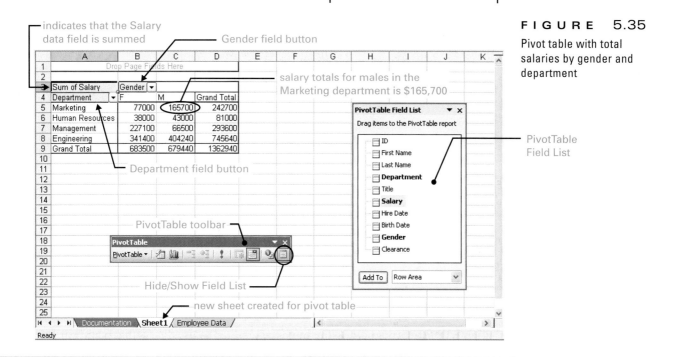

FIGURE 5.35

Pivot table with total salaries by gender and department

Selecting another pivot table summary function:

1. Click anywhere inside the pivot table framework and then click the **Field Settings** button on the PivotTable toolbar. The PivotTable Field dialog box opens

2. Click **Average** in the *Summarize by* list box (scroll the list box, if necessary) (see Figure 5.36)

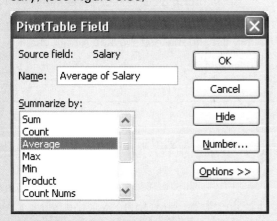

FIGURE 5.36

PivotTable Field dialog box

3. Click **OK** to return to the PivotTable report. The report displays the average salary by department and gender (see Figure 5.37)

4. Save the altered workbook under its current name, **Employee3.xls**

Changing the Formatting of a Pivot Table

The values in a pivot table are computed as part of the pivot table itself and cannot be changed manually. However, you can affect the formatting of the pivot table's contents. Additionally, you can change the calculations, field arrangement, and number of fields in a pivot table after it is created. One of the changes you may make to a pivot table's

FIGURE 5.37

Pivot table showing
average salaries by
gender and department

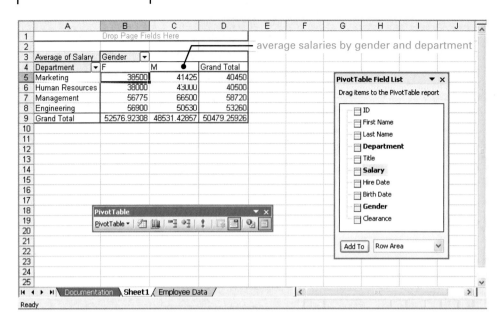

values is its formatting. While you might be tempted to use the Format menu bar command to modify the appearance of cells, be aware that Excel discards any formatting you apply through the Format menu whenever you rearrange a pivot table or refresh its contents. Instead, use the pivot table–supplied formatting commands. That way, Excel maintains the formatting even if you rearrange the table.

---

task reference   **Formatting Pivot Table Fields**

- Select any cell in the pivot table data item area

- Open the PivotTable toolbar, click **Field Settings**, and click the **Number** button

- Select a format from the Category list and make associated format choices

- Click **OK** to close the Format Cells dialog box and then click **OK** to close the PivotTable Field dialog box

---

Formatting pivot table values with a currency style:

1. Select cell range **B5:D9**

2. If necessary, display the PivotTable toolbar and then click the **Field Settings** button on the PivotTable toolbar. The PivotTable Field dialog box opens (see Figure 5.36)

3. Click the **Number** button on the PivotTable Field dialog box to open the Format Cells dialog box

4. Click **Accounting** in the Category list, double-click the **Decimal Places** spin box, type **0**, click the **Symbol** list box, and click **$**

5. Click **OK** to close the Format Cells dialog box, and then click **OK** to close the PivotTable Field dialog box

6. Click any cell within the pivot table to deselect the cell range. Excel formats the pivot table numeric entries (see Figure 5.38)

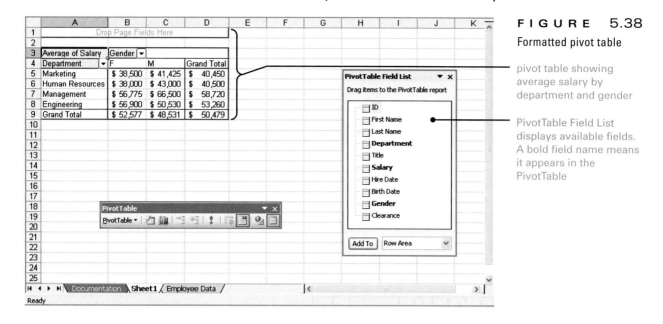

FIGURE 5.38

Formatted pivot table

pivot table showing average salary by department and gender

PivotTable Field List displays available fields. A bold field name means it appears in the PivotTable

The numbers in the pivot table look much better formatted, especially the Grand Total row (row 9), which contains averages rather than grand totals.

Rotating Pivot Table Fields

Perhaps the single most impressive feature of pivot tables is that you can rotate or pivot the values in pivot table column and row fields. By simply dragging a row or column button in a pivot table to a column or row position, you pivot the data to view it from a different perspective. For example, Alice wants to look at the departmental average salaries from a slightly different angle—with two rows for gender and the departments listed across four columns. She asks you to rotate the data so that she can see what new information the table reveals.

Rotating pivot table fields:

1. Move the mouse over the Gender field button appearing above cell B3 until the mouse changes to a four-headed arrow

2. Click the **Gender** field button and drag it below the Department field button—on top of the Marketing label in the PivotTable

3. Release the mouse button. The pivot table is reorganized so that the Gender is listed in the leftmost column and Department labels are listed in the column to the right

tip: Click **Edit** and then click **Undo** and repeat steps 2 and 3 if you do not get the described result

4. Hover the mouse over the Department field button in the PivotTable until the mouse changes to a four-headed arrow, click the **Department** field button, and then drag the field button up and just to the right of the Average of Salary label—over cell B3

5. Release the mouse button. Excel displays Gender in two rows and Departments in four columns. You may have to drag the PivotTable toolbar or the PivotTable Field List out of the way to see the entire PivotTable (see Figure 5.39)

EXCEL

FIGURE 5.39

Rearranged pivot table
fields

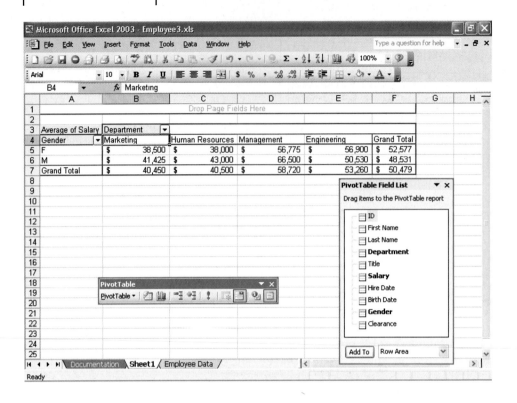

Removing and Adding Pivot Table Fields

You can change the composition of a pivot table anytime you want. If you decide that you want to see average salaries of males versus females regardless of the departments in which they work, you can remove the Department field from the pivot table. If you want to see finer details about salaries, you might want to examine average salaries by gender and clearance level among departments by adding the Clearance field to the pivot table. And, you can even examine salaries by age groups.

Removing a Pivot Table Field

Alice realizes that comparing salaries by considering only gender is misleading. There are a number of other factors that affect average salary of Comsec employees, such as seniority and clearance level. Nonetheless, she is interested in comparing the companywide difference between the average salaries of females versus males. Creating the pivot table to compute that value involves removing the Department data field from the pivot table.

Removing a field from a pivot table:

1. Click the **Department** field button and drag it to any cell *outside* the pivot table range. When the field button is no longer inside the pivot table, the mouse pointer changes to a small button displaying a red X below it—a symbol used throughout Microsoft Office to indicate *delete*

2. Release the mouse button. The pivot table is rearranged to display average salaries for males and females. When you remove a field, the original data remains unchanged—only the pivot table changes (see Figure 5.40)

Adding a Pivot Table Field

You can add any field to a pivot table that is identified as a column name and displays in the PivotTable toolbar. Simply click and drag one of the field buttons from the PivotTable toolbar to a row field, a column field, or a page field. Add the Clearance column to the column field in the pivot table and add the Department field to the row field to the left of the Gender button in the PivotTable.

FIGURE 5.40

Pivot table with field removed

	A	B	C
1	Drop Page Fields Here		
2			
3	Average of Salary		
4	Gender ▼	Total	
5	F	$52,577	
6	M	$48,531	
7	Grand Total	$50,479	
8			

Adding a field to a pivot table:

1. Click the **Clearance** field button found in the PivotTable Field List

tip: *If you do not have a PivotTable Field List visible, simply click the Hide/Show Field List button on the PivotTable toolbar (see Figure 5.35)*

2. Drag the **Clearance** field button to the column field in the pivot table (cell B3) and release the mouse button. Excel reorganizes the table to display average salaries with Gender in rows and Clearance across four columns

3. Click the **Department** field button, found in the PivotTable Field List, and drag it just to the right of the Gender button so that the mouse pointer hovers over the Gender list arrow and the large gray insertion I-beam appears to the right of the Gender field button (see Figure 5.41)

field button while being dragged to the pivot table

	A	B	C	D	E	F	G
1			Drop Page Fields Here				
2							
3	Average of Salary	Clearance ▼					
4	Gender	C	N	S	TS	Grand Total	
5	F	$ 75,700	$ 38,333	$ 57,433	$ 49,400	$ 52,577	
6	M	$ 38,900	$ 42,467	$ 54,657	$ 43,513	$ 48,531	
7	Grand Total	$ 57,300	$ 40,400	$ 55,938	$ 46,457	$ 50,479	
8							

gray I-beam indicates position of a proposed new field prior to releasing the mouse button

FIGURE 5.41

Adding a field to a pivot table

4. Release the mouse. Excel displays the newly rearranged format table, containing two row fields and one column field, to display average salaries broken out by Department, Gender, and Clearance level (see Figure 5.42). (You may want to drag the PivotTable Field list out of the way to see the pivot table)

You can sort a pivot table's row or column fields. Your pivot table Clearance fields may be listed in the same order as the custom sort order you created in Session 5.1: N, C, S, and TS. In any case, Alice wants the Clearance fields automatically sorted in ascending alphabetic order (C, N, S, and TS) each time the PivotTable report is updated. You do that next.

EXCEL

FIGURE 5.42

A three-field pivot table

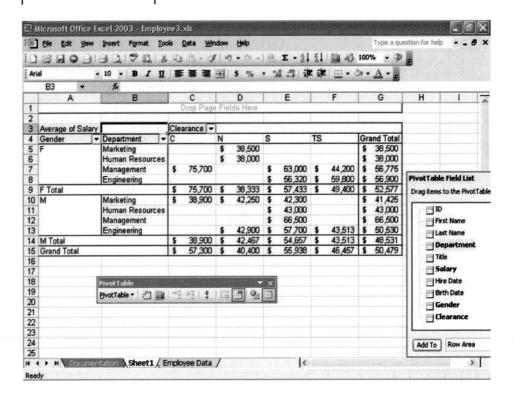

Sorting a pivot table by its column field:

1. Click any of the Clearance field column headers (N, C, S, or TS), and then click the **PivotTable** button located on the left end of the PivotTable toolbar. A menu of choices appears

2. Click **Sort and Top 10**. Excel displays the PivotTable Sort and Top 10 dialog box

3. Click the **Ascending** option button found in the AutoSort options panel, click the **Using field** list box, and click **Clearance** (if necessary). This designates the field that Excel will always keep in ascending order within a pivot table

4. Click **OK** to finalize your choices. Excel sorts the Clearance column labels and associated values into ascending order, left to right

Hiding Field Items

Perhaps the detail in a pivot table is too much, and you want to focus on one particular value. You can hide field items by clicking the list box arrow next to a field button and then select which items values you want to hide in a pivot table. Alice wants to produce two pivot table reports. The first one shows average salary by department and clearance level for males, hiding the information about females. The other report shows the same information for females, hiding the information about males. You produce the second report, female average salary information, next.

Hiding items in a pivot table:

1. Click the **Gender** list box arrow in the leftmost column of the pivot table to display a list of unique values constituting the Gender rank

2. Click the **M** check box to clear the checkmark and therefore hide the value of that item in the pivot table

3. Click **OK** to redisplay the pivot table with the male row information hidden

4. Print the report

5. Repeat steps 1 through 4, but in step 2 click the **M** check box to place a checkmark in it and click the **F** check box to clear that check box

After you complete the last step of the preceding series of steps, the pivot table displays average salaries for males only in each department at each of the four clearance levels.

Using Page Fields

You can use a pivot table's Page field to hide and unhide one or more data items. Page fields provide a slice, or cross section, of your data. You can look at the effect of one particular variable by placing the column in which it resides into a page field. While row or column fields allow you to select some or all items from a list of unique values by using check boxes, a page field allows you to select all values or one particular value, similar to option buttons. Page fields are a great choice when you want to view each unique field by itself.

Creating a pivot table containing a page field:

1. Click the **Employee Data** sheet tab to make that sheet active and click cell **D3** to make that cell active

2. Click **Data** on the menu bar and then click **PivotTable and PivotChart Report**. The first PivotTable Wizard dialog box opens

3. Click the **Microsoft Excel list or database** option, click the **PivotTable** option, and click the **Next** button

4. Click **Next** to accept the suggested cell range displayed in Step 2. An information dialog box opens explaining that a new report will use less memory if you base it on an existing report. Since this is unimportant for these two small pivot tables, click **No** to proceed

5. If necessary, click the **New worksheet** option to create the pivot table in a new worksheet, and then click the **Layout** button to specify the row, column, and page fields. The *PivotTable and PivotChart Wizard Layout* dialog box opens

6. Click the **Title** button and drag it to the **ROW** area of the layout in the dialog box, click the **Department** button and drag it to the **PAGE** area of the layout, and then click the **Salary** button and drag it to the **DATA** area of the layout. Excel labels it *Sum of Salary* (see Figure 5.43)

FIGURE 5.43

Selecting pivot table fields
in the PivotTable Wizard

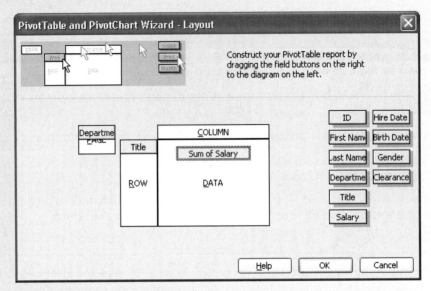

7. Double-click the **Sum of Salary** button in the DATA area of the pivot table layout to open the PivotTable Field dialog box, and click the **Average** function in the *Summarize by* list of functions

8. Format the entry by clicking the **Number** button, select **Accounting** in the Category list box, double-click the Decimal places text box, type **0**, select **$** in the Symbol list box, and click **OK** to close the Format Cells dialog box

9. Click **OK** to close the PivotTable Field dialog box, and then click **OK** to close the *PivotTable and PivotChart Wizard - Layout* dialog box

10. Click the **Finish** button. Excel creates a new worksheet containing the newly completed pivot table (see Figure 5.44)

FIGURE 5.44

Pivot table with a page
field

page field contains department names

row field displays
job titles

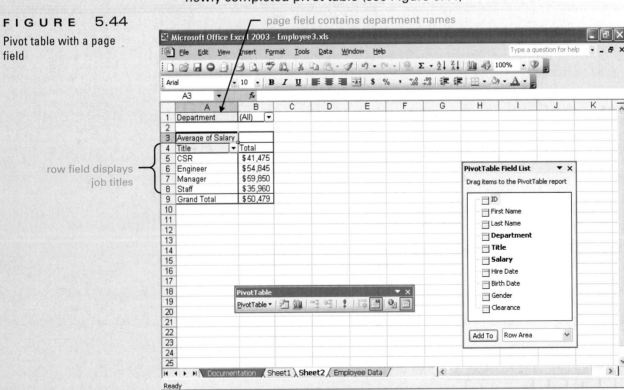

11. Click the **arrow** to the right of the Department button, click **Engineering**, and click the **OK** button located near the bottom of the list. The pivot table displays average salaries by job title for members of the Engineering department

12. Click the **arrow** to the right of the Department button, click **(All)**, and click the **OK** button located near the bottom of the list to redisplay the average salary by job title for all departments

Experiment with the page field by clicking the arrow and selecting other department names. Notice that you have two choices with a page field: All or a particular value. Unlike Row or Column fields, you cannot select two or three departments to display a salary summary.

Refreshing a Pivot Table

Pivot tables represent summary information computed from a data list. Because pivot table values are calculated from underlying data, you should not alter the pivot table values directly. However, any data list that underlies a pivot table is likely to change over time. Employees come and go, they get salary raises, and they are promoted. Perhaps you find it odd, but changing data in a pivot table's data list does not alter the values in the pivot table summarizing the list. Whenever you make a change to a data list that is summarized by a pivot table, you must *refresh* the pivot table, that is, make Excel recalculate the values in the pivot table based on the data list's current values.

First, look at Figure 5.44, cell B7, and observe that the average salary of all managers is $59,850. Melinda English has received a 10 percent salary increase following her very favorable semiannual performance review. Her new salary is $62,040. Update her salary and then observe the effect on the pivot table.

> **another word** ... **on Displaying Page Field Details**
>
> If you are ever curious about which rows of a data list make up a summary cell value appearing in a pivot table, you can double-click the cell in question. Excel will quickly create a copy of the source data—the list of all items in the source list that Excel used to calculate the value in a cell—in a separate worksheet. For example, the pivot table shown in Figure 5.44 indicates the average salary for managers is $59,850. Double-click cell B7 and Excel will provide a listing of all the managers' rows contributing to that statistic in a separate worksheet

Modifying a data list entry through a data form:

1. Click the **Employee Data** sheet tab to activate it, and then click cell **A3** to ensure that a cell within the data is active

2. Click **Data** on the menu bar and click **Form** to open the Employee Data form

3. Click the **Criteria** button, click in the **Last Name** text box, type **English**, and press the **Find Next** button. Excel displays the record for Melinda English

4. Double-click the **Salary** field, type **62040** to replace the old salary with the new one, and click the **Close** button to close the Employee Data form

5. Click the **Sheet2** sheet tab containing the pivot table displaying the average salary by job title. Notice that the average salary for managers—Melinda English has that job title—is unchanged at $59,850

EXCEL

It is clear that Excel does not automatically refresh a pivot table when the data in its underlying data list changes. You will have to do that manually.

anotherway
. . . to Refresh a
Pivot Table

Click any cell within the pivot table

Click **Data** on the menu bar and then click **Refresh Data**

Refreshing a pivot table:

1. Click any cell within the pivot table. (The pivot table *does not* include row 2 separating the Page field from the rest of the pivot table)

2. Click the **Refresh Data** [!] button on the PivotTable toolbar. Excel recalculates the pivot table values. Cell B7 displays $60,790, which is the updated average salary for all managers (see Figure 5.45). Cell B9 also changes because it is an overall average (though it is labeled "Grand Total")

FIGURE 5.45

Refreshed pivot table

	A	B	C
1	Department	(All) ▼	
2			
3	Average of Salary		
4	Title ▼	Total	
5	CSR	$41,475	
6	Engineer	$54,845	
7	Manager	$60,790	
8	Staff	$35,960	
9	Grand Total	$50,688	
10			

updated average salary value

Creating a Chart from a Pivot Table

Recall that one of the benefits of using pivot tables is that they display summaries such as averages, sums, and subtotals based on the current grouping you have defined. You can add a pivot chart to the report. Like the pivot table, a pivot chart changes as you change the pivot table to which it is linked. You can examine the impact of one data grouping of a data list by using a page field and plotting the results in a pivot chart.

You can create a chart from a pivot table just as you would with any other type of worksheet data by using the Chart Wizard or selecting the Chart command from the Insert menu. For convenience, the PivotTable toolbar contains a copy of the Chart Wizard button.

Alice wants to create a chart, which will graphically illustrate the differences in average salary among the four job titles currently held by Comsec employees. She also wants to examine average salaries between males and females with the same job title. Alice asks you to create a Clustered bar chart, based on the pivot table, displaying average salaries among those with the same job title.

Producing a chart from a pivot table:

1. Click any cell within the pivot table (probably on worksheet Sheet2) that you just created

2. Click the **Hide Field List** button on the PivotTable toolbar to hide the PivotTable Field List

3. Click the **Chart Wizard** button on the PivotTable toolbar. A Stacked column chart and Chart toolbar appear on a new chart sheet, Chart1

4. To see the chart without all the toolbars, click **View** on the menu bar and then click **Full Screen** (see Figure 5.46)

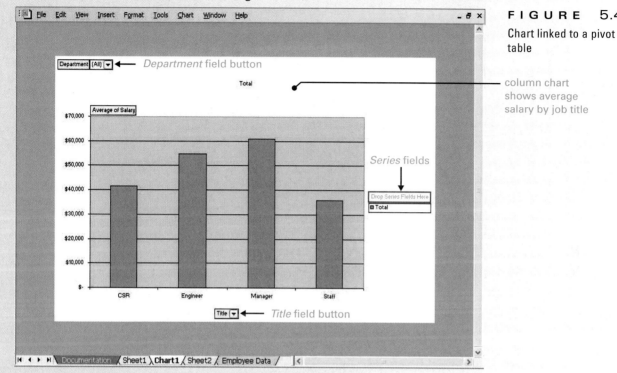

FIGURE 5.46

Chart linked to a pivot table

column chart shows average salary by job title

5. Restore the toolbars by clicking **View** on the menu bar and then clicking **Full Screen**

6. Click the **Chart Wizard** button on the PivotTable toolbar. The first of four Chart Wizard dialog boxes appears

7. Click **Bar** in the Chart type list box, click **Clustered Bar** (top row, first column) in the Chart subtype panel, and click the **Next** button. The *Chart Wizard - Step 3 of 4* dialog box appears

8. Double-click the **Chart title** text box to select all of its text, and then type **Average Salary by Department**

9. Click the **Category (X) axis** text box and type **Average Salary**, and then click the **Finish** button to complete the chart

10. Click the **Show Field List** button on the PivotTable toolbar to open the PivotTable Field List, and then click and drag the **Gender** field from the PivotTable Field List to the *Drop Series Fields Here* area on the right side of the chart

11. Click the **Hide Field List** button on the PivotTable toolbar to reveal more of the chart, right-click the PivotTable toolbar, and then click **PivotTable** in the list of toolbars to close it. Figure 5.47 shows the bar chart displaying average salaries by department

Pivot chart displaying
average salaries

click list arrow to display
data for all departments
or just one department

click list arrow to select
titles to hide or display

click arrow to
select *M, F,* or
(*Show All*)

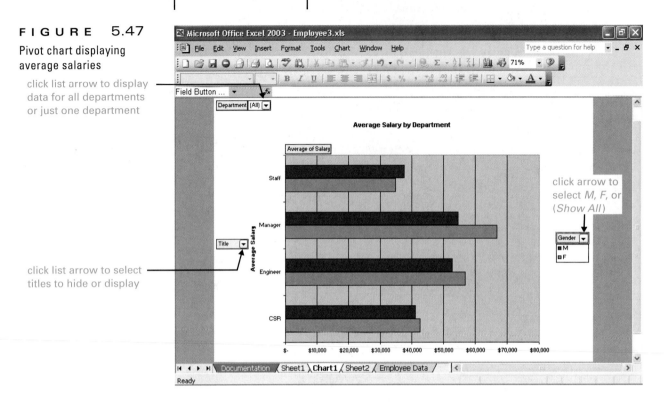

Finally, Alice wants you to print the entire workbook and save it.

Printing the Employee workbook and saving it in a new folder:

1. Click the **Documentation** sheet tab and type your name in cell C6 to the right of the label *Designer*

2. Click **File** on the menu bar, click **Print**, click the **Entire workbook** option button in the *Print what* panel, click the **Preview** button, adjust page margins, if necessary, and then click **Print** to print all worksheets in the Employee workbook

3. Click **File**, click **Save As**, and then click the **Create New Folder** button on the Save As toolbar to create a new folder

4. Type **Chapter5Complete** in the Name text box to create a folder name, click **OK**, click the **Save** button to save the workbook in the newly created folder

5. Click **File** and then click **Exit** to exit Excel

You show Alice your final workbook printouts. She is pleased with the results. Your pivot tables show the differences in average salaries by looking at different perspectives. The pivot table chart is an especially dramatic way to show the average salaries based on job titles and gender.

making the grade

1. Fields such as ID, LastName, Sex, and YearInSchool usually end up as _____ fields in a pivot table.

2. A field such as Salary, CommissionAmount, and Age usually ends up as _____ fields in a pivot table.

3. The default function that calculates pivot table summary information is what?

4. You can format a pivot table data field using the Format menu on the Standard toolbar or clicking the Number button on the PivotTable Field dialog box. Both format pivot table entries. Discuss the major advantage of using one method over the other.

5. You have created a pivot table from a list of products that you have sold during the week, but you discover a mistake in the sales price of two items. You make the change to the items in the list of sales. What else must you do to finalize your corrections?

SESSION 5.4 SUMMARY

An Excel list is a collection of data arranged in columns and rows in which each column displays one particular type of data. A label at the top of each column of the list identifies each column. To prevent the column-top labels from scrolling out of sight as you scroll down a long list, execute the Freeze Panes command on the Window menu. Using a data form facilitates adding, searching, and modifying a list. With the worksheet cursor inside the list, execute Form on the Data menu to create a form that uses the column labels for list box names.

Sort a data list on one column by making any cell in the column and in the list active and then clicking the Sort Ascending button or Sort Descending button on the Standard toolbar. More complicated sorts involving multiple columns require you to use the Sort command on the Data menu. You can sort data on up to three columns—a primary sort column and two tie-breaker columns. Blank fields always sort the corresponding row to the bottom of the list.

Apply an AutoFilter to a list to display rows satisfying criteria you select for one or more columns. Selecting match criteria on more than one column means multiple criteria must be true simultaneously for a row to remain in view. Excel hides other rows—those not matching the selection criteria. Criteria available through the AutoFilter list boxes are exact match criteria. More complex criteria such as selecting values greater than or equal to a particular value require the use of custom AutoFilters.

When you maintain data lists in order by one or more columns, you can use the Subtotal command to group and summarize the values in a group. Subtotal functions allow you to sum, average, and count values in numeric columns, and you can produce counts of character data. Using the outline buttons, you can expand or reduce the detail information visible in individual groups.

Pivot tables summarize lists by summarizing data based on one or more grouping criteria. You can choose from SUM, AVERAGE, COUNT, and several other aggregate functions in the data item area to summarize data based on row, column, and page fields consisting of columns. Pivot tables can reveal hidden information about groups of data in your lists. Pivot tables are also known as cross tabs or cross tab tables.

EXCEL

MICROSOFT OFFICE SPECIALIST OBJECTIVES SUMMARY

- Create and maintain a list—MOS XL03E-1-14
- Freeze rows and columns—MOS XL03S-5-6
- Create and use folders for workbook storage—MOS XL03S-5-9
- Sort a list on multiple sort keys—MOS XL03S-2-2
- Enter, search for, modify, and delete records in a list with a data form—MOS XL03S-1-2
- Group and outline structured data—MOS XL03E-1-3
- Create outlines and subtotals—MOS XL03E-1-1
- Create and apply conditional formatting—MOS XL03E-2-2
- Create filters and advanced filters with AutoFilter—MOS XL03E-1-2
- Use worksheet labels and names in formulas—MOS XL03E-1-14
- Create a pivot table and pivot chart—MOS XL03E-1-8

making the grade *answers*

SESSION 5.1

1. field

2. row

3. Freeze Panes

4. data form

5. custom

SESSION 5.2

1. Data, AutoFilter (and then filter the Location column with the address "Olin Hall").

2. Execute Data, Sort, select City in the Sort by list box, and select Bank Name in the Then by list box. The City (or whatever the column is labeled containing the city name) is the primary sort key, and Bank Name is the secondary sort key breaking ties in the City column.

3. Create an AutoFilter (Data, Filter, AutoFilter) and then create a custom filter (click Custom in the Salary list box) that reads "is less than or equal to" in the first Salary Custom AutoFilter text box and type "40000" in the second Salary Custom AutoFilter text box.

4. First, sort the customer list into order by customer name. Next, execute Data, Subtotals and specify "Customer" as the *At each change in* field on which subtotals are calculated. Click Sum in the *Use function* list box to produce a sum for each customer's sales. Check the Sales check box in the *Add subtotal to* list box to total the sales column.

5. The Conditional Formatting command found on the Format menu

SESSION 5.3

1. row, column, or page

2. data

3. SUM is the default function

4. Each time the pivot table refreshes data or changes, it "forgets' formatting applied through the Format menu. Formatting pivot table data cells within the PivotTable Wizard through the PivotTable Field dialog box applies formats that are not "forgotten" each time the pivot table is refreshed.

5. Refresh the pivot table

task reference summary

Task	Page #	Preferred Method
Freezing rows and columns	EX 5.5	• Select cell at upper-left corner • Click **Window**; click **Freeze Panes**
Adding a record to a list using a data form	EX 5.6	• Click list cell, click **Data**, click **Form** • Click **New**, type values in fields, press **Enter**, and click **Close**
Deleting a record from a list with a data form	EX 5.9	• Click list cell, click **Data**, click **Form** • Click **Criteria** button, Click **Find Next** as needed, click **Delete**, and click **OK**
Sorting a list on one column	EX 5.12	• Click cell in list • Click the **Sort Ascending** or **Sort Descending** button
Sorting a list on more than one field	EX 5.13	• Click list cell, click **Data**, click **Sort** • Specify Sort by and Ascending/Descending options • Repeat for up to two **Then by** fields • Click **OK**
Creating a custom sort order	EX 5.15	• Click **Tools**, click **Options**, click **Custom Lists** tab • Click **NEW LIST**, type each new member of the list in order • Click the **Add** button and click **OK**
Filtering a list with AutoFilter	EX 5.19	• Click list cell, click **Data** • Click **list arrow** on filtering column, click filter value from list
Clearing all AutoFilter filtering criteria	EX 5.21	• Click **Data**, point to **Filter** • Click **Show All** to remove all existing filters
Subtotaling a list's entries	EX 5.23	• Sort list by grouping column • Click a cell inside the list • Click **Data**, click **Subtotals** • Choose group column, choose aggregate function • Click **OK**
Displaying row or column headings on each page	EX 5.27	• Click **File**, click **Page Setup**, click the **Sheet** tab • Click **Collapse** dialog button on the **Specify Rows to repeat at top** or the **Specify Columns to repeat at left** • Specify row(s) or column(s) • Click **OK**
Applying a conditional format to cells	EX 5.30	• Click cell range to conditionally format • Click **Format**, Click **Conditional Formatting**, specify criteria • Click **Format** button on the Conditional Formatting dialog box and specify formatting options • Click **OK** • Click **OK**
Creating a pivot table with the PivotTable Wizard	EX 5.35	• Click **Data**, click the **PivotTable and PivotChart Report** • Specify the data's location • Select the **PivotTable** option and click the **Layout** button • Design pivot table layout by selecting row, column, data, and page fields and click **OK** • Designate location for pivot table as separate page or object on worksheet, click the **Finish** button
Selecting pivot table fields	EX 5.38	• Click and drag selected field(s) to summarize to Data Items area • Click and drag field buttons to Column, Row, and Page fields
Formatting pivot table fields	EX 5.40	• Select any cell in the pivot table data item area • Open the PivotTable toolbar, click **Field Settings**, and click the **Number** button • Select a format from the Category list and make associated format choices • Click **OK** to close the Format Cells dialog box and then click **OK** to close the PivotTable Field dialog box

EXCEL

TRUE OR FALSE

1. Never select the entire column you want to designate as the sort field.

2. The values of a pivot table can be changed manually.

3. Excel automatically refreshes a pivot table when the data in its underlying data list change.

4. You should resist the temptation to use the format menu bar command to alter a cell's appearance.

5. All, Top 10, and Custom are three filter choices that appear in all list columns.

FILL-IN

1. Pivot table fields correspond to _____ in a worksheet.

2. A(n) _____ sort key sorts the list on one column.

3. The easiest way to add a record to a long data list is to use a(n) _____ _____, which you access from the Data menu.

4. Use _____ (on the Data menu) to display only rows that match a particular value that you select from a list of values in the column's label list box.

5. You can display record groups on separate pages by inserting _____ _____(s) following each group in a list.

6. Use _____ _____ to format values in a special way for any values that match criteria for the cell range. For example, you can use this technique to display blue text for values less than $2,000.

MULTIPLE CHOICE

1. To which area would you not drag a field name button?
   a. Drop Row Fields Here
   b. Drop Column Fields Here
   c. Drop Page Fields Here
   d. Drop Data Items Here

2. A dialog box displaying one row of a list in text boxes is called a data
   a. label.
   b. marker.
   c. form.
   d. source.

3. The default Excel uses for numeric fields placed in the Drop Data Items Here area of a pivot table is
   a. AVERAGE.
   b. MAX.
   c. MIN.
   d. SUM.

4. What type of an operator compares two values?
   a. relational
   b. arithmetic
   c. mathematical
   d. comparison

5. The match criteria by which a field value matches a particular value are called
   a. primary.
   b. secondary.
   c. exact.
   d. object.

6. Sort form high to low order is called
   a. ascending.
   b. descending.
   c. primary.
   d. secondary.

REVIEW QUESTIONS

1. What is a list field and how is it related to record?

2. You have a long list of sales information including sales amount, salesperson, sale date, and customer city. What is a good way to create a worksheet showing total sales amount by city? Are there two different and equally good ways to approach this?

3. Explain why you must sort a list before using the Subtotals command. What would happen if you did not sort the list?

4. How is using a pivot table page field different from using a Row or Column field to select a particular value to summarize?

CREATE A QUESTION

For each of the following answers, create an appropriate, short question.

ANSWER	QUESTION
1. You have to sort the list first	_____
2. Click the Criteria button and type the field criteria	_____
3. Cells matching the criteria display with a special format	_____
4. Rows not matching the criteria are hidden	_____
5. Drag the field button to the Data Item area	_____
6. Drag the field button off the pivot table	_____

1. Filtering Fairmont Consulting's Charitable Contributions

Fairmont Consulting is a large computer consulting firm in northern California. Charles Fairmont, the CEO and founder of the firm, is well known for his philanthropic efforts. He believes that many of his employees also contribute to nonprofit organizations and wants to reward them for their efforts while encouraging others to contribute to charities. He started a program in which Fairmont Consulting matches 50 percent of each donation an employee makes to the charity of his or her choice. The only guidelines are that the charity must be a nonprofit organization and the firm's donation per employee may not exceed $500 a year.

Charles' assistant, Saundra, started an Excel file to record the firm's donations. Included are the day the request for a donation was submitted, the employee's name and ID number, the name of the charity, the dollar amount contributed by the firm, and the date the contribution was sent. Saundra wants you to give the completed record for December 2004 to the firm's accountants in order for the donations to be included in Fairmont's tax filings for the year.

1. Open the workbook **ex05Fairmont.xls** (see Figure 5.48) and save the workbook as **<yourname>Fairmont2.xls**

2. Add the following information:

Date Submitted:	**December 25, 2004**
Employee ID #:	**J24A**
Last Name:	**Greenburg**
First Name:	**Peter**
Organization:	**Leukemia Society**
Amount:	**$50**
Date Sent:	**December 29, 2004**
Date Submitted:	**December 27, 2004**
Employee ID #:	**1E5A**
Last Name:	**Taylor**
First Name:	**Steven**
Organization:	**Red Cross**
Amount:	**$200**
Date Sent:	**December 29, 2004**

3. Use the data form to determine how many organizations received single donations of over $100. Explain the steps you took

4. Sort the list alphabetically by organization and then by employee's last name. Include your name in the custom footer and then print the sorted list

5. Use the Subtotals command to total the contribution made per employee for the month of December. Print the sorted list

6. Use the AVERAGE function to determine the average donation made

7. Sort the list by donation value and compare these values to the average found in step 6. Include your name and print a list of all organizations that received a single donation above the average donation

FIGURE 5.48

Fairmont Consulting worksheet

	A	B	C	D	E	F	G	H
1	Submitted	Employee ID	Last Name	First Name	Organization	Amount	Donation Sent	
2	11/29/2004	688	Abbs	Don	Habitat for Humanity	$ 50	12/1/2004	
3	12/5/2004	08T	Adams	David	Red Cross	$ 100	12/6/2004	
4	12/9/2004	Y7CA	Ascott	Karen	Red Cross	$ 100	12/18/2004	
5	12/5/2004	M5NA	Bagby	Sharon	Rotary Club	$ 25	12/6/2004	
6	12/3/2004	39N	Butler	Barry	Rotary Club	$ 250	12/10/2004	
7	12/3/2004	0NNA	Clark	Jolene	Toastmasters	$ 20	12/5/2004	
8	12/2/2004	0NNA	Clark	Jolene	Make a Wish Foundation	$ 75	12/4/2004	
9	12/6/2004	0NNA	Clark	Jolene	Leukemia Society	$ 60	12/19/2004	
10	12/16/2004	CTBA	Donovan	Gary	Make a Wish Foundation	$ 130	12/21/2004	
11	12/12/2004	1XBA	Doster	Glenn	Amnesty International	$ 200	12/21/2004	
12	12/16/2004	L3H	Dunn	Elaine	Make a Wish Foundation	$ 225	12/29/2004	
13	12/4/2004	56NA	Foster	Scott	Rotary Club	$ 125	12/10/2004	
14	12/2/2004	56NA	Foster	Scott	Meals on Wheels	$ 125	12/26/2004	
15	12/17/2004	1F9A	Hughes	Gary	Red Cross	$ 50	12/22/2004	
16	12/27/2004	J5M	Johnson	Les	Foster Children's Fund	$ 25	12/30/2004	
17	12/10/2004	44JA	Kelleher	George	Romania Relief	$ 180	12/14/2004	
18	12/20/2004	57XA	Lomstein	Thomas	Meals on Wheels	$ 115	12/22/2004	
19	12/12/2004	FA5A	Peters	Roger	Toastmasters	$ 35	12/15/2004	
20	12/14/2004	FA5A	Peters	Roger	Foster Children's Fund	$ 80	12/19/2004	
21	12/6/2004	R9M	Simpson	Joseph	Red Cross	$ 50	12/19/2004	
22	12/13/2004	R9M	Simpson	Jospeh	Habitat for Humanity	$ 150	12/23/2004	
23	12/6/2004	08A	Thimsen	Timothy	Rotary Club	$ 50	12/14/2004	
24	12/3/2004	C3P	Warren	James	Lion's Club	$ 60	12/13/2004	
25	12/27/2004	R45A	Womak	Anthony	Habitat for Humanity	$ 100	12/29/2004	

Fairmont Data

Ready

2. Using Sorting and Filtering to Determine Top Students

Everingham Elementary School is preparing for the sixth-grade graduation ceremony. Part of the ceremony gives a special award for top students. One award is given to each male and female student with the highest scores in each of Math, English, and Science. Mrs. Moore is the only sixth-grade teacher, and she volunteered to compile a list of her students with grades above 95 percent in these subjects. She started the list, but fell ill and is unable to finish the list in time to prepare the awards.

You have been asked to finish the list and are given her work. Mrs. Moore has gathered the data in a spreadsheet called **ex05Grades.xls** (see Figure 5.49). Unfortunately, she also included all of her fifth-grade students with grades above 95 in these subjects.

1. Open the database **ex05Grades.xls**, save it as **<yourname>Grades2.xls** and begin by sorting by grades

2. Delete rows containing students in the fifth grade

3. Sort the list in descending order by Subject

4. Further sort the data within Subject by Grade in descending order. Include your name in a custom header and print the worksheet

5. Use the AutoFilter command to include only students whose Grade values are above 95. Print the worksheet

FIGURE 5.49

Everingham Elementary School Grades worksheet

	A	B	C	D	E	F	G	H	I	J	
1	Name	M/F	Grade Level	Subject	Grade						
2	Brewer, Patty	F	6	Math	99						
3	Carter, Gretchen	F	6	English	97						
4	Cox, Catherine	F	6	Science	96						
5	Dutton, Jennifer	F	5	Science	100						
6	Lawrence, Melanie	F	6	English	95						
7	Nichols, Saundra	F	6	Science	98						
8	Peters, Stephanie	F	5	Math	99						
9	Sharp, Susan	F	5	English	97						
10	Trotter, Megan	F	6	Math	100						
11	Vogel, Betsy	F	5	English	98						
12	Allen, David	M	6	Science	99						
13	Armstrong, Robert	M	5	Science	98						
14	Duran, Tony	M	6	English	100						
15	Fong, Peter	M	5	Math	95						
16	Hammer, Bill	M	5	English	95						
17	Jordan, Brian	M	6	Math	95						
18	Meyers, Phillip	M	6	Science	100						
19	Newman, Bruce	M	5	Math	98						
20	Silva, Paul	M	6	English	95						
21	Zappala, Chris	M	6	Math	100						
22											
23											
24											
25											

Grades

Ready

1. Filtering Soda Sales

Shores, Incorporated, manufactures and bottles 10 different types of soda, three of which are citrus noncola sodas. Shores decided a few years ago to focus on its citrus drinks division instead of colas, since its competition has been neglecting this area. Shores was expecting to capture a large portion of this market, but sales have not been strong in this area, and the company wants to focus its marketing efforts to further promote these drinks. The president of Shores feels that a factor in poor sales is that the firm has been spreading its efforts over the three different brands of citrus beverages. He wants to drop one of the brands. He has asked you to look at the drinks sales figures to help determine which drink of the three they should stop producing and which regions consume the most of Shore's noncola sodas.

You are given data for the past three months. It is sorted by month, brand of soda, in which region sold, and number of cases sold in thousands. Open the workbook **ex05Shores.xls** (see Figure 5.50) and use the Save As command in the File menu to save the workbook under the name **<yourname>Shores2.xls**. Improve the formatting of the data and bold the headers for each column. Sort the soda lists by product, within product by month, and within product and month by region. Use the Subtotals command to display total cases sold by brand of soda per region. Include your name in the custom header and print this list of subtotals. Sort the data by month and within month by region. The months should appear in order of March, April, and May. Print the list. Determine the firm's worst-selling brand of soda. Is this the brand that should no longer be produced? Determine which soda and region have the highest sales. Prepare a pivot table to provide you with this information. Summarize each month's sales using a pivot table. Use the Chart Wizard button on the PivotTable toolbar to create a bar chart of total cases sold by month. Print the pivot table and bar chart.

FIGURE 5.50

Shores, Incorporated, worksheet

	A	B	C	D	E	F	G	H	I	J	K
1	Month	Soda	Region	Cases Sold (thousands)							
2	March	Quench	Western	100							
3	March	Quench	Central	20							
4	March	Quench	Mountain	40							
5	March	Quench	Eastern	30							
6	March	Source	Western	80							
7	March	Source	Central	90							
8	March	Source	Mountain	90							
9	March	Source	Eastern	70							
10	March	Lucid	Western	25							
11	March	Lucid	Central	70							
12	March	Lucid	Mountain	60							
13	March	Lucid	Eastern	50							
14											
15	April	Quench	Western	120							
16	April	Quench	Central	40							
17	April	Quench	Mountain	30							
18	April	Quench	Eastern	30							
19	April	Source	Western	90							
20	April	Source	Central	70							
21	April	Source	Mountain	100							
22	April	Source	Eastern	60							
23	April	Lucid	Western	30							
24	April	Lucid	Central	40							

Shores Data

Ready

2. Analyzing Doctor's Information with Subtotals and Pivot Tables

Before choosing a doctor, several patients call Montgomery Hospital's Client Services office to get more information on the various doctors' backgrounds and experience. Since the hospital staff is overworked, the office manager, Alice Honeycutt, wants to prepare a database of information for quick reference in order to quickly answer questions. The most common questions from callers are about each doctor's specialty and the number of years that each doctor has been practicing medicine. Alice has compiled the necessary information, but needs help in making some corrections and summarizing the data. Open the workbook **ex05Doctors.xls** (see Figure 5.51) and use the Save As command in the File menu to save the workbook under the name **<yourname>Doctors2.xls**. Freeze the column headings for last and first name row labels.

Use the data form to find Robert Gordon's information. Change his years of experience to **20**. Find the information for Charlie Maxwell and change his years of experience to **27**. Sort the data by Specialty and within Specialty by years of experience (most to least). Add your name to the custom header and print the list. Apply conditional formatting so that the Experience field for doctors with fewer than eight years of experience is boldface. Print all doctors with less than eight years of experience, sorted by specialty. (*Hint:* Use AutoFilter.) Prepare a pivot table to summarize the average years of experience by specialty. Print the pivot table report. Format the average year's experience values to display two decimal places. Create a clustered bar chart showing the average years of experience by specialty (based on the pivot table you created). Place your name in the header and print the chart.

FIGURE 5.51

Montgomery Hospital Physician Data worksheet

	A	B	C	D	E	F	G	H	I
1	Last Name	First Name	Specialty	Years of Experience					
2	Conner	John	Pediatrician	10					
3	Simpson	Brad	Obstetrician	6					
4	Lordio	Marcus	Internal Medicine	8					
5	Gruber	Elliott	Pulmonologist	13					
6	Maxwell	Charlie	Surgeon	17					
7	Gonzolaz	Emilio	Pediatrician	28					
8	Wright	James	Pediatrician	22					
9	Cooper	Steven	Optometrist	35					
10	Carey	Michael	Cardiologist	5					
11	Bower	Martin	Orthopedist	9					
12	Sandler	John	Dermatologist	7					
13	Richards	Sean	Surgeon	27					
14	Newman	Christopher	Orthopedist	28					
15	Forrester	David	Pulmonologist	14					
16	Kelley	Michael	Obstetrician	11					
17	Schwartz	Edward	Internal Medicine	31					
18	Eaton	Adam	Dermatologist	4					
19	Nichols	Timothy	Cardiologist	29					
20	Peters	Scott	Internal Medicine	25					
21	Hodge	Dennis	Internal Medicine	21					
22	Barks	Louis	Surgeon	4					
23	Gordon	Robert	Orthopedist	18					
24	Johnson	Larry	Optometrist	18					
25	Bakker	Grant	Cardiologist	9					

Physician Data

Ready

1. Haller Electronics Online Store Initiative

Haller Electronics is an electronics manufacturer specializing in televisions, DVDs, and CD players. Haller Electronics targets the market of customers who know what they want to purchase and don't like the sales atmosphere of large electronics stores. Management decided to launch an online store for customers to buy their products. Brief descriptions and prices of each product would be included for a quick-and-easy purchasing experience. In attempting to stay truly Web based, Haller Electronics' Customer Service Department doesn't have a toll-free telephone number. Instead, customers can reach them through the firm's Web site or by sending e-mail to the department. Most customer service contacts are general inquiries. The manager of the Customer Service Department, Todd Felks, wants to ensure that customers are receiving timely responses from his staff.

Todd has taken a sampling of the customer requests and is looking at those received Monday and Tuesday of last week. Included are the date received, type of product the customer is inquiring about, whether the customer used the e-mail address or the Web site, date a response was sent, number of days it took to send the response, and name of the customer service specialist who handled it. To encourage staff to quickly expedite responses, a bonus program was started that rewards staff based on how quickly they respond. These figures are also included in the worksheet. Begin by opening **ex05Service.xls**, which includes all of this information (see Figure 5.52). Immediately save the worksheet as **<yourname>Service2.xls** to preserve the original worksheet.

Todd needs you to help organize this data for a presentation he must make to the board of the firm. First, sort the list in ascending order by the *Sent By* column. Within *Sent By*, further sort the ties in descending order by *Days*, and then sort in ascending order by *Specialist*. Include your name in the header and print the list.

Re-sort the data, first in ascending order by *Days* and then in ascending order by *Specialist* for matching *Days* field values. Print the list. From this, which method of inquiries is getting faster responses?

FIGURE 5.52

Haller Electronics worksheet

	A	B	C	D	E	F	G	H	I	J	K
1	**Received**	**Product**	**Sent By**	**Responded**	**Days**	**Specialist**	**Bonus ($)**				
2	Monday	CD	E-mail	Wednesday	2	Clark	10				
3	Monday	CD	E-mail	Thursday	3	Clark	5				
4	Monday	CD	E-mail	Tuesday	1	Gibbs	15				
5	Monday	CD	E-mail	Thursday	3	Newman	5				
6	Tuesday	CD	E-mail	Thursday	2	Newman	10				
7	Monday	CD	Web Site	Monday	0	Matus	20				
8	Tuesday	CD	Web Site	Wednesday	1	Clark	15				
9	Monday	DVD	E-mail	Wednesday	2	Kuhn	10				
10	Tuesday	DVD	E-mail	Thursday	2	Newman	10				
11	Monday	DVD	Web Site	Monday	0	Kuhn	20				
12	Monday	DVD	Web Site	Tuesday	1	Newman	15				
13	Monday	DVD	Web Site	Thursday	3	Clark	5				
14	Monday	DVD	Web Site	Monday	0	Gibbs	20				
15	Tuesday	DVD	Web Site	Tuesday	0	Gibbs	20				
16	Tuesday	DVD	Web Site	Wednesday	1	Kuhn	15				
17	Tuesday	DVD	Web Site	Tuesday	0	Gibbs	20				
18	Tuesday	DVD	Web Site	Wednesday	1	Gibbs	15				
19	Tuesday	DVD	Web Site	Wednesday	1	Kuhn	15				
20	Tuesday	DVD	Web Site	Tuesday	0	Matus	20				
21	Monday	DVD	E-mail	Wednesday	2	Matus	10				
22	Monday	TV	E-mail	Thursday	3	Gibbs	5				
23	Monday	TV	Web Site	Tuesday	1	Matus	15				
24	Monday	TV	Web Site	Monday	0	Newman	20				
25	Tuesday	TV	Web Site	Tuesday	0	Kuhn	20				

Service

Ready

2. Martin's Futures Trading

Martin's Futures Trading is one of the hottest online futures trading companies in the market today. The company's target clients are day traders, and Martin's offers direct access trading for real-time ordering. There are a vast number of tools and services that Martin's offers to its clients including technical resources, intraday charting, end-of-day charting, and simulated trading (for people just learning how the markets work). This organization specializes in developing and maintaining new client relations. Whether a new client is trading one contract on pork bellies or 1,000 contracts, George Cushing, director of Martin's client management organization, believes that the client needs to have knowledge and access to the tools and experts in that area of trade. Client management maintains all individual trading records for each client. Included in a trading record is client name, type of contracts, dollar value, number of trades per day, and tools utilized for that trade. George would like to personally review the new futures traders' transactions each week. Doing so allows him to contact those whom he thinks may benefit from expert direction or exposure to a new tool. He needs your help to accomplish this.

Begin by opening **ex05FuturesTrading.xls** (see Figure 5.53), which includes the previous week's trading records, and immediately save the worksheet as **<yourname>FuturesTrading.xls**. Create a filter that hides any clients who did not actually execute a trade (the Total Dollar Value column contains a zero). Next, sort the list in descending order by *Number of Contracts* and then by *Total Dollar Value*. Highlight light green any cell containing a dollar value that exceeds $50,000. Type your name into the header, print the worksheet, and print the worksheet formulas.

FIGURE 5.53

Martin's Futures Trading worksheet

	A	B	C	D	E
1	Name	Security Type	Number of Contracts	Total Dollar Value	Tools Utilized
2	White, George	Sugar	5	3570	Charts
3	Lee, Christopher	Treasury Bonds	8	88160	Consultation
4	Yang, Steve	Soybean Meal	2	3400	Literature
5	Peterson, Lance	Wheat	6	2436	Literature
6	Hogan, Barry	Hogs	10	43200	Charts
7	Nelson, Cindy	S&Ps	4	0	Consultation
8	Bonacci, Sam	British Pound	5	77100	Charts
9	Passero, Phil	Swiss Franc	8	54480	Charts
10	Stone, Julia	Copper	3	21090	Literature
11	Glander, Irene	Lumber	6	10200	Charts
12	Santoli, Timothy	Gold	7	2205	Consultation
13	Gorman, Dennis	S&Ps	23	20240	Literature
14	White, George	Wheat	9	3654	Charts
15	Lee, Christopher	Soybean Oil	6	9240	Consultation
16	Yang, Steve	Swiss Franc	7	47670	Literature
17	Peterson, Lance	Treasury Bonds	11	121220	Consultation
18	Hogan, Barry	Lumber	10	17000	Consultation
19	Nelson, Cindy	Copper	6	10380	Literature
20	Bonacci, Sam	Soybean Meal	3	5100	Charts
21	Passero, Phil	Wheat	7	2842	Charts
22	Stone, Julia	Soybeans	2	1114	Consultation
23	Glander, Irene	Wheat	7	2842	Literature
24	Santoli, Timothy	Lumber	8	13600	Charts
25	Gorman, Dennis	Gold	1	315	Consultation

EX 5.62

1. Analyzing California's Weather Patterns

Kevin Towers is the sales manager of the Kansas City office of a golfball manufacturing firm based in Michigan. For the past 18 months, his team has had record sales for its territory, and its sales were higher than any other offices. Management knows that Kevin's approach to teaching and motivating his staff has been greatly responsible for the phenomenal figures. To reward Kevin, and to hopefully spread his team's performance, he has been given the opportunity to spend four months in any of the firm's offices in California.

Kevin gladly accepts the offer and starts looking into where he wants to go. He decides he wants to be in a coastal city, and the firm has offices in San Diego, Los Angeles, and San Francisco. He will be in California from January 1 to April 30. Because he hasn't visited any of these three cities and wants to get in a lot of golf time, Kevin determines the main factor that will affect his decision is weather.

Begin by setting your browser to www. weather.com and locate the box in which you can enter the city or zip code for which you want information. Enter **San Diego, CA** and when the data appears, click the **Averages and Records** tab. Print this page and repeat this for Los Angeles and San Francisco. As Kevin is trying to predict the temperature and potential rainfall, focus on the Monthly Average and Records section on the top of the page. Do the following:

Create a spreadsheet to summarize the information you find. Record the temperature and rainfall in columns, and group the cities into four groups of rows labeled Average High, Average Low, Mean, and Average Precipitation. Fill in the appropriate data for each city and month. Because rain is Kevin's greatest concern, use conditional formatting to display the months with an average precipitation below 2.5 inches in blue and apply boldface. Place your name in a custom header and print the list. Prepare and format a pivot table summarizing total average precipitation by city. Print the pivot table. Print the new pivot table. Kevin also wants to be in the warmest weather possible while in California. Use conditional formatting to display the months with average high temperatures above 65 degrees in red and apply boldface. Print this worksheet. Looking at the average high temperatures above 65 degrees and average precipitation below 2 inches, to which city do you think Kevin should relocate? Explain your answer.

2. Analyzing Differences in Salaries

Howard Parker has just completed his MBA and has received several exciting job offers in the area of project management. He has lived in Austin, Texas, for most of his life and is looking to make a change. Since he received job offers from around the country, Howard has the opportunity to finally make a change and move to a new location. His problem is deciding which offer to take. All of his friends tell him to accept the job with the highest salary offer, but Howard knows it isn't that simple. Due to the great differences in cost of living, he knows he can't just look at the dollar figures; he must figure out which will give him the greatest standard of living. Howard decided that he must make the equivalent of a $65,000 salary in Austin—no matter where he moves.

Open **ex05Salaries.xls**, which contains information on the Howard's different job offers and save it as **<yourname>Salaries2.xls**. Go to www.homefair.com and click on the **moving** tab at the top of the page. Click the link **the salary calculator**™ found under the heading *Browse Categories*. This tool will enable you to help Howard figure out the equivalent of a $65,000 salary in each of the cities where he was offered a job. Follow the prompts on the Web site to enter Austin, Texas, as where moving from with a $65,000 salary. Run a calculation for each of the cities in which he was offered a job. Be sure to include that he wants to own a home, not rent. Input all of the salary equivalents in the Austin Eq. column. Type **Difference** in cell E1 and then create formulas in column E that calculate the difference between his offered salary and desired salary for each state. Include your name and print this spreadsheet.

Use the AutoFilter command to display only those offers that have a difference of $5,000 or more. Based on this, if Howard's main desire is having the greatest standard of living, which offer should he accept?

around the world

1. Analyzing Global Marketing Opportunities

Gretchen Kadletz had been a part-time tennis instructor for several years. As she had grown frustrated with the tennis equipment available in the market, she started her own company. With the aid of her attorneys and investors, she founded ProSwing to design tennis equipment and apparel.

Gretchen was able to develop a strong product line and was becoming successful in the United States. The area in which she was having trouble was the firm's international marketing strategy. One of her close friends, Susan Rawlings, suggested that Gretchen advertise the most effective way—by getting players to use and wear her products. While this was a good idea, Gretchen was not quite satisfied. She wanted to be sure that the players using her line were the players followed by the fans (her target market). She knew that this would bring ProSwing attention from tennis players around the world. She decided to concentrate on the tennis players with the highest current winnings, since they were likely to be very popular and visible to the fans. She would approach the top 25 international men and women players about using ProSwing products. She would then additionally advertise during tennis matches in the four countries most represented by the top 50 players in order to represent both the men and women top players.

Gretchen's assistant prepared a spreadsheet after finding recent sport statistics on the Web and compiled data on the top players. Included in the spreadsheet are the player's name, country of residence, most recent winnings, and gender. Currently, this database isn't very helpful to Gretchen and she needs your help to organize the data to plan her international strategy.

Begin by opening **ex05Tennis.xls** and then saving it as **<yourname>Tennis2.xls**. Sort the data in descending order by Winnings. Select and bold the data for the 25 players with the highest winnings. These are the players Gretchen will approach to use and wear ProSwing products. Include your name and print the data. Include your name in the worksheet header and print the worksheet. Remove bold from the 25 highest winners.

Next, sort the data in ascending order by Country and then in descending order by Winnings within each Country. Change the order of the columns so that Country is the first column, followed by Winnings, and then Player. Print the worksheet.

Use the Subtotals command to compute the total winnings for country. Collapse the subtotals so that only the country names and their totals appear, not the individual players or their genders. Ensure that all columns are wide enough. Print the Subtotaled worksheet.

2. Varoom Automotive Components

Julie Brown is Varoom's director of quality for worldwide motor manufacturing. Warranty issues are a major contributor to customer quality performance. Julie needs to track warranty claims for each manufacturing site. The customer quality engineers gather warranty information from the car manufacturers' database systems each month and then enter the data into a shared spreadsheet on the company's secure Web site. From the warranty information, Julie can decide which sites need her help in developing action plans to reduce warranty claims. Her sites' performance and action plans will then be presented at the quarterly director's meeting with Varoom's president.

Julie needs your help in organizing the data for her next meeting. Begin by opening **ex05Varoom.xls** and immediately save as **<yourname>Varoom.xls**. Begin by sorting the data in ascending order by these sort keys (simultaneously): Plant Location, Application, and Motor Description. Using the PivotTable Wizard, create a pivot table for Julie to show her an alternative approach to presenting the data. Within the PivotTable Wizard, drop *Motor Description* into the row field and drop *Plant Location* into the column field. Drop *% Defective* into the data items area. Finally, drop *Application* into the page field. Be sure to select **all** in the page field. Change the default SUM function to MAX for the numeric field using *Field Settings* in the *PivotTable* toolbar. Format the cells to display only two decimals. Before printing the document, format the data in the columns: Open the PivotTable toolbar, select **Table Options**, and click **Preserve formatting**. Next, right-align the column fields and data items. Select all worksheet tabs (press **Ctrl** and click each worksheet tab, in turn), type your name in all the worksheet headers, and print the entire workbook. Demonstrate to Julie the pivot table's flexibility by selecting *GM* as the only application's result to be displayed. Print this page also.

running project

Pro Golf Academy

Betty Carroll has obtained data from the cash registers showing sales for October of men's and women's golf shirts. She wants you to produce and print four reports described below. Each pivot table should be placed on a separate worksheet. Open **ex05ProGolf.xls** and save it as **<yourname>ProGolf5.xls**. Then do the following:

The first report is a pivot table listing total sales of all products broken out by *Item Name* and *Collection*. Figure 5.54 shows an example of this pivot table. The data item is the sum of the *Extended* column. The Row field is *Item Name*, and the Column field is either *women's* or *men's*. Format the sums to display the currency symbol and two decimal places. Produce column totals for men's and women's, but do not produce row totals. Rename the worksheet tab *Report 1.* Place your name in the worksheet header and print the worksheet containing this pivot table in landscape orientation.

The second report, also a pivot table, displays the sum of the *Total Sale* field for each Item Name and each Size. Place the *Item Name* in the Row field, the *Size* in the pivot table Column field, and

Collection in the Page field. Do not produce row totals in the pivot table, but allow column totals. Format the sums with currency symbols and two decimal places. Rename the worksheet tab *Report 2.* Place your name in the worksheet header and print this second pivot table worksheet in landscape orientation.

For the third report, Betty wants a list of all products in ascending order by Collection (1st), Item Name (2nd), and Date (3rd). Produce a subtotal of the Extended values for each unique Item Name, and ensure that each printed page prints the header row, which contains the column names. Place your name in the worksheet header, and print the third pivot table worksheet in landscape orientation. (*Hint:* Widen the column containing the grand total extended price.)

For the fourth report, use the Outline buttons to display only the subtotals by Item Name. Ensure that column A is wide enough to display the entire label for each product name—including the word *Total.* Print the summary report in landscape orientation. Based on this last report, which item has the largest dollar sales volume?

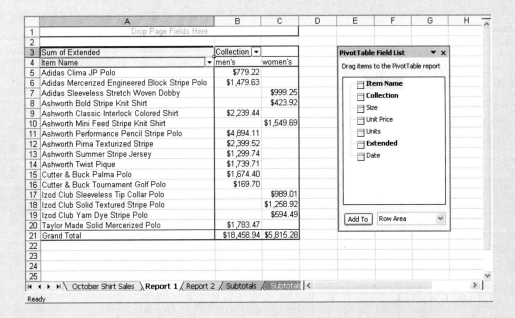

FIGURE 5.54

Pro Golf Academy example pivot table

1. Format? Format!

You have the choice of formatting a column of cells using the Conditional Formatting command or using the Cells command—both on the Format menu. Explain the difference between the two. For example, suppose you want to display all values in column A that are less than 40,000 in blue text. You could select the existing values meeting those requirements, select Format, Cells, and then apply a Font color. Or you could use conditional formatting to do the same thing. What is the advantage of conditional formatting over "conventional" formatting?

2. Pivot Table Revelations

What's the big deal about pivot tables? You have a long list of college alums and their donations. The list contains alums' names, addresses, cities, states, year of graduation, and last year's donation amount. There are over 25,000 alums in the list. What on earth does a pivot table provide that standard AVERAGE, SUM, and MAX functions do not? Describe a useful bit of information a pivot table could reveal from such a list that a fund-raiser might find helpful.

6

Employing Functions

know? *did you*

the *Ross Ice Shelf, a very small portion of Antarctica, is hundreds of feet thick and about the same size in land area as France.*

in *the United States before 1933, the dime was legal as payment only in transactions of $10 or less. In that year, Congress made the dime legal tender for all transactions.*

since *the Lego Group began manufacturing blocks in 1949, more than 189 billion pieces in 2,000 different shapes have been produced. This is enough for about 30 Lego pieces for every living person on Earth.*

you *can replace absolute cell references in expressions with what? Find out how in this chapter.*

Chapter Objectives

- Develop separate assumptions and output sections of a worksheet
- Use Insert Function to help write worksheet functions— MOS XL03S-2-3
- Provide data validation for selected worksheet cells— MOS XL03E-1-4
- Define and use names in functions in place of cell references— MOS XL03E-1-14
- Apply and modify cell styles—MOS XL03S-3-2
- Investigate the logical function IF—MOS XL03S-2-4
- Write the index function VLOOKUP—MOS XL03E-1-9
- Write financial functions including PV, PMT, PPMT, and IPMT— MOS XL03S-2-4
- Write and apply the NOW date function—MOS XL03S-2-4

Cal Whittington Automobiles

Cal Whittington, owner of Cal Whittington Automobiles, or "Cal's Cars," has a medium-sized automobile dealership in Muncie, Indiana. Cal's reputation for honesty and integrity is known throughout Indiana, and his funny (some say, silly) television advertising has helped spread the word about his automobiles. Cal has a trained staff of salespersons and sells both new and used automobiles. Each salesperson's desk contains a personal computer that the salespersons can use to request credit histories of customers, do worksheet calculations using Excel, and search a car database listing cars both on their lot and in neighboring cities. Having an Internet connection is handy for the salespersons, because they can locate a requested make and model of just about any car or truck from a network of dealerships that work together to provide cars to each other.

In addition to selling automobiles, Cal's dealership also provides financing for both the new and used vehicles they sell. By having their own financing within the dealership, Cal's makes a small profit through its increased interest rates and provides convenient, no-hassle financing for customers who might have difficulty obtaining a consumer loan elsewhere. Whenever a customer requests Cal's dealership to provide financing, the salesperson asks the customer to fill out a form and then the salesperson obtains the customer's credit history and rating from credit reporting agencies such as Equifax (www.Equifax.com),

TransUnion (www.transunion.com), or Experian (www.experian.com). Then, the salesperson fills out an online form with the finance details including the customer's down payment, car purchase price, and loan information and electronically transmits the information to another location for processing. It takes as much as 20 minutes to receive the loan information results back from the processing center.

The report shows loan details such as the customer's name, loan amount, and interest rate. In addition, it contains a loan payment and amortization schedule showing details about each loan payment throughout the life of the loan. Cal's salespersons want to provide the loan information more quickly and have asked Cal to look into eliminating the step of submitting information to the processing center and instead using an Excel template on each salesperson's computer to speed report production. Cal agrees that doing so would be a great time-saver.

Jessica Allison, Cal's financial manager, has asked you to produce a simple loan information and amortization worksheet that salespersons can use to show customers details about their loans whenever Cal's company provides the financing for a sale. Jessica has dubbed it the Loan Analysis worksheet. Figure 6.1 shows an example of a completed Loan Analysis worksheet. Use that as a guideline as you create the report and enhance it by following the steps in this chapter.

FIGURE 6.1

Completed Loan Analysis worksheet

	A	B	C	D	E	F	G	H	I
1	**Assumptions**				**External Data**				
2	Customer Name	Francis Parker			Credit Rating	Interest Rate			
3	FICO Credit Rating	755			500	10.75%			
4	Purchase Price	$ 21,000			600	8.50%			
5	Down Payment	$ 3,000			700	7.50%			
6	Loan Term	3	(years)		800	6.50%			
7	Application Date	6/14/2004							
8									
9	**Outputs**								
10	Payment:	$ 559.91	per month			Today's Date:	6/23/04		
11	Interest Rate:	7.50%	per year						
12	Loan Term:	3	years						
13	Loan Amount:	$ 18,000.00							
14	Assessment:	$ 300.00							
15	Payment	Beginning Balance	Principal Paid	Interest Paid	Total Principal	Total Interest	Ending Balance		
16	1	$ 18,000.00	$ 447.41	$ 112.50	$ 447.41	$ 112.50	$ 17,552.59		
17	2	17,552.59	450.21	109.70	897.62	222.20	17,102.38		
18	3	17,102.38	453.02	106.89	1,350.64	329.09	16,649.36		
19	4	16,649.36	455.85	104.06	1,806.50	433.15	16,193.50		
20	5	16,193.50	458.70	101.21	2,265.20	534.36	15,734.80		
21	6	15,734.80	461.57	98.34	2,726.77	632.70	15,273.23		
22	7	15,273.23	464.45	95.46	3,191.22	728.16	14,808.78		
23	8	14,808.78	467.36	92.55	3,658.58	820.72	14,341.42		
24	9	14,341.42	470.28	89.63	4,128.86	910.35	13,871.14		
25	10	13,871.14	473.22	86.69	4,602.07	997.05	13,397.93		
26	11	13,397.93	476.17	83.74	5,078.25	1,080.78	12,921.75		
27	12	12,921.75	479.15	80.76	5,557.40	1,161.54	12,442.60		
28	13	12,442.60	482.15	77.77	6,039.55	1,239.31	11,960.45		
29	14	11,960.45	485.16	74.75	6,524.70	1,314.06	11,475.30		

Documentation \ **Loan Analysis** /

Chapter 6 covers more Excel functions. Earlier chapters described a few mathematical functions such as SUM, AVERAGE, MIN, and MAX. Excel has several hundred functions, and it would be boring and difficult to cover all of them in this textbook. In this chapter, you will use several of the most common and important Excel functions including the financial functions, lookup functions, the NOW date function, and logical functions. In addition, you will learn how to create and use names and labels in formulas in place of cell references.

SESSION 6.1 USING DATA VALIDATION, NAMES, AND IF AND INDEX FUNCTIONS

In this section, you will learn how to create a data entry area of your worksheet separate from the output area—the area containing the formulas and calculations that depend on the assumptions portion of a worksheet. In addition, you will write functions to validate data entries to ensure that they are reasonable, use names to write formulas that reference names rather than cell addresses, and use an index function called VLOOKUP to search a table. This session emphasizes both the use and understanding of selected functions and how to validate data before you enter the data into a worksheet.

Introduction to Functions

Worksheet functions are special Excel built-in tools that perform complex calculations quickly and easily. Similar to special keys such as SQRT on a calculator, Excel functions compute square roots, loan amortizations, and a wide variety of statistical calculations. Excel has more than 240 built-in functions that perform calculations ranging from computing the absolute value (ABS) of a number to returning the two-tailed P-value of a z-test (ZTEST) and everything in between. Each Excel function is a member of one of

CHAPTER OUTLINE

FIGURE 6.2

Excel's function
categories

Function Group	Description
Database	Analyze data stored in lists or databases
Date and Time	Manipulate dates and times
Financial	Present value, amortization, and interest-related functions
Information	Determines the type of data in a cell (blank, numeric, empty)
Logical	AND, OR, NOT functions to calculate yes/no answers
Lookup and Reference	Search tables and return answers, determine row or column number of a cell
Math and Trigonometry	LOG, MOD, PI, COS, and other common math and trig functions
Statistical	Standard statistical functions including average, max, and standard deviation
Text	Character extraction, manipulation, and counting functions for text (labels)

several function groups. Figure 6.2 lists the function categories and briefly describes them. You are not going to learn about the 200-plus functions in this chapter. Instead, you will learn about some very important and often-used functions.

When you want to use a function with which you are not familiar, you can use Insert Function to select the function you need and simultaneously learn about the function and its arguments in the Wizard's steps. Alternatively, you can search for an appropriate function by typing a brief description of what you want to do. Excel then returns a list of function names and descriptions that you can browse.

Working with Functions

Recall that worksheet functions have two parts. The first part is the name of the function. The second part is a list of zero or more function *arguments* enclosed in parentheses, which are sometimes called *argument lists*. Of course, if a function is the first thing you write in an expression, it is preceded by an equals sign. Function names such as PMT describe, very briefly, what the function does (PayMenT, for example). Arguments specify the values, cells, or expressions that the function uses as input to compute its final value. All Office Excel 2003 functions return a single answer—the value of the function's evaluation. While most Excel functions have arguments, a few do not. Normally, a function without any arguments would be doomed to return the same value over and over because there are no input values (arguments) from which the function can compute a different answer. However, the few functions that have no arguments return different values each time they are used because they rely on outside values such as an ever-changing clock value or a random pattern to create a unique answer each time. Functions have the general form

```
function-name (argument list)
```

where "function name" is the function's name and "argument list" is zero or more arguments separated by commas forming the list placed inside of parentheses. Functions that have no arguments still must have opening and closing parentheses. The NOW() and RAND() functions are two examples. NOW returns the current date and time, but it has no argument list. Similarly, the RAND function returns a random number in the range of zero to one. If you were to accidentally omit the parentheses from any function that has no arguments, Excel would misinterpret your entry as a special user-defined name (discussed in this chapter) rather than a function name and would display an error message. Therefore it is important to always use parentheses following a function's name—either with or without arguments as required by the function.

Most functions have a particular number of arguments arranged in a particular order. An example is the date-category function DATE, which returns a number that represents, within Excel, a date and time. The function has the general form

```
DATE(year, month, day)
```

If you were to enter month information as the first argument, then the DATE function would return a spurious answer. Arguments like these are called *positional arguments* because their position in the argument list is important and inflexible. Other functions such as SUM, a function with which you are already familiar, have a maximum of 30 arguments. The arguments in the SUM function list are not positional. That is, the first argument has no particular significance different from any other arguments in the list. While 30 arguments may seem rather restrictive, one or more arguments can be a cell range and thus extend the total number of cells involved in the function. With the SUM function, for example, it is just as easy to sum 300,000 cells as it is to sum 30 in a single function. The trick is to use large cell ranges as individual arguments.

Organizing a Worksheet into Sections

For uncomplicated worksheets, it is common to divide them into at least two sections. More complex worksheets often consist of multiple worksheet pages woven together. For Cal's worksheet, it is helpful to divide the worksheet into sections. Doing so reduces or eliminates confusion about where a worksheet user is to enter values unique to each new customer. Cal's financial manager, Jessica Allison, has divided the *prototype* (a proposed model) worksheet into three sections called Assumptions, External Data, and Outputs. The Assumptions section contains input information unique to each customer and used by all the other formulas in the worksheet. They are called assumptions because the results of the worksheet in the output section depend upon the values of the assumptions. The external data section contains interest rate information, also used by formulas in the worksheet, whose values fluctuate based on the prime lending rate and other external factors. The outputs section performs calculations using the assumptions values and displays the results.

Providing an Assumptions Framework

Begin constructing the loan worksheet by opening the prototype worksheet that Jessica has constructed. Jessica has preformatted several worksheet cells to allow you to concentrate on the constants, formulas, and functions in the Loan Analysis worksheet that constitutes what you are learning.

Opening and saving the Loan Analysis workbook:

1. Start Excel

2. Open the workbook **ex06CalsCars.xls** and immediately save it as **CalsCars1.xls**

3. Click the **Loan Analysis** worksheet tab to display the loan details (see Figure 6.3)

FIGURE 6.3

Main Loan Analysis worksheet

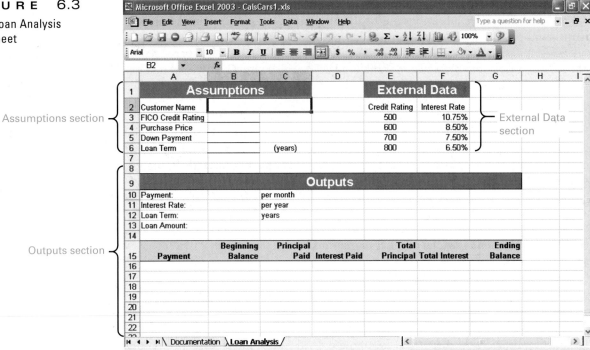

Assumptions section

External Data section

Outputs section

FIGURE 6.4

Initial Assumptions values and their meanings

Assumptions Cell	Description/Use	Value
B2	Customer's name	Francis Parker
B3	Credit rating number (obtained from credit report)	755
B4	Vehicle purchase price (negotiated)	21000
B5	Customer's down payment	3000
B6	Loan duration in years	3

Assumptions Data

With the general structure of the Loan Analysis worksheet in mind, you can enter the assumptions information—example data—that you will use to test the worksheet. In Session 6.2, you will add formulas to the Outputs section of the worksheet that depend on the assumptions values you are entering next. Later, when you are convinced that the worksheet works properly, you can erase the entries in the Assumptions section and save the workbook so that others can use it without erasing the data you have entered. Figure 6.4 lists the first set of values you will enter and briefly describes them.

Entering input values in the Assumptions area:

1. Click cell **B2** and type **Francis Parker**

2. Click cell **B3** and type **755**

3. Click cell **B4** and type **21000**

4. Click cell **B5** and type **3000**

5. Click cell **B6**, type **3**, and press **Enter** to complete the entry. Notice that the values in cells B4 and B5 display currency symbols (see Figure 6.5)

assumptions filled in

	A	B	C	D	E	F	G	H	I
1	Assumptions				External Data				
2	Customer Name	Francis Parker			Credit Rating	Interest Rate			
3	FICO Credit Rating	755			500	10.75%			
4	Purchase Price	$ 21,000			600	8.50%			
5	Down Payment	$ 3,000			700	7.50%			
6	Loan Term	3	(years)		800	6.50%			
7									
8									

FIGURE 6.5

Completed Assumptions section

External Data

The External Data section contains two completed columns of data. What do those represent? They are data that have been generated from external sources and entered here. The first column contains four values that the credit industry uses to report consumers' creditworthiness. The four values represent arbitrary groups of values. The first value, 500, is the lower limit of values ranging from 500 to 599. Second in the list, the value 600 is the lower limit of a range of values from 600 to 699. The third value, 700, is the smallest value in the range of values from 700 to 799. Finally, the value 800 represents any values from 800 up to infinity. While these credit ratings are similar to those used throughout the United States, they may not correspond to the lowest or highest possible credit rating scales or match current interest rates for the given credit rating range.

The second column in the External Data section represents interest rates that correspond to different credit rating groups. A person whose credit report shows a creditworthiness rating of 654 can qualify for a loan interest rate of 8.50 percent, because 654 falls in the category 600 to 699. Because a higher credit rating represents a lower risk that the consumer will default on the loan, higher credit ratings receive lower interest rates. You will later use the table to locate and assign a consumer a particular interest rate. The rate will be based on the consumer's reported credit rating obtained from one of the credit reporting agencies mentioned previously.

Supplying Data Validation

As a worksheet designer, you should always be aware that anyone using your worksheet could accidentally type the wrong data into one of the several input cells in the Assumptions area of your worksheet. Invalid entries include mistakes like entering text instead of a value or a value that is incorrect because it is too large or too small. Called *range errors*, values that are either too large or too small (negative or too close to zero, for example) do not make sense in the context of the application. For example, typing 50 in cell B6, the loan term duration in years, would be incorrect. Similarly, a negative value in cell B6 is incorrect. A credit rating value that is negative or larger than 800 is also incorrect. How can you detect or prevent range errors?

Excel can apply rules about the range of values and type of data that are allowed for one cell or a range of cells. Specifying data validation for individual cells allows you to restrict the type and value of information users enter into a worksheet. For example, you can specify that users must enter values in the range of 1 to 5 (years) in cell B6, the loan length in years. Similarly, you can restrict the values in cell B3 to values from 500 to 899.

Specifying Valid Data Value Ranges

Jessica wants you to restrict the value that a user can type into loan term cell B6 to values in the range of 1 to 5. Cal's does not offer loans for less than one year or more than five.

Restricting data values to a specific range and data type:

1. Click cell **B6** to select the cell to which you will apply data validation

2. Click **Data** and then click **Validation** to open the Data Validation dialog box

3. Click the **Settings** tab, if necessary, click the **Allow** list box to reveal the list of values, and click **Whole number**. The dialog box reveals several new text boxes, which depend on the value you select in the Allow list box (see Figure 6.6)

FIGURE 6.6

Partially completed Data Validation dialog box

select data type restriction from this list

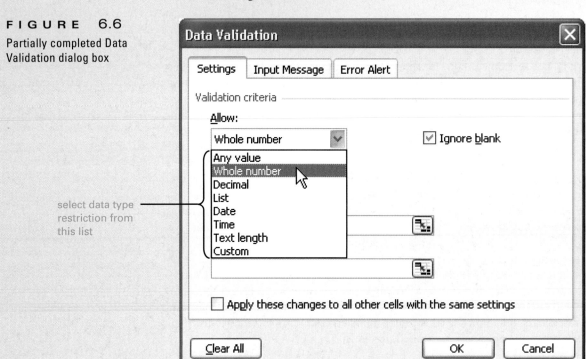

4. Click the **Data** list box to reveal a list of choices and click **Between** in the Data list box

5. Click the **Minimum** text box and type **1**

6. Click the **Maximum** text box and type **5**

tip: *If you clicked OK or pressed Enter by mistake and closed the Data Validation dialog box, don't worry. Simply reexecute steps 1 through 3 above and continue*

Providing a Data Entry Message

You can specify the message to display as someone begins to enter information into cell B6. The Data Validation dialog box should still be open as you do the following steps.

Entering an informative Data Validation input message:

1. Click the **Input Message** tab in the Data Validation dialog box, and ensure that the *Show input message when cell is selected* check box is checked

2. Click the **Title** text box and type **Valid Loan Term Value**

3. Click the **Input message** text box and type **Loan term must be from 1 to 5**

From now on, whenever anyone clicks cell B6, the Data Validation input message appears automatically. It will help reduce the risk that a user will enter an invalid value for the loan term.

Giving Data Entry Error Feedback

The Data Validation dialog box provides a third tab in which you can optionally specify an error message that Excel displays if the data in the cell does not meet the criteria specified on the Settings tab. This is the best way to bring data entry errors to a user's attention.

Entering an error alert message:

1. Click the **Error Alert** tab in the Data Validation dialog box, and ensure that the *Show error after invalid data is entered* check box is checked

2. Click the **Style** list box and click **Stop** (if necessary). Three levels of alert are available: Information, Warning, and Stop. The action each of the three alert levels causes appears in Figure 6.7

Type	Button Label	Action If Button Is Clicked
Information	OK	Value entered into the cell; processing continues normally
	Cancel	Value is not entered into the cell
Warning	Yes	Value entered in cell; processing continues normally
	No	Value placed in cell; Excel stops, waiting for you to enter another value
	Cancel	Value is not entered into the cell
Stop	Retry	Value remains; Excel stops and waits for you to enter another value
	Cancel	Value is not entered into the cell

FIGURE 6.7
Error Alert Style messages and actions

3. Click the **Title** text box and type **Error!** What you type in the Title text box appears at the top of the error message when Excel detects a data input error

EXCEL

4. Click the **Error message** text box and type **Loan term must be between 1 and 5. Your entry is incorrect. Please enter a correct value**. The message appears when Excel detects an invalid value in the cell

5. Click the **OK** button to close the Data Validation dialog box and finalize your settings

Testing Data Validation

After the Data Validation dialog box closes, you notice that the input message appears. That is because cell B6 is active. With the data validation rule intact, you can test it to ensure that invalid entries do not escape Excel's attention.

Testing data validation rules for cell B6:

1. Click cell **B5** to make it active momentarily, then click cell **B6**. The Data Validation input message appears indicating the range of valid data for the loan term (see Figure 6.8)

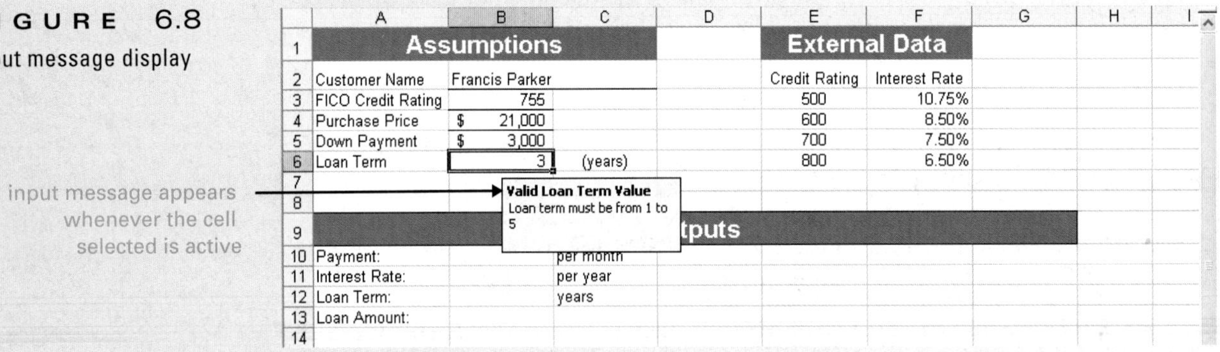

FIGURE 6.8

Input message display

input message appears
whenever the cell
selected is active

2. Type **17** and then press **Enter** to attempt to finalize the value and move to another worksheet cell. The error alert message you specified earlier in the Data Validation dialog box appears (see Figure 6.9)

You can click **Retry** to correct the mistake or you can click **Cancel** to erase your incorrect entry. Clicking Cancel restores cell B6 to the value it had prior to your incorrect entry

3. Click the **Retry** button

4. Type **3** and press **Enter**. Because this value is within the specified range of 1 to 5, Excel permits the entry and then makes cell B7 active

Defining Names

Until now, you have referenced cells using their addresses. In larger worksheets, it is easy to forget which cells contain particular values. When you are enhancing a worksheet someone else developed, you will likely examine the formulas to determine what calculations various parts of the worksheet are performing to better understand its flow and structure. Formulas such as =B4*C5−A7−C42 provide little information about the purpose of the expression. An alternative expression such as hoursworked*hourlyrate−statetax−federaltax is much easier to understand because the

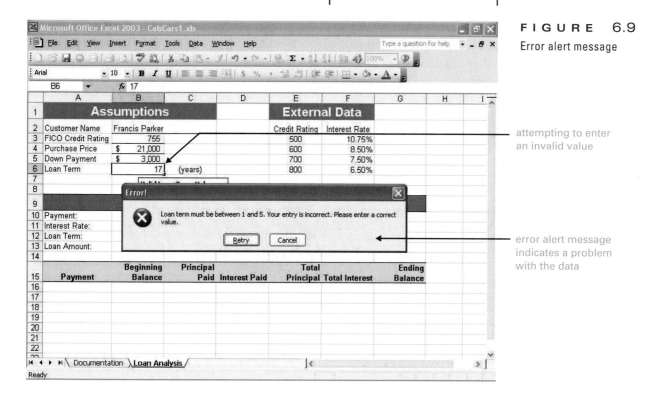

FIGURE   6.9
Error alert message

attempting to enter an invalid value

error alert message indicates a problem with the data

formula is built with names that infer their purpose. Excel provides an extremely helpful feature that allows you to assign a name to a cell or cell range and then use the name anywhere you would use the cell address. A ***name*** (also known as a ***range name***) is a name that you assign to a cell or cell range that can replace a cell address or cell range in expressions or functions. Names provide several benefits over using cell addresses.

- Names are easier to remember than cell addresses as you create formulas referencing cells
- Names provide documentation because the name reveals the purpose of the cell and clarifies formulas that contain names
- Excel treats names in copied formulas as though they are absolute cell references, which is an advantage when you clone a formula that you want to refer to a fixed location or cell

Names must be spelled in a particular way. Rules for names are the following:

- Names must begin with a letter or an underscore character
- The remaining characters in the name can be letters, numbers, periods, and underscore characters
- The maximum length of a name is 255 characters, although short and meaningful names are better
- Capitalization is ignored in names. (Excel considers the names "Payment" and "payment" as identical)
- Names can be words, but spaces are not allowed. Instead, use the underscore character in place of a space for multi-word names. (Gross_Pay is a legitimate name)
- Names can be single letters, with the exception of the letters R and C, but this is a bad idea
- Names that resemble cell references cannot be used. (For example, IR42 is not allowed)
- Simply stated, define names using six or more characters that contain letters and numbers and that are meaningful words

> **task reference**   Naming a Cell or Cell Range
>
> - Select the cell or cell range you want to name
> - Click the **Name box** in the formula bar
> - Type the name and press **Enter**

An alternative way to assign a name to a cell or cell range is to execute Insert, Name, Define, and type the name. You can use either method.

Defining a Name with a Menu Bar Command

Jessica wants you to assign names to key cells and cell ranges to make creating formulas easier. She suggests you define names for cells containing the purchase price, down payment, loan term, and the table containing the FICO (Fair, Isaac and Company) credit ratings and interest rates. (See www.fairisaac.com.) Defining names to key assumptions will make it easier to write formulas in the Outputs area that reference the cells in the Assumptions section of the worksheet.

help yourself *Press **F1**, type **name a cell** in the Search text box of the Microsoft Excel Help task pane, and press **Enter**. Click the hyperlink **Name cells in a workbook** and then click the **Name a cell or a range of cells** hyperlink to reveal information on naming cells. Maximize the Help screen if necessary. Click the Help screen **Close** button when you are finished, and close the task pane*

Defining a name:

1. Click cell **B3**

2. Click **Insert**, point to **Name**, and click **Define** to open the Define Name dialog box in which you define and delete names. Excel suggests the name FICO_Credit_Rating, which appears in the *Names in workbook* text box, because the label appears to the left of the selected cell

3. Type **CreditRating** (no spaces) in the *Names in workbook* text box to name cell B3 (see Figure 6.10), and then press **Enter**

4. Repeat steps 2 and 3 to name the following cells with the following names (Remember: Do not use spaces anywhere):

B4	**PurchasePrice**	B10	**PeriodicPayment**
B5	**DownPayment**	B11	**InterestRate**
B6	**LoanTerm**	B13	**LoanAmount**

With cell B13 still selected, look at the Name box located at the left end of the Formula bar. Notice that it displays the name you assigned cell B13—*LoanAmount.* Whenever you select a cell or cell range that has a defined name, the name appears in the Name box.

Note that when you define a name, the worksheet name is part of the definition and the cell reference is absolute. The name defined for cell B13, for example, is assigned to cell 'Loan Analysis'!$B$13. Loan Analysis is part of the name because it identifies the sheet on which the name is found—a true three-dimensional name.

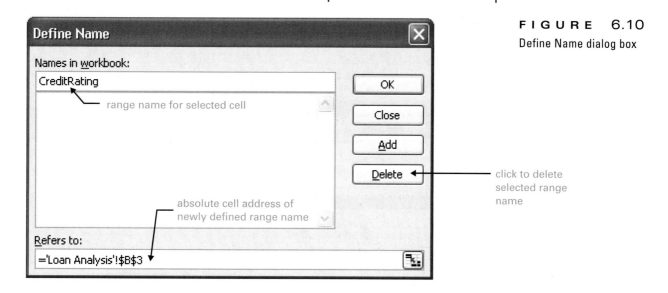

Defining a Name Using the Name Box

The most convenient way to assign a name is to use the Name box located on the left end of the formula bar. You can use the Name box either to define a name or to go to a named cell or cell range. A name defined in one worksheet is available to all worksheets in the workbook. If you have a large worksheet, clicking a name in the Name box list of names is a convenient way to move directly to a cell. For example, you could name the entire Assumptions area of the worksheet with the name Assumptions. Then, when you click the name Assumptions in the Name box, Excel goes to that section of the worksheet and highlights the name. In fact, whenever you want to know which cell or cell range is assigned a particular name, simply select the name from the Name box list.

---

*another*word   . . . on Names

Normally, names you define are workbook-level names. A **workbook-level name** (range name) is a name you define that is available for use in formulas from *any* worksheet in a workbook. You can create a **worksheet-level name**, which is a name that is available only on the worksheet in which it is defined. To define a worksheet-level name, precede the name with the name of the worksheet followed by an exclamation point. For example, you could define a worksheet-level name SalePrice on the worksheet Sheet12 by typing Sheet12!SalePrice as you define the name

---

Using the Name box to define a name:

1. Select cell range **E3:F6**, the cell range to which you want to assign a name

2. Click inside the Name box, type **CreditTable** (see Figure 6.11), and press **Enter**

tip: *If you accidentally enter the name in cell E3, then press the **Esc** key to nullify your action. Select cell range **E3:F6** again and be sure to click inside the Name box, which is on the left end of the formula bar. If you pressed **Enter** before discovering the mistake, click **Edit**, Undo, and repeat steps 1 and 2*

FIGURE 6.11
Defining a name with the Name box

Name box

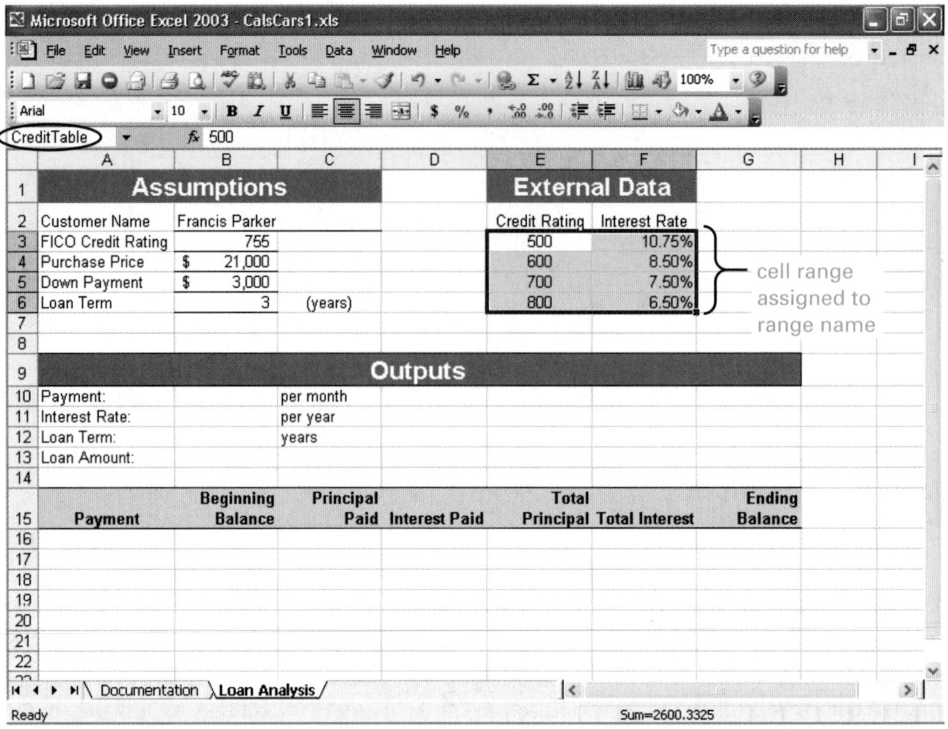

cell range assigned to range name

tip: *After you define a name for a range of cells, the name does not appear in the Name box unless you select the entire area*

Using Names in Formulas

The purpose of worksheet and workbook names is so that you can use them instead of cell addresses in formulas that you create to complete the loan analysis worksheet. When you use a name, Excel treats it like an absolute cell reference. You begin by writing the formula for cell B13 to compute the loan amount.

Creating a formula containing names:

1. Select cell **B13**, the cell that will contain the loan amount
2. Type =**PurchasePrice**−**DownPayment** and press **Enter**. The loan amount appears in cell B13
3. Click cell **B13** to make it active again and press the **F2** function key to edit the formula. Notice the names appearing in the formula (see Figure 6.12). They are color-coded to match the outlines around the independent cells that the formula references
4. Press the **Esc** key to cancel the edit cell request

task reference — Deleting a Name

- Click **Insert**, point to **Name**, and then click the **Define** button
- Click the name in the *Names in workbook* list that you want to delete
- Click the **Delete** button and then click the **OK** button

F I G U R E   6.12

Names appear in the formula

color-coded borders without square selection handles indicates a name is used in the referencing formula

formula contains names with colored outlines to identify referenced cells

Using IF and Index Functions

Making Alternative Choices with the IF Function

Last month, Cal's Cars began charging a special fee to any customer whose loan is over 80 percent of the purchase price of a car. Cal's management created the special assessment to cover the cost of insuring loans. The special assessment is $300. History has shown Cal and his managers that there is a much higher loan default rate among customers who finance more than 80 percent of a vehicle's purchase price than among those who do not. The special assessment, which Cal calls a "processing fee," will reduce Cal's risk with insurance to cover the balance of a loan should a customer simply quit making loan payments (default) on the loan. There is no special assessment for customers who finance 80 percent or less of their vehicle's purchase price.

Writing a formula to capture the preceding business rule requires a new statement —one in which there is one outcome from two possible choices. The two possible outcomes are a $300 fee for loans in which the ratio of loan amount to purchase price is greater than 0.8 or no fee for ratios less than or equal to 0.8. You will encounter many situations in which the formula you write in a cell can have two or more possible outcomes from which to choose depending on another cell or cells' value(s). Excel anticipates this and provides the function IF, belonging to the logical function category. The IF function has the following form:

```
IF(conditional test, expression if true, expression if false)
```

A **conditional test** is an equation that compares two values, functions, formula labels, or logical values. Every conditional test equation must include a **relational operator**, which compares two parts of a formula. The result of the comparison is either true or false. For example, in the conditional test A1>B2, the greater than symbol (>) relational operator compares the values in cells A1 and B2. IF A1 is greater than B2, then the result of the conditional test is true. Otherwise, it is false. Figure 6.13 shows a complete list of Excel's relational operators.

The second and third arguments of the IF function can be constants or arbitrarily complex expressions. The IF function displays the computed value of only one of the two argument expressions, depending on the evaluation of the conditional test. If the conditional test is true, Excel calculates and displays the value of the second argument. Otherwise (if the test is false), Excel calculates and displays the value of the third argument. Thus, you can create a formula whose output depends on a condition—a value in another cell.

In the Loan Analysis worksheet, the conditional expression you will write examines the ratio of the loan amount to the purchase price. You create a ratio simply by dividing one value by

F I G U R E   6.13

Excel's relational operators

Relational Operator	Meaning
<	Less than
>	Greater than
=	Equal to
<=	Less than or equal to
>=	Greater than or equal to
<>	Not equal to

FIGURE 6.14

Logic of the IF function

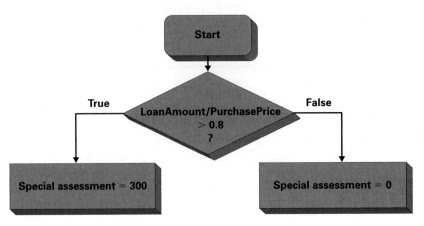

IF(LoanAmount/PurchasePrice > 0.8, 300, 0)

another. If the ratio is greater than 0.8, then the special assessment is $300. Otherwise, the special assessment is $0. Figure 6.14 shows the IF function and the logic of the expression.

Now you are ready to enter the IF function to determine whether the customer must pay the special assessment of $300 or not. In addition to the special assessment, you should conditionally display the label "Assessment" in cell A14 when processing fee appears in cell B14.

Writing an IF function:

1. Click cell **A14**, the cell that will display *Assessment* if the ratio of loan amount to purchase price is greater than 0.8—the same criteria for displaying (or not) an assessment fee of $300

2. Type =**IF(LoanAmount/PurchasePrice > 0.8, "Assessment:", "")** and press **Enter**

tip: *Notice that the second argument contains two quotation marks in a row without a blank between them. The IF function can display character string expressions such as "Assessment" as well as numeric expressions*

When you are unsure of a function and want help writing it, use the Insert Function button to the left of the formula bar or the Insert Function command. Executing Insert Function opens a dialog box that lists functions by categories and helps you build the function.

Using Insert Function to write an IF function:

1. Click cell **B14** to make it active

2. Click the **Insert Function** button next to the formula bar to open the Insert Function dialog box

3. Click the **Or select a category** list box to display its list of function categories

4. Click **Logical** in the list of function category choices, click **IF** in the *Select a function* list box, and then click **OK**. The Function Arguments dialog box opens

5. Click the **Logical_Test** text box and type
   LoanAmount/PurchasePrice > 0.8 (no spaces in this line). Notice that the
   moment you type 0.8, the label TRUE appears to the right of the box

6. Click the **Value_if_true** text box and type **300**, which is the value to return
   if the condition is true

7. Click the **Value_if_false** text box and type **0**, which is the value to return if
   the condition is false (see Figure 6.15)

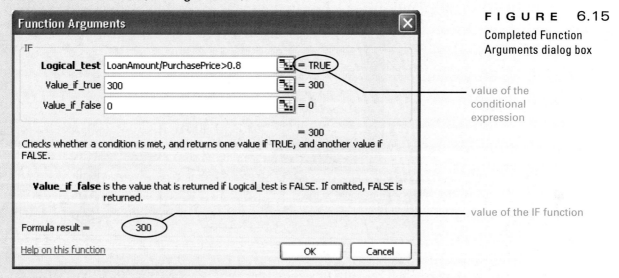

FIGURE   6.15

Completed Function
Arguments dialog box

value of the
conditional
expression

value of the IF function

8. Click **OK** to complete the function

Excel places the completed IF function into cell B14, calculates the value of the
function, and displays $300.00 because the ratio of the down payment to the purchase
price is greater than 0.8

Using the VLOOKUP Function

You will encounter many situations in which you need to look up an answer from a
table of possible answers. For example, an instructor needs a convenient way to look up
letter grades that correspond to students' percentage values, or an express shipping
company determines shipping prices by a package's weight and the location to which it
will be shipped. Or a tax consultant finds it convenient to look up the state or federal
tax rate for a client using the client's gross income and number of dependents.

Situations like the preceding ones call for a special class of functions called lookup
functions, also known as table lookup functions. Excel provides several ***lookup functions***, which use a search value to search a table—a range of cells—for a match or close
match and then return a value from the table as a result. The table that a lookup function searches is called the ***lookup table***, and the value being used to search the lookup
table is called the ***lookup value***. With Excel lookup functions, you specify the value or
cell address of the lookup value, the cell range of the lookup table, and the column or
row that contains the values you want to return as an answer.

Excel provides two lookup functions: HLOOKUP and VLOOKUP. You use the
HLOOKUP function, which stands for horizontal lookup, for lookup tables in which
the lookup column is in the first row of a multi-row table. You use the VLOOKUP function, which stands for vertical lookup, for a vertical lookup table—one in which the
search values are in the first column of the table. For either lookup function to work

FIGURE   6.16

VLOOKUP function syntax

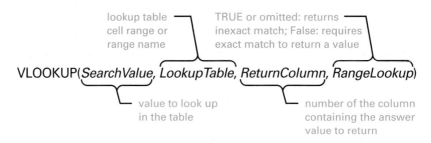

FIGURE   6.17

VLOOKUP function
searching a lookup table

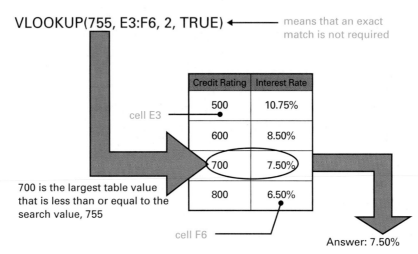

properly, the horizontal or vertical table must be sorted from low to high on the values in the first row (HLOOKUP) or first column (VLOOKUP). Otherwise, either function returns spurious results.

The VLOOKUP function has the general form shown in Figure 6.16. Before you apply the VLOOKUP function to the Loan Analysis worksheet, examine its parts for a better understanding of how it works.

The first argument of the function is the lookup value. The VLOOKUP function uses that value to search the lookup table. The second argument is the lookup table, which is the cell range or name specifying the lookup table's location. The third argument is the column containing the data you want VLOOKUP to retrieve. Finally, the fourth argument can be FALSE, TRUE, or omitted. If it is FALSE, VLOOKUP will look for an exact match in the lookup table. If it does not find a value in the first column exactly matching the lookup value, VLOOKUP returns #N/A error value. If the argument is TRUE or omitted (most people omit the argument), then VLOOKUP searches the first column looking for the largest value in the first column that is less than or equal to the search value. You can better understand this function by applying it to the Loan Analysis worksheet.

Cal's Loan Analysis worksheet can use a lookup function in cell B11 to retrieve the interest rate from a table by searching the table you named CreditTable (cells E3 through F6) using the FICO Credit Rating value in cell B3 as the lookup value. The CreditTable is arranged in columns, and it is sorted in ascending order on the first column—Credit Rating. With the lookup table arranged in this way, you will use the VLOOKUP function because the search values are in the first column. Figure 6.17 shows a graphical example of the VLOOKUP function and how it searches the lookup table and returns an applicable interest rate based on a customer's credit rating number.

task reference | Using the VLOOKUP Function

- Create a lookup table and sort the table in ascending order by the leftmost column
- Place in columns to the right of the search columns values you want to return as answers
- Write a VLOOKUP function referencing a cell containing the lookup value, the lookup table, and the column containing the answer

Jessica asks you to write a function in cell B11 that will use the customer's credit rating in the Assumptions section, cell B3, and look up and return the applicable interest rate from the lookup table.

Writing a VLOOKUP function:

1. Click cell **B11**
2. Click **Insert**, and then click **Function**
3. Click the **Or select a category**
4. Click **Lookup & Reference** in list of choices, scroll to the bottom of the *Select a function* list, click **VLOOKUP**, and click **OK**
5. Type **CreditRating** in the *Lookup_value* text box and press the **Tab** key
6. Type **CreditTable**, which is the name of the lookup table, and press the **Tab** key
7. Type **2** in the Col_index_num box because you want VLOOKUP to return an answer from the second column of the lookup table (see Figure 6.18)

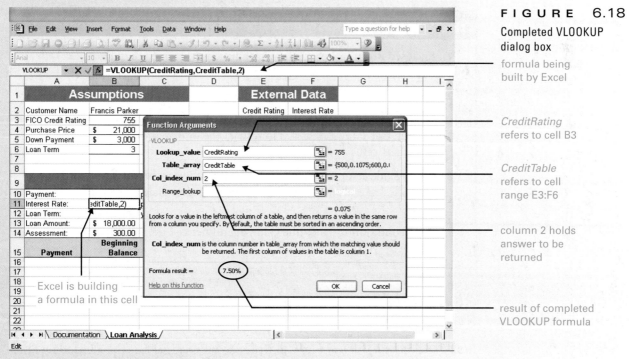

FIGURE 6.18
Completed VLOOKUP dialog box

formula being built by Excel

CreditRating refers to cell B3

CreditTable refers to cell range E3:F6

column 2 holds answer to be returned

result of completed VLOOKUP formula

8. Click **OK** to complete the function definition and close the VLOOKUP function dialog box. The function returns and displays the value 7.50%, which is the interest rate corresponding to the credit rating of 755

EXCEL

The last activity before ending this session is to write a simple formula in cell B12 that displays the loan term. While the loan term used in calculations is found in the Assumptions area, a second copy of it is handy to place in the Outputs section.

Writing the loan term formula:

1. Click cell **B12**

2. Type **=LoanTerm**

You have done a lot of work on the Loan Analysis worksheet in this session. Always save a worksheet before going on to the next session.

Saving the loan analysis worksheet:

1. Click **Save** button on the Standard toolbar to save the work you completed in this session

2. Click **File** on the menu bar and click **Exit**

Congratulations. You have learned a great deal about several important functions. In the next section, you will write several financial functions to produce a schedule of loan repayments that indicate how much you pay each month and how much of the payment reduces the loan balance and how much pays each month's interest.

SESSION 6.1

making *the grade*

1. Enclosed in parentheses following a function's name are one or more _____.

2. The _____ section of a worksheet contains input values used by other formulas in the worksheet.

3. You can use data _____ to restrict the information being entered into a worksheet cell.

4. You provide error messages with data validation techniques by specifying an error _____ message in the Data Validation dialog box.

5. When a cell can take on one of two possible values based on whether or not some condition is true—the value in another cell is 15 percent or greater, for instance—you should use the _____ function.

SESSION 6.2 USING FINANCIAL AND DATE FUNCTIONS

In this section, you will learn how to write several financial functions including PMT, PPMT, IPMT, and PV. You will also write dates and date functions. You will use AutoFill to copy an ascending series of values in a column and, later, to create several families of related formulas throughout your worksheet.

Using Financial Analysis Functions

Excel's financial functions allow you to extend your proficiency beyond the simpler functions of SUM, MIN, and MAX. You can use the financial and date functions to perform quite sophisticated financial and date calculations without the need to know the theory behind the functions. This session provides you with both the understanding of financial and date functions and experience using them in worksheets to see how they work. Excel's financial functions allow you to take control of many important monetary calculations such as the amount of a monthly payment of a mortgage, the present value of a future steady flow of revenue, or the amount of a loan payment that goes to pay off the principal and the amount that pays the periodic interest.

The financial functions you will encounter in this session all have a common basis. Each is in a family of functions that calculates basic rates of return and payment amounts. A fundamental concept in finance is the *time value of money*. In its simplest form, the **time value of money** means that receiving $100 today is more valuable than receiving it next year. Why? Because you could put the $100 in a bank and earn interest for a year and end up with more than $100 next year—perhaps $105 or $110. Financial functions answer questions such as this one: "How much money do I have to place in an investment that pays 5 percent per year in order to accumulate $10,000 in 10 years?" Other Excel financial functions answer the question "How much is my monthly payment for a $6,000 loan at 8 percent per year for three years?"

help yourself *Press **F1**, type **payment** in the Search text box of the Microsoft Excel Help task pane, and press **Enter**. Scroll down the list to locate and then click the hyperlink **PMT** and then read and scroll down the Help screen to read about the function. Maximize the Help screen if necessary. Click the Help screen **Close** button when you are finished, and then close the task pane*

Using the Payment Function, PMT

PMT is one of the Excel functions that calculates payments for a loan or investment that pays a fixed amount at a periodic rate. PMT, which stands for *payment*, is the most commonly used payment function. The PMT function calculates the periodic payment given three values: the periodic interest rate, the number of payments, and the loan amount (called the *present value*). Loan payments are amortized. **Amortization** is the process of distributing periodic payments over the life of a loan. The amount borrowed is the **principal**. The interest percentage is called the **rate**, and the time period over which you make periodic payments is the **term**.

A periodic payment is a fixed payment that you make on a regular basis—once every year, every month, every day, and so on. Part of the payment covers the interest on the loan and part of the payment repays a portion of the loan (principal). After the final loan payment, the loan's balance is zero—it is paid off. Over the life of a loan repayment, more of each monthly payment goes toward reducing the loan amount and less goes toward paying interest on the loan. The general form of the payment function, PMT, is shown in Figure 6.19.

Jessica wants you to work on the periodic payment function that will compute the monthly payment amounts for each customer and display that value in cell B10.

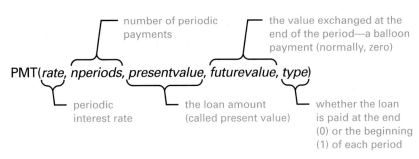

FIGURE 6.19

PMT function syntax

The PMT function references the InterestRate (cell B11), LoanTerm (cell B6), and LoanAmount (cell B13). All of Cal's customers make monthly payments. For example, in a three-year loan, a customer will make 36 payments—one per month. The frequency of the payment affects the interest rate. When you are dealing with *monthly* payments, remember to divide the annual interest rate by 12 (months) to yield a monthly interest rate.

Opening the loan workbook:

1. Start Excel and open the loan analysis workbook **CalsCars1.xls**

2. Immediately save workbook as **CalsCars2.xls** to preserve the original workbook in case you want to revert to the final version you saved in Session 6.1

Now you can write the formula for the monthly payment.

Writing the PMT function:

1. Click cell **B10**

2. Click **Insert**, click **Function**, type **periodic payment** in the *Search for a function* text box, click the **Go** button, ensure that **PMT** is highlighted in the *Select a function* list box, and click **OK**. The PMT function dialog box opens

3. If necessary, click the **Rate** text box and then type **InterestRate/12**. (You can write an arithmetic expression as a function argument)

4. Click the **Nper** text box and type **LoanTerm*12**. Making monthly payments means that you must multiply the number of years (in the cell named LoanTerm) by the number of payments per year (12)

5. Click the **Pv** text box and type **-LoanAmount**. The minus sign preceding LoanAmount reverses the sign of the function's result. Excel calculates the periodic (monthly) payment and displays it in the dialog box (see Figure 6.20)

6. Click **OK** to complete the function. The PMT function dialog box closes

The LoanAmount cell displays $559.91, which is the monthly payment on a loan of $18,000 for three years at 7.5 percent annual interest. The calculated result is not precise to the penny. Examine Figure 6.20 and you will see that the answer is actually 559.9119269 to seven decimal places. Formatting visually rounds that number to $559.91. Such a small difference will not affect what you do here, but you will learn to use the ROUND function in this session to counteract any cumulative effects such a number would have on a long-term loan or other investment.

Building a Loan Amortization Schedule

Jessica thinks that customers will want to know exactly how much of their loan payment is going toward repaying the loan and how much is going toward interest. She wants you to build a complete month-by-month amortization schedule. An *amortiza-*

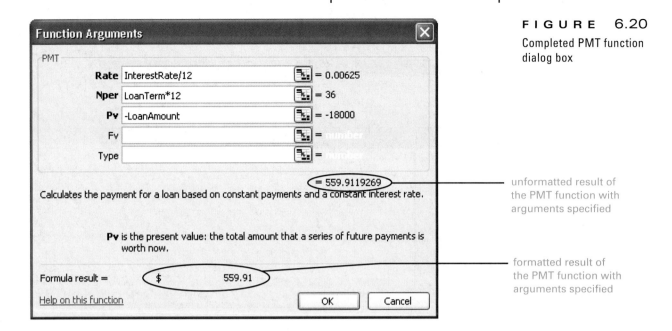

unformatted result of
the PMT function with
arguments specified

formatted result of
the PMT function with
arguments specified

tion schedule lists the monthly payment, the amount of the payment applied toward reducing the principal (loan amount), and the amount of the payment that pays the interest due each month. In addition, she wants you to display, each month, the beginning balance of the loan amount, the total paid so far toward the principal, and the total paid so far in interest charges. The column labels that appear in row 15 are the beginning of the amortization schedule.

There will be 36 rows of information in the amortization schedule for this example because it will take 36 payments to pay off the loan. Each row represents a month in the 36-month payout schedule. It would be nice if you could automatically allocate 12, 24, 36, or 48 rows in the amortization schedule based on the value in the LoanTerm cell.

Creating a Series of Constants with the Fill Handle

The Payment column is designed to hold the payment number beginning at 1 and ending, in this case, at 36. Although you could enter the values in cells A16 through A51 one at a time, it is much faster to enter the initial two values and then clone the remaining 34 values using the fill handle.

Creating and formatting an ascending number series:

1. Click cell **A16** and type **1**

2. Click cell **A17**, type **2**, and press **Enter**

3. Select the cell range **A16:A17**

4. Hover the mouse over the fill handle in the lower-right corner of cell **A17**, click and drag the fill handle down through cell **A51**, and release the mouse. The values 1 through 36 fill cells A16 through A51, and Excel displays the AutoFill Options Smart Tag

5. With cell range A16:A51 still selected, click the **Center** alignment button on the Formatting toolbar (see Figure 6.21) and click cell **B16**

EXCEL

FIGURE 6.21

Payment column
completed

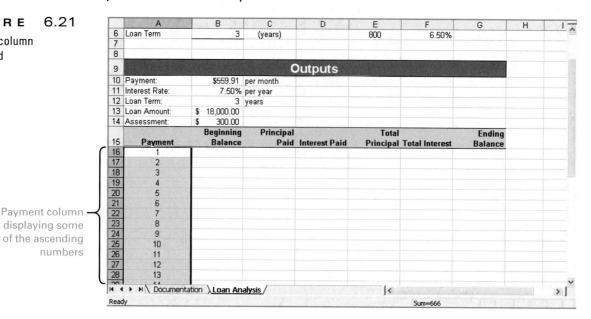

Payment column
displaying some
of the ascending
numbers

Writing a PV Function

The next formula you will write will appear in cell B16, the first of 36 that will display the beginning balance each month. The beginning balance is the amount of the loan left to pay after making the previous month's payment. The first month, the beginning balance is equal to the full loan amount. The beginning balance the second month is the original loan amount minus the amount of the payment applied in month one to pay off the loan. Although you could simply write the formula =LoanAmount (or the equivalent formula, =B13) in cell B16, you will use the present value function, PV, instead. Using the PMT value, interest rate, and loan term as arguments, the PV function returns the original loan amount as its computed result. If it does, that proves the periodic payment in cell B10 is correct. Otherwise, something is wrong.

Writing a PV function to compute the Beginning Balance:

1. If necessary, click cell **B16** to make it the active cell

2. Type **=PV(InterestRate/12,LoanTerm*12,-PeriodicPayment)** and press **Enter**. Remember to not include any spaces in the formula. Excel displays $18,000.00

tip: *One of the tricky things about financial functions, something mentioned earlier, is the sign of the resulting number. A negative sign means the money is flowing out of your pocket, and a positive sign means the money is flowing into your pocket. Because you want a positive value for the loan balance, be sure to type a minus sign preceding* PeriodicPayment.

The present value of a series of mortgage payments should equal the loan amount, because it represents the current value of a loan—far less than its value in the future as it collects interest.

Writing a PPMT Function

The amount of each loan payment that is applied to reduce the principal—eventually making it zero—varies throughout the term of the loan. For example, the amount of the $559.91 monthly payment that goes toward paying off the loan (the principal) is

F I G U R E   6.22

PPMT function syntax

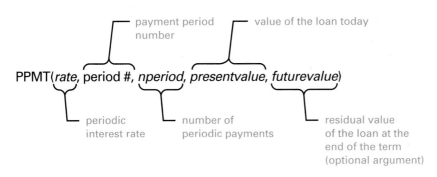

$447.41 the first month. The remainder of the payment, $112.50, is the interest on $18,000 for one month. When the last payment is due, the amount of the loan payment going toward paying off the loan is $556.43, whereas only $3.48 is due in interest. Thus, over the term of a loan, the payment toward reducing the loan increases, and the payment toward interest decreases.

Excel provides the PPMT function to compute the amount of a fixed periodic payment that goes to reduce the principal. Another function, IPMT, computes the interest portion of a payment, and you will learn about it after you investigate the PPMT function.

The PPMT function requires four arguments: the periodic interest rate, the particular period this payment is for, the total number of payments, and the present value of the loan. The fourth required argument, present value of the loan, is the total amount that a series of future payments is worth now—the loan principal. When creating a series of these formulas in a loan amortization schedule, the only argument of the four that changes is the second one. For the first period payment, it is 1; for the second period payment, it is 2 (or references a cell containing 2); and so on. The general form of the PPMT function appears in Figure 6.22.

Jessica wants each row of the amortization schedule to display the portion of the $559.91 payment that goes to pay off the loan. You code the function next.

Writing a PPMT function to compute the principal reduction amount:

1. Click cell **C16** to make it the active cell

2. Type **=PPMT(InterestRate/12,A16,LoanTerm*12,–LoanAmount)** and press **Enter**. Excel displays $447.41, which is the portion of the payment that reduces the principal this month

Be careful to place a minus sign just before typing LoanAmount in the fourth argument so Excel computes and displays a positive value.

Recall that using a name is the same as using the absolute reference of the cell address. This is particularly important because you will copy this formula and others down through the 35 other rows of the loan amortization schedule. You want all cell references to point to the original interest rate, loan term, and loan amount values throughout the amortization schedule. Using names instead of cell addresses guarantees that Excel will not change the references or adjust them in any way. The only cell reference that Excel will adjust when the formula is copied is the second argument, A16. Because you want the second argument to reference each of the individual payment numbers in column A, allowing the reference to remain a relative reference is perfect. Excel will adjust that reference as it copies the formula down through the amortization schedule rows.

Writing an IPMT Function

Cell D16 will contain a formula that computes the amount of the payment that is applied to pay the current month's interest. You will use the IPMT (Interest Payment) function to compute the interest payment. With this first formula as a guide, you will copy it down through all 36 months in the schedule in later steps. The general form of the IPMT function is similar to PPMT. Simply use the same form as PPMT but substitute IPMT for the function name preceding the opening parenthesis starting the function list.

Writing an IPMT function to compute the period's interest:

1. Click cell **D16** to make it the active cell

2. Type **=IPMT(InterestRate/12,A16,LoanTerm*12,–LoanAmount)** and click the **Enter** button on the left end of the formula bar to complete the formula and keep cell D16 the active cell (see Figure 6.23)

FIGURE 6.23

Worksheet with PPMT and IPMT functions

IPMT function and arguments

PPMT function result

IPMT function result

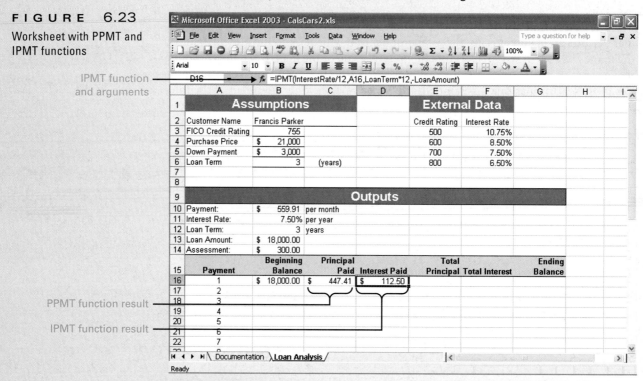

Building Principal, Interest, and Ending Balance Formulas

You have three formulas to build before the first row of the loan amortization schedule is complete. Once that line is done, the remaining 35 lines of the schedule will be simple to create. The Total Principal column holds a running sum of the payments to reduce the loan. The Total Interest column holds the sum of all the interest payments up to and including the current payment. In the last column is the Ending Balance. It is the amount of the principal left to pay. It is equal to the beginning balance for the month minus the Principal Paid amount. You will create these simple formulas in the next steps.

Writing Total Principal, Total Interest, and Ending Balance formulas:

1. Click cell **E16** and type **=C16**

2. Click cell **F16** and type **=D16**

3. Click cell **G16**, type **=B16-C16**, and press **Enter**. The value $17.552.59 appears and is the unpaid loan balance after the first payment is made

Cell E16 shows that of the $559.91 monthly payment, $112.50 is this month's interest payment and $447.41 reduces the loan balance. Each month, the sum of these two numbers is always the same—the monthly payment amount.

If creating formulas required you to write 36 rows of six formulas each, you'd be in for a lot of work. Thankfully, that is not the way worksheet products are designed. You can create a series of formulas that are unique and, often, clone them down or across worksheet cells to create an entire family of related but slightly different formulas.

Jessica tells you that you can create a unique formula for the beginning balance for the second payment and then clone the remainder of the first payment's formulas to the second payment row. With a few adjusting tweaks to selected second payment row formulas, you will have a model row that you can then copy to payment rows 3 through 36.

Writing a general-purpose Beginning Balance formula:

1. Click cell **B17**

2. Type **=G16**, and press **Enter**. The value $17552.59 appears in cell B17

The quickest way to create the formulas for the remainder of the second payment's row is to copy the corresponding formulas from the first payment's row and then make a couple of minor formula adjustments.

Using the fill handle to clone and then adjust selected formulas for the second payment row:

1. Select the cell range **C16:G16**

2. Click the **fill handle**, drag the mouse down one row until the AutoFill outline highlights the cell range C17:G17, and then release the mouse

3. Click cell **E17**, the Total Principal cell for the second payment, type **=C17+E16**, and press **Enter**. Excel displays $897.62

4. Click cell **F17**, the Total Interest cell for the second payment whose formula you are going to replace with a new one, type **=D17+F16**, and press **Enter**. Excel displays $222.20 (see Figure 6.24)

FIGURE **6.24**

Amortization schedule
with second payment's
row completed

	A	B	C	D	E	F	G	H	I
1	**Assumptions**				**External Data**				
2	Customer Name	Francis Parker			Credit Rating	Interest Rate			
3	FICO Credit Rating	755			500	10.75%			
4	Purchase Price	$ 21,000			600	8.50%			
5	Down Payment	$ 3,000			700	7.50%			
6	Loan Term	3	(years)		800	6.50%			
7									
8									
9	**Outputs**								
10	Payment:	$559.91	per month						
11	Interest Rate:	7.50%	per year						
12	Loan Term:	3	years						
13	Loan Amount:	$ 18,000.00							
14	Assessment:	$ 300.00							
15	Payment	Beginning Balance	Principal Paid	Interest Paid	Total Principal	Total Interest	Ending Balance		
16	1	$18,000.00	$447.41	$112.50	$447.41	$112.50	$17,552.59		
17	2	$17,552.59	$450.21	$109.70	$897.62	$222.20	$17,102.38		
18	3								
19	4								
20	5								
21	6								
22	7								

Documentation \ **Loan Analysis**

Ready

Format the first row so that it displays accounting-style currency symbols and then format the second payment row so that it does not display currency symbols at all. You will also format cell B10 containing the periodic payment to match formatting in other cells.

Adding a formatting style to the Style list:

1. Click cell **Format** and then click **Style**. The Style dialog box appears

2. Type **AcctSpecial** in the *Style name* list box to name the new formatting style you are creating, click the **Modify** button, click the **Number** tab (if necessary), and click **Accounting** in the Category list

3. Ensure that the Decimal places list box contains 2, click the **Symbol** list box, click **None** in the list of format choices, click **OK** to close the Format Cells dialog box, click **Add** to save the newly created style, and click **Close** to close the Style dialog box without applying the style

Once you have created a customized and named formatting style, you can apply it to any cells in any worksheet you open on the computer on which you created the style.

Formatting cells with the Format Painter and the Style list:

1. Click cell **B13** containing the loan amount. Cell B13 has the format you want to duplicate in other cells

2. Double-click the **Format Painter** button on the Standard toolbar to copy the format of cell B13. Double-clicking the Format Painter button turns it on until you click it again to turn it off. This allows you to paint a cell's format onto more than one cell or cell range

3. Click cell **B10**

4. Click and drag the cell range **B16:G16** and release the mouse. The first row takes on the same currency format as cell B13

5. Click the **Format Painter** button to deactivate it

6. Click and drag the cell range **B17:G17**, click **Format** on the menu bar, click **Style**, click the Style name list arrow, click AcctSpecial, and click OK. Excel applies the custom style you created in earlier steps to the selected cells (see Figure 6.25)

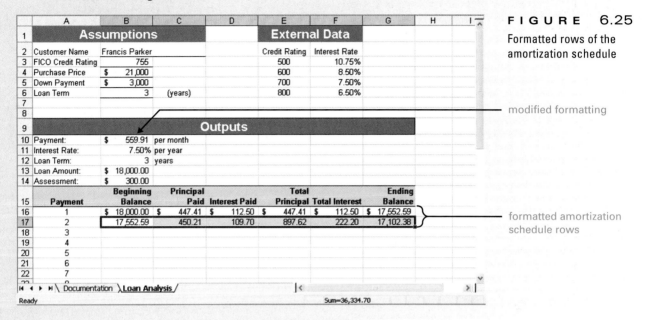

FIGURE 6.25

Formatted rows of the amortization schedule

modified formatting

formatted amortization schedule rows

Using AutoFill to Complete a Series of Related Formulas

Completing the amortization schedule will be surprisingly simple. Because you have created a model row—row 17—whose formulas contain cell references that use both absolute references (names) and relative references in the appropriate way, the row is a model row for the remaining rows. A ***model row*** contains distinct formulas that you can copy to other rows and not have to modify any copied cell formulas afterward.

You are ready to copy row 17 to rows 18 through 51.

Using the fill handle to copy formulas and complete the loan amortization schedule:

1. If necessary, select the cell range **B17:G17**

2. Move the mouse to the fill handle near the lower-right corner of cell **G17**. The mouse pointer changes to a small plus symbol

3. Click the mouse and slowly drag the fill handle down through row 51 so that Excel highlights the range **B17:G51** and then release the mouse (see Figure 6.26)

tip: *If you fill up too few rows, click and drag the fill handle to fill the remaining rows of the amortization schedule. If you fill up too many rows, delete the extra rows*

4. Scroll down the worksheet until you reach row 51. Notice that the final loan payment reduces the ending balance to zero. In other words, the last payment is just enough to pay off the remaining balance of $556.43 and pay the last month's interest of $3.48.

FIGURE 6.26

Completed amortization schedule

	A	B	C	D	E	F	G	H	I
28	13	12,442.60	482.15	77.77	6,039.55	1,239.31	11,960.45		
29	14	11,960.45	485.16	74.75	6,524.70	1,314.06	11,475.30		
30	15	11,475.30	488.19	71.72	7,012.90	1,385.78	10,987.10		
31	16	10,987.10	491.24	68.67	7,504.14	1,454.45	10,495.86		
32	17	10,495.86	494.31	65.60	7,998.45	1,520.05	10,001.55		
33	18	10,001.55	497.40	62.51	8,495.85	1,582.56	9,504.15		
34	19	9,504.15	500.51	59.40	8,996.36	1,641.96	9,003.64		
35	20	9,003.64	503.64	56.27	9,500.00	1,698.23	8,500.00		
36	21	8,500.00	506.79	53.12	10,006.79	1,751.36	7,993.21		
37	22	7,993.21	509.95	49.96	10,516.75	1,801.32	7,483.25		
38	23	7,483.25	513.14	46.77	11,029.89	1,848.09	6,970.11		
39	24	6,970.11	516.35	43.56	11,546.24	1,891.65	6,453.76		
40	25	6,453.76	519.58	40.34	12,065.81	1,931.99	5,934.19		
41	26	5,934.19	522.82	37.09	12,588.63	1,969.08	5,411.37		
42	27	5,411.37	526.09	33.82	13,114.73	2,002.90	4,885.27		
43	28	4,885.27	529.38	30.53	13,644.10	2,033.43	4,355.90		
44	29	4,355.90	532.69	27.22	14,176.79	2,060.65	3,823.21		
45	30	3,823.21	536.02	23.90	14,712.81	2,084.55	3,287.19		
46	31	3,287.19	539.37	20.54	15,252.18	2,105.09	2,747.82		
47	32	2,747.82	542.74	17.17	15,794.91	2,122.27	2,205.09		
48	33	2,205.09	546.13	13.78	16,341.04	2,136.05	1,658.96		
49	34	1,658.96	549.54	10.37	16,890.59	2,146.42	1,109.41		
50	35	1,109.41	552.98	6.93	17,443.57	2,153.35	556.43		
51	36	556.43	556.43	3.48	18,000.00	2,156.83	0.00		
52									

H ◄ ► H \ Documentation \ **Loan Analysis** /

Ready   Sum=1,028,571.16

ending loan balance is zero ——————

AutoFill Smart Tag appears after a copy operation ——

5. Click **Ctrl+Home** to deselect the cell range and make cell A1 active

6. Save the workbook

Working with Date Functions

Excel has 14 date and time functions available. When you enter a date manually, you simply type it in one of several acceptable forms. Excel recognizes that the information is a date and stores it in a special form. For example, if you type into a cell *10/17/2003* without an equal sign preceding it, Excel assumes you are entering the date October 17, 2003, and stores the date in a special date-valued form. The preceding form is called a ***date constant***. Similarly, you can type *October 17, 2003* and Excel will recognize the entry as a date and store it in the same, date-valued form. However, Excel recognizes *=10/17/2003* as an expression whose value is 0.000294, rounded to six decimal places.

There are occasions when you cannot or do not want to enter a fixed date because either it is unknown at the time or it varies with time. For instance, you might want to label a worksheet with the current date. If you type 6/14/2003 into a worksheet cell, the date is static—it never changes. If you want a date that is always current, you can use the Excel function NOW.

Jessica wants you to document the worksheet by adding two dates to the Outputs section of the worksheet: the date that the customer applied for the loan (the application date) and the current date each time the worksheet is printed. The former date is simply a date-valued expression such as 10/17/2003 whereas the latter date uses the NOW function to pick up the current date from the computer's internal clock/calendar. The loan application date requires a label as well as the date constant. Because the application date is an input value, you will place it in the Assumptions section.

Entering a date constant into a worksheet cell:

1. Click cell **A7**, type **Application Date**, and press **Enter**. Because you want to place an underline in cell B7 displaying the application date, you can copy the format from an existing cell, B6

2. Click cell **B6**, click the **Format Painter** button on the Standard toolbar, and click cell **B7**. Excel copies the format from cell B6 to cell B7. An underline displays in cell B7

tip: *If you accidentally paint the format on the wrong cell, simply click Undo Paste Special in the Edit menu to reverse the last action*

3. With B7 active, type **6/14/2004** and press **Enter**. Excel displays the date in cell B7. The underline in cell B7 emphasizes that it contains an input value—something an employee must type

4. If cell B7 displays a two-digit year, then execute step 5. If cell B7 displays a four-digit date, then skip step 5

tip: *If the date in cell B7 displays only two digits for the year, then the default date set for your machine may be set to show two years. You can change the date format by executing step 5*

5. Click cell **B7**, click **Format** on the menu bar, click **Cells**, click the **Number** tab, click **Date** in the Category list, scroll the Type list box until you locate the example date format 3/14/2001, click **3/14/2001**, and click **OK** to format cell B7 so it displays a four-digit year (see Figure 6.27)

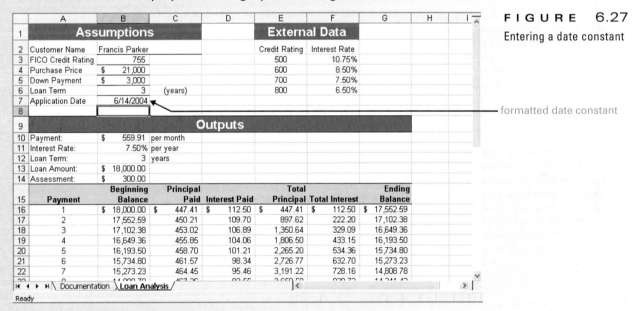

FIGURE 6.27

Entering a date constant

formatted date constant

Using the NOW Function

Several date functions use your computer's clock to determine the current date and time. The NOW function is the most commonly used of these functions. It is one of the Excel functions that has no arguments, but you must be sure to write it with both the opening and closing parentheses immediately following its name. Its form is simply

```
NOW()
```

If you forget the parentheses and type, instead, *=NOW* in a cell, Excel will generate and display the error message "#NAME?" The error message occurs because Excel thinks you are using a name called NOW, but you have not created that name. If you omit the pair of parentheses when you type the NOW function, simply edit the cell and include the opening and closing parentheses side by side.

Writing the NOW function:

1. Click cell **F10**, type **Today's Date:** and then press the **Tab** key
2. In cell G10, type **=NOW()** and press **Enter**. Depending on the exact width of column G, cell G10 displays either pound signs (#) or the date and time side by side in the cell

Regardless of which form displays in your worksheet (pound signs or the date and time), you will format the cell so that it displays the date but not the time in the next set of steps.

Formatting Date-Valued Cells

By default, the NOW function determines and displays both the current date and the current time. Jessica tells you that the time is unnecessary and distracting. She asks you to format the cell so that it displays the current date and omits the current time. To display the date only, you simply use one of the available date formats to exclude the time of day.

Formatting a date-valued cell to display only the date:

1. Right-click cell **G10**. A shortcut menu appears
2. Click **Format Cells** on the shortcut menu
3. If necessary, click the **Number** tab
4. Click **Date** in the Category list box,
5. Scroll the Type list to locate the example format 3/14/01, and click **3/14/01** in the Type list box (see Figure 6.28)

FIGURE 6.28

Formatting a date-valued cell

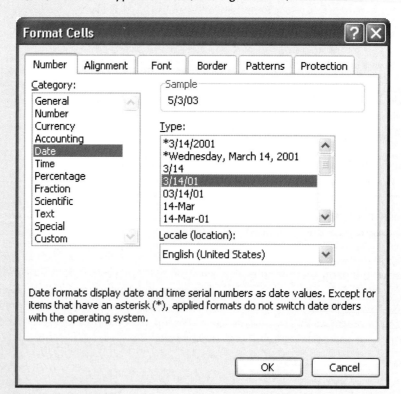

6. Click **OK** to finalize your choices and close the Format Cells dialog box (see Figure 6.29)

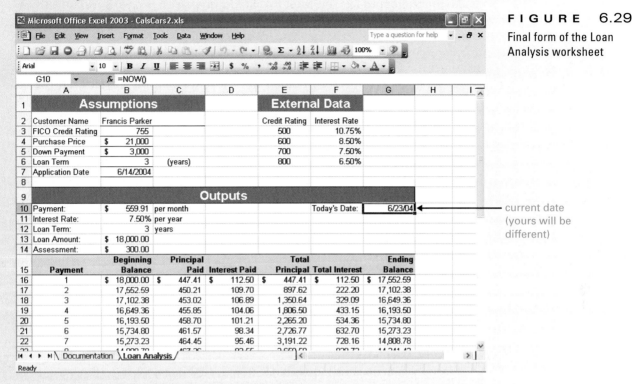

FIGURE 6.29

Final form of the Loan Analysis worksheet

Your worksheet's current date will be different from the date displayed in Figure 6.29

7. Save your workbook and exit Excel

You have completed a lot of work on the loan amortization workbook and learned about several important financial and date functions.

making the grade

SESSION 6.2

1. The process of distributing periodic payments over the life of a loan is called _____.

2. The Excel built-in function that computes the periodic payment is called _____.

3. A periodic payment includes money to repay the loan and money for _____ on the outstanding loan amount.

4. The _____ function computes today's value of a future series of cash flows. Today's value of the cash flow is called its _____ value.

5. The _____ function has no arguments, and you use it to retrieve the date and time from your computer's clock and display it.

EXCEL

SESSION 6.3 SUMMARY

Excel functions are built-in tools that perform calculations quickly and easily. Excel's functions are grouped by type. Most Excel functions have one or more arguments enclosed in parentheses following the function name. A function operates on the input values and expressions in its argument list enclosed in parentheses and it returns a single value. Most functions have positional arguments that must be arranged in a particular order.

Creating worksheets used by others often requires that you provide built-in tests for input data to ensure that they are reasonable and within range. Excel's data validation provides automatic input data checking and allows you to specify the range of allowed values in an input value, an input (help) message, and an error message.

Names allow you to assign a name to a cell or range of cells. They have an advantage over cell references because you can assign a meaningful and memorable name; you can remember names as you write expressions referencing the named cells. Secondly, names function as absolute cell references, making it simpler to copy formulas that reference named ranges.

The IF function allows you to create alternative expressions based on a condition. IF evaluates a condition, which is its first argument, and calculates and displays one expression's value if the condition is true or displays the other expression's value if the condition is false.

VLOOKUP is one of several index functions that does a table search with a search value and returns an answer from the table lookup operation. The two most popular lookup functions are VLOOKUP and HLOOKUP. Both are identical in function except for the arrangement of the lookup table—one uses a vertical lookup table and the other uses a horizontal lookup table.

Financial functions including PMT, PPMT, IPMT, and PV are all related. Each function operates on the theory of the time value of money: Money today is worth more than the same amount of money tomorrow. PMT computes a periodic payment given the interest rate, principal amount, and period. PPMT and IPMT compute the amount of the periodic payment for a particular period that pays off the principal (PPMT) and the amount that pays the interest due on the principal (IPMT). PV, or present value, computes today's value of a future steady stream of cash flows.

Worksheet date functions work with date-valued cells. The NOW function displays the current date and time. Special formats are available for formatting the NOW cell to display various forms of the date or to display various forms of the time. NOW obtains its information from the system clock, which also contains a calendar.

MICROSOFT OFFICE SPECIALIST OBJECTIVES SUMMARY

- Use Insert Function to help write worksheet functions—MOS XL03S-2-3
- Investigate the logical function IF—MOS XL03S-2-4
- Write financial functions including PV, PMT, PPMT, and IPMT—MOS XL03S-2-4
- Write and apply the NOW date function—MOS XL03S-2-4
- Apply and modify cell styles—MOS XL03S-3-2
- Provide data validation for selected worksheet cells—MOS XL03E-1-4
- Write the index function VLOOKUP—MOS XL03E-1-9
- Define and use names in functions in place of cell references—MOS XL03E-1-14

making the grade answers

SESSION 6.1

1. arguments

2. assumption(s) or input(s)

3. validation

4. alert

5. IF

SESSION 6.2

1. amortization

2. PMT

3. interest

4. PV; present value

5. NOW

task reference summary

Task	Page #	Preferred Method
Naming a cell or cell range	EX 6.12	• Select the cell or cell range you want to name • Click the **Name box** in the formula bar • Type the name and press **Enter**
Deleting a name	EX 6.14	• Click **Insert**, point to **Name**, and then click the **Define** button • Click the name in the *Names in workbook* list that you want to delete • Click the **Delete** button and then click the **OK** button
Using the VLOOKUP function	EX 6.19	• Create a lookup table and sort the table in ascending order by the leftmost column • Place in columns to the right of the search columns values you want to return as answers • Write a VLOOKUP function referencing a cell containing the lookup value, the lookup table, and the column containing the answer

EXCEL

TRUE OR FALSE

1. A range error indicates that a value is either too large or too small.

2. The time value of money states that $10 tomorrow is worth more than $10 today.

3. Excel functions operate on the input values and expressions in its argument list enclosed in parentheses.

4. The NOW function only returns and displays the current time.

5. By default all worksheet cells are locked.

FILL-IN

1. It is convenient to divide a worksheet into a(n) _____ section and an output section.

2. Use data _____ to ensure that a worksheet user enters an appropriate value into a cell or cell range.

3. A(n) _____ name acts like an absolute cell reference when you copy a formula containing it to other cells.

4. The _____ function has three arguments: a conditional expression and two alternative expressions. One expression displays if the condition is true, and the other displays otherwise.

5. Some functions have no arguments. An example is the _____ function, which returns the date and time.

6. To compute a periodic payment, use the PMT function. Its arguments are the _____, the number of periods, and the present value or loan amount.

MULTIPLE CHOICE

1. Which is not an argument of the VLOOKUP function?
   a. the match value
   b. the lookup table
   c. the return data
   d. the range lookup

2. Cells that you do not want Excel to protect when you apply worksheet protection are
   a. assumption cells.
   b. changing cells.
   c. unlocked cells.
   d. target cells.

3. Which of the following is not a financial function?
   a. PMT
   b. PVMT
   c. IPMT
   d. PV

4. The IF function has which of the following forms?
   a. IF(conditional test, expression if false, expression if true)
   b. IF(expression if false, expression if true, conditional test)
   c. IF(expression true, expression false, conditional test)
   d. IF(conditional test, expression true, expression false)

5. Cell references have an advantage over names. This is due to which of the following?
   a. A cell reference is more meaningful.
   b. A cell reference is more memorable.
   c. It is simpler to copy formulas that reference cell ranges.
   d. Cell names are easier to remember than cell references.

review of concepts

REVIEW QUESTIONS

1. Discuss how cell protection differs from data validation.

2. Suppose you want to write an expression in cell B7 that guarantees that a value a user enters into cell A1 is positive. Discuss how you would use an expression involving the IF function in cell B7 to return the positive value of any value entered in cell A1.

3. Describe the meaning of "the time value of money" and provide a concrete example using a savings account.

4. Explain the difference between these two expressions: **=7/21/2004** and **7/21/2004**.

5. Describe what happens if you type **=NOW** into a worksheet cell and press Enter. Assume that today's date is January 14, 2004.

6. Explain why locking or unlocking worksheet cells is not sufficient to protect or unprotect them.

CREATE THE QUESTION

For each of the following answers, create an appropriate short question.

ANSWER	QUESTION
1. It displays an error alert message	_____
2. The first argument of an IF function	_____
3. The greatest value that is less than or equal to the search value	_____
4. The Name box is the fastest way	_____
5. The IPMT function calculates and displays that value	_____
6. Double-click the tab, type a new name, and press Enter	_____

1. Determining Savings Match with Data Validation

Shelly Mueller has been studying German since her freshman year in high school. This summer, she has decided to participate in a study-abroad program sponsored by the German Club at her school. Her parents feel this will be a good learning experience for her and have agreed to pay for the cost of the program.

Shelly has a part-time job at a nearby stationery store where she earns $125 a week. She has two full months to save money for the trip before she leaves on the first of June. To encourage and help her with her savings, her grandfather has agreed to contribute to her savings. Shelly has kept track of her savings for each week and needs to send the summary to her grandfather. Since her grandfather is matching her savings, Shelly has decided to put in equal amounts for the "Match" row as she entered in the Savings row.

1. Open the workbook **ex06Savings.xls** (see Figure 6.30) and save it as **<yourname>Savings2.xls**

2. Click cell **A5** and type **Match**. Click cell **B5** and enter the formula **=B4**. Using the fill handle, copy this formula into the cell range **C5:I5**. Include your name in a custom header and print this sheet

3. Delete the formulas in the cell range **B5:I5**. Click cell **B5**, click **Data**, and then click **Validation** to activate the Data Validation dialog box. Use the data validation tool to ensure that no amount greater than $50 or less than $1 will be entered for the Match value

4. Type the title **Valid Amount** and type the input message **Valid amounts are less than or equal to $50**

5. Type an error alert message titled **Invalid Amount** and type the message **The amount you entered is greater than $50**. Use the stop style for this alert

6. Test the data validation by entering **$75** for the match value of cell B5. What happens?

7. Using the fill handle, copy these validation terms in cells **C5:I5**

8. Enter the correct match values, using the values in the Savings row and the $50 match limit as your guide

9. After the values for the fourth week of May, create a column titled **Totals**. (Type **Totals** in cell **J2**.) Write a SUM function in cell J4 to total the Savings row for both months

10. Using the fill handle, copy the formula into cell **J5** so that it includes the total matching contribution for her grandfather

11. Click cell **J6**, and then write a formula that displays the grand total amount Shelley will have for her trip. Label it **Grand Total** and adjust the cell widths, heights, and colors so that the worksheet is attractive

12. Include your name in the custom header, save the workbook, and print the worksheet

FIGURE 6.30

Savings match workbook

	A	B	C	D	E	F	G	H	I	J	K	L
1												
2	Month	April				May						
3	Week		1	2	3	4	1	2	3	4		
4	Savings	$75	$75	$50	$40	$40	$80	$75	$50			
5												

2. Deciding between Loan Options by Total Payment

James Thomas has been out of college for three years. Now that he has had the chance to put aside some of his income, he would like to look for a new car. He has been able to save $4,000 and has decided that he would like a car that is two years old with no more than 20,000 miles on it. He found a car that meets his criteria. The current owner wants $10,500 for the car. James will apply his savings to the purchase, but needs a loan for the remaining $6,500. He went to several local banks to find the best loan offer.

ABC Bank has a loan available at 9.5 percent interest for two years. The interest compounds monthly and James' payments would be due at the end of each month. XYZ Bank has a loan available at 9 percent interest for 2½ years. This loan also compounds monthly with payments due at the end of each month.

James needs your help to determine which loan alternative is best. He wants to determine which loan has the lowest monthly payment. He has entered each bank's offer in the worksheet called **ex06CarLoan.xls**.

1. Open **ex06CarLoan.xls** (see Figure 6.31) and save it as **<yourname>CarLoan2.xls** to preserve the original worksheet

2. Click cell **A6** and type **Periodic Payment**

3. Click cell **B6**, click **Insert** on the menu bar, and then click **Function**

4. Click **Financial** in the *Or select a category* list box, click **PMT** in the *Select a function* list box, and click **OK**

5. Based on the information given for ABC Bank, in the **Rate** text box write a formula referencing the interest rate cell, cell B4. Remember to divide the interest rate by the number of payments per year

6. Click the **Nper** text box and type the formula for the total number of payments you will make for the entire life of the loan. Remember to multiply the loan duration in years (a reference to the cell containing it) by the number of payments per year

7. Click the **Pv** text box, type − (minus) followed by the cell address containing the principal amount, **B3**, and then click **OK**

8. Copy the formula in cell **B6** to cell **C6** to also create the PMT function for the loan from XYZ Bank

9. Based on the monthly payment figures alone for each bank, which appears to be the better loan for James? Highlight this bank's information with a Light Green fill color. (Click the **Fill Color** list arrow on the Formatting toolbar and click the color **Light Green**)

10. Place your name in your worksheet's header, save the workbook, and print the worksheet

11. After examining your results, you decide to determine the total payments that James will make to each bank for their loan to make sure he chooses the right loan for his car. Title the row below Periodic Payment **Total Payments**. In cell **B7**, create a formula to multiply the monthly payment in B6 by the number of months in ABC Bank's loan term

12. Create a similar formula in cell **C7** using the monthly payment and months in the loan for XYZ Bank. Be sure the Total Payments display positive values

13. Based on the total payments, which loan should James take? Highlight the information for this bank and print the worksheet

14. Save the workbook

FIGURE 6.31

Loan options workbook

	A	B	C	D	E
1					
2		ABC Bank	XYZ Bank		
3	Loan Amount	$6,500	$6,500		
4	Interest Rate	9.50%	9%		
5	Term (years)	2	2.5		

challenge

1. Forecasting Interest Expense Using Amortization Schedules

Sharon Crowley has always wanted to blend her business savvy with her love of cooking. After college, she attended culinary school for two years specializing in pastries and desserts, and she decided to fulfill her lifelong dream to open her own dessert shop.

Sharon was able to qualify for a small business loan through her local credit union that would cover the costs of needed machinery and supplies and the first few payments of her lease for a total of $25,000. The loan rate is 8.75 percent and is to be paid monthly over a four-year period. Sharon wants to be able to forecast what her interest expenses will be for tax purposes. She has asked you to create an amortization schedule to detail the loan over its term.

Do the following. Open **ex06Desserts.xls** (see Figure 6.32) and save the workbook as **<yourname>Desserts2.xls**. Sharon has already figured out what her monthly payment would be using the PMT function, but she input the wrong rate for the loan. Change the interest rate in cell B4 to 8.75 percent. What happens to her monthly payment after the rate is adjusted? Enter the dates that each payment is due under the Date heading (cell A14), with the first payment due on March 31, 2004, in cell A15. Use the AutoFill feature to complete the sequential series April 30, 2004, through February 29, 2008. To represent the payment numbers, type **1** in cell B15 and **2** in cell B16. Use the AutoFill feature to complete the sequential series 3 through 48 in the Payment Number column. In cell C15, type the formula **=B3** to display the initial unpaid loan balance.

Click cell **D15**, click **Insert** on the menu bar, click **Function**, type **payment** in the *Search for a function* text box, click the **Go** button, and then click **PPMT** in the Function name. Enter the necessary information by typing cell references in each list box for the function. *Important:* Be sure to make cell references in the Rate, Nper, and Pv text boxes absolute references. The cell reference in the Per text box must be relative. Fill in the remaining information for Per (relative cell reference), Nper (absolute cell reference), and Pv (absolute cell reference), and then click **OK**. Change the formula, if necessary, so that the result is a positive number. Click cell **E15**, and write the formula

```
=-IPMT($B$4/12,B15,$B$5*12,$B$3)
```

To complete the information for the first payment due on March 31, 2004, the ending balance must be determined. Create a formula for cell **F15** that subtracts the Repayment of Principal from the Beginning Balance (cell **C15**). Create a formula for the Beginning Balance for cell C16 (payment 2) by referencing the Ending Balance of the previous month (using all relative references). Copy the remaining formulas from payment 1 (cells **D15:F15**) to the cells for payment 2 (to cells **D16:F16**). Now copy the formulas in cell range **C16:F16** to the cell range **C17:F62** to complete the schedule. What is the Ending Balance for payment 48? Include your name in the worksheet header and print the worksheet. Save the workbook.

	A	B	C	D	E	F	G	H	I	J
1	DTU Credit Union Loan									
2										
3	Loan Amount	$25,000								
4	Interest Rate	7.75%								
5	Term (years)	4								
6	Monthly Payment	$607.39								
7										
8										
9										
10										
11										
12										
13	Amortization Schedule									
14	Date	Payment Number	Beginning Balance	Repayment of Principal	Interest	Ending Balance				
15										
16										
17										
18										
19										
20										
21										
22										

Dessert Data
Ready

FIGURE 6.32
Sharon Crowley interest expense workbook

2. Computing Shipping Costs for West Coast Imports

West Coast Imports sells fine, imported gifts through the mail. The shipping manager tracks the shipping costs and total costs on a daily basis in a worksheet she maintains. At the end of each day, she erases the input data in preparation for the next day's orders. You will help the shipping manager by writing formulas that help her calculate the shipping cost for each package. You will employ data validation to ensure that the package weight and shipping zone are valid, thus providing a check on those values as the shipping manager enters them.

Shipping costs depend upon the weight of a package and the zone to which it is being shipped. For this problem, there are six shipping zones. Begin by opening the workbook **ex06Shipping.xls** (see Figure 6.33), save the workbook as **<yourname>Shipping2.xls**, and then make the changes specified in the following paragraphs.

Enter into cell C1 the function to display today's date. Format the cell to display the date (mm/dd/yy format) only. Select the cell range A4:A22 and use the Data Validation to ensure that a user can enter only whole numbers between 1 and 6. Type **Enter a value between 1 and 6.** for both the Input Message and Error Alert. Select the cell range D4:D22 and use the Data Validation to ensure that a user can enter only whole numbers between 1 and 100. Type **Enter a value between 1 and 100.** for both the Input Message and Error

Alert. Select the cell range A34:G68 (the shipping cost table) and assign it the name *Shipping*. Across the top of the table are the six zones and along the left edge are package weights. At the intersection of a zone and a weight is the shipping cost. For example, a 9-pound package shipped to zone 4 costs $10.60. Write in cell E4 the VLOOKUP expression that looks up the weight in the Shipping table and returns the cost. (*Hint:* Look up the weight in cell D4, write **Shipping** as the second argument, and reference the zone in cell A4 in a simple expression as the third argument to determine the lookup column returned—the zone number plus 1.) Clone the formula down through the rest of the column. Write the formula in F4 for the total cost—charge plus shipping cost—and copy it down the column. Form totals for the Charge, Weight, Shipping Expense, and Total columns in cells C24 through F24. Place the label *Total* in cell B24. Place a page break in cell A30 so the shipping table prints on a new page. Place your name in the worksheet header, print the worksheet, and print the formulas for cells E4 through F24 only. Sort the Orders by zone and use the Data Subtotal command to display subtotals of the Charge, Weight, Shipping Expense, and Total columns by zone. Ensure that column A is wide enough to display the newly inserted subtotal labels (particularly, "Grand Total"), then print the subtotal list of orders. (You do not need to print the second page containing the shipping table.)

FIGURE 6.33

Split screen showing order data and Shipping Costs table

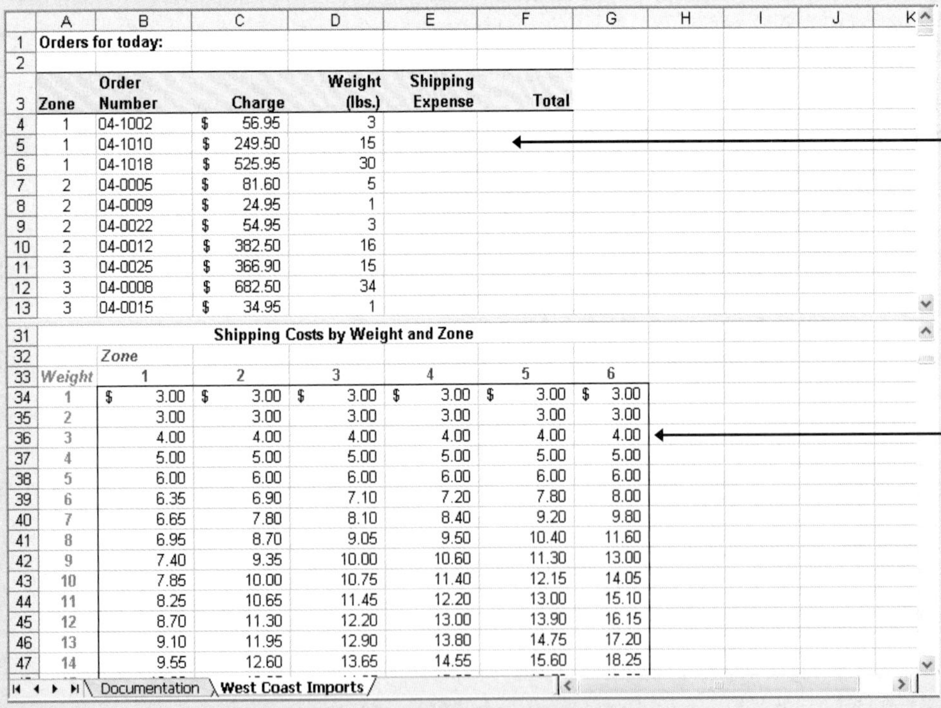

orders without formulas for shipping expense

Shipping Costs table containing cost based on weight and zone

1. Deciding between Investment Opportunities Using Payment

Jonathan Leitman owns a small, yet successful, custom furniture company. For the past few years, he has done little marketing since current customers refer most of his new customers to him. This past year, his business has greatly increased and he has decided to grow the business. He has already looked into opening a larger production facility, purchasing new machines and tools, and hiring a few carpenters to assist him. The initial cost of expanding the business will be $225,000, and Jonathan knows he will be able to raise this initial capital. Jonathan's problem is that he doesn't know how he should market his company.

A business consultant has recommended two options to him. The first option is that Jonathan hires a Web designer to create a Web site for the firm. The consultant feels this would be the best marketing opportunity since he could include pictures, dimensions, costs, and anything else a potential customer would want to know. The greatest advantage of the Web site is that orders could be placed directly through the Web site. The second option is to hire an advertising agency to design and implement a marketing campaign for the company. The main advantage of the advertising campaign option is that it would give the company exposure to a lot of potential customers who would not otherwise hear about the company's products.

Jonathan's consultant has estimated the additional initial cost for each of the options. The Web site will incur an additional initial cost of $250,000. Hiring an advertising agency will require an initial cost of $325,000. After meeting with his loan officer, Jonathan was approved for an additional $325,000 for his loan at a rate of 9.5 percent for three years with payments due monthly. In addition, the advertising agency has a relationship with the bank that would result in a reduction of the annual interest rate to 4.5 percent if Jonathan hires the agency.

Jonathan has asked you to help him decide which he should invest in—a Web site or an advertising campaign. He can choose only one of the options due to capital restraints. Open workbook **ex06Leitman.xls** and save it as **<yourname>Leitman6.xls**. Create a worksheet, titled **Payments**, that summarizes the initial cost and loan terms for each option. Remember to include in the initial cost the total of the initial costs of each investment and the initial cost of the facility, tools, and new carpenters. Using the Payment Function, determine the monthly payment and total payments for each investment option. Jonathan wants to compare interest and principal payments for each option since both the interest rates and principal amounts are different. He does not want to look at all 36 months, but has asked you to include in your worksheet a breakdown of the interest, principal, and total payments for the first and second month. If Jonathan's goal is to pay as little interest as possible, which option should he choose based on these results?

Improve the worksheet's appearance and make all payment amounts appear in red. Open the worksheet titled **Documentation** and, in row 4, enter Investment and Loan Options. In cell **B7**, enter **Prepared by: Jonathan Leitman**. In cell **B9**, enter **Analyzed by:** followed by your name. Click in cell **B11** and enter **Date:** followed by the current date. Make the appearance of the documentation sheet similar to the payments worksheet in font and color. Save the workbook again to preserve your work and print it.

2. Avante's Avocados

George Avante has been an avocado grower all his life. His great-grandfather started the family grove in Temecula, California. It has since been passed from generation to generation. Currently all his crops are sold to local grocery chains where Avante's gets approximately $0.25 each. The local grocery chains in turn sell the avocados for up to $1.00 each. George has decided that through the Internet, he can provide avocados, potentially nationwide, at a much better price to the consumer and achieve a higher profit for Avante's. His idea is based on the fact that so many other growers of oranges, grapefruits, apples, and exotic fruits have done the same by filling orders over the Internet and shipping directly to the private homes and businesses. With the romantic history behind the Avante grove, the beautiful location in the mountains of Temecula, the organic growth process, and the family involvement in actually personally picking avocados, an enticing Web site has been created and the market tested.

All the initial results look promising. However, George first must evaluate the financial implications of the costs associated with the new business. He will need to invest money in packaging equipment, new computers, and software, and remodel part of his current facilities to handle his own packaging operation. That will require a small business loan. Plus, there are many other new costs that Avante's will incur such as the actual packaging and shipping material, additional labor, Web site maintenance, and so on. George has already estimated these values and has added them to his current fixed and variable costs. George is uncertain where his breakeven point is, how the new loan payment impacts that point, and if he has the capacity to produce enough avocados to break even. If Avante's breakeven quantity exceeds the capacity, George still has options. He can adjust the sales price or change the terms of the loan. For now, though, he needs to base his decision on the established loan numbers and pricing.

Create a workbook that allows George to determine Avante's breakeven quantity. Open the workbook titled **ex06Avocado.xls**. Immediately save it as **<yourname>Avocado6.xls**. The Avante's Avocados worksheet has been broken into two sections: *Assumptions* and *Outputs*. In the Assumptions section you will see that George has already entered his estimates for costs, loan amount, capacity, etc. However, the Outputs section does not yet have any formulas. You need to create the formulas to perform the calculations so that George can make an informed decision. Start by naming each of the cells in the Assumptions section that contain values. Use the labels that appear to the left of the cells. (*Hint:* select the cell range **A2:B8**, click **Insert**, point to **Name**, click **Create**, ensure the **Left column** check box contains a checkmark, and click **OK**.) Next, write a payment function using PMT to calculate the *Loan Payment* per month in cell B11. Then write a formula to calculate the monthly *New Fixed Costs* (Current Fixed Costs + Loan Payment) in cell B12. Your formulas must use the cell names and not the actual values or cell address. Name both cells after the formulas are completed, as you did for the Assumptions section.

The last item that needs to be calculated is the *Breakeven Quantity*. For your worksheet, this is defined as the quantity of avocados that Avante's must sell each month to cover costs. Selling more avocados will result in a profit and selling less will result in a loss. The method for calculating the Breakeven Quantity is in the worksheet. You will have to rearrange the formula and solve for Quantity. (Breakeven Quantity equals the fixed cost divided by the result of the price less the variable cost per piece.) Finally, use an IF function to compare the *Breakeven Quantity* to the *Capacity* in cell B14. If the Breakeven Quantity is greater than the Capacity, display the phrase "Quantity Required Exceeds Capacity." If it is not greater than the Capacity, display the phrase "OK to Implement Project." Type your name in the header, save your workbook, and print it. Next print the worksheet formulas. Make sure you adjust the column widths so that the entire formula is displayed.

1. Using Future Values to Choose a Savings Vehicle

The Tallaricos' oldest son will be starting college in a little over a year. Since the tuition will be due at that time, they have decided to pull some of their money out of the stock market and invest in very conservative savings vehicles. They feel that they don't want to take any risks with this money. It must be available to pay for college. The first year's tuition will be approximately $24,000 and this is the amount for which the Tallaricoses want an alternative investment.

Open **ex06Conservative.xls** and save the workbook as **<yourname>Conservative2.xls**. First define the appropriate cells with the names **Rate**, **Years**, **Payment**, and **FutureValue**, as the columns are labeled. You have decided to go to www.bankrate.com to get the latest rates for each of these investments. When the Web page opens, click the **Rates** tab. In the box labeled **Overnight Averages**, click **Today's averages**. Once that page appears, scroll down until you see the Rates for Savings investments. Input these rates into the worksheet and input the information for Years and Payment. Remember that each investment will be for one year. For the money market account and checking account, Mr. Tallarico will make monthly contributions of $2,000 for the year period.

For the Future Value column, click cell **E5** and then click **Insert**, click **Function**, and locate the **Future Value** function. Use the given information to input the Future Value formula. Remember that the money market and checking accounts pay interest monthly. Once this is computed, use the fill handle to drag the formula into the needed cells in the Future Value column. Which savings vehicle should Mr. Tallarico use to invest $20,000? Include your name in the header, print the worksheet, and save the workbook.

2. Selling or Holding Stocks Using Lookup Tables

Professor Pasquale is a finance professor at the Stockdale City University. He started trading his own stocks a few years ago to illustrate how the stock market works for his class lectures. What started out as an experiment has become a hobby for the professor and he has his own online account in which he can place all of his trades and get any data on the stock market that he may need. He would like you to create a worksheet illustrating how each stock has performed for him, which he will use as an illustration in his finance class.

Open **ex06Stocks.xls** and save the workbook as **<yourname>Stocks2.xls**. Professor Pasquale wants you to look up the price of each stock on the day it was purchased three months ago from today's date and its price today. He then wants you to write formulas to calculate each stock's net change in price.

First, enter today's date in cell **C4**, and then copy it down through the cell range **C5:C10**. Next, ensure that the Date of Purchase and Current Date columns display dates with four-digit years by formatting them, if needed. Use your favorite browser and go to finance.yahoo.com (do not type www before finance). Click the **Stock Research** hyperlink, click the **Historical Quotes** link. For each stock, enter the ticker symbol, date of purchase, and today's date. The Web site will give you the price of the stock for each day during this period. Retrieve the closing price on the date of purchase and today's date and input these data into the worksheet for each stock. Write formulas in the Net Change column to subtract the purchase price from the current price.

Include your name in the worksheet header. Change the worksheet printing orientation to Landscape so that it prints on one page, print the worksheet, and save the workbook.

around the world

1. Comparing Semester Abroad Costs

Karen's university has a strong study abroad program. The university has developed relationships with many well-respected schools around the world and offers semester-length programs with course work completed at these schools. Karen is graduating next year and wants to spend the next semester in Europe.

You work in the office for study abroad programs and are friends with Karen. She has asked you to help her summarize the costs associated with each program so that she can make a decision. You need to design a worksheet for her and it needs to be clear and accurate. The program in Spain has the following costs: tuition $8,500, room and board $3,000, and airfare of $750. The France program has the following costs: tuition $7,200, room and board $4,500, and airfare of $975. The England program has the following costs: tuition $11,000, room and board $2,800 and airfare of $895. Karen also wants to take $2,000 with her for spending money, no matter which program she chooses. Open **ex06AbroadCosts.xls** and save it as **<yourname>AbroadCosts6.xls**. Input these costs into a worksheet and label the worksheet Abroad Costs. Create a column titled Total Costs and create the appropriate formula so the total cost of each program is included on the worksheet.

Based on your results, Karen has decided she must choose between Spain and France. A local French Club will loan Karen the full amount needed at an interest rate of 8.75 percent. She will need to make monthly payments on the loan for 10 years. For the Spanish program, she would take out a loan from the university at an interest rate of 9 percent. She would also have to make monthly payments on this loan, but for a total of seven years. Summarize this information on the Loan Costs worksheet. Create a column titled Monthly Payment and use the Payment function to calculate the monthly payment for each loan. Karen decides that she will choose the program with the lowest monthly payment because she feels it will cost her less overall. You think this way of thinking is incorrect and illustrate by showing her the Future Value of each loan, which is how much she really pays for each. Create a column for this information and input the appropriate financial formula to give the future value of each loan. Include your name in the header of both worksheets and print them both. Save your workbook.

2. Patrice Williams' Marathon Tours

Patrice Williams has been working as a group leader in an adventure racing company coordinating and escort-ing a group of 150 to 300 athletes from the United States to various race locations around the world. Patrice has developed what she thinks would be the ideal tour package for many great racing destinations. Typically, a package goes on sale one year in advance, and within six months the majority of the participants have signed up for the tour. Next year she will organize and implement a tour to London for the Flora London Marathon. Global Marathons offers a payment plan to attract enough customers to keep the event profitable. To avoid a loss associated with a dramatic change in the destination currency, she could borrow the final tour package amount and use that money to pay all the major costs up front.

Open the workbook titled **ex06Marathon.xls**. Immediately save the file as **<yourname>Marathon6.xls**. The worksheet has been broken into three sections: *Assumptions, External Data,* and *Outputs*. In the *Assumptions* section Patrice has supplied all the current information for you to perform the calculations.

Patrice gives a discount to all nonrunner participants traveling in the group. That discount is just the cost of the entry fee to the marathon. Patrice's margin for each participant is $250. She also requires a $200 deposit at the time the participant signs up for the tour. The hotels have provided their room rates based on occupancy level, which she has already converted to U.S. dollars (in the *External Data* section). You need to create the appropriate formulas for each variable in the *Outputs* section as well as an amortization schedule.

Start by naming each of the cells in the *Assumptions* section that contain values. Use the labels that appear to the left of the cells. It isn't necessary to label the hotel information. Complete the Hotel Calculations table, which is designed to figure the cost per hotel for the number of double rooms and single rooms and then total these values. Use the VLOOKUP function to calculate these costs. Total the results. In the *Totals* and *Deductions* section of *Outputs* create the appropriate functions to realize the *Total Package Costs*, as well as *Total Deposits* and *Total Margins*. Note the costs are total, not per person. Since Patrice doesn't need to take a loan out for the total amount, you need to reduce the *Total Package Costs* by those items under *Deductions*. This will give you the *Loan Amount*. Then, write a PMT function to calculate the *Monthly Payment*. Finally, complete the amortization schedule at the bottom of the worksheet. Compare the total interest paid with Patrice's *Total Margin*. Type your name in the header, save your workbook, and print it. Print the worksheet formulas. Adjust the column widths so that each formula is fully visible.

running project

Pro Golf Academy

Betty Carroll is worried about her cash flow this month. Each month she places her order for golf shirts by the 5th of the month to ensure delivery for the next month. January and February have been lean months this year, and she will need to order over $10,000 worth of golf shirts to carry her through next month. She has put together a worksheet containing her estimate of the number of each type of golf shirt she will need to purchase from her wholesale distributor and their individual unit (wholesale) costs. The total cost is over $10,000. She has calculated that she will be able to pay $2,000 cash, but she wants to obtain a loan for the balance to help her cash flow. She reasons that financing this next purchase over a one-year period will allow her enough cash and sales to pay off the loan and maintain a good cash flow. She asks you to put together a loan amortization schedule for the proposed loan's 12 payment periods beginning on March 1.

Begin by loading **ex06ProGolf.xls** and save it as **<yourname>ProGolf6.xls**. Type some documentation information on the Documentation worksheet such as the creation date, the author's name, the modification date, and the store's name.

Create the loan amortization information on this sheet. Model the worksheet after the loan analysis worksheet you created for this chapter, except omit the External Data section and use labels in the Assumptions area that are appropriate for her business (see Figure 6.34). (Use "Inventory Total Price" instead of "Purchase Price.") Omit the FICO® Credit Rating information. For the Application Date, write a function to display the current date and format the cell to display the date only. Assume the annual interest rate is 9.75 percent (inventory financing is more risky than automobile financing). Create the same columns in the amortization section as there are in the chapter case problem: Payment, Beginning Balance, Principal Paid, Interest Paid, Total Principal, Total Interest, and Ending Balance. The value in the Inventory Finance Amount should be the total order value (see the sum on the Purchases worksheet). The loan amount value is the Inventory Total Price minus $2,000 (Betty's down payment on the shirt purchase). Create names for the cells containing Inventory Total Price, Down Payment, Loan Term, Periodic Payment, Interest Rate, and Loan Amount. Move the Interest Rate label and the interest rate up into the Assumptions section, since it is now a user-input value. Unlike the chapter example, there is no special assessment fee. Use data validation for the cell containing the value of the Inventory Total Price so that a user can enter a value only in the range of $0 through $25,000. Format all the worksheet cells in an attractive way (see Figure 6.34).

Color the Documentation worksheet tab green, color the Purchases worksheet tab yellow, and color the Loan Amortization worksheet tab blue. Ensure that the Loan Amortization worksheet prints in landscape orientation. Write your name in each worksheet's header and print all three worksheets when you are done. Print the formulas for the Loan Amortization worksheet to demonstrate your use of names. Remember to save your finished workbook.

FIGURE 6.34

Example format for the Loan Amortization worksheet

	A	B	C	D	E	F	G	H
1	Assumptions							
2	Customer Name	Pro Golf Academy						
3	Inventory Finance Amount	$ 10,552.10						
4	Down Payment	$ 2,000.00						
5	Loan Term	1	year(s)					
6	Interest Rate	9.75%	per year					
7	Application Date	1/4/04						
8								
9	Outputs							
10	Periodic Payment:	$ xxxxxx.xx	per month					
11	Loan Term:	1	year(s)					
12	Loan Amt.	$ 8,552.10						
13								
14	Payment	Beginning Balance	Principal Paid	Interest Paid	Total Principal	Total Interest	Ending Balance	
15	1	$ xxxxxx.xx	$ xxxxxx.xx	$ xxxxxx.xx	$ xxxxxx.xx	$ xxxxxx.xx	$ xxxxxx.xx	
16	2	xxxxxx.xx	xxxxxx.xx	xxxxxx.xx	xxxxxx.xx	xxxxxx.xx	xxxxxx.xx	
17	3	xxxxxx.xx	xxxxxx.xx	xxxxxx.xx	xxxxxx.xx	xxxxxx.xx	xxxxxx.xx	
18	4	xxxxxx.xx	xxxxxx.xx	xxxxxx.xx	xxxxxx.xx	xxxxxx.xx	xxxxxx.xx	
19	5	xxxxxx.xx	xxxxxx.xx	xxxxxx.xx	xxxxxx.xx	xxxxxx.xx	xxxxxx.xx	
20	6	xxxxxx.xx	xxxxxx.xx	xxxxxx.xx	xxxxxx.xx	xxxxxx.xx	xxxxxx.xx	
21	7	xxxxxx.xx	xxxxxx.xx	xxxxxx.xx	xxxxxx.xx	xxxxxx.xx	xxxxxx.xx	
22	8	xxxxxx.xx	xxxxxx.xx	xxxxxx.xx	xxxxxx.xx	xxxxxx.xx	xxxxxx.xx	
23	9	xxxxxx.xx	xxxxxx.xx	xxxxxx.xx	xxxxxx.xx	xxxxxx.xx	xxxxxx.xx	
24	10	xxxxxx.xx	xxxxxx.xx	xxxxxx.xx	xxxxxx.xx	xxxxxx.xx	xxxxxx.xx	
25	11	xxxxxx.xx	xxxxxx.xx	xxxxxx.xx	xxxxxx.xx	xxxxxx.xx	xxxxxx.xx	
26	12	xxxxxx.xx	xxxxxx.xx	xxxxxx.xx	xxxxxx.xx	xxxxxx.xx	(0.00)	
27								
28								
29								

Documentation / Purchases / Loan Amortization

1. What's in a Name?

Explain the advantages and disadvantages of using a name in place of a cell or cell range in formulas. Begin by considering a VLOOKUP function similar to the one used in the chapter case. What advantage does using a table name instead of a cell range have?

2. Present Value

Suppose you won a cash prize for the most valuable cost-saving suggestion of the year, and your award is 10% of the probable savings, or $60,000. However, you do not get a lump sum payment of $60,000. Instead, the company will pay you the prize money in equal monthly installments of $1,000 per month for five years. You would like to have the money now to use as a down payment on a condominium. Your company agrees to pay you a lump sum next week. How do you figure out what is an equitable, reasonable amount? Describe how to arrive at a fair market value and what variables you must consider in determining the lump sum payment.

7

Developing Multiple Worksheet and Workbook Applications

did you know?

the *game of a cat's cradle—two players alternately stretch a looped string over their fingers to produce different designs—has been around since about 1760.*

there *are 110 calories per hour consumed during an hour of typing—only 30 more than those used while sleeping.*

Cleveland *spelled backwards is "DNA level C."*

as *of January 1998, American Express had not issued a single credit card with an expiration date past December 1999. The company hoped to protect cardholders from Y2K problems.*

ostriches *are the second fastest animal in the world. They can run at 40 miles per hour for at least 30 minutes.*

you *can reference worksheet cells that are stored on disk but not currently open. Learn more about this in the chapter.*

Chapter Objectives

- Design a multiple-sheet workbook and understand when it is useful
- Modify the onscreen window layout—MOS XL03S-5-6
- Set the default number of worksheets—MOS XL03E-5-3
- Insert, delete, and reposition worksheets in a workbook—MOS XL03S-5-4
- Creating a workbook template—MOS XL03E-4-4
- Rename a worksheet tab and color it—MOS XL03S-3-4
- Establish worksheet page settings—MOS XL03S-5-7
- Group worksheets in a workbook and enter data in multiple sheets at once
- Consolidate and summarize data using three-dimensional formulas
- Use cell Watch—MOS XL03E-1-13
- Reference cells in other workbooks using link formulas
- Maintain and update linked workbooks

Bridgewater Engineering Company (BECO)

Bridgewater Engineering Company (BECO) builds industrial tools and machines for heavy industry. Jack Leonard established the firm in 1951 in Somerville, New Jersey. After Jack retired, Stirling Leonard, Jack's son, took over as CEO. In addition to the plant in Somerville, BECO has plants in two other locations: Van Buren, Arkansas, and West Lafayette, Indiana.

The three plants collectively employ 175 people and 9 administrators. The workforce consists of trained, versatile mechanics led by professional engineers. BECO is experienced and equipped to build special machinery and equipment of all kinds including the installation of electrical, hydraulic, and pneumatic power components and their controls. Each spacious plant has over 10,000 square feet of workspace with 28 feet of headroom in all manufacturing areas. BECO's own facilities include lathes, vertical and horizontal boring mills, planers, and assorted machinery for milling, drilling, welding, and control assembly. BECO builds all machinery from scratch, using steel rods, sheet steel, and other sheet metals to fashion the custom-built machinery that customers order. Examples of machinery that BECO builds include lathes, surface grinders, drill presses, boring mills, band saws, and Turret mills—all products used in heavy manufacturing.

Stirling was slow to embrace computing, but two years ago he finally converted many of BECO's financial and job-bidding systems over to computer professionals who designed automated systems for him. He has maintained control and interest in tracking sales of machine tools and machines that BECO manufactures to give him a good overview of sales by machine type. He wants a summary of sales of machinery by all three plants in a handy, simple, easy-to-read format. Your job is to first study the three manufacturing plants' workbooks and then devise a workbook or workbooks that merge the data from the three plants together into a single overview worksheet. Figure 7.1 shows an example of the summary worksheet displaying total sales of the three BECO plants.

FIGURE 7.1

Summary of BECO
machine sales

	A	B	C	D	E	F
1		Qtr 1	Qtr 2	Qtr 3	Qtr 4	Totals
2	Danielli	745,633	937,044	514,510	684,618	2,881,805
3	Somerville	757,853	845,842	850,959	711,458	3,166,112
4	Van Buren	1,112,352	1,190,753	933,658	887,023	4,123,786
5	West Lafayette	1,661,436	1,771,758	1,123,607	1,402,665	5,959,466
6	Totals	4,277,274	4,745,397	3,422,734	3,685,764	16,131,169

expressions reference cells in other worksheets in this workbook

expressions reference cells in another workbook

Documentation \ Summary / Somerville / Van Buren / West Lafayette

Ready

Chapter 7 covers writing formulas that reference other worksheets in the workbook and other workbooks stored on your computer. In particular, you will learn about the benefits of using multiple worksheets to organize related data and how to create *three-dimensional formulas (3-D)*—formulas that reference other worksheets in the current workbook. When you create formulas that reference cells in other worksheets, you link the referenced workbooks to the worksheet containing the reference to other work-books. When you have completed this chapter, you will understand three-dimensional formulas and link formulas thoroughly.

SESSION 7.1 WORKING WITH MULTIPLE WORKSHEETS

In this section, you will learn why it is advantageous to keep related data in separate worksheets of a workbook, and you will write formulas that reference information on other worksheets in the same workbook. You will learn the benefits of grouping work-sheets before formatting them or typing text and values common to all grouped worksheets.

Using Multiple Worksheets

Using more than one worksheet in a workbook is one of the best ways to organize your data. Almost all of the Excel applications you have examined in the first six chapters of this textbook consisted of one worksheet with a few small exceptions. There are several advantages to storing data on separate worksheets of a workbook.

Why Multiple Worksheets Are Useful

Using multiple worksheets to store distinct, related information on separate worksheets makes sense for several reasons. Consider, for example, the Pro Golf Academy case that appears in each chapter. Suppose that Betty Carroll wanted to keep the sales of golf

sales for each machine
type by quarter

machines manufactured
in Somerville

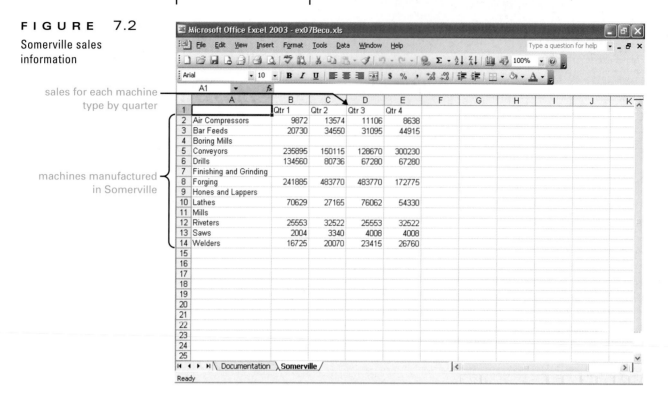

clubs separate from the sales of golf shirts. The simplest way to maintain a logical separation between product categories is by placing each on its own worksheet. Because each worksheet can have its own margin settings, unique page header and footer, print area, and other worksheet-specific settings, you can tailor print characteristics of each worksheet independently of other worksheets. Another advantage multiple worksheets provide is that you can protect individual worksheets in a workbook independently from others.

Designing a Multiple-Sheet Workbook

The BECO workbook, **ex07Beco.xls**, contains a documentation worksheet, which is the first worksheet in a workbook. Following the documentation worksheet is a worksheet containing sales data for BECO's Somerville plant. The worksheet lists the most recent four quarters of sales broken down by machine type (see Figure 7.2).

Sales information for BECO's other two plants is kept in separate workbooks. Sales data for the Van Buren plant are stored in the Excel workbook **ex07VanBuren.xls**, and sales data for the West Lafayette plant are in **ex07WestLafayette.xls**. When complete, the BECO workbook will contain worksheets from all three plants in one workbook. In addition to the detail worksheets, the workbook will contain a summary worksheet. A *summary worksheet*, sometimes called a *consolidation worksheet*, contains a digest or synopsis of the information contained in the individual worksheets. Frequently, the summary worksheet appears at the front of the workbook, either before the documentation worksheet or immediately after it. Figure 7.3 depicts the overall structure of the BECO workbook containing three plants' worksheets, a summary sheet, and a documentation sheet—all in one workbook.

Managing Worksheets

Stirling wants you to become familiar with creating, moving, deleting, and renaming worksheets in a workbook. He knows you will be called on to manipulate worksheets within a workbook. You will learn how to create, move, and rename a worksheet a few pages later. First, Stirling wants you to change the default number of worksheets in a workbook.

FIGURE 7.3

Structure of the BECO
workbook

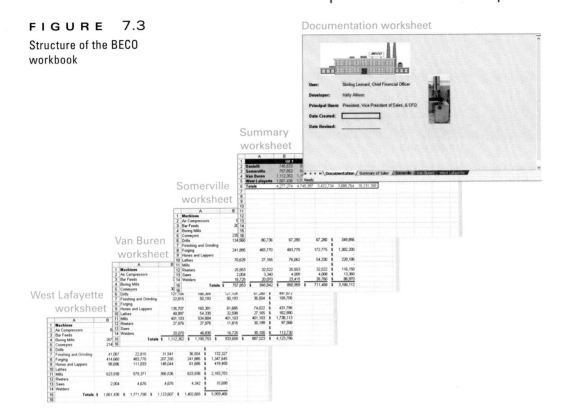

Setting the Number of Worksheets Created for a New Workbook

When you create a new workbook, an Excel Tools menu setting determines the number of worksheets in the workbook. Stirling asks you to set the default number of worksheets to two so that each *new* workbook you create on your computer will contain just two worksheets. You explain to Stirling that changing the number of worksheets does not alter any existing workbooks—either currently open or not.

Setting the number of worksheets in a new workbook:

1. Start Excel as usual, close the task pane, click **Tools**, click **Options**, and then click the **General** tab to display the general Excel settings

2. Drag the mouse across the value currently in the *Sheets in new workbook* spin control, type **2** (see Figure 7.4), and click **OK** to complete the selection and close the Options dialog box

Test the new setting by creating a new workbook. When you create a new workbook, Excel will create only two worksheets.

Testing the new worksheet number setting:

1. Click the **New** button on the Standard toolbar to create a new workbook. Notice that the new workbook has two worksheets, Sheet1 and Sheet2

EXCEL

FIGURE 7.4

Setting the initial number
of worksheets in a new
workbook

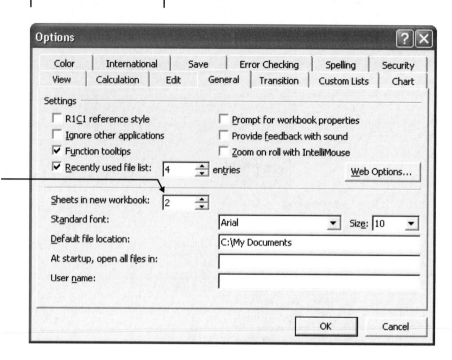

Initial number of
sheets created in a
new workbook

Deleting a Worksheet

You may wish to delete one or more worksheets in a workbook—especially "extra"
worksheets that are empty. Steps that follow show you how.

---

task *Reference*   Deleting a Worksheet

- Right-click the worksheet tab of the worksheet you want to delete

- Click **Delete** on the shortcut menu

Deleting a worksheet from a workbook:

1. Right-click the **Sheet2** worksheet tab. A shortcut menu appears (see
Figure 7.5)

FIGURE 7.5

Sheet tab shortcut menu

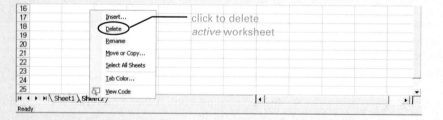

2. Click **Delete** to remove the worksheet from the workbook. Excel deletes
Sheet2 and displays Sheet1

tip: *If Excel displays the warning message "Data may exist in the sheet(s) selected for
deletion. To permanently delete the data, press Delete," that means you typed a value on the
empty worksheet Sheet3 at some point. Click **Delete** to delete the worksheet*

Because you are done with the current workbooks, you can close them. You can close all workbooks using one command.

Closing all open workbooks at once:

1. Close all workbooks but leave Excel running: Press and hold the **Shift** key, click **File**, and then release the **Shift** key

2. Click **Close all** on the File menu to close all workbooks

tip: *If a prompt appears asking if you want to save changes you made, click* ***No***

Creating a Template from a Workbook

Whenever several worksheets or workbooks will have the same structure and appearance, it is handy to create a general workbook that has the content and formatting that is common to worksheets you will be manipulating. Such a file is called a template. You can open a template whenever you want to create workbooks that are identical in structure and content.

task reference   Saving a Workbook as a Template

- Activate the workbook you want to save as a template, click **File** and then click **Save As**

- Type the template name (but not its extension) in the File name list box

- Click the **Save as type** list box, scroll the list box to locate and then click **Template (*.xlt)**

- Click the **Save** button

Stirling has a worksheet that has the contents and formatting he'd like you to use whenever you create a BECO style workbook. It is called **ex07BecoTemplate.xls** and he wants you to save it as an Excel template.

Opening a workbook and saving it as a template:

1. Open the workbook **ex07BecoTemplate.xls**

2. Click **File**, click **Save As**, and type **BecoTemplate** (no spaces) in the File name list box

3. Click the **Save as type** list box, locate and then click the entry **Template (*.xlt)** from the list, and click the **Save** button. Excel saves the workbook as a template in its Templates folder and displays its new name, **BecoTemplate.xlt**, on the title bar

4. Click **File**, and then **Close** to close the template

Combining Multiple Worksheets into One Workbook

One of BECO's administrators created the two-worksheet workbook containing the Documentation worksheet and sales information about the Somerville plant for four quarters and several machine types (see Figure 7.2). Data for the other two plants are in separate workbooks. Your first task is to open all three workbooks and then combine the three workbooks into one workbook.

Because Stirling wants you to combine all three workbooks into one workbook, you will open the Van Buren workbook and then copy the worksheet into the main BECO workbook by dragging the worksheet's tab.

---

task **reference**	Copying Worksheets from Other Workbooks

- Open the master workbook—the workbook into which you want to copy worksheets from other workbooks

- Open all other workbooks containing worksheets you want to copy to the master workbook

- In any of the open Excel workbooks, click **Window**, click **Arrange**, click the **Tiled** option button, and click **OK**

- Press and hold the **Ctrl** key, and then click and drag to the master workbook the tab of the worksheet you want to copy

- Release the mouse when the down-pointing arrow is in the correct tab location in the master workbook, and then release the **Ctrl** key

---

Copying the Van Buren worksheet to the BECO master workbook:

1. Open the workbook **ex07Beco.xls** and immediately save it as **Beco2.xls** to preserve the original workbook

2. Review the Documentation worksheet. Because all Documentation worksheet cells except C18 are locked, worksheet protection prevents you from selecting any cell except C18

3. Click the **Somerville** worksheet tab to make that worksheet active

4. Open the workbook **ex07VanBuren.xls**

5. Click **Window**, click **Arrange**, click (if necessary) the **Tiled** option button in the Arrange Windows dialog box, and click the **OK** button. The active worksheets of both workbooks appear side by side

6. Click the **ex07VanBuren.xls** title bar, if necessary, to ensure that the Van Buren workbook is active

7. Press and hold the **Ctrl** key, click and drag the **Van Buren** worksheet tab to the **Beco2.xls** workbook, and release the mouse when the worksheet position indicator, a down-pointing arrow, appears to the right of the Somerville tab (see Figure 7.6)

8. Release the **Ctrl** key. Excel copies the Van Buren worksheet to the Beco2 workbook and makes Van Buren the active worksheet

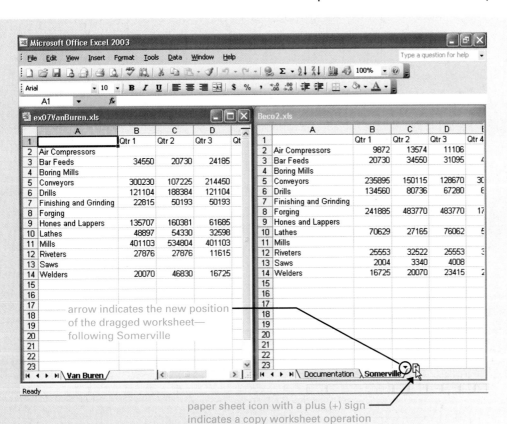

arrow indicates the new position
of the dragged worksheet—
following Somerville

paper sheet icon with a plus (+) sign
indicates a copy worksheet operation

9. Click the Title bar of the **ex07VanBuren.xls** workbook, click **File** on the menu bar, and click **Close** to close the workbook

tip: *If you attempt to close **Beco2.xls** by mistake, Excel will ask you if you want to save your changes. Click the **Cancel** button to leave **Beco2.xls** open. Then repeat step 9*

10. Click the **Maximize** button on the **Beco2.xls** Title bar to maximize it

---

another**word**

. . . on Dragging a Worksheet Tab to Another Workbook

When you press and hold the Ctrl key before you drag a worksheet tab to another workbook, you are copying it. If you simply drag a worksheet tab to another open workbook, the worksheet is cut from the original workbook and pasted into the destination workbook. If the worksheet you cut from a workbook is its only worksheet, Excel closes that workbook

---

Next, you copy the West Lafayette worksheet into the **Beco2.xls** workbook to complete the two-worksheet copy operation. This time, you will use a different method to copy the worksheet.

Copying the West Lafayette worksheet to the BECO master workbook:

1. Open the workbook **ex07WestLafayette.xls**

2. Click **Edit** and click **Move or Copy Sheet**. The Move or Copy dialog box opens

3. Click the **To book** list box to display the list of workbooks and click **Beco2.xls** from the list of workbook choices

4. Click the **(move to end)** choice in the *Before sheet* list box and click the **Create a copy** check box to *copy* the worksheet, making it the last worksheet in the destination workbook **Beco2.xls** (see Figure 7.7)

FIGURE 7.7

Move or Copy dialog box

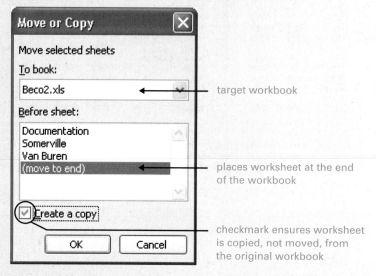

target workbook

places worksheet at the end of the workbook

checkmark ensures worksheet is copied, not moved, from the original workbook

5. Click **OK**. Excel copies the worksheet to **Beco2.xls** and makes it the active worksheet

6. Right-click the **ex07WestLafayette** button on the Taskbar and then click **Close** in the shortcut menu to close the workbook **ex07WestLafayette.xls**

7. Maximize the workbook and then save it

Now the BECO workbook contains four worksheets: Documentation, Somerville, Van Buren, and West Lafayette. The latter three worksheets contain sales information about all three BECO plants in one workbook.

Adding a Worksheet to a Workbook

Remembering that Stirling wants to summarize BECO's sales in a single worksheet that displays sales by machine across all three plants, you realize you will have to add a new worksheet to the BECO workbook. You will do that next.

Adding a new worksheet to a workbook:

1. With the West Lafayette worksheet of the **Beco2.xls** workbook active, click **Insert**

2. Click **Worksheet**. Excel adds a worksheet called Sheet1 in front of the West Lafayette worksheet. It makes the newly added worksheet active

tip: *If you practiced inserting a new worksheet more than once with an open workbook, the inserted worksheet name may be a different name such as Sheet2 or Sheet3, for example*

Moving a Worksheet

Because the worksheet will summarize the values in the three sales worksheets, you ask Stirling where he would like you to place a summary worksheet. Stirling tells you he prefers having a summary worksheet precede all the detail worksheets, but he wants the Documentation worksheet to remain the first worksheet in the workbook.

Move the new worksheet between the Documentation and Somerville worksheets:

1. Click **Edit**, and then click **Move or Copy Sheet**. The Move or Copy dialog box appears

2. Click **Somerville** in the *Before sheet* list box, and ensure that the Create a copy check box is cleared. (You do not want to create a copy of the worksheet.)

3. Click **OK** in the Move or Copy dialog box. Excel moves the worksheet to its new position between the Documentation and Somerville worksheets

Stirling wants you to become familiar with inserting a worksheet from a template. Because you created a template called BecoTemplate earlier, you will use that as the model for a new worksheet to insert into the BECO workbook.

Inserting a Worksheet Using a Template

When you create a template, you can create a workbook from the template by clicking File, clicking New, and then choosing the appropriate template from templates on your computer (the On my computer hyperlink) whose hyperlinks appear in the New Workbook task pane.

Inserting a worksheet from a template:

1. Right-click the **Somerville** worksheet tab. A shortcut menu appears

2. Click **Insert**, click the **BecoTemplate** icon in the Insert dialog box, and click **OK**. Excel inserts a worksheet from the template, complete with labels in column A and row 1

Because you will build a slightly different worksheet than what the template supplies, you will delete the newly added worksheet using a simple method not used before.

Deleting a worksheet using the shortcut menu:

1. Right-click the **Sheet1(2)** worksheet tab. A shortcut menu appears

2. Click **Delete**. Excel displays a delete confirmation dialog box

3. Click the **Delete** button in the confirmation dialog box to delete the worksheet

4. Click the **Sheet1** worksheet tab to activate that worksheet

---

anotherway
. . . to Insert a New Worksheet

Right-click the worksheet in front of which you want to insert a new worksheet

Click **Insert** on the pop-up menu

Ensure that the Worksheet icon is selected in the General tab and click the **OK** button

---

EXCEL

Renaming a Worksheet and Coloring a Worksheet Tab

The summary worksheet is an important one, and Stirling wants it to stand out. He asks you to rename the worksheet to Summary and to change the color of the tab to bright yellow.

Renaming a worksheet and coloring its tab:

1. Double-click the worksheet tab of the newly added worksheet (the tab name darkens), type **Summary**, and press **Enter**. Excel renames the worksheet

2. Right-click the **Summary** worksheet tab. A shortcut menu appears (see Figure 7.8)

FIGURE 7.8

Worksheet tab shortcut menu

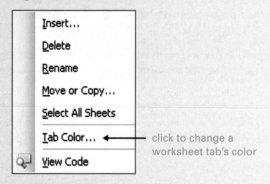

click to change a worksheet tab's color

3. Click **Tab Color**. The Format Tab Color dialog box appears

4. Click the **Yellow** color well (fourth row from the top, third column) (see Figure 7.9)

FIGURE 7.9

Selecting a worksheet tab color

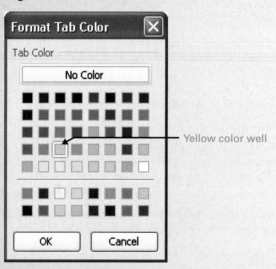

Yellow color well

5. Click **OK**. The dialog box closes and a fringe of yellow appears at the bottom of the Summary tab

6. Click the **Somerville** worksheet tab to make that worksheet active and notice the Summary tab—it is bright yellow (see Figure 7.10)

FIGURE 7.10

Brightly colored worksheet tab

yellow color adds emphasis to the worksheet tab

With all the worksheets in place, including the empty Summary worksheet, you are ready to create formulas that reference cells and cell ranges in other worksheets and to work with multiple worksheets as a group.

Grouping Worksheets

When you need to enter the same labels or formulas in several worksheets within a workbook, you can save a lot of time by grouping worksheets and then entering information common to multiple sheets in one operation. For instance, neither the summary worksheet nor any of the three other sales information worksheets have a column label identifying the contents of column A—machines. While you could type "Machines" in cell A1 in each worksheet separately, it saves time to group the worksheets and then type the label once. Grouping worksheets is also beneficial when you want to insert or delete rows common to all grouped worksheets or format cells, rows, or columns of all grouped worksheets in the same way.

help yourself *Press **F1**, type **group worksheets** in the Search text box of the Microsoft Excel Help task pane, and press **Enter**. Click the hyperlink **About viewing workbooks and worksheets**. Maximize the Help screen if necessary. Click the Help screen **Close** button when you are finished, and close the task pane*

Entering Text into Worksheet Groups

Although the three sales worksheets contain the labels Qtr 1, Qtr 2, Qtr 3, and Qtr 4 to indicate sales in each of the four calendar quarters, the Summary worksheet does not. Whenever you want to modify several worksheets simultaneously, you must first group them.

---

task reference **Grouping Contiguous Worksheets**

- Click the worksheet tab of the first worksheet in the group
- Use the tab scrolling buttons, if necessary, to bring the last worksheet tab of the proposed group into view
- Hold down the **Shift** key and click the last worksheet tab in the group

Grouping Noncontiguous Worksheets

- Click the worksheet tab of the first worksheet you want in the group
- Press and hold the **Ctrl** key and then click each worksheet you want to include in the group
- When you are done, release the **Ctrl** key

Stirling wants you to type "Machines" in cell A1 of each of the three manufacturing plants' worksheets. If you first group the worksheets into which you want to enter the label and then type it in one of them, Excel places the label in all worksheets in the group. Worksheet users sometimes call this ***drilling down***, because it changes several layers—grouped worksheets—in a workbook.

EXCEL

Grouping worksheets and entering a label in all of them at once:

1. With the **Somerville** worksheet active, press and hold down **Shift**, click the **West Lafayette** worksheet tab, and release the **Shift** key. Excel indicates the grouped worksheets by coloring their tabs (temporarily) white (see Figure 7.11)

FIGURE 7.11

Grouped worksheets

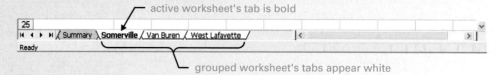

— active worksheet's tab is bold

— grouped worksheet's tabs appear white

2. Click cell **A1**, type **Machines**, and press **Enter**

3. Click the **Van Buren** worksheet tab and verify that cell A1 contains "Machines"

4. Click the **West Lafayette** worksheet tab and verify that cell A1 contains "Machines" Grouping worksheets and then entering data into one cell places data into the same cells in all grouped worksheets

Notice that the name of the active worksheet of a grouped set is bold. Clicking any of the worksheet tabs in the grouped set makes the worksheet active, but it does not ungroup them. This happens because there is at least one worksheet in the workbook that is *not* part of the worksheet group.

---

task reference   **Ungrouping Worksheets**

- Right-click any worksheet tab and click **Ungroup Sheets** from the shortcut menu

---

Ungroup the worksheets so that you can work independently on each worksheet.

Ungrouping worksheets:

1. Right-click the **Somerville** worksheet tab

2. Click **Ungroup Sheets** in the shortcut menu

Copying Formulas and Data into Worksheet Groups

Stirling tells you there are several ways to copy formulas from one worksheet to other worksheets. If you want to copy one or more formulas to more than one worksheet, the most efficient way is to copy the formulas to grouped worksheets rather than copying to individual sheets, one sheet at a time. In the next series of steps, you will create the sum of the columns for each quarter's sales and place the sums at the bottom of each column. You begin by creating a summation for sales at the Somerville plant. Then you will copy those formulas to the same cells in the Van Buren and West Lafayette worksheets.

Writing summation formulas in the Somerville worksheet:

1. Click the **Somerville** worksheet tab and then select the cell range **B2:E15**

2. Click the **AutoSum** button on the Standard toolbar. Excel places four SUM functions in the cell range B15:E15

3. Click cell **B15** to deselect the selected range and display the newly created SUM function in the formula bar (see Figure 7.12)

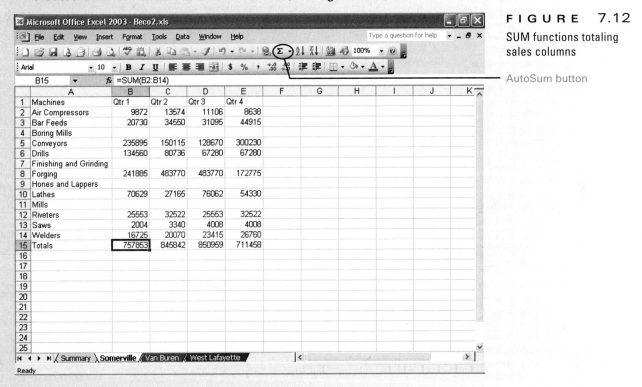

FIGURE 7.12
SUM functions totaling sales columns

AutoSum button

Copying formulas to other worksheets in a workbook:

1. Select the cell range **B15:E15**, which contains four SUM functions

2. Press and hold the **Shift** key and click the **West Lafayette** worksheet tab, and then release the **Shift** key. Excel groups the three sales worksheets

3. Click **Edit**, point to **Fill**, and click **Across Worksheets**. The Fill Across Worksheets dialog box appears (see Figure 7.13)

4. Click the **All** option button (if necessary) and then click **OK**

5. Click cell **A15** to deselect the cell range

6. Right-click any worksheet in the group and then click **Ungroup Sheets** in the shortcut menu. Excel ungroups the worksheets

EXCEL

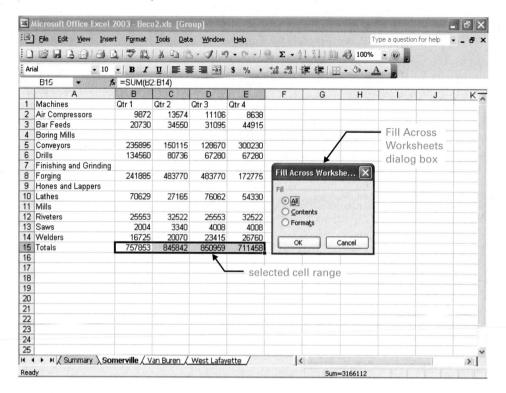

The Fill Across Worksheets command copies the selected cells to all other worksheets in the group to exactly the same cell range as the source cells. The All option copies both cells' contents and their formatting. Alternatively, you can choose to copy only contents or only formatting by selecting either Contents or Formats, respectively.

Writing Formulas and Data into Worksheet Groups

An alternative way to enter formulas and data into grouped worksheets is to group the worksheets first and then write the formulas and data. When you press Enter to complete a formula or execute a copy operation on one worksheet, Excel automatically copies formulas and data to other members of the worksheet group.

Writing formulas and labels to grouped worksheets:

1. Click the **Somerville** worksheet tab, hold down the **Shift** key, click the **West Lafayette** worksheet tab, and release the **Shift** key to group the three worksheets

2. Click cell **A15** and type **Totals**

3. Click cell **F1** and type **Totals**

4. Click cell **F2**, type **=SUM(B2:E2)**, and click the **Enter** checkmark (see Figure 7.14) on the formula bar to enter the formula and keep cell F2 active

5. Move the mouse to the fill handle in the lower-right corner of cell **F2**, click and drag it down through cell **F15**, and release the mouse. Excel fills in cells F3 through F15 with row totals. Cell F15 is a grand total because it sums cells B15 through E15, which are column totals

6. Click cell **F2** to deselect the cell range (see Figure 7.15) and make that cell active so that you can inspect its formula

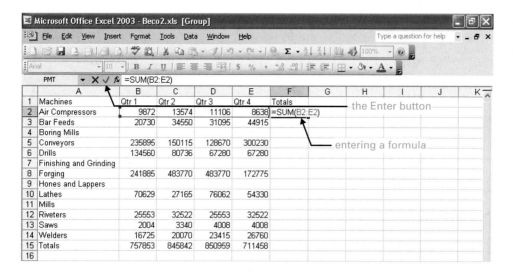

FIGURE 7.14
Entering a formula in three
worksheets simultaneously

FIGURE 7.15
Drill-down formulas
completed

Formatting Worksheet Groups

Formatting a cell or cell range in the active worksheet of a group of worksheets also formats the same cell or cell range in *all* group members. That is particularly handy when you want several worksheets to have the same appearance, helping to convey the message that similarly formatted worksheets are related to one another.

Stirling wants you to make several format changes to the three sales worksheets—Somerville, Van Buren, and West Lafayette. Because each of the three worksheets will be formatted in the same way, you will format the grouped worksheets and save time. By carefully selecting cell ranges, you can combine some of the preceding formatting steps to include more cells.

Formatting sales values with the accounting format:

1. With the three worksheets still grouped, click the **Somerville** worksheet tab, and then click and drag cell range **B2:F15**

2. Right-click anywhere inside the selected cells, click **Format Cells** on the shortcut menu, and click the **Number** tab

3. Click **Accounting** in the Category list, type **0** in the Decimal places spinner control, click the **Symbol** list box, click **None**, and click **OK**

EXCEL

4. Click and drag the cell range **F2:F15**

5. Press and hold the **Ctrl** key, click and drag the cell range **B15:E15**, and release the **Ctrl** key. Excel highlights the two cell ranges F2:F15 and B15:E15, the Totals column and row

6. Right-click any cell within the selected ranges, click **Format Cells** on the shortcut menu, and click the **Number** tab (if necessary)

tip: *If you right-click outside the range of selected cells, press **Esc**, reselect the two cell ranges, and repeat step 6*

7. Click the **Symbol** list box, click **$**, and click **OK**

8. Click cell **B1** to deselect the cell ranges and to prepare for the next steps (see Figure 7.16)

FIGURE 7.16

Applying the accounting format to grouped worksheets

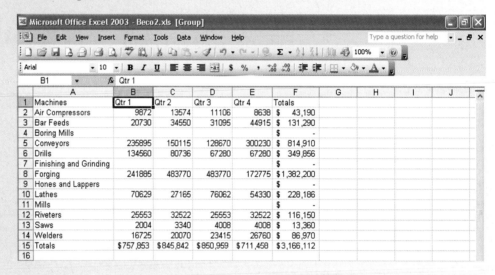

Next, you will right-align and boldface labels in cells B1 through F1 and the "Totals" label in cell A15, and you will boldface the label "Machines" in cell A1.

Right-aligning and bolding labels in grouped worksheets:

1. With the three worksheets still grouped and the Somerville worksheet active, select cell range **B1:F1**

2. Press and hold the **Ctrl** key, select cell **A15**, and release the **Ctrl** key

3. Click the **Align Right** button on the Formatting toolbar

4. Press and hold the **Ctrl** key, select cell **A1**, and release the **Ctrl** key. Cell A1 is added to the group of selected cells

5. Click the **Bold** button on the Formatting toolbar. Excel applies boldface to the 21 selected cells (seven cells in each of three worksheets comprising the grouped worksheets)

The last few formatting changes Stirling wants you to make are to place a double underline under the cell range B14:F14 to mark the bottom of the sales columns and then to widen columns B through F to 13 characters to accommodate the row totals and make the columns easier to distinguish from one another.

Applying underlining and increasing column widths:

1. Select the cell range **B14:F14**

2. Click **Format** and click **Cells**. The Format Cells dialog box opens

3. Click the **Font** tab, click the **Underline** list box (see Figure 7.17), and click **Double Accounting**. The Preview text box displays a facsimile of the double underline

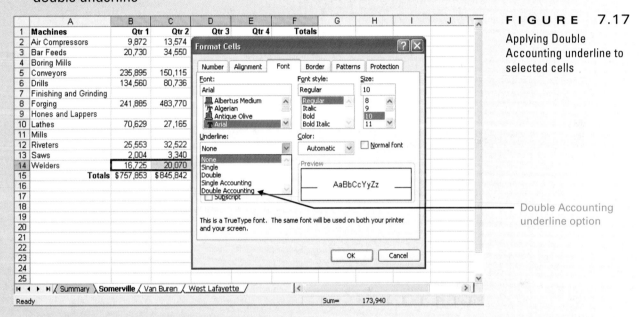

FIGURE 7.17

Applying Double Accounting underline to selected cells

Double Accounting underline option

4. Click **OK** to apply the formatting changes and close the Format Cells dialog box

5. Select columns **B** through **F** by dragging the mouse through their column heading buttons, right-click anywhere within the selected columns, click **Column Width**, type **13** in the Column Width text box, and click **OK**. Excel expands columns B through F on the three worksheets in the group to 13 characters in width

6. Click cell **A1** to deselect the column range (see Figure 7.18)

Satisfy yourself that the three worksheets all contain the same format changes by clicking the Van Buren and West Lafayette worksheet tabs and viewing their formats.

Establishing Worksheet Page Settings

After you format the worksheet, you give Stirling a copy of it on disk. He opens it and examines the worksheets over the weekend. Monday morning, he stops by your office and comments that some of the sales worksheets print on multiple pages and that the three plants' worksheets all have different print margins. He asks you to make all the sales worksheets page layouts uniform, including the print margins and page layout. In

FIGURE 7.18

Worksheet after modifying
column widths

	A	B	C	D	E	F	G	H
1	**Machines**	**Qtr 1**	**Qtr 2**	**Qtr 3**	**Qtr 4**	**Totals**		
2	Air Compressors	9,872	13,574	11,106	8,638	$ 43,190		
3	Bar Feeds	20,730	34,550	31,095	44,915	$ 131,290		
4	Boring Mills					$ -		
5	Conveyors	235,895	150,115	128,670	300,230	$ 814,910		
6	Drills	134,560	80,736	67,280	67,280	$ 349,856		
7	Finishing and Grinding					$ -		
8	Forging	241,885	483,770	483,770	172,775	$ 1,382,200		
9	Hones and Lappers					$ -		
10	Lathes	70,629	27,165	76,062	54,330	$ 228,186		
11	Mills					$ -		
12	Riveters	25,553	32,522	25,553	32,522	$ 116,150		
13	Saws	2,004	3,340	4,008	4,008	$ 13,360		
14	Welders	16,725	20,070	23,415	26,760	$ 86,970		
15	Totals $	757,853	$ 845,842	$ 850,959	$ 711,458	$ 3,166,112		
16								
17								
18	First Worksheet tab scroll button							
19								
20	Previous Worksheet tab scroll button							
21								
22	Next Worksheet tab scroll button							
23								
24	Last Worksheet tab scroll button							

Summary \ **Somerville** / Van Buren / West Lafayette /

Ready

worksheet tab scrolling buttons

addition, he would like you to place each worksheet's name (Somerville, Van Buren, or West Lafayette) in the left section of the footer so that each worksheet is identified by its tab name. Looking ahead, you decide to include the Summary worksheet in the worksheet grouping so that it will have the same page setup as the sales worksheets that it summarizes.

The best way to take care of the page setup and footer details Stirling requests is to work with grouped worksheets.

Adding a worksheet to an existing worksheet group:

1. With the three plants' worksheets grouped, press and hold the **Ctrl** key

2. Click the **Summary** worksheet tab to include it in the worksheet group and release the **Ctrl** key

Establishing page setup settings for grouped worksheets:

1. Click **File** and click **Page Setup**. The Page Setup dialog box opens

2. Click the **Margins** tab, double-click the **Left** margin spin control to select its current value, and type **0.75**

3. Double-click the **Right** margin spin control, and type **0.75**

4. Click the **Header/Footer** tab and click the **Custom Footer** button. The Footer dialog box appears

5. Click the **Center section** text box, type **Worksheet:**, press the **Spacebar**, and click the **Tab Name** button. The Tab Name button displays "&[Tab]" because it is a variable—Excel fills in each unique worksheet tab name depending on which worksheet is printed (see Figure 7.19)

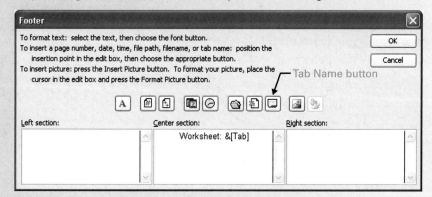

FIGURE 7.19

Setting the page footer for each worksheet in the group

6. Click **OK** to apply your page setting choices and close the Footer dialog box, and then click **OK** to close the Page Setup dialog box.

You probably notice that a dashed line appears to the right of column F on the active worksheet. The line is a page break indicator. It appears when you modify any of the page setup values such as the left or right margins. You can remove the page breaks by clicking Tools, clicking Options, clicking the View tab, and clearing the Page breaks check box in the Window options pane. Then click OK to apply your worksheet options.

Because you have completed your work with the worksheet group, you can ungroup them.

Ungrouping worksheets:

1. Right-click any of the worksheet tabs in the grouped worksheets

2. Click **Ungroup Sheets** in the shortcut menu. Excel ungroups the four-worksheet group

Consolidating and Summarizing Data with 3-D Formulas

Until now, you have written *two-dimensional formulas*, which are formulas that reference cells that are on the same worksheet. Now that you have information about the three BECO plants in multiple worksheets of a single workbook, you can create formulas on one worksheet that summarize the information found on three other worksheets. Formulas that reference cells in other worksheet cells are called three-dimensional (or 3-D) formulas. Each worksheet of a workbook is analogous to the board of a tic-tac-toe game.

Three-dimensional formulas can consolidate data from multiple worksheets. When you *consolidate* information, you are summarizing data from multiple worksheets. For example, you could write a formula in the Summary worksheet that totals sales by division. Or, you could write a function to average sales for the first quarter (Qtr 1) for all machines manufactured by all three plants. Consolidating information presents a simplified picture to someone who does not necessarily want to know all the details—a division manager or the president of a company, for example.

FIGURE 7.20

Consolidating sales information

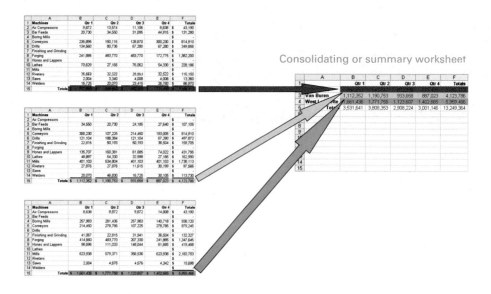

Figure 7.20 shows a graphical example of how you might summarize the sales worksheets for Bridgewater Engineering Company. The summary provides Stirling with a clear picture of sales by each of the plants without confusing details.

Before you write formulas that reference other worksheets' cells, look at the general form of a three-dimensional reference. It is

```
'sheetname'!cell-range
```

Sheetname is the name of the worksheet, and *cell-range* is the cell or cell range in the referenced worksheet. The exclamation point (called "bang" by programmers) separates the worksheet name from the cell range. When a worksheet name contains a space, such as *Van Buren* and *West Lafayette,* then the sheet name must be enclosed in apostrophes. For example, suppose you want cell B4 on the Summary worksheet to reference the sum of all first quarter sales at the Van Buren plant—cell B15 in the Van Buren worksheet. That 3-D formula is:

```
='Van Buren'!B15
```

To refer to cell B5 in the Somerville worksheet from another worksheet, you can omit the apostrophes because the sheet name does not contain spaces:

```
=Somerville!B5
```

How would you write a formula in the Summary worksheet to total the sales of all machines manufactured and sold by the West Lafayette plant? The West Lafayette plant's sales values are stored in the cell range B2:E14 on the West Lafayette worksheet. The Summary worksheet would refer to that cell range as an argument of the SUM function this way:

```
=SUM('West Lafayette'!B2:E14)
```

Naturally, whether you refer to a single cell or a cell range in a three-dimensional reference, that reference must make sense in the formula in which it is used. Otherwise, Excel will display an error in the cell. However, that would be illegal in an expression that does not allow a cell range—an expression such as

```
='West Lafayette'!B2:E14/52
```

You can specify a range of *worksheets* in a three-dimensional reference just as you can specify a range of cells in a two-dimensional reference. A reference to a range of sheets must include the first and last names of the worksheets in the range, and no other, separated by a colon, followed by an exclamation point, and then followed by a cell or cell range. For example, the 3-D reference 'Somerville:West Lafayette'!B10 refers to cell B10 found in each of three worksheets from Somerville through West Lafayette.

When would you ever use a sheet range in an expression? There are several cases where that type of 3-D reference is handy. The first quarter sales for each plant, conveniently, are found in the cell range B2:B14 on three worksheets (Somerville, Van Buren, and West Lafayette). You refer to the "silo" of cells in that 3-D range with the notation within the SUM function this way:

```
=SUM('Somerville:West Lafayette'!B2:B14)
```

When you include several worksheets in a sheet range, you do not enclose each worksheet name in its own apostrophes, even if some worksheet names contain spaces. Instead, enclose the entire range—the first worksheet name, the colon, and the final worksheet name—in apostrophes and follow the worksheet range with an exclamation point to mark the end of the worksheet range.

Writing 3-D Formulas

Happily, you have two choices when writing 3-D cell references. You can manually type the references, or you can use Excel's point mode to create a cell range expression automatically. If you use point mode, you must first select the *worksheet* range before you select the *cell* range, not the other way around.

task reference — Writing a Formula Containing a 3-D Reference

- After clicking the cell where you want the formula to appear, type =, type a function name, and type (. However, if you are not writing a function, then simply type =
- Click the sheet tab of the worksheet containing the cell or cell range you want to reference
- If a worksheet range is needed, then press and hold the **Shift** key and click the last worksheet tab in the range
- Click the cell or cell range you want to reference
- Complete the formula (type a concluding right parentheses for a function, for instance), and then press **Enter**

Placing formulas and labels in the Summary worksheet:

1. Right-click any of the worksheet tab scroll buttons (to the left of the leftmost worksheet tab) and then click **Summary**. The Summary worksheet becomes active

2. Click cell **B1**, type **='Somerville'!B1**, and press **Enter** to reference the Qtr 1 label on the Somerville worksheet. Naturally, you could type the label Qtr 1 too. Using a reference is better. If the label on the Somerville worksheet changes, then the label on the Summary worksheet automatically changes too

3. Click cell **B1**, drag its fill handle, and drag through the cell range **C1:F1**

4. Select the cell range **A2:A5**

5. Type **Somerville**, press **Enter**, type **Van Buren**, press **Enter**, type **West Lafayette**, press **Enter**, type **Totals**, and press **Enter**

6. Click the column A heading button, click **Format**, point to **Column**, and click **AutoFit Selection**. Excel resizes the column to fit the widest entry

7. Drag column heading buttons **B** through **F** to select the columns, right-click anywhere *within* the selected columns, click **Column Width**, type **13** in the Column width text box, and click **OK** to resize columns B through F

8. Click cell **B1** to deselect the column range and display the 3-D formula in the formula bar (see Figure 7.21)

FIGURE   7.21

Summary worksheet with 3-D formulas

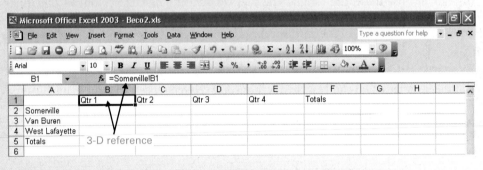

help yourself *Press **F1**, type **cell link** in the Search text box of the Microsoft Excel Help task pane, and press **Enter**. Click the hyperlink **Create a link to another cell, workbook, or program**. Finally, click **Create a link between cells in different workbooks**. Click the Help screen **Close** button when you are finished*

Now you are ready to write consolidating formulas. First, you will write a formula to sum the first quarter sales for the Somerville plant. Although the sum of Qtr 1 sales is in cell B15 on the Somerville worksheet, you prefer to write your own formula using a cell range in a 3-D reference as a double-check.

Writing formulas referencing other worksheets:

1. Click cell **B2** and type **=SUM(**

2. Click the **Somerville** worksheet tab

3. Click and drag the cell range **B2:B14**, and press **Enter**. Excel returns to the active worksheet, Summary, and displays the value 757,853 in cell B2

4. Click cell **B2**, drag the fill handle to cell **E2**, and release the mouse. Excel fills in the remainder of the Somerville total sales for each quarter, and it automatically adjusts the cell references (even for 3-D references) to reflect their location (see Figure 7.22)

Filling in the remaining SUM formulas is the same process as above. This time, however, you will create the first-quarter SUM formulas for the Van Buren and West Lafayette plants. Then you will copy that pair of formulas across their rows to save time.

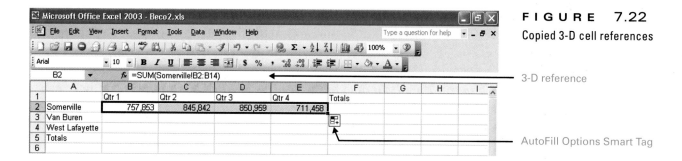

FIGURE 7.22
Copied 3-D cell references

3-D reference

AutoFill Options Smart Tag

Writing and copying the remaining 3-D SUM formulas:

1. Click cell **B3** and type **=SUM(**

2. Click the **Van Buren** worksheet tab. (You may have to scroll through the worksheet tabs to locate it)

3. Drag the mouse through the cell range **B2:B14**, and press **Enter**. Excel returns to the active worksheet and displays the value 1,112,352 in cell B3

4. In cell B4 type **=SUM(**

5. Click the **West Lafayette** worksheet tab. (You may have to scroll through the worksheet tabs to locate it)

6. Drag the mouse through the cell range **B2:B14**, and press **Enter**. Excel returns to the active worksheet, Summary, and displays the value 1,661,436 in cell B4

7. Select the cell range **B3:B4**, drag the cell pair's fill handle from cell **B4** to cell **E4**, and release the mouse. Excel copies the formulas and adjusts all cell references

Setting up a Watch Window

You can see the effect on any Qtr 1 sums on the Summary worksheet when you change a value on a dependent worksheet such as Somerville. Establishing a cell watch is a handy way to keep tabs on a formula in one worksheet while changing values in another worksheet. Displayed in a separate window, a cell Watch Window shows the current value of formula-containing cells that you identify.

Watching a cell and its formula in the Watch Window:

1. Click cell **B2**, which summarizes Somerville's first quarter

2. Click **Tools**, point to **Formula Auditing**, and click **Show Watch Window** to open the Watch Window

3. Click **Add Watch**, and then click **Add**. The Watch Window displays 757,853 in the Value column which is the current value of Summary worksheet cell B2

4. Click the **Somerville** worksheet tab, click cell **B9** (Hones and Lappers for Qtr 1), type **98765**, and press **Enter**. The value of the Watch Window cell B2 changes to 865,618

5. Click the **Undo** button on the Standard toolbar to reverse the change. Watch Window value reverts to its original value

6. Click the first row in the Watch Window, click the **Delete Watch** button on the Watch Window toolbar, and click the **Close** button on the Watch Window title bar to close the window

7. Click the **Summary** worksheet tab to reactivate that worksheet

Totaling Formulas Containing 3-D References

You can sum cells containing references to other worksheets just as you can any other cells. Now that you have summarized the sales from three other worksheets by calendar quarter and company, you can form row and column totals and compute a grand total. The row totals will appear in cells F2 through F4 of the Summary worksheet, and column totals will appear in cells B5 through E5. The grand total will appear at the intersection of the row totals and the column totals, in cell F5.

Using Excel's AutoSum button to write SUM functions:

1. On the Summary worksheet, click and drag the cell range **B2:F5**

2. Click the **AutoSum** button on the Standard toolbar. Row totals, column totals, and a grand total appear

3. Click any cell to deselect the range (see Figure 7.23)

FIGURE 7.23

AutoSum creates totals and a grand total

	A	B	C	D	E	F	G	H	I
1		Qtr 1	Qtr 2	Qtr 3	Qtr 4	Totals			
2	Somerville	757,853	845,842	850,959	711,458	3,166,112			
3	Van Buren	1,112,352	1,190,753	933,658	887,023	4,123,786			
4	West Lafayette	1,661,436	1,771,758	1,123,607	1,402,665	5,959,466			
5	Totals	3,531,641	3,808,353	2,908,224	3,001,146	13,249,364			
6									

Formatting the Summary Worksheet

With the summary formulas complete, you are ready to format the Summary worksheet for Stirling and the managers. You have already formatted the supporting worksheets. (*Supporting* worksheets are worksheets that are referenced by other worksheets and thus support those worksheets.) You can use Excel's AutoFormat command to format a range of cells.

Formatting the summary worksheet cells with AutoFormat:

1. Click and drag the cell range **A1:F5**

2. Click **Format** and then click **AutoFormat**. The AutoFormat dialog box appears

3. Drag the scroll button down until you see Classic 3 (see Figure 7.24)

4. Click **Classic 3** to select it, click **OK** to apply that format, and then click any cell to deselect the cell range

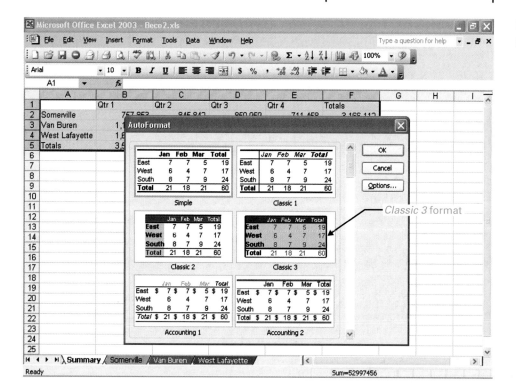

FIGURE 7.24
Selecting an AutoFormat

Printing Multiple Worksheets

Previously, when you printed out a worksheet that was part of a workbook of several worksheets, you simply clicked File, Print, and OK to print the worksheet. Printing more than one worksheet is just as easy. The only additional step is that you must first select (group) the worksheets and then print them.

---

task reference   Printing Multiple Worksheets

- Group the worksheets you want to print by pressing **Ctrl** and then clicking the worksheet tabs or by pressing **Shift** and clicking the first and last worksheets in a contiguous group

- Click **File**, click **Print**, ensure that the **Active sheet(s)** option button is selected, and click **OK**

You print the worksheets for Stirling—all sheets except the Documentation worksheet, as per Stirling's request.

Printing multiple worksheets:

1. Click the **Summary** worksheet tab, press and hold the **Shift** key, click the **West Lafayette** worksheet tab, and release the **Shift** key

2. Click **File**, click **Print**, ensure that the **Active sheet(s)** option button in the *Print what* panel is selected, click the **Preview** button, click the **Next** button repeatedly to examine each of the four pages, and then click the **Print** button

3. Right-click the **Summary** worksheet tab and then click **Ungroup Sheets** in the shortcut menu

Whenever you want to print *all* the worksheets in a workbook, you do not need to group the worksheets. Instead, click the *Entire workbook* option in the *Print what* panel. That option directs Excel to print all of a workbook's worksheets.

You have made a lot of changes to your workbook. Save it in case you want to take a break or return to work on the workbook another time.

Saving the BECO workbook:

1. Click the **Documentation** worksheet tab, and edit the Date Revised value (cell C18) to today's date

2. Click the **Save** button on the Standard toolbar to save the completed workbook

3. Click **File**, click **Save As** and type **Beco3.xls**, and then click the **Save** button to save an identical copy under a new name in preparation for Session 7.2

4. Click **File**, and then click **Close** to close the workbook

Deleting an Excel Template

Earlier in this session, you created a template called **BecoTemplate.xlt**, and Excel saved it in the Templates folder on the computer on which you are working. Now it is time to do a little housecleaning. You are going to remove the **BecoTemplate.xlt** template so that readers who might use this computer in the future will not encounter an error when they try to save the BecoTemplate template while reading the textbook.

---

task reference   Deleting an Excel Template

- Click **File** on the menu bar, click **New**, and click **On my computer** in the Templates panel of the task pane

- Right-click the template that you want to delete, and click **Delete**

- Click **OK** when asked if you want to send the template to the Recycle Bin

---

Deleting the BecoTemplate Template and closing Excel:

1. Click **File** on the menu bar and click **New** to open the task pane

2. Click **On my computer** in the Templates panel of the task pane

3. Right click the **BecoTemplate** template in the list of templates, click **Delete** in the pop-up menu, and click **Yes**. Excel deletes the BecoTemplate

4. Click the **Cancel** button to close the Templates dialog box

5. Click **File** and then click **Exit** to exit Excel

making *the grade*

1. You can view multiple workbooks on screen by clicking Window and then clicking the _____ command.

2. Group contiguous worksheets together by clicking the first worksheet tab, pressing the _____ key, and clicking the last worksheet tab in the series of tabs.

3. By default, a worksheet you add to a workbook appears where in the workbook?

4. Enter the same value in grouped worksheets by typing the expression and pressing Enter. That is also known as _____ down.

5. Perhaps the easiest way to select a particular tab in a workbook with many worksheets is to right-click any _____ scroll button and then click the worksheet tab name from the shortcut that appears.

SESSION 7.2 WORKING WITH MULTIPLE WORKBOOKS

In this section, you will learn how to write formulas that reference another *workbook*. You will learn how to instruct Excel to locate and retrieve information from another workbook stored on your computer, even when the referenced workbook is not open. You will create an Excel Workspace to preserve the onscreen relationship between open workbooks and worksheets.

Retrieving Data from Other Workbooks

In the previous session, you created 3-D formulas that referenced cells from other worksheets within the same workbook. Excel allows you to extend the concept of three-dimensional references to include other workbooks on your computer. For example, you could write a formula in the Summary worksheet in the BECO workbook that averages or totals a cell group in any workbook you worked on in Chapter 6.

Linking Workbooks

A three-dimensional reference to a cell in another workbook resembles a three-dimensional reference to another worksheet in the same workbook. The only difference is that any 3-D reference to another workbook must contain the workbook's location and name in addition to the worksheet name and cell address or cell range. The general form of a 3-D reference to another workbook—also called a ***link***, a ***dynamic link***, or an ***external reference***—is this:

```
'Location[workbook-name]worksheet-name'!cell-range
```

Location is the disk drive and folder name that contains the workbook. The folder may be within other folders, and the disk drive and folders that lead to the workbook are known as the ***path***. Enclose a workbook name in brackets to distinguish it from both the path preceding it and the worksheet name that follows it. The location, workbook name, and worksheet name or name range are enclosed in apostrophes. Following the worksheet name is an exclamation point and the cell reference, cell range, or cell name.

You notice that each part of the link becomes more specific from left to right. For example, suppose you are working on the Summary worksheet in the BECO workbook and you want to display the value of a cell in another workbook. The workbook you

FIGURE 7.25

Link workbook reference

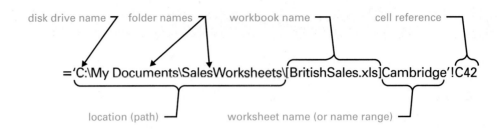

want to link to is on the drive and path C:\My Documents\SalesWorksheets\, the workbook name is **BritishSales.xls**, the worksheet name is Cambridge, and the cell containing the value you want to reference is C42. You would write the link reference to the cell as shown in Figure 7.25

You notice that apostrophes enclose the Location[workbook-name]worksheet-name part of the 3-D cell reference. This is required when the location, workbook name, or worksheet name contain spaces. If there are no spaces in the location, workbook name, or worksheet name, you can omit the apostrophes. You can drop the location portion of the 3-D reference if the workbook to which you are linking is in the same folder as the active workbook in which you are typing the link expression.

Advantages of Linked Workbooks

Workbook links are also called dynamic links because a change in a cell linked to another workbook automatically propagates to any expression that references the changed cell. This happens for links in open workbooks as well as workbooks that are not currently open or loaded. When you open a workbook containing a link to another workbook, Excel informs you that the worksheet contains dynamic links. If you approve, Excel opens referenced workbooks, inspects referenced cells, updates formulas containing the references to other worksheets' cells when necessary, and then closes the referenced workbooks. A workbook containing a worksheet to which a link formula refers is called a ***supporting workbook***. A workbook containing a link to a supporting worksheet is called a ***dependent workbook***, because one or more of its cells' value depend on the value stored in another workbook.

***task* reference**   **Building Link References by Pointing**

- Open the supporting workbook containing the cell or cells you will reference in another worksheet and workbook

- Make the workbook containing the link reference active and click the cell to contain the link reference

- Type the formula up to the point in which you reference the cell or cell range in another workbook

- Click the taskbar button corresponding to the supporting workbook to make it active

- Click the worksheet tab containing the cell or cell range to reference

- Click the cell or drag the cell range of the cell(s) you want to reference and press **Enter**

Creating a series of linked workbooks is often a better alternative than creating and using one larger workbook containing worksheets from all the referenced workbooks for several reasons. One of the most important advantages is that linked workbooks require less memory than a single multisheet workbook. Smaller workbooks containing dynamic links to other workbooks load and open faster than equivalent larger workbooks containing all the referenced worksheets.

Creating and Maintaining Linked Workbooks

Over the weekend, Stirling Leonard and members of BECO's board completed the paperwork to acquire a company called Danielli, Incorporated. Danielli is a small company that was a BECO competitor and manufactures some of the same types of machinery as BECO. While Stirling is busy with details of the merger, he wants you to incorporate some of the gross sales information Danielli keeps in its Excel workbook with the sales information in the BECO workbook. Danielli management wants to maintain physically separate workbooks for at least six months. To provide that separation, Stirling asks you to link to the Danielli workbook in order to summarize its sales in the BECO workbook. Both Stirling and Danielli's former CEO, Larry Sweet, agree that this is the best way to maintain a logical separation and yet have a consolidated sales statement.

Opening the Danielli workbook:

1. If you closed Excel at the end of the previous session, then start Excel

2. Open the workbook **ex07Danielli.xls** (see Figure 7.26)

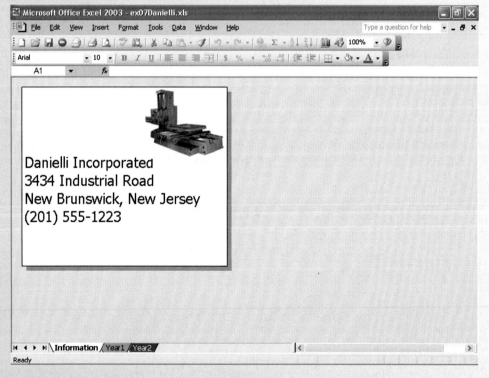

FIGURE 7.26

Danielli Information worksheet

3. Save the worksheet as **Danielli3.xls**. (There is no **Danielli2.xls** worksheet, but the digit *3* in the name will keep the worksheet synchronized with the BECO worksheet version 3)

4. Click the **Year1** worksheet tab and briefly review the worksheet's contents

5. Click the **Year2** worksheet tab and briefly review the worksheet's contents

6. Click the **Name** box list arrow and then click the name **Qtr2** from the list. Notice the name refers to the cell range C5:F5

7. Click the **Name** box list arrow and then click the name **Qtr4** from the list. Notice the name refers to the cell range C7:F7

You notice that the Danielli worksheet arranges sales in a manner different from BECO. Danielli's quarters are arranged in rows and products run across columns. BECO's quarter sales are in columns and products are stored in rows. This is a problem if you want to copy a link formula either down or across in the BECO worksheet. However, Danielli's workbook creator assigned names to each quarter to facilitate referencing the product sales values by a name rather than by a cell range.

With the Danielli supporting worksheet open, you are ready to write your first external or link formula. Stirling wants you to summarize sales of Danielli for the four quarters and include the summary in the Summary worksheet of the **Beco3.xls** workbook. The plant's names are listed in alphabetical order in the Summary worksheet, so Stirling wants Danielli listed at the top of the list—just above the Somerville summary row.

Opening the BECO workbook and entering a link formula:

1. Open the **Beco3.xls** workbook

2. Click the **Summary** worksheet tab, right-click cell **A2**, click **Insert** on the shortcut menu, click the **Entire row** option button, and click **OK** to insert a new row 2. Excel adds a new row and displays the Insert Options Smart Tag icon

3. Hover over the Insert Options Smart Tag until a list arrow appears, click the **Insert Options** list arrow (see Figure 7.27) and then click the **Format Same As Below** option button. Excel formats the newly added row the same as the other sales summary rows, not the header row

FIGURE 7.27

Formatting the new sales summary row

click to format row 2
to match row 3

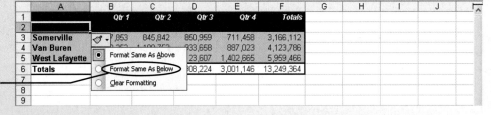

4. Click cell **A2**, type **Danielli**, and press the **Tab** key to make cell B2 active

5. In cell B2, type **=SUM(**

6. Click **Window** on the menu bar, click **Danielli3.xls** in the list of open workbooks, click the **Year2** worksheet tab, drag the mouse through the cell range **C4:F4** (see Figure 7.28), and press **Enter** to complete the formula

7. Click the **Danielli3.xls** button on the Taskbar to make that worksheet active, click **File** on the menu bar, and click **Close** to close **Danielli3.xls**. Excel makes BECO the active workbook again

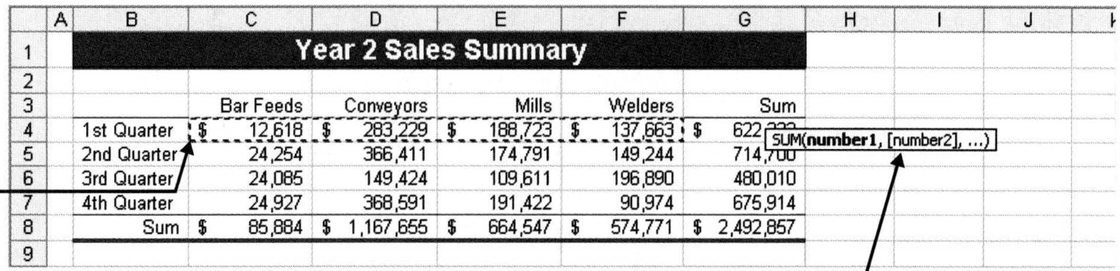

FIGURE 7.28

Selecting a cell range in an external workbook

dashed line outlines selected range

displays help about the SUM function and its arguments

You may be tempted to create the remaining Danielli formulas to be placed in cells C2 through E2 by copying the formula in cell B2. Unfortunately, the cells in the Danielli workbook are not arranged to accommodate a left-to-right copy as you did for the other BECO worksheets. Instead, you will have to build the remaining three link formulas by hand. In addition, you want a row total in cell F2, which you can copy from cell F3. Use the names Qtr2, Qtr3, and Qtr4 in the link formulas. The previous names are defined in the **Danielli3.xls** workbook for the three remaining cell ranges. Using names greatly simplifies your work because you do not need to worry about how the Danielli worksheet designer may have redesigned the worksheet—just as long as the names remain intact. That's why some worksheet designers call worksheets that use names "smart worksheets."

Creating the remaining link formulas by typing them:

1. Click cell **C2** in the Summary worksheet, type **=SUM('** (be sure to type the apostrophe following the left parenthesis)

2. Type the path to *your* Danielli worksheet, then type **[Danielli3.xls]Year2'!Qtr2)**, and press **Enter**. Excel displays the sum of Danielli's second quarter sales, 714,700

tip: *If you make a mistake in typing the link reference, Excel will display an error message such as "That name is not valid." If so, press the **Esc** key to go into edit mode, check the link formula very carefully, use your arrow keys to move to the mistake, correct it, and press **Enter***

3. Click cell **C2**, press **Ctrl+C** to place the formula on the Clipboard, click and drag the cell range **D2:E2**, and press **Ctrl+V** to paste in the two formulas

4. Click cell **D2**, press the **F2** function key to edit the cell, press the **Backspace** key twice to erase the last two characters in the formula, type **3)**, and press **Enter**

5. Click cell **E2**, press the **F2** function key to edit the cell, press the **Backspace** key twice to erase the last two characters in the formula, type **4)**, and press **Enter**

6. Click cell **F2** and then click the **AutoSum** button on the Standard toolbar, and press **Enter** to approve the AutoSum-suggested cell range and complete the formula (see Figure 7.29)

At first glance, all the values seem to be fine. However, you probably noticed that the totals in row 6 are unchanged. That is because Excel did not adjust the SUM functions in those rows after you added the Danielli row. Because the newly added row is out of range of the SUM functions in row 6, Excel does not know to automatically adjust the cell references to include the new row. Therefore, you need to fix those formulas before going on.

EXCEL

FIGURE 7.29

Worksheet after entering
four link formulas

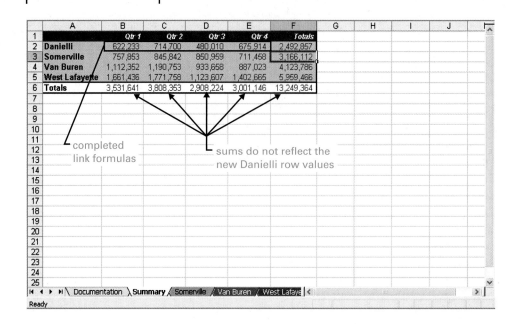

	A	B	C	D	E	F	G	H	I	J
1		Qtr 1	Qtr 2	Qtr 3	Qtr 4	Totals				
2	Danielli	622,233	714,700	480,010	675,914	2,492,857				
3	Somerville	757,853	845,842	850,959	711,458	3,166,112				
4	Van Buren	1,112,352	1,190,753	933,658	887,023	4,123,786				
5	West Lafayette	1,661,436	1,771,758	1,123,607	1,402,665	5,959,466				
6	Totals	3,531,641	3,808,353	2,908,224	3,001,146	13,249,364				

completed
link formulas

sums do not reflect the
new Danielli row values

Documentation \ **Summary** \ Somerville \ Van Buren \ West Lafaye

Ready

Modifying quarter summation formulas:

1. Select the cell range **B2:F6**, which includes the incorrect SUM function
   values in row 6 and the totals in column F

2. Click the **AutoSum** button on the Standard toolbar. Excel places updated
   SUM functions in cells B6 through F6

tip: *If any of the cells displays ######, widen the column in which the pound signs appear.
Simply double-click the right border of the column heading button to widen it to an optimal
width*

3. Click cell **A1** to deselect the range

Updating Linked Workbooks

When you save a workbook containing links to other workbooks, Excel stores the most
recent calculation of those results. If you later open a supporting workbook after closing the dependent workbook and make changes to various cells, the values of the dependent workbook are not updated until you open the dependent workbook. Excel
recognizes that the workbook contains formulas that are dependent on workbooks that
are closed and asks if you want to update the links. If you click the Update button, Excel
locates the supporting workbook, reads the link cell values from it, and updates the dependent workbook. If you click the Don't Update button, the workbook opens without
updating the linked cells. In that case, dependent formulas retain their values from the
last time the workbook was saved.

Erik Gepetti, Danielli's manager, just discovered an error in the **Danielli3.xls** workbook. The value in cell F7 (total sales of welders in the fourth quarter) is incorrect.
Instead of $90,974, the value should be zero. You agree to make the change and ensure
that Excel automatically updates the link value in the dependent workbook **Beco3.xls**.

task reference — Opening a Supporting Workbook from a Dependent Workbook

- Open the dependent workbook containing the link reference
- Click **Edit** and then click **Links**
- Click the name of the supporting workbook you want to open from the Links list
- Click the **Open Source** button

Modifying values in a supporting workbook:

1. Click **Edit** and click **Links**. The Edit Links dialog box appears (see Figure 7.30)

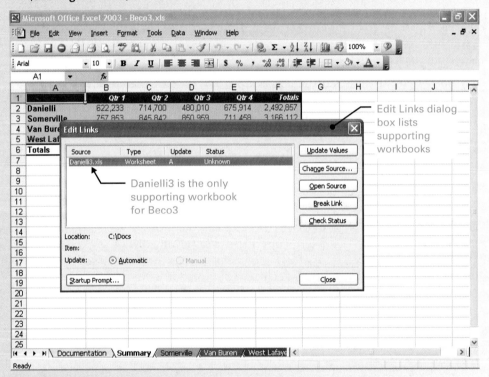

FIGURE 7.30

Edit Links dialog box

2. With the **Danielli3.xls** workbook name in the Edit Links list selected, click the **Open Source** button to open the selected workbook. Excel opens **Danielli3.xls** and makes it active

3. Click the **Year2** worksheet tab (if necessary), click cell **F7** and type **0** (zero), and press **Enter** to indicate no sales of welders in the fourth quarter

tip: You can also press the **Delete** key to empty the cell. In this case, either way is fine. If you were to compute averages or minimums on these sales figures, you should press Delete instead of typing zero

4. Click the **Save** button on the Standard toolbar to save the changed **Danielli3.xls** workbook, click **File** on the menu bar, and click **Close** to close the **Danielli3.xls** workbook. Excel makes **Beco3.xls** the active workbook. Notice that the value in cell E2 is now 584,940 (see Figure 7.31)

FIGURE 7.31

Updated link reference values

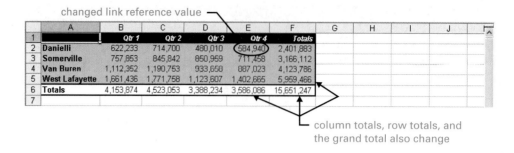

changed link reference value

column totals, row totals, and the grand total also change

Saving Linked Workbooks

You can save the dependent workbook, **Beco3.xls**, and the supporting workbook, **Danielli3.xls**, under names different from their original names by executing the Save As command in the File menu. For example, Stirling may want to save the supporting workbook **Danielli3.xls** under a name such as **DanielliPlant.xls**. Nothing prevents you or someone else from saving either workbook under a new name, but you must be careful when saving a supporting workbook under a new name.

Because these are common scenarios, Stirling wants to make sure both you and he know how to deal with them. Three cases highlight the different scenarios that arise based on which workbooks are open or closed:

1. Both **Bec03.xls** and **Danielli3.xls** are open and you save the *supporting* workbook, **Danielli3.xls**, under a different filename

2. Both **Bec03.xls** and **Danielli3.xls** are open and you save the *dependent* workbook, **Beco3.xls**, under a different filename

3. **Bec03.xls** is closed and **Danielli3.xls** is open and you save the *supporting* workbook, **Danielli3.xls**, under a different filename

What happens to all the links in the dependent workbook when you save (and optionally close) **Danielli3.xls** under a different name? Excel automatically and without notification alters all link formulas to reflect the new name under which you save a supporting workbook. For example, if you choose to save **Danielli3.xls** as **Acquisition.xls** after you execute File, Save As to save the supporting workbook, Excel changes all the links in cells B2:E2 to reflect that change. The link formula in cell B2, for example, becomes:

```
=SUM([Acquisition.xls]Year2!Qtr1)
```

Excel makes the change because the dependent workbook is open and available for change.

In case 2, nothing happens to the links in the dependent workbook. After all, you are changing the name of a workbook that is not a supporting workbook. All formulas remain the same.

Case 3 is the most interesting one. If you change the name of a supporting workbook when the dependent workbook to which it is linked is closed, then Excel cannot make changes to the links in the closed dependent workbook. When you later open **Beco3.xls**, the dependent workbook, Excel searches for **Danielli3.xls**. If you saved **Danielli3.xls** under the new name, **Acquisition.xls**, Excel will update **Beco3.xls** based on the old worksheet values stored in **Danielli3.xls**, not the new workbook **Acquisition.xls**. Worse yet, if you deleted **Danielli3.xls** after saving it under its new name, Excel will not be able to locate the workbook and thus will not be able to update link reference values in the dependent workbook. In this case, Excel issues an error message. Because you need to know how to handle this case—someone changes the names of one or more supporting workbooks—you will experience it firsthand.

In the steps that follow, you will experience just such a situation. It shows you that if you rename a supporting workbook or move it to another drive or directory, you must tell Excel the new name of the supporting workbook or where you moved it so that Excel can modify the link references, which is not the same as updating the *values* in a link reference.

Redirecting link references to a renamed supporting workbook:

1. Click **File** on the menu bar, click **Close**, and click **Yes** when asked if you want to save your changes to **Beco3.xls**. **Beco3.xls** closes, but Excel remains running

2. Click the **Open** button on the Standard toolbar. The Open dialog box opens

3. Navigate to the disk drive and folder containing the supporting workbook **Danielli3.xls**, right-click the filename in the Open dialog box, click **Rename** in the shortcut menu. Excel highlights the name **Danielli3.xls** in edit mode in the Open dialog box

4. Type the new name **Acquisition.xls**, press **Enter** to complete the file renaming process, but do not open the renamed dependent workbook

5. Navigate to the disk and folder containing **Beco3.xls** workbook and then double-click **Beco3.xls** to open the workbook. Excel opens the workbook and displays a dialog box asking if you want to update links

6. Click the **Update** button. Excel displays an alert box indicating it cannot update links (see Figure 7.32)

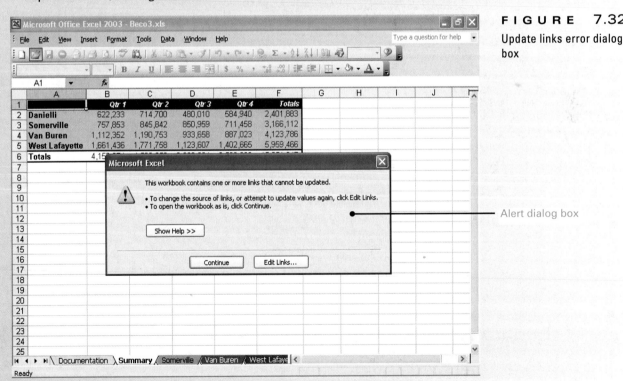

FIGURE 7.32

Update links error dialog box

Alert dialog box

7. Click the **Edit Links** button so that you can help Excel find the renamed supporting workbook. The Edit Links dialog box appears (see Figure 7.33)

FIGURE 7.33

Edit Links dialog box

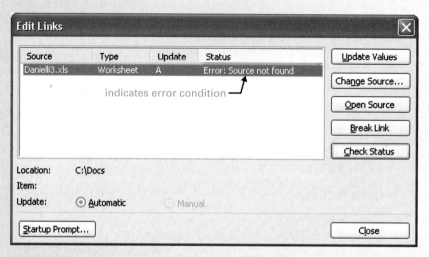

indicates error condition

8. Click the **Change Source** button in the Edit Links dialog box. The Change Source dialog box opens

9. Go to the folder containing the **Acquisition.xls** workbook, click the **Acquisition.xls** filename in the Change Source list of files and folders, and click the **OK** button. The Edit Links dialog box reappears and displays OK in the Status list (see Figure 7.34)

FIGURE 7.34

Edit Links dialog box with updated link locations

indicates new workbook name that Excel can locate

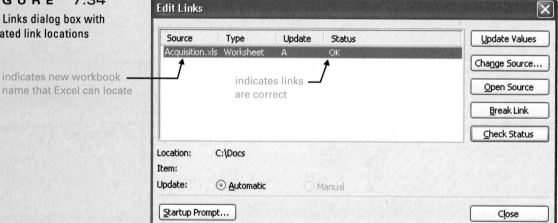

indicates links are correct

10. Click the **Update Values** button, and then click the **Close** button to close the Edit Links dialog box

You have done a lot of work and completed the workbook. Stirling is pleased. Save the workbook and exit Excel.

Saving your final BECO workbook and closing Excel:

1. Click the **Save** button on the Standard toolbar to save your changed **Beco3.xls** workbook

2. Click **File** on the menu bar and then click **Exit** to close Excel

making *the grade*

1. A reference to a cell in another workbook is called a _____, a dynamic _____, or a(n) _____ reference.

2. The disk drive and folders that lead to a workbook are known as the _____.

3. In an external reference, the workbook name is always enclosed in _____, even if it does not contain spaces.

4. The path, workbook name, and worksheet name of an external reference in which the path or the worksheet name contains a blank must be enclosed in what?

5. It is better to _____ worksheets when you want to type the same entry in the same location across multiple worksheets.

SESSION 7.3 SUMMARY

Three-dimensional formulas reference cells in other worksheets of a workbook. The cell references include the worksheet name enclosed in square brackets, an exclamation point, and a cell or cell range. A 3-D or link reference acts like any other cell reference.

You can combine worksheets from other workbooks into one workbook by opening all workbooks, clicking Window and then Arrange to display all workbooks on one screen. Then click and drag a worksheet tab from one window to a workbook in another window to cut and paste a worksheet. To copy a worksheet, press and hold Ctrl and then click and drag a worksheet tab to a workbook in another window.

You can group worksheets in a workbook by clicking the first worksheet tab and then shift-clicking (hold Shift and then click the mouse) the last worksheet of a contiguous set of worksheet tabs. Group noncontiguous worksheet tabs by Ctrl-clicking individual worksheet tabs. With worksheets grouped you can type text in one worksheet cell and the text is placed in all grouped worksheets in the same cell location. Similarly, you can format entries in the same cell(s) on grouped worksheets at the same time. Grouping allows you to establish the same page-level settings, such as page numbers and margins, for all worksheets in a group.

You can forge links between one workbook and a cell or cells of another workbook. Such cell references are called links, dynamic links, or external links. Workbooks containing external links are called dependent workbooks, and the workbooks to which they refer are called supporting workbooks. External links contain three parts: a path, a workbook name, and a cell or cell range. The combination of a path and a workbook name are enclosed in apostrophes if either the path or the workbook name contains spaces. If you rename a supporting workbook file, you have to reestablish the dependent program's link references to the renamed workbook. When one or more values in a supporting workbook change, the dependent workbook is updated with the new values the next time it is loaded.

MICROSOFT OFFICE SPECIALIST OBJECTIVES SUMMARY

- Insert and modify formulas—MOS XL03S-2-3
- Rename a worksheet tab and color it—MOS XL03S-3-4
- Insert, delete, and reposition worksheets in a workbook—MOS XL03S-5-4
- Modify the onscreen window layout—MOS XL03S-5-6

EXCEL

- Establish worksheet page settings—MOS XL03S-5-7
- Use cell Watch—MOS XL03E-1-13
- Define, modify, and use named ranges—MOS XL03E-1-14
- Create a workbook template—MOS XL03E-4-4
- Set the default number of worksheets—MOS XL03E-5-3

making the grade *answers*

SESSION 7.1

1. Arrange
2. Shift
3. Before the current, active worksheet
4. drilling
5. tab

SESSION 7.2

1. link, link, external
2. path
3. brackets, or square brackets
4. apostrophes
5. group

task reference *summary*

Task	Page #	Preferred Method
Deleting a worksheet	EX 7.6	• Right-click the tab of the worksheet to delete • Click **Delete** on the shortcut menu
Saving a Workbook as a Template	EX 7.7	• Activate the workbook you want to save as a template, click **File** and then click **Save As** • Type the template name in the File name list box, click the **Save as type** list box, scroll the list box to locate and then click **Template (*.xlt)**, and click **Save** button
Copying worksheets from other workbooks	EX 7.8	• Open the master workbook—the workbook into which you want to copy worksheets from other workbooks • Open all other workbooks containing worksheets you want to copy to the master workbook • In any of the open Excel workbooks, click **Window**, click **Arrange**, click the **Tiled** option button, and click **OK** • Press and hold the **Ctrl** key, and then click and drag to the master workbook the tab of the worksheet you want to copy • Release the mouse when the down-pointing arrow is in the correct tab location in the master workbook, and then release the **Ctrl** key
Grouping contiguous worksheets	EX 7.13	• Click the worksheet tab of the first worksheet in the group • Use the tab scrolling buttons if necessary to bring the last worksheet tab of the proposed group into view • Hold down the **Shift** key and click the last worksheet tab in the group
Grouping noncontiguous worksheets	EX 7.13	• Click the worksheet tab of the first worksheet you want in the group • Press and hold the **Ctrl** key and then click each worksheet you want to include in the group • When you are done, release the **Ctrl** key
Ungrouping worksheets	EX 7.14	• Click the worksheet tab of any worksheet not in the worksheet group • If all worksheets in the workbook are grouped, right-click any worksheet tab and click **Ungroup Sheets** from the shortcut menu

task reference summary

Task	Page #	Preferred Method
Writing a formula containing a 3-D reference	EX 7.23	• After clicking the cell where you want the formula to appear, type **=**, type a function name, and type the left parenthesis. If no function is needed, then type **=** • Click the sheet tab of the worksheet containing the cell or cell range you want to reference • If a worksheet range is needed, then press and hold the **Shift** key and click the last worksheet tab in the range • Click the cell or cell range you want to reference • Complete the formula (type a concluding right parenthesis for a function, for instance) and then press **Enter**
Printing multiple worksheets	EX 7.27	• Group the worksheets you want to print by pressing **Ctrl** and then clicking the worksheet tabs or pressing **Shift** and clicking the first and last worksheets in a contiguous group • Click **File**, click **Print**, ensure the **Active sheet(s)** option button is selected, and click **OK**
Deleting an Excel Template	EX 7.28	• Click **File** on the menu bar, click **New**, and click **On my computer** in the Templates panel of the task pane • Right-click the template which you want to delete, and click **Delete**, and click **OK** when asked if you want to send the template to the Recycle Bin
Building link references by pointing	EX 7.30	• Open the supporting workbook • Make active the workbook to contain the link reference and the cell to contain the link reference • Type the formula up to the point in which you reference the cell or cell range in another workbook • Click the Taskbar button corresponding to the supporting workbook to make it active • Click the worksheet tab containing the cell or cell range to reference • Click the cell or drag the cell range of the cell(s) you want to reference and press **Enter**
Opening a supporting workbook from a dependent workbook	EX 7.35	• Open the dependent workbook containing the link reference • Click **Edit** and then click **Links** • Click the name of the supporting workbook you want to open from the Links list • Click the **Open Source** button

EXCEL

TRUE OR FALSE

1. Linked workbooks require less memory than an equivalent multisheet workbook.

2. Formatting a cell in the active worksheet of a group of worksheets will format the same cell in all group members.

3. When you include several worksheets in a sheet range, enclose each worksheet name in its own apostrophes.

4. Workbooks containing external links are called dependent workbooks.

5. To print all the worksheets in a workbook, you must first group the worksheets.

FILL-IN

1. A(n) _____ worksheet is sometimes called a consolidation worksheet.

2. One way to copy a worksheet from one workbook to another is to display the source and target workbooks, press and hold the _____ key, and drag the worksheet from the source workbook to the target workbook.

3. Add a blank worksheet to a workbook by clicking Insert on the menu bar and then clicking _____.

4. When you press and hold the Ctrl key and then click two or more worksheet tabs in a workbook, you are _____ the worksheets.

5. In a workbook with many worksheets, you can speed up accessing worksheets by assigning a unique range _____ to cell A1 of each worksheet. Then you can access the _____ Box left of the formula bar to switch from one worksheet to another.

6. Worksheets that contain cells referenced by expressions in another workbook are called _____ worksheets.

MULTIPLE CHOICE

1. Which is not considered part of the general form of an external link?
   a. a workbook name
   b. a cell or cell range
   c. a path
   d. a cell value

2. A workbook containing a link to a supporting worksheet is called a
   a. supporting workbook.
   b. dependent workbook.
   c. summary workbook.
   d. consolidation workbook.

3. Entering data in the same cell of several workbooks simultaneously is called
   a. filling down.
   b. driving down.
   c. auto filling.
   d. drilling down.

4. When will dependent formulas retain their values from the last time the worksheet was saved?
   a. if the dependent workbook is opened without updating the links
   b. each time the dependent workbook is opened, regardless of the update status you chose
   c. if the supporting workbook's cells are changed and the dependent workbook is open
   d. if the dependent workbook is opened with an update to the links

5. What will Excel do if you save the dependent workbook under a different filename while the supporting and dependent workbooks are open?
   a. Nothing happens to the links in the dependent workbook. All formulas remain the same.
   b. Excel will issue an error message because it won't be able to locate the workbook.
   c. Excel automatically and without notification alters all link formulas to reflect the new name.
   d. Excel doesn't allow you to save a dependent workbook under a different filename without saving the supporting workbook under a different filename as well.

REVIEW QUESTIONS

1. Discuss the fastest way to enter the text **Acme Consolidated** in cell A12 of seven worksheets of the same workbook.

2. What is the advantage of a summary or consolidating worksheet?

3. Discuss what, if anything, is wrong with the following expression (assuming that the workbook exists and contains the referenced worksheet):

   `=SUM(C:\My Worksheets for Beco\[Danielli.xls]Sales!B4:B12)`

4. What happens if you change the name of a supporting workbook when the dependent workbook is closed?

CREATE A QUESTION

For each of the following answers, create an appropriate short question.

ANSWER	QUESTION
1. Click Edit, click Links, and then click the Change Source button	_____
2. =[SalesDetail]Sales!C12	_____
3. Click the Qtr1 worksheet tab, press the Ctrl key, click the Qtr2 worksheet tab, click cell A1, and type Sales Information	_____
4. Click File on the menu bar and then click Save Workspace	_____
5. Click and drag the worksheet tab from where it is to another location	_____

1. Summarizing Sales Data Using Reference Tools

Reed Lanterns makes specialty and custom lanterns and lamps. Its clients range from amusement parks to business buildings to private home builders. Reed currently has 11 sales representatives across the country to promote the firm and service its clients. Scott Reed, the owner of Reed Lanterns, has decided to promote one of the representatives to sales manager. Scott has asked you to help him determine which sales representative should be promoted to the management position. He would like you to summarize the sales reps' sales per quarter for the past two years in order to see which sales rep has sold the most.

Scott has reviewed the worksheets you have created and has given you some suggestions. He would like you to add a worksheet to summarize the sales representatives' figures for the past two years. There are also some formatting changes he would like you to complete to improve the appearance of the worksheet.

1. Open **ex07ReedReps.xls** and save it as **<yourname>ReedReps2.xls** (see Figure 7.35). These two worksheets are what you have created for Scott

2. Insert a Documentation sheet so that it is the first worksheet in the workbook. Enter the workbook name, **Reed Sales Representative Report**, your name, and the date

3. Insert a worksheet at the end of the workbook titled **Sales Summary**. Create the following column titles and place them in the cell range A1:D1: **Sales Rep**, **2003 Total Sales**, **2004 Total Sales**, and **Total Sales**

4. Use 3-D references to place the reps' names in the Sales Summary worksheet, cells **A2** through **A12**, by referring to their cell addresses in the 2004 Totals worksheet

5. In the Sales Summary worksheet, type a 3-D cell reference in cells **B2** and **C2** referring to cell **F3** in the 2003 Totals and 2004 Totals worksheets, respectively. Select cells **B2:C2** and drag the fill handle down through the cell range **B12:C12** to complete columns B and C

6. For the Total Sales column, select cell range **B2:D12** and then use the AutoSum button to create SUM functions in column D. Be sure that all currency figures display two decimal places and the Accounting format with the currency symbol

7. To improve the appearance of the worksheets, do the following. In the 2003 and 2004 Totals worksheets, make the font of the top row 14 point, bold, and blue. In these worksheets and the Sales Summary worksheet, make the column headings' font bold and blue, and fill the cells in light yellow

8. Format the column headings in the Sales Summary worksheet so that the cells are bordered as in the 2003 and 2004 Totals worksheets

9. In the Sales Summary worksheet, determine which rep had the greatest sales and should be promoted to manager. Display this rep by filling his information with a light green background. Remove the onscreen gridlines from the Documentation worksheet. Place your name in the worksheet header of each worksheet, save the workbook, and print all sheets in the workbook

FIGURE 7.35

Reed Lanterns workbook

	A	B	C	D	E	F	G	J	K
1			2003 Sales Representative Report						
2	Sales Reps	1st Qtr	2nd Qtr	3rd Qtr	4th Qtr	Rep Total	Rep Average		
3	Steve	$ 6,767.00	$ 5,656.00	$ 3,434.00	$ 3,432.00	$ 19,289.00	$ 4,822.25		
4	Darin	$ 7,878.00	$ 2,323.00	$ 3,433.00	$ 3,432.00	$ 17,066.00	$ 4,266.50		
5	Trevor	$ 4,323.00	$ 6,245.00	$ 6,256.00	$ 6,283.00	$ 23,107.00	$ 5,776.75		
6	Cindie	$ 7,878.00	$ 6,767.00	$ 7,667.00	$ 2,312.00	$ 24,624.00	$ 6,156.00		
7	Jason	$ 4,567.00	$ 7,876.00	$ 7,878.00	$ 2,123.00	$ 22,444.00	$ 5,611.00		
8	Kim	$ 4,238.00	$ 4,445.00	$ 4,876.00	$ 3,213.00	$ 16,772.00	$ 4,193.00		
9	Jessica	$ 6,218.00	$ 6,219.00	$ 6,072.00	$ 6,074.00	$ 24,583.00	$ 6,145.75		
10	Madison	$ 3,432.00	$ 5,550.00	$ 4,545.00	$ 6,245.00	$ 19,772.00	$ 4,943.00		
11	Brian	$ 7,878.00	$ 4,532.00	$ 3,434.00	$ 8,989.00	$ 24,833.00	$ 6,208.25		
12	Jon	$ 5,678.00	$ 9,997.00	$ 8,878.00	$ 7,778.00	$ 32,331.00	$ 8,082.75		
13	Dave	$ 7,878.00	$ 3,434.00	$ 7,899.00	$ 7,878.00	$ 27,089.00	$ 6,772.25		
14									
15									
16									
17									
18									
19									
20									
21									
22									
23									
24									

\ 2003 Totals / 2004 Totals /

Edit

2. Producing a Consolidated Income Statement for Delzura Machinery

Delzura Machinery firm builds glass-beveling machinery for both professional and hobbyist customers. It produces and sells a small lathe-style glass-beveling machine with four stations for $1,350 up through a large industrial-model beveling machine for $14,000.

Phyllis Dobkin, the executive vice president, wants you to create a one-page summary workbook that summarizes the key figures from each workbook. Each workbook contains a similar format because the same person created both of them. Key figures Phyllis wants you to place on a summary workbook are Net Sales, Cost of Goods Sold, Gross Profit, Total Operating Expenses, and Net Income.

1. Open the supporting workbooks **ex07DelzuraHawthorne.xls**, **ex07DelzuraPortland.xls**, and the main workbook you will alter and save called **ex07DelzuraMain.xls**

2. Make **ex07DelzuraMain.xls** active, save the workbook as **<yourname>DelzuraMain2.xls**, click the **Summary** worksheet tab, and type the following labels in the indicated cells: A1: **Consolidated Income Statement**; A4: **Net Sales**; A6: **Cost of Goods Sold**; A8: **Gross Profit**; A10: **Total Operating Expenses**; A12: **Net Income**; B3: **Hawthorne**; and C3: **Portland**

3. Bold cells **B3** and **C3**, select cell **A1** and drag the mouse across the cell range **A1:C1**, click the **Merge and Center** button, and format the merged cells to **Bold** and **12 pt**

4. Display portions of all three worksheets by clicking **Window** on the menu bar, click **Arrange**, click the **Tiled** option button, and click **OK**

5. In preparation for writing link formulas, click the **ex07DelzuraHawthorne.xls** Title bar to make it active and then click the **Hawthorne** worksheet tab

6. Click the **ex07DelzuraPortland.xls** Title bar to make it active, then click the **Portland** worksheet tab, and then click the **DelzuraMain2.xls** title bar to make it active

7. In the DelzuraMain2.xls worksheet, click cell **B4**, type **=SUM(**, click the **ex07DelzuraHawthorne.xls** Title bar, drag cell range **B4:E4** in the Hawthorne workbook, type **)**, and press **Enter**. (Excel displays the value $ 462,735 and formats the entry)

8. Click cell **C4**, type **=SUM(**, (don't type the comma) click the **ex07DelzuraPortland.xls** Title bar, drag cell range **B4:E4** in the Portland workbook, type **)**, and press **Enter**. (Excel displays the value $529,286 and formats the entry)

9. Click cell **B6**, type **=**, (don't type the comma) click the **ex07DelzuraHawthorne.xls** Title bar, click cell **F5** in the Hawthorne workbook, and press **Enter**

10. Click cell **C6**, type **=**, (don't type the comma) click the **ex07DelzuraPortland.xls** Title bar, click cell **F5** in the Portland workbook, and press **Enter**

11. Click cell **B8**, type **=B4–B6**, press **Enter**, and copy cell **B8** to cell **C8**

12. Click cell **B10**, type **=**, click the **ex07DelzuraHawthorne.xls** Title bar, click cell **F14** in the Hawthorne workbook, and press **Enter**

13. Click cell **C10**, type **=**, click the **ex07DelzuraPortland.xls** Title bar, click cell **F14** in the Portland workbook, and press **Enter**

14. Click cell **B12**, type **=B8–B10**, press **Enter**, and copy cell **B12** to cell **C12**

15. Format the eight cells displaying values to accounting format, zero decimal places, and currency symbols

16. Close the **ex07DelzuraHawthorne.xls** and **ex07DelzuraPortland.xls** workbooks, and click **No** if you are asked if you want to save changes

17. Click the **Maximize** button on the Title bar of **DelzuraMain2.xls**, click the **Comments** worksheet tab, fill in your name in the Developer text box, type in yesterday's date in the Date Created text box, and type in today's date in the Date Revised text box

18. Click the **Summary** worksheet tab of **DelzuraMain2.xls**, click **File**, click **Page Setup**, click **Header/Footer**, fill in your name in the header section, click **OK** to close the Page Setup dialog box, save the workbook, and print both worksheets of the workbook

1. Summarizing Contract Billing and Bonuses with Excel

Kelleher & MacCollum is an accounting firm that services large corporations in the northeastern United States. The main role of the firm's consultants, however, is not examining financial statements during audits or tax season; instead, the consultants at Kelleher & MacCollum are highly regarded as accounting experts. They are hired by corporations to come into their accounting offices, analyze current policies and procedures, recommend changes and improvements, and consult management on the best way to implement the needed changes.

The last three firms that hired Kelleher & MacCollum to recommend changes to their Accounting Departments specifically asked for the team led by Aaron Cole. These were the most successful contracts in the firm's history. The gross billing for each company was over $100,000, far exceeding any past contracts. The CEO of Kelleher & MacCollum, Dennis Kelleher, wants to reward Aaron and his team members for their excellent work. He has decided to give each team member a bonus of 5 percent of their gross billing for these three contracts. In addition to this 5 percent, Aaron Cole will also receive an additional 5 percent bonus on the total amount billed to all three contracts.

Currently, the amount billed per contract is by consultant name, hours billed, and charge per hour. The total charge for each consultant and the total charge for the contract are also included. Each consultant's charge per hour is based on his or her levels of education, experience, and knowledge. Dennis Kelleher needs a summary of all three contracts' figures in order to determine the appropriate bonus amounts. He has asked you to create a Summary worksheet of this information.

Open the workbook **ex07Kelleher.xls** and save as **<yourname>Kelleher2.xls**. (See Figure 7.36.) Insert a documentation worksheet, called *Documentation*, and enter the workbook name, your name, and the date in the first column. At the end of the workbook, insert a new sheet called **Total Billing**. Use the Fill Across Worksheets command in the Edit menu to copy the column titles from the Front & Leaf worksheet to the Total Billing worksheet and the consultants' names from the Front & Leaf worksheet. In the Hours Billed column of the Total Billing worksheet, insert the sum for each consultant's hours from the corresponding cells of the three contract worksheets. From the Front & Leaf worksheet, use the Edit, Fill Across Worksheets command to copy the dollar amounts from the Charge per Hour column to fill in the same column in the Total Billing worksheet.

In the Total Billing worksheet, title column D **Total Billed**. For each cell corresponding to each person's row, create a formula that multiplies the Hours Billed by the Charge per Hour. At the bottom of the Total Billed column, sum the consultant Total Billed values. Title column E **Bonus**. In this column, create formulas that multiply the Total Billed per consultant by 5 percent to determine their bonus amount. Remember that Aaron Cole receives a 5 percent bonus of his total hours billed and 5 percent of all hours billed. Total this column and bold the total value at the bottom of the column. Save your changes. Include your name in the header of each worksheet and print the Total Billing worksheet.

FIGURE 7.36

Kelleher & MacCollum initial workbook

	A	B	C	D	E	F	G	H
1	**Front & Leaf Publishing**							
2								
3	**Consultant**	**Hours Billed**	**Charge per Hour**					
4	Aaron Cole	40	$150	$6,000				
5	Cliff Sellers	40	$80	$3,200				
6	Brian Campbell	60	$95	$5,700				
7	Joseph Hackett	80	$100	$8,000				
8	Laurie Baker	120	$80	$9,600				
9	Joanna Sellis	80	$120	$9,600				
10	Karen Watson	65	$110	$7,150				
11	Susan Moore	95	$100	$9,500				
12	Angela Hall	55	$85	$4,675				
13	Tina Hunter	75	$75	$5,625				
14	Derek Yen	110	$120	$13,200				
15	Hector Martin	120	$110	$13,200				
16	Kelly Rosen	65	$85	$5,525				
17				$100,975				
18								
19								
20								
21								
22								
23								
24								

2. Consolidating Information for a Toy Robot Seller

Elizabeth Brodkin is the chief financial officer for Robotic Creations, a company that sells four categories of robot toys: educational robots, tin robots, transformers, and robot pets. She maintains two very simple workbooks. The main workbook contains four worksheets in which she keeps a summary of sales by quarter of three of the four categories of robot toys. Called **ex07Robot**, the workbook also contains a documentation worksheet on the front. The second workbook, called **ex07RobotPets**, tracks sales of the robot pet category of robots. She would like you to help her in two major ways. First, she wants you to copy the single worksheet in ex07RobotPets into the ex07Robot workbook and place it between the Tin Robots worksheet and the Transformers worksheet. Secondly, she wants you to insert a new worksheet after all the worksheets in the ex07Robot workbook. That worksheet should

summarize the sales of each of the robot categories. You should apply an attractive format to the summary worksheet and color the worksheet tabs of any worksheets you added to the workbook. The summary worksheet contains text with the four quarters listed in column A and labels in cells B1 through E1 containing the labels for the four categories of robots. Be sure to label each worksheet with your name in the header and the sheet name in the footer, and print all worksheets.

Begin by opening **ex07Robot.xls** and save the workbook as **<yourname>Robot2.xls**. Then open **ex07RobotPets.xls**. Copy the Robot Pets worksheet to the **<yourname>Robot2.xls** (see Figure 7.37) workbook. Add a new worksheet to the **<yourname>Robot2.xls** workbook and rename it *Sales Summary*. Create link formulas to the other worksheets to summarize sales. Save your finished work and print all worksheets in the **<yourname>Robot2.xls** workbook.

FIGURE 7.37
Robotic Creations workbook

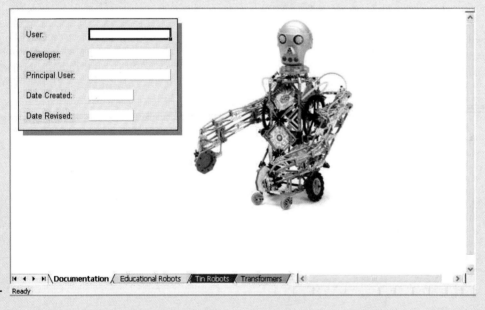

1. Summarizing Multiple Worksheets and Workbooks

Assist Insurance is a Web-based insurance company. Assist Insurance (AI) has advertised throughout the southern states as their office is in Tennessee. AI is a site that the public uses to find the best health care insurance plans for their individual needs. They pride themselves on their excellent customer service and low prices. The CFO of AI feels that there is a market segment that AI could dominate—students. Since AI's prices are so low, their services are attractive to the typical student. After several meetings, the board decided that in order to get more student clients, they plan to open a few test locations in selected cities. Recent studies have shown that Web-based businesses that are also in front of students and easily accessible are more successful than those with Web-only services. The board has approved the opening of six test locations.

As an intern at AI, you have been assigned to the project of determining the areas where AI should open an office. AI wants these offices to be in the six cities with the greatest amount of student awareness. In other words, AI needs to determine in which cities they are currently best known. Your manager has already narrowed it down to three states: Florida, Georgia, and Louisiana. Each state's figures for the past four quarters have been recorded in an individual notebook. Open **ex07AIFlorida.xls** and save as **AIFlorida2.xls**. Do the same for the worksheets **ex07AIGeorgia.xls** and **ex07AILouisiana.xls**—save the workbooks as **AIGeorgia2.xls** and **AILouisiana2.xls**, respectively. For each state, the following statistics are available for each quarter: the number of hits the Web site received from that city, the number of hits that resulted in purchases, the average age of site visitor, and the number of hits received from students. For each state, you will need to create a summary sheet to summarize the past four quarters' figures. Once each workbook is summarized, the information will need to be incorporated into a single summary workbook.

The board is only concerned with the number of hits and the number of hits received from students. Create a summary sheet for each state so that column A contains the same information on each worksheet for each individual state. Title Column B **Hits** and column C **Student Hits**. For column D, create the title **Percent from Students**. Create formulas for columns B and C, using 3-D cell references, so that they total the corresponding figures for each city from each quarter. For column D, create a formula that will divide the number of student hits by total hits. This will give the percentage of hits that were received from students. Fill the formulas for each city. Format this column in percentages with one decimal point.

Create a new workbook and name it **AISummaryReport**. Create a documentation worksheet and place on it the title of the workbook, the names of three states summarized, your name, and the date. Create a summary worksheet, called AI Summary Report, grouped into distinct rows by state. Use a light green color to highlight the three state names, below which are the cities within the state. Include within each state's group of cities the information from each state's summary sheet. Create columns to include the total number of hits, number of hits received from students, and total percentage of hits from students. Improve the appearance of the worksheet (bold column headings, use *Wrap text* alignment, etc.) and use a light yellow background color to highlight the rows of the four cities with the greatest response from students. (*Hint:* Sort all cities on percent, note the highest values, and click Edit, Undo to restore the rows to their original order.) Type your name in the AISummaryReport header. Print the AISummaryReport workbook and follow the summary worksheet with the summary worksheet for each state.

2. Pampered Paws

Pampered Paws is a pet store that sells pet products and provides a pet-sitting service for clients who do not want to board their animals in a kennel. Pampered Paws pet-sitting clients prefer to leave their pets at home—in surroundings that are familiar to their pets and comforting to them. For a reasonable daily fee, a Pampered Paws employee will visit a client's pet in its home twice daily. During each 15-minute visit, the employee plays with the client's pet and checks the pet's food and water. The employees walk dogs and, on occasion, cats as part of the service. (They draw the line at turtles, however.)

Pampered Paws has a thriving retail store selling a complete line of pet food and other products. Grace Jackson, Pampered Paws's owner, has hired a Web developer to create a Web store in which Pampered Paws will sell most of their products online. She wants you to help her analyze the profitability of the company's product offerings to estimate the profitability of a comparable online business.

Pampered Paws has captured the sales of the cat and dog food portion of their business and in an Excel workbook. Figure 7.38 shows one of the sales accumulation worksheets. The sales workbook contains six worksheets, one for each month, listing sales in date order for the first six months of the year. Grace wants you to add three worksheets to the workbook to summarize the two quarter and one half-year sales. Label the quarterly summary worksheets *Quarter 1* and *Quarter 2*, and label the half-year worksheet *Summary*.

Start by loading **ex07PamperedPaws.xls** and immediately saving it as **<yourname>Paws.xls**. Insert the

three new worksheets. Place the Quarter 1 worksheet before the January worksheet, place the Quarter 2 worksheet between the March and April worksheets, and place the Summary worksheet between the Documentation and Quarter 1 worksheets. Color both the Quarter 1 and Quarter 2 worksheet tabs green. Quarter 1 should summarize both the total number of bags sold and the total sales amount for January through March. Quarter 2 should be similar to Quarter 1, except it summarizes sales for April through June. Follow this model for both Quarter 1 and Quarter 2: Place the text **Total Bags** in **B1**, the text **Total Sales** in **C1**, the text **January** in **A2**, **February** in **A3**, and **March** in **A4**. Write link formulas in B2 to sum January's total bags sold and in C2 to sum January's total sales. Repeat these two formulas for February and March. Follow the same pattern for Quarter 2, but write the link formulas and month names for April through June.

Color the Summary worksheet's tab red. Its structure is as follows: Place the label **Quarter 1** in cell **A2**, the label **Quarter 2** in cell **A3**, the label **Total Bags** in **B1**, and the label **Total Sales** in **C1**. Write four link formulas that total bags sold and dollar sales from the Quarter 1 worksheet. Similarly, sum the bags and total the sales from the Quarter 2 worksheet. Format the three worksheets you added in an attractive manner. Place your name in the *Left section* of the three worksheets' headers, place the worksheet name in the *Center section* of the worksheets' headers, and save the workbook. Print only the three summary worksheets, Summary, Quarter 1, and Quarter 2. (*Hint:* group the three worksheets prior to printing.)

FIGURE 7.38

Example Pampered Paws pet food sales worksheet

	A	B	C	D	E	F	G	H
1	Item Name	Animal	Size (lb)	Unit Price	Bags	Total Sale	Date	
2	Eukanuba Kitten	cat	6.5	$ 15.99	3	$ 47.97	01/01/02	
3	Iams Chunks	dog	8	$ 8.99	8	$ 71.92	01/01/02	
4	Nutro Max Weight Control Formula	dog	5	$ 5.99	8	$ 47.92	01/02/02	
5	Nature's Recipe Puppy Lamb Meal & Rice Canine	dog	5	$ 5.99	10	$ 59.90	01/02/02	
6	Science Diet Canine Large Breed Growth	dog	5	$ 7.99	7	$ 55.93	01/02/02	
7	Natural Life Feline Adult Formula	cat	4	$ 5.99	9	$ 53.91	01/02/02	
8	Natural Life Kitten Formula	cat	4	$ 5.99	8	$ 47.92	01/03/02	
9	Eukanuba Premium Performance	dog	8	$ 11.49	5	$ 57.45	01/03/02	
10	Iams Chunks	dog	8	$ 8.99	6	$ 53.94	01/03/02	
11	Bil-Jac Cat Food	cat	7	$ 9.99	1	$ 9.99	01/03/02	
12	Iams Hairball Care Formula	cat	4	$ 7.99	6	$ 47.94	01/03/02	
13	Pro-Plan Senior Formula	dog	8	$ 8.49	9	$ 76.41	01/03/02	
14	Natural Life Feline Adult Formula	cat	4	$ 5.99	2	$ 11.98	01/03/02	
15	Nature's Recipe Puppy Lamb Meal & Rice Canine	dog	5	$ 5.99	5	$ 29.95	01/04/02	
16	Authority Puppy with Real Lamb	dog	5	$ 4.99	1	$ 4.99	01/04/02	
17	Natural Life Kitten Formula	cat	4	$ 5.99	3	$ 17.97	01/04/02	
18	Eukanuba Premium Performance	dog	8	$ 11.49	10	$ 114.90	01/04/02	
19	Authority Adult with Real Chicken	dog	5	$ 4.99	4	$ 19.96	01/05/02	
20	Bil-Jac Senior Dog Food	dog	7	$ 9.99	4	$ 39.96	01/05/02	
21	Iams Hairball Care Formula	cat	4	$ 7.99	10	$ 79.90	01/05/02	
22	Eukanuba Premium Performance	dog	8	$ 11.49	6	$ 68.94	01/06/02	
23	Natural Life Feline Adult Formula	cat	4	$ 5.99	4	$ 23.96	01/07/02	
24	Bil-Jac Puppy Food	dog	7	$ 9.99	9	$ 89.91	01/07/02	
25	Eukanuba Premium Performance	dog	8	$ 11.49	7	$ 80.43	01/08/02	

Documentation \ **January** / February / March / April / May / June /

Ready

1. Analyzing and Selecting the Best Law Schools Using the Web

Roger Thornburg graduated from college three years ago. He has been working for his father's law firm and has decided to pursue his law degree. Since Roger plans on returning home after he graduates to continue working with his father, he wants to spend his law school career far away from home. For the three years he will be in school, Roger has picked two states on opposite ends of the country where he wants to go to school—California and New York. Fortunately, both states are home to several of the top-tier law schools. Since Roger is working six days a week, he has asked you to help him in his application process by finding information online regarding law schools in these two states.

Because Roger is only interested in schools among the top 25, he suggests you go to a Web site that lists schools in order of ranking: www.usnews.com. (You may want to use Google or another search engine and search with the terms "law school rank".) When on the home page, select **Best Grad Schools** under **Rankings and Ratings**. Under Best Graduate Schools, look at the section titled **Law**. You will be using Top Law Schools for your information. Open **ex07LawSchools.xls** and save as **<yourname>LawSchools2.xls**. This is the workbook Roger has started in which you will record the information you find on the Web. He has created a worksheet for each state and created column headings to organize the criteria most important to him in choosing schools to apply to—each university's name, rank, overall score, average undergraduate GPA of in-coming students, and the average LSAT score of those students. For each worksheet, use the information from the Web to fill in the appropriate data for the schools in each state that appear in the top 25.

After glancing at the results, Roger asks you to add a column titled Diversity. He knows that he will best benefit from going away to school if he is part of a diverse student body. Go back to the Best Graduate Schools page, look under the Law heading, and select Diversity Rankings. Use these figures to fill in the needed data. To further narrow down Roger's choice of schools, he wants you to highlight the information for the top two schools in each state. To do this, under each column heading (rank/score/etc.) highlight the two cells with the highest score or ranking. Determine which two schools from each state have the greatest number of highlighted cells.

Create a worksheet titled Summary. In the summary worksheet, include the same column headings as in the state worksheets. Consolidate the information for the top two universities from each state in this worksheet so that it reflects the data for the top four schools. Again highlight the two cells under each column with the highest score or ranking. Conclude which two universities have the greatest scores for Roger's criteria. Highlight the names of those two universities. Create a documentation worksheet and on it include your name, the date, and the title **Law School Rankings**. Group all the worksheets and then place your name in the worksheet headers and place the worksheet name in the worksheet footers. Print the entire workbook.

around the world

1. Wilton Industries International Sales Consolidation Workbook

Wilton Industries International has sales offices in North America, Europe, the Pacific Basin, Latin America, and Asia. Jerry Parr keeps track of the sales in each region for each month. Currently he has collected sales, in millions of U.S. dollars, in a workbook named **ex07Wilton.xls**. Your task is to use link formulas to summarize data from the individual month's sales in both the summary worksheet and two quarterly worksheets you will add to the workbook.

Open **ex07Wilton.xls** and save it immediately as **<yourname>Wilton2.xls**. Next, add two new worksheets and rename them **Qtr1** and **Qtr2**. Rename the sheet called Sheet1 to **Summary**. Reorder the sequence of worksheets so that Summary is followed by these: Qtr1, Jan, Feb, Mar, Qtr2, Apr, May, and Jun. Place the label **Quarter 1 Sales** in cell **A1** on the **Qtr1** worksheet. Place the label **Quarter2 Sales** in cell **A1** on the **Qtr2** worksheet. Merge and Center format the Quarter 1 and Quarter 2 labels across cells A1 and B1 in each worksheet and then apply boldface to both labels. Write link formulas in cells A2 through A6 that will display the region labels on the Jan worksheet in cells A2 through A6. Do the same thing for the Qtr2 worksheet. On the Qtr1 worksheet in cells B2 through B7, write line formulas that sum the sales for each region in the first three months. Do the same thing for the Qtr2 worksheet: Write link formulas to sum sales for April through June by region. Group Qtr1 and Qtr2 and then format cell B2 with the Accounting format, display two decimal places, and display the currency symbol. Format cells B3 through B6 the same way, but omit the currency symbol. Click cell A1 and then ungroup the worksheets. Color the Qtr1 and Qtr2 worksheet tabs green. Color the Summary worksheet tab red.

The summary worksheet should summarize sales for the five regions for each quarter. Write link formulas that reference the total sales on the Qtr1 and Qtr2 summary worksheets for each region (e.g., =Qtr1!B3 for cell B4 on the summary worksheet). Remove the gridlines from the onscreen display of the Summary worksheet. Italicize the five region names on the Summary worksheet. Place your name in the header and place the worksheet names in the footer. Remember to use the code for the worksheet names. Save the workbook and print it.

2. Jump Start

Jump Start is a small family owned "functional food products" company. They have been producing, selling, and distributing sports drinks, energy bars, and energy gels for 15 years. Jump Start operates sales and distribution offices in Paris, Vancouver, Toronto, Minneapolis, Beijing, and Tokyo. Each site is responsible for managing product promotions, sales, ordering, and distribution for their region. As assistant to the vice president of Global Sales, you need to consolidate all the pertinent information from each region.

Begin by opening **ex07JumpStart.xls**. Save this file as **<yourname>JumpStart2.xls**. The workbook contains worksheets for four regions. (The Beijing and Tokyo offices send their information directly to you in separate files. You will open those files later.) First, insert a new worksheet and name it *Summary* and color the worksheet tab bright yellow. Next, group the original worksheets so that they can be formatted exactly the same. Begin by formatting all the original worksheets to have Boldface column titles and column widths of 12 Characters. Cells A7 and A14 should be Boldface as well. Right Align the column titles for each month and for the column *Totals*. In the Sales (Units) and Sales Revenue sections create the appropriate formulas for each Totals (column and row) cell. In the Sales Revenue section, format the cells to have an Accounting format with only the Totals cells containing a currency symbol and zero decimals. Add a Double Accounting underline to cells B13 through N13.

On the *Summary* worksheet, create two tables—one titled *Sales (Units)* and the other titled *Sales Revenue*. Merge the cells such that each section title is legible. In cells A3 and A13 type in the column title *Site*. Directly below Site add the name of each sales office (Tokyo, Vancouver, and so on). Make sure the site names are in Ascending order and the column title (Site) is in Boldface. In cells B3 through F3 add the column titles of *Q1* through *Q4* and *Totals*. Right Align these cells and Boldface them. Format cells B13 through F13 the same way. In cells A10 and A20 type in the row titles *Totals* and boldface them. Format the column widths to be 10 Characters. Now open the information files for Beijing and Tokyo, **ex07Beijing.xls** and **ex07Tokyo.xls**. Write link formulas to sum all the quarterly data. This will require links such as =SUM(Vancouver!B7:D7) and =[ex07Beijing.xls] Beijing!$B$7. Also sum each Totals cell and format the Sales Revenue section with the same Accounting format as the original worksheets. Place your name in the header and the worksheet names in the footer for all worksheets. Format the Page Setup to be Landscape and to fit on one page. Save your file, and print it. Next print the worksheet formulas.

Pro Golf Academy

Pro Golf Academy has tracked their sales of the men's and women's golf apparel and captured the sales data in a workbook called **ex07ProGolf.xls** (see Figure 7.39). It contains six worksheets, one for each month, listing sales in date order for the first six months of the year. Betty wants you to add three worksheets to the workbook, write link expressions to summarize the sales information, and print only the three worksheets you are about to add (*Summary, Quarter 1,* and *Quarter 2*). Two of the new worksheets are the quarterly summaries. Label the first of these worksheets **Quarter 1** and the second one **Quarter 2**. Place the worksheet Quarter 1 just before the January worksheet and place the worksheet Quarter 2 between the March and April worksheets. Quarter 1 should summarize both the total number of units sold and the total sales amount for the months of January, February, and March. Quarter 2 should be similar to Quarter 1, except it summarizes sales for April through June.

Start by loading **ex07ProGolf.xls** and save it as **<yourname>ProGolf7.xls**. Insert the three new worksheets and move them into their locations among the worksheets. The **Summary** worksheet should be the first worksheet in the workbook.

Color its worksheet tab red. It displays four numbers and four labels. The numbers are the total quarter 1 units sold, total quarter 1 sales, total quarter 2 units sold, and total quarter 2 sales. Color the two quarter worksheet tabs bright yellow. Next, follow this model for both Quarter 1 and Quarter 2: Place the text **Total Units** in **B1**, the text **Total Sales** in **C1**, the text **January** in **A2**, **February** in **A3**, and **March** in **A4**. Write link formulas in B2 to sum January's total units sold and in C2 to sum January's total sales. Repeat these two formulas for February and March. Follow the same pattern for Quarter 2, but write the link formulas and month names for April through June. The Summary worksheet is simple: Place the label **Quarter 1** in cell **A2**, the label **Quarter 2** in cell **A3**, the label **Total Units** in **B1**, and **Total Sales** in **C1**. Write four link formulas that sum quarter 1 total units and total sales from the Quarter 1 worksheet and sum quarter 2 total units and total sales from the Quarter 2 worksheet. Format the three newly added worksheets in an attractive manner, place your name in all nine worksheet headers, save the workbook, but print only the three summary worksheets—Summary, Quarter 1, and Quarter 2.

FIGURE 7.39

Pro Golf Academy apparel sales data workbook

	A	B	C	D	E	F	G	H
1	Item Name	Collection	Size	Unit Price	Units	Extended	Date	
2	Adidas Clima JP Polo	men's	M	$ 29.97	1	$ 29.97	1/1/2004	
3	Adidas Clima JP Polo	men's	M	$ 29.97	6	$ 179.82	1/1/2004	
4	Taylor Made Solid Mercerized Polo	men's	M	$ 34.97	6	$ 209.82	1/1/2004	
5	Adidas Mercerized Engineered Block Stripe Polo	men's	XL	$ 39.99	7	$ 279.93	1/2/2004	
6	Ashworth Performance Pencil Stripe Polo	men's	M	$ 54.99	8	$ 439.92	1/2/2004	
7	Izod Club Solid Textured Stripe Polo	women's	S	$ 34.97	8	$ 279.76	1/2/2004	
8	Taylor Made Solid Mercerized Polo	men's	M	$ 34.97	10	$ 349.70	1/4/2004	
9	Ashworth Summer Stripe Jersey	men's	XL	$ 49.99	1	$ 49.99	1/5/2004	
10	Ashworth Twist Pique	men's	XL	$ 59.99	7	$ 419.93	1/5/2004	
11	Cutter & Buck Palma Polo	men's	M	$ 29.90	7	$ 209.30	1/5/2004	
12	Cutter & Buck Palma Polo	men's	M	$ 29.90	8	$ 239.20	1/5/2004	
13	Izod Club Sleeveless Tip Collar Polo	women's	M	$ 29.97	5	$ 149.85	1/5/2004	
14	Ashworth Classic Interlock Colored Shirt	men's	M	$ 39.99	5	$ 199.95	1/6/2004	
15	Ashworth Pima Texturized Stripe	men's	L	$ 49.99	10	$ 499.90	1/6/2004	
16	Ashworth Summer Stripe Jersey	men's	XL	$ 49.99	3	$ 149.97	1/6/2004	
17	Ashworth Twist Pique	men's	XL	$ 59.99	5	$ 299.95	1/6/2004	
18	Ashworth Performance Pencil Stripe Polo	men's	M	$ 54.99	10	$ 549.90	1/7/2004	
19	Izod Club Solid Textured Stripe Polo	women's	S	$ 34.97	10	$ 349.70	1/7/2004	
20	Izod Club Yarn Dye Stripe Polo	women's	L	$ 34.97	5	$ 174.85	1/7/2004	
21	Ashworth Performance Pencil Stripe Polo	men's	M	$ 54.99	5	$ 274.95	1/8/2004	
22	Cutter & Buck Palma Polo	men's	M	$ 29.90	1	$ 29.90	1/8/2004	
23	Izod Club Sleeveless Tip Collar Polo	women's	M	$ 29.97	3	$ 89.91	1/8/2004	
24	Taylor Made Solid Mercerized Polo	men's	M	$ 34.97	4	$ 139.88	1/8/2004	
25	Adidas Mercerized Engineered Block Stripe Polo	men's	XL	$ 39.99	4	$ 159.96	1/9/2004	

January / February / March / April / May / June

Ready

analysis

LEVEL **FOUR**

CHAPTER SEVEN

1. Moving from One Worksheet to Another Quickly

Suppose a workbook contains 13 worksheets—one for each month and a summary worksheet. Each worksheet tab contains an appropriate label. If you write a lot of link formulas in the summary worksheet, you have to move to various worksheet tabs to "point" to the referenced cells on other pages. Come up with another method, besides right-clicking the worksheet tab scroll buttons, to select a worksheet name and move to it directly. Does the alternative way have any advantages such as the number of sheets or the ease with which you can jump to other worksheets?

2. Worksheet Groups and Link Formulas to External Workbooks

Provide insights describing why you might want to consolidate information from multiple workbooks on one worksheet of a separate workbook. In your discussion, provide reasons why a company would maintain information on distinct workbooks. In other words, why not simply place all the information on separate worksheets of a single workbook. Consider workgroups, team members, and so on, in your analysis.

Auditing, Sharing, Protecting, and Publishing Workbooks

did you know?

Cary *Grant's real name was Archibald Leach, for whom John Cleese's character in A Fish Called Wanda was named.*

a *fly can react to a perceived danger by changing direction in 30 milliseconds.*

one-*third of the solar energy hitting Earth evaporates water—about 95,000 cubic miles each year.*

in *the tenth century, the Grand Vizier of Persia, Abdul Kassem Ismael, ported his entire library with him wherever he went. Four hundred camels, trained to walk in alphabetical order, carried the entire 117,000-volume library.*

Excel *provides a rich variety of auditing and worksheet protection features. Read this chapter to learn more about those features.*

Chapter Objectives

- Use the Audit toolbar
- Locate a cell's precedent cells and dependent cells— MOS XL03E-1-11
- Display and clear tracer arrows—MOS XL03E-1-11
- Locate and correct errors using audit tools—MOS XL03E-1-12
- Share a workbook with other users—MOS XL03E-3-3
- Insert comments and review others' comments—MOS XL03S-4-1
- Track, accept, and reject changes made to a workbook— MOS XL03E-3-5
- Merge multiple versions of the same workbook— MOS XL03E-3-4
- Protect workbooks and worksheets—MOS XL03E-3-1
- Password protect a worksheet—MOS XL03E-3-2
- Hide worksheets—MOS XL03S-3-4
- Publish workbooks to the Web—MOS XL03E-4-3
- Insert hyperlinks—MOS XL03S-5-3

chapter case

Nivaca International Art Treasures

Nivaca International Art Treasures ("Nivaca") is a pure play e-commerce company—it has no storefront besides its Web site. Nivaca specializes in discovering, marketing, and making available to the public art that is produced by artists located in difficult-to-reach corners of the world. Nivaca agents and buyers trek to remote locations from the Andes Mountains to the rain forests of Africa seeking isolated villages—especially in communities where artists produce high quality objects that have very narrow distribution. Nivaca's noble mission is to encourage economic development in Third World countries, to promote artists located in particularly impoverished regions, and to provide customers with wonderful art at bargain prices.

While artists in isolated communities have always been able to sell their goods in small quantities to local residents, they have never been able to gain wider exposure for their goods. Shipping goods to other countries has been a problem for most artists in difficult to reach locations because they are not close to mass transportation. Some villages have had to rely on horses or mules to deliver their few goods to larger villages often hundreds of miles away. Occasionally an adventurous tourist would stumble onto a village producing a particular type of art, purchase and transport the artwork out of the country, and tell friends about the wonderful art he or she found. Typically, such art cannot be shipped to others without personally contacting the artists, so visiting the village in person has been the only way to purchase locally made art objects—until recently.

Nivaca is filling the void between local producers and world consumers. Their guiding rule is that the artists must earn more than the going local rates and the customer must pay less than market rate for the art. Nivaca arranges to pick up and ship objects to consumers who view and order art from their Web site.

Through **disintermediation**—eliminating the often-expensive "middleman" who traditionally charges up to 15 times the actual value—everyone benefits. Recently, for example, a large, upscale New York department store sold vases produced by artists in San Pedro, Peru, for $350 and more. Unlike large department stores, Nivaca is able to offer the same type of vase for $11 (plus shipping). What's more, the San Pedro producers make more profit from the $11 sale than they do from the $350 sale. That's exactly where Nivaca flourishes.

Naturally, Nivaca uses Excel in many capacities: to track sales, to provide managers with summary and detailed customer billing and retention information, and to provide a variety of other management reports. Lately, they have had some anomalies in their reports, where they suspect there are some errant formulas. John Lounsbury, Nivaca's chief financial officer (CFO), wants you to examine some of their Excel reports and locate any mistakes they contain. In addition, John wants you to provide worksheet protection on a field submission report so that their field representatives cannot accidentally overwrite critical formulas in the reporting worksheets they use. Finally, John wants to publish the workbook on the company's intranet so others can review it. Figure 8.1 shows one of those Excel worksheets that Nivaca managers use.

EX 8.2

FIGURE 8.1

Example worksheet used by Nivaca managers

	A	B	C	D	E	F	G	H	I	
1	**Monthly Sales**									
2		Retail								
3	Month / Region	January	February	March	April	May	June	July	August	Sep
4	Andes	122,911.42	157,762.52	46,866.36	45,665.37	49,405.82	50,461.99	58,624.02	165,627.33	167
5	Brazil	99,219.15	132,017.60	65,522.02	168,450.79	36,711.45	149,269.82	57,660.49	167,146.20	68
6	India	43,567.88	39,211.09	34,854.30	31,368.87	27,883.44	25,095.10	22,306.75	20,076.08	17
7	Indonesia	71,027.53	76,090.02	80,041.43	123,693.87	115,185.85	111,543.85	48,402.21	45,678.90	123
8	Mexico	93,151.71	57,914.09	125,387.37	72,551.89	54,858.28	94,175.32	63,076.07	134,811.55	95
9	Thailand	68,045.29	113,992.57	42,669.25	69,079.62	83,479.12	71,080.25	90,540.51	39,703.56	167
10	West Africa	152,135.72	46296.72	101,255.14	140,369.58	78,857.96	143,980.72	63,477.77	162,471.45	158
11	Subtotal	650,058.70	576,987.89	496,595.87	651,179.99	446,381.92	645,607.05	404,087.82	735,515.07	798
12										
13		Wholesale								
14	Month / Region	January	February	March	April	May	June	July	August	Sep
15	Andes	22,712.36	9,300.51	5,550.61	641.24	9,382.64	5,948.35	371.92	8,074.69	15
16	Brazil	3,665.10	39,383.83	17,456.22	27,677.58	3,311.74	18,562.27	2,142.46	10,026.49	4
17	India	3,981.74	6,117.35	4,498.82	6,966.94	3,179.90	179.64	1,758.23	551.66	2
18	Indonesia	9,364.86	5,376.28	14,459.45	562.60	31,793.61	2,022.40	10,371.94	3,328.37	23
19	Mexico	15,888.38	6,836.70	26,894.34	17,978.80	1,439.67	22,248.00	4,767.63	11,534.19	8
20	Thailand	15,927.15	22,834.76	12,386.68	108.88	7,968.73	11,386.04	6,815.19	2,418.21	30
21	West Africa	11,233.19	13,135.53	3,310.28	19,702.93	14,663.75	21,638.52	3,657.93	45,215.18	2
22	Subtotal	82,772.78	102,984.96	84,556.40	73,638.97	71,740.04	81,985.22	29,885.30	81,148.79	87
23										
24	Total	#REF!	679,972.85	581,152.27	724,818.96	518,121.96	727,592.27	433,973.12	816,663.86	886
25										
26										
27										
28										

Logo / Quarterly Summary / **Monthly Sales** / Commissions

INTRODUCTION

Chapter 8 covers the Excel auditing tools that allow you to locate precedent and dependent cells with tracer arrows, locate and correct errors, and erase cell-to-cell tracer arrows. You will learn how to share a workbook on a network with colleagues, review their comments and suggested changes, and insert your own comments. Using Excel's publishing tools, you will convert a workbook into HTML-based Web pages that you can place on the Web, allowing anyone with access to the pages the ability to review and modify the Web version of a workbook.

SESSION 8.1 AUDITING A WORKBOOK

In this session, you will learn how to use the rich set of Excel auditing tools to locate and correct errors in cells. You will use the Auditing toolbar to locate cells referenced by a particular cell and to locate cells that depend on a particular cell. Using the Trace Error tool, you will locate and examine several errant formulas that can cause other cells depending on the errant cells to be incorrect also.

CHAPTER OUTLINE

8.1 Auditing a Workbook, EX 8.3

8.2 Sharing a Workbook and Tracking Changes, EX 8.16

8.3 Protecting and Publishing Workbooks, EX 8.24

8.4 Summary, EX 8.42

EX 8.3

EXCEL

Using Audit Tools

Excel has several powerful features that can help you locate potential trouble spots in your workbook including locating cells whose value depends on a particular cell and finding errors. Worksheets can contain errors that are not obvious because the results appear to be reasonable. Close examination and spot testing can reveal errors. Excel recognizes potential trouble spots and displays symbols such as #VALUE! in cells that contain one or more references to cells whose value cannot be determined or calculated correctly. Excel goes further by marking more subtle potential mistakes such as numbers entered as strings or formulas that don't match similar ones nearby. In the latter case, Excel notes these with a warning flag in the corner of the suspect cell.

John senses that there are mistakes in the workbook containing Nivaca's summary of sales for the last year. He asks you to perform a quality check on the workbook to ensure the results are accurate. He's sensitive to stockholder criticism of other corporations' financial statements, and he wants no inaccuracies while he is at Nivaca's helm. You will use Excel's Formula Auditing toolbar to uncover the source of any errant formulas.

Excel's Formula Auditing toolbar provides tools to check worksheet formulas by using a graphical representation of the relationships between selected cells containing the formulas. You open the Formula Auditing toolbar to examine its contents. An *error indicator,* a small triangle, appears in the upper-left corner of a cell whenever Excel finds a formula that breaks one of its internal rules for valid formulas.

Opening the Nivaca workbook and displaying the Formula Auditing toolbar:

1. Start Excel as usual

2. Open the workbook **ex08Nivaca.xls** and immediately save it as **<yourname>Nivaca2.xls** to preserve the original workbook. Review the Cover Sheet worksheet

3. Click the **Quarterly Summary** worksheet tab. It summarizes the sales for the current year by quarter and region. Notice the seven regions containing art and artists whom Nivaca represents (see Figure 8.2). Several cells display error indicators

FIGURE 8.2

Nivaca's Quarterly Summary worksheet

	A	B	C	D	E	F	G	H
1	Quarterly Summary							
2								
3	Quarter Region	Qtr 1	Qtr 2	Qtr 3	Qtr 4			
4	Andes	365,103.78	161,505.41	415,373.24	372,834.03			
5	Brazil	357,263.92	403,983.65	309,704.15	205,761.26			
6	India	132,231.19	94,673.90	65,389.86	50,702.25			
7	Indonesia	256,359.57	384,802.18	255,331.42	424,576.55			
8	Mexico	326,072.59	263,251.96	317,822.12	451,081.07			
9	Thailand	275,855.70	243,102.64	337,314.18	337,789.33			
10	West Africa	281,069.86	419,213.46	436,273.34	349,269.30			
11								
12	Subtotal	$ 1,993,956.61	$ 1,551,319.74	$ 2,137,208.31	$ 2,192,013.79			
13								
14		Retail	Wholesale					
15	Total	$ 7,315,772.32	#REF!					
16								
17								
18								
19								
20								
21								
22								
23								

|◄ ◄ ► ►|\ Logo \ **Quarterly Summary** / Monthly Sales \ Commissions /

Ready

4. Click **Tools**, point to **Formula Auditing**, and then click **Show Formula Auditing Toolbar**. Excel displays the Formula Auditing toolbar (see Figure 8.3)

3. If necessary, click the list arrow next to the Who list box, and then click **Everyone but Me**

4. Click **OK**. Excel displays the Accept or Reject Changes dialog box and highlights cell B19 (see Figure 8.21). You will accept that change

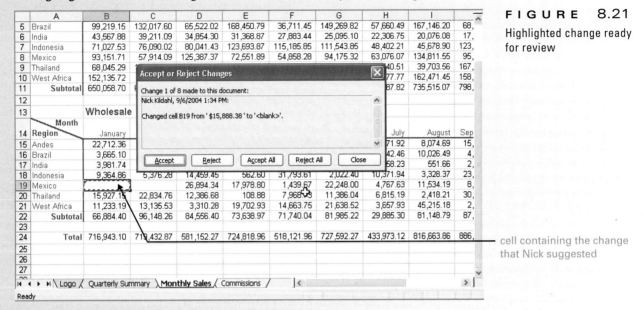

FIGURE 8.21

Highlighted change ready for review

cell containing the change that Nick suggested

5. Click the **Accept** button. Excel displays the next change

6. Click the **Accept** button to accept the suggested change to cell C19. Excel displays the change in which cells were moved from A13:C14 to C1:E2

7. Click the **Reject** button to revoke the change of moving the retail and wholesale summary values. Excel highlights the cell range A11:E11, indicating Nick deleted it

8. Click the **Accept** button five times in sequence to affirm the suggested deletion of the five cells in the cell range A11:E11. Excel closes the Accept or Reject Changes dialog box

You have reviewed changes and made your final decisions. You no longer need to share the workbook with Carol or Nick. Therefore, you will instruct Excel to stop Track Changes as you edit the workbook and then you will turn off workbook sharing.

Halting Track Changes and canceling the shared workbook session:

1. Click **Tools**, point to **Track Changes**, and click **Highlight Changes**. Excel opens the Highlight Changes dialog box

2. Click the **Track changes while editing** check box to clear its checkmark, and then click **OK**. If Excel displays a message indicating it will remove the workbook for shared use, then click **Yes**. Excel saves the workbook, clearing it for exclusive, nonshared use. Notice that the Title bar no longer displays "[Shared]" following the worksheet name

Merging Changes to Multiple Copies of a Workbook

An alternative method of consolidating changes made by multiple persons to the same workbook is to merge workbooks. In order to merge workbooks, several conditions must be met. First, you must distribute copies of the same workbook to anyone who wants to provide changes. Second, each copy of the workbook must have a name different from the other copies. Third, you cannot password protect the workbooks. Finally, the change history must be turned on. Suppose you have distributed three copies of the same workbook to three different people in your group (for comments) and you have named them **Nivaca1.xls**, **Nivaca2.xls**, and **Nivaca3.xls**. Assuming the original workbook, prior to saving copies, conforms to the conditions mentioned above, you can merge the multiple changes made by three groups as described in this Task Reference.

---

task reference — Merging Multiple Versions of the Same Workbook

- Open the workbook into which you want to merge changes

- Click **Tools** on the menu bar and click **Compare and Merge Workbooks**

- Press and hold the **Ctrl** key and click each workbook listed in the *Select Files to Merge Into Current Workbook* dialog box that you want to merge, and click **OK**

After you complete the Workbook Merge operation, be sure to Save the master copy to which you merged the changes.

Saving and closing the Nivaca workbook:

1. Click the **Close Window** button, and then click **Yes** when asked if you want to save your changes

2. Exit Excel

You, Carol, and Nick have completed editing the shared workbook. Next, you will take Nick's suggestion and hide the Commissions worksheet and protect the workbook.

SESSION 8.2

making the grade

1. More than one person can simultaneously open and modify a _____ workbook.

2. A _____ change occurs when two or more users make a change to the same worksheet cell. Excel recognizes this condition and displays a dialog box asking you to decide which change takes precedence.

3. Display the _____ toolbar to easily locate comments, one after another, in a workbook.

4. Excel tracks changes in a shared workbook only if you first check the *Track Changes While Editing* check box in the _____ Changes dialog box.

5. Excel stores any changes made to a shared workbook in a _____ _____ file.

SESSION 8.3 PROTECTING AND PUBLISHING WORKBOOKS

In this section, you will learn how to hide cell formulas, hide entire worksheets, and un-lock selected worksheet cells. In addition, you will learn how to enforce worksheet and workbook protection, and publish a complete workbook to the Web.

Protecting Workbooks and Worksheets

In a protected worksheet, you can apply the Hidden protection format to any cell whose formula you want to hide. Subsequently, when a user selects a hidden cell, its for-mula does not appear in the formula bar. One reason you might want to hide a cell's formula is that it is proprietary. That is, you don't want the actual calculation acciden-tally revealed to someone who might obtain a copy of the worksheet. When a cell's for-mula is hidden, the formula's results are still visible. For example, if you hide the formula $=Sum(A1:A42)*.42+.28*SalesTotals$, then the result of that formula (say, $42567.89) appears in the cell. Only the formula, itself, is invisible.

When you *protect a worksheet,* Excel disallows any changes to any cells that are locked. A user cannot delete columns or rows, change format, or change the contents of protected cells. Normally, a worksheet designer applies worksheet protection as the last step before releasing the workbook to the users or customers. Typically, worksheet formulas—cells displaying calculations that depend on other cells—receive protection. Cells that contain input values, which users must be able to change, must remain un-protected. Therefore, you will want to explicitly unlock those cells.

Excel offers many features allowing you to protect your work. You can protect a worksheet, an entire workbook, individual cells, graphics, charts, scenarios, and more. You can allow specific types of editing on protected worksheets and other objects.

Protection is a two-step process. First, you unlock cells for which you want users to be able to type new data. Second, you enforce Excel protection rules by explicitly turn-ing on worksheet protection through a menu. When a cell is *unlocked,* it is not pro-tected. Only locked cells are protected. By default, Excel locks *all* cells in a workbook.

After you enable protection, you cannot change a locked cell. If you attempt to do so, Excel issues an error message. Protection is available independently to each work-sheet in a workbook, so you can choose to protect some worksheets and not protect others in the same workbook.

help yourself *Press **F1**, type **protect a workbook** in the Search text box of the Microsoft Excel Help task pane, and press **Enter**. Click the hyperlink **About worksheet and workbook protection**. Maximize the Help screen, and then click the hyperlink **Protecting worksheet elements**. Click the Help screen **Close** button when you are finished, and close the task pane*

Hiding Cells and Worksheets

John wants you to hide the formulas located in the range B4:E10 on the Quarterly Summary worksheet. Recall that those formulas summarize sales by region and quar-ter. John simply does not want a casual viewer to see the formulas. You begin by open-ing the workbook you saved in the last session and saving it under a new name.

Opening the Nivaca workbook and saving it under a new name:

1. If you took a break at the end of the previous session, then ensure Excel is running and then open **<yourname>Nivaca3.xls**

2. Save the workbook as **<yourname>Nivaca4.xls**

Next, you can hide the formulas for the cell range B4:E10.

Hiding select cells' formulas:

1. Click the **Quarterly Summary** worksheet tab

2. Select the cell range **B4:E10**

3. Click **Format**, click **Cells**, and then click the **Protection** tab of the Format Cells dialog box

4. Click the **Hidden** check box to place a checkmark in it (see Figure 8.22), and then click **OK**

FIGURE 8.22

Hiding selected cell formulas

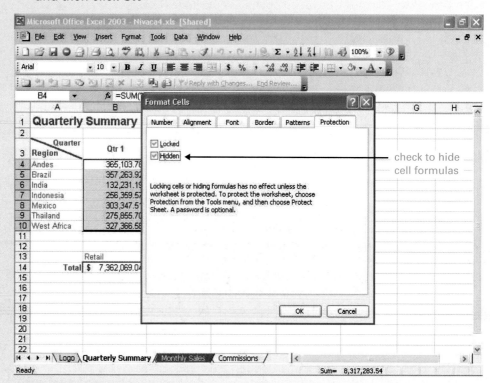

5. Click cell **B4** to make it active

Notice that the formula bar still displays the worksheet formula for cell B4. Excel does not actually hide the formulas until you enable worksheet protection. You will do that later in this session.

You can also hide entire worksheets of a workbook. All data and any calculations in a hidden workbook are still available to any other worksheets via references. Unlike hiding cell formulas, hiding a worksheet occurs immediately. Once a worksheet is hidden, the Unhide command is available in the Format Sheet command sequence.

---

task reference   **Hiding a Worksheet**

- Click the worksheet tab of the worksheet you want to hide
- Click **Format**, point to **Sheet**, and click **Hide**

FIGURE 8.3

The Formula Auditing toolbar

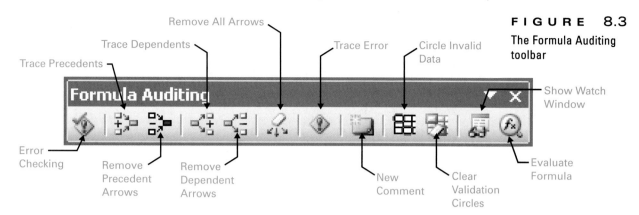

Several of the Formula Auditing tools draw graphical arrows on your worksheet called tracer arrows. A *tracer arrow* displays the relationship between the active cell and another cell related to it. Excel has two types of tracer arrows. One type of tracer arrow points to dependent cells. The other type of tracer arrow points to precedent cells. A *dependent cell* uses the value of the active cell in its formula. A *precedent cell* is one whose value is used (referenced) by the active cell. One way to visualize the relationship between a particular cell (the active cell) and other worksheet cells is to trace either its precedent cells or its dependent cells with the corresponding tools found in the Formula Auditing toolbar. For example, if the formula $=Max(A1:A5)$ is in cell A10, then cell A10 has precedent cells (A1:A5) and no obvious dependent cells. Cell A1 has a dependent cell, A10, but no apparent precedent cells. Any particular cell may have both precedent cells and dependent cells, however.

Tracing Precedent Cells

Cell C12 contains one clue John saw that might indicate the Quarterly Summary worksheet contains errors. Its value is 20 to 25 percent smaller than the subtotals for the first, third, and fourth quarters (see Figure 8.2). In addition, cell C12 and several other cells display error Smart Tag indicators in the upper-left corner of their cells. You begin your audit activities by auditing cell C12.

***task* reference**　　　　　　　**Tracing Precedent or Dependent Cells**

- Select the cell whose formula you want to trace

- Click the **Trace Precedents** button on the Formula Auditing toolbar to display tracer arrows pointing to the formula's precedent cells

or

- Click the **Trace Dependents** button on the Formula Auditing toolbar to display tracer arrows pointing to cells that are dependent on the formula's value

---

Tracing the precedent cells for a formula:

1. Click cell **C12**, and then click the **Trace Precedents** button on the Formula Auditing toolbar. Excel displays tracer arrows that point to a block of cells above it surrounded by a color border called a *range finder*. An error alert Smart Tag also appears

2. Hover the mouse over the error alert Smart Tag. A screen tip indicates the perceived anomaly (see Figure 8.4)

FIGURE 8.4

Precedent cell tracer arrows and the error alert Smart Tag

tracer arrow and box surrounding dependent cell range

error alert

screen tip indicating possible error cause

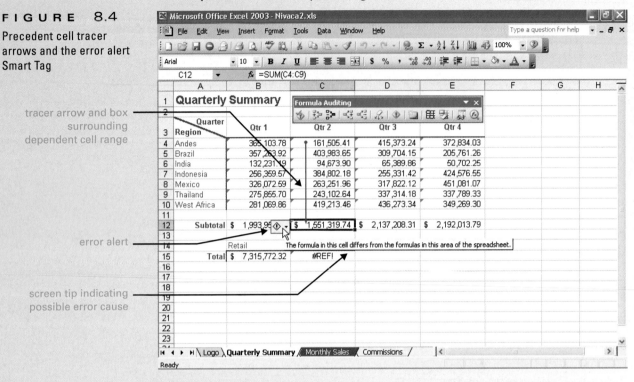

The tracer arrow indicates the group of precedent cells. A rectangle appears whenever the precedent cells are written as a cell range in the audited cell. The screen tip and the tracer arrow and rectangle indicate that the cell range in the formula stored in cell C12 omits cell C10 (West Africa). You correct that error next.

Correcting an incorrect SUM formula:

1. With cell **C12** still selected, click the formula bar

2. Change the formula to **=SUM(C4:C10)**, and press **Enter**. The tracer arrow disappears and the value of the second quarter sales has changed to $1,970,533.20. This is in line with other quarters' values

Another value that appears to be significantly different from other quarters' values is cell B10, which contains the first quarter sales from the region of West Africa. Notice that it is approximately 30 percent smaller than West Africa's other quarterly sales summary values. You audit that cell next.

Auditing West Africa's first quarter sales formula:

1. Click cell **B10**

2. Click the **Trace Precedents** button on the Formula Auditing toolbar. A tracer arrow appears pointing to a worksheet icon (see Figure 8.5)

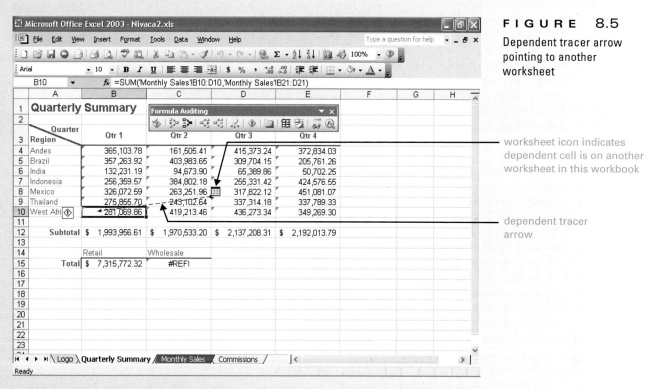

FIGURE 8.5

Dependent tracer arrow pointing to another worksheet

worksheet icon indicates dependent cell is on another worksheet in this workbook

dependent tracer arrow

3. Move the mouse pointer over the tracer arrow until it becomes an arrowhead, then double-click the **tracer arrow**. The Go To dialog box appears

4. Click '**[Nivaca2.xls]Monthly Sales'!B10$D$10** (Figure 8.6), and then click **OK** to open the Monthly Sales worksheet (Figure 8.6). Excel selects one of the cell ranges upon which cell B10 depends. Cell C10 looks suspicious, but you will investigate that one later

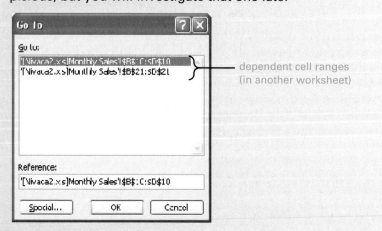

FIGURE 8.6

Go To dialog box

dependent cell ranges (in another worksheet)

tip: *Your filename will be slightly different. It will contain your name in addition to "Nivaca2.xls"*

5. Click the **Quarterly Summary** worksheet tab, hover over cell B10's error alert box, and then click the **error alert box** ◊ to reveal different options for revealing and dealing with the cell's error (see Figure 8.7)

F I G U R E   8.7

Error alert box option list

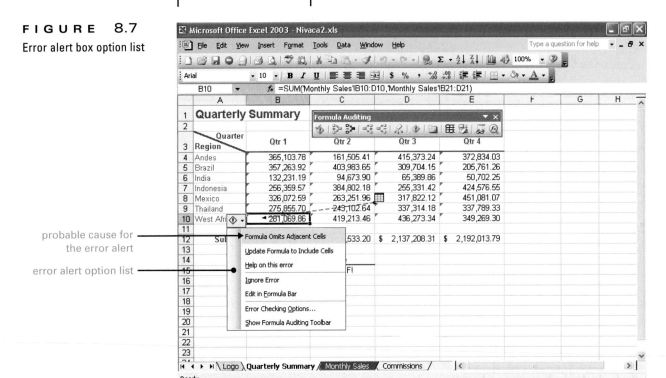

probable cause for
the error alert

error alert option list

---

anotherword   **. . . on Double-Clicking a Tracer Arrow**

Double-clicking a tracer arrow is handy for locating a dependent or precedent cell on another worksheet. It works equally well for locating dependent or precedent cells on the *same* worksheet. Double-clicking a tracer arrow makes the cell at the other end of the arrow active

---

The suspect error is at the top of the list "Formula Omits Adjacent Cells," and you understand the reason: the SUM formula references a partial row in the Monthly Sales worksheet. Excel suspects you meant to include adjacent cells in the row. While Excel is often correct about a partial-row sum, it is not a mistake in this case. Each sum in the range B4:D10 on the Quarterly Summary worksheet totals only 3 of the 12 months' values in the Monthly Sales worksheet. No doubt you have noticed that each cell in cell range B4:E10 contains an error indicator in the upper-left corner. If you click any other cell in that range and click its error alert box, you will see that Excel displays the same "Formula Omits…" error. You will clear these error indicators next.

Removing cells' error indicators:

1. Select the cell range **B4:E10**

2. Click the **error alert box** that appears to the left of cell B4

3. Click **Ignore Error** in the error alert box list. Excel removes all of the error indicators from the cells in the selection

4. Click any cell to deselect the cell range

help yourself *Press* **F1**, *type* **formula auditing** *in the Search text box of the Microsoft Excel Help task pane, and press* **Enter**. *Click the hyperlink* **Display the relationships between formulas and cells** *and then click the* **Show All** *hyperlink to helpful information on tracing precedent and dependent cells. Maximize the Help dialog box, if necessary. Click the Help screen* **Close** *button when you are finished, and close the task pane*

Tracing Dependent Cells

John notices two other apparent mistakes on the Monthly Sales worksheet and asks you to investigate it. Cell C10 contains an error indicator (unlike its neighboring cells), and cell B24 displays an obvious error, the text "#REF!." You begin by investigating cell C10.

Correcting an errant formula:

1. Click the **Monthly Sales** worksheet tab, and then click cell **C10**

2. Click the **error alert box**. The error message at the top of the error alert list, "Number Stored as Text," means that cell C10 contains text (whose value is zero) rather than a value. Look at the formula bar. The value begins with an apostrophe that someone apparently typed by mistake (see Figure 8.8)

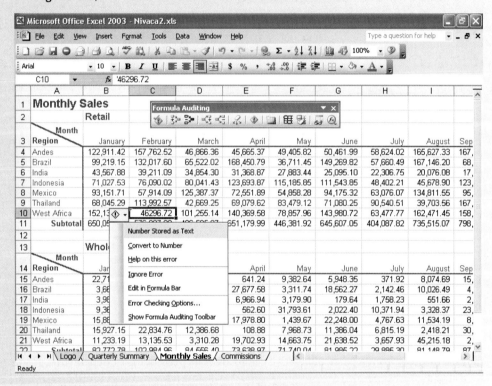

FIGURE 8.8

A "Number Stored as Text" error

Before correcting the error, you want to see what other cells are affected by the incorrect value in this formula. To see what cells reference a formula in error, you trace the cell's dependents.

Tracing a cell's dependents:

1. With cell C10 still selected, click the **Trace Dependents** button on the Formula Auditing toolbar. Excel creates tracer arrows pointing to cell C11, a subtotal, and to another worksheet

2. Hover over and double-click the **tracer arrow** pointing to another worksheet, click '[Nivaca2.xls]Quarterly Summary'!$B$10 in the Go To list box, and click **OK** to jump to the referenced worksheet. Cell B10, the selected cell, is dependent on the value in the errant cell, C10 on the Monthly Sales worksheet

tip: *Your filename will be slightly different. It will contain your name in addition to "Nivaca2.xls"*

3. With cell B10 on the Quarterly Summary worksheet still selected, click the **Trace Dependents** button. Excel draws a tracer arrow from cell B10 to cell B12 (see Figure 8.9). Notice that the subtotal for West Africa's first quarter is currently 281,069.86

FIGURE 8.9

Tracing dependent cells

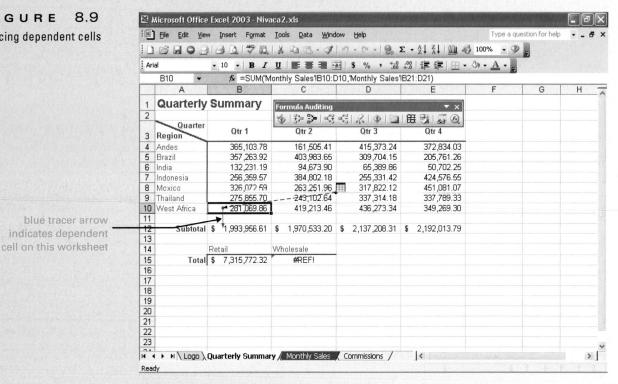

blue tracer arrow indicates dependent cell on this worksheet

Clearing Tracer Arrows

Each time you trace another cell's precedents or dependents, another set of tracer arrows appears. When the screen becomes cluttered with tracer arrows, it can be difficult to trace the flow from a particular active cell to all of its precedents or dependents. If so, then it is a good time to clear out all tracer arrows and trace a cell's precedents or dependents (or both) with a clean slate.

Removing tracer arrows from a display:

1. Click the **Remove All Arrows** button on the Formula Auditing toolbar. Excel removes the tracer arrow

2. Click the **Monthly Sales** worksheet tab, and then click the **Remove All Arrows** button on the Formula Auditing toolbar to remove the tracer arrows from that worksheet

Correcting Errors

The error in cell C10 persists, so you will correct it now that you have traced the affected cells on other worksheets.

Correcting an error using the error alert list:

1. Click cell **C10**, if necessary

2. Click the **error alert box**. An error alert list appears (see Figure 8.8)

3. Click **Convert to Number** in the list. Excel changes the text string into a numeric value

4. Clean up the formatting: click cell **C8**, click the **Format Painter** on the Standard toolbar, and click cell **C10**. Excel formats cell C10 to match the rest of the column

5. Click the **Quarterly Summary** worksheet tab, and examine cell B10. Notice its value is now 327,366.58—increased from its previous value of 281,069.86. Correcting the error modifies any dependent cells too, of course

For some less subtle errors, Excel displays an error value. An *error value* is the result of a formula that Excel cannot resolve and provides a clear warning that there is a problem. Figure 8.10 lists several of the error values and their descriptions. In addition to listing an error value in a cell, Excel attempts to discern the cause of the error, indicating, when possible, that a formula is dividing by zero or that a referenced cell has been deleted. One of these error values appears on the Monthly Sales worksheet, and you will fix it next.

Locating Other Errors

You can use the Error Checking button on the Formula Auditing toolbar to provide information about possible causes and remedies for error values.

Error Value	Description and Possible Error Source
#DIV/0!	A formula contains a division by a value or expression that is zero. Ensure the divisor is not a reference to an empty cell or does not evaluate to zero
#NAME?	The text in a formula is not a defined name. Check for typing mistakes
#N/A	No information is available for the calculation in your formula. Any cells that reference cells containing the #N/A value also return #N/A
#NULL!	Using two cell ranges in a formula that do not intersect
#NUM!	An argument in a function that requires a number but is, instead, text. It can also indicate that the result of a formula is too large or too small to be represented in a worksheet
#REF!	A formula referring to a cell that was deleted when the row containing it was deleted
#VALUE!	You have entered a formula that refers to a text entry. This can occur when you specify a range of cells for a function argument that requires a single value or cell reference

FIGURE 8.10

Excel error values and their meanings

EXCEL

Viewing error information:

1. With the Quarterly Summary worksheet still active, click cell **C15**

2. Click the **Error Checking** ![error checking button] button on the Formula Auditing toolbar. Excel opens the Error Checking dialog box

3. Click the **Help on this error** button in the Error Checking dialog box. Excel displays help and suggests some possible solutions (see Figure 8.11)

F I G U R E   8.11

Error alert help

4. After reviewing the Help window, close it by clicking the **Close** button

5. Click the **Resume** button on the Error Checking dialog box to restore its dimmed buttons (see Figure 8.12)

F I G U R E   8.12

Error Checking dialog box

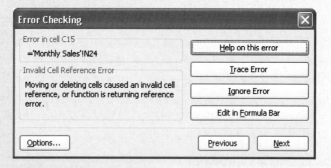

task reference   Tracing Errors

- Click the cell displaying an error value
- Click the **Trace Error** button on the Formula Auditing toolbar
- Follow any tracer arrows back to the error source

A possible cause of the #REF! error value is that the formula in cell C15 references a cell that subsequently was deleted—perhaps when the entire row containing it was deleted. Any other cells dependent on a cell displaying #REF! also display that error value. The Trace Error button on the Error Checking dialog box can help you locate the source of the error. It performs the same action as the Formula Auditing toolbar's Trace Error button.

Locating the error source:

1. Click the **Trace Error** button on the Error Checking dialog box, and then close the Error Checking dialog box. A tracer arrow appears pointing to a worksheet icon. This means the error source is on another worksheet

2. Move the mouse pointer over the tracer arrow until it becomes an arrow-head, then double-click the **tracer arrow**. The Go To dialog box appears

3. Click **'[Nivaca2.xls]Monthly Sales'!$N$24**, and click **OK** to activate the Monthly Sales worksheet. Cell N24 on the Monthly Sales worksheet be-comes active

4. Click the **Trace Error** button on the Formula Auditing toolbar. A red tracer arrow appears leading from cell B24 to cell N24 along with a blue tracer arrow leading from cell B22 to B24 (see Figure 8.13)

FIGURE 8.13

Locating the source of the #REF! error

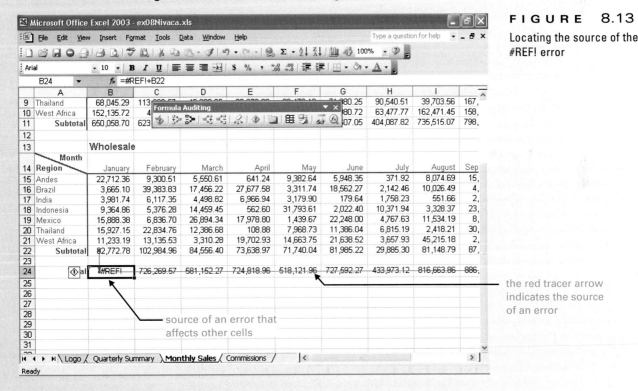

the red tracer arrow indicates the source of an error

source of an error that affects other cells

The red tracer arrow, indicating an error source, clearly points to cell B24. If you look at the formula bar, you will see the errant formula =#REF!+B22. This indicates that the formula is referencing a cell that was subsequently deleted—perhaps when the row or column containing it was deleted. Because cell B24 should total January Retail and Wholesale sales (cells B11 and B22), the correction is simple. Replace the #REF! in-dicator in the formula with a reference to cell B11.

Correcting an errant formula:

1. Click cell **B24**, if necessary, type **=B11+B22**, and press **Enter** to correct the formula

2. Click the **Remove All Arrows** ![button] button on the Formula Auditing toolbar to clear the display of all tracer arrows. Notice that the #REF! error value has disappeared from both cell B24 and (if you scroll to the right) cell N24

As you have seen earlier, not all formula errors display error values. They are more subtle, such as the numeric value that is stored as a string. Excel has a great tool for sniffing out more subtle errors—the Error Checking button on the Formula Auditing toolbar. The Error Checking button surveys the active worksheet looking for suspected mistakes, and it tags any suspect cells with green triangles in their upper-left corners. You can examine each tagged cell to determine if it needs to be corrected.

---

task reference   **Finding Subtle Errors**

- Click the worksheet tab of the worksheet whose integrity you want to check

- Click the **Error Checking** button on the Formula Auditing toolbar

- Use the options available in the Error Checking dialog box to correct the errant formula, or click the Next button to go to the next suspicious formula

---

Certifying that the worksheet is error-free means you should use the Error Checking tool to seek out any errors you may have overlooked. After completing the error-checking procedures, you can be confident that the worksheet is in good shape. You perform this final error check next.

Seeking out subtle errors in the workbook:

1. Click the **Error Checking** ![button] button on the Formula Auditing toolbar. Excel displays a message box indicating that no errors have been found on the Monthly Sales worksheet

2. Click **OK**

3. Click the **Quarterly Summary** worksheet tab, click the **Error Checking** button, and then click the **OK** button when the message box appears suggesting that Excel found no errors in the worksheet

4. Click the **Remove All Arrows** ![button] button on the Formula Auditing toolbar to clear the display of all tracer arrows

5. Click the **Commissions** worksheet tab, click the **Error Checking** button, and then click the **OK** button when the message box appears suggesting that Excel found no errors in the worksheet

Excel's tracer arrows and its rich set of error checking features allow you to quickly locate and correct errors in formulas.

Examining Worksheet Formulas

Sometimes the best way to get the larger view of a worksheet's formulas is to review them on screen simultaneously. Excel's *Formula Auditing Mode* displays all of a worksheet's formulas on screen rather than the values they represent. In selected exercises at the end of some previous chapters you have revealed worksheet formulas in order to print them. Printing worksheet formulas is an excellent way to document a workbook, and it provides an overall visual check for formula integrity. Review formulas by executing the steps that follow.

Displaying worksheet formulas:

1. Click the **Quarterly Summary** worksheet tab

2. Click **Tools**, point to **Formula Auditing**, and click **Formula Auditing Mode**. Excel displays each of the formulas of the Quarterly Summary worksheet

3. Click cell **B12** to display its precedent cells (see Figure 8.14)

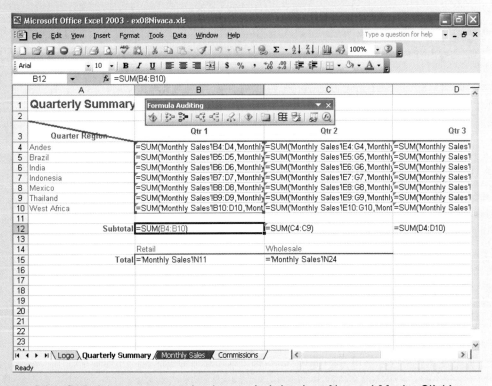

FIGURE 8.14

Displaying a worksheet's formulas

4. Click **Ctrl+`** (grave accent key) to switch back to Normal Mode. Clicking Ctrl+` toggles back and forth between Formula Auditing Mode and Normal Mode

tip: *The grave accent key is normally located above the Tab key. It is not the apostrophe key, which is next to the Enter key*

5. Close the Formula Auditing toolbar

Your error search-and-correct activities are complete. Therefore, you can save and close the workbook and close Excel.

EXCEL

Saving and closing the Nivaca workbook:

1. Press and hold the **Shift** key, click the **Commissions** worksheet tab, release the **Shift** key to group the worksheets, and click cell **A1** (this makes cell A1 the active cell on each selected worksheet)

2. Click the **Logo** worksheet tab to ungroup the worksheets and make Logo the active worksheet

3. Click the **Close Window** button, and then click **Yes** when asked if you want to save your changes

4. Exit Excel

John is pleased with the corrections you have made to the Nivaca workbook. He wants you to pass the shared workbook around to colleagues so they can review the workbook and make suggestions about its design and content. In the next sessions, you will learn how to use several collaboration tools and review the suggestions of others.

SESSION 8.1

making the grade

1. Excel displays the error value _____ when a cell contains a formula that references a cell whose value cannot be determined or calculated correctly.

2. A(n) _____ _____ appears in the left corner of a cell whenever Excel finds a formula that breaks one of its internal rules for formation of valid formulas.

3. A _____ cell is one whose value is referenced by the active cell.

4. A _____ _____ graphically displays the relationship between the active cell and another cell.

5. The _____ _____ toolbar contains buttons to aid you in locating errors in a workbook.

SESSION 8.2 SHARING A WORKBOOK AND TRACKING CHANGES

In this section, you will learn how to create a shared workbook stored on a network, how to insert hyperlinks, and how to locate and review team members' comments they make on a shared workbook. You will see how to accept or reject suggested changes, and how to resolve potential conflicts when more than one shared workbook user makes a change to the same cell.

Sharing a Workbook

Not so many years ago, if you wanted to share a workbook with a colleague, you had to copy it onto a floppy disk, carry it down the hall, and have the person with whom you want to share the workbook copy it to his or her computer. This "sneakernet" approach was used more than anyone wanted to admit. Today, infrastructure changes have all but done away with the sneakernet approach. Now, most organizations provide their employees or students with computers connected to a network. Usually, the network is also connected to the Internet. Sharing Excel workbooks is a lot easier due to networks. Microsoft Excel provides terrific tools that allow you to take advantage of network technology to share workbooks with other users in your organization.

A *shared workbook* is an Excel workbook that more than one person can open, modify, and save. Excel allows simultaneous modification of a workbook, which is not uncommon for workbooks stored on networks. Users sharing a workbook can also access it serially—one user after another. In this case, the work of one user who saves the shared workbook appears in the workbook loaded by a subsequent workbook user.

When you try to open a shared Excel workbook stored on a network drive while another user has it open for modifications, Excel permits you to do so. However, there are some restrictions on what you can do when you share a workbook. When you open a workbook for sharing, you can enter text, numbers, and cell formatting; modify formulas; and copy, paste, and move data by dragging the mouse. You can insert columns and rows. However, you *cannot* insert blocks of cells, merge cells, insert charts, create hyperlinks, create outlines, insert automatic subtotals, insert worksheets, or create data tables or pivot tables. In addition, the following are disabled in shared workbooks: Conditional Formatting, Data Validation commands, and Scenarios. Still, sharing a workbook has the obvious advantage that multiple people can access and modify a single, shared copy of a workbook. Sharing a workbook avoids a lot of hassles with determining how to consolidate multiple, independently modified versions of a workbook.

help yourself *Press* **F1**, *type* **sharing a workbook** *in the Search text box of the Microsoft Excel Help task pane, and press* **Enter**. *Click the hyperlink* **Edit a shared workbook**. *(You may have to scroll the Search Results list box.) Click the Help screen* **Close** *button when you are finished, and close the task pane*

Creating a Shared Workbook

Since you last saved the Nivaca workbook, John Lounsbury wants to circulate it to two other people for their review and comments: Carol Lloyd and Nick Kildahl. The first step is to open the workbook to be shared, establish a couple of sharing parameters, and save it on the network with a folder that all team members can access.

Establishing a shared Nivaca workbook:

1. If you took a break at the end of the previous session, ensure Excel is running and then open **<yourname>Nivaca2.xls**

2. Click **Tools**, click **Share Workbook**. Excel opens the Share Workbook dialog box

3. Click the **Allow changes by more than one user at the same time** check box so that multiple users can make simultaneous modifications to the workbook (see Figure 8.15)

4. Click **OK**. Excel displays a message indicating that the workbook will be saved and requesting your permission to continue

5. Click **OK** to save the shared workbook. Note that the text "[Shared]" appears on the Title bar following the workbook filename

EXCEL

John notifies Carol and Nick that the workbook is available for their review, and he tells them the folder and network address where he saved the workbook. He checks the shared workbook periodically to track changes that may occur to it.

Dealing with Conflicting Changes

Naturally, when more than one person work on a shared workbook, conflicts can arise. For example, one person could make a change to cell B7 and another person could later make a different change to the same cell. Whenever someone saves a workbook containing conflicting changes, Excel displays the Resolve Conflicts dialog box. The conflicting changes appear and allow the person saving the workbook to decide which changes to preserve and which not to preserve. Anyone sharing a workbook can choose to save or discard changes when there are conflicts. Excel stores rejected changes in a tracking log. The tracking log allows shared-workbook users to rescind rejected changes. In this case, the final authority on incorporating changes is John Lounsbury. John closes the workbook and waits for further comments and changes from Carol and Nick.

Saving your workbook:

1. Click the **Logo** worksheet tab, and then click cell **A1**

2. Click the **Close Window** button on the right end of the menu bar to close the worksheet

3. Click **Yes** when asked if you want to save your changes

Tracking Changes

Both Carol and Nick have had a chance to go over the workbook and make changes to it. They have inserted comments and edited formulas, and now it is time for you to review the comments and suggested changes. The last person to save the workbook, Nick Kildahl, has renamed it **ex08NivacaShared.xls**. You will open the latest version of the workbook and save it under a new name.

Opening the shared and modified Nivaca workbook:

1. Open the workbook **ex08NivacaShared.xls**

2. Save the workbook as **<yourname>Nivaca3.xls**

Locating, Reviewing, and Deleting Comments

Nick sent John an e-mail indicating that he has inserted some comments that he wants to make sure that John reviews. He's also made a couple of changes to cell formulas. John asks you to review the comments and then delete them when you are done.

Reviewing others' comments:

1. Click **View**, point to **Toolbars**, and then click **Reviewing** to open the Reviewing toolbar

2. Dock the Reviewing toolbar at the top of the screen and just below the Standard and Formatting toolbars

3. Click the **Next Comment** button on the Reviewing toolbar. Excel displays the first comment on the Logo worksheet (Figure 8.16)

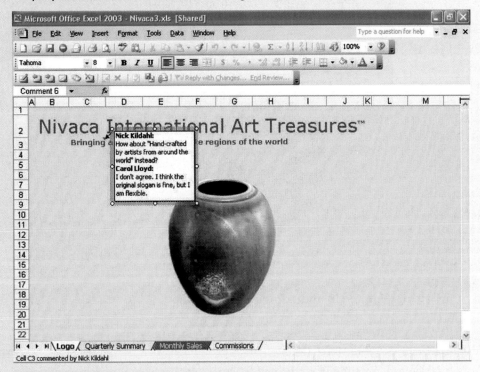

FIGURE 8.16
Reviewing a comment

4. Click the **Next Comment** button again to go to the next comment, which is located in cell B19. It indicates that Nivaca did not do wholesale business in Mexico for January or February

5. Click the **Next Comment** button once more to read the final comment, which is on the Commissions worksheet

6. Click the **Next Comment** button. Excel informs you that you have reached the end of the workbook

7. Click **OK** to redisplay the first comment on the Logo worksheet

    You report back to John about the comments' contents. He asks you to delete all of them before continuing your review process.

Deleting comments in a shared workbook:

1. With the first comment on the Logo worksheet displayed, click the **Delete Comment** button on the Reviewing toolbar

2. Click the **Next Comment** button to move to the second comment, and then click the **Delete Comment** button to remove it

3. Click the **Next Comment** button to move to the third comment, and then click the **Delete Comment** button to remove it

4. Right-click the empty area to the right of the menu bar (or any toolbar). Excel displays a list of toolbars (see Figure 8.17)

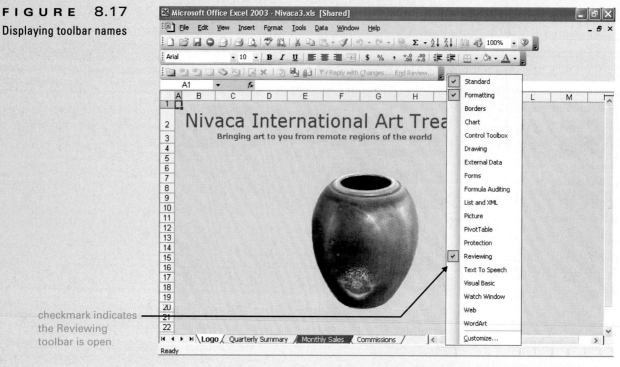

checkmark indicates
the Reviewing
toolbar is open

5. Click **Reviewing** to close the Reviewing toolbar

Evaluating Suggested Changes

You can decide at any time to go through a shared workbook and review the changes others have made to it. However, changes made by others to the worksheet are tracked (recorded) only if you select the Track Changes While Editing check box in the Highlight Changes dialog box prior to first saving the workbook for sharing. John took care of that, so all changes made since then have been recorded.

Excel stores any changes to a shared workbook in a tracking log file. The normal default for keeping the log file is 30 days, but you can change that value. Excel does not record some types of changes, such as format modifications, in the log file—a change that Carol made to the monthly retail and wholesale sales values, for instance. Excel facilitates tracking changes by displaying a change in a text box next to the changed cell and indicates who made the change and when it was made.

task reference	Tracking Worksheet Changes

- Click **Tools**, point to **Track Changes**, and click **Highlight Changes**
- Click the list arrow next to the When check box, and click one of the available time periods
- Click the list arrow next to the Who list box, and then click one of the available names whose changes you want to track
- Click the **Where** reference box and indicate which part of the workbook you want to review changes
- Click the **List changes on a new sheet** check box to collect and display the changes on a separate worksheet
- Click **OK** to finalize your choices

Display all changes anyone (except you) made to the Nivaca workbook next.

Highlighting shared workbook changes:

1. Click **Tools**, point to **Track Changes**, and click **Highlight Changes**. Excel displays the Highlight Changes dialog box

2. Click the list arrow next to the When check box, and then click **All**

3. Click the list arrow next to the Who check box, and then click **Everyone but Me**. Excel automatically checks the Who check box after you make a selection (see Figure 8.18)

4. Ensure your selections match Figure 8.18, and then click **OK**. If a dialog box appears indicating "No changes were found . . . ," then click the **OK** button to close the dialog box

FIGURE 8.18

Highlight Changes dialog box

Now you are ready to review the substantive changes others made to the workbook, one change at a time.

Reviewing changes made by others:

1. Click the **Quarterly Summary** worksheet tab

2. A comment indicator appears in cell C1. Hover the mouse pointer over cell C1. A comment appears indicating that Nick Kildahl moved cells A13:C14 to this current location on the date and time indicated in the comment (see Figure 8.19). Reviewing each change in this manner can be error-prone. Instead, have Excel place all changes on a separate worksheet in the following steps

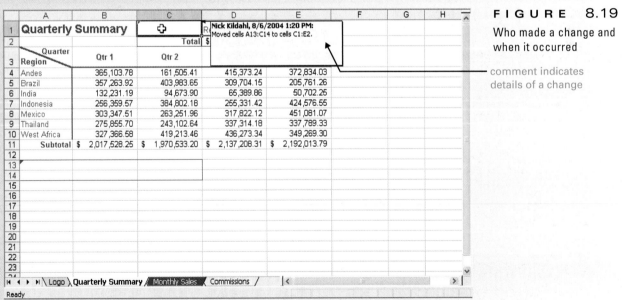

FIGURE 8.19

Who made a change and when it occurred

comment indicates details of a change

3. Click **Tools**, point to **Track Changes**, and click **Highlight Changes**. Excel opens the Highlight Changes dialog box

4. Click the **List changes on a new sheet** check box, and then click **OK**. Excel writes the tracking log to a separate worksheet, and then makes that worksheet active (see Figure 8.20)

FIGURE 8.20

Track Changes History worksheet

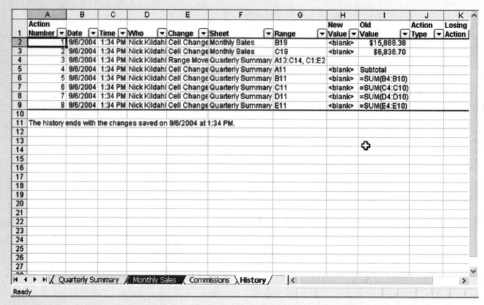

5. Examine the worksheet's contents. It details who made a change, when it was made, and old and new values

The track changes worksheet, labeled *History*, persists only until you close or save the workbook. When you reopen the workbook, the History worksheet and the log it contains disappear—even if you saved the workbook after Excel inserted the History worksheet.

Accepting or Rejecting Changes to a Shared Workbook

John reviews the change history, and asks you to reject some changes and accept others. He outlined the details in a note. You proceed to make the requested changes next.

---

task reference   **Accepting and Rejecting Suggested Changes to Cells**

- With a shared workbook open, click **Tools**, point to **Track Changes**, and click **Accept or Reject Changes**
- Click the list arrow next to the When check box, and click one of the available time periods
- Click the list arrow next to the Who list box, and then click one of the available names whose changes you want to accept or reject
- Click the **Where** reference box and indicate which part of the workbook you want to review changes
- Click **OK** to finalize your choices

Accepting and rejecting selected changes to a shared workbook:

1. Click **Tools**, point to **Track Changes**, and click **Accept or Reject Changes**. Excel opens the *Select Changes to Accept or Reject* dialog box

2. Click the **When** check box to clear its checkmark

> **task reference**   Unhiding a Worksheet
>
> - Click **Format**, point to **Sheet**, and click **Unhide**
> - In the Unhide dialog box, click the name of the worksheet you want to unhide from the list, and click **OK**

Next, you will hide the Commissions worksheet.

Hiding the Commissions worksheet:

1. Click the **Commissions** worksheet tab to make the worksheet active
2. Click **Format** on the menu bar, point to **Sheet**, and click **Hide**. Excel immediately removes the Commissions worksheet tab, effectively rendering the worksheet invisible, and makes the Monthly Sales worksheet active

Before moving on, ensure you know how to unhide a worksheet by locating the Unhide command. Because John wants the Commissions worksheet to remain hidden, you will stop short of actually unhiding the worksheet in the steps below.

Locating the Unhide command:

1. Click **Format**, point to **Sheet**, and click **Unhide**. Excel displays the Unhide dialog box and lists the only currently hidden worksheet (see Figure 8.23)

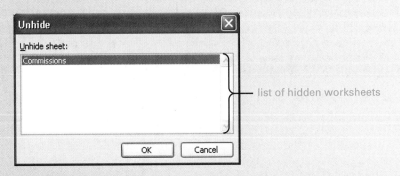

list of hidden worksheets

FIGURE 8.23

Unhide dialog box used to reveal hidden worksheets

2. Click the **Cancel** button to close the dialog box because you don't want to unhide the Commissions worksheet for the moment

Unlocking Worksheet Cells

You have learned from John that managers enter data into the Monthly Sales worksheet for each month's sales by region. Sometimes, the managers accidentally overwrite formulas in the worksheet that subtotal and total columns or rows. To prevent that from occurring in the future, John wants you to protect all worksheet formulas on the Monthly Sales worksheet, allowing managers to access only the cells holding both retail and wholesale sales values—cell ranges B4:M10 and B15:M21, respectively.

Excel has several features that allow you to protect individual cells. By default, Excel locks all cells in a workbook but disables protection. When enabled, protection prevents users from entering data into locked cells. If you try to alter a locked cell, Excel displays an error message. Therefore, you protect cells of a worksheet by *unlocking* any cells into which users can enter data or alter existing information. In most applications, a vast majority of a worksheet's cells remain locked.

---

task *reference*   **Unlocking Cells**

- Select the cell or cell range you want to be unlocked
- Click **Format**, click **Cells**, and then click the **Protection** tab
- Click the **Locked** check box to clear its checkmark and click **OK**

Preventing inadvertent modifications to formulas means that you unlock selected data entry cells in the Monthly Sales worksheet. Then, you enable worksheet protection.

Unlocking selected worksheet cells:

1. With the Monthly Sales worksheet active, click and drag the cell range **B4:M10**

2. Press and hold the **Ctrl** key, click and drag the cell range **B15:M21**, and release the **Ctrl** key

3. Click **Format** and then click **Cells**. The Format Cells dialog box opens

4. Click the **Protection** tab, if necessary. Notice that the Locked check box contains a checkmark, reinforcing the fact that cells are locked by default

5. Click the **Locked** check box to clear its checkmark (see Figure 8.24) and then click **OK**

F I G U R E   8.24

Unlocking selected cells

clear the Locked check box
to unlock selected cells

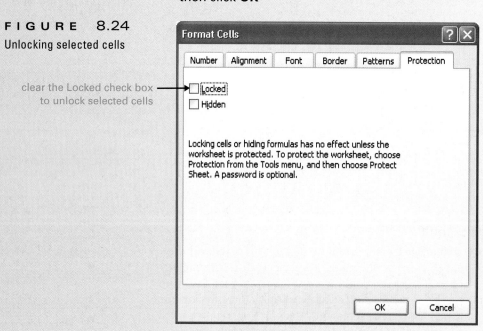

Although nothing appears to happen to the worksheet, you have removed the locks on two input cell ranges. Excel does not provide any visual clues that indicate which cells are locked and which are not. It is a good idea to provide the user with a hint by formatting unlocked cells with a background color or a border color. You do that next.

Color-coding unlocked cells:

1. With cell ranges B4:M10 and B15:M21 still selected, click **Format**, click **Cells**, and click the **Patterns** tab

2. Click the **Yellow** color square (row four, column three), and click **OK**

3. Click any cell to deselect the cell range

The yellow color reminds users that the cells are unlocked and available for input. Anyone wishing to use the worksheet will be alerted to the cells by their vibrant color.

Next, you will enforce worksheet protection for two worksheets: Monthly Sales and Quarterly Summary.

Enabling Worksheet Protection

Once you have unlocked selected cells, you can enable protection so that every locked cell is protected from modification. In addition, you can set a parameter so that the only cells that the user can click are unlocked cells in the protected worksheet. This means that if you later choose to make changes to your worksheet, you will have to turn off worksheet protection before making those modifications. If you do so, remember to enable protection again before releasing the modified worksheet for general use.

---

task reference   Enabling Worksheet Protection

- Select the worksheet on which you want to enable protection

- Click **Tools**, point to **Protection**, and click **Protect Sheet**

- Optionally enter (and remember) a password twice and click **OK**

Even though you have unlocked selected cells, anyone who opens the workbook can make changes to any cell in the Monthly Sales worksheet. You must tell Excel to enforce the protection by enabling protection for the Monthly Sales worksheet. Each worksheet in a workbook is independently protected. Therefore, you can enable protection in one or more worksheets in a given workbook and leave other worksheets unprotected. For example, no worksheet protection is enabled for the Logo worksheet, even though all of its cells are locked (by default). Excel also provides password protection so that anyone attempting to reverse worksheet-enabled protection must know the password you assigned before he or she can proceed to disable worksheet protection.

Enabling protection for two worksheets:

1. With the Monthly Sales worksheet active, click **Tools**, point to **Protection**, and click **Protect Sheet**. The Protect Sheet dialog box appears. Several detailed options, in the form of check boxes, are available. Two are checked by default. You can assign a password, so that a user is required to enter a password to make any worksheet protection changes

FIGURE 8.25

Protect Sheet dialog box

2. Click the **Select locked cells** check box to clear its check-mark (see Figure 8.25). This facilitates moving from one un-locked cell to another. The user merely presses the Tab key to select the next unlocked cell in the sequence

3. Click **OK**. The Monthly Sales worksheet is protected

4. Click the **Quarterly Summary** worksheet tab to make that worksheet active

5. Click **Tools**, point to **Protection**, click **Protect Sheet**, and click **OK**. There's no need to clear the Select locked cells check box because all cells on the Quarterly Summary are locked (by default)

Because you cleared the Select locked cells check box for the Monthly Sales worksheet in previous steps, you can press the Tab key to move between unprotected cells on that worksheet. That is, Excel will not allow a locked cell to become active on the protected worksheet.

Using the Tab key to move between unlocked cells:

1. Click the **Monthly Sales** worksheet tab to activate the worksheet

2. Attempt to click cell **A4**. Excel will not make that cell active because it is locked and protection is enabled

3. Click cell **B4**, one of the *unlocked* cells, and press **Tab**. Cell C4 becomes active

4. Press the **Tab** key two more times, slowly. Notice that cells D4 and then E4 become active, in turn. That's a handy feature of unlocked cells in protected worksheets

Protecting a Workbook

Recall that you hid the Commissions worksheet on John's request. Even though you protected the Monthly Sales worksheet and the Quarterly Summary worksheet, anyone could execute Format, Sheet, and click Unhide to reveal the hidden Commissions work-sheet. By protecting the entire workbook, you can prevent this from occurring. But anyone can unprotect the workbook and subsequently unhide the Commissions work-sheet. Preventing people from unhiding worksheets requires you to password protect the workbook. Specifying passwords to protect Excel objects, including workbooks, is serious business. Once an object is protected, there is no way to unprotect a worksheet or workbook without it. If you forget the password, not even Microsoft can help you. For that reason, John doesn't want to use a password to lock down the workbook. Besides, he thinks password protection is unnecessary in his company.

---

task reference   **Protecting a Workbook**

- Click **Tools**, point to **Protection**, and click **Protect Workbook**
- Check or clear check boxes to set options as needed
- Type an optional password
- Click **OK**
- If you entered a password, then you are asked to retype it and then click **OK**

Protecting the Nivaca workbook:

1. Click **Tools**, point to **Protection**, and click **Protect Workbook**. The Protect Workbook dialog box opens

2. Ensure the Structure check box is checked and that the Windows check box is clear. *Do not* type a password in the Password text box (see Figure 8.26)

3. Click **OK**. Excel protects the workbook

FIGURE 8.26
Protect Workbook dialog box

You can satisfy yourself that workbook protection disallows unhiding a worksheet. Try to unhide a worksheet by executing these steps:

Attempting to unhide a worksheet:

1. Click **Format** and point to **Sheet**. Notice that the Unhide command is dimmed and thus unavailable

2. Click cell **B4** to close the menu

3. Save the workbook

You demonstrate to John the worksheet protection built into the Nivaca workbook. He's pleased. But there is one more thing he wants. He would like to publish the entire workbook on the company's protected intranet so others in the company can view it and interact with it online.

Publishing a Workbook

Microsoft makes it easy to create Web pages from any Excel workbook. Once converted to one or more Web pages and placed on the Web, pages are available to anyone with a modern Web browser. Alternatively, you can place Web pages created from an Excel workbook on a private intranet allowing only selected individuals access (company employees, for example) to the pages. You can create two types of Web pages with Excel's converters: interactive and noninteractive. An *interactive Web page* creates a spreadsheet component enabled within the Web page. The spreadsheet component simulates an Excel workbook, allowing users to enter data, format entries, and edit data—just like an Excel workbook. Any change made to the Web-based worksheet object does not affect the original Excel workbook from which it is created. Any changes persist only for the Web session, but users can perform what-if analysis with the Web workbook.

A *noninteractive Web page* creates Web pages in HTML format and allows users to view the entire Excel workbook. However, they cannot make changes to the values or formulas appearing on the Web page. This type of read-only workbook is very handy for employees in far-flung locations that want a convenient, central source to review Excel-derived documents. Figure 8.27 shows the Nivaca workbook in both interactive and noninteractive Web versions.

Publishing a Noninteractive Web Page

John would like managers to view the Nivaca workbook online. After weighing the two alternative types of Web pages that Excel can create, he decides a noninteractive Web page is just right—at least for the foreseeable future. He asks you to create such a Web site on your computer to test the concept.

First, you will preview the Web pages before actually creating them.

EXCEL

FIGURE 8.27

Interactive and
noninteractive, Web-
based workbooks

interactive workbook
allows modification of
cells in the browser

noninteractive Web-based
workbook does not allow
modification of cells in the
browser

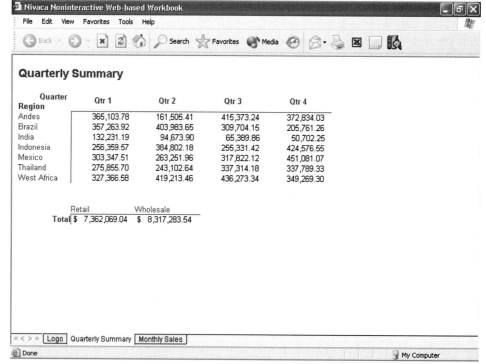

Previewing the Web pages prior to creation:

1. Click **File** and then click **Web Page Preview** on the File menu. Excel opens a Web browser and displays a Web version of the Nivaca workbook. Notice that the worksheet tabs appear at the bottom of the display

2. Click the browser **Maximize** button to see the entire Web page

3. Click the **Quarterly Summary** box near the bottom of the page. The browser displays the Quarterly Summary worksheet in a form that is almost indistinguishable from the Excel worksheet (see Figure 8.28)

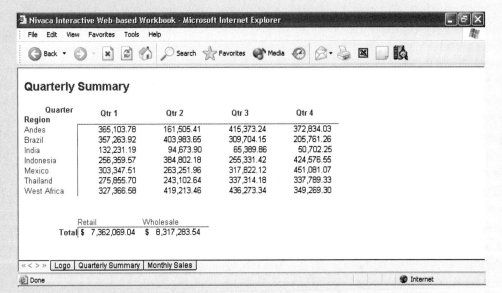

FIGURE 8.28

Web rendering of the Quarterly Summary worksheet

4. Hover the mouse over the Logo box. The Logo box turns white

5. Click the **Monthly Sales** box to view that Web page

6. Close your Web browser and return to the Nivaca workbook

The Web pages look good. You can build an actual Web page that you will later post to the company's intranet.

---

task reference   Publishing an Excel Workbook as a Noninteractive Web Page

- Click **File**, click **Save as Web Page**
- In the Save As dialog box, click **Entire Workbook** and clear the **Add interactivity** check box
- Type a filename in the File name list box
- Optionally, click the **Change Title** button, type a new Web page title, and click **OK**
- Click **Save**

Creating a noninteractive workbook:

1. Click **File**, then click **Save as Web Page**. The Save As dialog box appears

2. Ensure that the **Add interactivity** check box is cleared

3. Click the **Entire Workbook** option, if necessary

4. Click the **Change Title** button, type **Noninteractive Nivaca Workbook** in the Set Page Title text box, and click **OK**

5. Select all of the text in the File name list box and then type **NivacaSales**

6. Click the **Save as type** list box, click **Single File Web Page (*.mht; *.mhtml)**, and use the *Save in* list box to navigate to the folder where you want to create your Web page. Your Save As dialog box settings should match Figure 8.29, with the exception of the *Save in* list box

FIGURE 8.29
Save As dialog box

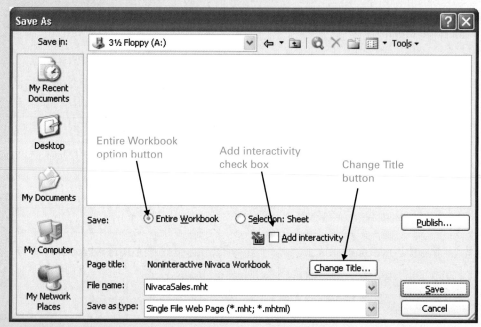

tip: *If you choose Web Page (*.htm; *.html) in the Save as type list box, then Excel creates an htm file and a large number of related files. The related files are stored in a folder. Creating an mht-style Web page (the Single File Web Page choice) saves space and reduces file proliferation*

7. Click the **Save** button

tip: *If Excel displays a warning dialog box stating that Custom views cannot be saved, click the **Yes** button. Excel creates a file called **NivacaSales.mht***

Check out your Web page. Remember where you created your Web page NivacaSales.htm. You will open it in your browser next.

Reviewing the Web Workbook with a Browser

Follow these steps to review the Web page that Excel created from your Excel workbook.

Reviewing a noninteractive Web workbook page:

1. Minimize Excel

2. Launch Internet Explorer, navigate to the folder containing **NivacaSales.mht**, and open the file **NivacaSales.mht**. Click **File**, click **Open**, click the **Browse** button, and navigate to the folder with the Look in list box, click **NivacaSales.mht**, click **Open**, and click **OK**

3. Examine each of the worksheets by clicking their respective worksheet boxes located at the bottom of the display

4. When you are done reviewing the Web page, close Internet Explorer

5. Maximize the Excel application to redisplay the Nivaca workbook

Publishing an Interactive Web Page

Publishing an Excel workbook with interactivity components allows anyone with access to the Web page to view and modify the Web version of the worksheet—even though the Web user does not have access to the original Excel workbook. John would like you to also publish an interactive version of the Nivaca workbook so he can evaluate both types of Web workbooks.

---

anotherword   . . . on Publishing an Excel Workbook to the Web

Saving a workbook as a Web page (html) results in many files: one HTML file for each worksheet, another HTML file for displaying worksheet tabs, and a host of other files. Unless required, it is better to save the entire workbook as a single Web archive (mht) file. The resulting file can be large, but you do not have to upload or maintain lots of separate folders and files

---

task reference   Publishing an Excel Workbook
                               as an Interactive Web Page

- Click **File**, click **Save as Web Page**
- In the Save As dialog box, click **Entire Workbook** and check the **Add interactivity** check box
- Click the **Publish** button
- Click the **Choose** list box and select the portions of the workbook you want to publish
- Click the **Change** button to change the Web page title
- Click the **Browse** button to specify a filename and folder location
- Click the **AutoRepublish every time this workbook is saved** check box (placing a checkmark in it)
- Click the **Open published web page in browser** check box (placing a checkmark in it)
- Click the **Publish** button

You are ready to publish an interactive version of the workbook so John can evaluate whether he prefers it over the noninteractive version.

Publishing an interactive workbook:

1. Click **File**, then click **Save as Web Page**. The Save As dialog box appears

2. Click the **Entire Workbook** option, if necessary, and click the **Add interactivity** check box to place a checkmark in it

3. Click the **Publish** button. The *Publish as Web Page* dialog box appears

4. Click the **Choose** list box and select **Entire Workbook**, if necessary

5. Click the **Change** button, type **Interactive Nivaca Workbook** in the Title text box, and click **OK**

6. Click the **Browse** button. The Publish As dialog box opens

7. Click the **Save in** list box and navigate to the folder where you want to store your Web pages

8. Select the suggested filename in the File name list box, type **NivacaSalesInteractive**, click the **Save as type** list box, select **Single File Web Page (*.mht; *.mhtml)**, and click **OK**

tip: *If Excel displays a warning dialog box stating that Custom views cannot be saved, click the **Yes** button*

9. Click the **AutoRepublish every time this workbook is saved** check box

10. If necessary, click the **Open published web page in browser** check box to place a checkmark in it. Your Publish as Web Page dialog box settings should match Figure 8.30, with the exception of the File name list box

FIGURE 8.30

Publish as Web Page dialog box

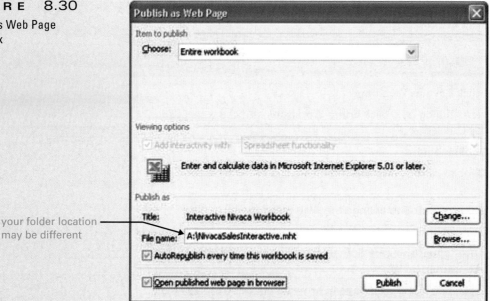

your folder location
may be different

11. Click the **Publish** button. Excel displays a warning message indicating that it cannot hide formulas. Click **OK**. Excel creates a Web page called **NivacaSalesInteractive.htm**

12. Click the **Maximize** button to view the whole page, click the **sheet selector** (it looks like a sheet tab), and select **Monthly Sales** (see Figure 8.31). Leave the browser open so you can complete another series of steps that follow

To prove to yourself that the interactive version of the worksheet is just that—interactive, you will make a few changes and view the results in your browser.

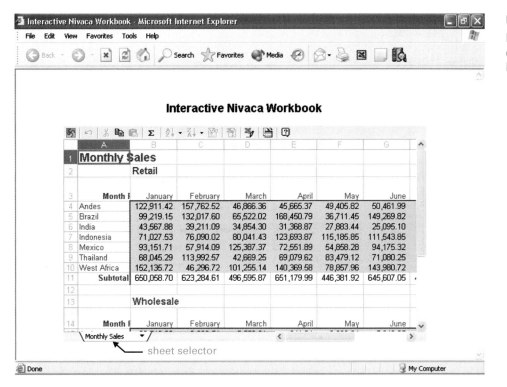

FIGURE 8.31
Monthly Sales worksheet displayed in a Web browser

Performing what-if analysis with an interactive Web workbook:

1. With your browser maximized and displaying the Monthly Sales worksheet, select the cell range **B4:B10**—January sales in all seven regions—and then press the **Delete** key.

2. Select cell range **C4:M4** (it may be easiest to click **C4**, press and hold **Shift**, and press the **right arrow** key repeatedly until you have selected the cell range), and then press the **Cut** ✂ button on the Office Web Components toolbar

3. Click cell **C7**, click the **Commands and Options** 📋 button on the Office Web Components toolbar, click the **Format** tab (if necessary), click the **Bold** button (see Figure 8.32), and click the Commands and Options **Close** button. Excel bolds the selected cell

4. Click the **sheet selector** (see Figure 8.32) and then click **Quarterly Summary**. Notice that the total for Retail is $5,646,786.22, which is less than its original value ($7,362,069.04). The Web version of the worksheet reacts to what-if changes

5. Close the browser, reopen the Nivaca workbook, and click the **Quarterly Summary** worksheet tab. Notice that the Retail total is unchanged from its original value, $5,646,786.22

The interactive workbook works just dandy. You can change values and the values are recalculated just like Excel does. Furthermore, changes to the Web version of the workbook do not affect the original Excel worksheet.

EXCEL

FIGURE 8.32

Formatting an interactive
Web worksheet

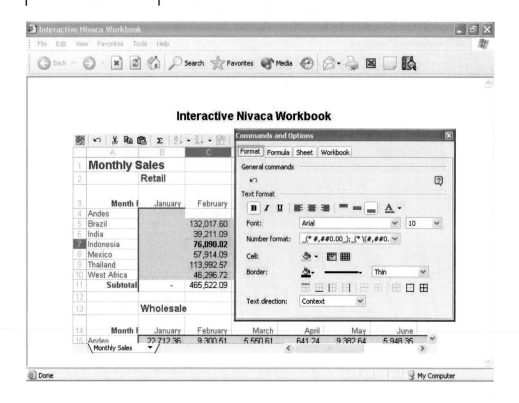

Inserting a Hyperlink to Another Resource

Excel permits you to insert hyperlinks to a variety of resources directly into any work-sheet cell. You can create a hyperlink to another worksheet in the same workbook, to a Web page on the World Wide Web, to a Word document, or to another document stored on your computer. The advantage of hyperlinks is that most everyone recognizes what they are, and they are simple to use—just click.

John wants you to insert a hyperlink to a Brazilian art museum that contains some of the same art objects as he sells. He would like you to use the text in cell A5 (*Brazil*) already on the Quarterly Summary worksheet as the hyperlink test. The Web address he wants you to reference is www.museuvirtual.com.br. First, you have to temporarily disengage worksheet protection before you can insert the hyperlink.

Disengaging worksheet protection:

1. With the Quarterly Summary worksheet active, click cell **A5** containing the label *Brazil*

2. Click **Tools**, point to **Protection**, and click **Unprotect Sheet**

With the worksheet unprotected, you can make a modification to cell A5 and then protect the worksheet again.

Inserting a hyperlink to a World Wide Web page:

1. With cell A5 selected, click **Insert** and click **Hyperlink**. The Insert Hyperlink dialog box opens

2. Click the **ScreenTip** button, type **Brazilian art** in the ScreenTip text box, and click **OK**

3. In the Address text box, type **www.museuvirtual.com.br**. Notice that Excel supplies the prefix text "http://" after you type "www." (see Figure 8.33)

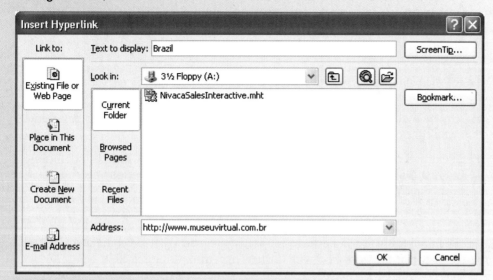

FIGURE 8.33
Insert Hyperlink dialog box

4. Click **OK**. Excel turns the text "Brazil" into a hyperlink

Reestablish worksheet protection before you save the altered worksheet.

Reestablishing worksheet protection and save the changed worksheet:

1. Click **Tools**, point to **Protection**, click **Protect Sheet**, and click **OK**

2. Click **File** and click **Save**. A dialog box appears asking if you want to enable the AutoRepublish feature

3. Click the **Enable the AutoRepublish feature** option button (see Figure 8.34), and then click **OK**. Excel takes a bit longer to save your file because it is also updating the interactive Web pages associated with the Excel file

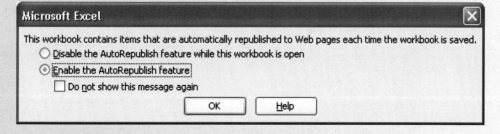

FIGURE 8.34
AutoRepublish query

4. Excel displays a warning about not being able to protect hidden formulas. Click **OK** to complete the update process

Next, you will test the hyperlink you just created.

Testing the Brazil hyperlink:

1. Hover the mouse over cell **A5** until it turns to a pointing finger (and the ScreenTip "Brazilian art" appears), and then click the hyperlink **Brazil**. Excel opens your browser and displays the Web page to which you have linked

    tip: *Opening the link may take time because the Web site is in Brazil. If you cannot open the link, then the site may be down. Don't worry. The process is the same regardless of the Web site you reference*

2. After viewing the site briefly, close your Web browser. Your Excel workbook reappears

3. Click the **Logo** worksheet tab, click **File**, and then click **Exit**. If Excel displays a dialog box asking if you want to save the changes you made, then click **Yes**

The final test you will perform is to satisfy yourself that Excel updated the Web-based version of the worksheet with the new hyperlink you inserted.

Testing the Web page Brazil hyperlink:

1. Open your Web browser, navigate to the Web page **NivacaSalesInteractive.mht**, open it, and maximize your browser window

2. Click the **sheet selector** and click **Quarterly Summary** (if necessary). Excel displays the Quarterly Summary page (see Figure 8.35)

3. Hover the mouse over cell **A5** until it turns to a pointing finger, and then click the hyperlink **Brazil**. Excel opens your browser, which displays the Web page to which you have linked. Maximize the browser window (see Figure 8.36)

4. Close all browser windows and your browser

You have completed your work. John is pleased with the results. After some days considering the two types of Web-enabled worksheets, John has decided to publish only the noninteractive version on his intranet that only managers can access.

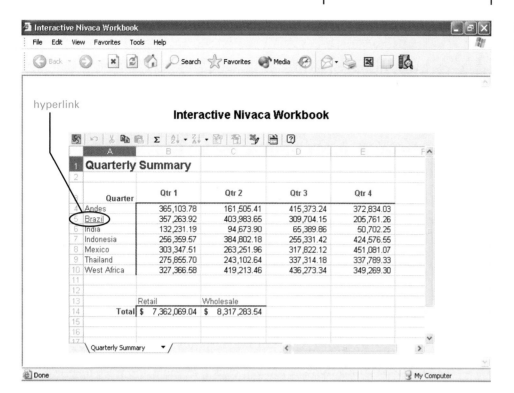

FIGURE 8.35
Updated Quarterly
Summary Web page

FIGURE 8.36
Brazilian art Web page

making the grade

1. By default, all workbook cells are _____, and those cells cannot be modified in any way as long as you enable worksheet protection.

2. To prevent users from unprotecting worksheets, you can type an optional _____.

3. Press the _____ key to move from one unlocked cell to another in a protected worksheet.

4. You can publish Excel workbooks on the Web as one of two general types. One type, called _____, allows no changes to the Web-based workbook. The other, called _____, allows the user to do what-if analysis on the Web-based workbook.

5. You can insert a _____ in an Excel cell to jump to any Web page you would like.

SESSION 8.4 SUMMARY

Using the built-in Auditing toolbar, you can click a formula and trace its precedent cells. Precedent cells are cells that the active cell's formula refers to. Tracer arrows lead from the active cell to all cells it references—including references to other worksheets. Tracing dependent cells of the active cell's formula draws tracer arrows from the active cell to any cells that reference, or depend upon, the active cell. Error indicators, appearing as small triangles in cells, indicate that there may be some inconsistency or error in the cell to which they are attached. An error alert box appears whenever a more serious error exists in a cell's formula such as division by zero or a reference to a cell that has been deleted.

Excel allows you to share a workbook so that multiple people can work on it simultaneously. If you set it up so that Excel tracks changes, then Excel will generate a log of changes identified by user names. Any one person can affirm or rescind changes identified by the shared workbook users. Conflicts arise when more than one person make a change to the same cell.

By default, Excel cells are locked. Using the Format menu, you can clear the Locked property for selected cells so that anyone can change the contents or formatting of the unlocked cells. Cell protection is enforced only if you choose to protect the worksheet. Protection is enforced independently on each worksheet. The strongest protection is provided when you supply a password, although no one can help you if you forget the password.

Excel allows you to publish a workbook on the Web. Through a very simple Save as Web Page command on the File menu, Excel produces either interactive Web pages or noninteractive Web pages. Users can modify interactive Web pages stored on a Web server, but they cannot change any cells or their formatting on a noninteractive Web worksheet. Hyperlinks in Excel workbooks allow you to open a variety of documents on your own computer or open Web pages located anywhere on the World Wide Web.

MICROSOFT OFFICE SPECIALIST
OBJECTIVES SUMMARY

- Insert comments and review others' comments—MOS XL03S-4-1
- Locate a cell's precedent cells and dependent cells—MOS XL03E-1-11
- Display and clear tracer arrows—MOS XL03E-1-11
- Locate and correct errors using audit tools—MOS XL03E-1-12
- Protect workbooks and worksheets—MOS XL03E-3-1
- Password protect a worksheet—MOS XL03E-3-2
- Share a workbook with other users—MOS XL03E-3-3
- Hide worksheets—MOS XL03S-3-4
- Merge multiple versions of the same workbook—MOS XL03E-3-4
- Track, accept, and reject changes made to a workbook—MOS XL03E-3-5
- Publish workbooks to the Web—MOS XL03E-4-3
- Insert hyperlinks—MOS XL03S-5-3

---

making the grade answers

SESSION 8.1

1. #VALUE!
2. error indicator
3. precedent
4. tracer arrow
5. Formula Auditing

SESSION 8.2

1. shared
2. conflicting

3. Reviewing
4. Highlight
5. tracking log

SESSION 8.3

1. locked
2. password
3. Tab
4. noninteractive, interactive
5. hyperlink

---

task reference summary

Task	Page #	Preferred Method
Tracing precedent or dependent cells	EX 8.5	• Select the cell whose formula you want to trace • Click the **Trace Precedents (Trace Dependents)** button on the Formula Auditing toolbar to display tracer arrows pointing to the formula's precedent (dependent) cells
Tracing errors	EX 8.12	• Click the cell displaying an error value • Click the **Trace Error** button on the Formula Auditing toolbar • Follow any tracer arrows back to the error source
Finding subtle errors	EX 8.14	• Click the worksheet tab of the worksheet whose integrity you want to check • Click the **Error Checking** button on the Formula Auditing toolbar • Use the options available in the Error Checking dialog box to correct the errant formula, or • Click the Next button to go to the next suspicious formula
Tracking worksheet changes	EX 8.20	• Click **Tools** • Point to **Track Changes** • Click **Highlight Changes** • Click the list arrow next to the When check box • Click one of the available time periods • Click the list arrow next to the Who list box • Click one of the available names whose changes you want to track • Click the **Where** reference box and indicate which part of the workbook you want to review changes • Click the **List changes on a new sheet** check box to collect • Display the changes on a separate worksheet • Click **OK** to finalize your choices
Accepting and rejecting suggested changes to cells	EX 8.22	• With a shared workbook open, click **Tools** • Point to **Track Changes** • Click **Accept or Reject Changes** • Click the list arrow next to the When check box • Click one of the available time periods • Click the list arrow next to the Who list box • Click one of the available names whose changes you want to accept or reject • Click the **Where** reference box and indicate which part of the workbook you want to review changes • Click **OK** to finalize your choices
Merging multiple versions of the same workbook	EX 8.24	• Open the workbook into which you want to merge changes • Click **Tools** on the menu bar and click **Compare and Merge Workbooks** • Press and hold the **Ctrl** key and click each workbook listed in the *Select Files to Merge Into Current Workbook* dialog box that you want to merge, and click **OK**
Hiding a worksheet	EX 8.26	• Click the worksheet tab of the worksheet you want to hide • Click **Format**, point to **Sheet** • Click **Hide**
Unhiding a worksheet	EX 8.26	• Click **Format**, point to **Sheet** • Click **Unhide** • In the Unhide dialog box, click the name of the worksheet you want to unhide from the list • Click **OK**
Unlocking cells	EX 8.27	• Select the cell or cell range you want to be unlocked • Click **Format**, click **Cells**, • Click the **Protection** tab • Click the **Locked** check box to clear its checkmark • Click **OK**

task reference summary

Task	Page #	Preferred Method
Enabling worksheet protection	EX 8.29	• Select the worksheet on which you want to enable protection • Click **Tools**, point to **Protection** • Click **Protect Sheet**. Optionally enter (and remember) a password twice • Click **OK**
Protecting a workbook	EX 8.30	• Click **Tools**, point to **Protection** • Click **Protect Workbook** • Check or clear check boxes to set options as needed, type an optional password • Click **OK** • If you entered a password, then you are asked to retype it and then click **OK**
Publishing an Excel workbook as a noninteractive Web page	EX 8.33	• Click **File** • Click **Save as Web Page** • In the Save As dialog box, click **Entire Workbook** and clear the **Add interactivity** check box • Type a filename in the Filename list box • Optionally, click the **Change Title** button, type a new Web page title, click **OK**, and click **Save**
Publishing an Excel workbook as an interactive Web page	EX 8.35	• Click **File** • Click **Save as Web Page** • In the Save As dialog box, click **Entire Workbook** and check the **Add interactivity** check box • Click the **Publish** button • Click the **Choose** list box and select the portions of the workbook you want to publish • Click the **Change** button to change the Web page title • Click the **Browse** button to specify a filename and folder location • Click the **AutoRepublish every time this workbook is saved** check box (placing a checkmark in it) • Click the **Open published web page in browser** check box (placing a checkmark in it) • Click the **Publish** button

TRUE OR FALSE

1. A precedent cell is one that uses (references) the active cell in its formula.

2. The Trace Precedents button is on the Formula Auditing toolbar.

3. A shared workbook, often stored on a network, is a workbook that more than one person can open and modify simultaneously with other users.

4. When using a shared workbook, a conflict can arise when two users each independently change the same worksheet cell.

5. You can prevent users from modifying formulas simply by locking the cell containing the formula.

6. An Excel workbook published as an interactive Web workbook allows users to produce what-if analysis. Furthermore, the changes a user makes to a worksheet persist from one Web session to another.

FILL-IN

1. Excel supplies a _____ _____(s) to graphically illustrate which cell(s) a formula references when you press the Trace Precedents button.

2. Press the _____ _____ button on the Formula Auditing toolbar to identify which cells depend on the active cell.

3. You must select the _____ (*hint:* four words) check box in the Highlight Changes dialog box prior to first saving the workbook for sharing. Then you can later decide which changes to keep and which to discard.

4. The _____ check box (always checked by default) is found on the _____ tab of the Format Cells dialog box allowing you to set or clear protection for one or more cells.

5. Click the _____ command on the Format Sheet to make it invisible.

6. Checking the _____ check box causes Excel to republish to the Web workbook any changes you make to the corresponding Excel workbook.

MULTIPLE CHOICE

1. Precedents are identified by which tracer arrow?
   a. Yellow arrow
   b. Blue arrow
   c. Black arrow
   d. Red arrow

2. To trace precedents, use the _____
   a. Trace Precedents button on the Formula Auditing toolbar.
   b. Trace Precedents button on the Standard toolbar.
   c. Trace Arrows command on the Formatting toolbar.
   d. Precedents command in the View menu.

3. The border surrounding a cell or cell range that appears when you trace a formula's dependent cells is called a _____
   a. dependent cell border.
   b. range finder.
   c. range editor.
   d. edit border.

4. When using a shared Excel workbook, you can enter numbers, but you *cannot*
   a. type formulas.
   b. format cells.
   c. insert columns and rows.
   d. merge cells.

5. Publishing an Excel workbook as an interactive Web page allows users to do all the following to the workbook except
   a. type new values into cells to perform what-if analysis.
   b. type formulas containing references to other cells in the same worksheet.
   c. format entries boldface.
   d. save an altered Web workbook for use in another Web session.

review of concepts

REVIEW QUESTIONS

1. Is it possible for a cell containing a value to have precedent cells? How about dependent cells? Explain.

2. Discuss what Excel would display if you typed the formula =C4+D7 in cell A1 (assuming C4 and D7 contain numbers) and then later deleted row 4. What type of error appears and how might you locate the source of the error?

3. Explain, very briefly, the advantages and disadvantages of creating a shared workbook. Start by explaining the purpose of a shared workbook.

4. Describe how to review changes suggested by various users of a shared workbook.

5. How do you keep secret a cell's formula and still display the result of that formula? Why would you want to hide a formula anyway?

6. Suppose you choose to hide a complete worksheet so that you can keep it invisible from all except you. Periodically, you may want to make changes to the hidden worksheet. Describe how to hide the worksheet and keep even experts from being able to see and print it.

CREATE THE QUESTION

For each of the following answers, create an appropriate, short question.

ANSWER	QUESTION
1. It displays worksheet formulas	_____
2. When using a shared workbook, Excel stores them in a tracking log	_____
3. Doing so makes a dependent cell active	_____
4. Click the Error Checking button on the Formula Auditing toolbar and then click Help on this error	_____
5. Click the Next Comment button on the Reviewing toolbar	_____
6. Click Format, click Cells, click the Protection tab, and place a checkmark in the check box called Hidden	_____

1. Scrip Order Form

Martha Peterson rows for Big Bay Rowing Club (BBRC), the oldest all-women's rowing club in the United States. She is also this year's chairman of finance. Funded completely by annual dues and fund-raising activities, BBRC members twice yearly hold rummage sales to raise money. This year, Martha has decided to try raising money using scrip, which is similar to a gift certificate. However, unlike a gift certificate, scrip issued by each merchant also provides a rebate to the club selling the scrip. The percentage rebate varies somewhat among merchants and ranges from 4 percent to as high as 16 percent. The typical rebate is approximately 5 percent. Customers buying scrip can exchange it for merchandise at face value. That means for every scrip "dollar" sold, the customer receives full dollar-for-dollar retail value and the club receives four to five cents.

Martha has developed a scrip order form. She prints copies to give to club members selling scrip to pass back to Martha. She uses the same form to total all scrip units from individual members and then mails the master form to Scrip Vantage for processing. Within a week, Scrip Vantage sends to Martha scrip from the merchants in the quantities and denominations on the master order form. Martha's form contains four additional formulas that detail the total money due Scrip Vantage, the gross credit, the shipping cost to send the scrip to Martha, and the net credit. The net credit is the rebate, after expenses, that she deposits into the Big Bay Rowing Club's account to help pay for new rowing equipment. There are several errors on her form, and she wants you to help locate and correct the errors, format the worksheet to make input cells obvious, and protect the worksheet so she cannot inadvertently alter formulas.

1. Open **ex08ScripVantage.xls** (see Figure 8.37) and save it as **<yourname>ScripVantage2.xls**

2. Click **Tools**, point to **Formula Auditing**, click **Show Formula Auditing Toolbar**, and move the Formula Auditing toolbar near the top of the screen without docking it

3. Click cell **F18**, click the **Trace Error** button, type =**SUM(F8:F17)**, and press **Enter** to correct the error

4. Click **F18** and then click the **Trace Precedents** button. Notice the tracer arrow shows the precedents are correct. Click the **Remove Precedent Arrows** button

5. Click cell **L21**, click the **Error Checking** button. Notice the error message: "A value used in the formula is of the wrong data type." Click the **Close** button on the Error Checking dialog box, click cell **K21**, and press the **Delete** key

6. Click cell **G29**, click the **Trace Error** button. Click the **Formula** bar, delete **+#REF!** from the formula, and press **Enter**

F I G U R E   8.37

Scrip Vantage workbook with errors

7. Click cell **G33**, click the **Error Alert** box, click **Trace Error**

8. Click the **Error Alert** box associated with cell G31, click **Edit in Formula Bar**, and delete the two occurrences of **+#REF!** from the formula, press **Enter**, and click the **Remove All Arrows** on the Formula Auditing toolbar

9. Select the cell range **G8:G18**, press and hold **Ctrl**, select the cell ranges **G21:G27** and **M8:M24**, release the **Ctrl** key, click **Format**, click **Cells**, click the **Protection** tab, click **Hidden**, and click **OK**

10. With the three cell ranges still selected, click **Format**, click **Cells**, click the **Number** tab, click **Custom** in the Category list, drag across the entry in the Type list box, type **;;;** (three semicolons), and click **OK**

11. Click the merged cell pair **C4** and **D4**, press and hold the **Ctrl** key, and select the following cells and cell ranges: **C5, I4, I5, E8:E17, E21:E26**, and **K8:K23**, and release the **Ctrl** key

12. With the cells still selected, click **Format**, click **Cells**, click the **Protection** tab, clear the **Locked** check box, and click **OK**

13. With the cells still selected, press the **Delete** key, click the **Fill Color** button list arrow (Formatting toolbar), click the **Light Yellow** color well (fifth row, third column), and click cell **C4** to deselect the cells

14. Click **Tools**, point to **Protection**, click **Protect Sheet**, click the **Select locked cells** check box (if necessary) to clear the check box, and click **OK**

15. Click **Tools**, click **Options**, click the **View** tab (if necessary), click **Row & column headers** to clear the check box, click the **Gridlines** check box to clear it, and click **OK**

16. Type your name in the worksheet header

17. Click cell **C4**, if necessary, to select the merged cell pair C4 and C5, press **Tab** four times, type **5**, press **Tab**, type **10**, press **Tab**, type **7**, and press **Enter**

18. Close the Formula Auditing toolbar, save the workbook, and print the worksheet

FIGURE 8.38

Grimwald Project Report published to the Web

2. Grimwald Project Management

Grimwald Project Management is a contractor doing work for various governmental bodies. It has a small staff of experts in the field of computer security who each work on more than one project. Each month, Grimwald tracks employees' labor hours and bills its customers based on the labor hours each employee works. Lately, Grimwald has been doing government contract work for the United States exclusively. Grimwald, like other contractors, can charge the U.S. government overhead to cover employee benefits, sick pay, and other costs in addition to the direct labor costs (hours times hourly rate for each employee). The government allows contractors to charge general and administrative costs (G & A) as well as earn a respectable profit. Unlike free enterprise, the government has rules on how much a contractor may charge for overhead, G & A, and profit. Overhead is 75 percent of direct labor, G & A is 12 percent of overhead plus direct labor, and profit may be no more than 12 percent of the total of direct labor, overhead, and G & A. Phil Herner, the projects coordinator, has cobbled together a workbook with the required formulas in place, but there are errors. He wants you to correct the errors, hide the cells containing the company proprietary percentages assumptions, and provide a set of unlocked cells in which to enter each month's labor hours. Furthermore, he wants you to publish an interactive workbook to the intranet so any Grimwald manager can perform what-if analysis using his or her browser.

1. Open **ex08Grimwald.xls**, save it immediately as **<yourname>Grimwald2.xls**, and click the **Project Report** worksheet tab

2. Select the cell range **C3:C5**, click **Format**, click **Cells**, click the **Protection** tab, and then click the **Hidden** check box, and click **OK**

3. With the cell range still selected, click **Format**, click **Cells**, click the **Number** tab, click the **Custom** selection in the Category list, select any text in the Type text box, type **;;;** (three semicolons), and click **OK**

4. Click cell **C7**, press and hold the **Ctrl** key, select cell range **B10:D15**, and release the **Ctrl** key

5. Click **Format**, click **Cells**, click the **Protection** tab, click the **Locked** check box to clear it, click **OK**, click the **Fill Color** list box arrow, and click the **Light Yellow** color well (fifth row, third column)

6. Click cell **C22** and press **F2**. The range finder in cell D3 highlights the error. Press **Esc**

7. Click cell **B22**, click the formula bar, move the insertion point to the left of **C3** in the formula, and press **F4**, and press **Enter**

8. Click Cell **B22**, then click and drag its fill handle to cell **D22** and release the mouse

9. Click cell **B23**, click the formula bar, move the insertion point to the left of **C4** in the formula, and press **F4**, and press **Enter**

10. Click cell **B23**, then click and drag its fill handle to cell **D23** and release the mouse

11. Click **Tools**, point to **Protection**, click **Protect Sheet**, click the **Select locked cells** check box to clear it, and click **OK**

12. Click the **Save** button on the Standard toolbar

13. Click **File**, click **Save as Web Page**, click the **Selection: Sheet** option button, click the **Add interactivity** check box, click the **Change Title** button, and type **Grimwald Project Management**, and click **OK**

14. Select all the text in the **File name** text box, type **Grimwald**, and click the **Save** button

15. Click **File**, click **Exit**, and click **Yes** if you are asked if you want to save your changes. Excel closes

16. Locate and open the Web page you created called **Grimwald.mht** in your browser (see Figure 8.38 on the previous page)

17. Click cell **B10**, type **100**, click cell **C11**, type **120**, click **D12**, type **130**, click **B13**, type **110**, click **C14**, type **140**, click **D15**, type **155**, and press **Enter**

18. Click cell **C7**, type your name, and print the Web page using your browser's Print command in the File menu, and close your browser

hands-on projects

challenge

1. Determining Total Cost of Ownership

The Indiana governor's special assistant for educational initiatives, Nancy Carroll, oversees purchases by secondary education institutions across the state. Her latest thrust has been to reduce the cost of printers—both laser and ink—purchased by schools. She knows that low prices for ink printers sometimes appear to be attractive, but the total cost of ownership is the real cost (TCO). TCO is based on the average cost per page of toner or ink plus the cost of a new printer based on its expected lifetime. Nancy assumes that the printers the schools purchase will last only three years. Her intern collected data about five typical laser printers and five typical ink printers. Data include the purchase cost of each printer, the cost for a laser cartridge and black and color ink cartridges, and the average coverage when printing a typical document. She notes that almost all documents cover either 5 or 8 percent of a page, where 100 percent represents a completely covered page (all black, for example).

Open the TCO worksheet **ex08PrinterTCO.xls** and save it as **<yourname>TCO2.xls**. On the Cover Sheet worksheet, make the words *Summary* and *Data* hyperlinks to like-named worksheets. Unlock those two cells, and protect the worksheet. Modify the page margins to one inch all around, and horizontally center the Cover Sheet on a portrait-oriented page when you later print it. Click the **Data** worksheet tab and examine the worksheet (see Figure 8.39). The 5 percent and 8 percent coverage columns indicate the number of pages that you can print with one cartridge—a cartridge's *yield*. Dividing the cartridge cost (column C) by the copies per cartridge (columns D and E for each printer) yields the cost per page—a formula you will write on the Summary worksheet. Protect the Data worksheet. Click the **Summary** worksheet tab, unlock cell **C4**, and locate the error source for cells B10 and E10. Correct those formulas. Type **10000** in cell C4, which contains your estimate of the number of pages printed each year. Write formulas for 5 percent and 8 percent cost per page cells for each of the 10 printers. (Studies for color printers found that about 4 percent of a page is black and 4 percent is colored.) Format cells B10:C14 and B16:C20 with the Number format, comma separator, and four decimal places. In columns E and F, write formulas for the total cost of ownership, which is the estimated pages printed times the cost per page plus the purchase cost of a printer—for 5 percent and 8 percent coverage. Format the TCO column values with the Accounting format, currency symbol, and two decimal places. Identify the best value at 5 percent and the best value at 8 percent by highlighting the two cells with a bright yellow background. Insert in those cells the comment **This is the best value**. Protect the Summary worksheet. Insert your name in all three worksheet headers, print the entire workbook, and then print the formulas for the Summary worksheet (landscape orientation). Save your final result.

FIGURE 8.39

Total cost of ownership data

	A	B	C	D	E	F	G	H	I
1	Description	Printer Purchase Cost[1]	Cost per Cartridge	Copies per Cartridge					
2				5% coverage	8% coverage				
3	**Laser Printers**								
4	HP LaserJet 1200	$ 340.00	$ 51.00	2,500	1,600				
5	Lexmark E322	$ 360.00	$ 112.00	6,000	3,750				
6	HP LaserJet 2200DN	$ 935.00	$ 84.00	5,000	3,160				
7	Lexmark T522N	$ 1,120.00	$ 256.86	20,000	12,500				
8	HP LaserJet 4200N	$ 1,370.00	$ 123.95	12,000	7,500				
9	**Ink Printers**								
10	HP DeskJet 5550	$ 125.00							
11	Black		$ 17.00	450	284				
12	Color		$ 28.00	390	246				
13	Epson Stylus C82 Inkjet	$ 135.00							
14	Black		$ 23.00	870	548				
15	Color		$ 25.00	1260	794				
16	Epson Stylus C80N	$ 300.00							
17	Black		$ 23.00	870	548				
18	Color		$ 25.00	1260	794				
19	HP PhotoSmart 7350	$ 167.00							
20	Black		$ 16.00	450	284				
21	Color		$ 27.00	390	246				
22	Epson Stylus Photo 925	$ 225.00							

Cover Sheet / Summary \ Data /

Ready

2. Professor O'Connell's Electronic Grade Book

Patrick O'Connell is a lecturer in the Accounting, Finance, and Information Systems Department at University College, Cork (www.ucc.ie) located in Cork, Ireland. In the last weeks of each semester, his students frequently ask him what he thinks their grade will be. Referring them to his course syllabus, he restates the percentage that each graded component of the course counts toward the final grade, and he asks them to do a rough calculation to determine their grades. It did not take Professor O'Connell long to determine that it would help both him and his students to post an electronic grade calculation worksheet allowing students to punch in their scores to see their expected course grade. The professor has asked you to help him create an Excel workbook that computes students' final grades given the three components of his course: exams, quizzes, and homework assignments. Once the Excel worksheet is complete, he wants to create an interactive Web worksheet, posted to the UCC server, so that students can use their browsers to access the password-protected Web site and compute their scores. Professor O'Connell has created a prototype worksheet that he wants you to use as a model to create an actual student grade worksheet (see Figure 8.40).

Begin by opening **ex08GradeCalc.xls** and save it as **<yourname>GradeCalc2.xls**. Professor O'Connell's requirements for the grading workbook include these.

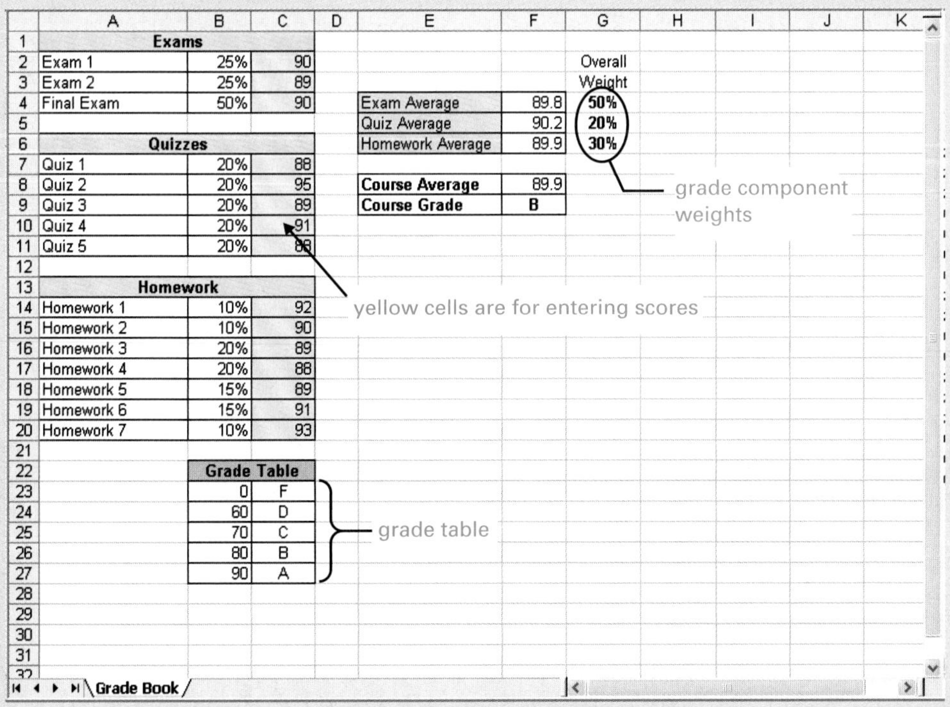

Format cells B2:B4, B7:B11, and B14:B20 as percentages displaying no decimal places. Format cells C2:C4, C7:C11, and C14:C20 as **Number** with zero decimal places and a light yellow fill color. Format cells F6:F8 and F10 as **Number** with one decimal place. Bold cell F9 and center align it. Write formulas in cells D2:D4, D7:D11, and D14:D20 that are the product of the two values to the left of each. For example, D2 contains B2*C2. Format the preceding 15 cells so they are invisible. These products create the weighted values for the exam, quiz, and homework averages. Write formulas for cells F4, F5, and F6 that sum the hidden products for their respective grade component (exams, for example). Cell F8 sums the product of the average for each component and its overall weight (cells G5, G6, and G7), resulting in a weighted course average. The course grade uses a VLOOKUP function, the grade table, and the course average to yield a grade. The formula should use the IF function to display a null string (two consecutive apostrophes) if the value in cell F8 is zero. Doing so allows you to erase all scores in the yellow-filled cells and not display an F in the Course Grade cell. Unlock the yellow-filled input cells, protect the worksheet (disallowing selecting locked cells), insert your name in the worksheet header, and save the workbook. Type scores shown in Figure 8.40 into the yellow-filled cells to check your results against the figure's results. Print the worksheet and then print the worksheet formulas. Clear all yellow-filled cells, then save the worksheet as an interactive Web page, changing the Web page title to **Grade Calculation Worksheet<yourname>** and changing the Web page name to **<yourname>index.html**. After saving the Web page, open your browser, display the worksheet, type in typical scores in the yellow input cells, and print the Web page.

FIGURE 8.40

Completed grade worksheet

e-business

1. The Incredible Cheesecake Company

Michelle Lindsay is the manager of one of three Incredible Cheesecake Company stores located in southern California. In addition to its flagship product, cheesecake, the bakery also sells muffins, scones, and a variety of fresh baked goods. They bake their products twice daily from a location not far from their two other stores.

Michelle has been tracking sales of their products using her accounting program. Yesterday, she exported the sales data for the first three months of the year to an Excel workbook. She has asked two key associates to analyze the Excel data and make comments on them. Both people have made sparse comments and saved the shared workbook on the server.

Because Michelle wants to expand her Internet business segment, she wants you to create a pivot table showing the business generated by online customers and the three other market segments; create a pie chart showing the dollar volume of the four market segments (Domestic, International, Mail Order, and Online); place the workbook, including the pivot table and chart, on the company's intranet; and allow others in the company to review it but not make changes to it—a noninteractive Web page.

Begin by opening **ex08IncredibleCheesecake.xls** and save it as **<yourname>ICC2.xls**. Locate and exam-ine any comments throughout the Sales worksheet, and then delete them. In column G, create and then clone formulas to calculate the product of Qty and Price. Label the new column (cell G1) **Extended**. Paste the Price column's format onto the Extended column, and widen the column as needed. Next, clear all comments and create a pivot table on a new worksheet showing total sales by Venue (*Venue* is the Row field and *Extended* is the Data field). Change the Excel-suggested Data field name *Sum of Extended* to **Total Sales**. Format the Total Sales field to display a currency symbol and zero decimal places. Rename the worksheet tab holding the PivotTable to **Pivot Table** (two words), and color the worksheet tab green. Select the PivotTable labels and values (eight cells) and create a three-dimensional pie chart (on its own worksheet) showing the total revenue of each of the four market segments. Label each slice with its corresponding category label and value. Rename the chart tab **Pie Chart** and color it Blue. Rearrange the worksheets in this order, left to right: Q1 Sales, Pivot Table, and Pie Chart. Place your name in the header of each worksheet. Save the workbook. Create noninter-active Web pages for the entire workbook, changing its title to your name. Print the Excel PivotTable worksheet page and print the first page of the raw data. Launch your browser and open the Web version of the ICC workbook and print the Pie Chart Web page and the PivotTable Web page.

2. Lathram and Associates' Online Invoice

Bob Lathram, cofounder of Lathram and Associates, provides Web hosting and electronic commerce services to a growing number of small and medium-sized online merchants. Potential merchants can commit for different levels of Web presence by selecting from an extensive list of services including simple Web hosting —providing a domain name online location for a customer's Web log, or "blog" (a frequent, chronological publication of personal thoughts and Web links)— advertising, or other catalog of products. Other services Lathram offers range from Web building tools that a merchant can use to build a simple store complete with shopping cart up to a complete, custombuilt Web site constructed by Lathram experts. Bob wants to develop an online invoice that his sales staff can fill out and mail to customers. The online invoice would be available only on a password-protected part of the Web site, and it would save time and money. Bob has crafted a prototype invoice, spending most of his time on formatting so that the online invoice resembles their paper invoice (including formatting numeric entries the way he likes them). He wants you to add the formulas to calculate extended price, subtotal, shipping, sales tax, and the total. In addition, he wants you to protect all cells not designated for data input and provide an online version of the invoice that he and the staff can test for a month before going live.

Open **ex08Lathram Invoice.xls** and save it as **<yourname>Lathram2.xls**. For your convenience, Bob has color-coded the data input cells on the invoice with a light yellow fill color. Begin by formatting the color-coded cells. Select them all (Ctrl-click all light yellow cells) and then unlock them, change the fill color to white to match the rest of the invoice, and change the font color to black. Write formulas in cells O19:O26 to form the product of Quantity and Unit Price for each row using the IF function so that nothing displays in an Extended Price cell if its corresponding Unit Price cell is empty. Write a formula for Subtotal, displaying the sum of all the Extended Price cells only if the sum is greater than zero; otherwise, it displays nothing (""). Shipping is simply 1.2 percent of the subtotal, but the cell displays a value only if subtotal is not empty. Be sure to use the ROUND function to round the result to two decimal places. The Sales Tax entry is empty if Subtotal is empty. Otherwise, the sales tax is 7.75 percent of Subtotal (sales tax is not charged on shipping). Use the ROUND function here too. *Total* is the sum of Subtotal, Shipping, and Sales Tax *unless* Subtotal is empty. In this case Total is empty. Set the Print Area to the cell range B2:Q35. Protect the worksheet, and then remove the row and column headers (click **Tools**, **Options**, **View** tab, clear **Row & column headers**). Fill in all unlocked cells—including at least three line items in the Quantity/Description/Unit Price portion of the invoice. Print the worksheet, and then print the worksheet formulas. Empty all unlocked cells, and then create an interactive, Web-based invoice, changing the title to your first and last names. Display the Web version of your invoice in your browser and print it.

on the web

1. Comparing Exotic Fruit Prices

Honor Fong has sold fresh, exotic fruit from her 500-square-foot store in San Francisco for 12 years. She sells her produce locally, and she has built a small but growing mail-order business that ships to customers all across the United States and Mexico. Although she has thought about opening an online store to increase her market reach, she is not quite ready to take on that added responsibility. Periodically, Honor compares her fresh fruit prices to Frieda's—one of her main competitors (www.friedas.com). Honor's daughter, Joanne, has developed a price comparison workbook. The Survey Data worksheet contains fruit prices from Frieda's online fruit store along with the weight of each. The Price per Pound Comparison worksheet contains formulas. The formulas in the Frieda's column refer to a fruit name, price, and weight found on the Survey Data worksheet. The price per pound formulas in Frieda's column are a fruit's price divided by its weight.

Open **ex08ExoticFruit.xls**, and save it as **<yourname>ExoticFruit2.xls**. Use Google (www.google.com) or other search engines to look up the prices and weight of the listed fruits from another Web store besides Frieda's. Enter the data into the Survey Data worksheet, and write formulas for the companion Price per Pound Comparison worksheet. (Restore the original row formatting after you copy formulas down the columns.) Replace the label "Store 2" (cell D1 on the Survey Data worksheet) with the name of the Web store, and turn the label in cell C2 on the Price per Pound Comparison worksheet into a hyperlink to the store's Web site. Protect the Price per Pound worksheet. Place your name in all worksheet headers, and place a field referencing the worksheet's name in the footer of each worksheet. Print the worksheet, and then save the Price per Pound Comparison worksheet as a noninteractive Web page. Change the Web page title to your first and last names, load the Web page into your browser, and print it.

2. Delightful Sunny Products

The Beverage division of Delightful Sunny Products distributes orange juice and its own beverage called *Thirst Delight* to grocery stores in the western United States. Sarah Masterson has created a consolidated operating budget showing the important numbers for sales of both drinks, the cost of sales, expenses, and before-tax earnings. The division ships products from plants in California and Florida. Each state's sales and expense information is on its own worksheet, with the consolidated information totaling all corresponding values from both states' worksheets on the Corporate worksheet. Open **ex08Sunny.xls** and save the workbook as **<yourname>Sunny2.xls**. Locate and correct any formula errors on the Corporate worksheet (*hint:* display the formulas and look for inconsistencies). Protect the Corporate worksheet. On the Documentation worksheet, change *Corporate*, *California*, and *Florida* entries into hyperlinks to their respective worksheets, and protect the Documentation worksheet (allowing users to select locked cells). Unlock all nonformula cells on the California and Florida worksheets, and protect both worksheets. Place your name in each worksheet's header, insert each worksheet's (tab) name in the worksheet footer, print the Documentation and Corporate worksheets, and print the Corporate worksheet formulas. Save the workbook. Publish the entire workbook (place your name in the Web page title) as a noninteractive Web Archive (see "Another Word" in Session 8.3). Open the Web workbook and print each page from your browser.

around the world

1. African Coffee Importers

African Coffee Importers (ACI) purchases green coffee beans from a dozen African countries. All purchases are top-quality Robusta and Arabica beans in 60-kilogram (kg) bags. ACI always pays the coffee farmers in their local currency, but ACI's accountant also records sales in U.S. dollars (USD).

Open **ex08AfricanCoffee.xls** and save it as **<yourname>AfricanCoffee2.xls**. Click the **Currency Information** worksheet tab. Click the cell range **B3:F14** and name it **CurrencyTable**. Insert a hyperlink in cell D16 to the Web page www.xe.com/ucc/full.shtml. Using that link, find the currency name, abbreviation, and exchange rate for currencies of Ethiopia, South Africa, and Tanzania. Insert the information you locate into the appropriate rows in the currency table. Remove all comments from all worksheets using the Reviewing toolbar. Protect the **Currency Information** worksheet. Click the **Purchase Quantities** worksheet tab. First, set the column widths of columns A through G to 13, 11, 11, 14, 11, 16, and 11, respectively. Next, write formulas in D3:D14 for purchase cost. Write formulas for the Cost per Pound column (look up the weight conversion for kilograms to pounds). Using the VLOOKUP function and the currency rates on the Currency Information worksheet, write formulas for the *Purchase Cost (country's currency)* column. Using VLOOKUP, write an expression to look up the country's currency name and insert it in the *Currency Name* column. Format all U.S. dollar cells with the Accounting format, $ currency symbol, and 2 decimal places. Format the *Purchase Cost (country's currency)* column with Accounting format, no currency symbol, and zero decimal places. Write formulas for total cost (cell D16) and average cost per bag (cell D17). Unlock cells B3:C14 and then protect the Purchase Quantities worksheet. Place your name in the header of all worksheets, print the entire workbook, print the formulas for the Purchase Quantities worksheet, and save the workbook again.

2. Xanthan Gum Company Income Statement

Keltrol Xanthan Gum Company produces xanthan gum, which is used in many consumer products ranging from chewing gum to paint. A thickening agent, xanthan gum is used in salad dressings as a stabilizer to keep ingredients suspended uniformly without imparting any masking flavor. Xanthan is found in seaweed, and Keltrol has two plants that process the seaweed to extract the xanthan. These plants are in Cork, Ireland, and Glouchester, England. Employees at the company headquarters, in San Diego, California, track the plants' production via proforma income statements for each plant. Each of the two proforma worksheets is stored in a workbook called **ex08Keltrol.xls**. The Cork worksheet records values in Euros, whereas the Glouchester worksheet records values in Pounds Sterling. Your task is to summarize both plants' values on the Summary worksheet, converting Euros and Pounds to U.S. Dollars. In addition, correct any errors on the Cork and Glouchester worksheets. Use those worksheets as a guide to writing formulas for the Summary worksheet.

Begin by opening **ex08Keltrol.xls** and saving it as **<yourname>Keltrol8.xls**. Create link formulas on the summary page to sum values from each plant (after values are converted to U.S. Dollars). Look up conversion rates for Euros to U.S. Dollars and Pounds to U.S. Dollars and place the values in cells B2 and B3, respectively, of the *Currency Conversion Rates* worksheet. Note these two cells are named E2USD and P2USD, respectively, to help you as you write conversion formulas on the Summary worksheet. When you are done, place your name in the header of *Summary*, *Cork*, and *Glouchester* worksheets, print the three worksheets, print their formulas, and publish only the Summary worksheet (noninteractive) to the Web. Display the published worksheet in Internet Explorer and print it.

running project

Pro Golf Academy

Betty Carroll has agreed to be one of the sponsors for the Tanglewood Golf Club's annual golf tournament. Instead of paying a sponsorship fee in exchange for tournament-day advertising in the registration tent, Pro Golf Academy has agreed to create a tournament budget workbook. Betty has nearly completed the workbook, and she wants you to check its formulas to ensure there are no errors. In addition, she wants you to post the worksheet to the Tanglewood's intranet (or your PC), so tournament organizers can perform what-if analysis using the Web-based version of the workbook. Betty expects 160 players to register for the tournament.

Begin by opening **ex08ProGolf.xls**, making the Tournament Planning worksheet active, and saving the worksheet as **<yourname>ProGolf8.xls**. Unlock all assumptions cells, then examine each of the subtotal formulas for errors and correct the error(s). Protect the worksheet so that users can select only unlocked cells.

All of the assumptions—cells into which anyone can type data and perform what-if analysis—

have a bright yellow background. Fill in the yellow assumptions cells with the following data: cost/golfer: $75; charge/player: $150; meal cost: $35; meal charge: $50; number of players: 160; meals only: 10; first, second, and third prizes are $4000, $2000, and $1000, respectively. Sponsor cells are as follows: expect one Grand sponsor at $5000, three Major sponsors at $3000 each, four Catering sponsors at $1000 each, six Box Lunch sponsors at $400 each, and seven Driving Range sponsors at $100 each.

Type your name in the worksheet header. Select all of the yellow, unlocked assumptions cells and open the Formula Auditing toolbar. With the yellow cells selected, repeat the following actions: click the **Trace Dependents** button and press **Enter**. Continue until all assumptions cells display tracer arrows. Print the worksheet. Clear all tracer arrows. Publish the Tournament Planning worksheet as an *interactive* Web worksheet. Title the Web page **Tournament Planning Worksheet**, and save it as **<yourname>Page.htm** (substitute your name for *<yourname>*). Display the Web-based worksheet in your browser (see Figure 8.41), and print the Web page.

FIGURE   8.41

Web–based Tournament Planning worksheet

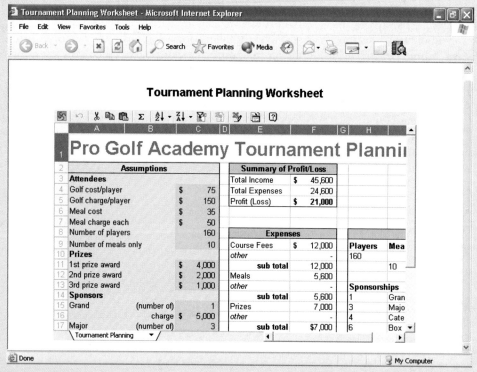

1. Sharing a Workbook

Discuss why someone would share a workbook. Include in the discussion at least three advantages and discuss when changes are selected or deleted and who does it. What settings, if any, must you turn on to locate changes and determine who made them?

2. Web Accessible Workbooks

Why would you publish an Excel workbook to the Web? Discuss why you would choose to publish an interactive versus a noninteractive workbook. How can you keep the Web version of a workbook synchronized with a stored copy on someone's PC?

9

Using Data Tables and Scenarios

did you know?

each *year, 9 million tons of salt, more than 10 percent of all the salt produced in the world, is applied to American highways for road deicing. The cost of buying and applying the salt adds up to $200 million.*

the *first VCR, or videocassette recorder, was made in 1956 and was the size of a piano.*

Rudyard *Kipling, living in Vermont in the 1890s, invented the game of snow golf. He painted his golf balls red so that they could be located in the snow.*

Denver *has the nation's largest city park system, with more than 200 parks within city limits and 20,000 acres of parks in the nearby mountains—an area larger than all of Manhattan Island.*

Queen *Elizabeth I of England, using a diamond, scratched the following message on her prison window: "Much suspected of me, Nothing proved can be."*

Excel *data tables and scenarios are related. Find out how in this chapter.*

Chapter Objectives

- Learn about the relationships between volume, cost, and profit
- Learn and use break-even analysis to determine production levels for profitability—MOS XL03S-1-3
- Create and use one-variable and two-variable data tables— MOS XL03E-1-7
- Create charts based on one-variable and two-variable data tables—MOS XL03S-1-4
- Create Excel scenarios—MOS XL03E-1-6
- Manage Excel scenarios with the Scenario Manager— MOS XL03E-1-6
- View, add, edit, and delete scenarios—MOS XL03E-1-6
- Create a scenario report—MOS XL03E-1-6

chapter case

Artistic Furniture Corporation

Artistic Furniture Corporation ("Artistic") was founded in 1985 in El Cajon, California, by its president, Dave Messer. Paul Messer, Artistic's vice president and Dave's son, is a 50 percent owner of the privately held corporation and actively participates in all facets of the business.

Artistic is a wholesale business and sells its custom home theater cabinet systems to retailers—most of whom are located in California. Artistic sells its systems to both furniture dealers and electronics retailers who sell large-screen televisions and complete, expensive stereo systems.

Artistic's typical home theater cabinet sells in the retail market for over $4,000. Retail customers with expensive entertainment systems often want attractive cabinets in which to house their equipment. Thus, retail electronics and big-screen stores like to have at least two of Artistic Furniture Corporation's home theater cabinetry in the showroom.

In addition to a management function, Artistic's operation contains seven manufacturing departments: panel processing, lumber milling, assembly, prefinishing, finishing, final assembly, and shipping. Artistic receives raw wood boards and panels at its receiving dock and sends the materials through each department, in turn, to produce a finished entertainment center. Panel processing and lumber milling prepare the panels, doors, and drawers for the cabinet from the blueprints. Assembly and prefinishing departments build and sand the cabinet. Members of the finishing and final assembly departments (most employees work in at least three of the departments) are responsible for applying the finish coat of paint or lacquer and installing all hardware and glass. Shipping is responsible for placing the furniture in containers in preparation for pickup and shipment.

There are two major categories of costs in building the home entertainment systems: fixed costs and variable costs. Fixed costs include rent, taxes, and utilities. Variable costs include the cost of raw materials, labor, and supplies used to manufacture the systems. Dave and anyone else in a profitable business must be aware of both costs in order to make a profit. Figure 9.1 shows a worksheet displaying examples of both fixed and variable costs, the number of units produced, the revenue generated, and profit. You will be helping Paul Messer improve the worksheet and do sophisticated what-if analysis by using two Office Excel 2003 tools: data tables and scenarios.

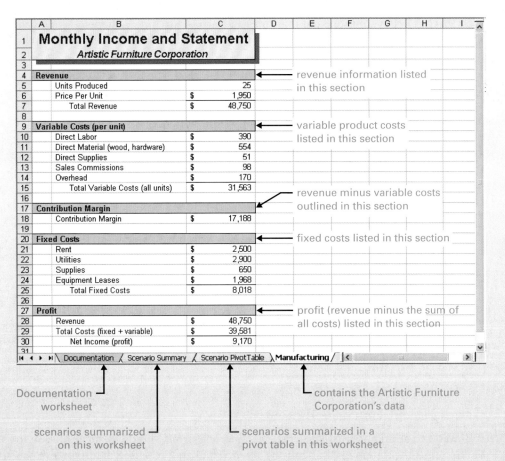

FIGURE 9.1

Artistic Furniture
Corporation completed
worksheet

Chapter 9 covers two very important what-if tools: one- and two-variable data tables and scenarios. In this chapter, you will learn how to use one-variable and two-variable tables to quickly and easily make changes and observe their effect on a series of values in a worksheet—changes to the profitability of a company, for example. You will consider the relationships among the important business terms of volume, cost, and profit. Called *Cost-Volume-Profit (CVP) analysis,* it examines the relationship between a product's expenses (cost), the number of units of the product produced (volume), revenue, and profit. Revenue, which is the total units produced multiplied by their sales price, determines profit. Profit is revenue minus total cost. CVP analysis helps managers make good decisions, including which products to make and sell, whether or not the company should change its pricing policy, and whether or not to purchase additional manufacturing facilities to increase productivity. Using CVP, managers focus on these five elements: production volume, product pricing, product mix, per unit variable costs, and total fixed costs.

A frequent problem in examining the effect of altering the sales price of a unit or another variable is keeping track of the various outcomes. Several worksheet cells aid in determining that all-important bottom line, profit. Frequently, business people want to examine several cases, or scenarios, each with a different combination of variables (unit cost, labor, volume, etc.) to observe the effect on profit. One solution is to create multiple worksheets, each with a different combination of variable values, and print out

CHAPTER OUTLINE

9.1 Using Data Tables
    EX 9.4

9.2 Using Scenarios
    EX 9.23

9.3 Summary EX 9.39

each sheet. A better solution, and one you will learn to use in this chapter, is to create several scenarios. Scenarios allow you to create sets of variable values you want to change as named groups.

SESSION 9.1 USING DATA TABLES

In this section, you will learn about the relationships among product cost, volume, and profit. You will build a worksheet to aid Dave in making manufacturing decisions such as whether to reduce unit costs, produce more units, and determine how many units they must sell to reach *break-even*—when profit is zero. Break-even analysis is particularly important because it illustrates the effects on profit from cutting variable and fixed costs or raising prices.

---

anotherword   . . . on Researching Topics You Encounter

Whenever you want to locate supporting information in local reference materials or on the Internet, use the Research tool: Click **Tools** and then click **Research** to open the Research task pane. Click the **Search for** text box, type **break even analysis**, click the drop-down arrow, and then click **All Research Sites** to the right of the *search services* text box. If necessary, begin or refresh a search by clicking the **Start searching** arrow. Click any of the results to open more information. Clicking a hyperlink opens a document, but some documents require additional fees. Click **MSN sources** for free information

---

Creating an Income Statement

Paul wants to examine ways that Artistic can increase profits. To do so, he wants you to build an income statement that conveys the revenue and expenses, at a high level, so that he can look for ways to increase revenue or cut expenses to achieve higher profitability. Paul has started a monthly income statement worksheet, but he has become quite busy and wants you to complete the worksheet. Once you have created the worksheet showing revenue, expenses, and profit, then Paul and you will discuss ways to use a worksheet with data tables and scenarios to review the effect of changes in production units and expense reductions. By generating a data table, you will be able to display a series of revenues, expenses, and profits based on changes to a couple of worksheet cells—units produced—to locate any critical inflection points where Artistic's profitability changes dramatically. First, Paul explains the relationships between cost, volume, and profit in general and then describes expenses that Artistic has when producing its line of entertainment center cabinets.

Revenue

One of the components of CVP analysis, *revenue*, is the money (or other items of value) that a company receives during a given period. Revenue can include sales, interest income, proceeds from the sale of a subsidiary, and so forth.

You will create the monthly income statement by building on the workbook that Paul created. Paul explains to you that the main source of revenue is, of course, wholesale sales of their entertainment centers. They sell for an average of $2,050 per unit. With its current pool of skilled labor, Artistic can produce up to 30 units per month. Paul asks you to continue his work by creating the revenue section of the income statement first, and he wants you to enter two values and a formula into three worksheet cells. One cell will display the number of units Artistic projects it will produce in a month and the second cell should contain $2,050—the sale price of each unit.

Opening the Artistic worksheet, entering revenue values and formulas, and applying a default numeric format:

1. Start Microsoft Office Excel 2003

2. Open the workbook **ex09Artistic.xls** and immediately save it as **Artistic1.xls** to preserve the original. Review the documentation worksheet, called Documentation (see Figure 9.2)

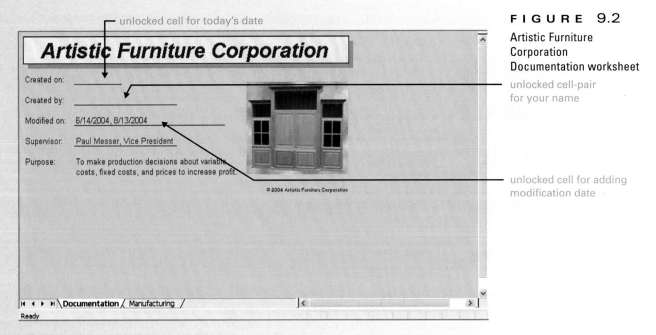

F I G U R E 9.2

Artistic Furniture Corporation Documentation worksheet

3. Click the **Manufacturing** tab to switch to that worksheet (see Figure 9.3)

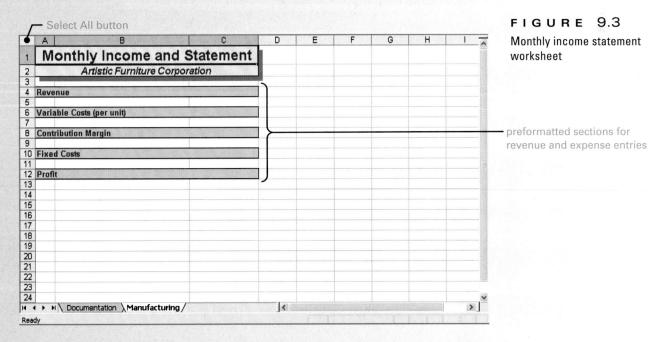

F I G U R E 9.3

Monthly income statement worksheet

preformatted sections for revenue and expense entries

4. Click the **Select All** button to select all the worksheet's cells, click **Format** on the menu bar, click **Cells**, click the **Number** tab, click **Accounting** in the Category panel, type **0** in the Decimal places spin control box, click the **Symbol** list box, select **$** (if necessary) from the list of choices, and click **OK** to apply your choices and close the Format Cells dialog box

5. Select cells **A5:A7**, click **Insert** and click **Rows**. Excel inserts three rows that are formatted to match row 4

6. Click the **Insert Options** Smart Tag, and click the **Format Same As Below** option

7. Click cell **B5**, type **Units Produced**, click cell **B6**, type **Price Per Unit**, click cell **B7**, type **Total Revenue**, press **Enter**, click cell **B7** again, and click the **Increase Indent** button *twice* to indent the label (see Figure 9.4)

FIGURE 9.4

Partially complete
Revenue section

label is indented ⟶

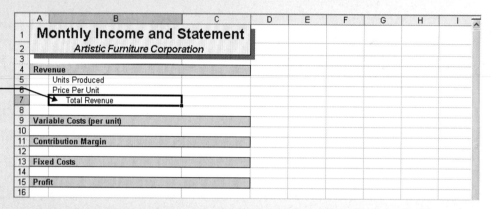

8. Click cell **C5**, click **Format**, click **Cells**, click the **Number** tab (if necessary), click **Accounting** in the Category panel, click the **Symbol** list box, click **None** in the list of choices, click **OK** to apply your choices and close the Format Cells dialog box, and type **3** in cell C5

9. Click cell **C6**, click the **Borders** list box arrow on the Formatting toolbar, click the **Bottom Border** button (row 1, column 2), and then type **2050**

10. Click cell **C7**, type **=C5*C6**, and press **Enter**. Excel computes the total revenue, which is the units produced times the price per unit (see Figure 9.5)

FIGURE 9.5

Computing revenue

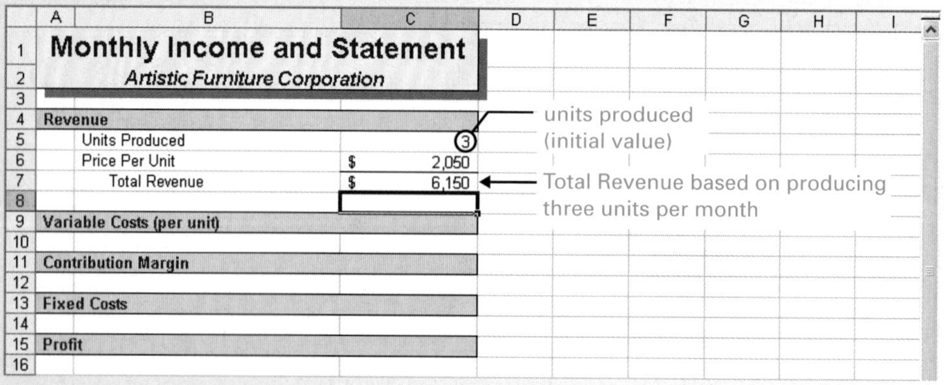

You have completed Artistic's revenue formula. It is very simple because Artistic is a one-product company. Were it to shift to producing several, slightly different entertainment center cabinets, then the Revenue section would list several pairs of values representing each product's projected number of units produced and the price. In that case, total revenue would simply be the sum of individual product revenues.

By changing cell C5, the number of units produced, you can conduct what-if analysis to project total revenue for various numbers of units. What-if analysis on this developing worksheet answers the question "How much revenue is generated if we produce x units per month?" Perform a few what-if examples to view the changes in revenue.

Performing what-if analysis of revenue:

1. Click cell **C5**, type **0**, and click the **Enter** ✔ button on the left end of the formula bar. Excel displays a hyphen in cell C5, which is the representation of zero formatted with the Accounting format

2. Type **20** in cell **C5** and click the **Enter** ✔ button found on the left end of the formula bar. Excel computes total revenue of $41,000

3. Type **10** in cell **C5** and press **Enter**. Cell C7 indicates that producing 10 units per month yields revenue of $20,500

If that were all there were to making money, businesses would hire lots of people and start producing products at maximum capacity. There's more to business than revenue, of course, because creating any product also involves costs.

Variable Costs

There are two categories of costs incurred when producing almost anything: variable costs and fixed costs.

A ***variable cost*** (or variable expense) is one that varies directly with the number of units of a product a company produces. If you increase the number of units you produce, variable costs increase. Decrease units produced, and the variable costs decrease correspondingly. Variable costs are sometimes called direct costs.

One variable cost at Artistic is direct material. The main direct material is wood. Artistic receives thousands of board-feet of wood each month (wood volume is measured in board-feet), which it uses to make its cabinets. Labor, mentioned previously, is another significant variable expense. Labor simply means the wages paid to employees who work each day to produce cabinets.

Other variable costs that are directly tied to the number of cabinets Artistic produces include direct supplies (sand paper, drill bits, and other supplies that are consumed during production), overhead (utilities directly attributable to production, for example), and sales commissions. Paul wants you to add rows to the Variable Costs section of the worksheet so that you can enter five categories of variable costs and a line that totals all variable costs.

Adding rows to the Variable Costs section:

1. Select the cell range **A10:A15**, click **Insert** and click **Rows**. Excel inserts six rows that are formatted to match row 9. The Insert Options Smart Tag appears

2. Click the **Insert Options** Smart Tag to display the list of options (see Figure 9.6), and click the **Format Same As Below** option

FIGURE 9.6

Insert Options Smart Tag

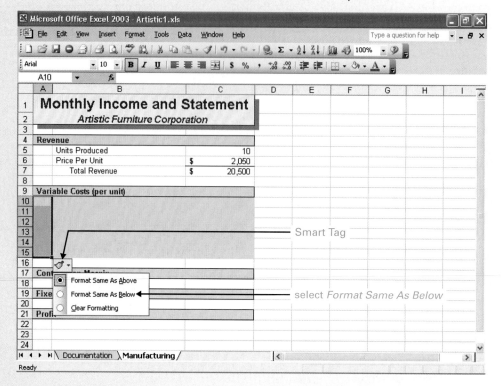

With ample room in the Variable Costs section of the worksheet, you can add the variable cost items and add a formula to subtotal the variable costs. Paul explains that the variable costs are each computed as a percentage of the wholesale price of each unit. Direct labor, the cost of production workers, is approximately 20 percent of sales. Direct material (wood and hardware) is approximately 30 percent of sales. The value for direct supplies is approximately 2.5 percent of sales. Sales commissions are exactly 5 percent of sales, and overhead is approximately 9 percent of sales.

Entering variable cost values and formulas:

1. Click cell **B10**, type **Direct Labor**, click cell **B11**, type **Direct Material (wood, hardware)**, click cell **B12**, and type **Direct Supplies**

2. Click cell **B13**, type **Sales Commissions**, click cell **B14**, type **Overhead**, click cell **B15**, type **Total Variable Costs (all units)**, and press **Enter**

3. Click cell **B15** and click *twice* the **Increase Indent** button on the Formatting toolbar to indent the label

4. Click cell **C10** and type **410**

5. Click cell **C11** and type **615**

6. Click cell **C12** and type **51**

7. Click cell **C13** and type **=5%*C6** (sales commissions vary directly with a sale and should be entered as a formula—in case the price changes)

8. Click cell **C14** and type **185**

9. Click cell **C15**, type **=SUM(C10:C14)*C5**, and press **Enter**

10. Click cell **C6**, click the **Format Painter** button on the Standard tool-bar, and click cell **C14** to copy the format (see Figure 9.7)

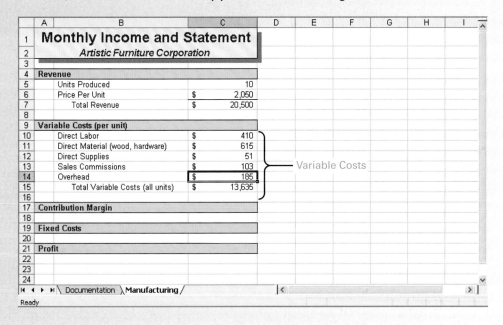

FIGURE 9.7
Completed Variable Costs section

Contribution Margin

Paul describes the contribution margin, another important concept in any business. *Contribution margin (CM)* is the amount remaining from revenue after you deduct all variable costs. Managers use contribution margin to first cover fixed expenses. Any remaining amount goes toward profits. If CM is not large enough to cover fixed expenses, then there is a loss for the reporting period. Simply stated, CM is revenue minus variable expenses. Paul asks you to write a simple formula that displays the contribution margin and to place that formula in the Contribution Margin section. Begin by inserting a new row and then write the label and formula for the contribution margin.

Adding a row for contribution margin and writing the CM formula:

1. Click cell **A18**, click **Insert**, and click **Rows**

2. Click the **Insert Options** Smart Tag to display the list of options, and click the **Format Same As Below** option

3. Click cell **B18** and type **Contribution Margin**

4. Click cell **C18**, type **=C7-C15**, and press **Enter** (see Figure 9.8)

The contribution margin indicates that if the company produces 10 entertainment centers, then the company's fixed costs (as yet to be determined) must be less than $6,865. What are Artistic Furniture Corporation's fixed costs and how do they reduce the profitability of the company?

FIGURE 9.8

Contribution Margin

	A	B	C	D	E	F	G	H	I
1	**Monthly Income and Statement**								
2	*Artistic Furniture Corporation*								
3									
4	**Revenue**								
5	Units Produced		10						
6	Price Per Unit	$	2,050						
7	Total Revenue	$	20,500						
8									
9	**Variable Costs (per unit)**								
10	Direct Labor	$	410						
11	Direct Material (wood, hardware)	$	615						
12	Direct Supplies	$	51						
13	Sales Commissions	$	103						
14	Overhead	$	185						
15	Total Variable Costs (all units)	$	13,635						
16									
17	**Contribution Margin**								
18	Contribution Margin	$	6,865	← contribution margin is revenue					
19				minus variable cost					
20	**Fixed Costs**								
21									
22	**Profit**								
23									
24									

|◄ ◄ ► ►|\ Documentation \Manufacturing /

Ready

Fixed Costs

A *fixed cost* (or fixed expense) is one that remains constant no matter how many or how few goods or services you manufacture and sell. Paul tells you that fixed costs include the rent on the building, heating and lighting (utilities), equipment leases, and supplies. If all the Artistic employees go on vacation for two weeks, the company must still pay the building rent. Artistic incurs other fixed expenses such as utilities, computers, computer supplies, and communication equipment. Paul asks you to add rows to the Fixed Costs section to hold the four fixed costs and the fixed cost total. The fixed costs are as follows. Rent is $2,500 per month; utilities average $3,280 per month; supplies are $845 per month, and equipment leases amount to $1,968 per month.

Adding rows for fixed costs, entering values, and totaling fixed costs:

1. Click the row selector button for row **22** and drag the mouse through row selector button **26**

2. Click **Insert** and then click **Rows**

3. Type the following labels in the indicated cells, pressing Enter after typing each entry:

    B21: **Rent**

    B22: **Utilities**

    B23: **Supplies**

    B24: **Equipment Leases**

    B25: **Total Fixed Costs**

4. Click cell **B15**, click the **Format Painter** ⬗ button on the Standard toolbar, and click cell **B25** to copy the format from cell B15 and apply it to cell B25

tip: *If you select the wrong cell—either to copy the format from or paint the format to—then click **Undo Paste Special** in the Edit menu and execute step 4 again*

5. Enter the following values and a formula in the indicated cells. Press the down arrow key after typing each entry

C21: **2500**

C22: **3280**

C23: **845**

C24: **1968**

C25: **=SUM(C21:C24)**

6. Click cell **C14**, click the **Format Painter** 🖌 button on the Standard toolbar, and click cell **C24** to copy the format from cell C14 and apply it to cell C24. Compare your results to Figure 9.9

	A	B	C	D	E	F	G	H	I
3									
4	**Revenue**								
5		Units Produced	10						
6		Price Per Unit	$ 2,050						
7		Total Revenue	$ 20,500						
8									
9	**Variable Costs (per unit)**								
10		Direct Labor	$ 410						
11		Direct Material (wood, hardware)	$ 615						
12		Direct Supplies	$ 51						
13		Sales Commissions	$ 103						
14		Overhead	$ 185						
15		Total Variable Costs (all units)	$ 13,635						
16									
17	**Contribution Margin**								
18		Contribution Margin	$ 6,865						
19									
20	**Fixed Costs**								
21		Rent	$ 2,500						
22		Utilities	$ 3,280						
23		Supplies	$ 845						
24		Equipment Leases	$ 1,968						
25		Total Fixed Costs	$ 8,593	← Total Fixed Costs					
26									
27	**Profit**								

Documentation \ Manufacturing /

Ready

FIGURE 9.9

Fixed costs

Profit

Profit is revenue minus the sum of all costs—both fixed and variable, which is the same as the contribution margin minus total fixed costs. The number of units in which profit is zero is called the ***break-even*** point. Naturally, a healthy company sells enough units to generate profits above the break-even point.

Entering labels and writing the profit formula:

1. Click cell **B28** and type **Revenue**

2. Click cell **B29** and type **Total Costs (fixed + variable)**

3. Click cell **B30** and type **Net Income (profit)**

4. Click cell **C28**, type **=C7**, and press **Enter**. Excel displays total revenue—the same value displayed in cell C7

5. In cell C29, type **=C15+C25**

6. Click cell **C30** and type =C28-C29

7. Click cell **C24**, click the **Format Painter** 🖌 button on the Standard tool-bar, and then click cell **C29**

8. Click cell **B25**, click the **Format Painter** 🖌 button, and then click cell **B30**. Cell C30 indicates that Artistic would lose money at the rate of $1,728 per month the way things stand now

9. To view more of the worksheet at once, click **View** on the menu bar and then click **Full Screen**. Excel displays more—perhaps all—of the active worksheet on the screen (see Figure 9.10)

FIGURE 9.10

Artistic loses money producing 10 units

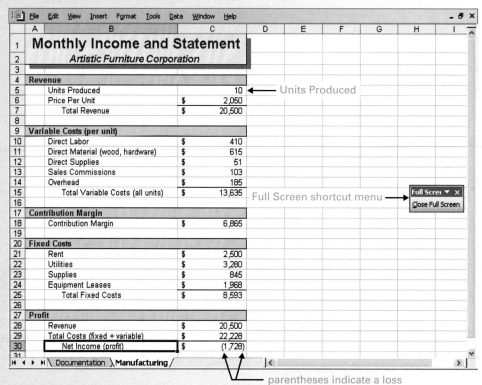

10. Click **Close Full Screen** on the Full Screen shortcut menu to return to normal display

Determining the Break-Even Point

You show Paul the completed Monthly Income and Statement worksheet. While he is not surprised that Artistic would lose money manufacturing and selling 10 units per month, he'd like you to know more about how many units to produce. Perhaps Artistic Furniture Corporation could reduce its production and thereby reduce its variable costs. Alternatively, it could hire more people, produce more units per month, and see what that does to the bottom line—profit.

Paul wants you to produce a worksheet showing the different values for profit by changing the number of units from zero to their current maximum capacity of 30 units.

Break-Even Analysis Using an Equation

You have created an income statement that allows you to change several key values and observe their change on profit. Paul wants to know how many entertainment units Artistic must produce in order to generate a profit.

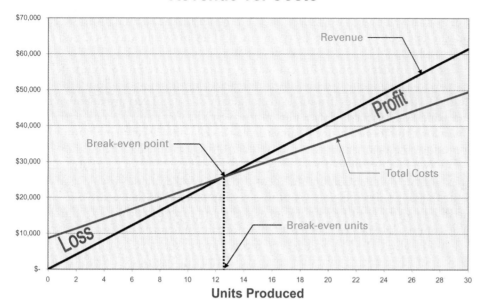

Break-even analysis can help you find the point at which you generate a profit, because it takes into account the relationships among cost, volume, and profit (CVP). The formula below captures the relationship between volume, cost, and profit.

```
Profit = Revenue - (Variable expenses + Fixed expenses)
```

You can rearrange this equation into one that is widely used in CVP analysis to this:

```
Revenue = Variable expenses + Fixed expenses + Profit
```

Break-even occurs when profit equals zero. So, in the case of Artistic concepts, you can rewrite the equation using the number of units produced as a variable and solve for it. In other words, you rewrite the preceding equation using the variable U to stand for the number of units produced (found in cell C5, Figure 9.10):

```
$2,050U = $1,364U + $8,593 + 0
```

If you were to solve the preceding equation for the variable U—the number of units to produce—the break-even production point would be approximately 12.5 units.

Break-Even Analysis Using a Chart

Rather than solve the preceding equation, you can use Excel to create a line chart and then observe the break-even point by locating the point where the revenue and total cost lines cross. Figure 9.11 illustrates the relationship between revenue and costs. Units appear along the X-axis. Values appear on the Y-axis. Notice that revenue is less than total costs up to 12 units. Above the break-even point where the revenue and total costs curves cross, revenue is above the cost curve and thus the company generates a profit.

A spreadsheet approach to determining the break-even point is to perform what-if analysis by changing the value in cell C5 (see Figure 9.10), beginning at zero. That is, you could enter 0 in cell C5 and observe the value in cell C30. Then, type 5 into cell C5 and observe the value for profit. Continuing in this manner is both time-consuming and error-prone. A better approach is to create an Excel data table.

Performing What-If Analysis with a One-Variable Data Table

Paul wants you to take advantage of Excel's quick recalculation and what-if ability to generate a series of results, one after the other. There will be many situations where you will want to perform what-if analysis on a worksheet by varying one or more cells' values repeatedly to see their effect on the entire worksheet. One approach is to type one or more values into worksheet cells and then print the resulting worksheet. Then, you can repeat the previous set by typing new values, observing the result, and printing the worksheet.

Excel provides a more efficient way to examine the results of multiple what-if analyses in a data table. A ***data table*** summarizes key input and output cell values of multiple what-if analyses in a single, rectangular cell range. Excel provides two types of data tables: one-variable data table and two-variable data table. A one-variable data table allows you to specify one input variable—a cell—that Excel changes automatically to produce the data table. As you can guess, a two-variable data table allows you to specify two distinct what-if variables and it generates a table of output values. Both types work in a similar fashion: You identify one or two key input variables and then indicate the range of values you want those key input variables to take on. The key input variable that you want Excel to change is called the ***input cell***. You execute the Data Table command to create a compact table of results. When you do, Excel steps through each input value (or pair of values) and records in the data table how the value changes the output (dependent) formulas you have identified. The ***result cell*** holds the result that is affected by a change in the input cell. It is a value you want to study closely.

help yourself *Press* **F1**, *type* **data table** *in the Search text box of the Microsoft Excel Help task pane, and press* **Enter***. Scroll down the list to locate and then click the hyperlink* **About data tables***. Maximize the Help screen if necessary. Read and optionally print the description of data tables and the examples shown. Click the Help screen* **Close** *button when you are finished. Close the task pane*

Examining a Simple One-Variable Data Table

Learn how a one-variable data table works by examining a simple example. Suppose you want to know how much revenue you will generate if you sell 2, 4, or more units of a product whose price is $24.50. Figure 9.12 shows a worksheet that illustrates a one-variable data table. Cell B4 contains the formula =B2*B3, the product of the number of units sold or produced times the per-unit price. The input cell is B2, the number of units produced. That is the value you will ask Excel to vary in increments of 2 to see the resulting revenues. The set of possible units produced, called the ***input values***, are located in cells D3 through D12. Cell E2 contains the result cell, which is the formula =B4 because it references the formula in cell B4. Below the result cell, in cells E3 through E12, are the result values. The ***result values*** are the computed answer for each input value that Excel uses. The cell range D2:E12 is the one-variable data table, which contains the input values and resulting output or result values. You can also construct a data table in two rows. In that case, the input values run along the first row and the result values appear in the second row. The input value must be placed in the first row or column.

While a one-variable data table can contain only one row or column of input values, you can specify several rows or columns of *result* values. You will see exactly how this works as you create a one-variable data table displaying several results for Artistic Furniture Corporation.

Creating a One-Variable Data Table

Paul wants you to create a one-variable data table in which you determine values for net income (profit) when varying the number of units produced from zero to 30 in increments of two units (0, 2, 4, etc.). When you create the data table, you will select C5 as the input cell, because it holds the number of units produced—the value that all other formulas in the Artistic worksheet depend on.

FIGURE 9.12
Simple example of a one-variable data table

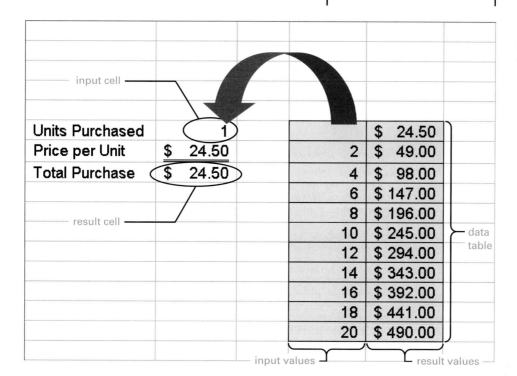

task reference Creating a One-Variable Data Table

- Decide whether you want values for the input cell to appear in a row or down a column

- If you arrange a data table in columns, then insert the input values in the first column beginning below the first row of the table and place a reference (a formula) to the result cell in the cell above and to the right of the column of input values

- If you arrange a data table in rows, then insert the input values in the first row beginning in the second column of the data table and place a reference (a formula) to the result cell in the cell below the input row and to its left

- Select the table, click **Data**, and then click **Table**

- Enter the cell reference of the input cell in the Row input cell box if input values are in a row or enter the cell reference of the input cell in the Column input cell box if the input values are in a column in the data table

- Click **OK**

Entering an input values column and results formulas:

1. Click cell **E4** and type **Units**

2. Click cell **E5**, type **0**, click cell **E6**, type **2**, and press **Enter**

3. Select the cell range **E5:E6**, click **Format** on the menu bar, click **Cells**, click the **Number** tab (if necessary), click **Number** in the Category list box, type **0** in the Decimal places spin control box (if necessary) and click **OK** to apply the formatting changes to the two cells

4. With cells **E5** and **E6** still selected, drag the fill handle down through cell **E20** and then release the mouse. Excel creates a series of ascending numbers from 0 to 30 in increments of 2

5. Click cell **F4** and type **=C28**, which is a reference to the revenue formula—one of the formulas for which you want to create a result values column

6. Click cell **G4** and type **=C29**, which is a reference to the total costs cell—another formula for which you want to create a series of result values

7. Click cell **H4** and type **=C30** (a reference to the profit formula) and press **Enter** (see Figure 9.13)

FIGURE 9.13

Input values and result cells in a data table

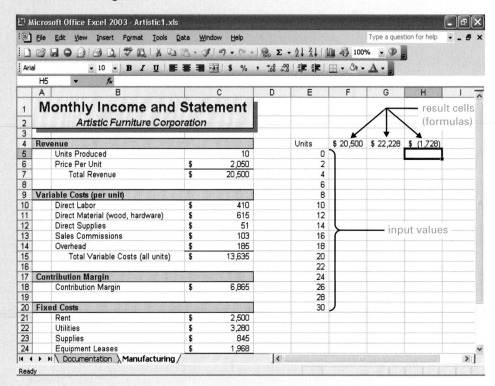

Before you create the data table, you can format the result cells so that they look like labels. That little trick keeps the formulas intact and simultaneously supplies labels for the columns of the data table. Reformatting does not affect the results in the data table. It simply makes the results easier to read.

Formatting formulas in the top row of the data table to look like labels:

1. Right-click cell **F4**

2. Click **Format**, click **Cells**, click **Custom** in the Category list box, and select all of the text in the Type text box

3. Type **"Revenue"**—be sure to type both quotation marks (see Figure 9.14), and then click **OK** to apply the text format

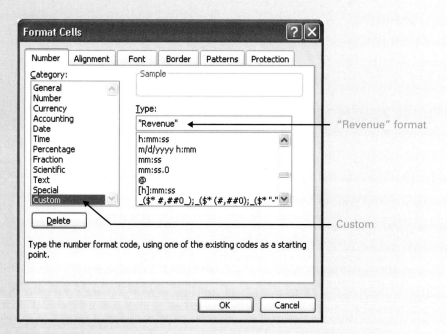

FIGURE 9.14
Applying a text format to a formula

4. Click cell **G4** and repeat steps 2 and 3, typing **"Costs"** (include the quotation marks) in step 3

5. Click cell **H4** and repeat step 2

6. Type **"Profit";"Profit"** and then click **OK** to apply the text format. You type the quoted string Profit twice, separated by a semicolon, so that Excel displays *Profit* for both positive and negative values. Notice the formula bar shows that the cell contains the formula =C30, whereas the format displays a label (see Figure 9.15)

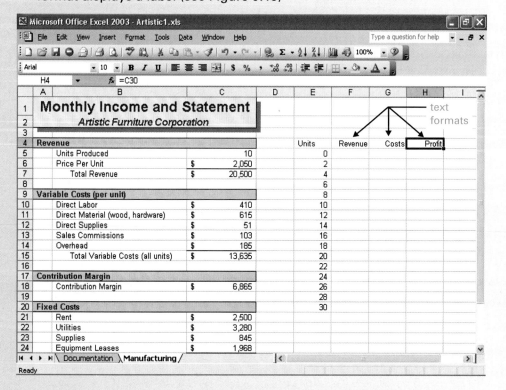

FIGURE 9.15
Completed text formats for result cells

With the input values and result cells in place along the edges of the as-yet imaginary table, you can create the data table to fill in result values for all listed input values.

Finishing the one-variable data table:

1. Select the cell range **E4:H20**

2. Click **Data** and then click **Table**

3. Click the **Column input cell** box and type **C5**, which is the input cell value that Excel will replace temporarily with each value in the input values column (see Figure 9.16)

FIGURE 9.16

Table dialog box

Column input cell holds the number of units produced

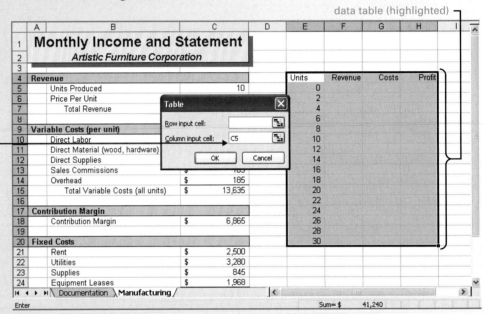

4. Click **OK** to complete the data table operation (see Figure 9.17)

FIGURE 9.17

Completed one-variable data table

results values for three separate formulas appear in three columns

					Units	Revenue	Costs	Profit
1	**Monthly Income and Statement**							
2	*Artistic Furniture Corporation*							
3								
4	**Revenue**							
5	Units Produced		10		0	$ -	$ 8,593	$ (8,593)
6	Price Per Unit	$	2,050		2	$ 4,100	$ 11,320	$ (7,220)
7	Total Revenue	$	20,500		4	$ 8,200	$ 14,047	$ (5,847)
8					6	$ 12,300	$ 16,774	$ (4,474)
9	**Variable Costs (per unit)**				8	$ 16,400	$ 19,501	$ (3,101)
10	Direct Labor	$	410		10	$ 20,500	$ 22,228	$ (1,728)
11	Direct Material (wood, hardware)	$	615		12	$ 24,600	$ 24,955	$ (355)
12	Direct Supplies	$	51		14	$ 28,700	$ 27,682	$ 1,018
13	Sales Commissions	$	103		16	$ 32,800	$ 30,409	$ 2,391
14	Overhead	$	185		18	$ 36,900	$ 33,136	$ 3,764
15	Total Variable Costs (all units)	$	13,635		20	$ 41,000	$ 35,863	$ 5,137
16					22	$ 45,100	$ 38,590	$ 6,510
17	**Contribution Margin**				24	$ 49,200	$ 41,317	$ 7,883
18	Contribution Margin	$	6,865		26	$ 53,300	$ 44,044	$ 9,256
19					28	$ 57,400	$ 46,771	$ 10,629
20	**Fixed Costs**				30	$ 61,500	$ 49,498	$ 12,002
21	Rent	$	2,500					
22	Utilities	$	3,280					
23	Supplies	$	845					
24	Equipment Leases	$	1,968					

Ready   Sum= $ 1,025,240

5. Click any cell to deselect the data table

The three columns of results in the cell range F5:H20 show the revenue, costs, and profit for units ranging from 0 to 30. By looking at the last column of the data table, you can see clearly that Artistic must manufacture and sell more than 12 units to be profitable.

Performing What-If Analysis with a Two-Variable Data Table

The data table you created above displays the effect on the company's profitability of changing a single variable, the number of units produced. You can create a *two-variable data table* that computes the effects of two variables on a single formula. Like a one-variable data table, a two-variable data table is rectangular and the results cells contain formulas that compute results values. However, a two-variable data table differs from a one-variable data table in several ways:

- The data table contains input values in the leftmost column (the first variable) and the topmost row (the second variable) of the table

- The formula that Excel uses to calculate the two-variable data table results must appear in the upper-left corner of the data table at the intersection of the row and column that contains the two sets of input values

- You can include only one output formula in a two-variable data table

Creating a Two-Variable Data Table

Paul anticipates slowing down production for the summer months as a number of his employees take vacation. By carefully scheduling when the employees take their two-week vacation, he will not have to shut down because there are enough skilled workers to build the entertainment centers. However, he determines that he cannot produce more than 10 to 12 entertainment units in the summer months. As you recall from the analysis earlier in this chapter, Artistic loses money if it produces fewer than 13 units per month at the current level of costs. Paul wants to investigate if there is any combination of units produced per month and sale prices that would yield a profit. In other words, is there a way to produce fewer units and perhaps raise the price per unit and still stay profitable? A two-variable data table answers that question.

---

task reference Creating a Two-Variable Data Table

- Type the formula or a reference to the input cell in the upper-left cell in the data table

- Type the first variable values in the row to the right of the formula

- Type the second variable values in the column below the formula

- Select a cell range that encompasses the formula, row values, and column values

- Click **Data** on the menu bar and then click **Table**

- Type the address of the input cell that corresponds to the row values in the Row input cell text box

- Type the address of the input cell that corresponds to the column values in the Column input cell text box

- Click **OK**

Filling in the labels, row values, and column values of the two-variable data table:

1. Save the workbook under the new name **Artistic2.xls**

2. Click cell **F22** and type **Units Produced**

3. Click cell **E24**, type **2000**, click cell **E25**, type **2100**, and press **Enter**

4. Select cells **E24:E25**, release the mouse, click the fill handle, drag it down through cell **E34**, and release the mouse. Excel creates a range of values from $2,000 through $3,000

5. Click cell **F23**, type **2**, and press **Enter**. Excel displays $2 because Accounting is the default format

6. Click cell **E20**, click the **Format Painter** button, and click cell **F23** to alter its format

7. Select the cell range **F23:K23**, click **Edit** on the menu bar, point to **Fill**, and click **Series**. Excel displays the Series dialog box (see Figure 9.18)

FIGURE 9.18

Series dialog box

type 2 for the Step value ——

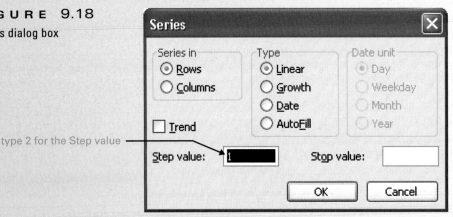

8. Type **2** in the Step value text box and then click the **OK** button to create the series of numbers from 2 through 12 (see Figure 9.19)

FIGURE 9.19

Completing a data table's column and row input values

	C	D	E	F	G	H	I	J	K	L	M
12	$ 51		14	$ 28,700	$ 27,682	$ 1,018					
13	$ 103		16	$ 32,800	$ 30,409	$ 2,391					
14	$ 185		18	$ 36,900	$ 33,136	$ 3,764					
15	$ 13,635		20	$ 41,000	$ 35,863	$ 5,137					
16			22	$ 45,100	$ 38,590	$ 6,510					
17			24	$ 49,200	$ 41,317	$ 7,883					
18	$ 6,865		26	$ 53,300	$ 44,044	$ 9,256					
19			28	$ 57,400	$ 46,771	$ 10,629					
20			30	$ 61,500	$ 49,498	$ 12,002				row input values	
21	$ 2,500										
22	$ 3,280			Units Produced							
23	$ 845			2	4	6	8	10	12		
24	$ 1,968		$ 2,000								
25	$ 8,593		$ 2,100								
26			$ 2,200								
27			$ 2,300								
28	$ 20,500		$ 2,400								
29	$ 22,228		$ 2,500		column input values						
30	$ (1,728)		$ 2,600								
31			$ 2,700								
32			$ 2,800								
33			$ 2,900								
34			$ 3,000								
35											
36											

Documentation \ Manufacturing /

Ready   Sum=42

The first row in the developing two-variable data table contains the series of production quantities you want Excel to plug into the revenue, costs, and profit equations to see if varying them, along with the price, generates a profit. The left-most column contains candidate prices for the entertainment center that has been priced at $2,050 up until now. The question that the two-variable data table will answer is this: What profit, if any, is created with the combinations of production quantities and prices. Each results cell will display the profit value for a single quantity-produced/price pair in the data table.

You are ready to create the profit formula and then complete the data table building process. First, you will write in the upper-left corner of the data table the formula referencing the profit cell—the model equation for which results will be created. Then, you will execute the Data Table command requesting Excel to fill in a series of results for the quantity/price variable pairs.

Completing the two-variable data table:

1. Click cell **E23** type **=C30** (a reference to the cell that calculates profit), and press **Enter**

2. Right-click cell **E23**, click **Format Cells** on the shortcut menu to open the Format Cells dialog box

3. Click the **Number** tab, if necessary, click **Custom** in the Category list, click the **Type** text box, press **Home**, press and hold the **Shift** key, press and release the **End** key, and release the **Shift** key to select the format appearing in the Type list box

4. Type **"Price";"Price"** including the quotation marks and the semicolon separating the identical character strings (see Figure 9.20)

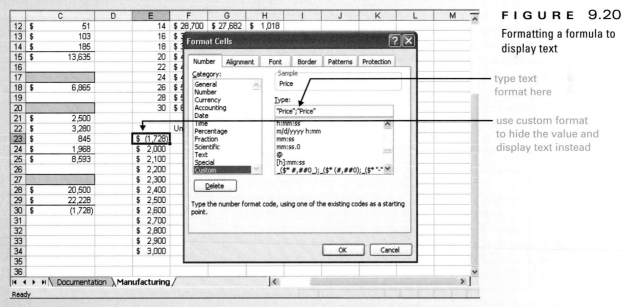

FIGURE 9.20

Formatting a formula to display text

type text format here

use custom format to hide the value and display text instead

5. Click **OK**

6. Select the cell range **E23:K34**, click **Data**, and click **Table**. The Table dialog box appears

7. Type **C5** in the *Row input cell* text box, because C5 contains the number of units produced in the original worksheet and corresponds to the changing values in the top row of the data table

8. Press the **Tab** key and type **C6** in the *Column input cell* text box. C6 holds the original sales price and is used in formulas throughout the worksheet. It corresponds to the column of changing sales price values

9. Click **OK** to complete the operation and generate the data table (see Figure 9.21), and click any cell to deselect the cell range

FIGURE 9.21

Completed two-variable data table

	C	D	E	F	G	H	I	J	K	L	M
12	$ 51		14	$ 28,700	$ 27,682	$ 1,018					
13	$ 103		16	$ 32,800	$ 30,409	$ 2,391					
14	$ 185		18	$ 36,900	$ 33,136	$ 3,764					
15	$ 13,635		20	$ 41,000	$ 35,863	$ 5,137					
16			22	$ 45,100	$ 38,590	$ 6,510					
17			24	$ 49,200	$ 41,317	$ 7,883					
18	$ 6,865		26	$ 53,300	$ 44,044	$ 9,256					
19			28	$ 57,400	$ 46,771	$ 10,629					
20			30	$ 61,500	$ 49,498	$ 12,002					
21	$ 2,500										
22	$ 3,280				Units Produced						
23	$ 845		Price	2	4	6	8	10	12		
24	$ 1,968		$ 2,000	$ (7,315)	$ (6,037)	$ (4,759)	$ (3,481)	$ (2,203)	$ (925)		
25	$ 8,593		$ 2,100	$ (7,125)	$ (5,657)	$ (4,189)	$ (2,721)	$ (1,253)	$ 215		
26			$ 2,200	$ (6,935)	$ (5,277)	$ (3,619)	$ (1,961)	$ (303)	$ 1,355		
27			$ 2,300	$ (6,745)	$ (4,897)	$ (3,049)	$ (1,201)	$ 647	$ 2,495		
28	$ 20,500		$ 2,400	$ (6,555)	$ (4,517)	$ (2,479)	$ (441)	$ 1,597	$ 3,635		
29	$ 22,228		$ 2,500	$ (6,365)	$ (4,137)	$ (1,909)	$ 319	$ 2,547	$ 4,775		
30	$ (1,728)		$ 2,600	$ (6,175)	$ (3,757)	$ (1,339)	$ 1,079	$ 3,497	$ 5,915		
31			$ 2,700	$ (5,985)	$ (3,377)	$ (769)	$ 1,839	$ 4,447	$ 7,055		
32			$ 2,800	$ (5,795)	$ (2,997)	$ (199)	$ 2,599	$ 5,397	$ 8,195		
33			$ 2,900	$ (5,605)	$ (2,617)	$ 371	$ 3,359	$ 6,347	$ 9,335		
34			$ 3,000	$ (5,415)	$ (2,237)	$ 941	$ 4,119	$ 7,297	$ 10,475		
35											
36											

M ◄ ► M \ Documentation \ Manufacturing /

Ready   Sum=-26656

10. Save the workbook by clicking the **Save** button on the Standard toolbar

What are Artistic's options? There are several. The lower right portion of the data table shows several positive values—profits—for combinations of production quantities and prices. For instance, Artistic Furniture Corporation can make a profit making and selling 12 units if it charges $2,100 for each unit.

Editing Data Tables

One-variable and two-variable data tables contain special formulas that compute and display the results values. These special formulas appearing in a data table are part of a related group called an *array formula*.

Deleting Data Table Result Values

If you try to delete any cell that is part of the array formula—cell G30 (see Figure 9.21) for example—Excel displays an alert box with the message *Cannot change part of a table*. If you decide to erase part of a data table and then re-create it, you must select all the results values and then delete the entire array of answers. Once you have deleted the results values, you can select the data table including the input values and formula(s) and then execute the Table command of the Data menu to regenerate the table.

Adding Data Table Input Values

Because the results values are, in fact, formulas, you can alter any of the input values in the input row or input column. After you do so, Excel automatically recalculates the results values to reflect the change in one or more input values. You can add new input values, but you must re-execute the Table command to add the new results values and update the formula array.

Copying Data Table Results

You can copy the table results to another location of the original worksheet. One reason you might want to do this is to preserve a data table's results before you change input values and generate different results values. You can copy all or any portion of the results values to another location using standard copy paste operations. For example, you can select the cell range F24:H30, press Ctrl+C to copy the results to the Clipboard, click cell E55, and press Ctrl+V to paste the cells to the new locations. When you copy array formulas out of the data table range, Excel changes the array formulas to constants.

---

making the grade

SESSION 9.1

1. The three-letter abbreviation for the process of examining the relationship between a product's cost, number of units produced, and profit is what?

2. When revenue is equal to total costs and profit is zero, this is called the _____ point.

3. A _____ cost is one that varies directly with the number of units that a company produces, whereas a _____ cost is one that remains constant no matter how many or how few goods or services a company sells.

4. A _____ table summarizes key input and output cell values of multiple what-if analyses in a single rectangular cell range.

5. The key input variable that you want Excel to change in a one-variable data table is called the _____ cell, and the _____ cell holds the computed answer that is affected by a change in the variable.

6. A _____-variable data table allows you to perform what-if analysis on more than one formula.

SESSION 9.2 USING SCENARIOS

In this section, you will learn how to use the Excel Scenario Manager, create scenarios, edit scenarios, delete and hide scenarios, and view scenario results.

Doing More Complex What-If Analysis

Data tables are fine for simple situations involving only one or two variables, but most managers' decisions involve many more variables. The combination of values assigned to one or more variable cells in a what-if analysis is called a *scenario*. A scenario consists of selected *variables*, which are cells in which Excel substitutes different values. A scenario identifies the cells that contain values you want to change as *changing cells*. *Scenario management* is the process of examining individual variables or changing cells and assigning a range of values to them. Excel's scenario manager allows you to create scenarios, alter existing scenarios, display individual scenarios, and produce a summary report, called a **scenario report**.

Paul carefully studied both your one-variable data table and the two-variable data table that clearly show the break-even point based on varying the number of units produced and the sale price of each unit. However, he wants to examine the effect of changing more of the cells in the Artistic worksheet. For example, Paul knows that there are other variables that Artistic Furniture Corporation can modify to change its profit picture. He has identified four distinct groups of variable values that he would like you to study—four scenarios. Figure 9.22 depicts the four scenarios.

EXCEL

FIGURE 9.22
Four scenarios

Cell and Meaning		Scenario Names and Cell Values			
		Current	Conserve	Efficient	High Cost
C5	Units Produced	10	25	20	28
C6	Price/Unit	$ 2,050	$ 1,950	$ 2,100	$ 2,400
C10	Labor/Unit	$ 410	$ 390	$ 425	$ 450
C11	Material/Unit	$ 615	$ 554	$ 615	$ 600
C14	Overhead/Unit	$ 185	$ 170	$ 200	$ 220
C22	Utilities	$ 3,280	$ 2,900	$ 3,400	$ 3,600
C23	Supplies	$ 845	$ 650	$ 900	$ 900

Paul believes that the values of 10 variables in the Artistic worksheet will have the largest effect on the company's profit. They include variable costs, revenue, fixed costs, units produced (production quantities per month), sales price per unit, labor per unit, material cost per unit, overhead, utilities, and supplies.

Paul wants you to work with the changes shown in Figure 9.22 to do a what-if analysis to see the result of each scenario. The best solution for evaluating these various proposals is to use scenarios with Excel's built-in Scenario Manager and produce a summary report that outlines each of the input or changing cells and displays output cells of your choice.

Opening the Artistic Furniture Corporation Workbook

Paul has prepared a worksheet for you to use that matches the one you created in Session 9.1 but omits the data tables. You will use the worksheet as you develop scenarios in this session. Begin by opening the newly created workbook and entering a few preliminary labels.

Opening the Artistic Furniture Corporation scenario workbook:

1. If you took a break since you completed the last session, ensure that Office Excel 2003 is running

2. Open the workbook **ex09ArtisticScenarios.xls** and immediately save it under the new name **Artistic3.xls** to preserve the original file

3. Click the **Name box** list arrow on the left end of the formula bar and click the name **CreateDate**

4. Type today's date and press **Enter**

5. Type your name and press **Enter**

6. Click the **Manufacturing** worksheet tab to make that sheet active

The worksheet is similar to the one you created in Session 9.1. Notice that cell C5 contains the current production assumption of 10 units per month, and cell C6 contains the selling price of each entertainment unit, $2,050. The remaining variable and fixed costs are the baseline values found in the Current scenario.

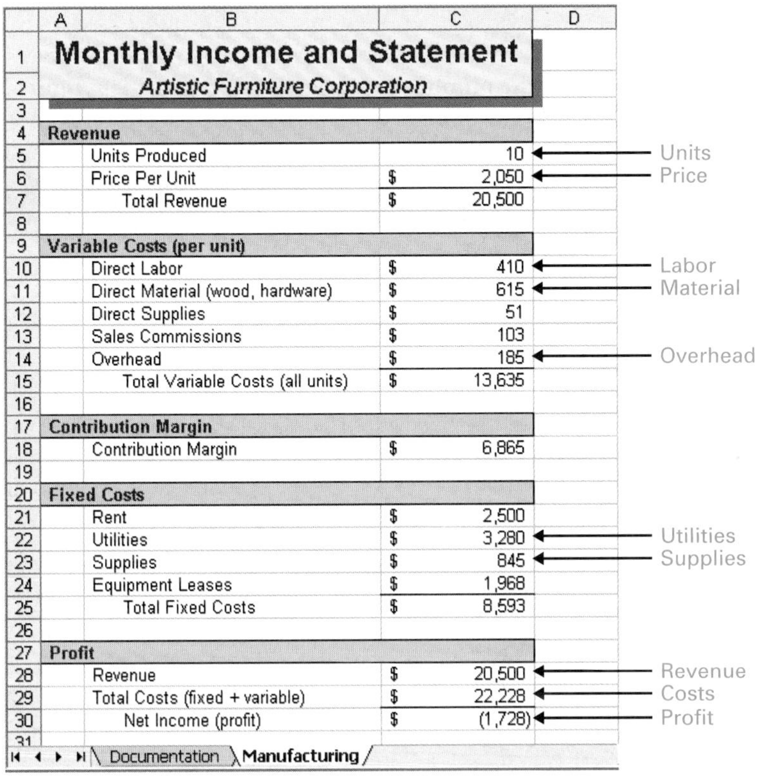

FIGURE 9.23

Input and results cells to receive names

	A	B	C	D	
1	**Monthly Income and Statement**				
2	*Artistic Furniture Corporation*				
3					
4	**Revenue**				
5		Units Produced		10	← Units
6		Price Per Unit	$	2,050	← Price
7		Total Revenue	$	20,500	
8					
9	**Variable Costs (per unit)**				
10		Direct Labor	$	410	← Labor
11		Direct Material (wood, hardware)	$	615	← Material
12		Direct Supplies	$	51	
13		Sales Commissions	$	103	
14		Overhead	$	185	← Overhead
15		Total Variable Costs (all units)	$	13,635	
16					
17	**Contribution Margin**				
18		Contribution Margin	$	6,865	
19					
20	**Fixed Costs**				
21		Rent	$	2,500	
22		Utilities	$	3,280	← Utilities
23		Supplies	$	845	← Supplies
24		Equipment Leases	$	1,968	
25		Total Fixed Costs	$	8,593	
26					
27	**Profit**				
28		Revenue	$	20,500	← Revenue
29		Total Costs (fixed + variable)	$	22,228	← Costs
30		Net Income (profit)	$	(1,728)	← Profit
31					

Documentation \ Manufacturing /

Before you create your first scenario, you will find it very helpful if you name each of the input cells in the scenario as well as the result cells. The reason to name these cells is that names appear in the scenario output when you produce a report, and associating names with input cells and result cells provides built-in documentation. Figure 9.23 shows the Manufacturing worksheet with pointers to the cells you will name and the suggested names you will assign in the exercise that follows.

Defining names for selected input and result cells:

1. Click cell **C5**, click the **Name box**, type **Units**, and press **Enter**

2. Repeat step 1, naming the following cells with the listed names. Remember to press Enter after typing each name:

   C6: **Price**

   C10: **Labor**

   C11: **Material**

   C14: **Overhead**

   C22: **Utilities**

   C23: **Supplies**

   C28: **Revenue**

   C29: **Costs**

   C30: **Profit**

tip: *Remember to press **Enter** before clicking another cell. Otherwise, Excel discards the name*

EXCEL

Creating Scenarios

You create one or more scenarios by using Excel's Scenario Manager. You can specify up to 32 cell values in each scenario, and the number of scenarios you can create is limited only by the amount of memory your computer has.

---

task reference   Creating a Scenario

- Click **Tools** and click **Scenarios** to open the Scenario Manager
- Click the **Add** button and type a scenario name
- Specify the changing (input) cells in the scenario
- Type commentary in the Comment text box and then click the **OK** button
- Type the values for each changing cell, scrolling the list if necessary, and then click **OK**
- Click **Close** to close the Scenario Manager

When you view your first scenario, Excel replaces all the changing cells with the values you specify in the scenario. If you want to preserve the original values in those cells, you should create a scenario that holds the current values in the worksheet. That way, you can quickly restore the worksheet to its original form using the scenario. That will be the first scenario you create—one you will call *Current*.

help yourself *Press **F1**, type **scenario** in the Search text box of the Microsoft Excel Help task pane, and press **Enter**. Click the hyperlink **About scenarios**. (You may have to scroll the Search Results list.) Maximize the Help screen if necessary. Read or print the description of scenarios. Click the Help screen **Close** button when you are finished, and close the task pane*

Creating a default scenario called Current and defining the changing cells:

1. Click **Tools** and then click **Scenarios**. The Scenario Manager dialog box appears (see Figure 9.24)

2. Click the **Add** button. Excel opens the Add Scenario dialog box

3. Type **Current** in the Scenario Name text box and press the **Tab** key to move to the Changing cells box

4. Click the **Collapse dialog box** 🔳 button to minimize the dialog box

5. Scroll to the top of the worksheet and then click cell **C5**

6. Press and hold the **Ctrl** key, click cell **C6** (Price Per Unit), click cell **C10** (Direct Labor), click cell **C11** (Direct Material), click cell **C14** (Overhead), click cell **C22** (Utilities), click cell **C23** (Supplies), release the Ctrl key, and press **Enter** to finalize your Changing cells selection

7. Press the **Tab** key to jump to the Comment text box and type **Profit for a typical production level**. This provides documentation for the set of values you are about to set for the selected cells (see Figure 9.25)

8. Ensure that the Prevent changes check box contains a check. This protects the scenario from being deleted inadvertently

9. Click the **OK** button. Excel displays the Scenario Values dialog box in which you specify the value to place in each changing cell

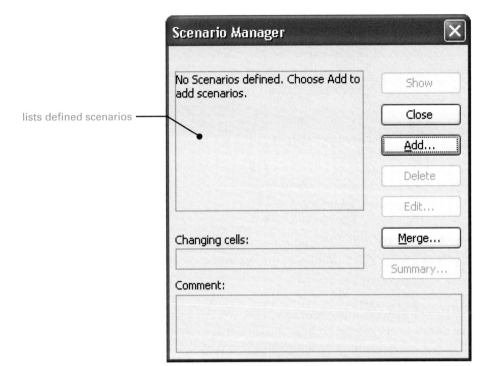

FIGURE 9.24
Scenario Manager dialog box

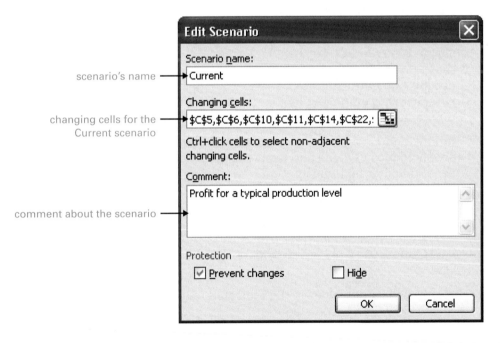

FIGURE 9.25
Specifying a scenario's changing cells

Once you have told Excel's Scenario Manager which cells Office Excel 2003 can change, you can specify the exact values for each changing cell for one or more scenarios. You define the values for the Current scenario next.

Specifying values for all changing cells in a scenario:

1. Click and drag the scroll box next to the changing cells values to view all seven of them (see Figure 9.26)

FIGURE 9.26
Scenario Values dialog
box

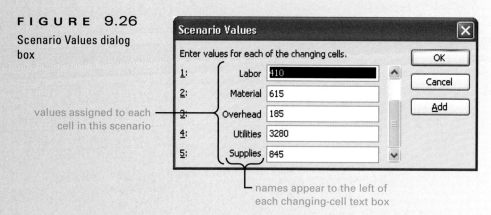

values assigned to each
cell in this scenario

names appear to the left of
each changing-cell text box

2. Click the **OK** button to add the scenario to the list of scenarios. Excel displays the Scenario Manager dialog box

Having defined one of four scenarios, you can proceed to define the other three. The difficult part is done, because you do not need to specify the changing cells again. Next, you will create three scenarios for the same set of changing cells by typing a complete new set of changing *values* for each scenario.

Adding three other scenarios:

1. Click the **Add** button in the Scenario Manager dialog box, type **Conserve** in the Scenario name text box, and press the **Tab** key *twice* to select the Comment text box

2. With the entire comment selected, type **Produce more units and simultaneously reduce variable and fixed costs**, and click **OK**. Excel displays the Scenario Values text box

3. Type **25** in the Units box and press **Tab**

tip: *If you accidentally press the Enter key after entering a value, Excel closes the Scenario Values dialog box. Simply click the **Edit** button in the Scenario Manager dialog box and then click the **OK** button in the Edit Scenario dialog box to continue entering values in the Scenario Values dialog box*

4. Type the following values in the indicated text boxes and press the **Tab** key after you type each value:

Price: **1950**

Labor: **390**

Material: **554**

Overhead: **170**

Utilities: **2900**

Supplies: **650**

5. Click **OK** in the Scenario Values dialog box to complete the scenario. Excel displays the Scenario Manager, which now contains two scenarios— *Current* and *Conserve*

6. Click the **Add** button in the Scenario Manager dialog box, type **Efficient** in the Scenario name text box, press the **Tab** key twice to move to the Comment text box, and type **Produce 20 units, sell each unit at a higher price, and increase costs**, and click **OK**

7. Type the following values in the indicated text boxes, pressing the **Tab** key after you finish typing each value:

Units: **20**

Price: **2100**

Labor: **425**

Material: **615**

Overhead: **200**

Utilities: **3400**

Supplies: **900**

8. Click **OK** to complete this scenario

9. Click the **Add** button in the Scenario Manager dialog box, type **High Cost** in the Scenario name text box, press **Tab** twice to move to the Comment text box, type **Produce 28 units, sell each unit at a very high price, and increase costs**, and click **OK**

10. Type the following values in the indicated text boxes, pressing the Tab key after you finish typing each value:

Units: **28**

Price: **2400**

Labor: **450**

Material: **600**

Overhead: **220**

Utilities: **3600**

Supplies: **900**

11. Click **OK** to complete this scenario. Excel displays Scenario Manager containing four scenarios (see Figure 9.27)

12. Click **Close** to close the Scenario Manager

With four scenarios defined and the Scenario Manager dialog box displayed, you have several choices. You can select a scenario by name and then click the Show button to request that Excel plug in the values you specified earlier into the changing cells. You can also delete a scenario, add a scenario, edit an existing scenario, merge scenarios together, or produce a summary report. In addition, you could click the close button to save all the scenarios you have created. Excel saves scenarios with the worksheet in which they have been created. Each worksheet in a workbook can have its own scenarios, all managed by the Scenario Manager. Each time you load a workbook, all of its scenarios are available to you.

Paul wants to see the consequences of applying these different scenario what-if values. He asks you to show him each one in turn.

FIGURE 9.27

Scenario Manager
containing four scenarios

four named scenarios ———

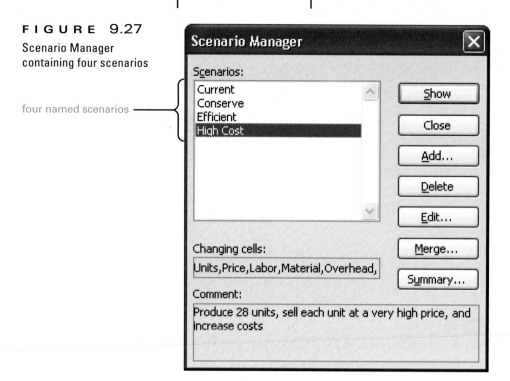

Showing Scenarios

After you create one or more scenarios, you can see their effect by opening the Scenario Manager, selecting a scenario, and requesting Excel to apply that scenario's values to their respective cells.

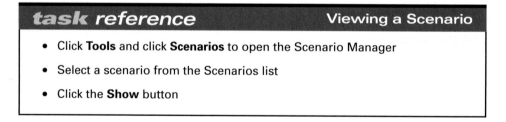

task *reference*   **Viewing a Scenario**

- Click **Tools** and click **Scenarios** to open the Scenario Manager
- Select a scenario from the Scenarios list
- Click the **Show** button

Next, you will open the scenario manager and view each scenario. Pay particular attention to cell C30, containing profit, after you apply each scenario. First, you will display the worksheet full screen to be able to see as much of it as possible before you apply different scenarios.

Viewing a scenario:

1. Click **View** and then click **Full Screen**. Excel opens the worksheet in full screen view and removes any previously visible toolbars

2. Scroll the worksheet so that you can see cells C5 through C30 on the screen at once. If it is not possible on your screen to see that range of cells, then scroll the worksheet up just enough to display cell C30 at the bottom of the screen

3. Click **Tools** and then click **Scenarios** to display the Scenario Manager dialog box

4. Move the dialog box to the right, if necessary, so it does not obscure column C

5. Click **Conserve** in the Scenarios list box and then click the **Show** button to apply the scenario's values. Excel inserts the values into the changing cells and recalculates the worksheet (see Figure 9.28). Notice that the Net Income (cell C30) contains $9,170

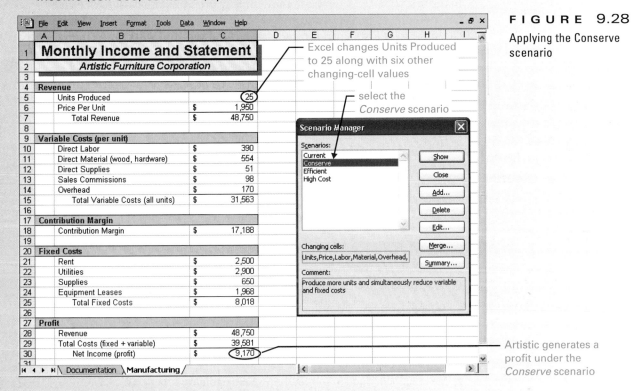

FIGURE 9.28

Applying the Conserve scenario

Excel places the value 25 into cell C5, the number of units produced. In addition, the other six changing-cell values appear in cells C6, C10, C11, C14, C22, and C23. Paul, who is looking at the worksheet on your computer, is pleased to see that the Conserve scenario produces a profit.

How does this scenario compare with the others? Which one creates the most profit? Apply the other scenarios to answer these questions.

Viewing Artistic's other scenarios:

1. With the Scenario Manager open, double-click the **Efficient** scenario in the Scenarios list box. Excel applies the seven changing-cell values to the worksheet and recalculates it. Profit is $5,312 under the Efficient scenario

2. Double-click the **High Cost** scenario in the Scenarios list box. Excel applies the seven changing-cell values of the High Cost scenario to the worksheet and recalculates it. Profit is $17,884 under the High Cost scenario—the highest value so far

3. Double-click the **Current** scenario in the Scenarios list box to restore the worksheet to its original values

4. Click the **Close** button to close the Scenario Manager dialog box

5. Click **View** on the menu bar, and then click **Full Screen** to restore the screen to its normal display

In the best scenario, High Cost, the company produces at near capacity, charges 20 percent more for its product, and incurs a slight increase in variable and fixed costs. Which course to follow depends on several factors, and Paul will have to mull over the consequences. Meanwhile, Paul wants you to make changes to the High Cost scenario by increasing the unit sale price to $2,250, increasing the utilities to $3,800, and increasing the supplies variable cost to $1,100. Then he wants you to rerun the scenario so that he can review it.

Editing a Scenario

To make changes to one or more scenarios, you click open the Scenario Manager, and then the Scenario Manager's Edit button. The Scenario Manager displays the Edit Scenario dialog box, which is identical to the Add Scenario dialog box. You can change the name of the scenario, remove existing changing cells, or specify a different set of changing cells.

---

task reference   **Editing a Scenario**

- Click **Tools** and click **Scenarios** to open the Scenario Manager

- Select a scenario from the Scenarios list

- Click the **Edit** button

- Make any changes in the Edit Scenario dialog box and click **OK**

- Make any changes in the Scenario Values dialog box and click **OK**

When anyone edits an existing scenario, Excel automatically adds text to the end of the commentary in the Comment box. You will find this information useful when you want to keep track of who is making changes to scenarios.

Editing Artistic's High Cost scenario:

1. Click **Tools** and then click **Scenarios** to open the Scenario Manager

2. Click **High Cost** in the Scenarios list box and click the **Edit** button. Notice that Excel adds a "Modified by..." message below the current comment in the Comment box (see Figure 9.29)

3. Click **OK**, because you do not need to modify the Scenario name, Changing cells, or Comment. The Scenario Values dialog box appears

4. Press the **Tab** key to select the value in the Price box, and then type **2250**

5. Press the **Tab** key *four times* to select the Utilities box, and then type **3800**

6. Press the **Tab** key to select the Supplies box, type **1100**, and click **OK**. Excel redisplays the Scenario Manager

FIGURE 9.29
Excel's comment in the
Comment list box

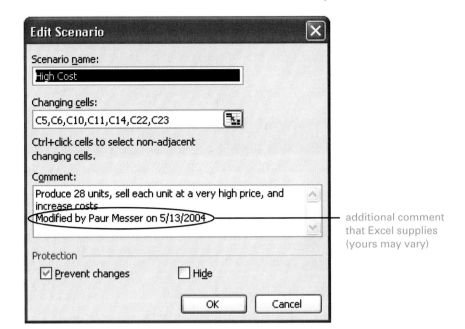

With the changes in place, you can view the newly edited scenario, High Cost, to review its effects.

Viewing an edited scenario:

1. With the Scenario Manager open, double-click the **High Cost** scenario to apply that scenario's values to the designated changing cells

2. Click the **Close** button to close the Scenario Manager, and then scroll the worksheet so that you can see cell C30, Net Income (profit), near the bottom of the screen (see Figure 9.30). Notice that profit has dropped to $13,494, which is probably a more realistic projection

3. Click the **Save** button on the Standard toolbar to save the workbook and the scenarios it contains

Deleting a Scenario

After much thought, Paul has decided that the Current scenario, which you created to preserve the original values of the worksheet, is no longer needed.

---

task reference   Deleting a Scenario

- Click **Tools** and click **Scenarios** to open the Scenario Manager
- Select a scenario from the Scenarios list
- Click the **Delete** button

Delete the *Current* scenario from the list of defined scenarios. Be aware that you cannot revive a scenario once you have deleted it.

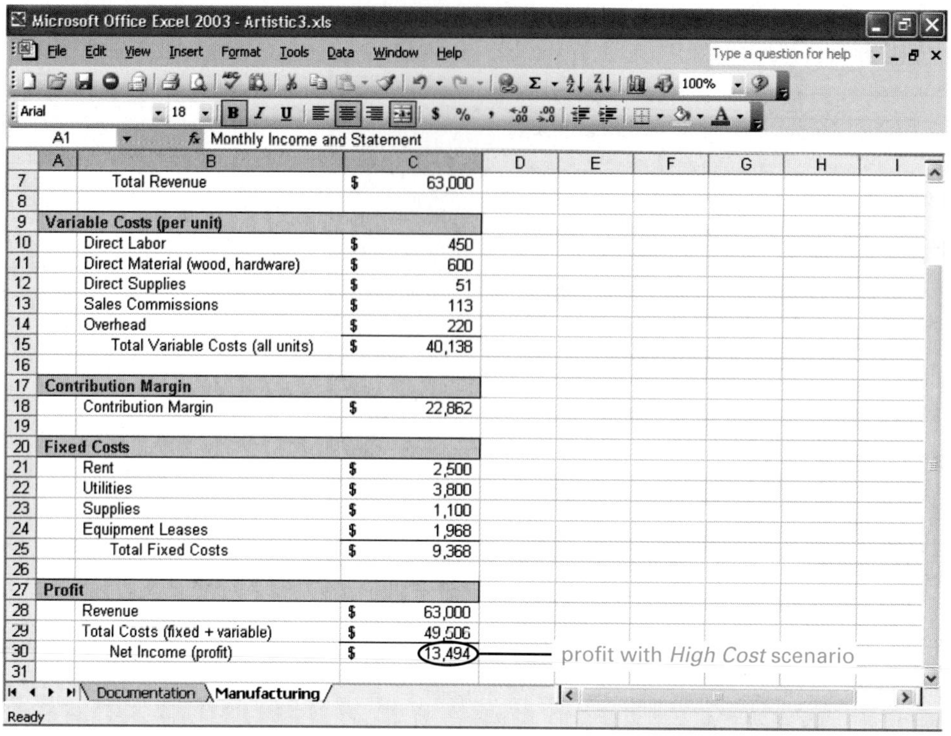

FIGURE 9.30
New results from edited
High Cost scenario

profit with *High Cost* scenario

Deleting a scenario:

1. Click **Tools** and then click **Scenarios** to open the Scenario Manager
2. Click **Current**, if necessary, in the Scenarios list
3. Click the **Delete** button. Excel deletes the Current scenario, removes its name from the list of scenarios, and redisplays the Scenario Manager dialog box (see Figure 9.31)

FIGURE 9.31

The Scenario Manager after deleting the Current scenario

Creating Scenario Reports

While scenarios have many benefits, the main drawback is that you cannot view the results of all the scenarios at once. That is, it is difficult to view the results of three or four scenarios side-by-side. Fortunately, Excel provides a way for you to view a condensation or summary allowing you to compare different scenarios. A *scenario summary* outlines each scenario by displaying changing cells and result cells in a separate worksheet. You can produce two types of summary reports: a scenario summary report and a scenario PivotTable report.

Producing a Scenario Summary Report

A scenario summary report helps managers make decisions about which course of action to take. You produce the report using the Scenario Manager. The Scenario Manager automatically includes all changing cells in the report, but you must select the result cells you want to include. Otherwise, the Scenario Manager includes in the report any cells whose value depends on any of the changing cells.

task reference	Producing a Scenario Summary Report

- Click **Tools** and click **Scenarios** to open the Scenario Manager
- Click the **Summary** button
- Click the **Scenario Summary** option button
- Type the cell addresses in the *Result cells* box of all result cells you want to display in the report
- Click **OK**

Paul wants a summary report for the three scenarios that lists the changing cells and the result cells C28, C29, and C30. The three result cells—named Revenue, Costs, and Profit, respectively—are the key values that will help Paul make a production decision.

Creating a Scenario Summary report:

1. With the Scenario Manager dialog box still open, click the **Summary** button. The Scenario Summary dialog box opens. You can produce either a *scenario summary* or a *scenario PivotTable* report

2. If necessary, click the **Scenario Summary** option button

3. Type **C28,C29,C30** in the *Result cells* box (see Figure 9.32). (You do not need to type spaces between the cell references)

4. Click **OK**. Excel's Scenario Manager creates a Scenario Summary report on a separate worksheet called Scenario Summary (see Figure 9.33). Notice the outlining symbols above and to the left of the summary report, allowing you to show and hide details

The Scenario Summary report is chock full of information. The first column contains the names (or cell addresses) of the changing and result cells. The names of the scenarios appear in the order in which you created them. The summary report's second column (labeled "Current Values") lists the contents of the changing cells and result

FIGURE 9.32

Selecting result cells for
the Scenario Summary
report

click for a Scenario
summary report

type addresses of
results cells here

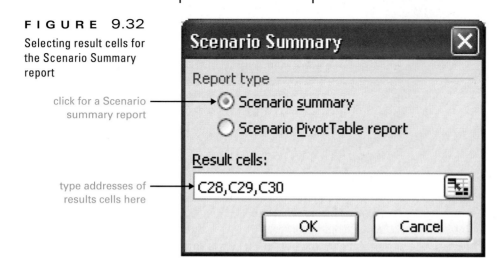

FIGURE 9.33

Scenario Summary
worksheet

outlining symbols allow
you to hide or reveal
details

Show Details symbol
(scenario comments)

Excel automatically
inserts a *Scenario
Summary* worksheet page

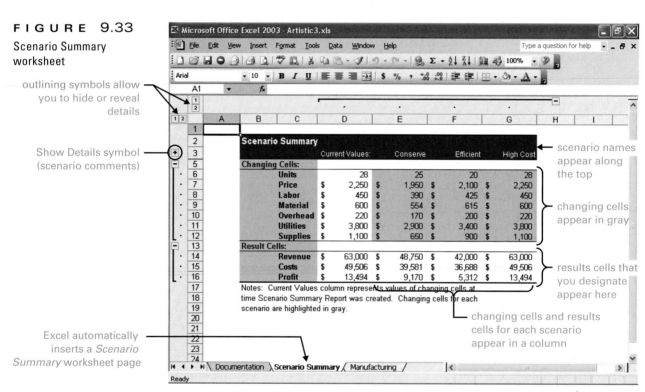

cells currently in the worksheet. The third through fifth columns show both changing cells and result cells for the Conserve, Efficient, and High Cost scenarios. The changing cells—the cells you designated in the Add Scenario dialog box—are shaded so that you can tell quickly which scenarios control which changing cells. The *show details* symbol to the left of row 3 indicates that Excel has hidden something there. Clicking that symbol reveals the contents of the Comment box that you filled in when creating the scenario. You can hide the Changing Cells rows, the Result Cells rows, or both by clicking the Show Detail symbols in the left portion of the worksheet.

Showing scenario comments:

1. With the Scenario Summary worksheet displayed, click the **Show Details** outline symbol next to row 3. Excel displays the previously hidden scenario comments (see Figure 9.34)

FIGURE 9.34

Showing scenario comments

click this Hide (Show) Details symbol to hide (show) scenario comments

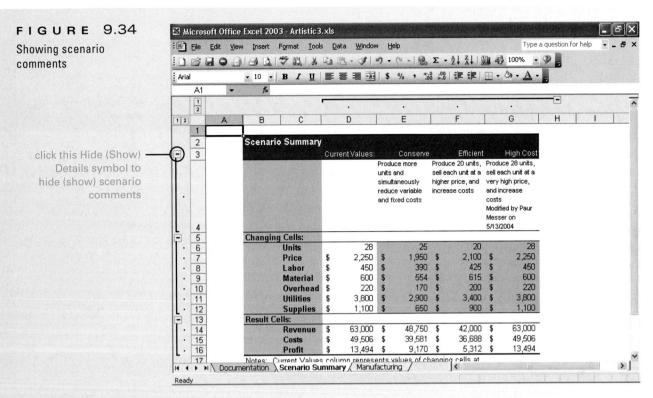

2. Click the **Hide Details** outline symbol adjacent to row 3 to hide the comments

Producing a PivotTable Report

The other report you can create with the Scenario Manager is the Scenario PivotTable. The Scenario PivotTable option inserts a new worksheet into your workbook. Unlike a Scenario Summary report, a PivotTable report is a what-if tool in its own right. You can use the mouse to drag and drop cells and cell ranges onto the pivot table and manipulate it just like any other pivot table. You can mix and match distinct scenarios to review their effects on result cells.

---

task reference   Producing a PivotTable Report

- Click **Tools** and click **Scenarios** to open the Scenario Manager

- Click the **Summary** button

- Click the **Scenario PivotTable** option button

- Type the cell addresses in the Result cells of all result cells you want to display in the report

- Click **OK**

Paul wants you to create a simple PivotTable report so that he can review it and decide if it is useful to him.

Creating a Scenario PivotTable report:

1. Click the **Manufacturing** worksheet tab to make that worksheet active

tip: *Because each worksheet holds the scenarios you created for it, you cannot create a Scenario Summary report or a PivotTable report from the Scenario Summary worksheet*

2. Click **Tools**, click **Scenarios**, and click the **Summary** button. The Scenario Manager displays the Scenario Summary dialog box

3. Click the **Scenario PivotTable report** option button, ensure that the Result Cells box contains the cell addresses C28, C29, and C30, and then click **OK** to create the PivotTable report (see Figure 9.35)

FIGURE 9.35

Creating a PivotTable report

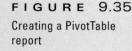
scenario names

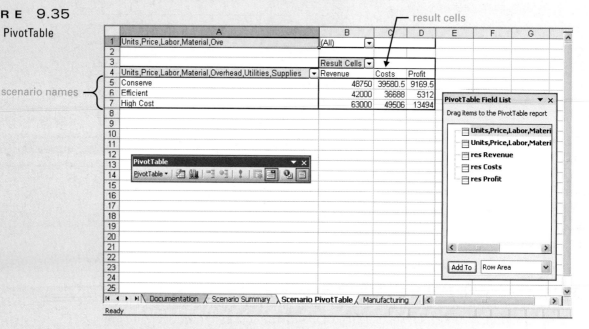

tip: *Your display may not show the PivotTable Field List or the PivotTable toolbar. Display the PivotTable toolbar: Click **Tools**, point to **Toolbars**, and click **PivotTable**. Click the **Show Field** List button (see Figure 9.35) on the PivotTable toolbar to display the PivotTable Field List*

4. Click the **Documentation** worksheet tab to make that worksheet active

5. Save the completed Artistic Furniture Corporation workbook

6. Exit Excel

Paul is very pleased with you for creating the data tables, scenarios, and scenario reports. By using these feature-rich what-if analysis tools, Paul will be able to fine-tune the Artistic Furniture Corporation production and maximize the company's profit.

making *the grade*

1. A _____ consists of selected variables, which are cells in which you substitute different values.

2. The cells whose values change in a scenario are called _____ cells.

3. Begin creating a scenario by clicking _____ on the Tools menu.

4. Every scenario you create must have a scenario _____.

5. A collection of scenarios is organized by the Scenario _____.

6. Scenarios are associated with an individual _____ and are only accessible when it is active.

7. You can create either a Scenario _____ report or a Scenario _____ to summarize all of a worksheet's scenarios.

SESSION 9.3 SUMMARY

Cost-Volume-Profit (CVP) analysis examines the relationship between a product's expenses, the number of units produced, revenue, and profit. Two feature-rich Excel tools help you perform what-if analysis by automating substitution of different values in key cells to help you perform CVP analysis. The two tools are data tables and scenarios. With Excel's one- and two-variable data table feature, you can determine the break-even point of a business—the number of units or mix of products and services a company produces in order for profit to be zero. A one-variable data table summarizes key input and output cell values in a what-if analysis by substituting a series of values for an input cell from a choice of several input values. Output of a one-variable data table is one or more rows or columns containing result cells (profits, for example) that display an output value for each input value substituted into the worksheet. Using a one-variable data table, you can view the effects of changing an input value on multiple output formulas. A two-variable data table computes the effects of two variables on a single formula. Excel substitutes values into selected cells of a worksheet to produce a result value for each pair of input values. For example, with a two-variable data table, you can study the effects of altering both the interest rate and the number of months in the period on a loan's monthly payment amount. Similarly, you could perform what-if analysis on the effect of changing the production volume of a product and the selling price of a product on the company's profitability.

Complex what-if analyses on more than two variables require more power than either one- or two-variable data tables provide. Using Excel's Scenario Manager, you can substitute up to 32 input values into the same number of selected input cells and analyze the results on key output cells. A group of values and changing cells is called a scenario, and you can define as many scenarios for a single worksheet as you would like. Once you have created one or more scenarios, you can click the Show button to plug the values of the scenario into the worksheet. Excel recalculates its values and displays the results of the scenario.

The Scenario Manager provides two types of reports: a Scenario Summary report or a Scenario PivotTable report. A scenario summary creates a separate worksheet with an overview of the changing cell values and result values for each scenario. PivotTable reports summarize scenarios on a separate worksheet also. Unlike scenario summaries, PivotTable reports are what-if tools. You can drag and drop cells and cell ranges into a pivot table and change it as you would any other pivot table.

EXCEL

MICROSOFT OFFICE SPECIALIST
OBJECTIVES SUMMARY

- Learn and use break-even analysis to determine production levels for profitability—MOS XL03S-1-3
- Create charts based on one-variable and two-variable data tables—MOS XL03S-1-4
- Create Excel scenarios—MOS XL03E-1-6
- Manage Excel scenarios with the Scenario Manager—MOS XL03E-1-6
- View, add, edit, and delete scenarios—MOS XL03E-1-6
- Create a scenario report—MOS XL03E-1-6
- Create and use one-variable and two-variable data tables—MOS XL03E-1-7

making the grade answers

SESSION 9.1	SESSION 9.2
1. CVP	**1.** scenario
2. break-even	**2.** changing
3. variable; fixed	**3.** Scenarios
4. data	**4.** name
5. input; result	**5.** Manager
6. one	**6.** worksheet
	7. Summary; PivotTable

task reference summary

Task	Page #	Preferred Method
Creating a one-variable data table	EX 9.15	• Decide if you want values for the input cell to appear in a row or down a column • If you arrange a data table in columns, then insert the input values in the first column beginning below the first row of the table and place a reference (a formula) to the result cell in the cell above and to the right of the column of input values • If you arrange a data table in rows, then insert the input values in the first row beginning in the second column of the data table and place a reference (a formula) to the result cell in the cell below the input row and to its left • Select the table, click **Data**, and then click **Table** • Enter the cell reference of the input cell in the Row input cell box if input values are in a row or enter the cell reference of the input cell in the Column input cell box if the input values are in a column in the data table • Click **OK**

task reference *summary*

Task	Page #	Preferred Method
Creating a two-variable data table	EX 9.19	• Type the formula or a reference to the input cell in the upper-left cell in the data table • Type the first variable values in the row to the right of the formula • Type the second variable values in the column below the formula • Select a cell range that encompasses the formula, row values, and column values • Click **Data** on the menu bar and then click **Table** • Type the address of the input cell that corresponds to the row values in the Row input cell text box • Type the address of the input cell that corresponds to the column values in the Column input cell text box • Click **OK**
Creating a scenario	EX 9.26	• Click **Tools** and click **Scenarios** to open the Scenario Manager • Click the **Add** button and type a scenario name • Specify the changing (input) cells in the scenario • Type commentary in the Comment text box and then click the **OK** button • Type the values for each changing cell, scrolling the list if necessary, and then click **OK** • Click **Close** to close the Scenario Manager
Viewing a scenario	EX 9.30	• Click **Tools** and click **Scenarios** to open the Scenario Manager • Select a scenario from the Scenarios list • Click the **Show** button
Editing a scenario	EX 9.32	• Click **Tools** and click **Scenarios** to open the Scenario Manager • Select a scenario from the Scenarios list • Click the **Edit** button • Make any changes in the Edit Scenario dialog box and click **OK** • Make any changes in the Scenario Values dialog box and click **OK**
Deleting a scenario	EX 9.33	• Click **Tools** and click **Scenarios** to open the Scenario Manager • Select a scenario from the Scenarios list • Click the **Delete** button
Producing a Scenario Summary report	EX 9.35	• Click **Tools** and click **Scenarios** to open the Scenario Manager • Click the **Summary** button • Click the **Scenario Summary** option button • Type the cell addresses in the *Result cells* box of all result cells you want to display in the report • Click **OK**
Producing a PivotTable report	EX 9.37	• Click **Tools** and click **Scenarios** to open the Scenario Manager • Click the **Summary** button • Click the **Scenario PivotTable** option button • Type the cell addresses in the Result cells box of all result cells you want to display in the report • Click **OK**

EXCEL

TRUE OR FALSE

1. A variable cost is one that varies directly with the number of units a company produces.

2. Break-even analysis can help you find the point at which you generate a profit, because it takes into account the relationship among cost, volume, and profit.

3. Profit = revenue + variable expenses + fixed expenses.

4. Excel provides two types of variable data tables called single and double variable data tables.

5. You cannot alter any of the input values in the input row or input column.

6. The combination of values assigned to one or more variable cells in a what-if analysis is called a scenario.

FILL-IN

1. Typically, there are two major categories of costs in building: _____ costs and _____ costs.

2. The point where profits are zero is called the _____ point.

3. A _____ variable data table can evaluate multiple result cells and produce result values.

4. In a two-variable data table, you always place the reference to the result cell in the _____ corner of the table—at the intersection of the row input values and the _____ input values.

5. The Excel _____ Manager allows you to create what-if analyses for more than two variables.

6. Unlike the Scenario summary, the _____ report is, itself, a what-if tool that allows you to drag input cells into it.

MULTIPLE CHOICE

1. A scenario identifies the cells that contain values you want to change as
   a. active cells.
   b. result cells.
   c. precedent cells.
   d. changing cells.

2. How many cell values can you specify in a scenario?
   a. up to 30
   b. up to 32
   c. up to 36
   d. unlimited

3. When anyone edits an existing scenario, Excel
   a. only allows you the option of manually adding comments to the comment box.
   b. does not allow you to track changes made to scenarios.
   c. automatically adds text to the end of the commentary in the comment box.
   d. automatically adds text to the end of the commentary in the edit tracking box.

4. Which type of summary report can you produce?
   a. a scenario PivotTable report
   b. a scenario Result Cells report
   c. a scenario Changing Cells report
   d. a scenario Comments report

5. A two-variable data table computes the effects of two variables on
   a. two formulas.
   b. one formula.
   c. one or two formulas.
   d. multiple formulas.

review of concepts

REVIEW QUESTIONS

1. Describe, briefly, the difference between fixed costs and variable costs in a manufacturing environment where the company is building products for sale.

2. Describe why a one- or two-variable data table is a good what-if tool compared to a worksheet without the ability to create data tables or similar analyses.

3. From what you have read in this chapter, what would you do if you wanted to see the effect of changing, say, four variables in a what-if analysis? Explain how you might automate the what-if analysis.

4. Explain what happens if you try to delete one of the result values in a two-variable data table.

CREATE THE QUESTION

For each of the following answers, create an appropriate, short question.

ANSWER	QUESTION
1. variable cost	_____
2. the upper-left corner of the data table	_____
3. array formula	_____
4. Scenario Manager	_____
5. result cell	_____
6. PivotTable report	_____

1. Considering Several Scenarios for Outdoor Adventures

Outdoor Adventures manufactures a line of outdoor camping and hiking equipment. Bill Hoskins, the president of Outdoor Adventures, has prepared a preliminary budget and he wants you to create three scenarios for him. He would like to see the effect of changing the labor, materials, and production revenues on the operating income—revenues minus expenses. He would like you to prepare a Scenario Summary report for him.

1. Open **ex09Outdoor.xls** and save it as **OutdoorAdventures.xls**

2. Click the **May** tab to make that sheet active (see Figure 9.36)

3. Click cell **B6**, type **=SUM(B3:B5)**, click cell **B18**, click the **AutoSum** button on the Standard toolbar, and press **Enter** to sum expenses

4. Click cell **B20** and type **=B6-B18**, press **Enter** to compute Operating Income (or net income).

5. Select the cell range **A3:B5**, click **Insert**, point to **Name**, click **Create**, and ensure that the **Left column check box** is checked, click **OK**, and click any cell to deselect the range

   Next, create three scenarios

6. Click **Tools**, click **Scenarios**, and click the **Add** button

7. Type **Current budget** in the Scenario name box, press the **Tab** key, type **B3:B5** in the Changing Cells box, press **Tab**, type **Current budget figures for the baseline**, click **OK** in the Add Scenario dialog box, and click **Add** in the Scenario Values dialog box to accept the current values and add another scenario

8. Type **Increase labor** in the Scenario name box, press **Tab** twice, type **Increase labor only**, click the **OK** button, type **72000** in the Labor box, and then click **Add** in the Scenario Values dialog box to add another scenario

9. Type **Increase materials** in the Scenario name box, press **Tab** twice, type **Increase materials only**, click the **OK** button, double-click the **Materials** box, type **2456**, and then click **Add** in the Scenario Values dialog box to add another scenario

10. Type **Increase production** in the Scenario name box, press **Tab** twice, type **Increase production only**, click the **OK** button, double-click the **Production** box, type **7800**, and then click **OK**

11. Click the **Summary** button on the Scenario Manager dialog box, ensure that the **Scenario summary** option button is selected, and click **OK**

12. When the Scenario Summary worksheet appears, click **File** on the menu bar, click **Page Setup**, click the **Page** tab (if necessary), click the **Landscape** option button in the Orientation panel, and click **OK**

13. Click the **Save** button on the Standard toolbar to save your workbook

14. Identify your workbook by placing your name in all three pages' headers, and then print all three worksheets

FIGURE 9.36

Outdoor Adventures workbook

	A	B	C	D	E	F	G	H
1	**Budget - May**							
2	*Revenues*							
3	Labor	$ 69,544						
4	Materials	1,319						
5	Production	6,556						
6	**Revenues total**							
7								
8	*Expenses*							
9	Commissions	$ 7,348						
10	Equipment	1,118						
11	Insurance	1,043						
12	Office Supplies	1,072						
13	Rent	2,046						
14	Salaries	51,194						
15	Telephone	939						
16	Travel	2,824						
17	Utilities	1,153						
18	**Expenses Total**							
19								
20	*Operating Income*							
21								
22								
23								
24								

Documentation \ May /

Ready

2. Using Two Variables to Determine Optimal Numbers

Parson City Community Recreation Center (PCCRC) is getting ready to open its doors. After years of fund-raising and two years of construction, the Center will soon be ready for use by the public. The only income the PCCRC will have to cover all expenses is membership dues that will be collected on a monthly basis. Since the Center has state-of-the-art teaching, and theater and sports facilities, the board expects membership to be high. The board must now decide what the Center will charge for monthly dues. Since the PCCRC is a nonprofit organization, it is crucial that the Center be as close as possible to break-even each year. In determining what the membership dues will be, the Center has to work around one restriction placed on it by the city—due to the size of the Center, there may be no more than 4,500 members.

Open **PCCRC.xls** (see Figure 9.37) and save it as **<yourname>PCCRC2.xls**. This is the budget determined by the board. A one-variable data table has already been completed with different possible numbers of members with dues set at $25. As you can see, these possible scenarios will not allow the PCCRC to even cover its expenses. In order to decide what to charge for monthly dues, it needs your help in creating a two-variable data table. It wants you to work with monthly dues in the range of $25 to $35, in increments of $2, and number of members from 4,000 to 4,500, in increments of 100.

1. In cell **J18**, enter **$25** as the lowest possible charge for dues. Enter **$27** in **K18**, **$29** in **L18**, and so on, up to **$35**

2. In cells **I19** through **I24**, copy the membership numbers from the one-variable data table

3. Since this is a two-variable data table, in cell **I18**, enter **=D21** for Income. Since a currency value appears, format the cell to display **Members**

4. In cell **L17**, type **Dues** and align it to the right of the cell. Apply Bold and Italic to *Members* and *Dues* and change the typeface to a green color

5. Select the range **I18:O24**, select **Data** in the menu bar, and then click **Table**

6. In the table dialog box, type **D15** in the Row Input box to reference membership dues

7. For the Column input box, type **D14** to reference the number of members. Click **OK**

8. After the table is filled, analyze the data. Look for the cell with positive income closest to $0. How many members paying what amount of dues yield this result? Highlight the cell and its corresponding member and dues figures with a bright yellow background color

9. Select the cell range **I17:O24**, press **Ctrl+X** to cut the cell range, click cell **F17**, press **Ctrl+V** to move the selected cells. Right-click the column header for column F, click **Column Width**, type **11**, click **OK**, and press **Ctrl+Home** to select cell A1

10. Click **File**, click **Page Setup**, click **Page** tab, click the **Landscape** option button, and click **OK**

11. Include your name in the worksheet header, print the worksheet, and save the changed workbook.

FIGURE 9.37

Parson City Community Recreation Center workbook

	A	B	C	D	E	F	G	H	I	J	K	L
1	PCCRC Budget											
2												
3	Monthly Expenses											
4	Lease			$18,300					Members	Revenues	Expenses	Income
5	Overhead			$6,745					4,000	100,000	130,100	-30,100
6	Supplies			$7,585					4,100	102,500	130,100	-27,600
7	Salaries			$90,120					4,200	105,000	130,100	-25,100
8	Theater Programs			$3,000					4,300	107,500	130,100	-22,600
9	Sports Facilities			$4,350					4,400	110,000	130,100	-20,100
10	Total Expenses			$130,100					4,500	112,500	130,100	-17,600
11												
12												
13	Monthly Revenues											
14	Members			4000								
15	Dues			$25								
16	Total Revenues			$100,000								
17												
18	Budget											
19	Total Revenues			$100,000								
20	Total Expenses			$130,100								
21	Income			-$30,100								
22												
23												
24												
25												
26												
27												

PCCRC Budget

Ready

challenge

1. Reviewing Best and Worst Case Scenarios for Abel-Massey Corporation

Abel-Massey's president, Bert Abel, has produced a pro forma income statement in which he is projecting expenses and income for his business. The worksheet, called **ex09AbelMassey.xls**, is preformatted and contains revenue and expenses for the current year and projections for the next two years. Bert wants you to create three scenarios and then create a Scenario Summary report that outlines the results of the scenario analysis. To make the analysis easier to understand, Bert has named all the changing cells and the three result cells so that they are self-documenting in the summary report. The changing cells are specially formatted with a gray background so that both the worksheet reader and anyone who creates scenarios can easily identify them. Most of the changing cells represent a percentage of product sales. For example, cell B7 contains 30 percent. That is a what-if estimate of the contract revenues as a percentage of product sales in this model.

Your job is to create three scenarios called Base, Worst, and Best. Start by opening **ex09AbelMassey.xls** and save it as **<yourname>AbelMassey.xls** to preserve the original workbook. Use the values shown in Figure 9.38 and the corresponding scenario values for the three scenarios. When you have completed the three scenarios, produce a Scenario Summary report—an additional worksheet. Select cells **C22**, **D22**, and **E22** as the Result cells in the Scenario Summary dialog box when you produce the summary report. Click the Scenario Summary worksheet and then select landscape orientation for the page in the Page Setup dialog box. The other pages print suitably in portrait orientation.

Either print the three Abel-Massey worksheets comprising the workbook or execute File, Save As, depending on your instructor's direction. Here are the three scenarios' values and the cells and names to which they correspond (see Figure 9.38).

FIGURE 9.38
Abel-Massey scenarios and their values

Changing Cell	Name	Base	Worst	Best
C6	SalesYear1	$1000	$1000	$1200
D6	SalesYear2	$1200	$1200	$1400
E6	SalesYear3	$1400	$1400	$1600
B7	ContractRevenue	30%	25%	35%
B11	ProductCost	50%	55%	45%
B12	SubcontCost	18%	21%	15%
B16	Equipment	9%	10%	8%
B17	Payroll	25%	28%	22%
B18	Rent	25%	28%	22%
B19	Supplies	2%	2%	2%

2. Examining Car Financing Options with a Two-Variable Data Table

Nancy Webber graduates from college in three months, and she has received three terrific job offers. Having a job in hand and the promise of a good salary, Nancy wants to purchase a new car. She figures she will need a $10,000 loan to buy the car she wants. She's not sure what interest rate she will be able to lock in, but Nancy knows she cannot afford a payment of more than $315 per month. In order to find the best combination of loan duration (years) and interest rate, Nancy wants to build a two-variable data table with interest rates from 6 percent to 10 percent as column values in the table and years—from 1 to 5—along the top of the table.

Begin by opening **ex09Loan.xls** and save it as **<yourname>Loan2.xls**. The loan worksheet contains the loan amount in cell B1, an interest rate in cell B2, the loan length in years in cell B3, and the monthly payment (a PMT function) in cell B5. Create a two-variable data table whose upper-left corner, containing a reference to

cell B5, is cell D2. In cells E2 through I2, type the values **1** through **5** representing the duration in years of the loan. In cells D3 and D4, type **6.00%** and **6.25%**, respectively. Select cells **D3** and **D4**, and then drag the fill handle down through cell D19. In cell D2, type **=ABS(B5)**, which is the absolute value of the cell B5 containing the monthly payment. Create a two-variable data table for the cell range D2:I19. Format the values in the resulting data table to display currency symbols and two decimal places. Format cell D2 to display the text "**Interest**" instead of the formula result. In cell E1, type **Years** to label the top row. Conditionally format the cell range **E3:I19** (see Figure 9.39) so that any value less than or equal to $315 is red in color. For added interest, select the entire table, open the Drawing toolbar, and select a drop shadow. Identify your worksheet by placing your name in the header. Select the landscape orientation. Either print the worksheet or execute Save As, according to your instructor's direction.

FIGURE 9.39

Car Financing Options workbook

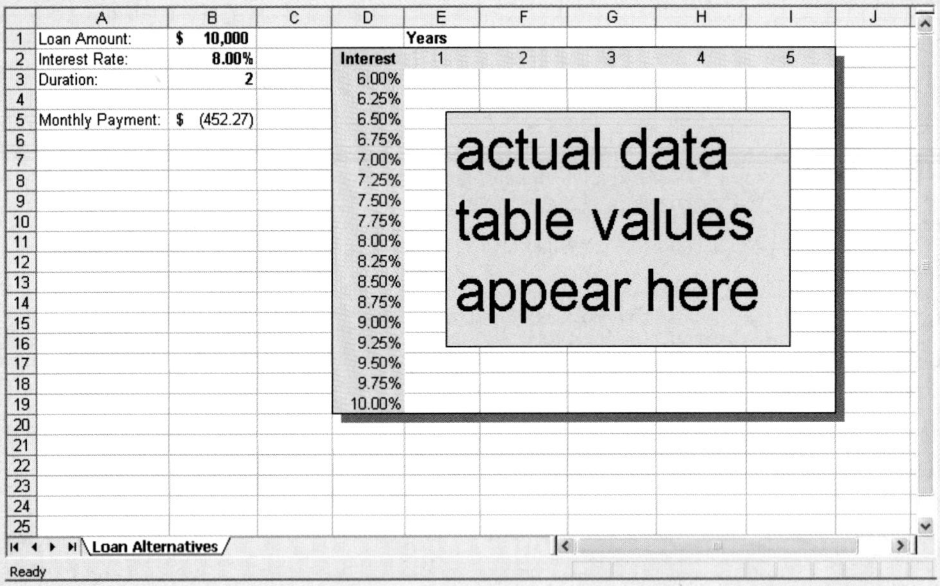

1. Determining Whether a Project will Produce Income Using Tables

G. Mercer is a retailer with stores throughout the northeast. Sales have been strong for the past few years and the company is thinking about expanding its operations to include locations in large western cities. Before investing in actual store locations, G. Mercer needed to figure out a way to determine the level of demand for its products in areas outside the northeast. An online store will allow the company to record where customers are located throughout the country, help gain name recognition in new areas, and increase sales. While there are many benefits to launching a Web site, G. Mercer wants to be sure that the new project will at least bring in enough total income over the first six months to cover costs for the project.

A local designer has agreed to design the Web site for $30,000. G. Mercer will spread this cost over six months, for $5,000 each month. The online store will use currently unused office space to house a Technology Department that will run and update the Web site and also a customer service team to assist online customers. Estimated salaries for the Technology Department total $12,000 a month. New equipment and computers will total $7,000 a month and customer service salaries will be $26,000.

G. Mercer will use its current warehouses and distributors to handle the online orders. However, each order will cost an additional $2.00 in labor and $1.00 in packaging. The customer pays for all shipping costs. In order to determine whether this venture will be profitable in the first six months, the following estimates have been made for number of orders. For January: 245 orders; February: 298 orders; March: 362 orders; April: 403 orders; May: 476 orders; and June: 495 orders. The company wants to use conservative estimates and believes orders will average $156 in sales during this preliminary period.

Stephanie Peters is director of the Finance Department and needs you to summarize these figures for a presentation. Open **ex09GMercer.xls** (see Figure 9.40) and save as **<yourname>GMercer2.xls**. This is the spreadsheet Stephanie designed to analyze sales, costs, and income. She has already calculated the results for January, and she wants you to complete the information for February through June. To supply these figures, you will need to create a one-variable data table

in cells G6:J11. For the column headings, use **Orders**, **Revenue**, **Costs**, and **Income** in cells G5:J5. For these column cells, enter references to the appropriate cells in the current worksheet created by Stephanie. (Be sure to use the cell for Total Costs.) Title the column before Orders as **Month** and fill in **January** through **June**. Be sure not to include this column when creating the table. In the Units column, enter the estimates given to you. When the Table dialog box opens, specify the input cell as **D6** and that the table is in column format.

Chart this data table to illustrate when G. Mercer will break even. To create the chart, use the data table you created and the figures for Orders, Revenues, and Costs. Use the XY Scatter Chart without markers on the lines. Title the chart **G. Mercer Break-Even** and type **Orders** in the X-axis box. Select for the chart to appear on a new sheet and title the sheet **BE Chart**. Should G. Mercer take on the Web site project? In which month will the company begin to cover its costs? Include your name in the worksheet header. Execute either Print or Save As, according to your instructor's direction.

FIGURE 9.40

G. Mercer workbook

	A	B	C	D	E
1	G. Mercer				
2	Online Store Forecasts				
3	January through June				
4					
5	*Revenues*				
6	Number of Orders			245	
7	Average Order Sales		$	156	
8	*Total Revenues*		$	38,220	
9					
10					
11	*Fixed Costs*				
12	Web Site Design		$	5,000	
13	Equipment			7,000	
14	Tech Salaries			12,000	
15	Customer Service Salaries			26,000	
16	*Total Fixed Costs per Month*		$	50,000	
17					
18	*Variable Costs*				
19	Labor		$	2	
20	Packaging			1	
21	*Total Variable Costs per Order*		$	3	
22	Orders for Month			245	
23	*Total Variable Costs for Month*		$	735	
24					

G. Mercer \ **Store Forecasts** /

Ready

2. Examining Options to Decrease Fixed Costs

WebVideo is one of the best online stores for movies and videos. Its products range from new releases to hard-to-find and rare videos. The site is easy to navigate and offers competitive prices coupled with quick delivery—all of which contributed greatly to WebVideo's popularity. Since the company has no retail locations, all videos are housed in a single warehouse and distribution center. In order to meet customers' requests and maintain its reputation for service, WebVideo has always maintained large inventories of each movie, resulting in hundreds of thousands of videos. While this has enabled WebVideo to quickly locate and deliver videos, it is a very costly way to operate. All of the videos had to be bought by WebVideo and are an enormous investment. WebVideo receives income from each sale, but since its initial and replenishment costs are so high, the company has not been able to show a profit.

Open **WebVideo.xls** (see Figure 9.41) and save as **<yourname>WebVideo2.xls**. This workbook contains the company's income statement for the past two months. Enter formulas in cells C13 and D13 that compute the contribution margins for the first two months' values (revenues minus variable costs). WebVideo clearly has enough revenue to cover variable expenses, so management has decided that it must decrease fixed costs. Upper management has determined that the best way to achieve this is to sell off some inventory and move to a smaller facility. First, WebVideo manager Sally Cunnard wants you to determine, using a one-variable data table, how an estimated increase in

video sales might affect variable costs, fixed costs, and operating income.

Cells F5:I13 contain the outline of a one-variable data table with monthly video sales estimates in cells F6:F13 (in increments of 500). In cell F5, type =D3, in cell G5, type =D11; in cell H5 type =C20, and for cell I5 type =D22. Select the table range **G5:I13**, click **Data**, and then click **Table**. Click the **Column input cell** text box, enter **D3** and click **OK**. Format the cell range G6:I13 with the currency symbol and two decimal places.

According to your data table, at what number of videos sold (approximately) will WebVideo receive positive income? Bold this number and make its font red. Include your name in the worksheet header, save the workbook, and print the worksheet.

Next, WebVideo wants you to examine what its income would be if it moved to another facility. The company needs to determine if it will receive positive income sooner by choosing this option. Another facility will give the firm the following decreased costs: Lease $5,350, Overhead $1,860, Salaries $96,000, and Maintenance $700. Since WebVideo will carry a smaller inventory, some videos ordered by customers online will have to be sent to WebVideo from an outside supplier. This is going to cause an increase in shipping costs to $2.55. This $1.40 increase will be partially passed on to the customer through an increase in video prices to $15.99. WebVideo expects this increase in price to cause some of its customer to choose its competitors to order videos. But WebVideo also believes that its superior customer service will retain a large number of its clients and expects 8,400 videos to sell in April. Create a new worksheet in your same workbook, name the worksheet tab Option 2, and create an income statement similar to the Video Analysis worksheet and use all of the forecasted costs and revenues for WebVideo moving to a new facility. Will this option bring positive income for WebVideo in the month of April? Type your name in the worksheet header. Save this latest version of your workbook, and print the Option 2 worksheet.

FIGURE 9.41

WebVideo workbook

	A	B	C	D	E	F	G	H	I	J	K
1			February	March		Data table:					
2		**Revenues**									
3		Videos Sold	7370	8410							
4		Price per Video	$14.99	$14.99		Videos Sold	Variable Costs	Fixed Costs	Operating Income		
5		Total Revenues	$110,476.30	$126,065.90		8000					
6						8500					
7		**Variable Costs (per unit)**				9000					
8		Shipping	$1.15	$1.15		9500					
9		Packaging/Handling	$0.72	$0.72		10000					
10						10500					
11		Total Variable Costs	$13,781.90	$15,726.70		11000					
12						11500					
13		**Contribution Margin**				12000					
14											
15		**Fixed Costs**									
16		Lease	$7,350.00								
17		Overhead	$2,980.00								
18		Salaries	$125,000.00								
19		Maintenance	$1,500.00								
20		Total Fixed Costs	$136,830.00								
21											
22		**Operating Income**	-$40,135.60	-$26,490.80							
23											
24											

Video Analysis

Ready

on the web

1. Using Scenarios to Forecast Stock Prices

Travis Lewis inherited his grandfather's investments years ago. Travis has decided to analyze his holdings and sell some of the stocks. Since the stocks were inherited, the cost basis used for tax purposes will be the price of each stock at his grandfather's death. Travis will have to pay capital gains tax on the profit of each stock, which his advisor estimates will be 20 percent. He will also have to pay a flat $250 commission to his broker for each stock sold.

Travis has decided to sell the following stocks: Nokia, Siebel Systems, Wells Fargo, Disney, and Baxter International. Open **ex09TravisStock.xls** and save as **<yourname>TravisStock2.xls**. This workbook records the information Travis needs to determine which stocks to sell now that at least break even. Use the Web to determine the cost basis for each stock and its current price. Go to www.finance.yahoo.com. Under Research & Education, select **Historical Quotes** to find the cost basis and current price of each stock. Once these are determined, enter the gain or loss per share. For total gain or loss, create a formula to multiply the number of shares held by the amount of gain or loss per share. The capital gains tax amount formula will multiply this total by 20 percent (cells H3:H7). Simply reference negative numbers as stocks that should not be sold. Fill the profit column with a formula that will subtract tax and commission for total gain per stock. Which stocks should Travis currently sell? Include your name in the worksheet header. Execute Print or Save As, according to your instructor's direction.

Travis is debating waiting to see how the market changes over the next few years. He asked his advisor to come up with four possible scenarios for the stock market five years from now. Travis needs you to use the Scenario Manager to see what the possible status of his stock holdings will be in five years. Using the four possible forecasts, add a scenario for each possible outcome, using current price and capital gains tax as the changing cells. Create a Scenario Summary report for Travis, using profit as the result cells. Include your name in the header and print the report.

2. Analyzing College Expenses

Karen Roman will be an incoming freshman at the University of California, Santa Barbara, next fall. She has been busy preparing for her new school and the big move across country. She is expecting to receive an academic scholarship for $7,750 and her parents have agreed to give Karen an additional $8,000 a year to go toward expenses. Karen will need to use student loans to cover any additional needs at UCSB.

Using her Web browser, Karen went to www.ucsb.edu to locate more information on what her expenses will be once she starts school. Once on the home page, select **Current Students** and then click **Financial Aid**. Click **Cost of Attendance** to display an outline of expenses. Open **ex09UCexpenses.xls**, save the workbook as **<yourname>UCexpenses.xls**, and fill in the current undergraduate expenses for Karen. Remember to note expenses for being an out-of-state student. In cells D5 and D21, create formulas to compute the total sources and expenses. In cell **D24**, enter **=D5** and in cell **D25**, enter **=D21**. Create a formula in cell **D26** for Amount Needed to subtract D25 from D24. Format this row boldface.

Create a one-variable data table to reflect the different possible amounts of scholarships she may receive. Her different possibilities are the current amount of $7,750, $8,500, $11,800, $14,500, and $15,200. In the cell range **G3:I3**, enter the following headings: **Scholarships**, **Total Sources**, and **Amount Needed**. Under scholarships, enter the five possibilities for Karen. In cells **G4:I4**, enter references to the appropriate cells in the expense statement. Select the range of the title, click on **Data**, and then click **Table**. Enter **D3** as the column input cell. Format the table so that each cell has a dollar sign and no decimals. Format the Amount Needed cells to be positive numbers in red. Title the worksheet tab **Loan Amounts**. Type your name in the worksheet header. Print the entire workbook.

around the world

1. Using Scenario Manager to Forecast Income

Jeff Livingston owns Leaf Furniture, a large store that sells imported furniture from around the world. Jeff has been busy preparing for the summer and has attended several trade shows where teak furniture was the new trend. He has decided to carry an initial line of teak patio furniture—specifically, sets of a table and four chairs. Jeff contacted many teak furniture makers around the world to inquire about their prices and to see samples of their teak pieces. Based on quality of craftsmanship, Jeff has narrowed it down to four manufacturers located in Zaire, Brazil, the United States, and Thailand. Since each seller's location causes the shipping and tariff charges to vary greatly, Jeff needs to be sure to include these numbers and not look at just the cost per set. After looking at the differences in these additional charges, Jeff has asked you to help him determine from which manufacturer he should purchase the furniture.

Open **ex09Teak.xls** and then save as **<yourname>Teak2.xls**. Jeff expects to charge $1,200 per furniture set based on his competitors' prices. His first order will be for 30 sets of furniture and he will order more though the summer based on sales. Jeff has already started the worksheet by entering revenue information and expects to make $36,000 in sales from the first 30 sets. Jeff has also entered each seller's charge per set (product cost), shipping charge, and surcharge. Complete the Income Statement by entering **Income** in cell A15. Enter the appropriate formula in this row's cells to compute income received after costs are subtracted from revenues. Bold this row. Based on this information, which seller should Jeff use? Include your name and print the Income Statement.

Jeff has looked over these figures and agrees with your recommendation. He wants to consider different options for the sales price and number of units sold. His current scenario would be to charge $1,200 per set, to sell 30 sets, and for his costs to remain the same. The worst case would be if he sold 15 sets, sold them for $1,200 each, and his product cost increased by $30 per set. The best case would be if he sold 30 sets, was able to increase the price to $1,500 each, and his product cost dropped by $20 each. Use the Scenario Manager to enter the Best Case, Current Case, and Worst Case scenarios. For changing cells, be sure to include the cell ranges for Price per Set, Number of Sets Sold, and Product Cost. Specify the values for these changing cells based on the three scenarios Jeff gave you. Next, create a Scenario Summary report, using the cells that represent Income as the result cells. Include your name in all worksheet headers, and print the Scenario Summary and the Income worksheets.

2. Katrina Cosmetics

Katrina Cosmetics purchases makeup that is produced in Malaysia. The makeup is sold in Katrina Cosmetic shops throughout Europe, Canada, and the United States. For the past three years sales have been stagnant at nearly $25 million. Katrina Cosmetics' board has set the revenue goal for next year at $30 million. Currently all sales representatives in the shops are paid a flat salary. They do not receive any commissions. The board has asked that a different sales program be initiated to help achieve the new revenue goal. Your boss, the head of sales, has asked for your assistance in pulling together a few scenarios that would show how this goal could be achieved and how it would influence the bottom line. The new scenarios will include commissions for the sales representatives, not flat salaries.

Begin by opening **ex09Katrina.xls**. Immediately save this file as **<yourname>Katrina2.xls**. In this file you will find a partially completed income statement. Modify the worksheet in three ways. First, in the *Variable Costs* section you must add a row for the cost of *Commissions*. Because the current scenario does not include Commissions, enter zero as the value. Make sure you modify the formula for the *Total Variable Costs* to now include Commissions. Next write a formula to calculate the *Contribution Margin*. Then create a *Profit* section that calculates *Net Income*. Now you are ready to pull together the scenarios. The first is the current situation where revenues are at $25,000,000, commissions are $0, and salaries are $7,000,000. The next is a straight commission proposal. Use the new goal of $30,000,000 for revenue, $8,400,000 for commissions, and $0 for salaries. The final scenario is a combination of commission and salary, with revenue at $30,000,000, commissions at $4,200,000, and salary at $3,500,000. Make sure that the changing cells are named accordingly (*Revenue, Commissions,* and *Salaries*). Name C24 and C25 *Costs* and *Profit,* respectively. Use the Scenario Manager to enter the Straight Commission, Combined Commission & Salary, and Current scenarios. Create a Scenario Summary report that shows the results for Costs and Profit. Optimize the widths of the scenario columns so the scenario names appear but the columns are not too wide. Set up the scenario page to print with 1-inch margins and in landscape orientation. Save your file, include your name in the header of both worksheet pages, and print both pages of the workbook.

running project

Pro Golf Academy

Pro Golf Academy manager, Betty Carroll, knows a significant portion of her revenue is from golf ball sales. She speculates that having the right mix of golf ball brands for sale can greatly improve Pro Golf's profitability. Betty knows that examining the number of the different golf ball brands she sells is one way she can perform an extensive what-if analysis to increase the store's profitability. Betty has put together a preliminary worksheet, called **ex09ProGolf.xls**, containing Pro Golf's per unit wholesale cost (what she pays) for various golf ball brands (all are per dozen prices) and Pro Golf's typical retail price (the price Pro Golf charges its customers). She has created additional columns indicating typical sales in units of each brand per month. She wants you to complete the worksheet by writing formulas for the Total Cost, Total Sales, and Profit columns. Begin by opening **ex09ProGolf.xls** (see Figure 9.42) and saving the worksheet immediately as **<yourname>ProGolf9.xls**. Then, make the changes indicated in the paragraphs that follow.

The Total Cost formula for each golf ball brand is its wholesale cost times the units sold. The Total Sales formula for each golf ball brand is the product of the units sold and the retail price. The profit for each golf ball brand is the Total Sales minus Total Cost.

Write SUM functions in cells E10 through G10 for the Total Cost, Total Sales, and Profit columns. Format cell range E4:G10 with the Accounting format, two decimal places, and the currency symbol. Assign the names *TotalCost* to cell E10, *TotalSales* to cell F10, and *TotalProfit* to cell G10. Next, use the Scenario Manager to create three scenarios with changing cells D4 through D8 (unit sales of each golf ball brand). The result cells you should include in the scenario are the sums in the cell range E10:G10. Figure 9.43 lists the details of the three scenarios you are to create. Create a Scenario Summary report, move the Scenario Summary worksheet to the right of the Golf Ball Sales Analysis worksheet, and format the worksheet tab bright yellow. On the Scenario Summary worksheet, format the 12 Result Cells values in cells D12 through G14 with the Accounting format, zero decimal places, and the currency symbol.

Place your name in the worksheet header of all three worksheets. Place the worksheet tab name in the Center section of each worksheet's footer. Go to the Documentation worksheet and type today's date in the cell to the right of the label "Created on." Type your name next to the label "Created by." Save the workbook, and then print all three worksheets.

FIGURE 9.42

Pro Golf sales analysis worksheet

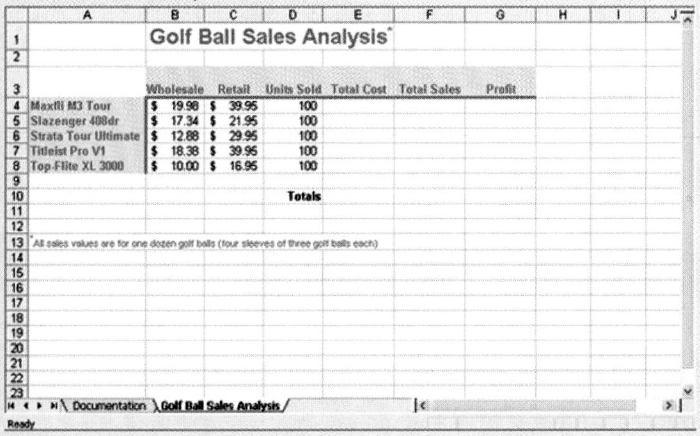

FIGURE 9.43

Pro Golf scenarios

Changing Cells	Scenarios		
	Typical	One	Two
D4	100	100	300
D5	266	200	100
D6	221	100	150
D7	314	300	200
D8	222	240	100

1. Break What?

Describe *break-even analysis* and explain why managers use it. In particular, suppose you charge your customers $500 for a bicycle and your manufacturing costs are as follows: variable cost per unit is $250 and fixed costs (per month) are $7,000. Calculate how many bicycles you must manufacture each month to break even. Be sure to include the equation and all analysis you use to determine the value.

2. Scenarios

Excel's scenarios allow you to perform what-if analysis. Describe succinctly how scenarios are advantageous. That is, how would an equivalent manual method be more difficult (or not) if Excel did not supply the ability to create scenarios?

Using the Solver

did you know?

some *Chinese typewriters have 5,700 characters. The keyboard on some models is almost three feet wide, and the fastest someone can type on these machines is 11 words per minute.*

the *colloquial term "mackintosh" for a raincoat comes from Charles Mackintosh, the Scottish chemist who invented and patented the first practical waterproof cloth in 1823.*

the *Chinese invented eyeglasses, and Marco Polo reported seeing many pairs worn by the Chinese as early as 1275.*

there *are more telephones than people in Washington, D.C.*

that *a company other than Microsoft created the Solver add-in for Microsoft Excel? Read this chapter to find out the name of that company.*

Chapter Objectives

- Learn how to use Excel's goal-seeking tools and concisely state a goal-seeking objective
- Try to attain a desired goal by trial and error
- Implement goal-seeking by using a graph—MOS XL03S-1-4
- Create goal-seeking reports
- Install the Excel Solver tool—MOS XL03E-1-7
- Format and resize graphics—MOS XL03E-2-3
- Use Excel's Solver to unravel more complex problems—MOS XL03E-1-7
- Identify the formula to be optimized—MOS XL03E-1-7
- Specify constraints on the problem that the Solver must satisfy—MOS XL03E-1-7
- Learn how to create Solver Answer, Limits, and Sensitivity reports—MOS XL03E-1-7

chapter case

ExerCycle

John Laskowski is an exercise enthusiast whose favorite form of exercise is to ride his bicycle on long weekend trips. John was the manager of a Chicago-area bicycle shop called Bikes4U. More than a few of John's bicycle customers commented how much they missed riding their bicycles during the often bitterly cold winter months. Although many of those customers suggested that the bicycle shop also sell stationary bicycles, Bikes4U owners wanted to maintain their focus on outdoor bikes of all types. John felt there was a big potential market in stationary bikes, so last year he left Bikes4U to open his own store and sell stationary exercise bicycles. He drew up a business plan, found several small retail locations in small shopping centers near his home, and then settled on one model of exercise bicycle that he felt would be a best-seller. In his busi-

ness plan, John outlined the retail and wholesale prices of a particular exercise bike that he wanted to sell exclusively.

John needs financing to purchase a quantity of the exercise bicycles and wants your help to calculate how many bicycles he can purchase. The bank has looked over John's business plan and agreed to loan him $58,000. If his business proves to be successful over the coming months, the bank has promised him additional financing. John wants you to help him determine how many exercise bicycles he can purchase. Later, John will sell an additional exercise bicycle model and would like your help to determine the best product mix to maximize his profit. Figure 10.1 shows the completed Exercise Bicycle Data worksheet of the ExerCycle workbook.

FIGURE 10.1

Completed Exercise
Bicycle Data worksheet

	A	B	C	D	E	F	G	H	I	J
1	**Single unit information**									
2	Model	**Upright 961**	**Recumbent 268**							
3	Item retail price	$2,400	$2,555							
4	Item wholesale cost	$1,800	$1,855							
5	Item profit	$600	$700							
6										
7	Assembly time (hrs)	4.5	5.5							
8										
9	**Total production information**				**Totals**		**Resources**			
10	Number of units	14	17		31		Available	Slack		
11	Cost	$25,200	$31,535		$56,735		$58,000	$1,265		
12	Profit	$8,400	$11,900		**$20,300**					
13	Assembly time (hrs)	63.0	93.5		156.5		160.0	3.5		
14										
15			$20,300							
16			$2							
17			TRUE							
18			TRUE							
19			TRUE							
20			TRUE							
21			$100							
22										
23										
24										
25										

Documentation / Solver Answer Report / **Exercise Bicycle Products**

Ready

Chapter 10 covers two sophisticated tools that work backward from a desired solution to determine the values needed to optimize the result. The first of these two tools is the Goal Seek command. The second tool is called the Solver. First, you will learn how to use the Goal Seek command to determine how many products you can purchase from a distributor given an upper limit on the loan you received from a bank. The *Goal Seek* command works backward in a worksheet to compute an unknown value that produces the final optimized result you desire.

Excel's Solver is a more powerful and capable tool than goal seeking. The Solver can minimize or maximize the value in the result cell by manipulating the values in more than one cell to achieve a desired end result. The Solver can answer the question "How can I allocate my limited resources (time, money, labor, or supplies) among several alternative options to achieve the best result?" You can use the Solver to figure out what *product mix*, or quantities of each product to sell, will generate the greatest profit. In decision analysis, the types of problems that the Solver works with are called *linear programming problems*, which involve one or more unknowns and several equations and inequalities.

SESSION 10.1 USING GOAL SEEK

In this section, you will learn how to use the Goal Seek command to solve a problem by working backward from a desired outcome. You will begin by opening a workbook, formatting and protecting a documentation worksheet, and then entering preliminary values for a product that John wants to sell. Once you have set up the values and formulas in the data portion of the workbook, you will try solving the problem by hand by substituting values into independent cells that affect the final result. Then, you will use Goal Seek to find the values that create the desired result. You will use a graphical method of goal seeking by selecting a chart element and stretching it to the outcome you want. Excel invokes the Goal Seek command to help you.

Designing a Goal Seek Workbook

John wants to design the goal-seeking worksheet so that it has two sections. The upper section includes the exercise bicycle's name, its selling or retail price, John's cost to purchase a single exercise bike, and the profit per bike. The lower section of the worksheet describes aggregate information about all the exercise bikes that John hopes to sell, including the total number of units for sale, their cumulative profit, their total cost, and the total time to assemble all bicycles. John has developed a rough sketch of the layout of the worksheet (see Figure 10.2).

John also wants the workbook to contain a documentation worksheet that precedes the data worksheet. It will contain the simple ExerCycle logo, the designer's name, a design date, and modification dates.

Formatting and Protecting the Documentation Worksheet

Start by modifying the documentation worksheet, the first worksheet in the ExerCycle workbook. You will format the background color of the worksheet, change its tab name to Documentation, modify the tab's color, insert data validation into two cells to display messages, eliminate the row and column headers on the Documentation worksheet, and protect the worksheet so that users can change only three cells on the Documentation worksheet.

FIGURE 10.2

Design of the Goal Seek worksheet

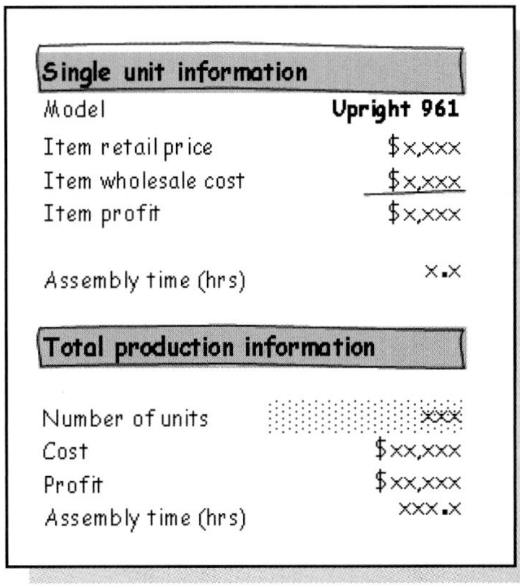

Single unit information	
Model	**Upright 961**
Item retail price	$x,xxx
Item wholesale cost	$x,xxx
Item profit	$x,xxx
Assembly time (hrs)	x.x

Total production information	
Number of units	xxx
Cost	$xx,xxx
Profit	$xx,xxx
Assembly time (hrs)	xxx.x

Renaming and Coloring a Worksheet Tab

First, you will rename a worksheet tab and then apply a color to it.

Opening the ExerCycle workbook and modifying the worksheet tab:

1. Start Excel as usual

2. Open the workbook **ex10ExerCycle.xls** and immediately save it as **ExerCycle2.xls**

3. Right-click the **Sheet1** worksheet tab, click **Tab Color** in the shortcut menu, click the **Light Turquoise** color square (fifth row from the top, fifth column), and click **OK** to close the Format Tab Color dialog box

4. Double-click the **Sheet1** worksheet tab to select its name, type **Documentation**, and press **Enter** to rename the worksheet tab

Unlocking Selected Cells

Now that you have given the worksheet tab a meaningful name and colored it the same color as the worksheet itself, you can work with three cells that the user enters data into. You will unlock them, provide data validation, and then protect the entire worksheet. John wants any worksheet user to be able to enter his or her name in the designer cell, enter the current date, and type a modification date in cells C12, C14, and C16. A message telling the user what he or she can type into each cell is a helpful addition to the Documentation worksheet.

Unlocking data input cells:

1. Click cell **C12** on the Documentation worksheet

2. Press and hold the **Ctrl** key, click cells **C14** and **C16** in turn to select them, and then release the **Ctrl** key

3. Click **Format**, click **Cells**, click the **Protection** tab of the Format Cells dialog box, click the **Locked** check box to clear its checkmark, and click **OK**

Adding Simple Data Validation to Selected Cells

Next, you will supply data validation for the three input cells (C12, C14, and C16) on the Documentation worksheet to remind the user about what information he or she can type in the cells.

Providing data validation for the three data input cells:

1. Click cell **C12**, click **Data**, click **Validation**, and click the **Input Message** tab

2. Click the **Input message** text box, type the message **Type your first and last names**, and then click **OK** to close the Data Validation dialog box

3. Click cell **C14**, click **Data** on the menu bar, and click **Validation**

4. Click the **Input message** text box, type the message **Type today's date (mm/dd/yy)**, and then click **OK** to close the Data Validation dialog box

5. Click cell **C16**, click **Data** on the menu bar, and click **Validation**

6. Click the **Input message** text box, type the message **Press F2 and then type the latest modification date. Use a comma to separate the latest date from previous ones.** (include the terminating period), and then click **OK** to close the Data Validation dialog box (see Figure 10.3)

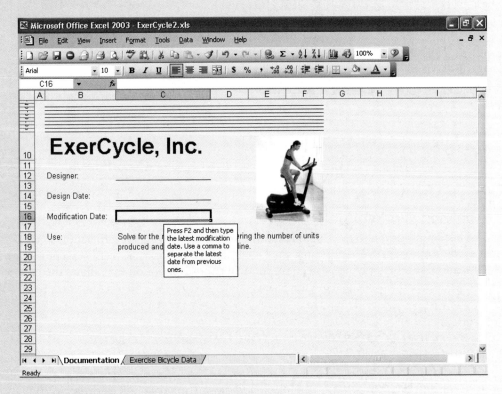

F I G U R E   10.3

Data validation message on the Documentation worksheet

Photo courtesy of Precor, Inc.

Eliminating Row and Column Headers

Spreadsheet row and column headers are not useful for this Documentation worksheet, so John wants you to eliminate them.

Hiding a worksheet's row and column headers:

1. Click **Tools**, and then click **Options** (at the bottom of the menu)

2. Click the **View** tab, if necessary, and then click the **Row & column headers** check box, found in the Window options panel, to clear its checkmark (see Figure 10.4)

3. Click **OK** to complete the operation and close the Options dialog box. Excel eliminates the row and column headers from the Documentation worksheet. Other worksheets are unaffected

FIGURE 10.4
Removing a worksheet's
row and column headers

clear the *Row & column*
headers check box ———

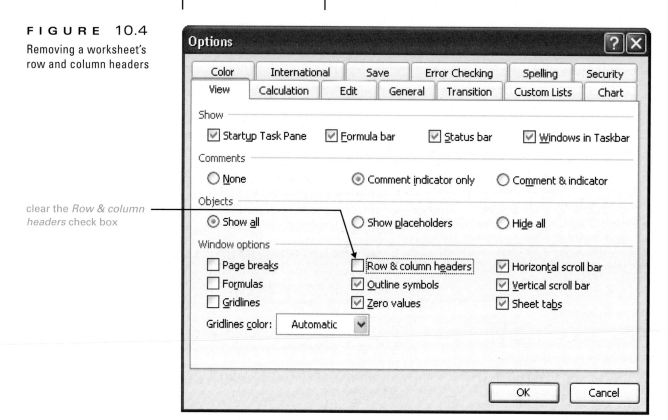

Applying Worksheet Protection

The last modification to the Documentation worksheet is to engage protection so that
the user cannot inadvertently alter any Documentation worksheet cells (except C12,
C14, and C16). In applying protection, you will choose an option that allows the user
to make active only cells that are unlocked.

Enforcing protection on the Documentation worksheet:

1. Click cell **B12** containing the label *Designer:* (observe cell address in the
   Name box; it will display B12 when you click the correct cell)

2. Click **Tools** on the menu bar and point to **Protection**

3. Click **Protect Sheet**. The Protect Sheet dialog box opens

4. Click the **Select locked cells** check box, located at the top of the list of
   labeled check boxes, to clear its checkmark. Clearing the check box
   prevents users from selecting any *locked* cell in the worksheet (see
   Figure 10.5)

5. Click **OK** to complete the process and close the Protect Sheet dialog box.
   Observe that cell C12 becomes the active cell

6. Click the **Save** button on the Standard toolbar

See the effect of exempting any locked cell on the Documentation worksheet from
becoming active by following the steps below. The steps attempt to make several ineli-
gible cells active.

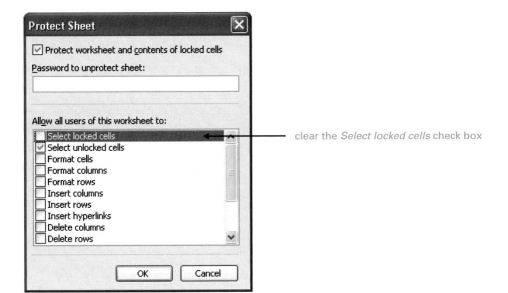

FIGURE 10.5
Setting protection
features

Experimenting with the newly applied protection:

1. Press and release the **Tab** key four times, *slowly*. Notice that cells C14, C16, C12, and C14, in turn, become active. That means that you can use the Tab key to move from one unlocked cell to another

2. Using the mouse, try to click any cell in the Documentation worksheet *except* cell C12, C14, or C16. Nothing happens. The active cell remains cell C14 (assuming you executed step 1 above)

You show the newly formatted worksheet to John and illustrate how Excel enforces cell protection. John is pleased and suggests you now move to the goal seek worksheet to add the necessary values, labels, and formulas.

Creating a Goal Seek Worksheet

Using the Goal Seek command, you can compute an unknown value that yields the result you want. In the case of ExerCycle, John wants to know how many exercise bicycles he can purchase with the $58,000 loan he obtained from the bank.

Entering Values and Writing Formulas

You begin building the goal seek worksheet by entering data, labels, and formulas for the upright exercise bicycle called the Upright 961.

Entering labels and values in the Exercise Bicycle Data worksheet:

1. Click the **Exercise Bicycle Data** worksheet tab

2. Click cell **B1**, click the **Bold** button on the Formatting toolbar, click the **Align Right** button on the Formatting toolbar, and type **Upright 961**

3. Click cell **B2** and type **2400**, which is the suggested retail price of the upright exercise bicycle

4. Click cell **B3** and type **1800**, which is John's wholesale cost

5. Click cell **B6** and type **4.5**, which is the number of hours John estimates it will take to assemble the exercise bicycle and prepare it for sale

6. Click cell **B8** and type **3**, and then press **Enter** (see Figure 10.6). Cell B8 contains John's initial estimate of the number of bicycles he will buy, assemble, and sell

FIGURE 10.6

Worksheet with price, cost, and labor hours entered

	A	B	C	D
1	Model	Upright 961		
2	Item retail price	2400		
3	Item wholesale cost	1800		
4	Item profit			
5				
6	Assembly time (hrs)	4.5		
7				
8	Number of units	3		
9	Cost			
10	Profit			
11	Assembly time (hrs)			
12				

The values you entered in four cells represent known constants in the worksheet that will represent John's simple business of buying, assembling, and selling a single product. Next, you write the formulas that depend on these numeric constants. The formulas include the profit on the sale of a single exercise bicycle—its item profit, total cost, total profit, and total assembly time based on the number of units John can sell. In addition, you will assign a name to the very important cell B8, which contains the number of units to sell. Near the end of this section, you will use the Goal Seek command to determine the value of that cell if you purchase as many bicycles as your loan allows you to buy.

Entering formulas and naming a cell:

1. Click cell **B4**, type **=B2-B3**, and press **Enter**

2. Click cell **B8**, click in the **Name box** to the left of the formula bar, type **UprightUnits** (no spaces), and press **Enter**

3. Click cell **B9**, type **=B3*UprightUnits**, and press **Enter**

4. In cell **B10**, type **=B4*UprightUnits**, and press **Enter**. The value 1800 appears. It is the profit John will realize if he sells all the bicycles

5. In cell **B11**, type **=B6*UprightUnits**, and press **Enter**. The value 13.5 appears. That is the total number of hours needed to assemble all the bicycles (see Figure 10.7)

	A	B	C	D
1	Model	Upright 961		
2	Item retail price	2400		
3	Item wholesale cost	1800		
4	Item profit	600		
5				
6	Assembly time (hrs)	4.5		
7				
8	Number of units	3		
9	Cost	5400		
10	Profit	1800		
11	Assembly time (hrs)	13.5		
12				

FIGURE 10.7
Goal Seek worksheet with formulas

Setting a Default Format and Formatting Individual Cells

With the basic goal seek worksheet set up, you can establish the default numeric format and then apply other formatting to dress up the worksheet. First, set the format for all numeric cells in the worksheet to currency with zero decimal places.

Setting a default numeric format:

1. Press **Ctrl+A** to select all the worksheet's cells

2. Click **Format**, click **Cells**, click the **Number** tab, click **Currency** in the Category list, type **0** in the Decimal places box, click the **Symbol** list box, click **$**, click (**$1,234**) in the Negative numbers list (third row from the top), and click **OK** to close the Format Cells dialog box

Next, you will format cell B3 with an underline and then change the format on numeric cells that are not currency values.

Underlining a cell and modifying the format of other numeric cells:

1. Click cell **B3**, click **Format**, click **Cells**, click the **Font** tab, click the **Underline** list box, click **Single Accounting** in the list, and click **OK**

2. Click cell **B6**, press and hold **Ctrl**, click cell **B8**, click cell **B11**, and release the **Ctrl** key

3. Click the **Comma Style** button on the Formatting toolbar, and then click the **Decrease Decimal** button on the Formatting toolbar

4. Click cell **B8**, and click the **Decrease Decimal** button on the Formatting toolbar (see Figure 10.8)

All the numeric entries are formatted in attractive ways, and values that represent currencies are obvious. John is pleased with the way the worksheet is shaping up.

EXCEL

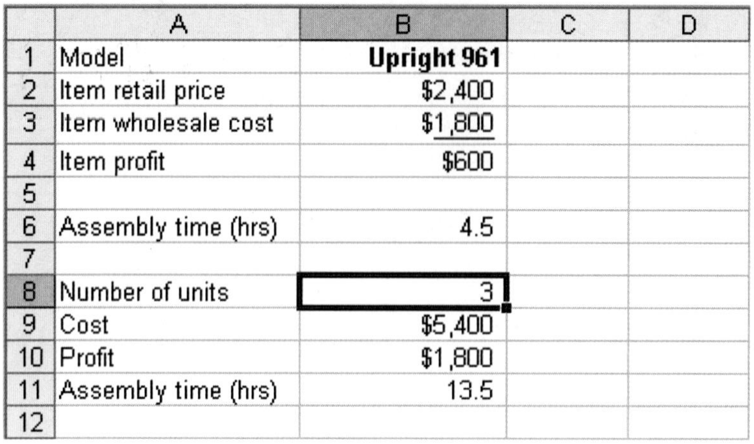

FIGURE 10.8

Worksheet with numeric entries formatted

	A	B	C	D
1	Model	**Upright 961**		
2	Item retail price	$2,400		
3	Item wholesale cost	$1,800		
4	Item profit	$600		
5				
6	Assembly time (hrs)	4.5		
7				
8	Number of units	3		
9	Cost	$5,400		
10	Profit	$1,800		
11	Assembly time (hrs)	13.5		
12				

Inserting Rows and Adding Section Banners

John would like you to provide visual headings about the two sections that display "Single unit information" and "Total production information" so that the sections are clearly distinguished. He wants the first heading above the label *Model* in row 1, and he wants the second heading marking the total production information just above the label *Number of units* found in cell A8.

anotherway

... to Insert a Row

Right-click the row header

Click **Insert** on the shortcut menu

Inserting rows and adding section banners:

1. Click cell **A1**, click **Insert**, and then click **Rows**. Excel inserts a new row 1

2. In cell A1, type **Single unit information** and press **Enter**

3. Click cell **A9**, click **Insert**, and then click **Rows**. Excel inserts a new row 9

4. In cell A9, type **Total production information** and press **Enter**

Applying Fill Colors to Selected Cells

With the two section headings in place, you can apply fill colors to them and to cell B10 containing the number of units to sell.

Applying fill colors to selected cells:

1. Click and drag cell range **A1:B1** and click the **Fill Color** button list arrow on the Formatting toolbar to display a palette of color selections

tip: *If you click the **Fill Color** button instead of its list arrow, then click the **Undo** button on the Standard toolbar and repeat step 1*

2. Click the **Light Turquoise** color square in the fifth column of the bottom row in the Fill Color palette.

tip: *If you hover the mouse over any color square, its name appears in a ScreenTip. That ensures you are about to click the correct color square*

3. With cells A1 and B1 still selected, click the **Bold** button on the Formatting toolbar, click the **Borders** button list arrow, and then click the **Outside Borders** button to place an outline around the cell pair

4. With cells A1 and B1 still selected, click the **Format Painter** button on the Standard toolbar

5. Click and drag the cell range **A9:B9**. Excel pastes all the formatting from cells A1:B1 onto the cell range A9:B9

6. Click cell **B10**, click the **Fill Color** button list arrow on the Formatting toolbar, and click the **Light Yellow** color square in the third column of the bottom row in the Fill Color palette (see Figure 10.9)

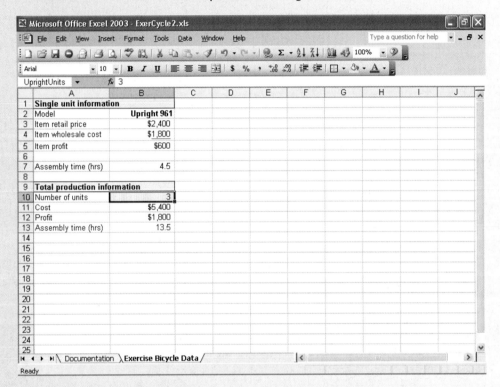

FIGURE 10.9

After applying fill colors

With the formatting complete and formulas in place, you are ready to use the Goal Seek command.

Using the Goal Seek Command

Recall that the purpose of the worksheet you are developing is to determine how many upright exercise bicycles John can purchase with his $58,000 loan. That is the *Goal Seek objective*—the end result you want to achieve. Now you can focus on the main goal: maximizing John's profit on the sale of exercise bicycles. John stops by your desk and you show him the work you have done so far on the workbook. You ask John why assembly time for each bicycle and total assembly time are part of the worksheet. He tells you that in order to figure out the maximum profit the store can generate, you must consider two constraints in his business model. (A *constraint* is limitation on the values that a cell can have.) As you remember, John has a loan for $58,000. That limits how many bicycles he can purchase from the manufacturer.

There is another restriction that John has not mentioned yet. Because John is ExerCycle's only employee, his time is split between running the store, selling bicycles, and assembling bicycles. John figures that he has only 160 hours for assembling bicycles each month, and he wants to sell all he can in order to stay in business. He explains that if he had an unlimited supply of money and time, his profit would be enormous. However, you have to help him figure out his profit given the time and money restrictions.

You can use the trial-and-error method to see how many units John can purchase with his loan. Sometimes the solution is relatively easy to find that way. Other times, it is very difficult.

Generating Solutions by Trial and Error

One method to calculate profit John can realize from selling bicycles is to enter different numbers in cell B10, which is the quantity he purchases and sells, and then observe the recalculated values for total cost, total profit, and total assembly time. Doing this is typical what-if analysis. In other words, you can ask what-if questions by typing the value 25, then 35, and then 40 in turn into cell B10 and examining the resulting values of those substitutions. That is the traditional approach you have used so far in this textbook.

Using what-if techniques to examine cost, profit, and assembly time values:

1. With cell **B10** selected, type **25**, and press **Enter**. Cell B12 displays the profit, $15,000. Notice that the cost is $45,000, and assembly time for 25 units is 112.5 hours

2. Click cell **B10**, type **40**, and press **Enter**. Although profit has risen to $24,000, the purchase cost for 40 units is $72,000 (cell B11). Figure 10.10 shows the first two analyses side by side

FIGURE 10.10

Comparing two what-if results

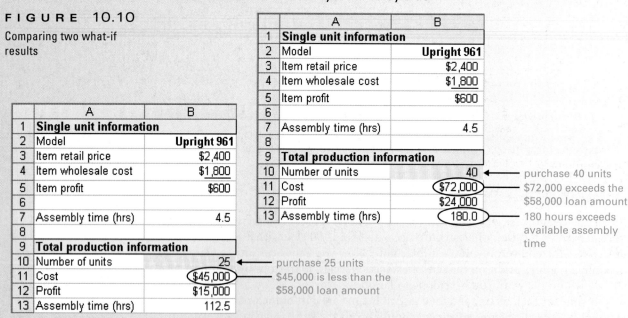

3. Click cell **B10**, type **35**, and press **Enter**. Profit is $21,000. While assembly time for 35 units, 157.5 hours, is within the constraint limit, the total wholesale cost of $63,000 is still larger than the bank loan

The previous what-if analyses reveal that the number of units John can sell to maximize his profits under the constraints of time and money is between 25 units and 35 units. You could continue using this trial-and-error method, but using this method—even for this relatively simple problem—would waste a lot of time. Excel provides a better approach.

help yourself *Press **F1**, type **goal seek** in the Search text box of the Microsoft Excel Help task pane, and press **Enter**. From the Search Results list, click the hyperlink **About Goal Seek**. Maximize the Help screen if necessary. Read and optionally print the description of the Goal Seek command. Click the Help screen **Close** button when you are finished, and close the task pane*

Generating a Solution with the Goal Seek Command

By using the Excel Goal Seek command, you can short-circuit the trial-and-error process to find a solution. Goal seeking starts with the end result that you want and then backtracks from the formula to a precedent value that satisfies the desired result. A *precedent value* is the value on which a formula, or result, is directly (or indirectly) based. In this case, the end result you are seeking is a total wholesale cost (cell B11) that is less than or equal to the loan amount of $58,000. The precedent value, quantity to purchase and then sell, is stored in cell B10. Excel can repeatedly change the value of the precedent value until the end result is less than or equal to the goal value you specify. The difference between what-if analysis and goal seek analysis is the way John asks the question(s). John could ask "*What* would it cost *if* I purchased 25 bicycles?" Using goal seek analysis, the question John would pose is "If I can spend $58,000 on bicycles, how many can I purchase?"

You can use goal seek to answer the question of how many bicycles can be purchased for $58,000. Another goal-seeking question is "How many bicycles can be assembled under the time constraint of 160 hours?" Goal seek *cannot* answer both questions at the same time. You have to choose either purchase cost or assembling hours as the result and then use goal seeking to determine the maximum precedent value that satisfies either constraint.

---

task reference   **Using Goal Seek**

- Click **Tools** and then click **Goal Seek**

- Click the **Set cell** box and type the cell address of the result cell

- Click the **To value** box and type the result value you want

- Click the **By changing** cell box and type the address of the changing cell

- Click **OK** to solve the problem, and then click **OK** to close the Goal Seek Status dialog box

---

To use the Goal Seek command, you first identify the changing cell and the result cell. The changing cell is the precedent cell whose value Excel changes to reach the result you want. The result cell, which always contains a formula, is the cell holding your goal. In this case, the goal is cell B11 containing the formula to calculate the total purchase price. Your goal is to set this value as close to $58,000 without going over that value, which will maximize John's profit. Because goal seeking solves for one precedent value only, you must inspect cell B13 to make sure Excel's solution does not force the assembly time above 160.

Using Goal Seek to find how many bicycles John can purchase:

1. Click **Tools** and then click **Goal Seek**. The Goal Seek dialog box opens

2. Drag the Goal Seek dialog box to the right so that you can see cells B10 and B11

3. Type **B11** in the *Set cell* box, and then press **Tab** to move to the *To value* box

4. In the *To value* box, type **58000** and press **Tab**. $58,000 is John's loan amount and, thus, his spending limit

5. In the *By changing cell* box, type **B10**. Cell B10 is the precedent cell that Excel can change in its attempt to reach the $58,000 cost goal. See Figure 10.11

FIGURE 10.11

Completed Goal Seek dialog box

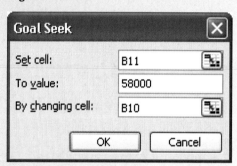

6. Click **OK** to launch the Goal Seek process. The Goal Seek Status dialog box opens and indicates that it found a solution

7. Drag the Goal Seek Status dialog box to the right so that you can see cells B10 and B11. Notice that cell B10 contains the answer, 32 bicycles (see Figure 10.12)

FIGURE 10.12

Goal Seek has found an answer

this is the quantity to purchase in order to ...

... spend $58,000

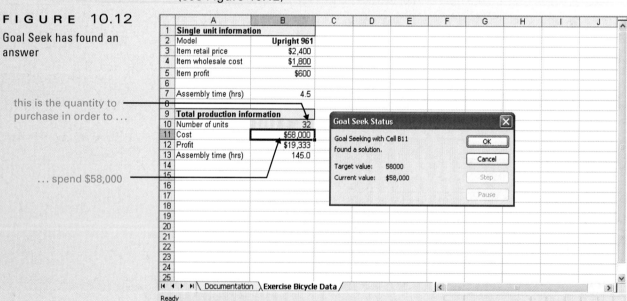

8. Click **OK** to accept the result and close the Goal Seek Status dialog box

tip: *If you want to reject the answer that Excel has found, click the Cancel button to restore the original values for the precedent and result cells*

If you click cell B10 and examine the formula bar, you will see Goal Seek actually determined 32.222222 bicycles can be produced. Of course, you cannot purchase or sell a fraction of a bicycle, so you discard any fraction in the answer and settle on 32 bicycles. The value for the assembly time, 145.0 hours, is less than the available time, so that constraint is met simultaneously. If you are curious about the quantity of bicycles John could assemble in 160 hours, regardless of their cost, you can run another Goal Seek command to see the answer.

Using Goal Seek to find how many bicycles John can assemble in 160 hours:

1. Click **Tools** and then click **Goal Seek**. The Goal Seek dialog box opens

2. Type **B13** in the *Set cell* box, and then press **Tab** to move to the *To value* box

3. In the *To value* box, type **160** and press **Tab**. 160 is the maximum hours John has available to assemble bicycles

4. In the *By changing cell* box, type **B10**. Cell B10 is the precedent cell that Excel can change in its attempt to reach the 160-hour goal

5. Click **OK**. The Goal Seek Status dialog box opens and indicates that it found a solution. Notice that cell B10 contains the answer, 36 bicycles (see Figure 10.13)

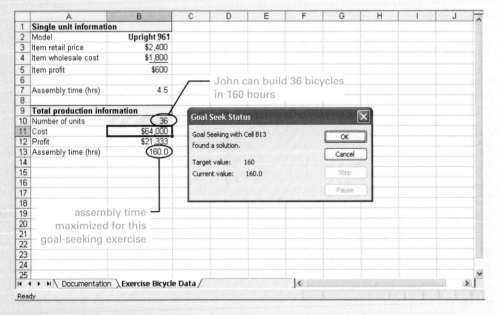

FIGURE 10.13

Goal Seek maximizes assembly hours

6. Click **OK** to accept the result and close the Goal Seek Status dialog box

Though goal seeking has demonstrated that John could assemble 36 (35.555, actually) bicycles in the allotted 160 hours, the purchase cost of the bicycles, $64,000, exceeds the loan amount. In this case it is clear to you that the real constraint John will have to observe is total cash available to purchase bicycles from the manufacturer, not the labor hours available.

Graphic Goal Seeking

Excel also allows you to do goal seeking graphically. For example, you can create a simple column chart of total profit and total cost. Once you have constructed the two-column chart, you can perform that goal-seeking procedure by selecting the graph's profit data marker and then dragging the column up to the $50,000 mark on the Y-axis. Dragging the data markers automatically launches the Goal Seek command.

Creating a simple column chart:

1. Select cell range **A11:B12**, click the **Chart Wizard** button on the Standard toolbar, click **Next**, click **Next** again, click the **Legend** tab, click the **Show legend** check box to clear it, and click **Finish**. Excel creates an embedded column chart

2. Move the chart to the right, if necessary, so that you can see both the chart and worksheet columns A and B

With the embedded chart built, you can perform goal seeking by manipulating either of the chart's columns.

Goal seeking by resizing a chart data marker:

1. Click the **Profit** data marker, which is the short blue bar with the label "Profit" below it, and then click the **Profit** data marker again to select just that column

2. Move the mouse to the large selection handle in the top middle of the data marker. The mouse changes to a double-headed arrow pointing up and down

3. Click and drag the selection handle up toward the $50,000 horizontal rule until the ScreenTip indicates that the value is approximately $50,000 (see Figure 10.14), and then release the mouse. This takes patience and a steady hand. Excel opens the Goal Seek dialog box

4. With the insertion point in the *By changing cell* box, type **B10**

5. If you were unable to drag the data marker to exactly $50,000, then press **Shift+Tab** to move back to the *To value* box and type **50000**. Your Goal Seek dialog box should look like the one in Figure 10.15

6. Click **OK** to accept your values and cell addresses. Excel finds a solution

7. Click **OK** to accept the solution and close the Goal Seek Status dialog box (see Figure 10.16)

8. Click any worksheet cell to deselect the range and corresponding data marker in the chart

The Goal Seek command invoked through a chart indicates that John must sell more than 83 exercise bicycles to yield a profit of $50,000.

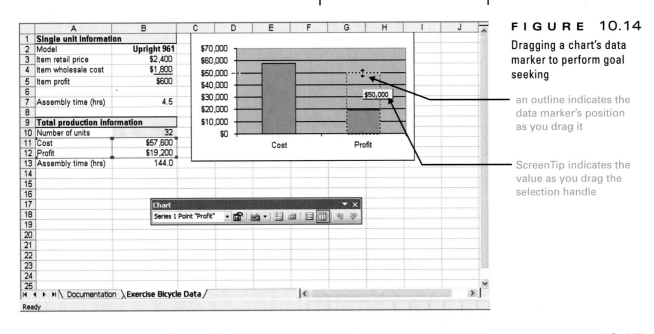

FIGURE 10.14

Dragging a chart's data marker to perform goal seeking

an outline indicates the data marker's position as you drag it

ScreenTip indicates the value as you drag the selection handle

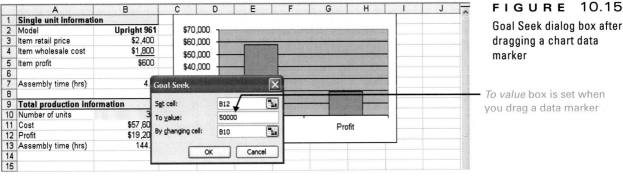

FIGURE 10.15

Goal Seek dialog box after dragging a chart data marker

To value box is set when you drag a data marker

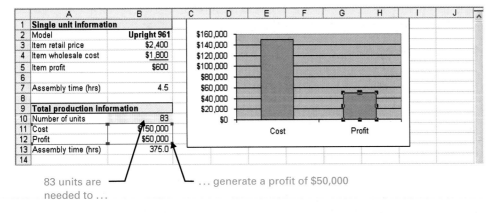

FIGURE 10.16

Graphic goal-seeking results

83 units are needed to ...

... generate a profit of $50,000

Deleting the chart and restoring the number of units to its original value:

1. Click the **Chart Area** (the white area near the outermost rectangle surrounding the chart) to select the embedded chart, and then press the **Delete** key. Excel removes the chart

2. Click cell **B10**, type **32**, and press **Enter**

John is pleased with your results and can see that he can purchase enough bicycles with his first round of financing to start his business with sufficient stock.

Saving and closing the workbook:

1. Type your first and last names in the Exercise Bicycle Data worksheet header (*Hint:* Click **View**, click **Header and Footer**)

2. Click the **Documentation** worksheet tab, click **C12** next to the Designer label, type your first and last names, press **Tab**, type today's date, and press **Enter**

3. Click **File** on the menu bar and then click **Exit**

4. Click the **Yes** button when Excel asks you if you want to save the changes you made to **ExerCycle2.xls**

SESSION 10.1

making the grade

1. Goal seeking works backward from the _____ to determine an answer.

2. A Goal Seek _____ is another name for the result you want to achieve.

3. In goal seeking, a _____ limits the values that a cell can have.

4. The _____ value is the value on which a formula, or result, is directly (or indirectly) based.

SESSION 10.2 SOLVING COMPLEX PROBLEMS

In this section, you will learn how to install the Solver tool and how to use the Solver to determine a solution to a more complex problem involving multiple products and multiple constraints. You will use the Solver to decide the best combination of exercise bicycle products to sell in order to maximize profits. You will learn about the three Solver reports: Answer, Limits, and Sensitivity.

Introducing the Problem

Recently, John received a letter from Biking Industries, the manufacturer from whom John purchases the Upright 961 exercise bicycle. In the letter, Biking Industries' vice president of marketing informed John that one of the recumbent exercise bicycles they manufacture is on sale for the next three months. John can purchase the recumbent bicycle, called the Recumbent 268, at the wholesale price of $1,855. Its suggested retail price is $2,555. John wants to offer more than one exercise bicycle for sale to give customers more choice and so that his sales success does not depend on one exercise bicycle alone. He tells you that the bank is not willing to increase the loan amount from its original $58,000. Thus, John will have to determine how many of each type of exercise bicycle he can purchase for $58,000. You ask John about assembly time for the recumbent model. He asks you to call the manufacturer and find out an estimate of the time it takes to assemble the Recumbent 268.

You find out from Biking Industries that the estimated assembly time for the Recumbent 268, assuming an experienced person is performing the work, is 5.5 hours. That is an hour more than the assembly time for the Upright 961, but the recumbent model is slightly more complex than the upright version.

The data you have learned here, though relatively simple, illustrates the type of problem that you encounter frequently in business. John wants to maximize total profit selling the two bicycles, yet he is restricted by both time and money. Time and money are the problem's constraints—time to assemble the bicycles and the total amount he can spend to acquire the disassembled exercise bicycles. You can't help but wonder exactly how many of each type of exercise bicycle John should sell in order to maximize his profits.

help yourself *Press **F1**, type **solver** in the Search text box of the Microsoft Excel Help task pane, and press **Enter**. Scroll down the Search Results list to locate and then click the hyperlink **Define and solve a problem by using Solver**. Maximize the Help screen if necessary. Read and optionally print the description of the Solver command. Click the **How?** hyperlink in step 2 and notice that it opens an explanation of how to install the Solver. Click the Help screen **Close** button when you are finished, and close the task pane*

Introducing the Solver

The Goal Seek command is suitable for problems that involve an exact result value that depends on one precedent value. For more complex problems, the Solver is your best choice. You can use the Solver for *equation-solving* in which you use goal seeking or back solving like the Goal Seek command and *constrained optimization* in which you specify a set of constraints and an outcome or result that you want optimized (minimized or maximized). Unlike the Goal Seek command, the Solver can change the value of several cells at once, not just one, to reach the desired final result.

What applications use the Solver? Most often, the Solver is the tool of choice when you need to solve a resource allocation problem. A *resource allocation problem* is one in which productive resources (people, raw materials, time, and so on) can be used in a variety of places or in different products, and in which those resources must be distributed in the best way possible. "Best" usually implies minimizing costs, maximizing profits, or reducing risk to a very low level. For example, a Solver could solve for the best allocation of a fixed number of labor hours between multiple products manufactured by a company. Similarly, the Solver could determine how many of each of several products to sell to maximize profit, which is a *product mix* problem. Determining the best way to ship a variety of packages across different available routes to destination warehouses is another example of a problem that the Solver can disentangle.

Solver problems involve precedent cells, also known as decision variables, and an objective function. Excel's Solver can change decision variables to cause changes in the *object function*, which is the cell containing a function whose value you want to optimize and whose value is affected by a change in the decision variables.

The Solver is an Excel add-in, which means that it might not be available in the Tools menu. An *add-in* is a specialized feature of Excel that not everyone uses on a regular basis. Therefore, it is not necessarily included automatically as one of the available programs on the Tools menu. To see whether or not you have Solver installed, look in the Tools menu. If Solver is not in the menu, you can install it easily by following installation steps provided in this chapter.

Microsoft did not develop the Microsoft Excel Solver. Instead, Frontline Systems, headquartered in Incline Village, Nevada, first produced it for Microsoft after winning a competition among third-party solver developers in 1990. Frontline Systems has continued to work with Microsoft to supply the enhanced Solver add-in that is available for Office Excel 2003.

EXCEL

Installing the Solver

In order to work with the steps in this session, you need the Excel Solver. First, determine if the Solver is installed on the computer you are using.

Determining if the Solver Add-in is installed on your computer:

1. Start Excel as usual. Excel opens and displays a new workbook and empty worksheet

2. Click **Tools**

3. Scan the Tools command list for "Solver . . ." If present, Solver is about three-fourths of the way down the list of commands—just after the Formula Auditing command

4. Press the **Esc** key to close the Tools menu

If the Solver command is not in the Tools menu, the Solver Add-in was not installed when Excel was installed. Check with your instructor to ensure that it is okay to install the Solver. If so, execute the following steps to install the Solver. If the Solver is installed in Excel, skip the next steps labeled "Installing the Solver on your computer."

Installing the Solver on your computer:

1. Click **Tools** and then click **Add-Ins**. The Add-Ins dialog box opens

2. Click the **Solver Add-in** check box to place a checkmark in it (see Figure 10.17)

F I G U R E 10.17

Adding the Solver to the Tools menu

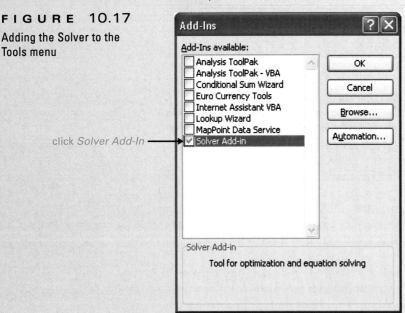

click *Solver Add-In*

3. Click **OK** to add the Solver to the Tools menu and close the Add-Ins dialog box

Formulating the Problem Concisely

With the Solver available in the Tools menu, you can turn your attention to examining the problem and reviewing a worksheet partially set up to solve the problem. John has created a revised worksheet with formatting already established so that you can focus on solving the asset allocation problem at hand. Begin by opening the product mix workbook and saving it under a new name.

Opening the product mix worksheet:

1. Open the workbook **ex10ExerCycleMix.xls** and immediately save it as **ExerCycleMix2.xls**. The Documentation worksheet appears

2. Click cell **C12**, if necessary, to make it active. Cell C12 is the cell to the right of the label *Designer*

tip: *Remember that the cell address of the active cell appears in the Name box to the left of the formula bar*

John wants you to add a picture to the documentation sheet. The picture is a man riding the Recumbent 268. You will insert the picture and resize it to fit within the white rectangle on the Documentation sheet.

Inserting and resizing a graphic:

1. Click **Insert**, point to **Picture**, and click **From File**

2. Use the *Look in* list box to navigate to the folder containing the file **ex10Recumbent268.jpg**, click **ex10Recumbent268.jpg**, and click the Insert button to embed the picture in the worksheet

3. Hover the mouse over the picture's green rotate handle, which is located at the top, center of the picture, and drag it to the right and down until the picture is upright

4. Resize the picture by clicking any *corner* sizing handle and dragging toward the center of the picture until it is approximately the size of the white rectangle on the Documentation sheet

5. Click in the middle of the picture and drag it so that the upper left corner of the picture is aligned with the upper left corner of the white rectangle and release the mouse

6. Repeat step 4 above, clicking and dragging the lower right sizing handle until the picture just covers the white rectangle. Release the mouse and resize the picture so it just covers the rectangle

7. Once the picture matches the size of the white rectangle, right-click the picture, point to **Order** in the pop-up menu, and click **Send to Back**

8. Click the **white rectangle** so sizing handles surround it, and press the **Delete** key to delete it (see Figure 10.18)

tip: *if you omit step 8 and accidentally delete the picture, click Undo and repeat step 8*

EXCEL

FIGURE 10.18

Documentation worksheet of the product mix workbook

Photo courtesy of Precor, Inc.

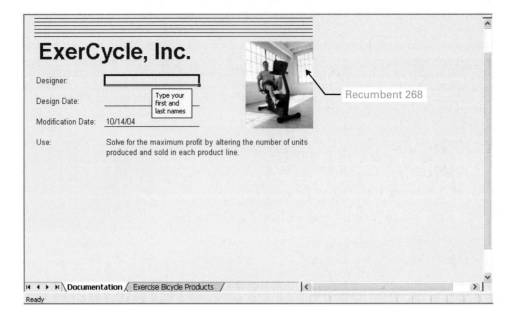

Finally, protect the worksheet so that the picture stays in place and only unlocked cells on the Documentation worksheet are accessible to workbook users.

Protecting the Documentation worksheet and typing documentation:

1. Click **Tools**, point to **Protection**, and click **Protect Sheet**

2. Ensure that the Protect worksheet and contents of locked cells check box is checked, and ensure that the Select locked cells check box is clear

3. Click **OK**

4. Type your first and last names in cell C12 and then press **Tab** to move to the next unlocked cell in the worksheet, cell C14

5. Type today's date and then press **Tab** to move to cell C16

6. Press **F2**, type a comma and a space, type today's date, and then press **Enter**. Cell C12 becomes active

7. Click the **Exercise Bicycle Products** worksheet tab to make that worksheet active. The retail prices, costs, and item profits for the two exercise bicycles are filled in already (see Figure 10.19)

The Exercise Bicycle Products worksheet is similar in structure to the Exercise Bicycle Data worksheet of the goal-seeking workbook you completed in the last session. The main difference is that there are two product columns, columns B and C.

John has asked you to complete the formulas and values for three areas highlighted in Figure 10.19. First, you are to write formulas for the total cost, total profit, and total assembly time for the Recumbent 268—cells C11 through C13. Then, you can fill in row totals in the cell range E10:E13. Finally, you can fill in the resource restrictions in cells G11 and G13 as well as the accompanying formulas for slack in cells H11 and H13. *Slack* is the quantity of a resource that has not been used or allocated. A synonym for slack is "unused," but *slack* is the term you will most often see in applications like this one.

FIGURE 10.19

Exercise Bicycle Products
worksheet

product unit cost and
price information

aggregate production
information about
multiple units of both
products

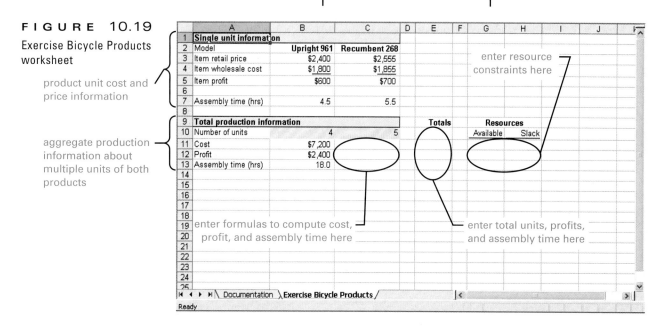

You are ready to write the missing equations and values to complete the worksheet
prior to applying the Solver.

Writing formulas for the recumbent exercise bicycle:

1. Click cell **C10** and observe the Name box. Notice that part of a cell name appears there

2. Click cell **C11**, type **=C4*RecumbentUnits**, and press **Enter**. The formula calculates the total cost of recumbent exercise bicycles, $9,275 in this case

3. In cell C12, type **=C5*RecumbentUnits** and press **Enter**. Excel calculates the total profit and displays $3,500

4. In cell C13, type **=C7*RecumbentUnits** and press **Enter**. Excel calculates the total assembly time for five recumbent exercise bicycles, which is 27.5 hours (see Figure 10.20)

	A	B	C	D	E	F	G	H	I	J
1	**Single unit information**									
2	Model	Upright 961	Recumbent 268							
3	Item retail price	$2,400	$2,555							
4	Item wholesale cost	$1,800	$1,855							
5	Item profit	$600	$700							
6										
7	Assembly time (hrs)	4.5	5.5							
8										
9	**Total production information**						Totals	Resources		
10	Number of units	4	5					Available	Slack	
11	Cost	$7,200	$9,275							
12	Profit	$2,400	$3,500							
13	Assembly time (hrs)	18.0	27.5							
14										
15										

values for recumbent
bicycle product

FIGURE 10.20

Recumbent exercise
bicycle aggregate values
displayed

An important series of formulas are the totals you will place into the cell range E10:E13. The values total the number of units purchased and sold, cost, profit, and assembly time. Two of those totals, total number of units and total assembly time, are especially important. They will help you determine the best product mix based on the allocation of limited resources. You enter the totals next.

Writing formulas to sum values for all products:

1. Select the cell range **E10:E13**

2. Click the **AutoSum** button on the Standard toolbar. Excel places SUM functions in cells E10 through E13 totaling the partial rows to the left of each SUM function

3. Click cell **E10** and then examine the formula bar. Notice the summed cell range, B10:D10, includes the extra cell D10 (see Figure 10.21)

FIGURE 10.21

Product summation formulas completed

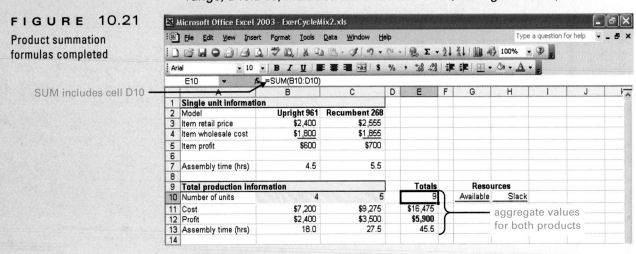

SUM includes cell D10

aggregate values for both products

Normally the extra cell in a sum formula would be a problem. In this case, it is a *feature*. If John ever asks you to insert a column to accommodate another product, you would click the column D header and then insert a column.

The only formulas and values needed to complete the Exercise Bicycle Products worksheet prior to using the Solver are the constraints. Part of formulating the problem correctly is knowing all the problem's constraints and stating them precisely in a worksheet. Recall that the constraints in this problem are the number of assembly hours available and the cash (loan amount) available to purchase the bicycles.

You will enter the total cash available into cell G11 and the total assembly hours into cell G13. In cells H11 and H13, you will enter a simple formula that shows the slack available. Prior to executing the Solver, slack resources will be equal to the total available resources. Once the Solver has completed its work, the slack resources will be the available resources minus the used resources. Execute the following steps to complete the Resources section of the worksheet.

Entering the available resources values (constraints):

1. Click cell **G11**, which is in the same row as total cost, and type **58000**. That amount is the total available to purchase bicycles

2. Click cell **G13**, type **160**, and press **Enter**. John has available a total of 160 hours of assembly time

Next, enter formulas that indicate how much of the resources remain after they are allocated to building the bicycles. Initially the slack values are equal to the available resources because the resources are unconsumed. When you employ the Solver, the values for slack resources should decline. In an ideal situation, you have exactly the resources needed for an optimal outcome, and the values for *all* slack resources are zero. That is, all resources would be completely consumed with no inventory or idle time remaining. In reality, this rarely occurs for all resources.

Next, write the formulas to compute slack values, which are the total available resources minus the consumed resources—represented by totals in column E for total cost and total assembly time.

Entering formulas for slack resources:

1. Click cell **H11**, type **=G11-E11**, and press **Enter**. The value $41,525 appears and indicates that building 4 upright and 5 recumbent exercise bicycles leaves $41,525 available for purchasing more bicycles

2. Click cell **H13**, type **=G13-E13**, and press **Enter**. The slack hours available for building additional bicycles, 114.5, appears (see Figure 10.22)

	A	B	C	D	E	F	G	H	I	J	
1	Single unit information										
2	Model	Upright 961	Recumbent 268								
3	Item retail price	$2,400	$2,555								
4	Item wholesale cost	$1,800	$1,855								
5	Item profit	$600	$700								
6											
7	Assembly time (hrs)	4.5	5.5								
8											
9	Total production information				Totals		Resources				
10	Number of units	4	5		9		Available	Slack			
11	Cost	$7,200	$9,275		$16,475		$58,000	$41,525			
12	Profit	$2,400	$3,500		$5,900						
13	Assembly time (hrs)	18.0	27.5		45.5		160.0	114.5			
14											
15											

constraints are complete

profit under this scenario

FIGURE 10.22

Worksheet with constraints complete

Solving More Difficult Problems Using Trial and Error

You have helped John create a worksheet in which you will be able to find the combination of upright and recumbent bicycles to sell that will maximize John's profit and stay within the cost and assembly time limitations. As with goal seek problems, you can solve more complex problems with multiple constraints using trial and error.

EXCEL

In the next steps, you will enter different values for the *Number of units* and then note the total profit and the slack values. Carefully examine each of the slack values to ensure that none of them becomes negative. Negative resources indicate a solution is not feasible. That is, you cannot use resources you do not have. Finally, you will graph the results to see if you can detect a pattern.

Entering various quantities and searching for an optimal solution:

1. Select the cell range cell **B10:C10**, the two precedent cells upon which both profit and slack formulas depend

2. Type **10**, press **Enter**, type **12**, and press **Enter**. In this scenario, you propose that John sells 10 upright bicycles and 12 recumbent bicycles. Total profit is $14,400 and there are positive slack values for resources

3. Type **18**, press **Enter**, type **20**, and press **Enter**. Total profit is $24,800, which is better than the previous scenario. However, both the cost and assembly slack values are negative, which means the procedure requires more resources than you have available (see Figure 10.23)

FIGURE 10.23

Infeasible solution

	A	B	C	D	E	F	G	H	I		
1	Single unit information										
2	Model	Upright 961	Recumbent 268								
3	Item retail price	$2,400	$2,555								
4	Item wholesale cost	$1,800	$1,855								
5	Item profit	$600	$700								
6											
7	Assembly time (hrs)	4.5	5.5								
8											
9	Total production information				Totals		Resources				
10	Number of units	18	20		38		Available	Slack			
11	Cost	$32,400	$37,100		$69,500		$58,000	($11,500)			
12	Profit	$10,800	$14,000		**$24,800**						
13	Assembly time (hrs)	81.0	110.0		191.0		160.0	(31.0)			
14											
15											

negative cost indicates a cost overrun

profit is almost $25,000 under these assumptions

negative assembly hours indicate more time used than is available

4. Type **20**, press **Enter**, type **12**, and press **Enter**. The total profit is $20,400 and the assembly slack time is positive—some assembly time is still available—but the slack value for cost (cell H11) is negative $260. This is an infeasible solution because it would require additional cash

5. Type **4**, press **Enter**, type **5**, and press **Enter** to return the purchase quantities back to their original values

6. Click any cell to deselect the two-cell cell range

You have tried three pairs of numbers and found two solutions that would work, but did you find the best solution? Looking at the answer, you can't help but wonder if the proposed solution of 10 upright and 12 recumbent units is the best solution. The Excel Solver can answer that question for you. It is designed to help you solve constrained optimization problems like this.

Using the Solver

Excel's Solver attempts to find the best solution for the optimization problem. You identify to the Solver the object function (or target cell), the precedent cells (or changing cells), and all constraints that apply to the problem. Solver then goes to work to find the maximum or minimum value for the object function by changing the precedent cells' values. The solution must satisfy all specified constraints, such as a limit on resources. In this case, the constraints are the upper limit on funds available to purchase unassembled exercise bicycles and the total number of hours available to assemble them.

First, make sure you understand how to identify all the important cells that the Solver will either examine or alter. The object function is total profit whose result appears in cell E12. It is a simple expression that sums the profits of the two bicycles.

The precedent cells, which the Solver can change in its search for an optimal solution, are cells B10 and C10. Those are the same cells you modified in your manual search for a solution to the product mix that optimized profit.

The only two constraints for this problem are values, not formulas, found in cells G11 and G13. Cell G11 contains the maximum total cost of all products, $58,000, that John can purchase, and cell G13 holds the maximum hours available for product assembly—160 hours.

With all of the important components identified, you can set up Excel's solver and then have it determine a solution.

---

task reference   Using the Solver

- Click **Tools** and then click **Solver**

- In the *Set Target Cell* box, type the address of the cell containing the objective function

- Click one of the **Equal To** option buttons and, if necessary, type a value in the *Value of* box

- In the *By Changing Cells* box, type the cell addresses of all cells that Excel can change

- Click the **Add** button to add constraints to the Subject to the Constraints box

- Click the **Solve** button to create a solution

- Click the **OK** button

Opening the Solver Parameters dialog box to enter parameters:

1. Click **Tools** and then click **Solver**. The Solver Parameters dialog box opens

2. Click the **Set Target Cell** box and type **E12**. Cell E12 contains the object function, total profit

3. If necessary, click the **Max** option button to indicate to the Solver that you want to maximize the value in cell E12

4. Click the Solver Parameters dialog box Title bar and drag the dialog box so that it is below row 13 of your worksheet

5. Click the **By Changing Cells** box and then click and drag the cell range **B10:C10** to select the two changing cells (see Figure 10.24)

FIGURE 10.24

Partially complete Solver Parameters dialog box

enter changing-cell addresses here

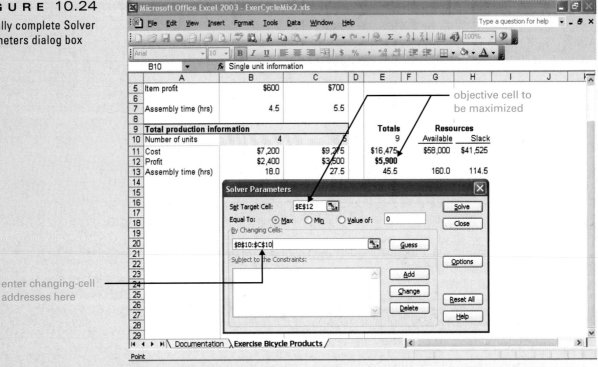

Now you are ready to have Solver look for a solution. John wants the right mix of products to maximize profit.

Solving for maximum profit:

1. Click the **Solve** button on the Solver Parameters dialog box. Solver quickly solves the problem. After a short time, Solver opens the Solver Results dialog box with a message "Set Cell values do not converge" (see Figure 10.25). Notice the enormous number of units in cell E10— over 465 million bicycles!

2. Click the **Cancel** button in the Solver Results dialog box to discard the proposed solution and restore the worksheet cells to their original values

The Solver issued the error message shown above because it has no constraints. The Solver calculated the obvious answer to maximizing profits: Build a few billion bicycles!

The Solver attempts to solve the problem by repeatedly substituting values for the changing cells and examining the target cell value. After a large number of substitutions, the Solver recognizes that it is not getting any closer to a solution. It halts and issues the error message you see above. To reach a feasible solution, you have to specify constraints.

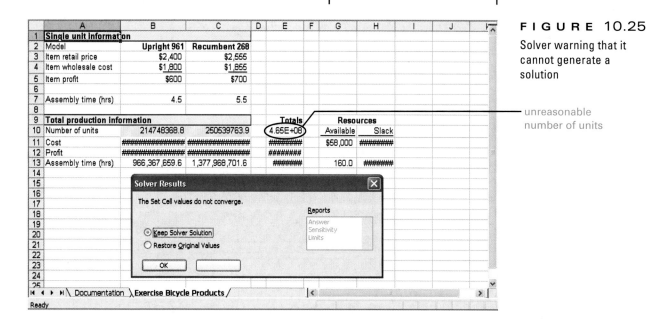

FIGURE 10.25

Solver warning that it cannot generate a solution

unreasonable number of units

Adding Constraints

With the target cell and changing cells identified, you next identify the problem's constraints. One constraint is that the total amount available to purchase exercise bicycles—the wholesale purchase amount—is $58,000. That value you placed in cell G11. Cell E11 contains a formula that calculates the total cost of all bicycles to be purchased. You express the constraint that the purchase price must be less than $58,000 by writing an expression, called an *inequality*, this way:

    E11 <= G11

The second and final constraint is that the total assembly time (cell E13) must be less than 160 hours (cell G13). Just as above, you write the second constraint as an inequality too. The inequality is:

    E13 <= G13

You express all Solver constraints by clicking the Add button in the Solver Parameters dialog box and then writing the constraint expression. You can add as many constraints as you need.

Entering Solver constraints:

1. Click **Tools** and then click **Solver**. The Solver Parameters dialog box opens and displays the same Set Target Cell, E12

2. Click the **Add** button in the *Subject to the Constraints* panel. The Add Constraint dialog box opens

3. Type **E11**, the total value of all bicycles purchased, in the Cell Reference box

4. Click the list box in the center of the Add Constraint dialog box, and then click **<=** in the list

5. Click the **Constraint** box and type **G11** to establish the upper limit of $58,000 (see Figure 10.26)

EXCEL

FIGURE 10.26

Adding a spending constraint

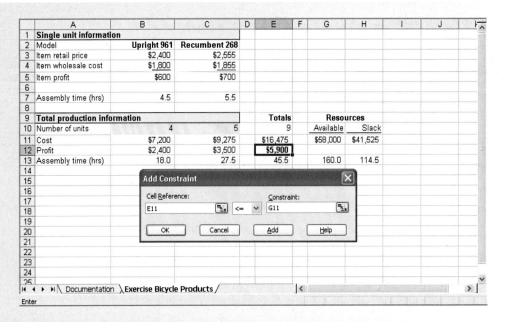

anotherway

...to Add a Cell Reference Box or the Constraints Box

Click the **Cell Reference** box or the **Constraints** box

Click the **Collapse Dialog Box** button

Click the cell whose address you want in the Cell Reference box or Constraint box

tip: *Although you could type 58000 in the Constraint cell, it is better to type a cell reference or a cell name. That way, you can change a constraint by typing a new value in a cell*

6. Click the **Add** button in the Add Constraint dialog box. The Solver stores the first constraint and then clears the list and text boxes in preparation for you to enter another constraint

7. In the Cell Reference box, type **E13**. Cell E13 contains the total assembly used, so far, to build the bicycles

8. If necessary, click the list box in the center of the Add Constraint dialog box, and then click the <= relational operator in the list

9. Click the **Constraint** box and type **G13** to establish the upper limit of 160 hours

10. Click **OK** to close the Add Constraint dialog box and return to the Solver Parameters dialog box (see Figure 10.27)

FIGURE 10.27

Solver Parameters dialog box with newly added constraints

target cell, whose value is to be maximized

changing cells

two constraints

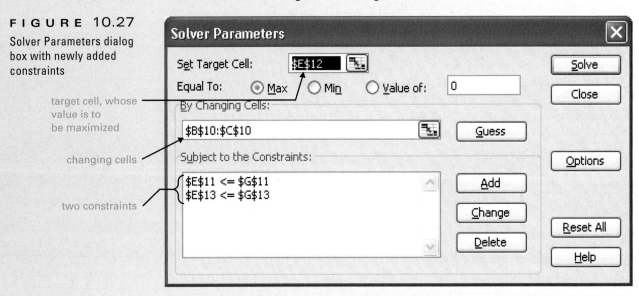

The constraints that you just specified appear in the *Subject to the Constraints* text box. Notice that Excel uses absolute cell references. Had you named the cells that are involved in the constraints, their names would appear instead of their cell references.

If your constraints do not match Figure 10.27, you can delete the incorrect one(s) and then click the Add button to enter the correct restraints.

With the target cell, changing cells, and constraints specified, the Solver is ready to attempt to solve the problem. Keep in mind what it is you want: the product mix that yields the maximum profit given the limited supply of money and assembly time.

Generating a solution using the Solver:

1. Click the **Solve** button on the Solver Parameters dialog box. The Solver reports that it has found a solution and that all constraints and optimality conditions are satisfied (see Figure 10.28)

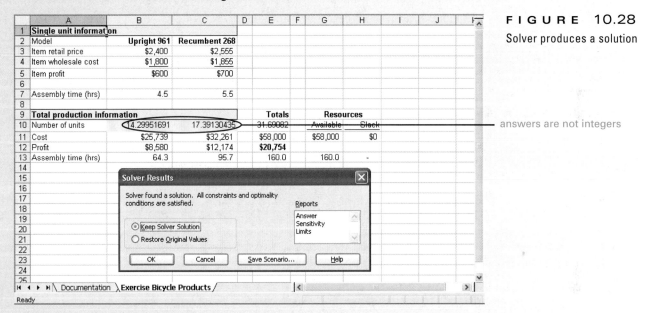

FIGURE 10.28
Solver produces a solution

answers are not integers

2. If the Solver Results dialog box obscures part of the active worksheet, drag it out of the way. Leave it open so that you can use it in the steps that follow

Insisting on Positive Integer Answers

Notice that cells H11 and H13 indicate that all of the resources are completely used. There are exactly zero dollars left (cell H11) and the assembly process has consumed precisely 160 hours (cell H13). The maximized profit, displayed in cell E12, is $20,754. What product mix of upright and recumbent bicycles yields that profit? Cells B10 and C10 contain the answer. They indicate that John must assemble and sell 14.29951691 Upright 961 bicycles and 17.39130435 Recumbent 268 bicycles to maximize profit. However, you cannot assemble a fraction of an exercise bicycle.

Occasionally, the Solver will make changing cells negative to arrive at an answer. Negative values for production quantities are rarely an acceptable way to solve an optimization problem. Next, you add constraints that prevent the Solver from generating solutions that are either negative or contain fractional values.

Constraining changing cell values to positive numbers:

1. Click the **Restore Original Values** option, and then click **OK** to close the Solver Results dialog box and restore the original worksheet values

2. Click **Tools**, click **Solver**, and then click the **Add** button in the *Subject to the Constraints* panel. The Add Constraint dialog box opens

3. With the insertion point in the Cell Reference box, click and drag the worksheet cell range **B10:C10**. Excel enters $B$10:$C$10 in the Cell Reference box

4. Click the list box in the middle of the dialog box, and then click the >= choice in the list

5. Type **0** in the Constraint box. This constraint indicates that you will only accept values for the changing cells that are greater than or equal to zero (see Figure 10.29)

FIGURE 10.29

Limiting changing cells to positive values

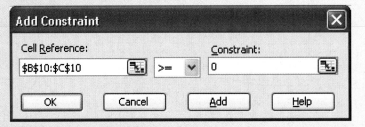

6. Click the **Add** button to add the previously created constraints and clear the Add Constraint boxes for the next entry

Finally, you limit the changing cell values to integer numbers, because John can only assemble whole bicycles.

Constraining changing cell values to integers:

1. With insertion point in the Cell Reference box, type **B10:C10**

2. Click the list box in the middle of the dialog box, and then click the **int** choice in the list (*int* is an abbreviation for integer and forces the Solver to return solutions that are whole numbers)

3. Click **OK** to save this constraint and close the Add Constraint dialog box. The Solver Parameters dialog box reappears (see Figure 10.30)

Your constraints should match those shown in Figure 10.30. If an individual constraint does not match, delete it and then insert the correct constraint expression.

FIGURE 10.30

Solver Parameters dialog box with additional constraints

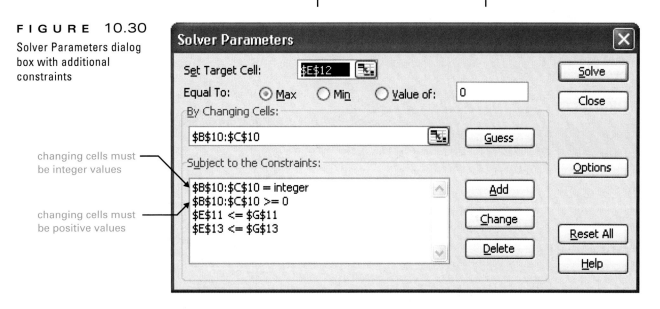

changing cells must be integer values

changing cells must be positive values

---

task *reference* Deleting a Solver Constraint

- Click **Tools** and then click **Solver**
- Click the constraint you want to delete
- Click the **Delete** button

If you were to create a scatter chart with two lines showing the cost and assembly hours constraint, it would look like Figure 10.31. The Y-axis is the number of recumbent bicycles that John can purchase and assemble, and the X-axis is the number of upright exercise bicycles that John can purchase and assemble. The blue line represents the assembly hours constraint, and the red line represents the cost constraint. Observe where the red line—the cost constraint—intersects the Y-axis. That chart point indicates that John could build 29 recumbent exercise bicycles and zero upright exercise bicycles—based on the cost constraint alone. Look at the point where the assembly hours constraint line intersects the X-axis. The data point indicates that under the assembly hours constraint, John has time to assemble approximately 32 upright exercise bicycles and zero recumbent bicycles. Other points on either of the cost lines represent mixtures of both bicycles.

The smallest chart area that is bounded by the assembly line, the cost line, the X-axis, and the Y-axis represents product mix data points that are feasible. The point in which the two curves cross represents the optimal product mix. The dashed line from the crossover point to the X-axis shows the optimal number of upright units subject to both constraints, while the horizontal dashed line from the optimal production point to the Y-axis shows the optimal number of recumbent units subject to both constraints.

While graphic solutions are a convenient way to visualize a solution, the Solver does a faster job of determining the optimal product mix under the constraints you have set forth.

FIGURE 10.31

Chart showing optimal
product mix with
constraints

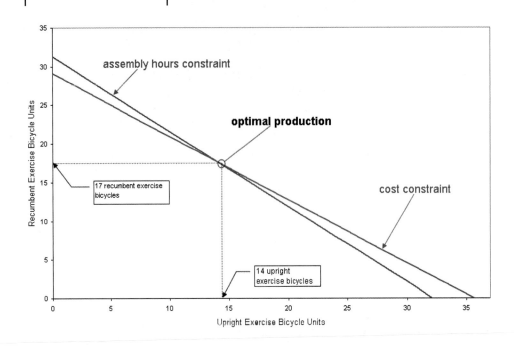

Solving the product mix problem with corrected restraints in place:

1. Click the **Solve** button in the Solver Parameters dialog box. The Solver
   returns an answer with positive integer values for the changing cells B10
   and C10 (see Figure 10.32). The Solver determines that John should
   build and sell 14 upright bicycles and 17 recumbent bicycles

FIGURE 10.32

Solver finds a suitable
product mix

product mix to maximize
profit given the constraints

maximized profit given
the constraints

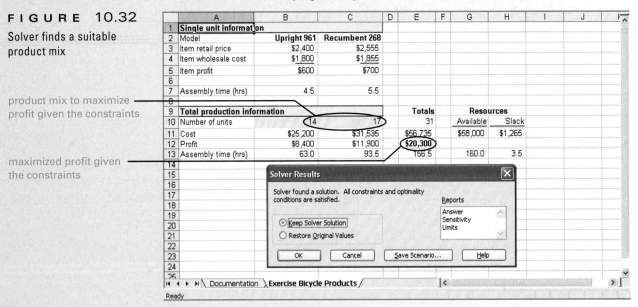

2. Click **OK** to accept the solution and close the Solver Results dialog box

You show the worksheet to John, who happens to be walking past your desk as you
complete the preceding exercise. He's very happy and notices that his $58,000 covers his

wholesale cost to purchase the exercise bicycles with $1,265 to spare. The total assembly time is 156.5 hours, which is just under the maximum allowed of 160 hours.

Saving Solver Parameters

When you save a workbook after using the Solver, Excel saves all the values you specify in the Solver Parameters dialog box along with the workbook. Therefore, you do not need to reenter the Solver parameters if you want to work with the Solver later. Each *worksheet* can store one set of Solver Parameter values. Conversely, a worksheet cannot store more than one set of Solver parameters. In order to save more than one set of Solver parameters within a worksheet, you must use the Solver's Save Model option.

   Although John does not anticipate that the constraints or any other Solver parameters will change, he asks you to save the current Solver Parameters values so that either you or he can investigate other constraints and find alternative product mix solutions.

---

task reference   Saving Solver Parameters

- Click **Tools** and then click **Solver**

- Click **Options** and then click **Save Model**

- Select an empty cell range into which Excel can store the Solver's parameters, and then click **OK**

- Click **Cancel** in the Solver Options dialog box, and then click **Close**

Saving Solver parameters and naming them:

1. Click **Tools** and then click **Solver**. The Solver Parameters dialog box opens and displays the parameters you established earlier

2. Click the **Options** button. The Solver Options dialog box opens (see Figure 10.33)

3. Click the **Save Model** button. The Save Model dialog box opens and prompts you for a cell range in which to store the Solver parameters in the worksheet

4. Click cell **C15**, because that cell is empty as are the cells below it, and then click **OK**. Excel stores parameter values in the cell range C15:C21. Then the Solver Options dialog box reappears

5. Click **Cancel** to close the Solver Options dialog box, and then click the **Close** button to close the Solver Parameters dialog box. Solver parameters are saved (see Figure 10.34)

6. Select the cell range **C15:C21**, click the **Name box** to the left of the formula bar, type **SolverModel1417**, and press **Enter**

7. Click any cell to deselect the cell range

Creating Reports with the Solver

In addition to printing out the worksheet, John wants you to produce an answer report—one of three reports available with the Solver.

EXCEL

FIGURE 10.33

Solver Options dialog box

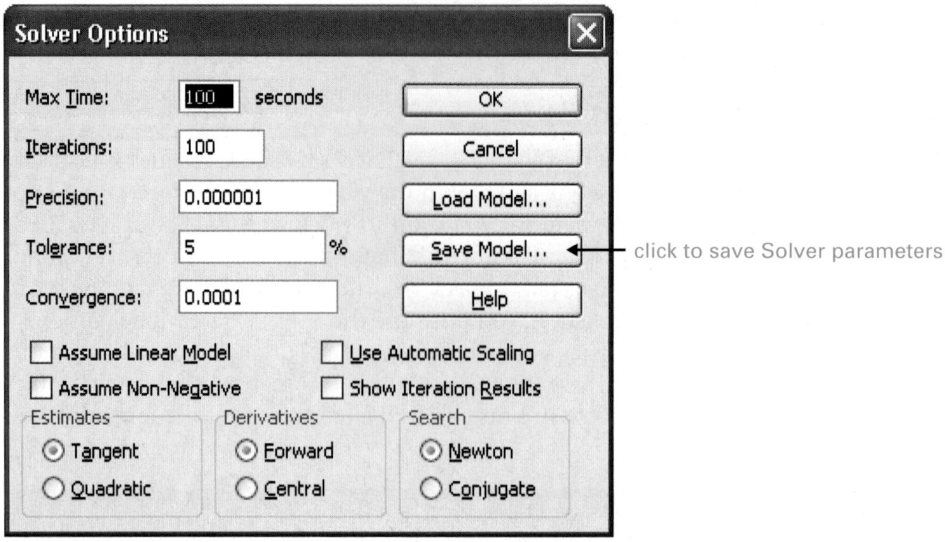

FIGURE 10.34

Saved Solver parameters

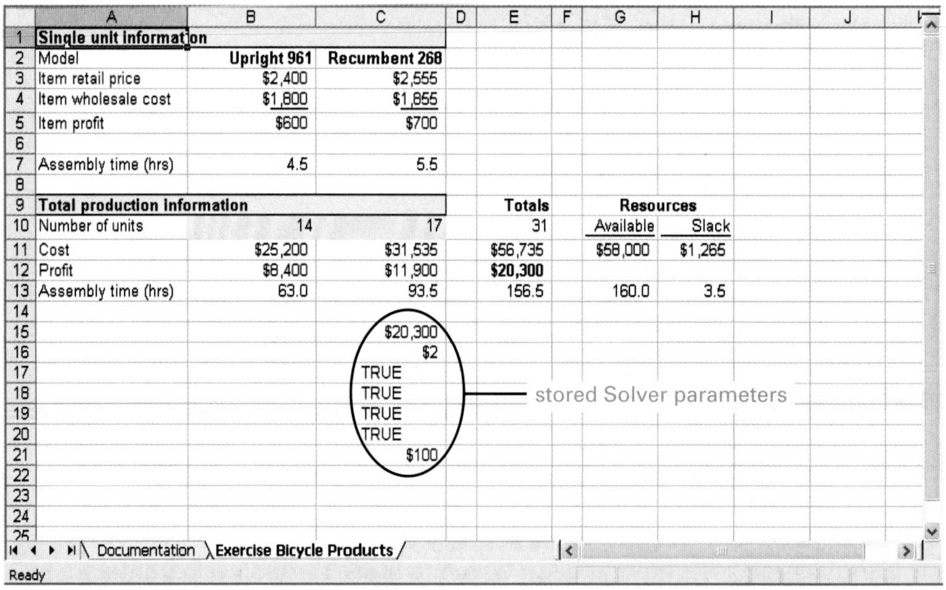

The Solver allows you to create three types of reports that you can analyze to better understand the results that the Solver has created. The three reports are the Answer report, Sensitivity report, and Limits report. An *Answer report*, the most popular and useful of the three reports, lists the target cell, the changing cells with their original and final values, constraints, and data about the constraints. The most useful part of an answer report lists the constraints and indicates which constraints are binding and the amount of slack in the constraints that are not binding. A *Sensitivity report* tells how sensitive the current solution is to changes in the adjustable cells. A *Limits report* displays the range of values that the changing cells can assume based on the constraints you have defined. Both the Sensitivity report and the Limits report allow the user to specify the reliability of the results. However, both reports are available only when the problem does not contain integer constraints. Because both the assembly hours and the total cost constraints are integer constraints, you cannot use the latter two reports. Therefore, you will request the Solver to produce an Answer report and you will then examine its contents.

Producing an Answer report:

1. Restore the changing cells to their original values: Click cell **B10**, type **4**, click cell **C10**, type **5**, and press **Enter**

2. Click **Tools**, click **Solver**, and then click the **Solve** button. The Excel Solver creates the same solution as before: Purchase, assemble, and sell 14 upright and 17 recumbent exercise bicycles

3. Click **Answer** in the Reports list box and ensure that the **Keep Solver Solution** option is selected (see Figure 10.35)

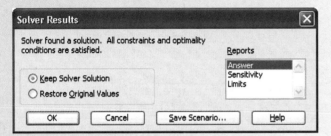

FIGURE 10.35

Preparing to create an Answer report

4. Click **OK**. Excel produces an Answer report

Excel places the Answer report on its own worksheet and names it *Answer Report 1*. Each time you create another Answer report, Excel increases the report number by one (Answer Report 2 would be the name of the next worksheet). Execute the steps that follow to examine the Answer report.

Examining an Answer report:

1. Click the **Answer Report 1** worksheet tab to view the Answer report that the Solver created (see Figure 10.36)

The report contains four parts. The first section contains the report title, workbook and worksheet names, and the date and time when the report was created (rows 1 through 3 of Figure 10.36). The second section describes the characteristics of the target cell. The description includes the optimization (max, min, or value), the cell location, the cell name, its original value, and its final value. In the third section are all of the changing cells, labeled Adjustable Cells in the Answer report. They indicate the cells' address, names, original values, and final values. The fourth section lists all of the constraints. The columns in the constraint list display each constraint's cell address, name, final value, constraint expression, status (Binding or Not Binding), and slack value.

The constraint list reveals which of the constraints were limiting factors, indicated by the status of *Binding*, and cells with final values less than the constraint values, indicated by *Not Binding*. The only binding constraints are those requiring that the changing cells be integer values. Although the final values of both the Cost Totals and the Assembly Time constraints are close to their limit values, neither has reached their respective limit values. For example, the Cost Totals row indicates that the total cost of $56,735 is less than the limit value of $58,000 by the slack listed, 1265. Notice that the slack assembly time of 3.5 hours, though not binding, is less than the time needed to assemble one more recumbent or upright exercise bicycle. Even though there is enough slack time to make one more bicycle, the slack of the other constraint, available money, is not enough to purchase another bicycle.

FIGURE 10.36

Viewing an Answer report

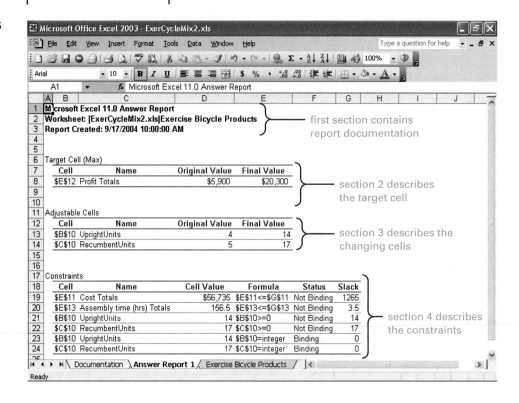

You are ready to print the final report for John, including the Answer report. First, rename the Answer Report 1 worksheet tab, then add a worksheet header to that page, print the three worksheets, and save the workbook.

Printing and saving the ExerCycleMix2 workbook:

1. Double-click the **Answer Report 1** worksheet tab, type **Solver Answer Report**, and press **Enter**. That readily identifies the report the worksheet contains

2. Right-click the worksheet tab, click **Tab Color**, click any green color in the Format Tab Color dialog box, and click **OK**

3. Press and hold the **Ctrl** key, click the **Exercise Bicycle Products** worksheet tab, release the **Ctrl** key, click **View** on the menu bar, click **Header and Footer**, click the **Custom Header** button, type your first and last names in the Left section, click **OK**, and click **OK** again

4. Click the **Documentation** worksheet tab and then click the **Save** button on the Standard toolbar to save the workbook and preserve all of the changes you made in this session

5. Exit Excel

You show John the printed worksheets. He is glad to know exactly how many of each of the two products he can produce to maximize his profits given his labor and money constraints. John could not have done this work without your help.

making **the grade**

1. You can use the Solver for constrained _____ in which you specify a set of constraints and an outcome that you want minimized or maximized.

2. The Solver changes decision variables, or changing cells, to cause changes in the object _____, which is the cell containing a function whose value you want to optimize.

3. The Solver goes to work to find the maximum or minimum value for the target cell or object function by changing the value of the _____ cell(s).

4. A(n) _____ is a limitation on the value that a cell can have.

5. A(n) _____ report displays the range of values that the changing cells can assume based on your constraints.

SESSION 10.3 SUMMARY

The Goal Seek command works backward from a single-valued solution to produce a final, desired result. The Goal Seek finds a solution by repeatedly changing one cell's value until the specified result cell contains the desired result value, called the Goal Seek objective. A constraint, or limitation, is a cell that limits the values that a cell can have. By modifying a cell's value within its allowed limits, Goal Seek can produce an optimal result. Goal Seek is useful to determine the maximum profit for a product given a constraint on the number of hours required to sell or manufacture each product. Similarly, Goal Seek can determine a least cost solution to a wide variety of cost minimization problems in wide ranges of disciplines from agriculture to zoology. Without tools such as the Goal Seek command, only the unattractive alternative of exhaustive trial-and-error is available. Using trial-and-error, you can repeatedly substitute values into independent cells and then examine their effect on the objective cell. This is an error-prone and laborious technique at best.

For more complex optimization problems, Excel provides the Solver. You can use the Solver for equation solving in which you use goal seeking or back solving and for constrained optimization in which you specify a set of constraints and an outcome that you want to optimize. Unlike the Goal Seek command, the Solver provides a solution, where possible, that involves multiple resources that affect the outcome. The Solver can determine the best way to use consumable resources such as energy and raw materials to create one or more products. A slack resource is the quantity of a resource required to produce an optimal result that is unused or unallocated. You can add constraints to limit solutions to values within a range, to positive values, to negative values, and to integer values. Integer value Solver constraints limit a result to integral values and eliminate answers containing fractions.

MICROSOFT OFFICE SPECIALIST OBJECTIVES SUMMARY

- Implement goal seeking by using a graph—MOS XL03S-1-4
- Install the Excel Solver tool—MOS XL03E-1-7
- Use Excel's Solver to unravel more complex problems—MOS XL03E-1-7
- Identify the formula to be optimized—MOS XL03E-1-7

- Specify constraints on the problem that the Solver must satisfy—MOS XL03E-1-7
- Learn how to create Solver Answer, Limits, and Sensitivity reports—MOS XL03E-1-7
- Format and resize graphics—MOS XL03E-2-3

making the grade *answers*

SESSION 10.1

1. solution or result

2. objective

3. constraint

4. precedent or changing

SESSION 10.2

1. optimization

2. function

3. changing (or precedent)

4. constraint

5. Answer

task reference *summary*

Task	Page #	Preferred Method
Using Goal Seek	EX 10.13	• Click **Tools** and then click **Goal Seek** • Click the **Set cell** box and type the cell address of the result cell • Click the **To value** box and type the result value you want • Click the **By changing** cell box and type the address of the changing cell • Click **OK** to solve the problem, and then click **OK** to close the Goal Seek Status dialog box
Using the Solver	EX 10.27	• Click **Tools** and then click **Solver** • In the *Set Target Cell* box, type the address of the cell containing the objective function • Click one of the **Equal To** option buttons and, if necessary, type a value in the *Value of* box • In the *By Changing Cells* box, type the cell addresses of all cells that Excel can change • Click the **Add** button to add constraints to the Subject to the Constraints box • Click the **Solve** button to create a solution • Click the **OK** button
Deleting a Solver constraint	EX 10.33	• Click **Tools** and then click **Solver** • Click the constraint you want to delete • Click the **Delete** button
Saving Solver parameters	EX 10.35	• Click **Tools** and then click **Solver** • Click **Options** and then click **Save Model** • Select an empty cell range and then click **OK** • Click **Cancel** and then click **Close**

TRUE OR FALSE

1. The Goal Seek objective is the end result you want to achieve.

2. A nonbinding constraint is when the constraint is the limiting factor.

3. The Goal Seek command finds a solution changing multiple cells' values.

4. The precedent cells are also known as the target cells.

5. Solver will not make changing cells negative to arrive at an answer.

6. Unfortunately, a worksheet cannot store more than one set of Solver parameters.

FILL-IN

1. The _____ _____ command works backward to compute an unknown value that produces a result you want.

2. You specify a(n) _____ when you indicate a limitation on the values that a cell can have.

3. A(n) _____ value is a cell value upon which a formula is directly or indirectly dependent.

4. Excel's _____ is the best choice, instead of Goal Seek command, when you do not know the desired end result—only that you want to minimize or maximize a value.

5. A specialized feature in Excel that is not automatically included when you install Excel is called a(n) _____.

6. You can create a(n) _____ report that displays which constraints are binding and which are not.

MULTIPLE CHOICE

1. This function is the cell containing a function whose value you want to optimize.
   a. optimize
   b. object
   c. results
   d. value

2. This Solver report shows how sensitive the current solution is to the changes in the changing cells.
   a. Answer
   b. Sensitivity
   c. Limits
   d. Changing

3. What is a slack resource?
   a. the quantity of a resource that is undesirable
   b. the quantity of a resource required to produce an optimal result that is currently being used
   c. the quantity of a resource required to produce an optimal result that is unused or unallocated
   d. the quantity of a resource that cannot be allocated or used

4. In decision analysis, the types of problems that the Solver works with are called
   a. regression analysis problems.
   b. simulation problems.
   c. linear programming problems.
   d. net present value problems.

5. The value on which a formula is based is a
   a. result value.
   b. reference value.
   c. base value.
   d. precedent value.

review of concepts

REVIEW QUESTIONS

1. Explain briefly when you would use Goal Seek techniques versus the Solver.

2. Discuss whether you would use the Goal Seek command or the Solver command to determine what grade you need on the final exam to achieve an overall course average of 90 percent.

3. Discuss why the target cell must always be a formula, not a constant value, when you use the Solver.

4. Discuss what happens if you use the Solver but specify no constraints.

CREATE THE QUESTION

For each of the following answers, create an appropriate, short question.

ANSWER	QUESTION
1. This type of constraint is binding	_____
2. The Goal Seek objective	_____
3. A limitation on the values that a cell can have	_____
4. A precedent value	_____
5. The quantity of resources that are not used or allocated	_____
6. A Sensitivity report	_____

1. Maximizing Ocean Pacific Spas' Profit

Ocean Pacific Spas manufactures and sells two spa models: the Infinity and the Classic. Ocean Pacific Spas receives spa bodies from another manufacturer and then adds a pump and tubing to circulate the water. The Infinity Spa takes, on average, 15.5 hours of labor to fit a pump and tubing and 14.5 feet of tubing. The Classic model requires 10.5 hours of labor and uses 20 feet of tubing. Based on selling patterns, George Millovich (Ocean Pacific Spas' owner) has determined that the Infinity spa generates a profit of $400 per unit, and the Classic spa generates $345 profit. While George would like a large labor capacity and sufficient tubing and motors to build any number of spas, his resources are limited. For the next production period, George has 2,650 labor hours, 3,450 feet of tubing, and 231 pumps available. Help George figure out how many Infinity spas and Classic spas to build in order to maximize his profit.

1. Open **ex10OceanSpas.xls**, save it as **<yourname>OceanSpas2.xls**, and type your name to the right of the Modified By label on the Documentation worksheet, press **Tab**, and type today's date near the Modification Date label, press **Enter**, and then click the **Spa Data** tab to display that worksheet

2. Click **D5**, type **=C2*C3+D2*D3**, and press **Enter**. The expression sums the profit for both types of spas

3. Click and drag cell range **C8:D10**, type **15.5**, press **Enter**, type **14.5**, press **Enter**, type **1**, press **Enter**, type **10.5**, press **Enter**, type **20.0**, press **Enter**, type **1**, and press **Enter**. That completes the material and labor constraints for each spa type. Next, enter the systemwide constraints—overall materials and labor available for all products

4. Click cell **C14**, type **=C8*C2+D8*D2**, click cell **C15**, type **=C9*C2+D9*D2**, click cell **C16**, and type **=C10*C2+D10*D2**. These equations multiply the resources per spa type and the number of units of each type produced to display the total resources used to manufacture all units. At first, these display zero because no units are being produced (cells C2 and D2)

5. Click cell **D14**, type **2650**, click cell **D15**, type **3450**, click cell **D16**, type **231**, and press **Enter**. These values are the total number of labor hours, total length of pipe, and total number of pumps available for producing all spas. Now you are ready to solve for the maximum profit and determine how many Infinity units and Classic units to produce

6. Click **Tools** on the menu bar, click **Solver**, click the **Set Target Cell** box, and type **D5**

7. Click the **Max** option button, click the **By Changing Cells** box, and type **C2:D2**

8. Click the **Add** button, and move the Add Constraint dialog box to the right so that you can see all the entries in column D through row 16. Then click the **Cell Reference** box, click and drag the cell range **C14:C16**, click the **relationships** list box, click **<=**, click the **Constraint** box, click and drag the cell range **D14:D16**, and click the **Add button**

9. Click the **Cell Reference** box, click and drag the cell range **C2:D2**, click the **relationships** list box, click **>=** (greater than or equal to), click the **Constraint** box, type **0**, and click the **Add** button

10. Click the **Cell Reference** box, click and drag the cell range **C2:D2**, click the **Relationships** list box, click **int**, and click **OK**

11. Click the **Solve** button, then click the **Answer** in the Reports box, and click **OK**

12. Format the values representing dollar amounts with the currency symbols and zero decimal places. How many units of the Infinity and the Classic spa should Ocean Pacific Spas manufacture to maximize its profits given the constraints you entered?

13. Place your name in the Header of all three worksheets, save your workbook, and either print all worksheets or execute Save As, according to your instructor's direction

2. Finding a Monthly Payment that Fits the Budget

Jessica Engstrom wants to purchase a newer model automobile to replace her decrepit 1984 car. The bank where Jessica has a checking account, Washington Mutual, is advertising an annual interest rate of 7.75 percent for three-year loans on used cars. By selling her old car and using some cash she has accumulated, Jessica has $3,000 available as a down payment. Under her current budget, Jessica figures that the maximum monthly loan payment she can afford is $300. She wants to find out the maximum car price she can afford and keep the monthly payment no higher than $300. She cannot alter the interest rate, and the three-year term is part of the loan package that cannot be changed either. Use the Excel Goal Seek command to figure out the highest purchase price Jessica can afford.

Jessica has started a worksheet, but you must help her fill in the remaining details. Do the following to complete the worksheet and find Jessica's answer.

1. Open **ex10LoanGoal.xls**, save it as **<yourname>LoanGoal2.xls**, and type your name near the Modified By label on the Documentation worksheet, press **Tab**, type today's date near the Modification Date label, and click the **Sheet1** tab to open that worksheet

2. Rename Sheet1 to **Loan Analysis** (see Figure 10.37), change the Loan Analysis sheet tab color to Green, and delete the Sheet2 worksheet

3. Type the following values in the corresponding cells: In cell B3, type **19000**; in cell B4, type **3000**; in cell E3, type **7.75%**; in cell, E4 type **3**

4. Click cell **B5** and type the formula to calculate the loan amount **=B3-B4**

5. Click cell **B7** and enter the monthly payment formula **=–PMT(E3/12,E4*12,B5)**. Be sure to place the minus sign following the equal sign so the calculated answer is positive

6. Format cells B3, B4, B5, and B7 to display currency symbols and two decimal places

7. Now Goal Seek the highest purchase price for $300 per month: Click cell **B7**, then click **Tools**, and click **Goal Seek**

8. Ensure that the Set cell text box contains B7, press **Tab**, type **300**, press **Tab**, type **B3**, and click the **OK** button to perform the Goal Seek

9. Click **OK** to close the Goal Seek Status dialog box

10. Type your name in the worksheet header of the Loan Analysis worksheet, and print or Save As according to the direction of your instructor

FIGURE 10.37

Jessica Engstrom's Loan Analysis workbook

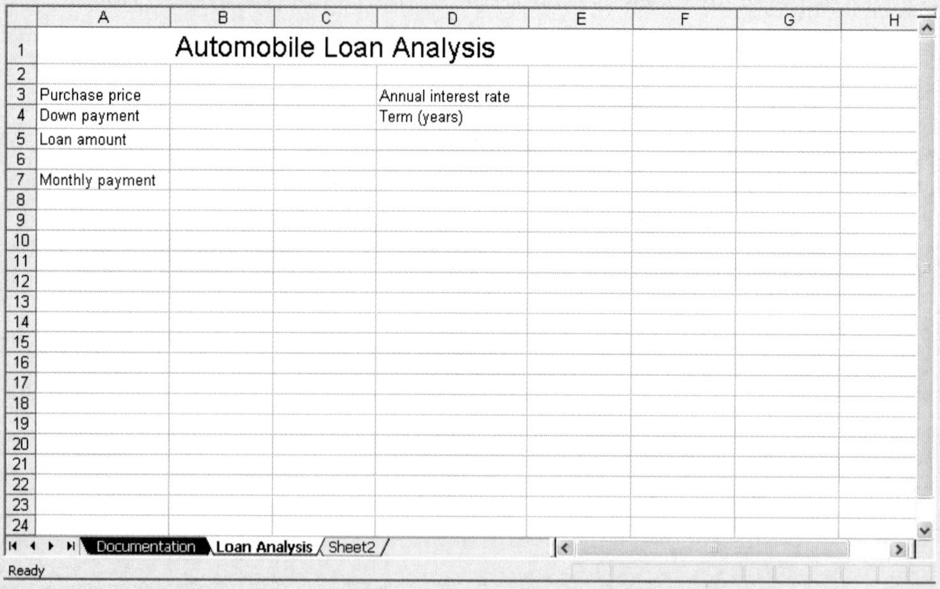

1. University Employees Credit Union Investments

The State University Employee Credit Union (SUECU) is projecting how it will allocate funds for investments next fiscal year. The credit union makes four types of loans to its members-only organization. Besides loans, SUECU also invests members' money in risk-free investments. The projected loan and risk-free investment annual rates of return are as follows:

Loan or Investment Type	Annual Rate of Return
Automobile loans	10%
Furniture loans	10%
Other secured loans	9%
Signature loans	12%
Risk-free investments	5%

This year, the credit union will have $2,000,000 available to invest in loans and risk-free investments. State laws and the credit union association laws restrict the allocation of funds to loans and investments in the following ways:

- Signature loans cannot exceed 10 percent of the funds invested in all loans (automobile, furniture, other, and signature)

- Risk-free investments cannot exceed 30 percent of the total funds available for investment ($2,000,000)
- Total auto loans cannot exceed $1,000,000
- Furniture loans cannot total more than $750,000

Use the Solver add-in to determine how much money should be allocated to each of the five types of investments to maximize the total annual return. Request that the Solver create an Answer Report worksheet.

Begin by opening **ex10CreditUnion.xls** (see Figure 10.38) and save the workbook as **<yourname>CreditUnion2.xls**. Format all numeric currency entries to zero decimal places and the Accounting format. Ensure that the Solver cannot use negative values for any of the investments. Format all interest rates using the percentage format with zero decimal places. Start the initial allocations of each of the five investments at $100,000, and optimize the amount of interest. Type your name next to the Modified By label on the Documentation sheet, and enter today's date next to the Modification Date label on the Documentation sheet. Place your name in the worksheet header of the Data and Answer Report worksheets. Either print all worksheets or execute Save As, according to the direction of your instructor. Print the Answer report in landscape orientation, if you choose to print your worksheets.

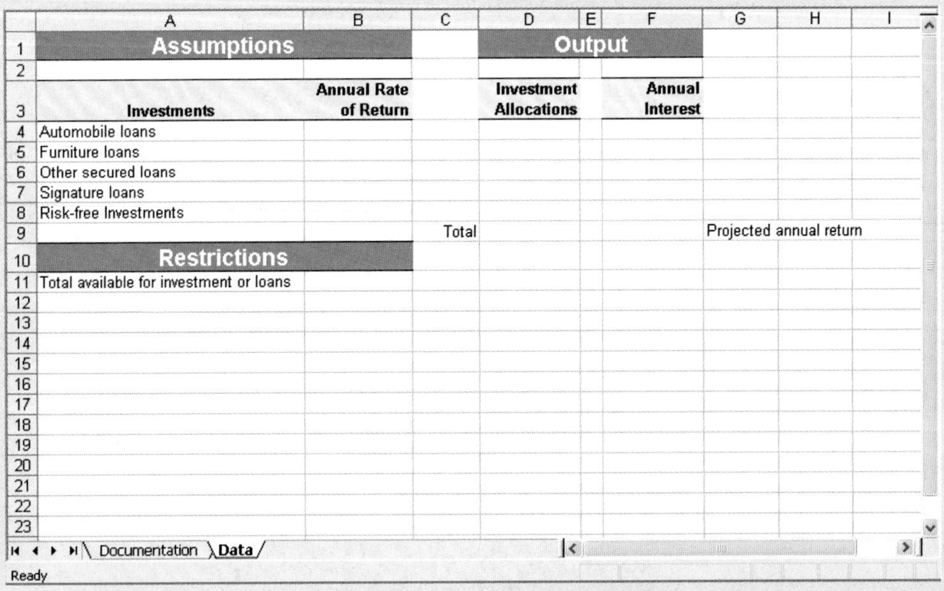

FIGURE 10.38

University Employee's Credit Union workbook

2. Maximizing Profit for Green Creek Bevels

Green Creek Bevels manufactures linear glass bevels for the art glass industry using a fully automated series of beveling machines. Unlike custom bevel artisans, Green Creek does not produce bevels with curves. Starting with a rectangular piece of glass, a series of four processes are required to produce a finished bevel. The first process is grinding using a steel wheel and steel grit. Following this, a machine smoothes the bevel using a Newcastle stone. Then a cork wheel coated with pumice buffs each bevel. Finally, a felt wheel coated with jeweler's rouge restores the glistening surface to a bevel. Green Creek produces two grades of bevels: Premium and Standard. Premium bevels require more care and time on the machines to produce than standard bevels. The profit for a premium bevel is $10, whereas the profit for a standard bevel is $7.

Tobias Carling wants to use Excel's Solver to compute the number of each bevel type he should produce to maximize his profit. Begin by opening the worksheet, called **ex10GreenCreek.xls** (see Figure 10.39), and save it as **<yourname>GreenCreek2.xls**. It contains columns for the Premium and Standard bevel information. Under *Steps to Complete*, in cell A5, are the time units needed to grind, smooth, buff, and polish a bevel per hour, along with the maximum time units available for each machine in cells G6 through G9. Write formulas for total profit (premium profit per unit times premium units produced plus standard profit per unit times standard units), and total time units for grinding, smoothing, buffing, and polishing the bevels. Total polish time, for example, is the formula =C9*C2+D9*D2.

Name cell C2 **PremiumUnits**; name cell D2 **StandardUnits**; name cell E3 **TotalProfit**. Format cells appropriately to display currency values (or not). Write formulas for slack time in H6:H9. Use the Solver to maximize profit, cell E3, with changing cells C2:D2 and constraints that total time in E6:E9 must be less than the constraints in the cell range G6:G9. Produce an Answer report. How many units of Premium and Standard bevels should Tobias produce each hour? Write your name and date in the underlined cells on the Documentation worksheet and in the worksheet headers for the Answer Report worksheet and the Production Data worksheet. Print the workbook, or execute Save As, according to the direction of your instructor.

FIGURE 10.39

Green Creek Bevels Production Data worksheet

	A	B	C	D	E	F	G	H	I	J	K	L	M
1			Premium	Standard	Totals								
2		Units	1	1									
3		Profit	10	7									
4													
5	Steps to Complete						Constraints	Slack					
6	1	Grind	3	2			20						
7	2	Smooth	4	4			30						
8	3	Buff	7	6			40						
9	4	Polish	8	7			49						
10													
11													
12													
13													
14													
15													
16													
17													
18													
19													
20													
21													
22													
23													
24													
25													

Documentation | Production Data

Ready

e-business

1. Computing Profit for a Hosted Web Site Store

Otis Toadvine wants to bring his brick-and-mortar coffee bean store online. Investigating online Web hosting packages, he locates Yahoo!® Small Business (store.yahoo.com). Using the Excel Goal Seek tool, determine what total dollar volume of credit card sales Otis needs in order to realize a monthly profit of $30,000.

Otis has created a rudimentary workbook called **ex10WebHosting.xls** (see Figure 10.40). Save the file as **<yourname>WebHosting2.xls** to preserve the original file. Next, use your Web browser to display the Dynamic Store Front Web page, click the **Pricing** link, and print the page so that you have the pricing information at hand. Then, fill in cell **C11** with the one-time application fee, cell **C14** with the monthly hosting fee (minimum), and cell **C17** with the monthly statement fee. Cell C16 contains a formula 1.89 percent times the total sales value from credit card sales plus $0.25 times the number of credit card swipes (see the Web page). Write a formula in cell C21 for profit: total sales minus total variable costs minus the application fee. (Otis has decided to expense the one-time application fee the first month.) Using Goal Seek, determine the value that credit card sales (cell C5) must be in order to achieve a profit of $30,000. Enter your name and today's date in the appropriate cells on the Documentation worksheet, and place your name in the Hosting Cost Calculation worksheet header. Either Print or Save As, according to the direction of your instructor.

FIGURE 10.40

Hosting Cost Calculation worksheet

2. Rug Weaving Specialists

Oscar Rubenstein is the owner of Rug Weaving Specialists, which weaves Oriental-style rugs for the American market. Although rugs are available in various sizes, Oscar's company produces only the most popular size—6 feet by 9 feet. He is considering offering his rugs through the Internet, and he wants to determine how many rugs he can manufacture of each type to meet the anticipated increased demand, maximize his profit, and stay within his budget.

Oscar's weavers produce two types of rugs: Qum and Tabriz. Both types of rugs contain wool, but a Qum rug also contains silk. Labor costs are higher for a Qum rug, and profits are correspondingly higher too. Profit on a typical Qum rug is approximately $2,500, and profit on a typical Tabriz rug is roughly $1,300. Each rug requires processing by each one of three departments before being completed, and the labor hours required by each department or process are as follows:

Department/ Process	Qum Rug	Tabriz Rug
Weaving	2,000	1,000
Cutting	30	10
Binding/finishing	30	30

Examining the table, you can see that a Tabriz rug requires 1,000 hours to weave, 10 hours to cut, and 30 hours to bind and finish.

With its current labor force, Oscar's production supervisor estimates the following hours are available next month: 8,000 weaving hours, 160 cutting hours, and 200 binding and finishing hours. Oscar wants to know how many of each rug type he can produce next month to maximize his profits. In addition, he wants to know the total number of rugs that his company can produce and the total number of hours required in each department to produce the rugs.

Begin by opening the workbook **ex10Rugs.xls** (see Figure 10.41), and then save it immediately as **<yourname>Rugs10.xls**. Oscar has already formatted most of the worksheet, suggested locations for various formulas and constants, and provided a preliminary layout. Write in cell B3 the formula for profit, which is the sum of the profit for each of two rug types. Name that cell **TotalProfit**. Cells B7 and C7 contain the constant 1, which is the initial guess of how many rugs to produce in a month. Place labor hour requirements in cells B11 through C13, which correspond to the two rug types named in cells B5 and B6. Write formulas for total hours required for weaving, cutting, and binding/finishing for each rug type. Sum, in cells D16:E18, labor hours for departments. Place labor hour constraints in cells E16:E18, and name them **WeavingRequired**, **CuttingRequired**, and **BindingRequired**, respectively. Name cells G16:G18 **WeavingLimit**, **CuttingLimit**, and **BindingLimit**, respectively. Using the Solver, enter **B3** as the target cell, click **Max**, set cells **B7:B8** as the changing cells, and set up the three labor constraints. In addition, ensure that the changing cells are integers that are greater than zero. Solve to maximize profit. After Solver finds a solution, create an Answer report, move the report so it follows the Rug Weaving Model worksheet tab, place your name in the header of both worksheets, and print both worksheets. Plug in 3 and 4 for the changing cells and print the Rug Weaving Model worksheet again. Examine unused labor. Is that a feasible solution?

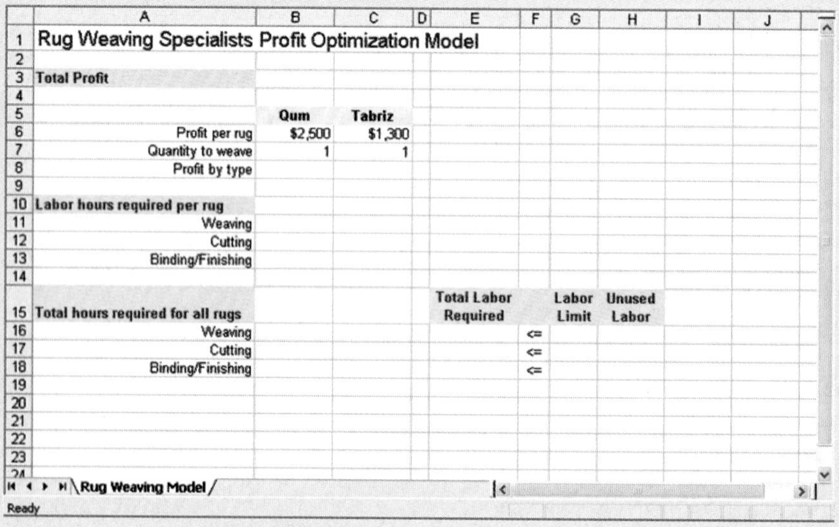

FIGURE 10.41

Rug Weaving worksheet with initial production volumes

1. Finding the Highest Profit on DVD Sales

Allison Gonzales, the sales manager for DVDs and More, wants to maximize her profit on the sale of portable DVD players. She has created a worksheet with some formatting in place called **ex10DVD.xls**. She would like you to use the Web to locate the retail price of two other portable DVD players and add their data in rows 4 and 5 (items 3 and 4 in the list). Use www.Hotbot.com or a similar Web search engine to find prices for portable DVD players. For the wholesale price of each unit (cells D4 and D5), write a formula that computes 55 percent of the retail price for both units you find. Fill the cells in rows 4 and 5 with appropriate formulas.

The only constraint is that Allison has $200,000 to purchase new DVD players. So, the total wholesale cost of the four types of DVD units must be less than $200,000. Place formulas in cells G6 through I6 that sum the number of units, cost, and profit. You want to maximize total profit, which is in cell I6. Cell H8 contains the slack value (any cash left over after you purchase the proposed units of each product). Name cell H6 **TotalCost**, cell I6 **TotalProfit**, and cell C8 **PurchaseCash**. Solve for maximum profit under the cost constraint, limiting the number of units to positive integers. Produce an Answer report. Place your name in all worksheet headers and include today's date. Print or Save As according to your instructor's direction.

2. Slick Suits

Wendy Potter is the top professional personal trainer for female triathletes in the world. Recently, she decided to begin a partnership with Slick Suits. Slicks Suits is a one-person operation that produces custom full-body wetsuits for athletes. Wendy has helped promote Slicks Suits through her personal training business for five years. Wendy will have to dedicate at least 20 hours per week to Slick Suits, and her personal training business may suffer as a consequence. Therefore, her Slick Suits revenue must offset the income she will lose from her personal training business if she is to continue. The profits for Slick Suits will have to be at least $4,000 per week and the initial costs can't exceed $2,000 per week. Using Excel, help Wendy determine if this business is worth her time and money. Because Wendy does not want to jeopardize quality or her name with uncontrolled growth, she has asked Slick Suits to limit its production time to 80 hours per week using only two operators.

The pricing strategy has not yet been finalized. Using your Internet browser and a good search engine, do a search for *Orca wetsuit sales*. Web sites such as www.fitness-stuff.com contain prices for both Orca™ Predator 2 full and sleeveless wetsuits, which are comparable to Slick Suits. Begin by opening **ex10SlickSuits.xls**. Immediately save this file as **<yourname>SlickSuits10.xls**. Enter in cells B3 and C3 the wetsuit prices you find on the Web. Under the *Totals* heading write the formulas to calculate the total for each row. In the *Resources* section type in values as stated above under *Available* (that is, $2000 for *Cost*, $4000 for *Profit*, and 80 for *Manufacturing Time*). These are also the constraints for *Cost, Profit,* and *Manufacturing Time.* Enter the formulas to calculate *Slack* as well. The only additional constraint is that each week at least five of each wetsuit style will be produced. This is based on Slick Suits' historical demand. Solve for maximum profit under these constraints, remembering that Wendy's goal is a profit of at least $4,000 per week. Therefore the slack will appear as a negative number for profit. Ensure your constraints include that the number of units be positive integers. Produce an Answer report. Save your file, include your name in the header of all worksheets, and print all the worksheets.

around the world

1. Shipping Solutions

Shipping Solutions has manufacturing plants in Philadelphia and Los Angeles. It manufactures doors and ships them to its four warehouses. Its warehouses are located in Philadelphia, Buenos Aires, London, and Tokyo. Each warehouse has a limited amount of storage space for the doors—one of the constraints. The two manufacturing plants each have a maximum capacity to produce doors. The manufacturing facilities can produce more doors than the warehouses can store. The problem is to find the cheapest way to ship doors from both the Philadelphia and Los Angeles facilities to each of the four warehouses and supply them with the number of doors each warehouse requires.

Two tables appear in the worksheet that Winnie Holyoke, the resident Excel expert, created. The topmost table lists the shipping costs in cost unit from each manufacturing facility to each warehouse. The second table—the one whose solution you are going to find—lists the numbers of units shipped from each manufacturing facility to each warehouse. Those numbers start out at zero. Your job is to minimize the total cost of shipping units to each of the warehouses.

Open the worksheet **ex10Shipping.xls**. Cell C16 contains the SUMPRODUCT function, which you may not have used yet. Briefly, it multiplies two cell ranges, one cell at a time, and sums the products. In this case, SUMPRODUCT multiplies the shipping cost per unit and a corresponding number of shipping units for each of eight cell pairs and forms the sum of the products. Cell C16, the total shipping cost, is the value to minimize. All constraints are colored light green so that they are easy to spot. There are two sets: maximum production capacity by manufacturing plant (cells H10:H11) and the warehouse storage limits found in cells C13:F13. The changing cell range, which Solver can manipulate, is C10:F11. Solve for the minimal cost that satisfies all constraints. Produce an Answer report. Identify the worksheets by placing your name in the worksheets' header. Print all worksheets.

2. Trading Education

Trading Education is a firm that promotes, organizes, and operates two-day training seminars for individuals who want to learn how to trade stocks and commodities. A team of three experts have been teaching at the seminars for several years and have achieved an outstanding reputation in the trading world. Currently, all of the seminars are held in the United States and Canada. Typically they average 120 attendees. Australia has long been a country with strong activity in trading the U.S. markets as has Singapore. Therefore, Trading Education would like to evaluate those two countries as its next expansion targets. The proposal is to hold two seminars in Singapore and four in Australia. Since the seminars are held only on weekends, each additional seminar will result in an additional week of travel expenses and wages for the crew. The remaining employees, including the experts, are on salary, but they will receive a bonus should profits exceed $750,000. The firm needs your help in evaluating this proposal. The marketing team needs to have an idea of the right mix of attendees that can help them achieve their goal of keeping costs down while maximizing profits. The constraints are that the profits must be at least $500,000; a maximum of 280 attendees can be accommodated in Singapore and 560 in Australia; and costs cannot exceed $650,000. The maximum cost is based on what six seminars would cost in the United States in similar locations.

Begin by opening **ex10TradingEducation.xls**. Immediately save this file as **<yourname>Trading2.xls**. Note the values that are currently in cells B11 and C11. If attendance falls below these levels, Trading Education will lose money. Therefore, these values need to be included in your constraints. Write the formulas to determine *Cost* and *Profit* for each seminar plan. Cost is equal to the fixed cost plus the variable cost (attendee cost times the number of attendees). Under the *Totals* heading write the formulas to calculate the total for each row. In the *Resources* section type in values as stated above under *Available* (that is, $650,000 for Cost and $500,000 for Profit). You need to create the formulas to calculate *Slack* as well. Now you are ready to enter all the appropriate constraints in *Solver*. Ensure your constraints include that the Number of Attendees is an integer for each country. Solve for maximum profit under these constraints. Produce an Answer report. Save your file, include your name in the header, and print the entire workbook.

running project

Pro Golf Academy

In Chapter 9, Betty created several different scenarios in order to investigate the best mix of golf ball brands to sell. While the scenario analysis allowed her to evaluate her profit under the scenarios in which she varied the amount of each product she sold, she was not able to determine the best product mix. She would like to take the Chapter 9 scenario analysis to the next step and determine how many dozens of sleeves of each of the five golf ball brands she needs to sell to *maximize* her profit. Open **ex10ProGolf.xls**, save it immediately as **<yourname>ProGolf10.xls**, and then click the **Golf Ball Sales Analysis** worksheet tab. The golf ball brands appear in alphabetical order (see Figure 10.42). Betty has changed the retail price on all five golf balls. The new retail price is a 50 percent markup of the wholesale price for each golf ball brand.

Betty wants to use the Solver to optimize total profit by having the Solver change the values in cell range D4:D8. Write formulas for total cost, total sales, and profit and place them in cell ranges E4:E8, F4:F8, and G4:G8, respectively. Place SUM functions in cells D10 through G10 to sum the Units Sold, Total Cost, Total Sales, and Profit columns. One Solver constraint is that the total cash Betty has available to purchase golf ball 12-ball sleeves at wholesale (column E's sum) is $6,000 (cell B15). The second and last condition is that there is shelf space for no more than 400 dozen sleeves of golf balls (cell B16). Name cell B15 *TotalCashAvailable,* name cell E10 *TotalCost,* and name cell G10 *TotalProfit* so the names appear in the Solver results. Write formulas in cells E15 and E16 to represent slack for both constraints. Using the Solver, solve for the optimal number of units to sell of each golf ball brand, and create an Answer report. Fill in your name and today's date in the Documentation worksheet, place your name in each worksheet's header, and print all three worksheets.

FIGURE 10.42

Pro Golf Academy Golf Ball Sales Analysis worksheet

	A	B	C	D	E	F	G	H	I	J
1		Golf Ball Sales Analysis								
2										
3		Wholesale	Retail	Units Sold	Total Cost	Total Sales	Profit			
4	Maxfli M3 Tour	$ 19.98	$ 29.97	100						
5	Slazenger 408dr	$ 17.34	$ 26.01	100						
6	Strata Tour Ultimate	$ 12.88	$ 19.32	100						
7	Titleist Pro V1	$ 18.38	$ 27.57	100						
8	Top-Flite XL 3000	$ 10.00	$ 15.00	100						
9										
10			Totals							
11										
12										
13										
14	Constraint				Slack					
15	Cash for purchase									
16	Storage space									
17										
18										
19										
20										
21										
22										
23										

Documentation | Golf Ball Sales Analysis

Ready

1. Finding the Shortest Feasible Loan Repayment Period

Suppose you want to purchase a car for $10,000, and you have $3,000 for the down payment. You know you can obtain a loan for $7,000. Assume that the annual interest rate for this type of car loan is 7.0 percent. You know that the bank will allow you to repay the loan over 2, 3, 4, or 5 years. However, your budget allows you to make a monthly payment no larger than $140. What technique, short of trial and error, could you use to determine the loan duration? Are there any constraints? If so, be sure to describe them. Also, use Excel to determine if you should request a 2-, 3-, 4-, or 5-year loan to meet the previous monthly payment cap.

2. More Complex Problems

Describe when you might use the Excel Solver tool. In particular, mention what type(s) of problems are suited for the Solver and discuss the meaning of "constraint" and why it exists. Discuss what happens, for example, if you simply tell the Solver that you want to maximize profit, specify changing cells, and do not specify constraints.

Importing Data

did you

know?

Nolan *Bushnell, who invented Pong, is credited as the father of video games.*

about *three percent of the metal in a typical personal computer is precious, and a third of that is gold.*

Bell *Labs originally conceived of the idea of the cellular phone in 1947.*

Nieman Marcus *was the first mail-order catalog to offer a home computer for sale—a Honeywell H316 in 1969 for $10,600.*

the *first digital computer in the world, the ENIAC, had 18,000 vacuum tubes.*

the *Hayes company created the first modem, which set the AT command set standard for modem communications.*

prior *to founding Apple Computer, Steve Jobs and Steve Wozniak wrote a game for Atari called Breakout.*

Chapter Objectives

- Import text files into Excel with the Text Import Wizard—MOS XL03E-4-1

- Move a worksheet from one workbook to another one—MOS XL03S-5-4

- Import database information into Excel using the Query Wizard—MOS XL03E-4-1

- Export data from Excel—MOS XL03E-4-2

- Use Microsoft Query to create a query to filter, sort, and retrieve database records—MOS XL03E-4-1

- Write a database query that joins two related database tables and returns values from each table—MOS XL03E-4-1

- Edit and save database queries—MOS XL03E-4-1

- Write an aggregate query to summarize imported data—MOS XL03E-4-1

Mission Bay Boat Works

Mission Bay Boat Works builds some of the world's fastest racing shells and a wide range of recreational shells. Headquartered in Vancouver, British Columbia, Mission Bay Boat Works (MBBW) has a small inside sales office in Seattle, Washington, to serve its U.S. customers. Building boats with patented hull designs, MBBW racing shells are available in sizes ranging from singles to eight-person models. MBBW shells are noted for their durability as well as their lightweight and sleek design. Mission Bay's recreational shells, though slightly heavier than their racing shell counterparts, are carefully crafted for durability, low maintenance, and low water resistance.

Bob Plimpton, who is the manager of inside sales for Mission Bay Boat Works, wants to consoli-

date information about his inside salespersons into an Excel workbook. Unfortunately, the information sources he needs are located in disparate locations and are in text and database formats. He wants you to help him bring together the information into an Excel workbook so that he can print, modify, and study it. Employee inside sales information is in text format, and customer information is in an Access database. After you translate the information into Excel format, Bob wants to place some of it on the company Web server so that inside salespersons can access it using a Web browser. Figure 11.1 shows the Documentation worksheet of the completed Mission Bay Boat Works workbook.

FIGURE 11.1
Completed Mission Bay
Boat Works workbook

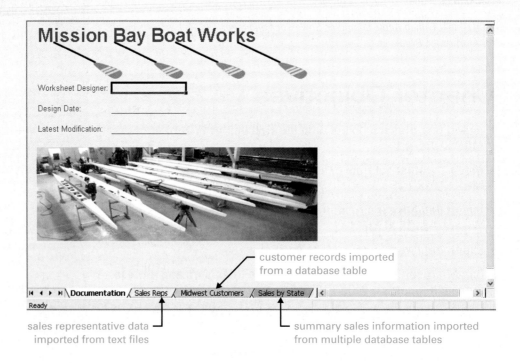

customer records imported from a database table

sales representative data imported from text files

summary sales information imported from multiple database tables

Chapter 11 covers importing data from sources other than Excel workbooks and producing worksheets and charts that you store on the World Wide Web. External data sources from which you will import data into Excel include comma-delimited text files produced by programs such as Notepad, Web-based data files found on the Internet, and information stored in Microsoft Access databases including tables and information produced by executing Access queries. You will import into an Excel worksheet text data whose fixed-length data are stored in columns. Excel can import data whose individual values are separated from one another by commas or another of several possible field separators. Using copy-paste techniques, you can copy data displayed in your Web browser and paste the data into an Excel worksheet. This is particularly handy because a large percentage of the data available on the Web are in text format, not worksheet format.

Excel can import and dissect data stored in Microsoft Access databases as well as in a variety of other database formats. Excel uses structure information about the database's tables to separate distinct fields into Excel columns, and you can choose to use the table column names as column headers in an Excel worksheet. An Excel *query* combines related information from one or more database tables, based on your search and sort criteria, and returns a table as a result. A *database table* is arranged in rows and columns and holds data.

SESSION 11.1 IMPORTING TEXT DATA

In this section, you will learn how to import data from a text file, using an Excel Wizard to guide you in converting the data into Excel format. You will learn about text file formats including delimited text and fixed-width text and how to import data from each format. In addition, you will learn about modifying data with formulas and then converting the formulas to values. You will learn how to import XML data also.

help yourself *Press **F1**, type **import** in the Search text box of the Microsoft Excel Help task pane, and press **Enter**. From the Search Results list, click the hyperlink **Import a text file**. Maximize the Help screen if necessary. Read and optionally print the information. Click the Help screen **Close** button when you are finished, and close the task pane*

Importing Text Files into Excel

Bob knows that pulling together all of the data he needs will be a big task. Data that he wants you to locate and import into an Excel workbook include information about the sales representatives he manages, and products he sells.

Mission Bay Boat Works Data Sources

The data you need to complete the workbook are in several locations. The sales representative information is stored in two text files that Bob's predecessor compiled. Some of the parts and accessories that MBBW sells are on Web pages; however, Bob wants them in his Excel workbook so that he can refer to the items easily. The third location for critical business information—customer sales data—is in a Microsoft Access database. The company captures sales information including each customer's name, address, and the sale amount. In the same Access database are records of people who have not yet made a purchase but who have indicated interest in receiving a catalog or further information. People on this list represent possible future sales, and Bob wants the marketing staff to contact people in the database to see if MBBW can assist them in purchasing products. Figure 11.2 shows the three data sources you will help Bob pull together into one workbook.

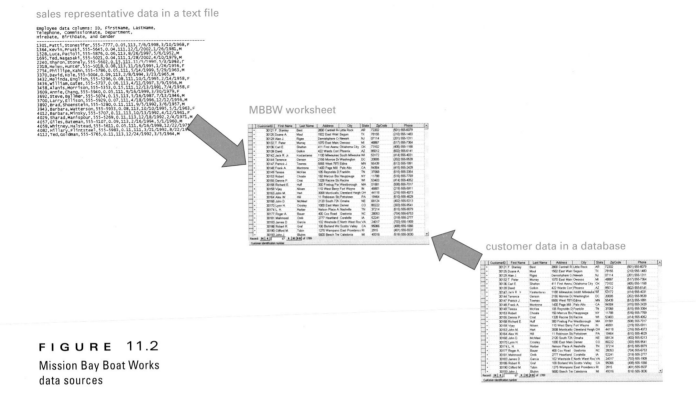

FIGURE 11.2

Mission Bay Boat Works
data sources

Understanding Text Files and Data Separation Choices

Text data consists only of characters (letters, digits, and special characters) that you can type on a keyboard—devoid of any special formatting (boldface, italic, etc.). Text data is the most common data format because just about every program that exists today can store your data in text format regardless of the product's native format. Excel, for example, allows you to store worksheet data in text format in addition to the default Excel worksheet format. Similarly, Word provides a "plain text" output format for Word documents.

As text data have no internal markers to indicate where data begin and end, text files and programs that read text files rely on delimiters to separate data fields from one another. A *delimiter* is a character or group of characters that separates two pieces of data. Delimiters are used in almost every computer application. Common delimiters you will encounter include blanks, commas, semicolons, quotation marks, brackets, and braces—any character(s) that does not normally occur in the data it is delimiting.

An alternative to delimited data is to arrange data into specific locations or starting positions. Such an arrangement is known as *fixed-width* data. An individual unit of data, either fixed length or separated from others by a delimiter, is called a data *field*.

Programs read data from particular locations in a record and store each of the data groups, called fields, in different locations within the program for processing. Figure 11.3 shows an example of fixed-length data in which distinct information about several salespersons begins in the same column for each data field. Figure 11.4 shows comma-separated data fields in a Notepad window. Values separated from one another by commas are called *comma-separated values*, abbreviated *CSV*.

Excel can import either fixed-length data fields or delimited data fields. With either type of file, Excel knows where each field begins and ends and assigns each field to its own column when you open either type of file in preparation to import data. Excel places each record in a data file in successive rows of a worksheet. If you choose to import text data beginning in cell B2, then Excel will place the first record into cell row 2,

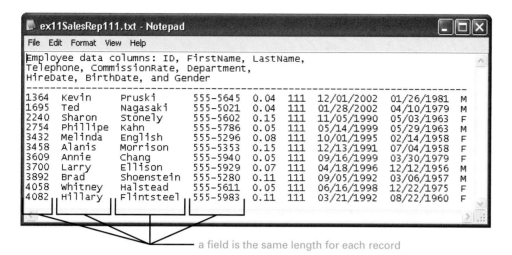

FIGURE 11.3

Text file with fixed-length fields

a field is the same length for each record

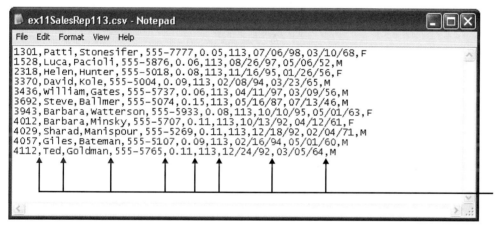

FIGURE 11.4

Text file with comma-separated fields

commas separate fields from each other

the second record into row 3, and so on. Similarly, the first field of each record goes into column B of its row. The second field of each record goes into column C, and so on.

Working with a Fixed-Length Data File

The employee records file contains information about the inside sales representatives located in the Seattle office who call customers and potential customers around the United States. Bob is not sure about the data's structure, but the office manager who gave him the file assures Bob that it is a text file containing no special characters.

The file extension .txt indicates that the file is a text file. Whenever Excel opens a file whose extension is .txt, it automatically launches the ***Text Import Wizard*** to lead you through a process to convert the text format data into Excel format. The Text Import Wizard displays the first few lines of the file and asks you to determine if the data are delimited or fixed length and which row is the first row you want Excel to import. Step 2 asks you to indicate where each data field in the incoming data begins. You can add a line, called a ***column break***, to indicate the beginning of a field, or you can move or remove column breaks as needed to properly identify where columns begin. In step 3, you can optionally designate a column data format for each field, and you can indicate which text fields to omit from the Excel worksheet.

Opening the Text Import Wizard

Bob wants you to import into Excel the sales representative information found in the two text files called **ex11SalesRep111.txt** and **ex11SalesRep113.csv**. There are two text files because the sales employees once worked in two different divisions, each with a different manager. The manager of division 111 kept the sales representative information in a fixed-length text file, whereas the manager of division 113 kept information about his sales representatives in a comma-separated text file. Because the two divisions' sales representatives now work in one division, you will import the files into Excel and then merge the two sets of records into one Excel worksheet. You begin by importing the employee records in the fixed-length text file.

There are two ways to launch the Text Import Wizard: You can open an existing workbook and then execute Import External Data found in the Data menu, or you can open a text file directly in Excel.

---

task reference   **Importing Fixed-Length Data Using the Text Import Wizard**

- Click **File** and then click **Open**

- In the Files of type list box of the Open dialog box, select **Text Files**

- Using the *Look in* list box, navigate to the folder containing the text file, click the filename in the list of files, and click the **Open** button

- Click the **Fixed Width** option button in the Original data type panel

- Click the **Start import at row** spin box to select the first row to import, and click the **Next** button

- In step 2, click to the left of each field to add a break line, double-click a break line to remove it, or drag a break line to its correct position at the beginning of a column as needed. Then click the **Next** button to proceed

- In step 3, for each column, click a **Column data format** option button to select a column format or click the **Do not import column** option button to skip the column, and then click the **Finish** button

---

Opening the fixed-length sales representatives text file:

1. Start Excel and close the Getting Started task pane, if necessary

2. Click the **Open** button on the Standard toolbar, click the **Files of type** list arrow, click the **Text Files (*.prn; *.txt; *.csv)** entry, navigate to the disk and folder containing the sales representatives text file **ex11SalesRep111.txt**, click **ex11SalesRep111.txt**, and click the **Open** button. The Text Import Wizard—Step 1 of 3 dialog box opens (see Figure 11.5)

3. Click the **Fixed width** option button, if necessary, to indicate that the text file contains fixed-width data

Specifying the Starting Row

Notice in Figure 11.5 that the text file contains commentary in the first four lines indicating the names of the columns and their ordering. A dashed line follows the three

FIGURE 11.5

Text Import Wizard Step 1 of 3 dialog box

select one of two formats based on the text data

the first few rows of the text file appear in the *Preview of file* panel

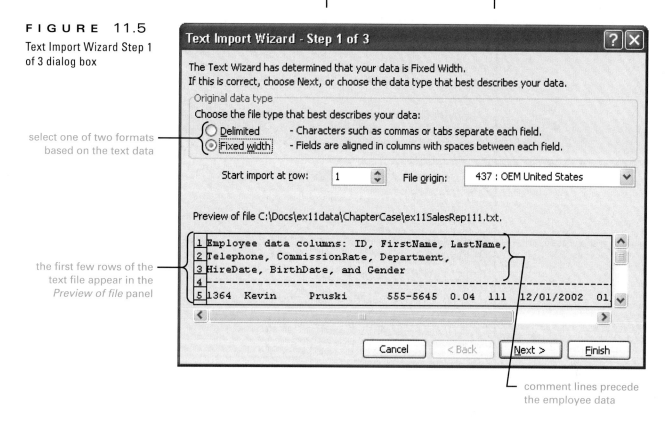

comment lines precede the employee data

rows of field description information and separates the comments from the data. Comment lines in the beginning of a text file describing the text file's contents and column format are common in many text files.

Because you do not want to import the first four rows of the **ex11SalesRep111.txt** file into the Excel worksheet, you will tell the Text Import Wizard to skip them.

Specifying the first row to import:

1. Click the **Start import at row** spin box up arrow repeatedly until the value 5 appears in the box. This causes Excel to import rows beginning with row 5 (see Figure 11.6)

2. Click the **Next** button to go to the second Text Import Wizard step

Altering Column Breaks and Adding New Ones

The Text Import Wizard examines the text file and places vertical lines, called **column breaks,** in the data where it believes new columns begin. Sometimes the Wizard is correct and places all breaks where they belong, but occasionally the Wizard doesn't place enough column breaks or places them in the wrong locations. Always check each column break to ensure that it is in the correct location. If necessary, you can drag a line break to move it, delete unneeded line breaks, or add new ones. Remember to drag the horizontal scroll box to view the entire breadth of the text, if needed.

The Wizard does its best to place the column breaks where columns begin. It uses the vertical lines to mark the positions of its proposed column breaks. You observe the line breaks that the Text Import Wizard suggests and see that there are several missing column breaks. In addition, one line break is out of place (see Figure 11.7).

EXCEL

FIGURE 11.6

Setting the starting row

Start import at row spin box indicates the first row to import

row 5 will be the first of several rows imported

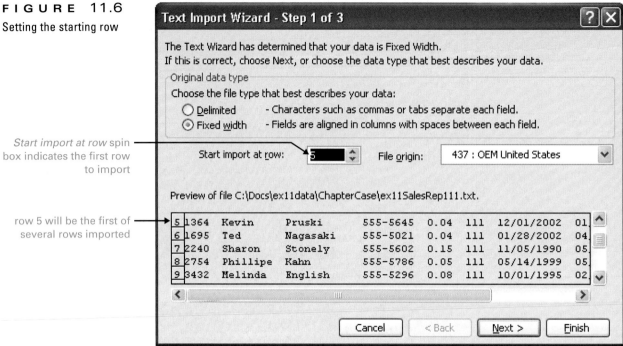

FIGURE 11.7

Wizard-suggested column breaks

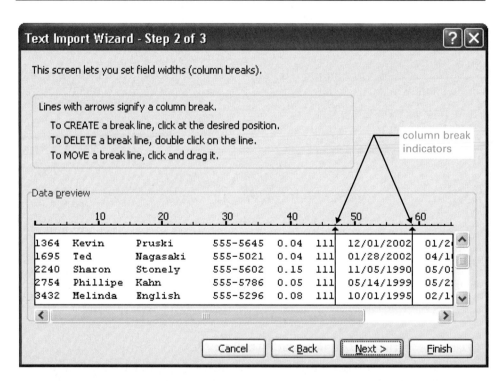

task reference   Adding, Moving, and Deleting Column Breaks Using the Text Import Wizard

- Add a column break by clicking the position just above the ruler in the Data preview panel where you want the column break to appear

- Move a column break by clicking it and then dragging it to its new position

- Delete a column break by double-clicking it

Add new column breaks and move the one misplaced column break so that Excel correctly interprets the data.

Modifying Text Import Wizard column breaks:

1. Click the space immediately to the left of the first name *Kevin* (position 6 on the ruler) to create a column break at the beginning of the first name column. Be sure the line does not cross any data

tip: *Don't worry if you place a column break in the wrong location. You can move it easily by clicking and dragging the line to its proper location*

2. Click the space immediately to the left of the last name *Pruski* (position 16) to create a column break at the beginning of the last name column

3. Click the space immediately to the left of the telephone number beginning in position 28 (see the ruler above the data in the Data preview panel) to create a column break

4. Click the space immediately to the left of the commission rate (0.04 in the first record) to create a column break at position 38

5. Click the space immediately to the left of the department number, 111, to create a column break at position 44

6. Click and drag the column break line that is in position 47 (between the department number and the hire date) to position 49—immediately to the left of the hire date column (see Figure 11.8)

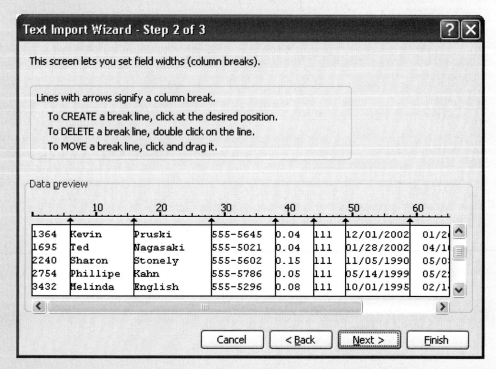

FIGURE 11.8

Adjusted column breaks

7. Click and drag the column break line in column 59 to column 61

8. Click and drag the Data preview horizontal scroll box to check the rightmost text fields. The column breaks are fine for the rightmost fields

Specifying Data Formats and Skipping Selected Columns

The third and final step of the Text Import Wizard lets you specify the data type of each column you are importing. You are limited to General, Text, Date, and Do Not Import columns. The General option treats text as text and numbers as numbers, the default for all imported columns. The Text option treats all entries in a column as text, even if some entries appear to be numbers. The Date option treats entries as dates. The Do Not Import column option provides a convenient way to skip a data column.

In the third and final Wizard step, you will set the data format for two columns and tell the Wizard to skip the department number column.

Setting the data format for selected columns:

1. Click the **Next** button to go to the last Text Import Wizard step. The Text Import Wizard—Step 3 of 3 dialog box appears (see Figure 11.9)

FIGURE 11.9

Text Import Wizard Step 3 of 3 dialog box

data format options

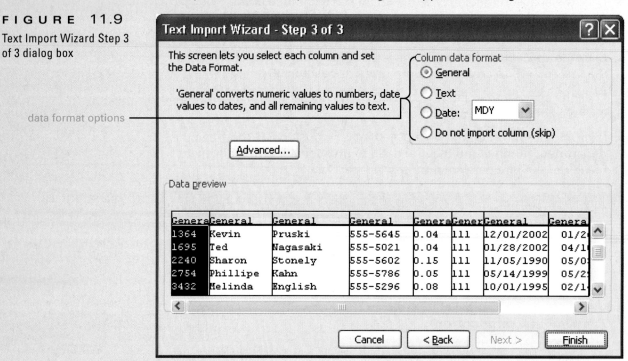

2. Click anywhere within the sixth column from the left, containing the values 111, and then click the **Do not import column (skip)** option button located in the Column data format panel

3. Click anywhere within the seventh column containing dates, and then click the **Date** option button to ensure that Excel interprets the dates correctly

4. Click the eighth column containing employees' birth dates, and then click the **Date** option button to ensure that Excel interprets the dates correctly.
   Notice that the column headers above the three columns whose format option you changed are now Skip, MDY, and MDY, respectively (see Figure 11.10)

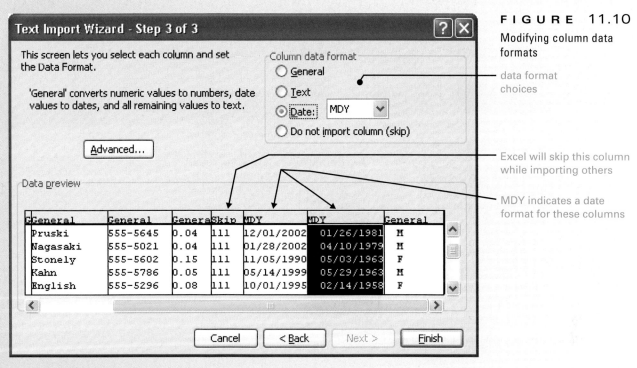

FIGURE 11.10

Modifying column data formats

data format choices

Excel will skip this column while importing others

MDY indicates a date format for these columns

5. Click **Finish** to import the data into an Excel worksheet. Excel creates a new workbook whose tab and workbook name are the same name as the text file you imported

6. Double-click the worksheet tab, type **Sales Reps**, and press **Enter** to rename it

7. Insert a new row 1 at the top of the worksheet and enter the following text in cells **A1** through **H1**, respectively: **ID**, **First Name**, **Last Name**, **Phone**, **Commission Rate**, **Hire Date**, **Birth Date**, and **Gender**

8. Select cell range **A1:H1**, click **Format**, click **Cells**, click the **Alignment** tab, click the **Wrap text** check box (found in the Text control panel), click the **Font** tab, click **Bold** in the Font style list, and click the **OK** button to format the column labels

9. Drag the mouse through the column headings for columns **A** through **H** and then double-click the right dividing line between any two selected column headings to optimize the width of the selected columns

10. Select column **E** (click its column heading), and then drag the dividing line between columns E and F until the word *Commission* in cell E1 appears on one line

11. Click cell **A1** to deselect the cell range (see Figure 11.11)

Saving Imported Data as an Excel Workbook

Look carefully at the Excel Title bar. Notice that the name *ex11SalesRep111.txt* appears in the Title bar. This indicates Excel still believes the file you are viewing is a text file—even though it is in an Excel workbook. Save the imported data as an Excel workbook.

EXCEL

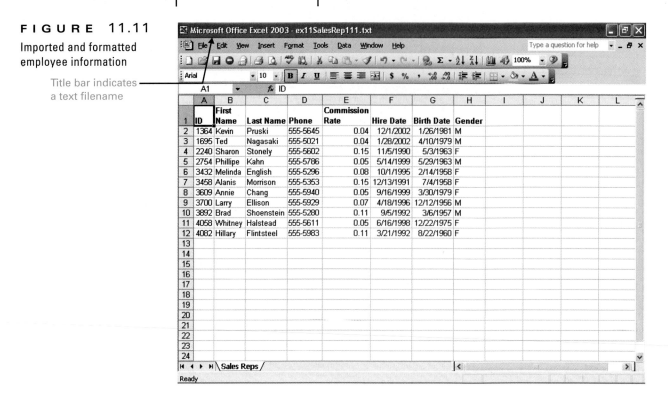

Saving the imported employee text file as an Excel workbook:

1. Click **File** and click **Save As**

2. Click the **Save as type** list box, and then click **Microsoft Excel Workbook (*.xls)** in the list

3. Type **SalesReps2** in the File name list box and click the **Save** button

4. Close the workbook

Bob is pleased when you show him your work. With one of the two sales representative text files imported, you are ready to import the second one.

Working with a Comma-Separated Values Text File

The data file **ex11SalesRep113.csv** contains sales representative information from the old Division 113 of Mission Bay Boat Works. You know that the division's manager kept the sales representative information in a comma-separated, or CSV, format. Excel is particularly adept at importing CSV files because each field is delimited with a comma. That is, a comma occurs following each field except for the last field in a record. There is no ambiguity about where one field ends and another one begins. Naturally, using CSV formatted files means that numeric field values cannot contain commas, because the comma is a field separator. A value such as 10,761.34 is written without a comma in the CSV file: 10761.34.

You are ready to import the CSV file **ex11SalesRep113.csv** into Excel. When you are finished importing the data, you will combine the two sales representative worksheets into the main worksheet, **ex11MBBW.xls**.

Importing comma-separated values into Excel:

1. With Excel open, click the **Open** button on the Standard toolbar, click the **Files of type** list arrow, and click **Text Files (*.prn; *.txt; *.csv)** from the list of file types

2. Using the *Look in* list box, navigate to the folder containing the file **ex11SalesRep113.csv**, click **ex11SalesRep113.csv**, and click the **Open** button. Excel imports the CSV file and displays it in a new workbook (see Figure 11.12)

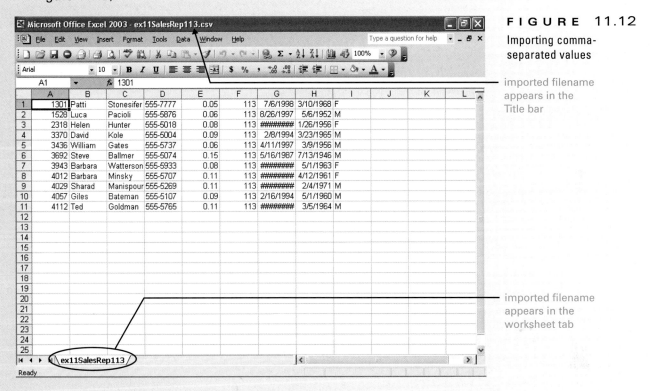

FIGURE 11.12
Importing comma-separated values

imported filename appears in the Title bar

imported filename appears in the worksheet tab

You can eliminate the column containing the old department number, column F. After eliminating that column, the worksheet will be ready to copy into the main workbook.

Eliminating an unwanted column:

1. Right-click column F's column heading. Excel selects column F and displays a shortcut menu

2. Click **Delete** in the shortcut menu to delete the column, and then click cell **A1** to deselect column F

Moving, Copying, and Pasting Data between Workbooks

Bob wants the imported employee data from both files placed into the workbook **ex11MBBW.xls**. In this section, you will open **ex11MBBW.xls** and **SalesReps2.xls**, and then move the Sales Reps worksheet to the **ex11MBBW.xls** workbook. Next, you will copy the data from **ex11SalesRep113.csv** and paste the data into the Sales Reps worksheet—just below the existing sales rep information. Finally, you will close the **ex11SalesRep113.csv** workbook and tidy up the consolidated Sales Reps worksheet by sorting the data and saving the workbook under a new name.

Opening Other Workbooks

In order to consolidate the two imported text files into the main Mission Bay Boat Works worksheet, open all three workbooks to facilitate moving and copying data between them.

Opening two other workbooks:

1. With the **ex11SalesRep113.csv** workbook open, click the **Open** button on the Standard toolbar

2. Click the **Files of type** list arrow, and click **Microsoft Excel Files** from the list of file types

3. Using the *Look in* list box, navigate to the folder containing the file **SalesReps2.xls**, click **SalesReps2.xls**, and click the **Open** button

4. Click the **Open** button on the Standard toolbar, navigate to the folder containing the file **ex11MBBW.xls**, click **ex11MBBW.xls**, and click the **Open** button

Three workbooks are open in Excel: **SalesReps2.xls**, **ex11MBBW.xls**, and **ex11SalesRep113.csv**.

Moving a Worksheet to Another Workbook

Now you can move the **SalesReps2.xls** worksheet over to the **ex11MBBW.xls** workbook.

Moving a worksheet to another workbook:

1. Click **Window**, and then click **SalesReps2.xls** in the list of active workbooks to make it active

2. Click **Edit** and click **Move or Copy Sheet**. The Move or Copy dialog box opens

3. Click the **To book** list box arrow and click **ex11MBBW.xls** in the list of open workbooks

4. In the *Before sheet* list box, click **(move to end)**. Figure 11.13 shows the completed Move or Copy dialog box

5. Click the **OK** button. Excel *moves* the Sales Reps worksheet to **ex11MBBW.xls**, closes the **SalesReps2.xls** workbook, and displays the newly moved worksheet (see Figure 11.14)

6. Click **File**, click **Save As**, type the name **MissionBoats2** in the File name list box, and click the **Save** button to save the workbook under its new name

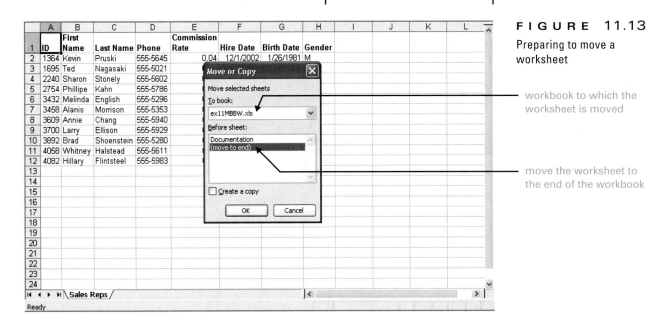

FIGURE 11.13

Preparing to move a worksheet

workbook to which the worksheet is moved

move the worksheet to the end of the workbook

FIGURE 11.14

Moved Sales Reps worksheet

Copying and Pasting Data to Another Workbook

Next, you will copy and paste a worksheet from **ex11SalesRep113.csv** into the Sales Reps workbook.

Copying and pasting worksheet data:

1. Click **Window** and then click **ex11SalesRep113.csv** to make that workbook and accompanying worksheet active

2. Click and drag the cell range **A1:H11**, and click the **Copy** button on the Standard toolbar. Excel places the selected cell range onto the Clipboard

3. Click **File** and then click **Close**. When Excel displays a dialog box asking if you want to save the changes you made to ex11SalesRep113.csv, click **No**. The worksheet **MissionBoats2.xls** becomes active

EXCEL

4. Click cell **A13** and then click the **Paste** button on the Standard toolbar. Excel pastes the data into rows 13 through 23

5. Click Cell **A1** to deselect the range, and click the **Save** button on the Standard toolbar to preserve your latest changes (see Figure 11.15)

FIGURE 11.15

Completed Sales Reps worksheet

	A	B	C	D	E	F	G	H	I	J	K	L
1	ID	First Name	Last Name	Phone	Commission Rate	Hire Date	Birth Date	Gender				
2	1364	Kevin	Pruski	555-5645	0.04	12/1/2002	1/26/1981	M				
3	1695	Ted	Nagasaki	555-5021	0.04	1/28/2002	4/10/1979	M				
4	2240	Sharon	Stonely	555-5602	0.15	11/5/1990	5/3/1963	F				
5	2754	Phillipe	Kahn	555-5786	0.05	5/14/1999	5/29/1963	M				
6	3432	Melinda	English	555-5296	0.08	10/1/1995	2/14/1958	F				
7	3458	Alanis	Morrison	555-5353	0.15	12/13/1991	7/4/1958	F				
8	3609	Annie	Chang	555-5940	0.05	9/16/1999	3/30/1979	F				
9	3700	Larry	Ellison	555-5929	0.07	4/18/1996	12/12/1956	M				
10	3892	Brad	Shoenstein	555-5280	0.11	9/5/1992	3/6/1957	M				
11	4058	Whitney	Halstead	555-5611	0.05	6/16/1998	12/22/1975	F				
12	4082	Hillary	Flintsteel	555-5983	0.11	3/21/1992	8/22/1960	F				
13	1301	Patti	Stonesifer	555-7777	0.05	7/6/1998	3/10/1968	F				
14	1528	Luca	Pacioli	555-5876	0.06	8/26/1997	5/6/1952	M				
15	2318	Helen	Hunter	555-5018	0.08	11/16/1995	1/26/1956	F				
16	3370	David	Kole	555-5004	0.09	2/8/1994	3/23/1965	M				
17	3436	William	Gates	555-5737	0.06	4/11/1997	3/9/1956	M				
18	3692	Steve	Ballmer	555-5074	0.15	5/16/1987	7/13/1946	M				
19	3943	Barbara	Watterson	555-5933	0.08	10/10/1995	5/1/1963	F				
20	4012	Barbara	Minsky	555-5707	0.11	10/13/1992	4/12/1961	F				
21	4029	Sharad	Manispour	555-5269	0.11	12/18/1992	2/4/1971	M				
22	4057	Giles	Bateman	555-5107	0.09	2/16/1994	5/1/1960	M				
23	4112	Ted	Goldman	555-5765	0.11	12/24/1992	3/5/1964	M				
24												

Documentation \ Sales Reps /

Ready

Formatting and Sorting the Imported Data

Bob wants the sales rep rows to be sorted by last name and then first name so that he can easily locate any particular employee. He also wants you to format the commission rate column so that the rates display a percentage with two decimal places and to center the values in the Gender column. You agree that will make the list easier to use, and you also decide to color the column label backgrounds and color-code the worksheet tab.

Sorting and formatting the Sales Reps worksheet:

1. Click **Data**, click **Sort**, click the **Sort by** list box arrow, and click **Last Name**

2. Click the **Then by** list box arrow and then click **First Name**

3. Ensure that the **Ascending** option button is selected for both sort fields, and then click **OK** to sort the rows

4. Select cell range **E2:E23**, click the **Percent Style** button on the Formatting toolbar, and click the **Increase Decimal** button on the Formatting toolbar *twice* so that the commission rates display two decimal places

5. Select cell range **H2:H23** and click the **Center** alignment button on the Formatting toolbar. Excel centers the Gender column values

tip: *Recall that you can select a filled cell range by clicking the first cell in the range, holding down the **Shift** key, tapping the **End** key, pressing an arrow key, and then releasing the **Shift** key. Excel will select the cell range in the direction of the arrow you pressed until it encounters an empty cell*

6. Select cell range **A1:H1**, click the **Fill Color** list arrow on the Formatting toolbar, click the **Light Yellow** color square (fifth row from the top, third column) from the drop-down color palette, and click cell **A1** to deselect the cell range

7. Right-click the **Sales Reps** worksheet tab, click **Tab Color** in the shortcut menu, click the **Light Yellow** color square, and click **OK** (see Figure 11.16)

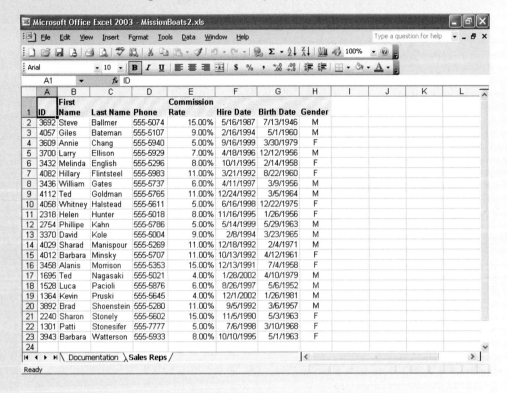

FIGURE 11.16

Sorted and formatted
Sales Reps worksheet

Now you have the two text files containing sales representative information imported into a single worksheet called Sales Reps. It is a simple matter for Bob to review or alter the inside sales reps by consulting his master workbook.

Saving your workbook:

1. Click the **Documentation** worksheet tab to make that worksheet active

2. Click the **Save** button on the Standard toolbar

Not only does Excel support importing a wide variety of data formats, it also supports exporting several widely-recognized data formats including extensible markup language (XML), Web pages, tab delimited text, several older Excel workbook formats, and comma delimited (CSV)—to name just a few. Bob suggests you save the Sales Reps worksheet, but not the Documentation worksheet, in a form that other sales persons can easily import into a variety of computer products. He thinks that the comma delimited file format is a good choice.

Exporting a worksheet as a CSV format:

1. With the Sales Reps worksheet active, click **File**, click **Save As**, and navigate to the folder where you want to save the exported Sales Reps data by using the *Save in* list box

2. Click the **Save as type** list box, scroll the list to locate *CSV (Comma delimited) (*.csv)*, click CSV (Comma delimited) (*.csv)

3. Click the **Save** button. If Excel displays a warning message about multiple sheet support, then click **OK** to continue creating the CSV-format worksheet. If a second message appears indicating selected features are not compatible with the CSV format, click the Yes button to continue. Excel exports the file and saves it as **MissionBoats2.csv**

4. Click the **File** and then click **Exit** to exit Excel. If a message appears asking if you want to save your changes, click **No**

SESSION 11.1

making *the grade*

1. _____ data consists only of characters that you can type on a keyboard and does not contain any special formatting.

2. Groups or fields of data often are separated from one another with a _____ character that does not otherwise occur in the data.

3. When the Excel Text Import Wizard imports text data, it indicates the beginning of each new column of data with what?

4. Text files in which values are separated from one another with commas have the special name _____ - _____ values. People often use the abbreviation _____ to refer to these types of files.

SESSION 11.2 USING QUERIES TO IMPORT DATABASE DATA

In this section, you will learn how to import data from a Microsoft Access database using both the Query Wizard and Microsoft Query. You will select columns from a database table to import, specify which rows to import using criteria, and sort information prior to importing it into Excel—all with the Query Wizard. Using the more powerful Microsoft Query, you will import information from multiple related database tables that compute a summation of grouped records, and you will save queries for later use.

Retrieving Data from Databases

It is common for companies to store their important data such as customer names and addresses, invoices, product catalogs, and employee information in corporate databases. A *database* is a collection of information organized so that a computer program can select requested information from it quickly—a sophisticated electronic filing system. Special software called *database management systems*, or *DBMSs*, take in user requests and comb through a database to deliver requested information, update information, or delete information.

Excel is incapable of storing millions of database records because of worksheet row limits and computer memory limitations. However, Excel can tap into the power of database systems through a query. Excel passes a query you specify in Excel to database software that translates the query, retrieves the data, and passes the data back to the Excel program. Special software installed with Excel, called a **database driver**, translates Excel information requests into database commands. Database drivers allow you to retrieve data from Access databases, Web pages, text files, Paradox databases, dBASE databases, and a host of other files and database systems.

In this chapter, you will use two different methods to create a database query: Excel's Query Wizard and Microsoft Query. The Query Wizard, like other Excel Wizards, displays a series of dialog boxes that lead you through the process of locating a database, forming a query based on the table you select from the database, and importing data from a database system into Excel.

Microsoft Query is a more powerful tool for importing database information into Excel. It allows you to specify more complex database queries, perform calculations within a query that the Query Wizard cannot perform, join together related tables, and retrieve information from several tables at once.

help yourself *Press **F1**, type **import query** in the Search text box of the Microsoft Excel Help task pane, and press **Enter**. From the Search Results list, click the hyperlink **About importing data**. Click the **Show All** hyperlink to open all the collapsed Help paragraphs so you can scan them. Maximize the Help screen if necessary. Read and optionally print the information. Click the Help screen **Close** button when you are finished, and close the task pane*

Using the Excel Query Wizard

Bob tells you that Mission Bay Boat Works sales information is kept in a Microsoft Access database. He wants to analyze sales information in Excel, and there are two tables in the Access database that will help do that.

Bob wants to mail out a marketing brochure especially designed for customers living in Illinois, Indiana, or Michigan who have purchased racing shells or merely made an inquiry about the price and availability of boats. The information is in the Access database called **ex11MBBW.mdb**. Bob wants you to import the customer names and addresses of the customers from each of the three U.S. states into Excel. Bob tells you that each customer's information is stored in its own **record**, which is a collection of related information about one object (a person in this case) that is stored in a database table.

There are two general steps to get data out of a database and into an Excel worksheet. The first step is to specify a data source, which is the name and location of the database. The second step is to define a query that is responsible for searching the database and returning information to Excel.

Creating a Data Source Definition

First, you will open your Mission Bay Boat Works workbook, and then you will insert a new worksheet into it.

Opening a workbook and inserting a worksheet:

1. Open the workbook **MissionBoats2.xls** and then immediately save it under the new name **MissionBoats3.xls**

2. Click **Insert**, click **Worksheet**, drag the newly added worksheet tab to the right of the Sales Reps worksheet, double-click the newly added worksheet tab, type **Midwest Customers**, and press **Enter**

3. Right-click the **Midwest Customers** worksheet tab, click **Tab Color**, click the **Tan** color square (fifth row from the top, second from the left) in the Format Tab Color dialog box, and click **OK**

EXCEL

The first step to import database data into Excel is to choose a data source—the database from which you will import data. Once you have chosen a data source, you can refer to the named data source for other queries you will build in this session.

Creating a connection to a data source:

1. With the Midwest Customers worksheet active, click **Data**, point to **Import External Data**, and click **New Database Query**. The Choose Data Source dialog box opens (see Figure 11.17)

FIGURE 11.17

Choose Data Source dialog box

double-click to define a new data source

very important: make sure that this check box contains a checkmark. If it does not, then click it to place a checkmark in it

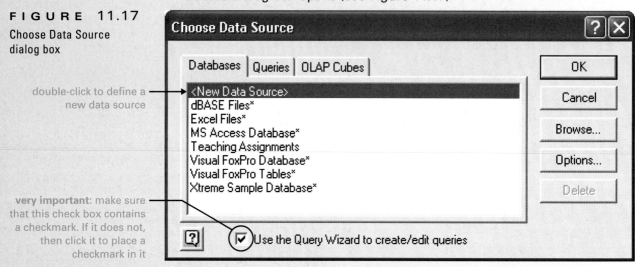

2. Ensure that the **Use the Query Wizard to create/edit queries** check box contains a checkmark, and then double-click the **<New Data Source>** selection

3. Type **<yourname>MBBW**, substituting your name for "<yourname>" in text box number 1 to name your data source, and then click in list box number 2 and select **Microsoft Access Driver (*.mdb)** (see Figure 11.18)

FIGURE 11.18

Create New Data Source dialog box

select *Microsoft Access Driver*

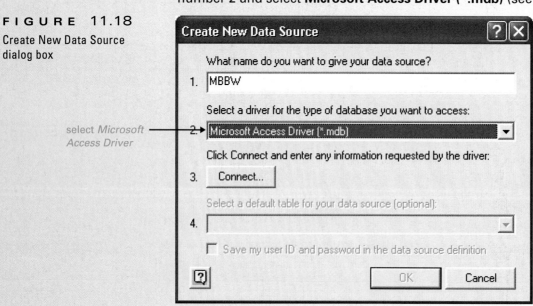

4. Click the **Connect** button that appears next to the number 3. This displays a new dialog box in which you select a specific database by name (see Figure 11.19)

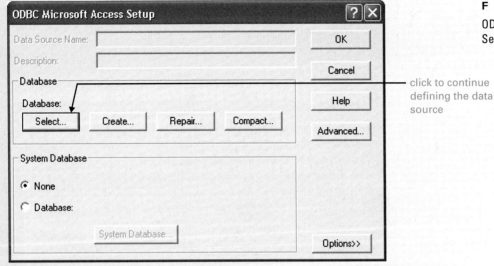

click to continue defining the data source

FIGURE 11.19

ODBC Microsoft Access Setup dialog box

5. Click the **Select** button in the Database panel. The Select Database dialog box opens

6. Use the Directories list box to navigate to the folder in which the file **ex11MBBW.mdb** appears, click **ex11MBBW.mdb** in the Database Name list box (see Figure 11.20), and click the **OK** button. The ODBC Microsoft Access Setup dialog box reappears

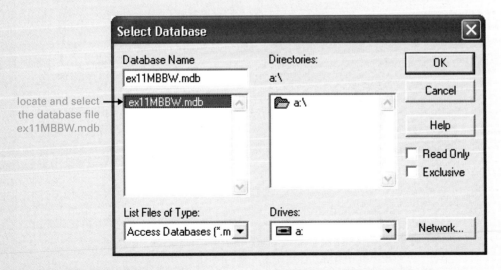

locate and select the database file ex11MBBW.mdb

FIGURE 11.20

Select Database dialog box

7. Click **OK** in the ODBC Microsoft Access Setup dialog box. The Create New Data Source dialog box reappears

8. Click the **OK** button in the Create New Data Source dialog box to complete the database connection procedure. The Choose Data Source dialog box reappears. It contains a new entry—the new data source you have defined

Choosing and Arranging Columns

After creating the data source, which you named with your own name followed by *MBBW* in this case, you can launch the actual Query Wizard. Then you will be able to specify which table(s) and which column(s) of the database table you want the query to import into your Excel worksheet. Bob tells you that the customer information is stored in a database table named tblCustomers. He wants you to import all the data columns, *except* CustomerID, for customers who live in Illinois, Indiana, or Michigan.

Choosing the table and table columns to import:

1. In the Choose Data Source dialog box, click **<yourname>MBBW** in the list of data sources to select it and then click the **OK** button. The Query Wizard executes and then displays the Query Wizard—Choose Columns dialog box listing tables and queries stored in the database (see Figure 11.21)

FIGURE 11.21

Query Wizard—Choose
Columns dialog box

click the expand button (+)
to display the *tblCustomers*
table's columns

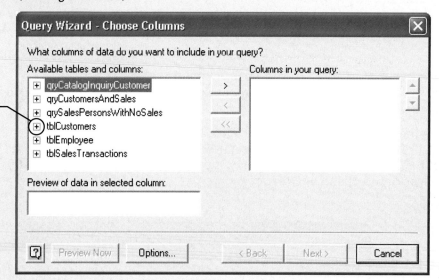

tip: *In large databases, the list of tables and queries may be very long. You can sort the table names and query names into alphabetical order by clicking the **Options** button and then checking the **List Tables and Columns in alphabetical order** check box in the Table Options dialog box that appears*

2. Click the **plus symbol** (+) to the left of tblCustomers in the *Available tables and columns* list box. The table's list of columns appears below the table name

3. Click the **FirstName** column name, and then click the > button to place the column name in the *Columns in your query* list.
   Notice that a column name is moved from one list to another, disappears from the available column list, and the Query Wizard highlights the next name in the list

4. Click the > button repeatedly to move the **LastName, Address, City, State, ZipCode,** and **PhoneNumber** columns, in turn, to the *Columns in your query* list box (see Figure 11.22)

tip: *If you aren't sure what information is in a particular column, highlight the column name and then click the **Preview Now** button to display a sample of the actual data in the Preview of data in selected column box*

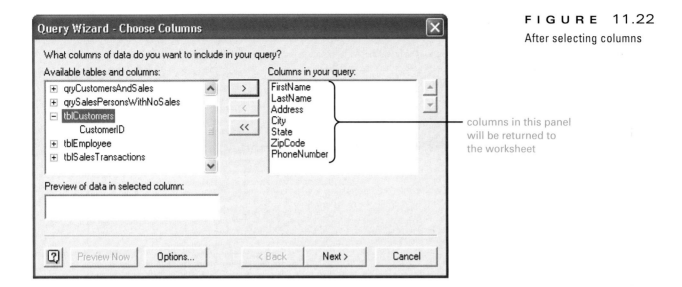

FIGURE 11.22
After selecting columns

columns in this panel
will be returned to
the worksheet

Filtering Data

You have specified the columns from the tblCustomers table that you want to import into Excel. Next, you must specify record *selection criteria*, also called a *filter*, which limits the records retrieved from a table. In this case, the process of limiting records, called filtering data, means you will restrict the retrieved customer records to three states: Illinois, Indiana, or Michigan.

Limiting retrieved records to those matching selection criteria:

1. Click the **Next** button. The Query Wizard—Filter Data dialog box opens

2. Click **State** in the *Column to filter* list. The first list box, located in the *Only include rows where* group, lightens

3. Click the leftmost list box in the first row of the *Only include rows where* group and click **equals** from the list of relational operations

4. Type **IL** (the abbreviation for Illinois) in the rightmost list box in the first row of the *Only include rows where* group

5. Click the **Or** option button below the first condition in the *Only include rows where* group

6. Click the leftmost list box in the second row and select **equals**

7. Click the list box arrow in the rightmost list box in the second row. Then scroll down the list box to locate and then click the entry **IN** (the abbreviation for Indiana)

8. Click the **Or** option button below the second condition in the *Only include rows where* group

9. Click the leftmost list box in the third row and select **equals**

10. Click the list box arrow in the rightmost list box in the third row. Then scroll down the list box to locate and then click the entry **MI** (see Figure 11.23)

FIGURE 11.23
Query Wizard—Filter Data
dialog box completed

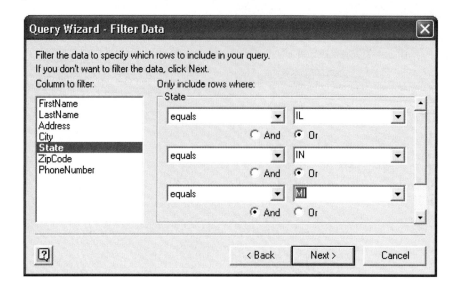

The filtering criteria tell the Query Wizard to only retrieve records in which the customer's State column has the value IL, IN, or MI. The query will exclude all other rows.

Sorting the Resulting Set

The Query Wizard's next to the last step is simple and quick. You can select up to three columns to sort the retrieved data, and you can sort each column in either ascending or descending order. Although you can sort the data after they are retrieved into Excel, it usually saves time to let the query do the work. The sort columns you specify must be among the columns returned by the query. For example, you cannot ask the Query Wizard to sort the CustomerID data, because that is not one of the columns that the query will return.

Sorting the data in the query:

1. Click the **Next** button to display the Query Wizard—Sort Order dialog box
2. Click the **Sort by** list box and then click **State** in the list that appears. The Query Wizard automatically selects the Ascending sort option for the column
3. Click the topmost **Then by** list box and then click **City** from the list of sort fields (see Figure 11.24)

Returning Data to Microsoft Excel and Saving a Query for Later Use

Now the query is complete and there is only one more step remaining. You can instruct the Query Wizard to retrieve the data from the database table and return the data to Excel. Additionally, you can save the query so that you can rerun it later. Why would you ever want to rerun a query? The answer is that the database data will probably change over time as more customers are added to the table and others place orders. If you rerun the query in two weeks, you are likely to retrieve a slightly different set of customer records. In other words, it is always a good idea to save your query so that you have the option of rerunning it again in the future.

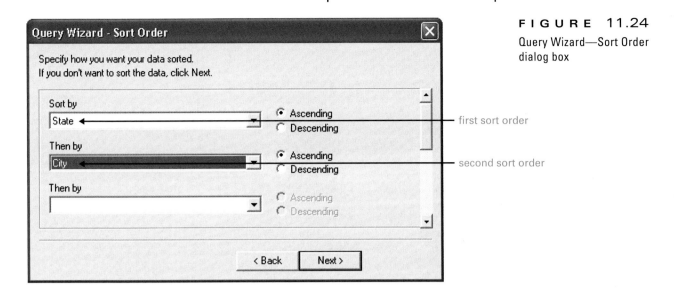

FIGURE 11.24

Query Wizard—Sort Order
dialog box

Bob wants to run this particular query four times in the next month—once each week—to analyze the customer data.

Saving the customer query:

1. Click the **Next** button to display the Query Wizard—Finish dialog box

2. Click the **Save Query** button, type **<yourname>MidwestCustomers** (substitute your first and last names for "<yourname>") in the File name list box, and click **Save**. The Query Wizard saves the query in a special folder called Queries and then redisplays the Finish dialog box. The External Data toolbar probably appears also (see Figure 11.25)

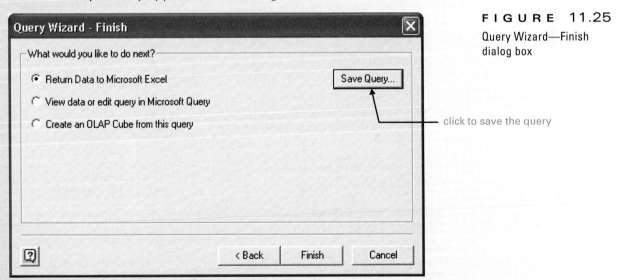

FIGURE 11.25

Query Wizard—Finish
dialog box

3. If the External Data toolbar appears, click the **Close** button on its Title bar to remove the toolbar

Now you can retrieve the customer information with the query you created and return it to the Excel worksheet.

Returning query results to a worksheet:

1. Ensure that the **Return Data to Microsoft Excel** option button is selected in the Query Wizard—Finish dialog box. Then click the **Finish** button. The Import Data dialog box appears asking where you want to place the data (see Figure 11.26)

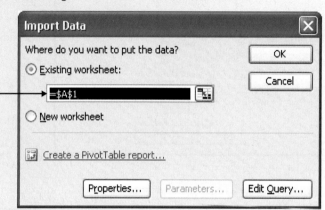

FIGURE 11.26

Import Data dialog box

listed cell is the upper-left corner where the query will return the data to the worksheet

2. Ensure that the **Existing worksheet** option button is selected and that =$A$1 appears in the location text box below the option button, and then click **OK**. Within a few seconds, the query retrieves the data from the tblCustomers table in the database and places it in consecutive rows of the Midwest Customers worksheet (see Figure 11.27)

FIGURE 11.27

Data returned by the query

External Data toolbar may appear

	A	B	C	D	E	F	G	H
1	FirstName	LastName	Address	City	State	ZipCode	PhoneNumber	
2	Anne	Levy	219 Piasa Street	Alton	IL	62002	(618) 555-7515	
3	Thomas E.	Cuneo	3040 West Salt Creek Lane	Arlington Heights	IL	60005	(708) 555-7058	
4	Robert C.	Shaich	Amsouth-Sonat Tower	Arlington Heights	IL	60004	(708) 555-4613	
5	Wayne	Weintraub	780 Mcclure Road	Aurora	IL	60504	(708) 555-7413	
6	William M.	Powell	6581 Revlon Drive	Belvidere			5) 555-5146	
7	Jeffrey A.	Diaz	2550 Huntington Avenue	Buffalo G			8) 555-8327	
8	Kim G.	Wyant	2150 East Lake Cook Road	Buffalo G			8) 555-3029	
9	S.	Franklin	500 East North Avenue	Carol Stream	IL	60188	(708) 555-6175	
10	Michael A.	Vokey	900 North Michigan Avenue	Chicago	IL	60611	(312) 555-4865	
11	C. Stokes	Pickett	900 North Michigan Avenue	Chicago	IL	60611	(312) 555-2458	
12	Bernard	Tiwana	Two North Riverside Plaza	Chicago	IL	60606	(312) 555-1953	
13	Michael R.	Stuart	23456 Hawthorne Boulevard	Chicago	IL	60601	(312) 555-2024	
14	Mary S.	Stettinius	130 East Randolph Drive	Chicago	IL	60601	(312) 555-4056	
15	James A.	Biggi	332 South Michigan Avenue	Chicago	IL	60604	(312) 555-1243	
16	Gregory P.	Mork	500 West Madison	Chicago	IL	60661	(312) 555-6013	
17	Ibrahim	Nichols	19345 U.S. 19 North	Chicago	IL	60604	(312) 555-3851	
18	Earl W.	Powell	3000 West 51St Street	Chicago	IL	60632	(312) 555-3831	
19	Daniel R.	Stern	1348 Merchandise Mart	Chicago	IL	60654	(312) 555-3627	
20	Robert F.	Wallace	1615 West Chicago Avenue	Chicago	IL	60622	(312) 555-8029	
21	Myron E.	Gosa	1618 Terminal Road	Chicago	IL	60611	(312) 555-8882	
22	R. Kent	Young	One Mediq Plaza	Chicago	IL	60631	(312) 555-8949	
23	David P.	McManus	10 South Riverside Plaza	Chicago	IL	60606	(312) 555-1082	
24	David	Gant	7401 South Cicero Avenue	Chicago	IL	60629	(312) 555-3427	
25	Roger A.	Reagan	500 West Monroe Street	Chicago	IL	60661	(312) 555-6234	

Documentation / Sales Reps \ **Midwest Customers** /

Ready

Editing Queries

If you work with Excel's Query Wizard quite a bit, you may create a large collection of saved queries. You can rerun any of your saved queries. Suppose you have created a query and discover that you forgot an important column from the database table you imported. That's not a problem since you can simply edit the query and then rerun it.

Bob wants you to remove the PhoneNumber column from the query and thus the column's imported data. Although you could simply delete the PhoneNumber column from the worksheet, the query would continue to import the PhoneNumber column whenever the query is run. For long-term results, it is better to edit the database query.

task reference   Editing a Query

- Make sure that one of the cells containing imported database data is active
- Click **Data**, point to **Import External Data**, and click **Edit Query**
- Step through each of the Query Wizard's steps, make any necessary changes at each step, and then press **Next** to go to the next step
- On the Query Wizard's final step, click the **Save Query** button to save your changes and then click the **Finish** button to refresh the imported data

Editing the MidwestCustomers query to delete an unwanted column:

1. Click cell **A1** to ensure that the active cell is one of the imported data elements

2. Click **Data**, point to **Import External Data**, and click **Edit Query**. The Query Wizard—Choose Columns dialog box opens

3. Click **PhoneNumber** in the *Columns in your query* list box (see Figure 11.28), and then click the < button to move the column name back to the tblCustomers table

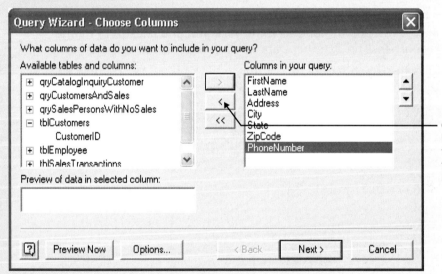

FIGURE 11.28

Preparing to remove a column from a query definition

click to move the highlighted column from the right panel to the left—to delete it from a query

4. Click **Next** to go to the Filter Data step, click **Next** again to go to the Sort Order step, and click **Next** once again to go to the Finish step

5. Click the **Save Query** button to save the modified query. The Save As dialog box opens

6. Click the **Save** button, and then click the **Yes** button when you are asked if you want to replace the query that already exists. The Query Wizard—Finish dialog box reappears

7. Click the **Finish** button to requery the database and import the new data into your Excel worksheet. Notice that the PhoneNumber column does not appear in the refreshed data

Refreshing Data

Databases are continuously changing as database personnel add new customers and delete existing ones. That's why it is important to refresh data whenever you are working with an Excel worksheet of imported database data. Excel displays a static picture of the data taken sometime in the past. To ensure that your Excel data are current, you refresh the data. You can set up a query so that it automatically refreshes the spreadsheet data each time a user opens the workbook. Bob thinks that's a good idea and asks you to do that next.

---

task reference   **Automatically Refreshing Data Each Time a Workbook Is Opened**

- Ensure that the active worksheet cell is one of the imported data values
- Click **Data**, click **Import External Data**, click **Data Range Properties**
- Click the **Refresh data on file open** check box to place a checkmark in it
- Click **OK**

Forcing a query to automatically refresh data:

1. If necessary, click cell **A1** to ensure that the active cell is one of the imported data elements
2. Click **Data**, point to **Import External Data**, and click **Data Range Properties**. The External Data Range Properties dialog box opens
3. Click the **Refresh data on file open** check box in the Refresh control section to place a checkmark in it (see Figure 11.29)

FIGURE 11.29

Ensuring a query refreshes the data

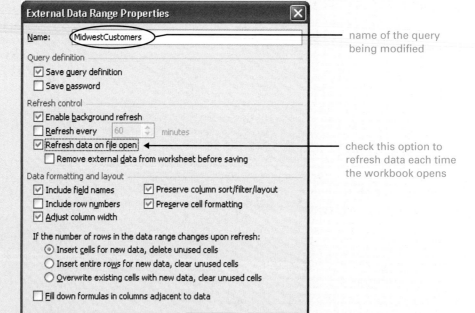

name of the query being modified

check this option to refresh data each time the workbook opens

tip: *The next time you open this workbook, Excel will display a Query Refresh dialog box indicating that the workbook contains queries to external data that refresh automatically. Click the* **Enable automatic refresh** *button to refresh the data*

4. Click **OK**

Each time someone opens the **MissionBoats3.xls** workbook, the query you created with Microsoft Query will import the latest database table data into the Midwest Customers worksheet.

What about creating more complicated queries involving more criteria or more than one database table? You have to use software that is more powerful than the Query Wizard.

Using Microsoft Query

Bob wants to analyze sales amounts for the last six months. In particular, he would like to see the total sales for the states of Illinois, Indiana, and Michigan to determine any pattern in customer demand by state. Some of the information Bob wants is in the tblCustomer table—the state in which each customer resides. Other information, total sales for each customer transaction, is in another table in the same database called tblSalesTransactions. Pulling information from two tables requires the database system to perform a join operation on the two tables. A *join* operation matches records in two tables based on a common field, such as a customer number or an inventory number. Joining two tables together in Query Wizard is difficult at best. The more powerful query tool you will use is called Microsoft Query.

When to Use Microsoft Query

Microsoft Query is a powerful database query tool that is included with Excel. It allows you to take full advantage of all the capabilities of your database system—including joining two or more tables together. The price you pay for this power is a slightly more complex and less intuitive query-building interface than the Query Wizard. Microsoft Query is a more powerful tool than the Query Wizard because Microsoft Query allows you to:

- Add more criteria to restrict which rows are returned to your worksheet
- Perform calculations on groups of information—calculations such as summing values, averaging values, or counting unique values
- Write SQL (pronounced "sequel") statements. *SQL* is an abbreviation for structured query language and is a standard language for requesting information from a database
- Join multiple database tables together

Whenever you need to do any of the preceding, then Microsoft Query is a better choice than using the Query Wizard.

Starting Microsoft Query

You ask Bob how to execute Microsoft Query instead of using the Query Wizard. He tells you to clear the checkmark from the *Use the Query Wizard to create/edit queries* check box in the Choose Data Source dialog box. Once you clear the check box, Microsoft Query dialog boxes appear as you define a new query. You are ready to create the new query to extract summary data by state that Bob wants. First, create a new worksheet and name its tab Sales by State.

Creating a new worksheet to hold the sales summary by state:

1. Click **Insert**, click **Worksheet**, click and drag the newly added worksheet to a new position following the Midwest Customers worksheet

2. Double-click the new worksheet tab, type **Sales by State**, and press **Enter**

3. Right-click the **Sales by State** worksheet tab, click **Tab Color**, click the **Rose** color square (fifth row from the top, leftmost column), and click **OK**

Choosing Database Tables and Joining Them

With the new worksheet available to hold the imported summary sales information, you begin to build the query.

Joining two tables together with Microsoft Query:

1. Click **Data**, point to **Import External Data**, and click **New Database Query**. The Choose Data Source dialog box appears

2. Click **<yourname>MBBW**, which is the name of the data source you created in previous steps

3. Click the **Use the Query Wizard to create/edit queries** check box to clear its checkmark (see Figure 11.30)

FIGURE 11.30

Choose Data Source dialog box for Microsoft Query

use the same MBBW data source you defined earlier (your data source name will be different but will end with "MBBW")

very important: make sure that this check box *does not* contain a checkmark

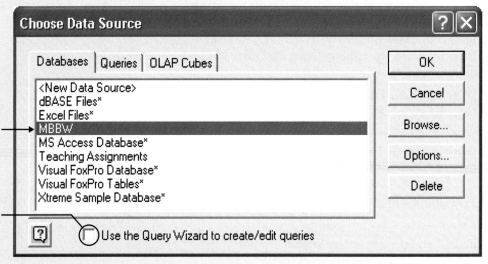

4. Click **OK**. The Add Tables dialog box appears

5. Double-click the **tblCustomers** table name in the Table list box

6. Double-click the **tblSalesTransactions** table name.
Microsoft Query displays a small panel in its query pane listing the columns in each table and shows a connection between the two tables. The join operation links the CustomerID field in tblCustomers table to the CustomerID field in the tblSalesTransactions table (see Figure 11.31)

7. Click the **Close** button in the Add Tables dialog box to close the dialog box

Microsoft Query automatically joins two tables when it determines that one table has a column name that is identical to a special column in another table called a primary key. A ***primary key*** is a table column whose values are unique for each record in

lists the columns in each table

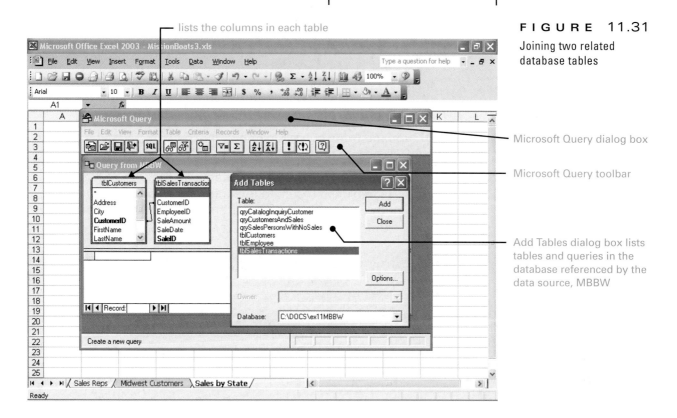

Microsoft Query dialog box

Microsoft Query toolbar

Add Tables dialog box lists
tables and queries in the
database referenced by the
data source, MBBW

a table. If the two tables had different common, or join, column names, you would have
to join the two tables together. To do so, you would drag and drop a primary key column from one table to its counterpart, called a **foreign key**, in the other table. Microsoft
then draws a line between the two column names indicating it has joined the two tables
on their primary key and foreign key pairs.

---

task reference   Manually Joining
                                                      Two Tables in a Query

- Drag and drop the primary key from one table to the corresponding foreign
  key in the second table

Selecting Table Columns

Now that you have selected the correct tables containing the State and Sales Amount
columns and joined the tables together, you are ready to select the columns you want to
retrieve from the database tables and return to your Excel worksheet.

---

task reference   Adding a Column to a Query

- Double-click a column name to add it to the lower half of the query window

or

- Drag and drop the column name to the lower half of the query window

---

EXCEL

Adding the State and SaleAmount columns to the query:

1. Scroll the column names in the tblCustomer field roster until you see the State column name

2. Drag and drop the **State** column name to the lower panel of the query. State names appear in the first column of the lower panel

3. Drag and drop the **SaleAmount** column name, in the tblSalesTransactions field roster, to the first row, second column in the lower panel of the query. Values for sale amounts appear in the second column (see Figure 11.32)

F I G U R E 11.32

Query with two column names from two tables

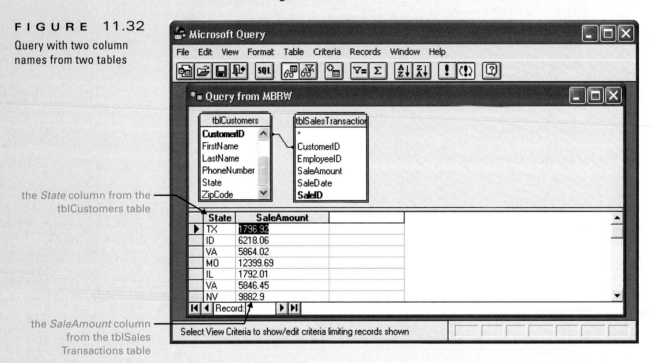

the *State* column from the tblCustomers table

the *SaleAmount* column from the tblSales Transactions table

---

anotherway
. . . to Add a Table Column to a Query

Double-click the column name in the table's list of column names

---

task reference   Removing a Column from a Query

- Move the mouse pointer over the column name in the lower panel of the query

- When the pointer changes to a down arrow, click to select the column

- Press the **Delete** key

Limiting Which Rows the Query Returns

You restrict which rows a query returns by adding *criteria* to the query. You used criteria before with the Query Wizard. The effects are the same when you apply criteria using Microsoft Query. Simply specify examples of the values for a particular column that you want to appear in the result, and Microsoft Query will return only records satisfying the criteria for those column(s).

---

task reference	Adding Criteria to a Query Using Microsoft Query

- Click **Criteria** on the Microsoft Query menu bar and then click **Add Criteria**
- Fill in the list and text boxes in the Add Criteria dialog box
- Click the **Add** button to add the criteria to the query
- Continue adding additional criteria, if needed
- Click the **Close** button when the criteria are complete

Limiting values returned by the query to the states of Illinois, Indiana, or Michigan means you must add the criteria to limit rows to those states.

Adding criteria to a query:

1. Click **Criteria** on the Microsoft Query menu bar, and then click **Add Criteria**. The Add Criteria dialog box appears

2. Click the **Field** list box arrow, scroll the list until you see tblCustomers.State, and then click the entry **tblCustomers.State**

3. Double-click the **Value** field text box to select its value, type **IL**, and click the **Add** button to add the criteria to the query

4. Click the **Or** option button at the top of the Add Criteria dialog box (see Figure 11.33)

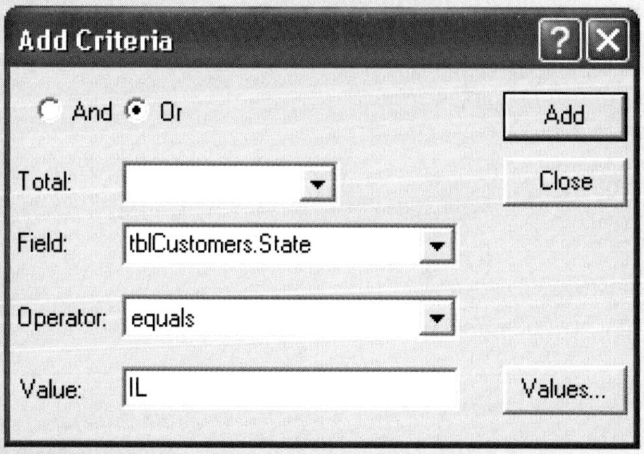

FIGURE 11.33

Adding criteria to a query

5. Double-click the **Value** field text box to select its value, type **IN**, and click the **Add** button to add the criteria to the query

6. Double-click the **Value** field text box to select its value, type **MI**, and click the **Add** button to add the criteria to the query

7. Click the **Close** button to close the Add Criteria dialog box

8. Click the **Maximize** button on the Query from . . . dialog box Title bar, and then click the **Maximize** button in the Microsoft Query dialog box (see Figure 11.34)

EXCEL

FIGURE 11.34

Previewing filtered results

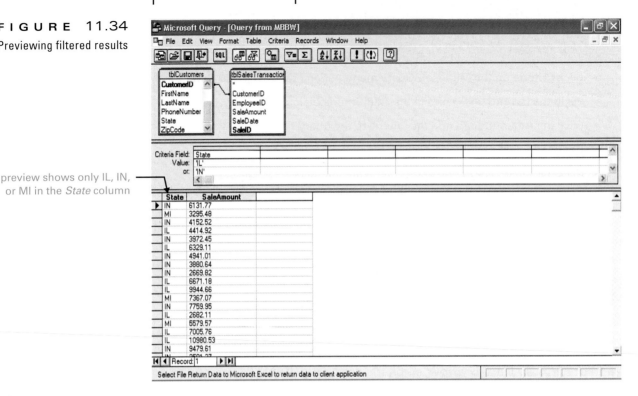

preview shows only IL, IN,
or MI in the *State* column

Adding Totals

Bob wants a summary of sales in the three states, not the details. He asks you to figure out a way to have the query display total sales for each of the three states.

You discover that Microsoft Query can provide five types of calculations on query data. They are average, count, maximum, minimum, and sum. The calculations are called *aggregate* calculations because they cumulate information about groups of data. The sum calculation, when used with the SaleAmount column in the query, will group all the sales results by State value and then sum the values within each group.

---

task reference   Summing a Value Column
                                                  in a Query

- Click any result in the column you want to sum

- Click the **Cycle Through Totals** button

Summing the SaleAmount column by State:

1. Click the first value in the SaleAmount column in the lower panel of the query

2. Click the **Cycle Through Totals** button (see Figure 11.35). The SaleAmount column header changes to *Sum of SaleAmount,* and the preview list of results shrinks to just three entries—one for each state that Bob wants to review (see Figure 11.35)

tip: *If some other aggregate title appears such as Avg of SaleAmount or Min of SaleAmount, then repeatedly click the **Cycle Through Totals** button until Sum of SaleAmount appears in the columns header of the second column in the lower query panel*

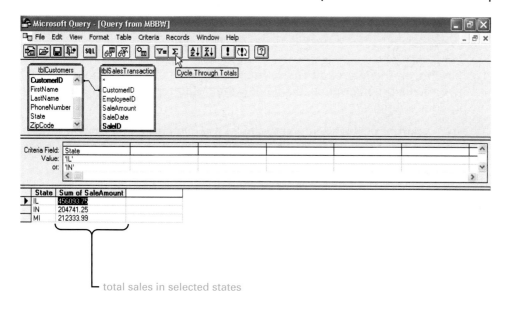

FIGURE 11.35

Preview of query results after summing

— total sales in selected states

Editing a Query's Column Name

Whenever you return results from a query that calculates sums, averages, minimums, maximums, or counts, Query creates a column name prefix indicating the type of calculation that appears in the column. Notice, for example, that the states' total values appear in a column named Sum of SaleAmount.

You can change the name in the query or you can change it in Excel. The problem with changing a returned column's name in Excel is that Query changes it back to the original name when you refresh the query. It is best to change a column's name in the query.

Bob wants the sum of sales column to be named *Total Sales*. He asks you to make the change.

FIGURE 11.36

Changing a query column's name

Renaming a query column:

1. Click any value in the Sum of SaleAmount column

2. Click **Records** on the Microsoft Query menu bar and then click **Edit Column**. The Edit Column dialog box appears

3. Drag the mouse through the text in the **Column heading** text box and then type **Total Sales** (see Figure 11.36)

4. Click **OK** to complete the column name change

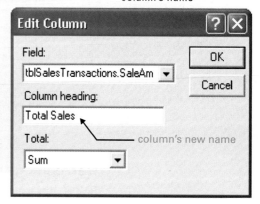

Saving a Microsoft Query

Before returning the results to your Excel worksheet, save the query in case Bob wants to rerun it periodically.

Saving a query with Microsoft Query:

1. Click **File** on the Microsoft Query menu bar, and then click **Save As**. The Save As dialog box opens, displaying the default folder Queries for holding your queries

2. Type **<yourname>TotalMidwestSales** in the File name text box and then click the **Save** button. Microsoft Query saves the newly built query

Returning Results to Excel

You have defined the query completely and are ready to transfer the query results from database tables.

Returning query results to Excel:

1. Click **File** on the Microsoft Query menu bar

2. Click **Return Data to Microsoft Excel**. Microsoft Query closes and the Import Data dialog box appears—exactly like the one shown earlier in Figure 11.26

3. Click **OK**. Microsoft Query places the database query results in cells A1 through B4 (see Figure 11.37)

FIGURE 11.37

Returned results

total sales by state for three states

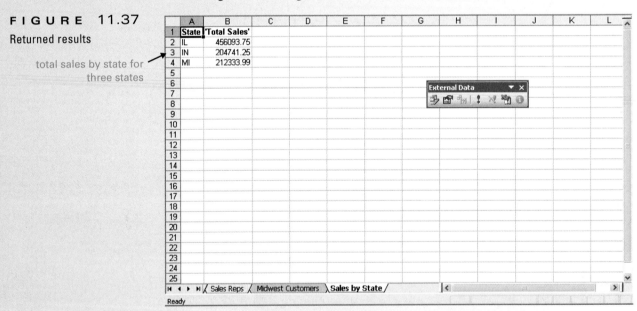

Refreshing Query Data

Bob is concerned that the customer data in the database are ever changing, but that his Excel summary worksheet is a static picture of the database. He asks you how he can be sure the data are accurate. You remind him that he can simply refresh the data.

Manually refreshing query data:

1. Right-click anywhere in the returned data set

2. Click **Refresh External Data**. Excel sends the query you created to the database and the updated results appear in your worksheet. Of course, none of the database table data are altered, so the Excel cells remain unchanged

Save your workbook, because you have completed your work on the Mission Bay Boat Works workbook and you want to preserve all your changes.

Saving your workbook and exiting Excel:

1. Right-click the **tab scrolling** buttons located left of the worksheet tabs and then click **Documentation** in the shortcut menu

2. Click the **Save** button on the Standard toolbar to save the workbook

3. Click **File** and then click **Exit**. Excel closes

Bob is pleased with your work. He can review the data in his Excel workbook, manipulating the numbers any way he wants, and refresh the data periodically when necessary.

---

making *the grade*

SESSION 11.2

1. A _____ is a collection of related information about one object that is stored in a database table.

2. By using _____ _____, also called filtering, you limit the records retrieved from a table to those matching certain characteristics.

3. When Excel reruns a database query, it retrieves the most recent information from a database table. You can right-click anywhere in the imported data and then click the _____ Data command to obtain the latest information.

4. To use a query to import information from two related tables, you must first link two tables based on a column found in both tables. You (or Microsoft Query) perform a(n) _____ operation to link the tables.

SESSION 11.3 IMPORTING XML DATA

In this section, you will learn how to import XML data from a file. Because data is being shared from such a wide variety of sources, many companies are sharing their data files in the format independent XML form. XML, or Extensible Markup Language, describes the structure of data instead of its format. XML is one of the most popular ways to share data, in part, because its data is in plain text format and both naming data elements and listing their values is straightforward.

Understanding XML

Extensible Markup Language provides the mechanism for describing data, such as that found in a worksheet, an Access database, or a Visio diagram, in a text file following published standards. These XML guidelines are maintained by the World Wide Web Consortium (www.w3.com). Data in XML form can be read by a variety of applications, and designers. XML provides a way to organize Excel workbooks that was previously very difficult, if not impossible. Because XML describes the data and not its format, it is used as the method of choice to pass data from one program to another. Excel is no exception. It contains tools to import XML data into workbooks easily and quickly. Similarly, Excel can export workbooks as XML data files.

Importing XML data into an Excel workbook requires you to attach an XML map, which defines the structure of the data, to the workbook. Excel can do this directly from the XML data, itself. Once the XML map is available to a workbook, you can drag its named elements to the worksheet cells. When you import XML data of the same structure, Excel matches the element names and positions data in their indicated worksheet cells without using wizards or requiring you to indicate data element boundaries. Figure 11.38 shows an example of an XML file displayed in Notepad. The XML data file contains information about racing shells including the manufacturers' names, types, models, and prices. The basic unit, which repeats for each different racing shell, is named *ShellItem.* That item contains begin/end XML tags identifying four fields. For example, the XML tag <Manufacturer> marks the beginning of a manufacturer's name, and its termination tag, </Manufacturer>, marks the end of the field. Notice the XML file contains no formatting information, and all data is text—including the XML tags.

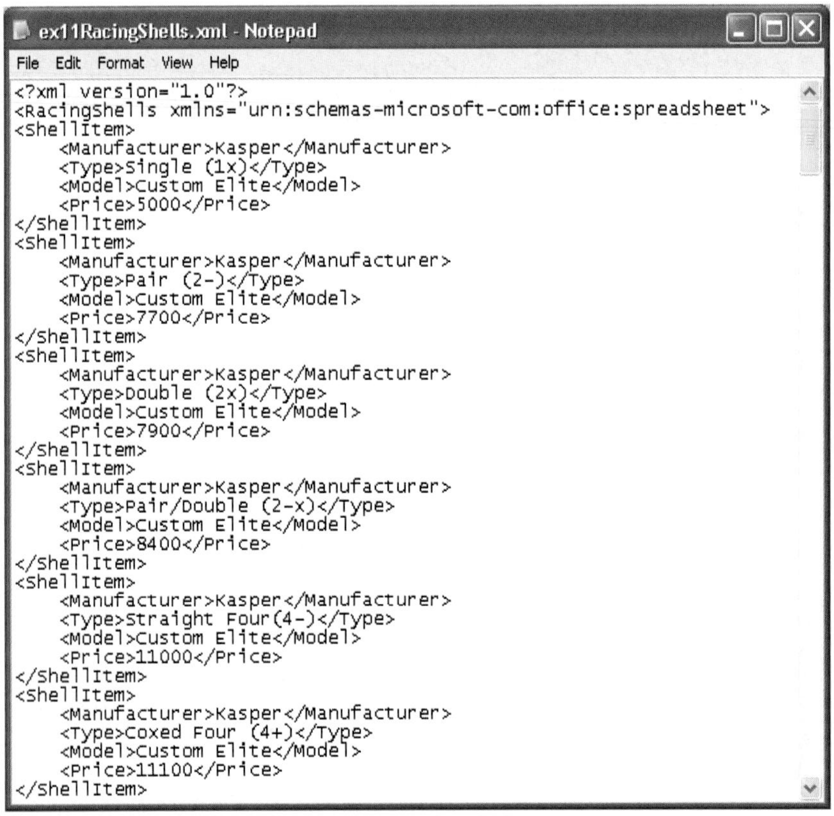


```
<?xml version="1.0"?>
<RacingShells xmlns="urn:schemas-microsoft-com:office:spreadsheet">
<ShellItem>
    <Manufacturer>Kasper</Manufacturer>
    <Type>Single (1x)</Type>
    <Model>Custom Elite</Model>
    <Price>5000</Price>
</ShellItem>
<ShellItem>
    <Manufacturer>Kasper</Manufacturer>
    <Type>Pair (2-)</Type>
    <Model>Custom Elite</Model>
    <Price>7700</Price>
</ShellItem>
<ShellItem>
    <Manufacturer>Kasper</Manufacturer>
    <Type>Double (2x)</Type>
    <Model>Custom Elite</Model>
    <Price>7900</Price>
</ShellItem>
<ShellItem>
    <Manufacturer>Kasper</Manufacturer>
    <Type>Pair/Double (2-x)</Type>
    <Model>Custom Elite</Model>
    <Price>8400</Price>
</ShellItem>
<ShellItem>
    <Manufacturer>Kasper</Manufacturer>
    <Type>Straight Four(4-)</Type>
    <Model>Custom Elite</Model>
    <Price>11000</Price>
</ShellItem>
<ShellItem>
    <Manufacturer>Kasper</Manufacturer>
    <Type>Coxed Four (4+)</Type>
    <Model>Custom Elite</Model>
    <Price>11100</Price>
</ShellItem>
```

FIGURE 11.38
XML data example

Adding an XML Map to a Workbook

Racing shell manufacturing information is in an XML file that Bob has downloaded from the Internet. He wants you to import that file into the MissionBoats workbook as the last worksheet. After you open the workbook, you will add a worksheet Bob has created and then attach an XML map to it.

Opening the workbook and copying a worksheet:

1. Open Excel, open the workbook **MissionBoats3.xls**, and click the **Enable automatic refresh** button if the Query Refresh dialog box appears

2. Immediately save the workbook under the name **MissionBoats4.xls**

3. Click the **Sales by State** worksheet tab, click **Insert**, and click **Worksheet**

4. Double-click the newly inserted worksheet's tab, type **Racing Shells** (with a space between the words), press **Enter**, right-click the tab, click **Tab Color**, and click the **Lime Green** color square (third row, third column)

5. Click the **Racing Shells** worksheet tab and drag it to the right of the Sales by State worksheet—so Racing Shells is the rightmost worksheet

6. Click cell **A1**, type **Manufacturer**, press **Tab**, type **Type**, press **Tab**, type **Model**, press **Tab**, type **Price**, and press **Enter**

7. Widen columns A through D so they are 15 characters wide

Now you can open an XML file to first obtain its map and attach that map to your worksheet to aid in later placing XML data elements in the appropriate Excel worksheet cells

Adding an XML map to a workbook:

1. Click **Data** on the menu bar, point to **XML**, and click **XML Source**. The XML Source task pane appears

2. Click the **XML Maps** button at the bottom of the task pane. The XML Maps dialog box appears

3. Click the **Add** button, and then navigate to the folder containing the file **ex11RacingShells.xml**, click **ex11RacingShells.xml**, and click **Open**. If a dialog box appears indicating that "...the specified XML source does not refer to a schema," then click its **OK** button

4. Click **OK** to close the XML maps dialog box. The XML map appears in the XML source task pane (see Figure 11.39)

5. Click **Manufacturer** in the XML maps task pane and drag it to cell **A2**

6. Click **Type** in the XML maps task pane and drag it to cell **B2**

7. Click **Model** in the XML maps task pane and drag it to cell **C2**

8. Click **Price** in the XML maps task pane and drag it to cell **D2** (see Figure 11.40)

FIGURE 11.39
XML map

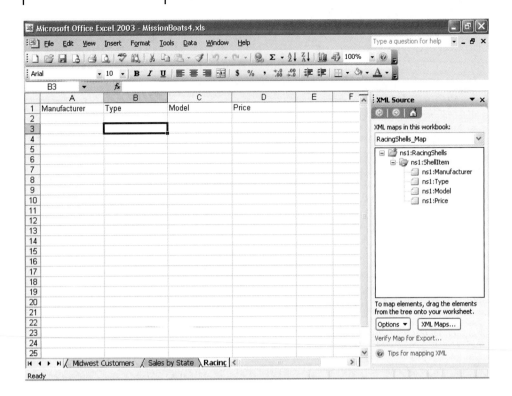

FIGURE 11.40
Mapping XML data

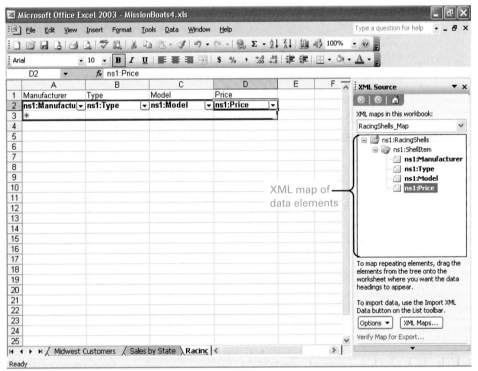

Importing an XML Document into an existing mapping

By dragging the XML elements into the worksheet, you indicate to Excel where you would like similarly named XML elements placed. In other words, you have mapped the data to the worksheet. All that is left is to import XML data into the worksheet.

Importing an XML document using an existing XML map:

1. Click the **Close** button on the XML Source task pane to close it

2. Click **View**, point to **Toolbar**, and click **List** (if necessary) to open the List toolbar

3. Click the **Import XML Data** button on the list toolbar, navigate to the **ex11RacingShells.xml** file, click **ex11RacingShells.xml**, and click the **Import** button. Excel imports the data, placing each element in its mapped location (see Figure 11.41)

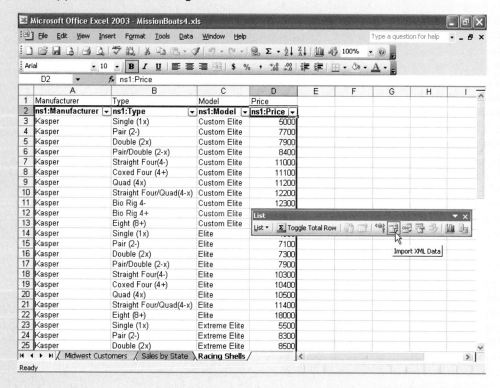

FIGURE 11.41
Mapping XML data

With the XML data successfully imported, you can save the workbook and exit Excel.

Saving your workbook and exiting Excel:

1. Right-click the **tab scrolling** buttons located left of the worksheet tabs and then click **Documentation** in the shortcut menu

2. Click the **Save** button on the Standard toolbar to save the workbook

3. Click **File** on the menu bar and then click **Exit**. Excel closes

making the grade

1. The XML guidelines are maintained by the _____ _____ _____ _____.

2. You use an XML _____ to define the location in an Excel worksheet where XML data is imported.

3. XML data elements are delimited with beginning and terminating XML _____.

4. The _____ toolbar contains the Import XML Data button.

SESSION 11.4 SUMMARY

Excel can import data in a variety of formats including delimited text. Text data have no internal structure to indicate where data for one column end and another column begin. Excel relies on a delimiter character or characters to distinguish one column from another when importing text data into a worksheet. Possible delimiters include commas, semicolons, spaces, or tabs. Text data columns that occur in specific locations for each record are called fixed-length data fields, and Excel can import this text file format also. The Text Import Wizard automatically opens whenever you open a file whose name ends with .prn, .txt, or .csv. The Text Import Wizard guides you through the three-step import process.

You can double-click a comma-separated values data file in Windows Explorer to open the file directly into Excel. The Text Import Wizard does not appear, because Excel knows how to import CSV files quickly.

Databases are the most popular choice for corporate data storage. Both large and small organizations use databases to hold customer, invoice, and employee information. Excel can import data from a wide variety of popular database systems including Microsoft Access, Oracle, Microsoft SQL Server, FoxPro, and IBM's DB2. You can use either Excel's built-in Query Wizard or Microsoft's separate Query program to import data from database systems. The Excel Query Wizard is slightly easier to use, but it is not quite as powerful as Microsoft Query. Using either product is a two-step process: You define and connect to a database data source and then you build a query that Excel sends to the database to retrieve information and return it to an Excel worksheet.

MICROSOFT OFFICE SPECIALIST OBJECTIVES SUMMARY

- Import text files into Excel with the Text Import Wizard—MOS XL03E-4-1
- Move a worksheet from one workbook to another one—MOS XL03S-5-4
- Import database information into Excel using the Query Wizard—MOS XL03E-4-1
- Use Microsoft Query to create a query to filter, sort, and retrieve database records—MOS XL03E-4-1
- Write a database query that joins two related database tables and returns values from each table—MOS XL03E-4-1
- Edit and save database queries—MOS XL03E-4-1
- Write an aggregate query to summarize imported data—MOS XL03E-4-1
- Export data from Excel—MOS XL03E-4-2

making the grade *answers*

SESSION 11.1

1. Text

2. delimiter

3. column break

4. comma-separated; CSV

SESSION 11.2

1. record

2. selection criteria

3. Refresh

4. join

SESSION 11.3

1. World Wide Web Consortium

2. map

3. tags

4. List

task reference *summary*

Task	Page #	Preferred Method
Importing fixed-length data using the Text Import Wizard	EX 11.6	• Click **File** and then click **Open** • In the Files of type list box of the Open dialog box, select **Text Files** • Using the *Look in* list box, navigate to the folder containing the text file, click the filename in the list of files, and click the **Open** button • Click the **Fixed Width** option button in the Original data type panel • Click the **Start import at row** spin box to select the first row to import, and click the **Next** button • In step 2, click to the left of each field to add a break line, double-click a break line to remove it, or drag a break line to its correct position at the beginning of a column as needed. Then click the **Next** button to proceed • In step 3, for each column, click a **Column data format** option button to select a column format, or click the **Do not import column** option button to skip the column, and click the **Finish** button
Adding, moving, and deleting column breaks using the Text Import Wizard	EX 11.8	• Add a column break by clicking the position just above the ruler in the Data preview panel where you want the column break to appear • Move a column break by clicking it and then dragging it to its new position • Delete a column break by double-clicking it
Editing a query	EX 11.27	• Make sure that one of the cells containing imported database data is active • Click **Data**, point to **Import External Data**, and click **Edit Query** • Step through each of the Query Wizard's steps, make any necessary changes at each step, and then press **Next** to go to the next step • On the Query Wizard's final step, click the **Save Query** button to save your changes and then click the **Finish** button to refresh the imported data
Automatically refreshing data each time a workbook is opened	EX 11.28	• Ensure that the active worksheet cell is one of the imported data values • Click **Data**, click **Import External Data**, click **Data Range Properties** • Click the **Refresh data on file open** check box to place a checkmark in it • Click **OK**
Manually joining two tables in a query	EX 11.31	• Drag and drop the primary key from one table to the corresponding foreign key in the second table
Adding a column to a query	EX 11.31	• Double-click a column name to add it to the lower half of the query window or • Drag and drop the column name to the lower half of the query window

EXCEL

task reference *summary*

Task	Page #	Preferred Method
Removing a column from a query	EX 11.32	• Move the mouse pointer over the column name in the lower panel of the query • When the pointer changes to a down arrow, click to select the column • Press the **Delete** key
Adding criteria to a query using Microsoft Query	EX 11.33	• Click **Criteria** on the Microsoft Query menu bar and then click **Add Criteria** • Fill in the list and text boxes in the Add Criteria dialog box • Click the **Add** button to add the criteria to the query • Continue adding additional criteria, if needed • Click the **Close** button when the criteria are complete
Summing a value column in a query	EX 11.34	• Click any result in the column you want to sum • Click the **Cycle Through Totals** button

TRUE OR FALSE

1. A database driver translates Excel information requests into database commands.

2. The only way to launch Text Import Wizard is to open a text file directly within Excel.

3. Excel has worksheet row limits and computer memory limits that render it incapable of storing unlimited database records.

4. You can retrieve data from a database by first creating a query and then submitting the query to the database system.

5. Excel's Query Wizard is more powerful for importing database information than Microsoft Query.

FILL-IN

1. The _____ _____ Wizard appears when you open a text file in Excel.

2. Text data appearing in the same columns throughout the data are called _____ length data.

3. Data in which fields are separated by commas are called _____ separated _____, or CSVs.

4. Double-click a column break in the Text Import Wizard to _____ the column break.

5. Before you can use Microsoft Query to retrieve information from a database, you must first define a _____ source.

6. The standard language for sending commands to databases is called SQL, which stands for _____ Query _____.

MULTIPLE CHOICE

1. The "R" in RTF stands for what? (Check on the Web.)
   a. Reserve
   b. Recall
   c. Rich
   d. Right

2. This operation links two related tables together.
   a. bond
   b. match
   c. join
   d. link

3. What type of data consist only of characters that you can type on a keyboard?
   a. numeric data
   b. character data
   c. field data
   d. text data

4. This is the abbreviation for text data whose values are separated by commas.
   a. TSV
   b. CSV
   c. TSC
   d. VSC

5. After a text file is opened in Excel, what will the file extension be prior to saving it?
   a. xls
   b. txt
   c. doc
   d. rtf

REVIEW QUESTIONS

1. Explain why you have to use an import Wizard to import a text file into Excel.

2. Explain why you might ask a database query to sort data, using Microsoft Query, before returning the data to the Excel worksheet. After all, you could perform a sort in Excel after the data is returned. (*Hint:* Think of a large amount of data.)

3. Explain why you might want to save a query. Once you have returned data into an Excel worksheet, is that it?

4. What does the term "aggregate data" mean when considering a database query?

CREATE THE QUESTION

For each of the following answers, create an appropriate, short question.

ANSWER	QUESTION
1. Comma-separated values	_____
2. Column break	_____
3. General, Text, Date, and Do Not Import column	_____
4. Edit, Paste Special, Values	_____
5. Filter	_____
6. The Refresh command	_____

1. Importing Faculty Teaching Assignments from a Database

Lincoln College, located in Lincoln, Nebraska, teaches a full range of business courses including undergraduate and graduate accounting, general business, and economics courses. Each semester, Dean Nancy Rivetti produces a list of faculty and the courses that they teach. Recently, the registrar placed all information about faculty, students, schedules, and course catalogs into an Access database. Nancy just received a database containing faculty teaching assignments, class scheduling table, and the School of Business course catalog table in an Access database. Nancy is not comfortable using an Access database and wants you to import this coming semester's teaching assignments into an Excel worksheet so that she can print and post it around the campus.

1. Open **ex11LincolnCollege.xls** and save the workbook as **<yourname>LincolnCollege2.xls**

2. Click the **Teaching Assignments** worksheet tab

3. Click **Data**, point to **Import External Data**, click **New Database Query**, ensure **<New Data Source>** is highlighted in the Choose Data Source dialog box, and then click **OK**. The Create New Data Source dialog box opens

4. Type **Teaching Assignments** in the first text box; click the second text box, and then click **Microsoft Access Driver (*.mdb)**; click the **Connect** button to open the ODBC Microsoft Access Setup dialog box

5. Click the **Select** button, navigate to the **ex11LincolnCollege.mdb** database in the Select Database dialog box, click **ex11LincolnCollege.mdb**, click **OK**, and click **OK** again to close the ODBC Microsoft Access Setup dialog box

6. Click **OK** to close the Create New Data Source dia log box

7. Clear the **Use the Query Wizard to create/edit queries** check box, if necessary, to use Microsoft Query; click **OK**

8. In the Add Tables dialog box, double-click **tblFacultyNames**, double-click **tblFacultyCourseAssignments**, double-click **tblCourseNames**, and click the **Close** button

9. Drag the **FacultyID** field name from the tblFacultyNames field roster and drop it on the **ProfessorID** field name in tblFacultyCourseAssignments field roster to join the two tables

10. To add fields to the lower portion of the query, double-click the following fields in the order listed: **FirstName**, **LastName**, **Name**, **Number**, and **Title**

11. Click any entry in the **LastName** column in the lower portion of the query, and then click the **Sort Ascending** button on the Microsoft Query toolbar

12. Click **File** on the Microsoft Query menu bar, and then click **Return Data to Microsoft Excel**

13. Click **OK** to approve the choices presented in the Import Data dialog box (see Figure 11.42)

14. Place your name in both worksheet headers, type your name in the Designed by location on the Documentation worksheet, and type today's date in the Design date cell. Save the workbook and then print both worksheets

FIGURE 11.42

Lincoln College data returned by query

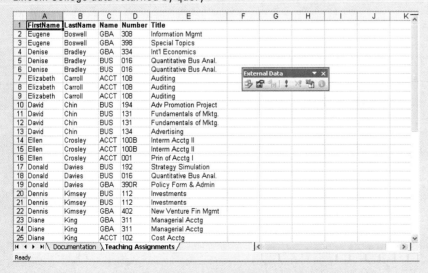

2. Importing U.S. Population Data from a Text File

Alicia Spencer, an editor with the Lafayette Journal and Courier newspaper, is writing an article about population shifts in the United States during the period 1999 through 2002. She would like to display population information in an Excel worksheet and develop percentages to show net inflow or outflow of population. Alicia tells you that a summer intern looked up information on the U.S. Census Bureau Web site and downloaded the information into a text file. The intern has gone back to college, and Alicia does not know how to move the data into an Excel worksheet. She asks you to help her.

1. Open a new Excel workbook, click the **Open** button on the Standard toolbar, click the **Files of type list box arrow**, and click the entry **Text Files (*.prn; *.txt; *.csv)**

2. With the Look in list box, navigate to the folder containing the file **ex11StatePopulation.txt**, click **ex11StatePopulation.txt**, and click the **Open** button

3. Double-click the **Start import at row** spin control box, type **6** to start the import at row 6, and click the **Next** button

4. Ensure that only the **Tab** check box is checked and then click the **Finish** button

5. Click cell **F1**, type **% Change**, and press **Enter**

6. Bold the column labels in the cell range **A1:F1**

7. Click cell **F2**, type the formula **=(E2-B2)/B2**, and press **Enter**

8. Click cell **F2**, drag its fill handle down through cell **F52**, and release the mouse

9. With the cell range F2:F52 selected, click the **Percent Style** button on the Formatting toolbar, and click the Formatting toolbar **Increase Decimal** button *twice*

10. Click any cell in column **F** and then click the **Sort Descending** button on the Standard toolbar

11. Select cell range **B2:E52**, click the **Comma Style** button, and click the **Decrease Decimal** button *twice*. (Both buttons are on the Formatting toolbar)

12. Click cell **A1**, press **Ctrl+A**, click **Format**, point to **Column**, click **AutoFit Selection**, and click cell **A1** to deselect the cell range

13. Double-click the **ex11StatePopulation** worksheet tab, type **State Population**, and press **Enter** (see Figure 11.43)

14. Place your name in the worksheet header

15. Click **File**, click **Page Setup**, click the **Page** tab, and click the **Fit to** option button in the Scaling section, click the **Print** button, and click **OK**

16. Click **File**, click **Save As**, click the **Save as type** list box arrow, scroll to the top of the list and click **Microsoft Excel Workbook (*.xls)**, drag through the text in the **File name** list box, type **<yourname>StatePopulation2,** and click the **Save** button

FIGURE 11.43

Importing state population data

	A	B	C	D	E	F	G	H	I	J
1	**State**	**1999**	**2000**	**2001**	**2002**	**% Change**				
2	Nevada	1,809,253	2,018,828	2,097,722	2,173,491	20.13%				
3	Arizona	4,778,332	5,167,142	5,306,966	5,456,453	14.19%				
4	Colorado	4,056,133	4,326,758	4,430,989	4,506,542	11.10%				
5	Florida	15,111,244	16,051,395	16,373,330	16,713,149	10.60%				
6	District of Columbia	519,000	571,641	573,822	570,898	10.00%				
7	Georgia	7,788,240	8,234,373	8,405,677	8,560,310	9.91%				
8	Utah	2,129,836	2,243,406	2,278,712	2,316,256	8.75%				
9	North Carolina	7,650,789	8,082,261	8,206,105	8,320,146	8.75%				
10	Texas	20,044,141	20,955,248	21,370,983	21,779,893	8.66%				
11	Rhode Island	990,819	1,050,698	1,059,659	1,069,725	7.96%				
12	Delaware	753,538	786,512	796,599	807,385	7.15%				
13	Idaho	1,251,700	1,299,721	1,320,585	1,341,131	7.14%				
14	New Mexico	1,739,844	1,821,767	1,830,935	1,855,059	6.62%				
15	Arkansas	2,551,373	2,678,668	2,694,698	2,710,079	6.22%				
16	Oregon	3,316,154	3,431,137	3,473,441	3,521,515	6.19%				
17	New Hampshire	1,201,134	1,240,472	1,259,359	1,275,056	6.15%				
18	Virginia	6,872,912	7,105,900	7,196,750	7,293,542	6.12%				
19	California	33,145,121	34,010,375	34,600,463	35,116,033	5.95%				
20	Tennessee	5,483,535	5,703,246	5,749,398	5,797,289	5.72%				
21	South Carolina	3,885,736	4,023,725	4,062,125	4,107,183	5.70%				
22	Maryland	5,171,634	5,312,461	5,386,079	5,458,137	5.54%				
23	New Jersey	8,143,412	8,433,276	8,511,116	8,590,300	5.49%				
24	Connecticut	3,282,031	3,411,956	3,434,602	3,460,503	5.44%				
25	Washington	5,756,361	5,911,803	5,993,390	6,068,996	5.43%				

State Population

Ready

challenge

1. Importing Text and Pivot Tables to Consolidate Purchasing and Sales Data

Off the Wall is an eclectic home furnishings store in Hollywood, California. The store has clients ranging from young to old and classic to modern, all looking for unique pieces for their home. Joe Bradley, the store owner, recently started carrying a new line of sofas, Maripa, featuring bright colors and patterns. Joe wants to determine how well the line is selling and which of his salespeople are successfully moving the line. Joe currently maintains ordering information on the Maripa line in a text file and employee sales information in an Excel workbook. He assigned each of his top six salespeople a model of the Maripa line so that it would be easier to track employee sales. He wants a single Excel worksheet that details Maripa sales information.

Open **ex11OTWSales.xls**, which is Joe's record of the number of Maripa sofas sold in June, sorted by employee ID number. Using Excel, open the file **ex11MaripaOrders.txt** to invoke the Text Import Wizard. The file **ex11MaripaOrders.txt** is Joe's record of Maripa sofas ordered, including both purchase price and sales price. Joe wants you to create an Excel worksheet, titled **June Maripa Sales**, using information from these two data sources. He wants the column headings to be **Item Number**, **Number ordered**, **Purchase Price**, **Sales Price**, **Number Sold**, and **Employee Name**. Begin by opening a new Excel workbook. Then use the Text Import Wizard to import the **ex11MaripaOrder.txt** data. Data are in fixed width columns. Import the labels in row 3 along with the data. Be sure to adjust columns, if needed, in Step 2 of the Text Import Wizard. Adjust columns in the Excel worksheet, if needed, to display all data adequately. Sort the infor-

mation in ascending order by the values in the Item Number column. From the **ex11OTWSales.xls** workbook, copy the number sold and employee name columns and paste them in the appropriate cells in the Maripa Sales worksheet. (*Hint:* Sort the **ex11OTWSales.xls** columns into Item Number order, and then copy cells by matching Item Number values in the two worksheets.) Joe asks you to insert a column to the right of Purchase Price with the heading **Total Cost** and another column to the right of Sold with the heading **Total Sales**. Use formulas to fill these columns with the total cost and sales for each item number.

Next, create a pivot table for Joe, sorted by item number, which includes the number of items purchased and sold as well as the total cost and total sales. Allow Joe to either view all of the data, or just by one item number at a time. Improve the appearance of the worksheet and then create a Documentation sheet as the first sheet of the workbook. Include the title **June Maripa Sales** in cell A2. Type **Created by:** followed by your name in cells A5 and B6. Type **Date:** in cell A7 followed by the current date in cell B7. Type **Re:** in cell A9, and type **Ordering and Sales Figures** in cell B9. Insert column headers in all worksheets. Save the workbook as **JuneMaripaSales.xls** and print all worksheets.

Joe's assistant has just given him the updated sales figures for July. He wants you to change the current workbook of June sales to include July sales. Make the Maripa Sales worksheet active and fill the Number Sold column with the following figures, from the first row to the last, in order: **7, 3, 7, 3, 6**, and **11**. Refresh your pivot table to reflect the new sales and change the Documentation sheet title to **July Maripa Sales**. Save your workbook and print the Maripa Sales worksheet again.

2. Selecting Products from a Database with a Database Query

Oriental Rug Specialists sells oriental rugs. Located in San Diego, Oriental Rug Specialists sells rugs made in China, India, Iran, Pakistan, Tibet, and Turkey. Each country is the exclusive producer of some types of rugs. For example, Iran weavers produce rugs called Nain and Tabriz. Several other countries such as Pakistan and Turkey also produce Tabriz rugs. Customers who want to purchase a Tabriz rug, for example, can choose either one produced in Iran or one produced in Turkey. Oriental Rug Specialists offers rugs in a wide range of sizes from as small as 1 foot by 1 foot to full-room carpets that are 10 feet by 14 feet and larger.

Fred Jacobsen, the store's manager, has cataloged all the rugs in his extensive inventory in a Microsoft Access database table called *tblOrientalRugs* (see Figure 11.44). Information in the database about each rug consists of a unique identification number (ID), the country of origin (Country), the rug type (Nain, Kirman, and so on, stored in the Description field), the width in inches (WidthInches), the length in inches (LengthInches), the retail price (Price), and the size (Size) stated in convention terms (for example, 6′ 2″ × 9′ 7″).

Fred wants to be able to import the database information into Excel and analyze it. However, he does not want to import the entire database table for analysis. Instead, he would like you to create a database query to import just selected rows and columns of information. Sometimes, he may want to import information about all Iranian Tabriz rugs in the inventory. Other times, he may want to know the total value of all Turkish rugs in stock.

Begin by opening **ex11RugSpecialists.xls**, an Excel workbook with a Documentation worksheet and an empty Data Analysis worksheet. Save the workbook as **<yourname>Rugs11.xls**, where "<yourname>" is your name. Fred wants you to import data from the *tblOrientalRugs* table in the database **ex11RugSpecialists.mdb**. In particular, he wants you to create a database query to import rugs manufactured in Iran whose type (Description) is either Tabriz or Kirman, and whose price is less than or equal to $3,500. Import only the Country, Description, and Price fields from the database. Sort the data in the query in ascending order on the Description field and ascending order on the Price field within matching Description fields. After you form the query, import the data (you do not need to save the query). Place your name in the worksheet header of both worksheets, fill in information in the Documentation worksheet, and print the entire workbook.

FIGURE 11.44

Oriental Rug Specialists rug database

	ID	Country	Description	WidthInches	LengthInches	Price	Size
	1002	Turkey	Azeri	16	19	$155	1′ 4″ x 1′ 7″
	1005	Turkey	Pillow	18	18	$95	1′ 6″ x 1′ 6″
	1008	Iran	Herez	120	152	$5,350	10′ 0″ x 12′ 8″
	1011	Iran	Herez	120	152	$2,950	10′ 0″ x 12′ 8″
	1014	Turkey	Herez	120	152	$3,950	10′ 0″ x 12′ 8″
	1017	Iran	Herez	120	157	$3,590	10′ 0″ x 13′ 1″
	1020	Iran	Kerman	120	186	$3,550	10′ 0″ x 15′ 6″
	1023	Iran	Herez	121	153	$4,290	10′ 1″ x 12′ 9″
	1026	Iran	Herez	122	146	$4,350	10′ 2″ x 12′ 2″
	1029	China	Little River	122	171	$10,900	10′ 2″ x 14′ 3″
	1032	Turkey	Azeri	123	154	$9,690	10′ 3″ x 12′ 10″
	1035	Turkey	Smyrna	124	150	$6,450	10′ 4″ x 12′ 6″
	1038	Iran	Kasvin	126	170	$10,000	10′ 6″ x 14′ 2″
	1041	Iran	Bibikabad	127	178	$1,875	10′ 7″ x 14′ 10″
	1044	Iran	Kasvin	142	234	$4,750	11′ 10″ x 19′ 6″
	1047	Iran	Semi-Antique Kasvin	134	206	$7,500	11′ 2″ x 17′ 2″
	1050	Turkey	Kilim	34	123	$310	2′ 10″ x 10′ 3″
	1053	China	Kashan	29	95	$495	2′ 5″ x 7′ 11″
	1056	Turkey	Yagcibedir	33	50	$340	2′ 9″ x 4′ 2″
	1059	China	American Hooked Rug	33	73	$650	2′ 9″ x 6′ 1″
	1062	Turkey	Yahyali	37	71	$675	3′ 1″ x 5′ 11″

Record: 33 of 475

1. Retrieving and Using Queries Regarding Web Auction Clients

Kellson's auction house in Maine has held public auctions of fine antiques and collectibles for over 40 years. Damion Kellson, president of the company, wanted to expand Kellson's client base, but its location in Maine made it difficult to attract clients from the western and central states. Instead of opening another auction house in the West, Damion thought it would be best to expand the firm's operations with a Web site. The site was designed to include detailed information and photographs of all items being auctioned and the capability for clients to place bids for items through the Web site. After one year, the Web division of the company has been very successful. Kellson's has been able to establish a solid client base in several new areas.

In two months, Kellson's will be holding the largest fine art auction in its history. All East Coast clients will be receiving mailers previewing the auction. In order to ensure that Kellson's Web clients know about the auction, Damion will send e-mails to all clients who have previously purchased art through Kellson's Web site. In addition, he will send an attachment with scanned pictures of all the art to clients whose most recent art purchase was over $50,000. Damion's assistant, Ruth, has started retrieving the information for the mailing by summarizing July's Web sales, based on Damion's criteria. Unfortunately, Ruth incorrectly included information on too many clients and saved her records in both a text document and Access. Damion needs you to import the correct information into Excel so that he can easily view all necessary information for the auction announcement. Open **ex11KWeb.xls**, the Excel workbook into which Damion wants you to import the data, and save it as **<yourname>KWeb2.xls**. Ruth has already formatted the Documentation sheet and labeled the worksheets for you. Select the **WebEMail** worksheet and import all of Kellson's Web clients' information from **ex11KWebMail.txt** (see Figure 11.45). Be sure to use the correct delimited format and do not import any state or profession information. This will give Damion the e-mail addresses he needs to send the auction announcements to everyone. Select the Priority worksheet, which will include data on clients who are to receive the additional attachment. For this worksheet, use the Query Wizard to retrieve information from the **KWebSales** table within the **ex11Kellson.mdb** database. Be sure to save your query. Do not include the columns ID, Age, or Purchases data, and filter your query to only include clients whose last purchase was *Art* that cost at least $50,000. (Only use numbers or letters when defining your query.) Copy and paste the e-mail addresses of these clients into column **D** and give it the column heading **E-mail Addresses**. Improve the format and appearance of both worksheets and enter your name and date into the Documentation worksheet. Save your workbook, insert your name in all worksheet headers, and print all worksheets.

FIGURE 11.45

WebEMail worksheet

	A	B	C
1	**Last Name**	**First Name**	**e-mail address**
2			
3	Bauer	Kevin	kevman@bauer.org
4	Connor	James	jamie2@connor.com
5	Cull	Gretchen	cull12@cull.net
6	Devin	Grant	grantmail@devin.com
7	Donaldson	Jason	jasonlee@donaldson.com
8	Durment	Christopher	coolchris@durment.org
9	Frotter	George	george@frotter.net
10	Goldman	Robin	robinl@goldman.com
11	Hammond	Michelle	shelly@hammond.org
12	Hess	Steven	steve@2hess.com
13	Jacobs	Lianne	lianne15@jacobs.org
14	Kinsky	Kyle	kyle34@kinsky.net
15	Mercier	Jennifer	jenn17@mercier.net
16	Pore	Melanie	mel@pore.net
17	Roberts	Jacob	jake@roberts.net
18	Robinson	Todd	amtodd@robinson.org
19	Simmons	David	davidb3@simmons.com
20	Todds	Scott	scotty@todds.net
21	Truman	Irene	irenet@truman.net
22	Webb	Joshua	joshster@webb.org
23			
24			
25			

Documentation / **WebEMail** / Priority

Ready

2. Creating a Database Query to Retrieve Customer Survey Data

Established in 1992, Hydroponics Universal specializes in the design, manufacture, and installation of commercial hydroponics systems. (Hydroponics is the growing of plants in nutrient solutions without an inert medium, such as soil, to provide mechanical support.) Past projects include growing units for the Canadian government, and the installation of several research greenhouses for educational institutions in the western United States.

Lloyd Carroll, the managing director, initiated the e-commerce strategy in 1998. He maintains that e-commerce is an essential tool for maintaining future business growth and provides a cost savings and significant additional revenue for the company. A customer is asked to complete a survey about the Web site after he or she completes an online purchase. The five-question survey uses a simple scale from 1 to 5, where 1 is "extremely dissatisfied" or "not at all," and 5 is "excellent" or "very easy." A score of 1 means the item needs immediate attention, whereas a score of 5 is superior service or exemplary. The data are captured from the Web site survey into an Access database.

Lloyd wants you to import selected portions of the database into an Excel worksheet. Create a database query to import the following fields from the database table, *tblCustomer,* to the worksheet: *State, Q-FindIt, Q-UsefulInfo, Q-EasyToNavigate,* and *Q-ReturnPolicy.* The latter four fields—all beginning with Q—are responses to these survey questions:

- Q-FindIt: Did you find what you wanted? (1=not at all; 5=exactly)
- Q-UsefulInfo: How useful is the information on our site? (1=not at all; 5=very useful)
- Q-EasyToNavigate: How easy is our site to navigate? (1=very difficult; 5=very easy)
- Q-ReturnPolicy: How do you like our return policy? (1=it is awful; 5=it is excellent)

Begin by opening the workbook **ex11Hydroponics.xls** and then save it as **<yourname>Hydroponics11.xls.** Click the **Data Analysis** worksheet tab, and then form a query to import data to that worksheet. Lloyd wants you to import customer rows only for customers who live in Missouri, Indiana, Ohio, Illinois, or Michigan. The query should sort the data in descending order by the value of the Q-UsefulInfo field and then in ascending order on state name abbreviations for matching Q-UsefulInfo values. Import the data beginning in cell A3 (see Figure 11.46), leaving two open rows at the top of the worksheet. In the top row, write expressions to average the values returned for each of the Q-questions, placing the AVERAGE function directly above the column it is averaging. Display the averages to two decimal places. Insert your name in the Data Analysis worksheet header, and print only the first page of the Data Analysis worksheet. Save the altered workbook under a unique name of your own choosing.

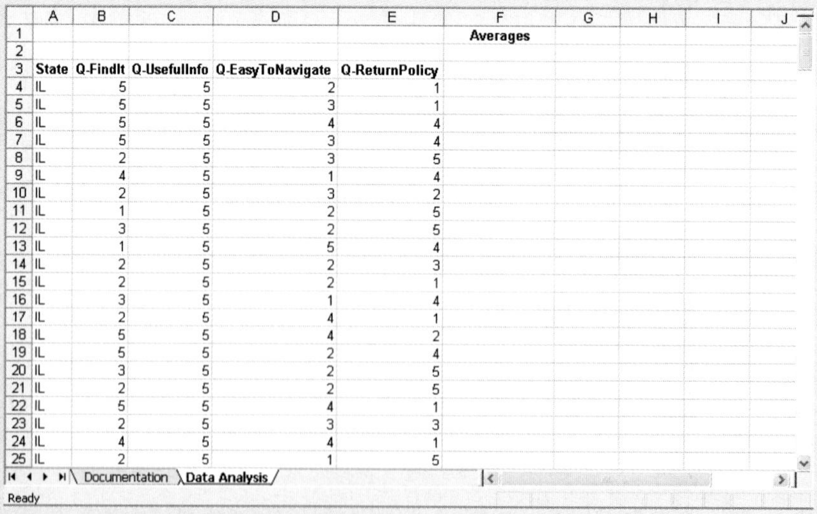

	A	B	C	D	E	F	G	H	I	J
1						Averages				
2										
3	State	Q-FindIt	Q-UsefulInfo	Q-EasyToNavigate	Q-ReturnPolicy					
4	IL	5	5	2	1					
5	IL	5	5	3	1					
6	IL	5	5	4	4					
7	IL	5	5	3	4					
8	IL	2	5	3	5					
9	IL	4	5	1	4					
10	IL	2	5	3	2					
11	IL	1	5	2	5					
12	IL	3	5	2	5					
13	IL	1	5	5	4					
14	IL	2	5	2	3					
15	IL	2	5	2	1					
16	IL	3	5	1	4					
17	IL	2	5	4	1					
18	IL	5	5	4	2					
19	IL	5	5	2	4					
20	IL	3	5	2	5					
21	IL	2	5	2	5					
22	IL	5	5	4	1					
23	IL	2	5	3	3					
24	IL	4	5	4	1					
25	IL	2	5	1	5					

FIGURE 11.46
Imported survey data, page 1

1. Importing and Using Queries to Summarize Presidential Data

Mrs. Borstel is a third-grade teacher at East Ridge Elementary School in Virginia. The class is learning about the U.S. government. She asked her aide to gather a variety of information on all of the U.S. presidents that will be stored in an Excel worksheet. To make it more interesting, she also asked her aide to gather more specific information on presidents who were born in Virginia.

Mrs. Borstel's aide placed the data in an Access database. It contains one table, called Presidents. The table contains these columns: PresidentID, LastName, FirstName, Party, Term, BirthState, InaugurationAge, and Height. PresidentID is a number indicating order in which the Presidents were elected. The Height field is each President's height in inches. The remaining fields are self-explanatory. The second table, called VirginiaPresidents, is supposed to contain data for those presidents born in Virginia. Mrs. Borstel wants you to organize this information in an Excel workbook.

Begin by opening Excel and saving a new workbook as **<yourname>Presidents.xls**. Use the Query Wizard to import data from the Presidents table in the **ex11Presidents.mdb** database. Specify in the Query Wizard that you *do not* want to import the Height column. Once all the President rows are imported, sort the Excel data in ascending order by the LastName field and then by the FirstName field for matching LastName field values. Name a worksheet **All Presidents**. Insert a new worksheet into the workbook and name it **Virginia Details**. Use the Query Wizard again to retrieve information from the **VirginiaPresidents** table. Import all fields and then sort the table by the President field.

As you can see, three columns of information are missing from the VirginiaPresidents table: the Vice President's name, the President's birth date, and the President's date of death. Go to a reference Web site, such as www.ipl.com (Internet Public Library), or use a search engine, such as www.dogpile.com or www.hotbot.com, to find the needed information on these presidents. Insert the missing information into the VirginiaPresidents worksheet.

Create a new first worksheet titled **Documentation** in the workbook. In row 3, enter **Presidents of the United States of America**. Below this title, enter **Created for: Mrs. Borstel**, **Created by:** followed with your name, **Date:** followed by the date, and **Details: Presidents from Virginia**. Make the appearance of the workbook uniform and attractive using colors and formatting. Remember that this will be given to the students and needs to get their attention. Place your name in all worksheet headers, save your workbook, and print the workbook.

2. Importing Data and Creating Pivot Charts to Compare Racing Records

Jackson Raceway is a racetrack in Kentucky built by Samuel B. Jackson. Sam was a fan of car races as a child and eventually built his own oval 2.5-mile racetrack, modeled after the Daytona International Speedway.

A friend of Samuel is chair of a charity. He approached Samuel about hosting a fund-raising event.

Begin work for Samuel by opening Excel and then importing **ex11Racers.txt** using the Text Import Wizard. The text file contains the information on each driver who will be included in the event program: name of the driver, car number, make of car, record laps for 2000, and record laps for 2001. A semicolon separates one data item from another. Import data beginning in row 3. Save your workbook.

Go to www.nascar.com and click the **Drivers and Teams** hyperlink on the left-hand side, and click the **Drivers** hyperlink. Use this page to gather information on four additional racers and the number of laps each completed at the Daytona 500 in the years 2000 and 2001 to complete the worksheet.

In order to clearly compare past records for the program, Samuel wants you to prepare a pivot table and pivot chart comparing each driver's record for 2000 and 2001. Place the racers' names in the column section and the sum of 2000 and 2001 figures in the data section. Insert the pivot chart, in a line chart format, on a new worksheet titled **Racer Chart** and move this worksheet to the end of the workbook. Specify the Y-axis scale values as follows: Min 100, Max 200, Major Unit 10, and Category X Axis Crosses at 100. Add a Documentation worksheet to the beginning of the workbook with the title **Jackson Raceway Charity Program Information**. Include your name and date, place your name in all worksheet headers, save your work, and print the workbook.

around the world

1. Using a Pivot Table to Summarize Imported Software Sales Figures

ModelWare is a software company based in Cambridge, England, specializing in designing software for the construction industry. Its programs range from those that design machinery to graphics programs that simulate new neighborhoods. Due to the European Union and introduction of the euro, expanding business across European nations has become easier than ever before. ModelWare's president, Richard Hearn, believes that the future of the company's success rests upon how well the firm capitalizes on the new opportunities in Europe.

Recently, management established sales operations in France, Germany, Ireland, Sweden, and Italy. Instead of sending only current English ModelWare employees to these markets, management also hired native representatives from each of the countries. The goal of this was to determine whether English or native representatives were able to more quickly build rapport with clients, establish client relationships, and sell software programs.

It has been four months since ModelWare began its new sales divisions in France, Germany, Ireland, and Sweden and Richard wants to analyze the representatives' sales. The sales manager, Connie Triffit, was supposed to give him sales information for the last four months, organized by country. For Richard's purposes, no representatives were named; instead English and Native are used to represent the sum for each type of representatives' sales. Open **ex11EuropeanSales.txt** using Excel. Be sure to scroll through the data while using the Text Import Wizard to ensure that the proper delimiter(s) is selected. Improve the appearance of the worksheet and ensure that there are no blank rows between data. Name the worksheet **EuropeanSales**. Richard has asked you to now create a pivot table and pivot chart reflecting each country's data. Using the data in the European Sales worksheet you just created, create a pivot table that allows Richard to look at all of the data either at once or by individual country, sorted by representative type. Select rep type for the column area and sums of the monthly figures for the data section.

Create the pivot chart in a line format on a new worksheet labeled **CountrySales**. Be sure that each representative type has its own line showing sales for each month. Create a Documentation sheet to be the first page of the workbook. Include the title, **ModelWare European Sales**, **Requested by: Richard Hearn**, **Created by:** followed by your name, and **Presented on:** followed by today's date. Place your name in the header of each worksheet. Save your workbook as **ModelWareSales.xls** and print all worksheets.

2. Listing Golf Courses for Irish Golf Holidays

Irish Golf Holidays is an Irish golf reservation system. Golfers can call the Irish Golf Holidays toll-free number to reserve tee times at any of over 150 golf clubs in Ireland. Billing is by credit card or charge card, and Irish Golf Holidays e-mails a guaranteed golf reservation confirmation back to the golfer. Paddy O'Hanlon, Irish Golf Holidays' director of marketing wants to automate the system and become a member of the SelectTeeTimes.com golf reservation network. In preparation for that automation, Paddy has created a list of golf clubs where Irish Golf Holidays can schedule tee times. The list contains the names of over 150 golf clubs, the county in which they are located, the type of golf course (links or inland), the number of holes in the course, course par, and total course length in meters. Paddy wants you to create two database queries to import the golf course information from the Access database in which it is stored into two separate Excel worksheets.

Open the workbook **ex11IrishGolf.xls**, save it as **<yourname>Irish.xls**, make the *Links* worksheet active, and create a database query to import information from the database file **ex11IrishGolf.mdb**. Import the fields County, Club Name, Type, Holes, Par, and Meters for golf courses whose Type is "links" (any golf course that is within four miles of the coast), 18-hole courses (Holes = 18), and courses whose length is less than 6,000 meters (Meters field is less than 6,000). The query should sort the results by County (ascending) and then Club Name (ascending) within matching County. Click the **CorkOrGalway** worksheet tab and then create a database query to import the County, Club Name, Type, and Meters fields for any golf clubs in either Cork County or Galway County (all must be inland courses) whose total length is greater than 6,000 meters. The query should sort the rows in ascending order by County and then descending order by Meters within County. Type your name in all worksheet headers and print the entire workbook.

Pro Golf Academy

Betty Carroll learned that the American Pro Golf Manufacturers Association (APGMA), Inc., has published an Access database containing a small survey detailing shopping outlets where people shop for golf products. The survey compares four types of stores and shows the percentage of people who claim to shop in each store type. (Row totals do not equal 100 percent, because people shop at combinations of store types.) The stores types listed in the survey instrument APGMA sent out are discount store, outlet store, pro shop, and sport superstore. In addition, the survey asked whether or not the customer actually purchased an item and which type of item it was. (The survey lists 14 categories of golf products.) Betty wants you to import the database table, called *OutletsShopped,* from the database, called **ex11ProGolf.mdb**, and place the data in the second worksheet, called *Outlets Shopped Analysis.*

Begin by opening the workbook **ex11ProGolf.xls**. Then, make the *Outlets Shopped Analysis* worksheet active, click cell **A2**, and import the data from the database to the worksheet. In row 18, write expressions to average each of the five columns containing numeric information.

Type **Average** in A18, and right-align and bold it. Edit any column labels to contain spaces between words. For example, change "OutletStore" to "Outlet Store" (two words). Select the alignment "wrap text" for all column labels (row 2). Format all numeric values as percentages with one decimal place (for example, 13.8%). Change the column width of columns B through G to 11. Create a pie chart of the shopping averages (row 18), and use the column labels as the legend. Place the percentage as a data label on each pie slice (step 3 of the Chart Wizard). Place the chart on a separate sheet, and rename the chart sheet tab **Average by Store Type**. Color the chart sheet tab red. Move to the Documentation worksheet, type any date last year in the "Created on" cell, type your name in the "Created by" cell, and type today's date in the "Modified on" cell.

Identify all worksheets by typing your name in the worksheet headers, save the workbook as **<yourname>ProGolf11.xls** (see Figure 11.47), print the Analysis worksheet and the chart sheet in landscape orientation, and print the Documentation worksheet in portrait orientation.

	A	B	C	D	E	F	G
1	**Outlets Shopped for Golf Products**						
2	Product	Purchased	ProShop	GolfSuperStore	DiscountStore	MallStore	OnlineGolfStore
3	Accessories	19.0%	6.0%	25.0%	24.0%	2.0%	41.0%
4	Apparel	38.0%	12.0%	38.0%	43.0%	16.0%	21.0%
5	Bags	23.0%	5.0%	28.0%	45.0%	3.0%	25.0%
6	Balls	7.0%	0.0%	22.0%	22.0%	6.0%	57.0%
7	Books and Videos	9.0%	4.0%	29.0%	21.0%	0.0%	29.0%
8	Footwear	54.0%	14.0%	19.0%	49.0%	10.0%	24.0%
9	Gift Certificate	17.0%	4.0%	29.0%	27.0%	20.0%	1.0%
10	Gloves	12.0%	0.0%	31.0%	38.0%	9.0%	25.0%
11	Irons	22.0%	5.0%	29.0%	38.0%	7.0%	28.0%
12	Lessons, instructor-led	14.0%	11.0%	33.0%	28.0%	3.0%	28.0%
13	Putters	12.0%	7.0%	19.0%	23.0%	3.0%	42.0%
14	Training aids	49.0%	7.0%	30.0%	38.0%	2.0%	24.0%
15	Wedges	20.0%	4.0%	28.0%	24.0%	6.0%	24.0%
16	Woods	29.0%	8.0%	36.0%	30.0%	3.0%	24.0%
17							
18	Average	23.2%	6.2%	28.3%	32.1%	6.4%	28.1%

Sheet tabs: Average by Store Type / Outlets Shopped Analysis

FIGURE 11.47
Completed shopping outlet survey

1. Create a Query or Import Data?

With Excel you can execute Data, Import External Data, and then Import Data commands to import information from a database. Why would you bother with a database query, which takes more time to design and is more complicated to create?

2. Save That Data

Describe how saving a query is different (or is it?) from saving the data that the query imports.

12

Automating Applications with Visual Basic

did you know?

during *Ronald Reagan's presidency, the White House purchased 12 tons of jelly beans.*

there *are more than 15,000 different varieties of rice.*

when *a piece of glass cracks, the crack travels faster than 3,000 miles per hour.*

during *a severe windstorm or rainstorm, the Empire State Building may sway several feet to either side.*

swimming *pools in the United States contain enough water to cover the city of San Francisco with a layer of water about 7 feet deep.*

Greece's *national anthem has 158 verses.*

Chapter Objectives

- Record a macro instruction—MOS XL03E-5-2
- Examine and use the Visual Basic Editor—MOS XL03E-5-2
- Run macro instructions using a dialog box and a command button—MOS XL03E-5-2
- Add and remove buttons from toolbars—MOS XL03E-5-1
- Save a macro in your Personal Macro Workbook
- Set the macro security level—MOS XL03E-3-2
- Create and modify Visual Basic code in the Visual Basic Editor—MOS XL03E-5-2
- Use Visual Basic objects, methods, properties, and variables—MOS XL03E-5-2
- Create a macro that automatically executes when you open a workbook—MOS XL03E-5-2
- Hide the Personal Macro Workbook—MOS XL03S-3-4
- Create custom functions—MOS XL03E-5-2
- Protect a worksheet to preserve its integrity—MOS XL03E-3-1

King's Stained Glass Studio

Mike King is the owner and creative designer of King's Stained Glass Studio, a small stained glass store and design studio, stocking art glass, glass bevels, and art glass-working supplies. Mike's only full-time employee, his wife Charlotte, works in the store selling glass and supplies. When time permits, she also helps Mike construct art glass windows. Mike spends almost all of his time designing and building stained glass panels commissioned by churches, businesses, and individuals. Mike and Charlotte's 1,200-square-foot store provides enough room for both Mike's studio and the retail store. Over 70 percent of the revenue is derived from store sales of glass and supplies.

Mike wants to make it easier for shoppers to locate the glass and supplies he sells and to list their prices. He envisions using his computer and Excel to provide a list of items and their prices that will make it simple for customers to quickly find what they want. Although he cannot afford to hire another full-time person to help Charlotte run the store, he has enough money to hire a part-time student to implement his in-store glass and supplies locator program. He has asked you to use the information already entered into an Excel workbook to create a simple interface that anyone can use to look up glass and supplies prices—whether he or she is familiar with Excel or not. Figure 12.1 shows the first page of a menu-based Excel workbook that allows customers to choose from three types of art glass or examine the supplies on hand in Mike's store.

F I G U R E   12.1

King's Stained Glass Store main menu

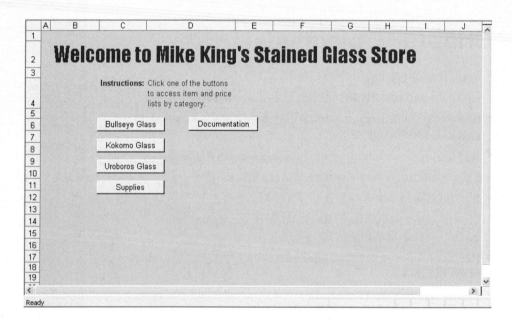

Chapter 12 covers creating Visual Basic macro instructions and functions to automate Excel. Office XP products employ a powerful programming language called Visual Basic for Applications (VBA) that allows you to write macro instructions to automate procedures and create procedures and functions. Fortunately, you do not have to be a programmer to create a macro. You can create a VBA macro by turning on the Macro Recorder, executing Excel commands and using the mouse as you would to manually accomplish a task, and then saving the recorded instructions to a named macro instruction. Once you have saved a sequence of instructions that Excel writes for you in VBA code, you can play back the macro instruction anytime you want to reproduce the sequence of instructions. When you store macro instructions in Excel's Personal Macro Workbook, Excel makes them available to all workbooks you open.

Excel provides the Visual Basic Editor in which you can write instructions that go beyond what macros provide. For example, you can write a sub procedure of VBA instructions to repeat a series of instructions such as examining a group of selected cells to determine which contain negative values—a procedure you could record with the macro instruction recorder. When you use a particular formula frequently in a workbook, you can turn it into a custom function that returns a value when you write an expression using the custom function. Saving a procedure or macro instruction as auto_open causes it to execute automatically when you first open the workbook to which it is attached.

SESSION 12.1 CREATING MACROS

In this section, you will learn how to record and save macro instructions using the Macro Recorder. Then you will view a macro instruction using the Visual Basic Editor and learn alternative ways to run a macro. You will learn how to run macros with the Macro dialog box and by assigning a macro to a command button. Finally, you will store a macro instruction so that the workbook containing it will execute the macro whenever the workbook opens.

What Is a Macro?

Mike knows that many of his customers do not have finely honed computer skills. If his idea of placing products and prices in an Excel workbook is to be successful, he cannot rely on customers knowing how to use Excel. For example, he knows he cannot assume a customer will know how to move from one worksheet of stained glass prices to another worksheet containing art glass tools. Therefore, he will have to automate the *Art Glass Catalog* (or AGC), as Mike calls the proposed workbook, so that it is as simple to operate as a television set. To do so, Mike reasons, will require the use of macro instructions to move from one worksheet to another when the customer clicks a clearly marked button on a worksheet. In addition, Mike would like to automate some parts of his customer information system using macro instructions and custom Excel functions.

A ***macro instruction***, or ***macro***, is a ***VBA procedure***, which is a group of VBA statements that collectively performs a particular task or returns a result. You can create two types of VBA procedures: functions and sub procedures. A ***VBA function*** is a procedure that returns a result, similar to the way Excel's built-in functions such as SUM and PMT return values. A ***VBA sub procedure*** is a procedure that performs a particular task. A macro is a VBA procedure, because a macro does not return a value. It does accomplish a task by executing the steps that the macro contains, though. Figure 12.2 shows a VBA macro procedure called *PrintFormulas* that prints a worksheet's formulas.

Using the Visual Basic Editor, you can write your own Excel custom functions. Functions begin with the word *Function* and end with *End Function*. Between them are the lines of Visual Basic statements that define the function. Functions usually have

FIGURE 12.2

A macro to print a worksheet's formulas

Excel automatically adds these comments

VBA statements to display formulas and print the worksheet

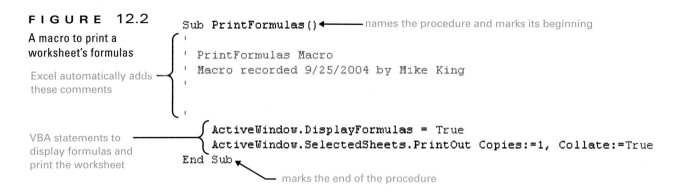

```
Sub PrintFormulas()          names the procedure and marks its beginning
'
' PrintFormulas Macro
' Macro recorded 9/25/2004 by Mike King
'
'
    ActiveWindow.DisplayFormulas = True
    ActiveWindow.SelectedSheets.PrintOut Copies:=1, Collate:=True
End Sub          marks the end of the procedure
```

arguments, which are symbolic names for values, expressions, and cell references that are passed to the function for its use in calculating an answer. Figure 12.3 shows the Bonus function that computes the bonus a salesperson earns based on the sale price of the item he or she sold. The salesperson earns a bonus if the sale is over $5,000. The bonus amount is 12 percent of the difference between the sale amount and $5,000.

Why Bother Creating a Macro?

Macros allow you to create your own commands. Doing so can save you a lot of time and effort—especially for tasks you perform repeatedly in a workbook or a few times in many workbooks. Some of the examples of time-consuming and somewhat tedious tasks that you can automate and simplify by using macros are:

- Place your name in a worksheet header
- Apply an AutoFormat to a range of worksheet cells
- Print a worksheet, print its formulas, and then redisplay the workbook in nonformula view
- Trace the precedent cells for each of a group of worksheet cells using one command
- Assign a group of instructions that accomplish a particular task to a command button

Deciding Which Macros You Need

You meet with Mike on Tuesday to discuss which macros you should write to automate the workbook so that customers can view the glass and supplies available at Mike's store. Mike's workbook currently contains six worksheets: Documentation, Welcome,

FIGURE 12.3

A function to calculate sales bonus

the function's name

an argument

```
Function Bonus(SalesAmount) As Single
    ' Compute sales bonus: 12% of sales over $5000
    If SalesAmount > 5000 Then
        Bonus = (SalesAmount - 5000) * 0.12
    Else
        Bonus = 0                    'No bonus if sale < $5001
    End If
End Function
```

a comment is formatted green and begins with an apostrophe

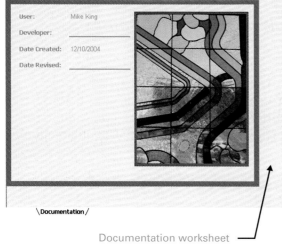

Documentation worksheet

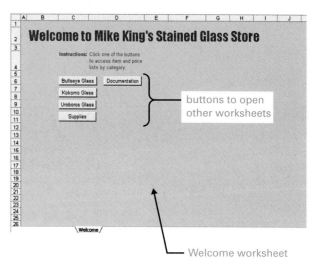

Welcome worksheet

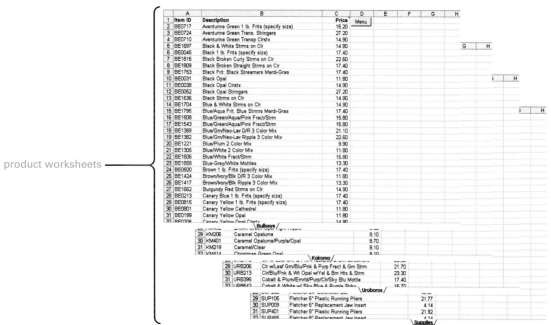

product worksheets

F I G U R E 12.4

Worksheets comprising King's product catalog workbook

Bullseye, Kokomo, Uroboros, and Supplies (see Figure 12.4). The Documentation worksheet contains brief comments about the workbook including the date when it was created. On the Welcome worksheet, Mike wants several buttons that open different product pages of the workbook when customers click them. In addition, Mike wants the Welcome worksheet to appear when anyone opens the workbook, because it is the main page from which customers go to product pages. The Bullseye, Kokomo, and Uroboros worksheets contain stained glass products from three like-named glass manufacturers. On the Supplies worksheet is a list of all the supplies Mike carries including copper foil, glass cutters of all descriptions, lead, solder, and so forth.

You discover that you can create a complete Excel application with Excel macro instructions written in VBA that will encapsulate instructions that you can assign to buttons you place on the worksheet surface. This user interface, forming the communication between the Excel workbook and customers using it, makes it easy for anyone to use the Excel application without knowing anything about Excel.

EXCEL

Opening the workbook and saving it under a new name:

1. Start Excel

2. Open the workbook **ex12ArtGlass.xls** and immediately save it as **Catalog2.xls** to preserve the original workbook in case you want to revert to that version. Excel displays the first worksheet, Documentation (see Figure 12.5)

FIGURE 12.5

Documentation worksheet

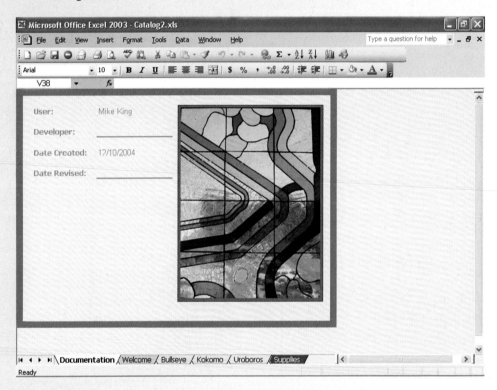

3. Click the other worksheet tabs to review the worksheets that comprise the Art Glass Catalog, and then click the **Welcome** worksheet tab

The Welcome worksheet will hold all of the buttons that customers will click to display the product worksheets. For example, a customer will examine the prices of Bullseye glass by clicking a button labeled Bullseye.

Recording a Macro

Excel provides an efficient tool for creating macros called the *Excel Macro Recorder.* As its name implies, the Macro Recorder records your actions. Recording a macro involves three steps. First, you start the Macro Recorder, and then you perform the actions you want Excel to record including clicking menus and commands and typing information into cells. Finally, you stop the recorder. Excel saves the recorded actions, including any mistakes you may make, in a macro instruction. Subsequently, you can replay the macro instruction any time you want to reproduce the results. Naturally, a macro's playback facility is particularly useful for long and often-used procedures, because a macro repeats the series of instructions exactly the same way you do manually in a fraction of the time.

Macros are saved in a special Excel object called a *module*. A module can contain many macros, and a workbook can hold an unlimited number of modules.

help yourself *Press **F1**, type **macro** in the Search text box of the Microsoft Excel Help task pane, and press **Enter**. Scroll the Search Results list to locate and then click the hyperlink **Create a macro**, and then click the hyperlink **Record a macro**. Maximize the Help screen if necessary. Take a moment to read the Help information on creating macro instructions. Click the Help screen **Close** button when you are finished, and close the task pane*

Macro Storage Choices

You can instruct Excel to save your macros in one of three locations: the current workbook, the Personal Macro Workbook, or a new workbook. Excel's ***Personal Macro Workbook*** is a workbook that Excel *always* loads, and subsequently hides, whenever you launch Excel. Macros stored in the Personal Macro Workbook are available for any workbook. The option to store a macro in a new workbook is less commonly used. The most common storage option is the current workbook, which is the default choice. If you store macros in the current workbook, you can execute them whenever the workbook is open. This is the option you will use in this chapter.

Choosing between Absolute and Relative Cell References

When the macro recorder is active, it records all commands you execute as well as the addresses of any cells you click. For example, if you click cell B4 while recording a macro, the recorder stores the instruction

```
Range("B4").Select
```

When the macro recorder stores the actual cell reference in recorded code, it is storing an absolute cell reference. An alternative way to record cell references in a macro instruction is to store cells' relative cell references. A relative cell reference refers to a clicked cell's location relative to the previously active cell. If cell B8 is active and you click cell C4 while recording a macro using relative cell reference, Excel stores the instruction

```
ActiveCell.Offset(-4,1).Range("A1").Select
```

"ActiveCell.Offset" is a relative reference, or offset, from the previously active cell, B8. That is, the notation "(−4,1)" indicates that cell C4 is −4 rows (up) and 1 column to the right of the previously active cell.

When you replay a macro recorded using absolute cell references, the macro affects the same cells every time it is played. When you record a macro using relative cell references, the cells affected are all relative to the cell that was active prior to executing the macro instruction. In other words, using relative cell references in macro instructions results in more versatile macros because they are not tied to particular worksheet cells.

Because the macros you record in this chapter do not need to take advantage of relative cell references, you will record all macros using absolute cell references. Next, you will learn how to ensure that the Macro Recorder uses absolute references.

Recording a Macro

Your first macro simply selects and displays the Bullseye worksheet and then selects cell A1 on that worksheet. Although it is a simple procedure and hardly seems worthy of a macro, keep in mind that you are automating a process for people who may not know anything about worksheets or the programs that display them.

EXCEL

---

task reference   Recording a Macro Instruction

- Click **Tools**, point to **Macro**, click **Record New Macro**
- Type a macro name in the Macro name text box
- Type a description in the Description text box
- Click **OK**
- Execute the tasks you want to record
- Click the **Stop Recording** button

Set up to begin recording the BullseyeWorksheet macro:

1. Click **Tools**, point to **Macro**, and then click **Record New Macro**. The Record Macro dialog box appears

2. Type **BullseyeWorksheet** in the *Macro name* text box, replacing the suggested name. (The suggested name is usually Macro1, Macro2, and so forth)

   tip: *Make sure you spell all macro names without spaces. The macro name above, BullseyeWorksheet, is one word*

3. Drag the mouse through the text in the **Description** text box, and then type **Make the Bullseye worksheet active** (see Figure 12.6)

FIGURE 12.6
Record Macro dialog box

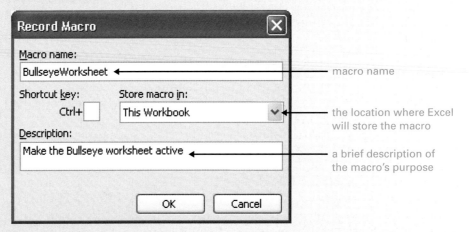

4. Click **OK** to begin the actual macro recording process. The floating Stop Recording toolbar appears

   tip: *Be careful what you do from now until you stop the Macro Recorder because it records every action you take. The Macro Recorder does not record mouse movements, so you can move the mouse to the menu bar or around the screen. Be sure not to click any commands unless you want your actions recorded—the recorder does not miss anything*

With the Macro Recorder active, you will record the commands that make the Bullseye worksheet active and make cell A1 active. Like a faithful scribe, the Macro Recorder will write down every action you perform.

Recording the BullseyeWorksheet macro:

1. Ensure that the Relative Reference button on the Stop Recording toolbar is not pressed in. If it is, then click the **Relative Reference** button to pop it out (see Figure 12.7)

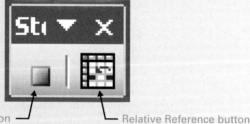

Stop Recording button — — Relative Reference button

FIGURE 12.7

The Stop Recording toolbar

2. Click the **Bullseye** worksheet tab to make that worksheet active, and then click cell **A1**

3. Click the **Stop Recording** button (see Figure 12.7). The Macro Recorder stops and places the BullseyeWorksheet macro in a module

4. Click the **Save** button on the Standard toolbar to save the workbook and its macro

Running a Macro

There are a variety of ways to play back a macro. You can run a macro by

- Assigning it to a keyboard shortcut
- Assigning it to a graphic object on a worksheet
- Assigning it to a toolbar button
- Assigning it to a menu
- Selecting it from a list of macros in the Macro dialog box

Some methods are more convenient than others, and you can decide which method works best for you. Users who are not accustomed to Office Excel 2003 probably will prefer either a toolbar button or a graphic object to launch a macro.

Using the Macro Dialog Box

Test the macro instruction by running it from the Macro dialog box to ensure that it works properly. After determining the macro works properly, you can consider a simpler method to execute macros.

Testing the BullseyeWorksheet macro:

1. Click the **Welcome** worksheet tab to make that worksheet active

2. Click **Tools**, point to **Macro**, click **Macros**, and ensure that **BullseyeWorksheet** is selected in the list of macro names (see Figure 12.8)

FIGURE 12.8

Macro dialog box

select macro to run from the list

click to run the selected macro

tip: *You can click* ***Alt+F8*** *to open the Macro dialog box*

3. Click the **Run** button to execute the macro. The Bullseye worksheet appears

Assigning a Macro to a Button

Perhaps the most convenient way to replay a macro instruction is by clicking a button or other graphic object it is assigned to. The most common graphic object to assign to a macro is a button, but you can choose any graphic object created with the Forms or Drawing toolbar.

task *reference*   Assigning a Macro to a Button

- Click **View**, point to **Toolbars**, click **Forms**
- Click the **Button** tool in the Forms toolbar
- Click a worksheet cell to place a button on the worksheet
- Select the macro to assign to the button from the Macro name list
- Click **OK**
- Drag the mouse across the button's caption and type a descriptive name
- Click any cell to deselect the button

Creating a button and assigning a macro to it:

1. Click the **Welcome** worksheet tab

2. Click **View**, point to **Toolbars**, and click **Forms** to open the Forms toolbar (see Figure 12.9)

tip: *The exact shape of your toolbar may be different from the figure*

3. If necessary, drag the Forms toolbar out of the way so that you can see cell C6

4. Click the **Button** tool in the Forms toolbar, and then click worksheet cell **C6**. (It is not important to be exactly in cell C6—just close to it.) Excel places a default-named button on the worksheet and opens the Assign Macro dialog box

5. Click **BullseyeWorksheet** in the *Macro name* list (see Figure 12.10) and then click **OK**. Excel closes the Assign Macro dialog box

Button tool

FIGURE 12.9
Forms toolbar

FIGURE 12.10
Assign Macro dialog box

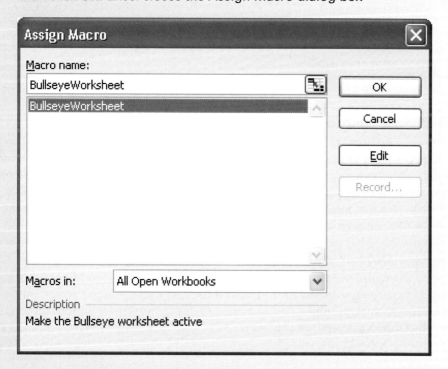

6. With the newly added button still selected, drag the mouse through the button's caption to select its characters. (The exact default name assigned depends on how many objects you have created so far)

7. Type **Bullseye Glass** (place a space between the two words)

8. If you cannot see the button's entire caption, move the mouse to the center selection handle on the right edge. When the mouse pointer changes to a double-headed arrow, click the selection handle and drag it to the right. Release the mouse when you think the button is wide enough.

9. Repeat step 8, as needed, to fine-tune the button's width until the button is sufficiently wide

EXCEL

10. Click any worksheet cell to deselect the button (see Figure 12.11)

FIGURE 12.11

The Bullseye worksheet button

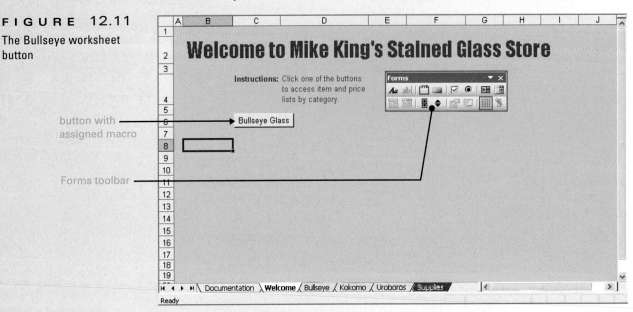

button with assigned macro

Forms toolbar

11. Close the Forms toolbar

Assigning a Macro to a Graphic

You can assign a macro to any graphic object in a way that is similar to the method you follow for a button. The difference is that the Assign Macro dialog box does not appear automatically after you draw the object. For example, you can place a Horizontal Scroll object, found in the AutoShapes section of the Drawing toolbar, on the worksheet. Then right-click the object and proceed as you did in steps 5 through 10 above to assign a macro to the graphic.

Making a Button Visible on Printouts

Buttons are designed for onscreen use, and they are convenient for worksheet users. By default, buttons *do not* display on a printed worksheet because users cannot interact with printed buttons. However, you may want to display worksheet buttons on printouts so that others can evaluate your work.

task reference	Making Buttons Visible on a Printout

- Right-click the button you want to display on a printout
- Click **Format Control** on the shortcut menu
- Click the **Properties** tab
- Click the **Print object** check box, and then click **OK**

Making a button visible on a printout:

1. Right-click the **Bullseye Glass** button. A shortcut menu appears

2. Click **Format Control**. The Format Control dialog box opens

tip: *If the Format Control dialog box only has a Font tab, chances are that you have clicked inside the button after it is already selected. In that case, click any worksheet cell and then repeat steps 1 and 2*

3. Click the **Properties** tab, and then click the **Print object** check box to place a checkmark in it (see Figure 12.12)

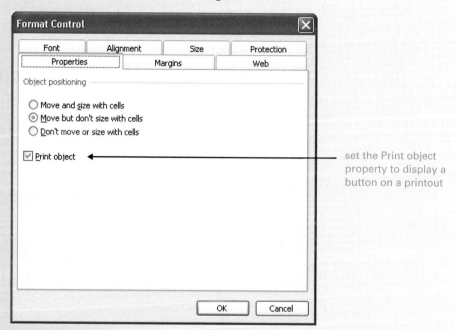

FIGURE 12.12

Setting a button's Print object property

4. Click the **OK** button

Recording Macros for the Other Product Worksheets

Mike points out that you will need to create three more buttons and three more macros to display the Kokomo, Uroboros, and Supplies worksheets.

Recording the Kokomo, Uroboros, and Supplies Macros

Creating macros to go to the three other glass and supplies worksheets is a snap. You've done the process recently. Here, you will record three new macros and assign buttons to them, although there are alternative approaches available for seasoned macro writers. These alternatives include copying and pasting code and making small changes to the clones, but doing so incurs some risk of mistake. It's best to stick to tried-and-true methods.

Recording additional macros:

1. If necessary, click the **Welcome** worksheet tab

2. Click **Tools**, point to **Macro**, and click **Record New Macro**

3. Type **KokomoWorksheet** in the Macro name text box, replacing the suggested name. Remember: No spaces in macro names

4. Drag the mouse through the text in the Description text box to select it, type **Make the Kokomo worksheet active**, and click **OK** to begin the actual macro recording process

5. Click the **Kokomo** worksheet tab, click cell **A1**, and then click the **Stop Recording** button

6. Click the **Welcome** worksheet tab to make the worksheet active

7. Repeat steps 2 through 6 to create the UroborosWorksheet macro, substituting **UroborosWorksheet** in step 3, **Make the Uroboros worksheet active** in step 4, and **Uroboros** in step 5

8. Repeat steps 2 through 6 to create the SuppliesWorksheet macro, substituting **SuppliesWorksheet** in step 3, **Make the Supplies worksheet active** in step 4, and **Supplies** in step 5

9. Save the workbook

Attaching Buttons to the Kokomo, Uroboros, and Supplies Macros

Next, you place buttons on the Welcome worksheet and attach them to the macros you created above.

Creating and assigning buttons to the Kokomo, Uroboros, and Supplies worksheets:

1. Click the **Welcome** worksheet tab, if necessary, to make that worksheet active, and click cell **A1**

2. Click **View**, point to **Toolbars**, click **Forms** to open the Forms toolbar, and drag it to the right so that you can see column C

3. Click the **Button** tool in the Forms toolbar, click the cell below the last button, drag the mouse pointer down and to the right so that the button outline is approximately the same size as the button above it, and release the mouse. The Assign Macro dialog box opens

4. Click **KokomoWorksheet** in the Macro name list (see Figure 12.13), and then click **OK**

5. Drag the mouse through the button's caption and type **Kokomo Glass** (two words)

6. If necessary, resize the button so that you can see the entire caption

7. Click any worksheet cell to deselect the button

8. Repeat steps 3 through 7, substituting **UroborosWorksheet** in step 4 and **Uroboros Glass** in step 5

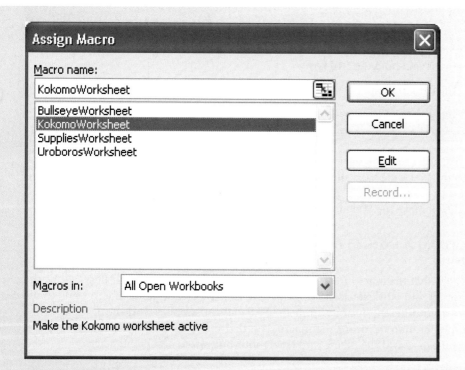

FIGURE 12.13
Assigning the
KokomoWorksheet macro
to a button

9. Repeat steps 3 through 7, substituting **SuppliesWorksheet** in step 4 and **Supplies** in step 5

10. Close the Forms toolbar (see Figure 12.14)

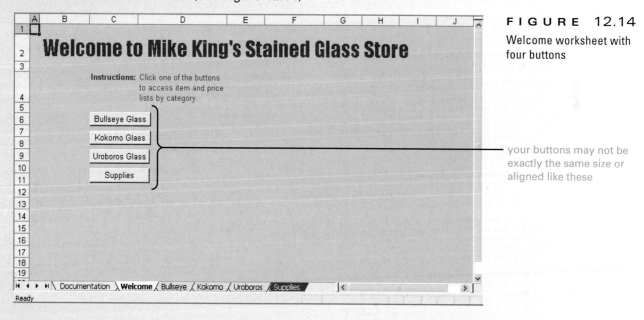

FIGURE 12.14
Welcome worksheet with
four buttons

your buttons may not be
exactly the same size or
aligned like these

tip: *If your worksheet buttons are not all uniform in size, don't worry. They still work fine when you click them*

You may want to alter a button's properties. One of the only tricky parts of doing that is selecting the button *without* clicking it.

EXCEL

---

task reference — Selecting a Button Control without Activating It

- Press and hold the **Ctrl** key
- Click the button
- Release the **Ctrl** key

Mike notes that you have not provided an obvious or easy way for a customer to return to the Welcome worksheet after opening one of the other worksheets. He would like you to place a button on each of the glass and supplies worksheets that, when pushed, will make the Welcome worksheet active.

Recording a Return Macro and Assigning It to Multiple Buttons

You realize that the macro instruction to return to the Welcome worksheet will be the same for all four worksheets, so you can save time by creating one macro that is activated by four different buttons—one on each glass or supplies worksheet.

In preparation to record the macro, you first make the Bullseye worksheet active. Then you can record the macro and create four buttons to access the macro.

Creating a Return to Menu macro:

1. Click the **Bullseye Glass** button to make the Bullseye worksheet active

2. Click **Tools**, point to **Macro**, and click **Record New Macro**

3. Type **ReturnToMenu** in the Macro name text box

4. Press **Tab** three times to move to the Description text box, type **Make the Welcome worksheet active**, and click **OK** to begin the actual macro recording process

5. Click the **Welcome** worksheet tab and then click the **Stop Recording** button

Next, you will create a button to activate the new macro and place it on the Bullseye worksheet. Then you can copy the button to the glass and supplies worksheets using a simple copy-and-paste technique.

Assigning the ReturnToMenu macro to a button and copying it to other worksheets:

1. Click the **Bullseye Glass** button to make the Bullseye worksheet active

2. Click **View**, point to **Toolbars**, click **Forms** to open the Forms toolbar, and drag it to the right, if necessary, so that you can see cell D1

3. Click the **Button** tool in the Forms toolbar, move the plus-shaped mouse to the upper-left corner of cell **D1**, and click the mouse. Excel places a button on the worksheet and opens the Assign Macro dialog box.

4. Click **ReturnToMenu** in the list of macro names, and then click **OK**

5. Drag the mouse through the button's caption and type **Menu**

6. Move the mouse to the border around the button. When the mouse pointer becomes a four-headed arrow, click the button's border to select the button. The border changes from a series of slash marks (/////) to dots, indicating that you have selected the button object and not the button's caption

7. Press **Ctrl+C** to copy the button to the Clipboard, and click cell **A1** to deselect the button

tip: *If you accidentally deselect the button, you can select it by pressing **Ctrl**, clicking the button, and releasing the **Ctrl** key. If you simply click the button without first holding down the Ctrl key, then you activate the attached macro*

8. Click the **Documentation** worksheet tab, click cell **C10** (below the entry *Date Revised*), press **Ctrl+V** to paste the button on the Documentation worksheet, and click the underlined cell to the right of the label *Developer* to deselect the button

9. Click the **Kokomo** worksheet tab, click cell **D1**, press **Ctrl+V** to paste the button near cell D1 on the Kokomo worksheet, and click cell **A1** to deselect the button

10. Click the **Uroboros** worksheet tab, click cell **D1**, press **Ctrl+V** to paste the button near cell D1 on the Uroboros worksheet, and click cell **A1** to deselect the button

11. Click the **Supplies** worksheet tab, click cell **D1**, press **Ctrl+V** to paste the button near cell D1 on the Supplies worksheet, and click cell **A1** to deselect the button

12. Click the Forms toolbar **Close** button (see Figure 12.15)

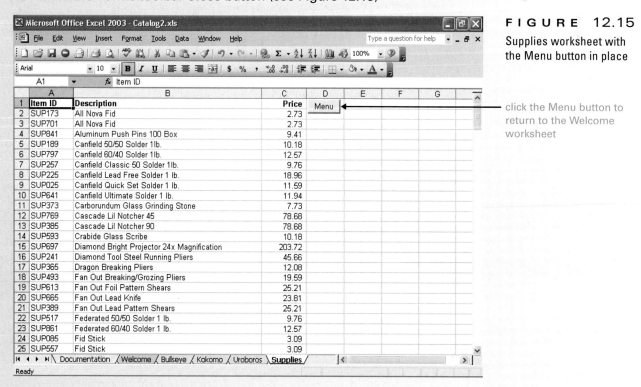

FIGURE 12.15

Supplies worksheet with the Menu button in place

click the Menu button to return to the Welcome worksheet

Adding a Button to a Toolbar

Sometimes it is convenient to add a frequently used button to one of the Excel toolbars such as the Standard or Formatting toolbars. That way, the button is always available no matter what workbook or worksheet is active. However, the button you add to a toolbar is available only on that computer and no other.

Adding a button to a toolbar:

1. Ensure that the Standard toolbar is visible. If it is not, then click **View**, point to **Toolbars**, and click **Standard**

2. Click **Tools**, click **Customize**, and click the **Commands** tab of the Customize dialog box

3. Scroll the Categories list until you see *Macros* (near the bottom), and click **Macros** in the Categories list

4. Click and drag **Custom Button** in the Commands panel to the leftmost position on the Standard toolbar, and release the mouse. Excel places the button, a happy face, on the Standard toolbar

5. Click the **Close** button to close the Customize dialog box

With the button on the Standard toolbar, you can assign the ReturnToMenu macro to it.

Assigning a macro to a custom toolbar button:

1. Click the **Smiley Face** button you added to the toolbar. The Assign Macro dialog box opens

2. Click **ReturnToMenu** in the list of macro names, and click **OK**. Excel closes the dialog box and assigns the macro

3. Click the **Smiley Face** button to ensure it works. Excel makes the Welcome worksheet active

4. Click the **Supplies** worksheet tab to activate that worksheet

Of course, you also can add buttons from other toolbars and menus to any toolbar. It is also important to know how to remove any button you add to the toolbar or to restore any toolbar to its original, factory-fresh condition.

Removing a toolbar button from a toolbar:

1. Click **Tools**, click **Customize**, and click the **Toolbars** tab of the Customize dialog box

tip: *If you want to reset the toolbar to its original condition as shipped from Microsoft, then click the Reset button*

2. Click and drag the **Smiley Face** button off of the toolbar. When you release the mouse, Excel removes the button

3. Click the **Close** button to close the Customize dialog box

Creating and Running Macros Stored in the Personal Macro Workbook

Excel placed all the macros you have recorded so far in a module that belongs to the current (active) workbook. A macro recorded in a workbook is available only when the workbook containing it is open, including any other open workbooks on a given computer.

Creating and Saving a Macro in the Personal Macro Workbook

A solution that makes macros you choose available whenever Office Excel 2003 is running is to store macros in the Personal Macro Workbook. Excel automatically creates the Personal Macro Workbook the first time you choose that option for macro storage. Excel stores the workbook, called **Personal.xls**, in the **XLStart** folder. Excel automatically opens and hides the **Personal.xls** workbook each time you start Excel, thereby making all macros stored in it available to all Excel workbooks you open.

Creating a macro and storing it in the Personal Macro Workbook:

1. With the Supplies worksheet still active, click **Tools**, point to **Macro**, and click **Record New Macro**

2. Type **KingHeaderFooter** in the Macro name text box, replacing the suggested name

3. Click the **Store macro in** list box to display a list of locations where you can store macros

4. Click the **Personal Macro Workbook** choice, press the **Tab** key to select the Description text box, type **Enter King's header and footer into a worksheet** to replace the existing description text (see Figure 12.16), and click **OK**. Excel starts the Macro Recorder

FIGURE 12.16

Creating a Personal Macro Workbook macro

save this macro in the Personal Macro Workbook

5. Click **View**, click **Header and Footer**, click the **Custom Header** button, click in the **Right section** panel, type **King's Stained Glass Studio**, and click **OK**

6. Click the **Custom Footer** button, click in the **Center section** panel, click the **Page number** button in the Footer toolbar, and click **OK**. The Page Setup dialog box reveals your choices (see Figure 12.17)

FIGURE 12.17
The Page Setup dialog box

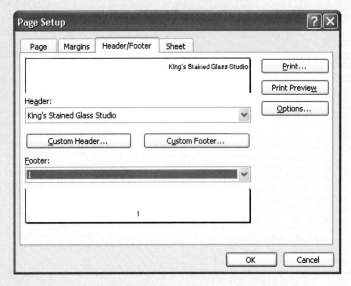

7. Click **OK** in the Page Setup dialog box to complete the procedure

8. Click the **Stop Recording** button. Excel stops recording the macro

Unhiding the Personal Macro Workbook

In case you want to examine or delete macros stored in the Personal Macro Workbook, you must first *unhide* the workbook. Then you can examine the macro instructions it contains. Although you will not unhide the **Personal.xls** workbook here, you should know how to do it.

task reference	Unhiding a Workbook

- Click **Window** on the menu bar
- Click **Unhide**
- Click a workbook in the Unhide workbook list and then click **OK**

Similarly, you can hide any active workbook by reversing the previous procedure.

task reference	Hiding a Workbook

- Make active any worksheet of the workbook you want to hide
- Click **Window** on the menu bar
- Click **Hide**

Setting the Macro Security Level

Viruses can exist in the form of macro instructions attached to Excel workbooks. If you download workbooks from the Internet, you want to beware of the potential viruses hidden in Excel workbooks. To guard against viruses or unwanted macro instructions in Excel workbooks, you can use any number of antivirus software packages. In addition, Excel provides a measure of security in the form of *security levels*. Three security levels are available in Excel: Low, Medium, and High. You should set your macro security level to Medium, at least. When Excel macro security is Medium, Excel will display a warning dialog box whenever you open a workbook containing macros.

Mike wants you to determine the macro security level he has, and he wants you to set it to Medium. Then you will save, close, and re-open the **Catalog2.xls** workbook to review the warning dialog box that Excel displays.

---

task reference   Setting the Macro Security Level

- Click **Tools**, click **Options**, and click the **Security** tab
- Click the **Macro Security** button
- Click the security level option button of your choice
- Click **OK** to close the Security dialog box and then click **OK** to close the Options dialog box

---

Setting the Excel macro security level:

1. Click **Tools**, click **Options**, and then click the **Security** tab

2. Click the **Macro Security** button near the bottom of the Security panel. Excel opens the Security dialog box

3. Click the **Medium** option button, if necessary (see Figure 12.18), to set the security level to Medium

FIGURE 12.18

Setting the macro security level to Medium

4. Click **OK** to close the Security dialog box and then click **OK** to close the Options dialog box

Opening a Workbook Containing Macros

You have made a lot of changes to the **Catalog2.xls** workbook since you last saved it, so you should save it now to preserve all the work you have done so far.

Saving your workbook and closing Excel:

1. Click the **Save** button on the Standard toolbar

2. Click **File**, and then click **Exit** to close the workbook and exit Excel. Excel displays a dialog box with the message "Do you want to save the changes you made to the Personal Macro Workbook?" (see Figure 12.19)

FIGURE 12.19

Saving the Personal
Macro Workbook

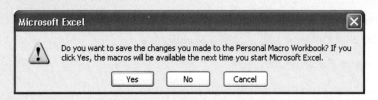

3. Click **Yes** to save the altered Personal Macro Workbook, **Personal.xls**

Now you can reopen the **Catalog2.xls** workbook and observe the macro security warning that Excel displays.

Opening a workbook containing a macro:

1. Start Excel

2. Click **File** and then click **Open**

3. Click the **Catalog2.xls** workbook in the list of workbooks and then click **Open**. Excel displays a warning indicating that the workbook contains macros (see Figure 12.20)

FIGURE 12.20

Excel macro warning

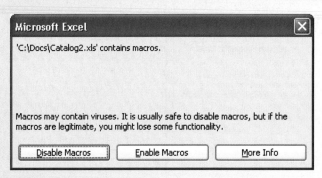

4. Click the **Enable Macros** button to open the workbook and allow its attached macros. Excel loads the workbook and displays the Supplies worksheet

tip: *If you click the Disable Macros button, Excel will open the workbook but disallow use of any of the macros it contains. The macros remain stored in the workbook's module(s)*

Mike is pleased with the macro instructions. He tries out each of the buttons on the menu bar and is delighted with them. The Menu button on each worksheet makes the Welcome worksheet active. You close the workbook, save the workbook under a new name, exit Excel, and take a break.

Saving the workbook under a new name and exiting Excel:

1. Click the **Menu** button on the *Supplies* worksheet and then click cell **A1**

2. Click **File** and then click **Save As**

3. Type **Catalog3** in the File name text box and then click the **Save** button

4. Close Excel

making the grade

1. A _____ is a VBA procedure that performs a particular task or returns a result.

2. A VBA _____ is a procedure that returns a result similar to Excel's built-in functions.

3. Excel's _____ _____ Workbook is a workbook that automatically loads whenever you load any Excel workbook.

4. Excel saves macros in a special object called a _____, which is stored with the workbook.

5. You can assign a macro to a _____ to facilitate running the macro by those unaccustomed to using Excel commands.

SESSION 12.2 WRITING SUB PROCEDURES AND CUSTOM FUNCTIONS

In this section, you will learn about the Visual Basic Editor, how to edit macros in the Visual Basic Editor, how to create and name a macro that automatically executes when you open a workbook, how to write code to gather data from a user with an input box, how to display special message boxes to a user signaling errors and posting information, and how to write iteration structures that repeat a sequence of instructions.

Examining the Visual Basic Editor

Having recorded several macros, you may wonder where Excel stores the macro instructions and exactly what they look like. As you recall, Excel writes macros in VBA, or Visual Basic for Applications. When you recorded your first macro, Excel created an object called a *module* in the active workbook. Recall that a module is where Excel stores VBA code. As you created the BullseyeWorksheet macro, for example, Excel recorded your keystrokes and commands and placed the VBA code in the Bullseyeworksheet and saved it in a module. Modules do not appear in the workbook along with worksheets. To view a module and the VBA procedures it contains, you have to open the Visual Basic Editor (VBE). The **Visual Basic Editor** is a program that contains multiple windows and allows you to view objects, VBA Code, and objects' properties in a convenient development environment. The editor is identical in all Office products.

The Visual Basic Editor provides an easy way for you to print, view, or modify any macros you have recorded.

Viewing a Macro with the Visual Basic Editor

---

task reference   **Opening the Visual Basic Editor**

- Click **Tools**, point to **Macro**, and click **Visual Basic Editor**

or

- Press **Alt+F11**

or

- Click **Tools**, point to **Macro**, and click **Macros**
- Select the name of the macro you want to edit
- Click the **Edit** button

Mike notices that there is no automated way to view the Documentation worksheet. You have created buttons to open the glass and supplies worksheets, so Mike would like a button on the Welcome worksheet that opens the Documentation worksheet. You realize that the code to open the Documentation worksheet will be similar to the code to open any of the other worksheets. The only difference is that the target worksheet's name is different. You decide to use the Visual Basic Editor to copy an existing macro, rename it, and then assign it to a button on the Welcome worksheet. Using this technique is faster than recording a new macro to do the job. Before creating the new macro, you want to become familiar with the Visual Basic Editor. First, you open the workbook **Catalog3.xls**.

Opening the workbook:

1. Start Excel

2. Open the workbook **Catalog3.xls**

3. Click the **Enable Macros** button when the Microsoft Excel dialog box appears

Now you can open the Visual Basic Editor and investigate its several windows.

Opening the Visual Basic Editor:

1. Ensure that the **Welcome** worksheet is active

2. Click **Tools**, point to **Macro**, and click **Visual Basic Editor**. Maximize the Visual Basic Editor window. The Visual Basic Editor opens (see Figure 12.21)

tip: *Your window contents and arrangement may be different from Figure 12.21*

tip: *The Project Explorer window displays "Project—VBAProject" in its Title bar. If the Project Explorer window does not appear on your screen (see Figure 12.21), press **Ctrl+R** to open it*

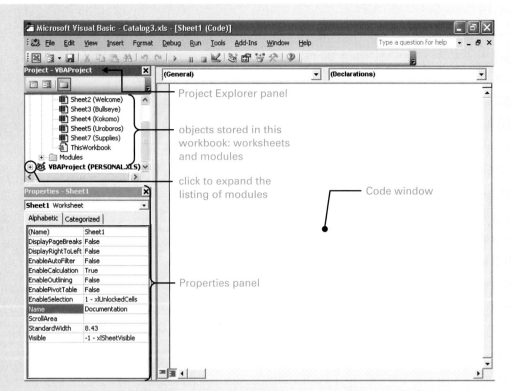

FIGURE 12.21

The Visual Basic Editor window

3. Click and drag down the Project Explorer window's vertical scroll box to reveal the object labeled *Modules* (see Figure 12.21)

4. If necessary, click the expand button (the **+** symbol) to the left of the Modules folder in the Project Explorer window to reveal Module1, which contains the macros you recorded

5. Right-click **Module1** and then click **View Code** to display the right panel of the Visual Basic Editor in the Code window (see Figure 12.22)

6. If necessary, click the **Maximize** button in the Code window to enlarge the Code window

Editing a Macro with the Visual Basic Editor

The Visual Basic Editor displays several windows that allow you to review and alter various parts of your Excel project. A **project** contains forms, modules, and the Excel workbook objects. You can see two of these elements, a workbook with its worksheets and a module, in the Project Explorer window. **Workbook objects** are a workbook's worksheets and chart sheets. A special object called ThisWorkbook provides a convenient way to refer to all of the workbook's objects with one name (see Figure 12.22). A project may contain one or more forms. A **form** is a dialog box that appears in response to a user-defined command key click or other event. Clicking one of the workbook's sheet names in the Project Explorer window activates its properties in the Properties window. In the Properties window, for example, you can change a worksheet's name. Double-clicking a module or form in the Project Explorer reveals its properties in the Properties window and reveals module code in the Code window.

FIGURE 12.22

Visual Basic Editor with
Module1 code visible

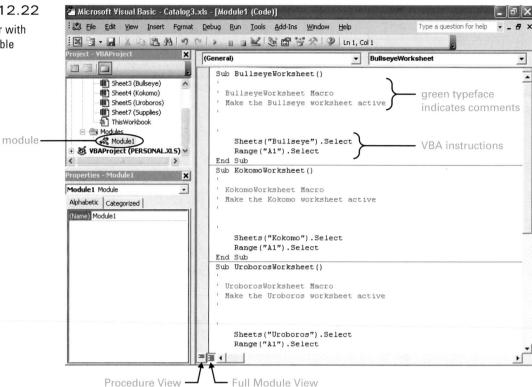

Procedure View ——|—— Full Module View

Creating a sub procedure and copying code from another sub procedure:

1. Drag the Code window scroll button down until you can see the ReturnToMenu code in the Code window, and then click anywhere *inside* the ReturnToMenu sub procedure code

2. Click the **Procedure View** button located in the lower-left corner of the Code window. Only the ReturnToMenu code is visible in the Code window

3. Press **Ctrl+A** to select all of the ReturnToMenu code, and then press **Ctrl+C** to copy the code to the Clipboard

4. Click the **Full Module View** button in the lower-left corner of the Code window, and then click anywhere *below* the "End Sub" statement of the ReturnToMenu macro to deselect the code and position the insertion point

5. Click **Ctrl+V** to paste the code into the Code window. The Code window displays both the original ReturnToMenu code and the newly inserted copy

6. Drag the mouse through the code line **ReturnToMenu()** in the copy of the sub procedure

7. Type **DocWorksheet()** to rename the sub procedure

8. Double-click **ReturnToMenu** in the comment line of the DocWorksheet sub procedure and type **DocWorksheet**

9. Double-click **Welcome** in the second comment line of the DocWorksheet sub procedure and type **Documentation**

10. Double-click the word **Welcome** in the DocWorksheet sub procedure code line *Sheets("Welcome").Select* and then type **Documentation** (see Figure 12.23)

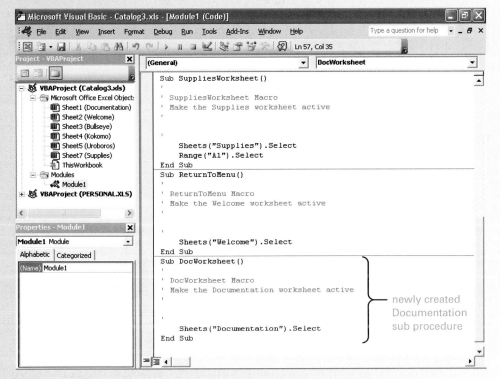

FIGURE 12.23
Modifying a copied sub procedure

11. Press **Alt+Q** to close the Visual Basic Editor window

Now you have code that you can execute to make the Documentation worksheet active. To finish this work, you will create a new button and attach the cloned code to it.

Creating a Documentation button and attaching code to it:

1. Press and hold the **Ctrl** key, click the **Bullseye Glass** button on the Welcome worksheet, release the **Ctrl** key, press **Ctrl+C** to copy the button to the Clipboard, and press **Ctrl+V** to paste the button onto the worksheet

2. Drag the copied button to the right of the original Bullseye Glass button until the bottom edges of the two buttons are aligned

3. Drag the mouse through the copied button's caption and then type **Documentation**

4. Move the mouse to the border of the Documentation button. When it changes to a four-headed arrow, right-click the button, click **Assign Macro** in the shortcut menu, click **DocWorksheet** in the list of macro names, and click **OK**

5. Click cell **A1** to deselect the Documentation button

Deleting a Macro

If you make a mistake while recording a macro and don't want to bother editing the recorded macro to correct it, you can delete a macro and start over. Although you do not need to delete any macros you have recorded in this session, you should know how to do so.

---

task *reference*   Deleting a Macro

- Click **Tools**, point to **Macro**, and click **Macros**
- Click the name of the macro in the Macro name list that you want to delete
- Click the **Delete** button
- Click **Yes** to confirm the deletion

Writing Sub Procedures

With the exception of the DocWorksheet procedure, you have created VBA sub procedures using the macro recorder. Using the macro recorder to create sub procedures has the advantage of precisely reproducing your keystrokes and commands. However, there are a number of situations where the macro recorder falls short. You cannot use the macro recorder to create a sub procedure that repetitively executes a series of instructions. Such a structure, called *repetition* or *looping* by programmers, repeats a series of steps until a special condition is recognized to halt the repetition. Excel applications developers use looping frequently. Another feature that the macro recorder is incapable of recording is branching. *Branching*, or *selection*, is a program structure that evaluates a condition and then takes one of two actions based on the outcome of condition evaluation. Selection is vital to writing robust VBA sub procedures. It allows you to evaluate whether the user's response is appropriate or not. Similar in design to the IF function, selection allows you to write an unlimited number of VBA statements for each of the two possible outcomes of a test—true or false. By writing your own sub procedures, or subroutines, you can take advantage of the full power of VBA and break the limits imposed by using the macro recorder alone.

help yourself *Press **Alt+F11** to open the Visual Basic Editor (VBE) and maximize its window. Press **F1**, type **writing sub procedures** in the Search text box of the Microsoft Visual Basic Help task pane, and press **Enter**. Click the hyperlink **Writing a Sub Procedure**. Maximize the Help screen if necessary. Take a moment to read the Help information. Click the Help screen **Close** button when you are finished, and press **Alt+Q** to close the Visual Basic Editor window and return to your Excel worksheet*

Writing a Sub Procedure That Executes Whenever the Workbook Opens

Mike would like to have the Welcome worksheet active whenever the Catalog workbook opens regardless of which worksheet was active when the workbook was closed. In addition, he would like to remove the worksheet tabs so that customers have to use the buttons you created to move from one worksheet to another.

To run a VBA sub procedure automatically whenever you open the **Catalog3.xls** workbook, you create an event procedure. An *event procedure* is one that executes whenever a particular event occurs. For example, a click event occurs when a user clicks a button, a worksheet becomes active, or the user presses the Enter key when completing an Excel formula. There are a large number of events to which Excel can react. The workbook open event, which occurs whenever a workbook opens, is the event for which you will write a sub procedure. You write the workbook open sub procedure next.

Writing a Workbook_Open event procedure:

1. Press **Alt+F11** to open the Visual Basic Editor

2. In the Project Explorer window, double-click the **ThisWorkbook** entry in *VBAProject(Catalog3.xls) Microsoft Excel Objects.* An empty Code window opens, and a blinking cursor appears in the Code window

tip: *If necessary, click the + outline control to open the ThisWorkbook heading if it is not visible*

3. Click the leftmost list box at the top of the Code window and then click **Workbook.** The rightmost list box at the top of the Code window displays *Open,* and two code lines automatically appear in the Code window

4. Between the two code lines, type the following code. Press **Tab** at the beginning of the first line—before typing it—to indent the comment line four spaces. (Excel automatically indents subsequent lines by the same amount.) Press **Enter** after typing each line (see Figure 12.24). Type *no* spaces in the second and fourth lines below

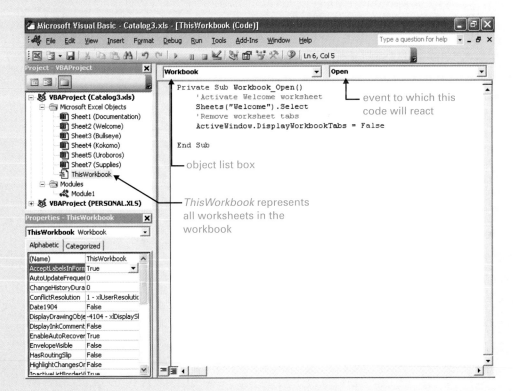

F I G U R E 12.24

Workbook_Open event procedure

'**Activate Welcome worksheet**

Sheets("Welcome").Select

'**Remove worksheet tabs**

ActiveWindow.DisplayWorkbookTabs = False

5. Press **Alt+Q** to close the Visual Basic Editor window and return to the workbook. The Welcome worksheet appears

EXCEL

---

*another**word***

. . . on Adding Code to the Workbook_Open Event Procedure

If you want to include additional code in the Workbook_Open event procedure but are not sure how to write the code, record the steps and copy them to the Workbook Open procedure

---

You decide to test the new code. It will be easy to spot any mistakes in short code segments like this.

Testing the Workbook_Open event procedure:

1. Click the **Supplies** worksheet tab to activate that worksheet prior to saving the workbook. Doing this will help you determine whether the Workbook_Open event procedure is working properly

2. Save the changed workbook

3. Close the **Catalog3.xls** workbook

4. Click the **Open** button on the Standard toolbar, locate and click the **Catalog3.xls** workbook in the Open dialog box, and click the **Open** button to open the workbook

5. Click the **Enable Macros** button. Excel opens the workbook, makes the Welcome worksheet active, and removes all worksheet tabs (see Figure 12.25)

FIGURE 12.25

Testing the Workbook_Open event procedure

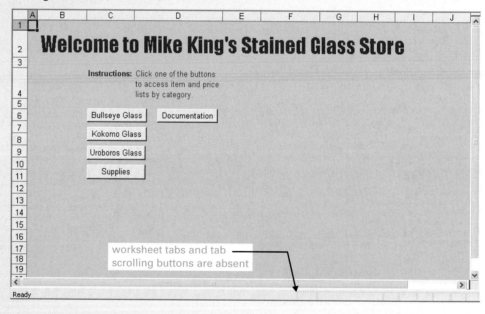

Getting Data with the InputBox Function

Mike wants to add a little security to the Catalog workbook by requiring a workbook user to enter a password before the workbook opens. The password that Mike has selected is the word *Excel*. Later, you can change the password if you want. Remember the password!

The logical location for the password code is in the Workbook_Open event code— the VBA code that Excel executes first when you attempt to open a workbook. Inserting

FIGURE 12.26

Example InputBox display

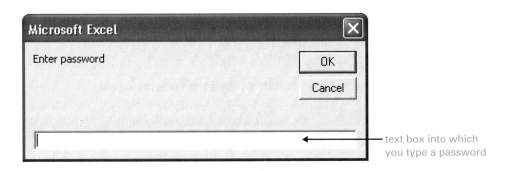

text box into which
you type a password

password protection in VBA code requires just a few new elements including the InputBox function and the If-Then-Else selection structure.

The InputBox function displays a dialog box with a text box, into which a user can type a string of characters and two buttons: OK and Cancel. The InputBox function has the following form:

InputBox (prompt, title)

Prompt is the message displayed within the dialog box, and it explains what the user is to input. *Title* is the title that appears in the dialog box's Title bar. Figure 12.26 shows the InputBox display that Mike wants you to create.

You modify the Workbook_Open code with code to implement the password requirement.

Writing an InputBox function:

1. Press **Alt+F11** to open the Visual Basic Editor

2. In the Project Explorer window, double-click the **ThisWorkbook** entry in *VBAProject(Catalog3.xls)\Microsoft Excel Objects.* The Workbook_Open event procedure appears in the Code window

3. Click the empty line above End Sub, ensuring that the blinking insertion point is indented four characters, and then press **Enter** to open up another blank line

4. Type **strAnswer = InputBox("Enter password")** and then press **Enter** (see Figure 12.27)

```
Private Sub Workbook_Open()
    'Activate Welcome worksheet
    Sheets("Welcome").Select
    'Remove worksheet tabs
    ActiveWindow.DisplayWorkbookTabs = False

    strAnswer = InputBox("Enter password")

End Sub
```

FIGURE 12.27

Completed InputBox
function code

5. Press **Alt+Q** to close the Visual Basic Editor, and then save and close the workbook

6. Click the **Open** button on the Standard toolbar, click **Catalog3.xls** in the Open dialog box, click **Open**, and click **Enable Macros**. Excel displays an input box with the prompt Enter password

7. Type your last name in the text box and then click the **OK** button. The dialog box disappears

The InputBox function works correctly. The next step is to add VBA code to process the information a user enters in the InputBox text box, ensuring that it is the prescribed password.

Controlling Program Flow with a Selection Structure

VBA provides several selection structures for testing conditions and executing alternative sets of instructions based on the outcome of the test. The most frequently used selection structure is If-Then. The form of the If-Then structure you will use, with its optional Else clause, is as follows:

```
If <condition to test> Then
    <true statement code lines>
Else
    <false statement code lines>
End if
```

Where <condition to test> is an expression that results in true or false (such as Name = "Fred", or C15 < 12). Expressions usually involve using comparison operators (<, <=, >, >=, =, <>) to compare the left side of the expression with the right side. The <true statement code lines> are one or more VBA statements that are executed if the condition is true. The <false statement code lines> contain the code lines that are executed if the condition is false. Only one set of code statements can be executed.

You will enhance the password enforcement code by adding an If-Then-Else selection structure to test whether the user has entered the correct password.

Writing an If-Then-Else selection structure:

1. Press **Alt+F11** to open the Visual Basic Editor

2. In the Project Explorer window, double-click **ThisWorkbook**

3. Click the empty line above End Sub, ensuring that the blinking insertion point is indented four characters

4. Type the following lines, pressing **Enter** at the end of each line. Press **Tab**, when needed, to indent the lines to match the code shown here and in Figure 12.28

   If UCase(strAnswer) <> "EXCEL" Then

      MsgBox "Incorrect password", vbOKOnly, "Error"

   Else

      Exit Sub

   End if

   tip: *Make sure you have spelled EXCEL correctly in the above code. When you complete this code, you will find it almost impossible to open the workbook if you forget the password or misspell it in the code above*

5. Press **Alt+Q** to close the Visual Basic Editor, and then save and close the workbook

6. Open **Catalog3.xls** and click **Enable Macros**. Excel displays an input box with the prompt Enter password

7. Type **excel** (lowercase is fine) in the text box and then click the **OK** button. The dialog box disappears

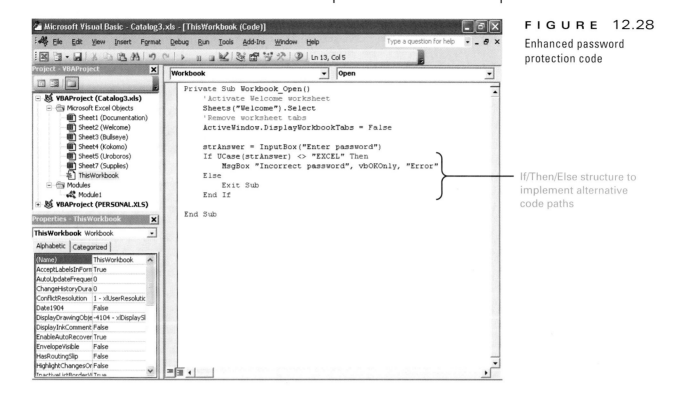

FIGURE 12.28

Enhanced password protection code

If/Then/Else structure to implement alternative code paths

The condition part of the If statement is

```
UCase(strAnswer) <> "EXCEL"
```

UCase is a function that converts the string stored in strAnswer to uppercase, holding the user's input password. Excel compares it to the uppercase string EXCEL. The relational operator <> means "not equal to." So the condition determines whether the uppercase version of the input password is not equal to EXCEL. If that is true, then the MsgBox statement executes. The MsgBox statement displays a dialog box and allows the user to click the OK button. (vbOKOnly places only the OK button on the dialog box.) If the condition is false, then the statement Exit Sub executes. It exits the sub procedure without further processing—the statement executed for a correct password.

Writing an Iteration Structure

The password checking code you have written does not actively prevent a user from opening the workbook. The code displays an error message when it detects an incorrect password and then exits the sub procedure, allowing the workbook to open. Because typing mistakes can occur, Mike wants the password procedure to allow the user up to three attempts to enter a correct password. On the third failed attempt, the workbook will close. Your task in finishing up the password protection scheme is to implement two new features.

First, you will create an *iteration* structure—one or more statements that execute a series of VBA instructions repeatedly *until* a condition is true or *while* a condition is true. (Iteration structures are also called loops.) Second, you will code a VBA statement that closes the workbook following the third incorrect attempt to enter a password.

Excel provides several ways to repeatedly execute a section of code. The one you will use is the For-Next structure, which has the following form:

```
For <counter> = <start value> To <end value>
   Statement₁
   Statement₂
   . . .
   Statementₙ

Next <counter>
```

The <counter> is the initial value of a counter that keeps track of how many times the statements within the loop, Statement$_1$, Statement$_2$, and so on, are executed. The <start value> is the first value that the counter takes on, and <end value> is the highest value, or limit, that the counter takes on. Statements between the For and Next statements are executed until the value of the <counter> exceeds the <end value> or until code within the loop exits the looping structure. To allow someone three attempts to enter a password, you will code a loop using the following For statement:

```
For intCount = 1 To 3
```

where intCount is the name you will give to the counter variable that keeps track of the number of times a loop executes.

Writing an iteration structure:

1. Press **Alt+F11** to open the Visual Basic Editor

2. In the Project Explorer window, double-click the **ThisWorkbook** entry

3. In the Code window, click immediately to the left of the first letter in the code line strAnswer = InputBox("Enter password"), and then press **Enter** to open a new line

4. Press the **up arrow** key to move to the line above the InputBox code line and type **For intCount = 1 To 3**

5. Press the **down arrow** key, press the **Home** key to move the insertion point in front of the first letter of the InputBox line, and then press **Tab** to indent the line

6. Repeat step 5 for the next five lines to indent each of them to the next tab stop

7. With the insertion point at the beginning of *End If,* press the **down arrow** key, ensure that the insertion point is lined up with the letter *F* in the For statement seven lines above it, and type **Next intCount** (two words)

8. Press **Enter**

9. Type **'Exhausted loop means allowable attempts exceeded** and then press **Enter**. Notice that Excel colors comments green

tip: *Be sure to type an apostrophe as the first character in the preceding line so that Excel interprets the line as commentary, not code. Your Workbook_Open event procedure should match Figure 12.29*

```
Private Sub Workbook_Open()
    'Activate Welcome worksheet
    Sheets("Welcome").Select
    'Remove worksheet tabs
    ActiveWindow.DisplayWorkbookTabs = False

    For intCount = 1 To 3
        strAnswer = InputBox("Enter password")
        If UCase(strAnswer) <> "EXCEL" Then
            MsgBox "Incorrect password", vbOKOnly, "Error"
        Else
            Exit Sub
        End If
    Next intCount
    'Exhausted loop means allowable attempts exceeded

End Sub
```

iteration structure statements

F I G U R E 12.29

Workbook_Open event procedure with iteration structure

The preceding code executes the InputBox code line and the If-Then-Else code lines up to three times, if necessary. On the third unsuccessful attempt, the MsgBox code executes and displays the error message to the user and then jumps to the line of code following the Next statement.

Closing a Workbook with VBA Code

The line following the "Exhausted loop" comment is where you will place a code line to close the workbook. That works because the only possible way to reach the line following the Next statement is looping three times and filling in the incorrect password each of the three times. Otherwise, if the user enters the correct password—even on the third attempt, then control transfers outside the Workbook_Open event procedure entirely. The statement to close the current workbook is

```
ThisWorkbook.Close
```

ThisWorkbook is the symbolic name for the entire workbook, an object, and *Close* is a method that operates on the object ThisWorkbook. A ***method*** is an action that takes place on behalf of the object to which it is attached.

You make the final modification to the Workbook_Open event procedure by adding the statement to close the workbook when the user fails after three times to enter a correct password.

Modifying the Workbook_Open event:

1. With the Visual Basic Editor open and the Workbook_Open event procedure displayed in the Code window, ensure that the insertion point is below the "Exhausted loop" comment line

2. Type **ThisWorkbook.Close** (see Figure 12.30)

tip: *As you type statements such as the preceding one, you will notice that Excel displays pop-up help, called IntelliSense showing allowed choices to add to the code. Simply ignore the help and continue typing*

3. Press **Alt+Q** to close the Visual Basic Editor

4. Click the **Save** button on the Standard toolbar to save your changes

5. Close the workbook, but leave Excel running

EXCEL

FIGURE 12.30

Completed
Workbook_Open
event procedure

```
Private Sub Workbook_Open()
    'Activate Welcome worksheet
    Sheets("Welcome").Select
    'Remove worksheet tabs
    ActiveWindow.DisplayWorkbookTabs = False

    For intCount = 1 To 3
        strAnswer = InputBox("Enter password")
        If UCase(strAnswer) <> "EXCEL" Then
            MsgBox "Incorrect password", vbOKOnly, "Error"
        Else
            Exit Sub
        End If
    Next intCount
    'Exhausted loop means allowable attempts exceeded
    ThisWorkbook.Close
End Sub
```

closes the current workbook, ——→ (points to `ThisWorkbook.Close`)
but leaves Excel running

Now you can test your work. First, you will pretend to forget the password and observe what Excel does to protect the workbook. In the second test, you will enter the correct password (Excel) the first time and observe the workbook open.

Testing password protection:

1. Open **Catalog3.xls** and click the **Enable Macros** button

2. Type **mcgraw** in the text box and press **Enter**. (Pressing the Enter key is the same as clicking the OK button in this case.) The Error dialog box appears

3. Press **Enter** to dismiss the Error dialog box

4. Repeat steps 2 and 3 two more times, typing **macros** and then **testing** in step 2 for the second and third attempts, respectively. After you enter the third incorrect password and press Enter, Excel closes the workbook

Wonderful! Entering an incorrect password three times in a row works correctly—the workbook closes. Now, try entering the correct password, Excel, to ensure that it opens the workbook.

Entering the correct password:

1. Open **Catalog3.xls** and click the **Enable Macros** button. The Microsoft Excel password dialog box appears

tip: *To prove that the password is case insensitive, you will use odd capitalization but correct spelling of the password in the next step*

2. Type **excEL** (three lowercase letters followed by two uppercase letters) in the text box and press **Enter**. The workbook opens and displays the Welcome worksheet. Notice that the worksheet tabs and tab scroll buttons are absent

3. Close the **Catalog3.xls** workbook

Writing Custom Functions

Although Microsoft Excel has a large number of built-in functions, chances are that Excel does not have a few functions you work with regularly. If this is the case, you can create your own custom functions using VBA code. Any function you create is called a *user-defined function*, or *UDF*. Like sub procedures, you place user-defined functions in modules.

Mike wants you to insert a customer invoice worksheet as the last worksheet in the Catalog workbook. Mike has created the basic invoice worksheet in a workbook called ex12ArtGlassInvoice. He will use the invoice worksheet to create and print invoices for his large accounts. Excel does not supply two functions in its built-in functions that Mike needs to complete his invoice worksheet. One of the missing functions computes a discount percentage for qualifying customer orders based on the number of units ordered for each item. A second function that Mike wants determines whether the customer's order is tax exempt or not. If not, then it calculates the tax owed based on the tax rate in his home state, Nebraska, and charges the customer accordingly.

Differentiating between Functions and Sub Procedures

A function and a sub procedure are similar because they both contain a sequence of VBA code lines. They both appear in a module attached to a workbook. Their purposes are different, however. A sub procedure contains VBA statements that affect a worksheet or workbook. On the other hand, custom function cannot delete a worksheet column, format worksheet cells, insert a worksheet, or perform an action that alters a workbook. Unlike a sub procedure, a custom function can only return a value to a worksheet formula.

Custom functions contain VBA statements that start with *Function* instead of *Sub*. The end of a function is marked with *End Function*, instead of *End Sub*. At least one statement in a function must assign the function name to a value or expression that is the result of the function prior to the end of the function. The general form of a custom function is the following:

```
Private Function <function name> (argument₁,...,argumentₙ) _
As <function data type>
    <one or more VBA statements>
    <function name> = <expression>

    . . .

End Function
```

Opening the Invoice Workbook

Before writing any custom functions, you will open the invoice worksheet (**ex12ArtGlassInvoice.xls**) that Mike has created and then write functions to perform the invoicing operation. He also mentions that another person wrote a VBA sub procedure to clear the invoice entries that do not contain formulas. The workbook has protection turned on so that anyone entering data can press the Tab key to move from one cell to another. There are some cells that require formulas that you are to write. You open the ex12ArtGlassInvoice worksheet next.

Opening the Invoice workbook:

1. Locate and open **ex12ArtGlassInvoice.xls**

2. Click the **Enable macros** button in the dialog box that appears warning you that the workbook contains macros

The workbook opens (see Figure 12.31)

FIGURE 12.31

Invoice workbook

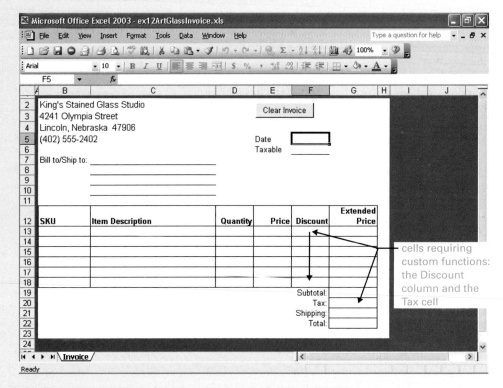

3. Save the workbook as **Invoice2** (see Figure 12.31)

4. Press the **Tab** key a dozen times. Notice which cells Excel activates. Excel moves to the next unlocked cell on the Invoice page, making it convenient for anyone to fill out the invoice row by row

Creating Custom Functions

Mike points out that the custom function you will write computes a discount based on the quantity ordered for each item. The custom function, to be called Discount, will occupy the cell range F13:F18. Cell G20 will hold the custom formula that computes tax, if any, on the sale. The custom function will be called *Tax*.

Mike explains how he calculates a discount, if any, for each invoice line. Discounts are based on the quantity of each item a customer purchases. If a customer purchases three items, for example, there are three entries on the invoice, one for each item, in cells B13 through G15. If the item quantity is less than 50, there is no discount. The purchase price of any item in which the quantity is between 50 and 99 receives a 5 percent discount. The discount for a quantity greater than 99 of any one item is 10 percent.

Rather than write a formula to implement this three-tier discount scheme, Mike wants you to write a custom function called Discount. The Discount function will have two arguments. The function uses the values in cells passed as arguments to calculate an answer that the function returns to the cell containing the function. The answer returned by a function can be any of several data types allowed by VBA. You indicate the function answer's data type with a type that follows the As phrase at the right end of the function's prototype statement (see Figure 12.32). The ***prototype statement*** is the first line of the function definition.

The ***data type*** of a variable reveals the type of information that is stored in the memory space.

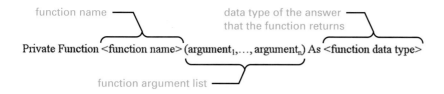

Writing a custom function to calculate a discount percentage:

1. Press **Alt+F11** to open the Visual Basic Editor, click **Insert** on the menu bar, and then click **Module** to create a new module. The Visual Basic Editor creates Module1 and places it below the module InvoiceModules

2. In the code window, type the following VBA code (press **Enter** at the end of each line except the last line, End If). Press the **Tab** key before typing the second line (a comment) to indent it, and press the **Tab** key, as needed, to match the indentation of the code below

```
Private Function Discount(Quantity) As Single
    'Calculate the discount percentage
    If Quantity > = 100 Then
        Discount = 0.1
    ElseIf Quantity > = 50 Then
        Discount = 0.05
    Else
        Discount = 0
    End If
```

tip: *When you complete the Private Function line, Excel automatically adds* End Function *to the last line in the function*

Next, you will implement the second function called *Tax.* The Tax function will compute sales tax for any sale that is taxable. If a sale is not taxable, the computed tax will be zero. If a sale is taxable, then cell F6 will contain Y (for yes). If it is not, then cell F6 will contain N (for no). The taxable status can be either uppercase or lowercase, because the Tax function will recognize either one.

Writing a custom function to compute sales tax:

1. Move the blinking cursor in the Code window to the end of the End Function line and press **Enter** to move to the beginning of a new line

2. Type the following VBA code (press **Enter** at the end of each line except the last line, End If):

```
Private Function Tax(Subtotal, Taxable) As Currency
    'Calculate Tax
    If UCase(Taxable) = "N" Or UCase(Taxable) = "NO" Then
        Tax = 0
    Else
        Tax = Subtotal * 0.075
    End If
```

Figure 12.33 shows the completed Discount and Tax custom functions

FIGURE 12.33

Completed Tax custom
function

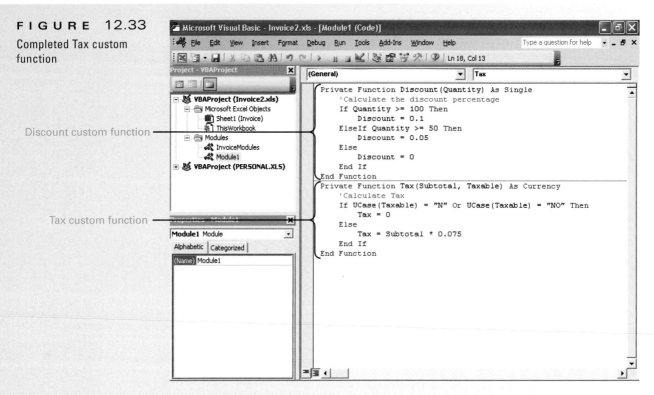

Discount custom function

Tax custom function

3. Press **Alt+Q** to close the Visual Basic Editor and display the Invoice
worksheet

Using Custom Functions

Once you have defined one or more functions, you can activate a worksheet cell and
write an expression containing the function and any arguments, such as cell references,
that you pass to the function. Suppose that you entered information about a purchased
item in the first row, row 13, of the invoice list of line items. You enter the SKU, or
stockkeeping unit, of the item in cell B13, the item description in cell C13, the quantity
(sheets of glass) in cell D13, and the price per unit in cell E13. In the cell range F13:F18
are expressions that reference the Discount function you defined to compute the percentage discount. (All the cells in the invoice are formatted to display percentages, currency, or integers as needed.) In cell F13, for example, you would write the expression

```
=Discount(D13)
```

The argument, cell D13, references the cell containing the quantity of that item ordered. When Excel computes the discount using your Discount function, the reference
to cell D13 is passed to the function and, in effect, is substituted for every occurrence of
the word Quantity in the function definition. The function returns the result, zero in
this case, to the cell containing the expression.

In order to make changes to the Invoice worksheet, you first disengage protection
so that you can alter the contents of cells.

Removing worksheet protection:

1. Click **Tools** and point to **Protection**

2. Click **Unprotect Sheet**. Excel removes protection from the Invoice
worksheet

With protection removed, you are free to write the Discount expression in a locked cell. Once all new formulas are in place, you will reestablish worksheet protection.

Using a custom function in a worksheet cell:

1. Click cell **F13** and type **=Discount(D13)** (see Figure 12.34)

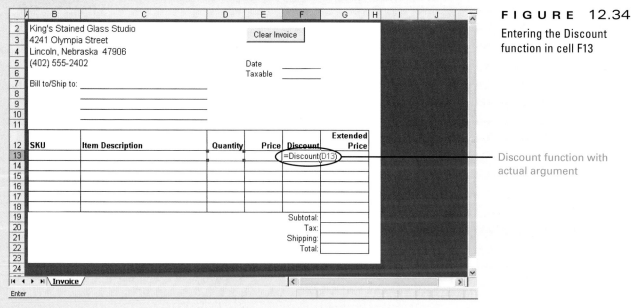

FIGURE 12.34

Entering the Discount function in cell F13

Discount function with actual argument

2. Press **Enter** to complete the expression

3. Click cell **F13**, click and drag the fill handle through the cell range **F14:F18**, and then release the mouse. The Discount expression appears in cell range F13:F18, though no value appears in the cells because the argument of each function refers to an empty cell

The final function you will write is the one to calculate tax, if any. The Tax function will appear in cell G20. The Tax function contains two arguments. The first argument refers to cell G19, which contains the subtotal. The second argument refers to cell F6, which indicates whether the transaction is taxable or not. When an invoice is completed, cell F6 will contain *Yes* or *No*, which indicates the taxable status. In other words, if cell F6 contains either "n" or "no," then the taxable amount returned by the Tax function is zero. Otherwise, tax is computed at 7.5 percent of the subtotal.

Writing the worksheet expression containing the Tax function:

1. Click cell **G20** and type **=Tax(G19,F6)** (see Figure 12.35)

2. Press **Enter** to complete the expression. Excel displays nothing in cell G20 because the subtotal is empty, so the tax is currently zero

FIGURE 12.35

Entering the Tax function in cell G20

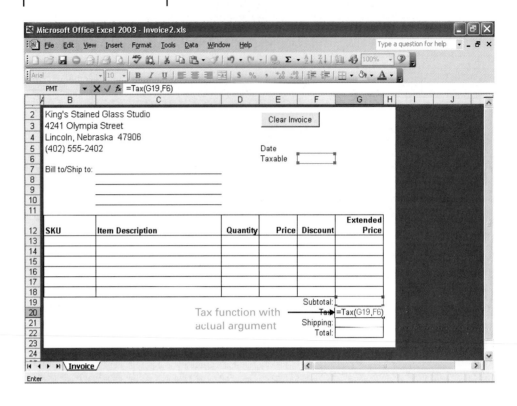

Cells in the fill-in fields such as Date, Taxable, Bill to/Ship to, the invoice lines, and Shipping are unlocked so that you can enter data into them. All other cells are locked to protect the formulas and labels they hold. With all formulas in place, protect your worksheet.

Restoring worksheet protection:

1. Click **Tools** and point to **Protection**

2. Click **Protect Sheet**. Excel displays the Protect Sheet dialog box

3. Click **OK** to finalize protection and accept the dialog box protection values displayed

4. Save the workbook

Testing Custom Functions

A simple way to test the worksheet is to type a few test values into a blank invoice.

Testing the Discount and Tax functions:

1. Click cell **F5**, type today's date, and press **Tab** to move to the next unlocked cell

2. In cell **F6**, type **yes**, and press **Tab** to move to the next unlocked cell—the first Bill to/Ship to entry

3. Fill out the shipping address with the following three lines, pressing **Tab** after finishing each line to move to the next line

Tobias Carling
12843 Glider Port Road
La Jolla, CA 92111

4. Press **Tab** to move to the first row just below the SKU label and enter the following lines for three items purchased. When you are finished, your invoice should match the one in Figure 12.36

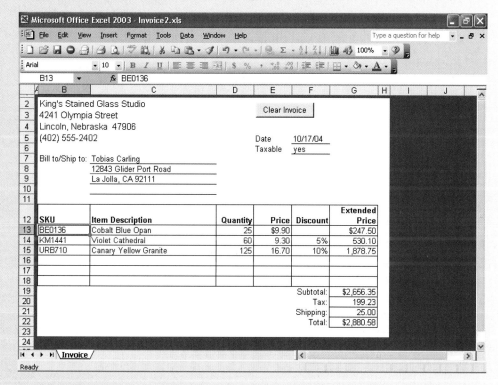

F I G U R E   12.36
Completed test invoice

5. Type **BE0136**, press **Tab**, type **Cobalt Blue Opal**, press **Tab**, type **25**, press **Tab**, type **9.9**, and press **Tab** to complete the first line and move to the beginning of the second one

6. In cell B14, type **KM1441**, press **Tab**, type **Violet Cathedral**, press **Tab**, type **60**, press **Tab**, type **9.3**, and press **Tab** to complete the second line and move to the beginning of the third one

7. In cell B15, type **URB710**, press **Tab**, type **Canary Yellow Granite**, press **Tab**, type **125**, press **Tab**, type **16.7**, and press **Tab** to complete the third invoice item line

8. Click cell **G21**, the Shipping cell, type **25**, and press **Enter**. Figure 12.36 shows the completed invoice. Compare your results to the figure

tip: *If the figure and your calculations do not match, recheck the values you entered and make changes where needed*

tip: *If you think your custom functions are incorrect, press **Alt+F11** and then compare your two functions to Figure 12.33. Make any necessary changes, press **Alt+Q** to move back to the worksheet, and press function key **F9** to recalculate the worksheet*

9. Clear the data you just entered by pressing the **Clear Invoice** button found near cell E2

Printing VBA Code

Printing your VBA code is an excellent way to document your work and preserve a hard copy of it.

---

task reference   **Printing VBA code**

- Click **Alt+F11**

- Double-click the module in the Project Explorer window containing the VBA code you want to print

- Click **File**, click the **Code** check box in the *Print What* panel

- Click the **Current Project** option button in the Range panel to select all of the code in a project, or click the **Current Module** option button in the Range panel to select only the current module

- Click **OK**

Printing the Discount and Tax function code:

1. Press **Alt+F11**

2. Double-click the **Module1** module in the Project Explorer window to reveal the Discount and Tax functions in the Code window

3. Click **File** and then click **Print**. The *Print—VBAProject* dialog box appears

4. Ensure that the **Current Module** option in the Range panel is selected, and ensure that the **Code** check box contains a checkmark (see Figure 12.37)

FIGURE 12.37

Preparing to print a code module

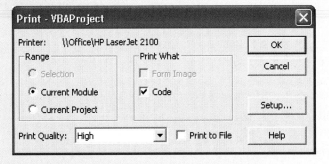

5. Click **OK**. Excel prints the code contained in the module

6. Press **Alt+Q** to close Visual Basic Editor and return to the worksheet

You are done with your work on the Invoice workbook, so save it and close Excel.

Saving the workbook and exiting Excel:

1. Click the **Save** button on the Standard toolbar

2. Click **File** and then click **Exit** to close Excel

making the grade

1. A _____ is where Excel stores VBA code.

2. A _____ contains forms, modules, and the Excel workbook objects.

3. You can use a _____ or repetition structure to repeat a series of VBA instructions.

4. The instruction that makes a decision to do one action or another is called a _____ structure.

5. You can pass a cell reference to a custom function through one of its _____.

SESSION 12.3 SUMMARY

Visual Basic for Applications, or VBA, is a powerful programming language that allows you to automate Excel procedures and create custom functions. Using the macro recorder, you can record your commands and keystrokes and capture them in a macro that you can replay whenever you need to. Alternatively, you can use the Visual Basic Editor to write macro instructions and custom functions by hand. Sub procedures that you create using the macro recorder are more limited than those that you code by hand. Recorded macros cannot perform If tests, and they cannot create code that loops. When you require selection (If) or iteration (loop) structures, you can manually write VBA code to implement sub procedures.

Sub procedures affect Excel objects in some way such as deleting columns, making a cell active, selecting a worksheet, and so on. Using the form menu, you can attach sub procedures to command buttons. By clicking a command button, the associated sub procedure executes. A specially named sub procedure, called Workbook_Open, automatically executes whenever the workbook containing it opens. The Workbook_Open sub procedure is a handy location for initialization procedures or welcome messages. Sub procedures in any open workbook are available to all open workbooks. Sub procedures that you want to be available to all workbooks should be saved in the Personal Macro Workbook.

Unlike sub procedures, custom functions cannot affect Excel objects. Instead, they return a value, or answer, to the cell containing the function. Functions return a value in VBA code by assigning the function name to the value or expression that computes a value.

MICROSOFT OFFICE SPECIALIST OBJECTIVES SUMMARY

- Protect a worksheet to preserve its integrity—MOS XL03E-3-1
- Hide the Personal Macro Workbook—MOS XL03S-3-4
- Set the macro security level—MOS XL03E-3-2
- Add and remove buttons from toolbars—MOS XL03E-5-1
- Record a macro instruction—MOS XL03E-5-2
- Examine and use the Visual Basic Editor—MOS XL03E-5-2

EXCEL

- Run macro instructions using a dialog box and a command button—MOS XL03E-5-2
- Create and modify Visual Basic code in the Visual Basic Editor—MOS XL03E-5-2
- Use Visual Basic objects, methods, properties, and variables—MOS XL03E-5-2
- Create a macro that automatically executes when you open a workbook—MOS XL03E-5-2
- Create custom functions—MOS XL03E-5-2

making the grade *answers*

SESSION 12.1

1. macro

2. function

3. Personal Macro

4. module

5. button

SESSION 12.2

1. module

2. project

3. looping or iteration

4. branching or selection

5. arguments

task reference *summary*

Task	Page #	Preferred Method
Recording a macro instruction	EX 12.8	• Click **Tools**, point to **Macro**, click **Record New Macro** • Type a macro name in the Macro name text box • Type a description in the Description text box • Click **OK** • Execute the tasks you want to record • Click the **Stop Recording** button
Assigning a macro to a button	EX 12.10	• Click **View,** point to **Toolbars,** click **Forms** • Click the **Button** tool in the Forms toolbar • Click a worksheet cell to place a button on the worksheet • Select the macro to assign to the button from the Macro name list • Click **OK** • Drag the mouse across the button's caption and type a descriptive name • Click any cell to deselect the button
Making buttons visible on a printout	EX 12.12	• Right-click the button you want to display on a printout • Click **Format Control** on the shortcut menu • Click the **Properties** tab • Click the **Print object** check box, and click **OK**
Selecting a button control without activating it	EX 12.16	• Press and hold the **Ctrl** key • Click the button on the worksheet • Release the **Ctrl** key
Unhiding a workbook	EX 12.20	• Click **Window** on the menu bar • Click **Unhide** • Click a workbook in the Unhide workbook list and then click **OK**

task reference summary

Task	Page #	Preferred Method
Hiding a workbook	EX 12.20	• Make active any worksheet of the workbook you want to hide • Click **Window** on the menu bar • Click **Hide**
Setting the macro security level	EX 12.21	• Click **Tools**, click **Options**, and click the **Security** tab • Click the **Macro Security** button • Click the security level option button of your choice • Click **OK** to close the Security dialog box, and click **OK** to close the Options dialog box
Opening the Visual Basic Editor	EX 12.24	• Click **Tools**, point to **Macro**, and click **Visual Basic Editor** or • Press **Alt+F11** or • Click **Tools**, point to **Macro**, and click **Macros** • Select the name of the macro you want to edit • Click the **Edit** button
Deleting a macro	EX 12.28	• Click **Tools**, point to **Macro**, and click **Macros** • Click the name of the macro in the Macro name list that you want to delete • Click the **Delete** button • Click **Yes** to confirm the deletion
Printing VBA Code	EX 12.44	• Click **Alt+F11** to open the Visual Basic Editor • Double-click the module in the Project Explorer containing the VBA code you want to print • Click **File** on the menu bar • Click the **Code** check box in the *Print What* panel • Click the **Current Project** option button in the Range panel to select all of the code in a project, or click the **Current Module** option button in the Range panel to select only the current module • Click **OK**

EXCEL

TRUE OR FALSE

1. Custom functions can affect Excel objects.

2. Recorded macros cannot perform IF tests and cannot create code that loops.

3. Sub procedures in any open workbook are available to all open workbooks.

4. A workbook can hold an unlimited number of modules.

5. Workbook objects are a workbook's worksheets and chart sheets.

6. You can set the Macro Security Level through Options found in the Tools menu bar.

FILL-IN

1. Excel stores in a(n) _____ all macros and user-defined functions.

2. Store a macro in Excel's _____ _____ workbook to make it available to any workbook you open.

3. A variable's _____ _____ restricts the type of information it holds.

4. You pass a cell reference to a sub procedure or a function through a(n) _____.

5. A(n) _____ is an action that takes place on behalf of the object to which it is attached.

6. The _____ statement is the first line of a function or sub procedure definition.

MULTIPLE CHOICE

1. When you create your own Excel function, it is called a
   a. new function.
   b. user-defined function.
   c. uniquely defined function.
   d. universally defined function.

2. How can you attach sub procedures to command buttons?
   a. by using the insert menu
   b. by using the attach menu
   c. by using the options menu
   d. by using the form menu

3. You cannot run a macro by
   a. assigning it to a keyboard shortcut.
   b. assigning it to a menu.
   c. assigning it to a toolbar button.
   d. assigning it to a cell.

4. "Single" data types are
   a. not defined. "Single" data type does not exist.
   b. single digit integers.
   c. whole numbers.
   d. single-precision numbers with decimal amounts.

5. An iteration structure is also called a(n)
   a. execution statement.
   b. loop.
   c. subroutine.
   d. code section.

review of concepts

REVIEW QUESTIONS

1. Buttons you add to an Excel worksheet to launch sub procedures normally do not appear on printouts. Why not?

2. You can create a macro by using the macro recorder or by creating it yourself in the Visual Basic Editor. Using the macro recorder is usually a simpler way to create a macro. Why would you use the Visual Basic Editor to create a sub procedure?

3. What is the main difference between a sub procedure and a user-defined (custom) function?

4. Why does Excel display a warning dialog box when you open a workbook containing macros?

CREATE THE QUESTION

For each of the following answers, create an appropriate, short question.

ANSWER	QUESTION
1. The macro recorder	_____
2. Save it in the Personal Macro Workbook	_____
3. A function can, but a sub procedure cannot	_____
4. The Visual Basic Editor	_____
5. The Project Explorer	_____
6. A selection structure	_____

1. The Voice of the Midwest, Radio Station WWWA

WWWA is a radio station in the Midwest that plays classical music. The station reaches an estimated audience of 1.5 million listeners. Seven full-time sales and marketing people are responsible for obtaining new advertisers to keep the station afloat. The station pays each salesperson a base salary ($2,000 per month), a commission on their month's sale amounts, and a bonus when applicable. The company awards a bonus to salespersons who sell more than $10,000 in new advertising each month. The bonus is 10 percent of the sales revenue over $10,000.

Margaret Perkins, the sales manager, wants you to help her create a worksheet to compute salespersons' commissions and bonuses with VBA code.

1. Open **ex12SalesQuota.xls** and save it as **<yourname>SalesQuota2.xls**. Click the **Documentation** tab. Type your name in the underlined cell to the right of the *User* label. Press the **Tab** key and type the current date adjacent to the *Date Revised* label

2. Click the **January Sales** worksheet tab, click cell **B8**, click the **Sort Ascending** button on the Standard toolbar, select cell range **C8:G8**, press and hold the **Ctrl** key, select cell range **C15:G15**, release the **Ctrl** key, and click the **Currency Style** button on the Formatting toolbar

3. Select cell range **C9:G14**, click the **Comma Style** button on the Formatting toolbar, select cell range **D8:D14**, click the **Percent Style** button on the Formatting toolbar, and click **Increase Decimal** button (also on the Formatting toolbar) *twice*

4. Press **Alt+F11** to open the Visual Basic Editor. Maximize the code window, if necessary. Click **Insert** on the menu bar, and click **Module** to insert a code module to the workbook

5. Click the code window and type the following code (indent as shown but write the function header on one line)

   Function Commission(TotalSales, CommRate As Currency) As Currency

   Commission = TotalSales * CommRate

   End Function

   Function Bonus(TotalSales, BonusRate, BonusFloor As Currency) As Currency

```
If TotalSales < BonusFloor Then
    Bonus = 0
Else
    Bonus = (TotalSales − BonusFloor) * BonusRate
End If
End Function
```

6. Press **Alt+Q** to close the Visual Basic Editor and return to the worksheet

7. Click **Tools**, click **Options**, click the **Security** tab, click the **Macro Security** button, click the **Medium** option button, click **OK**, and click **OK** again

8. Click cell **E8**, type **=Commission(C8,D8)**

9. Click cell **F8**, type **=Bonus(C8,B$3,B$4)**

10. Click cell **G8**, type **=B$2+E8+F8**, and press **Enter**

11. Select cell range **E8:G8**, press **Ctrl+C**, select cell range **E9:E14**, press **Ctrl+V**, click the **Paste Options** Smart Tag, and click the **Match Destination Formatting** option in the Paste Options list

12. Click cell **B15**, press **Ctrl+B**, click the **Align Right** button on the Formatting toolbar, type **Totals**, and press **Enter**

13. Select cell range **C8:C15**, click the **AutoSum** button on the Standard toolbar, select cell range **E8:G15**, click the **AutoSum** button on the Standard toolbar, and click any cell to deselect the cell range

14. Place your name in the January Sales worksheet header, print both the Documentation and January Sales worksheets, and print the January Sales worksheet formulas. (Click **Tools**, click **Options**, click the **View** tab, and click the **Formulas** check box, and click **OK**.) Remember to reverse the Formulas setting once you have printed the worksheet formulas

15. Press **Alt+F11**, and with the two functions displayed in the code window click **File**, click **Print**, click **OK**, and press **Alt+Q** to close the VB editor

16. Save your workbook and exit Excel

2. Creating a Macro to Trace Precedents of a Cell Range

Dr. Phil Hinman sometimes has difficulty tracking down errors in formulas he writes for various Excel workbooks he uses. For example, he believes there is a mistake in the formulas he has written for the grade book he maintains for his Philosophy 101 class, but he is having trouble locating it. He knows he can use the Formula Auditing command to locate cells that a formula references. He would like to generalize formula auditing so that he can select several cells and locate their precedent cells in one operation—something that Excel's Formula Auditing command cannot do. He has asked you to help him create a macro instruction he can call from any Excel workbook to audit one or more cell formulas. You will create a macro instruction and store it in your Personal Macro Workbook.

1. Open **ex12GradeBook.xls** and briefly review the Documentation page, and then click the **Phil 101** worksheet tab to move to that worksheet. Save the workbook as **<yourname>GradeBook2.xls**

2. Click cell **B16**, which contains a formula computing the lowest score for Exam 1

3. Click **Tools** on the menu bar, point to **Macro**, and then click **Record New Macro**

4. Type **PointOutPrecedents** in the *Macro name* text box, press **Tab**, hold down the **Shift** key and type **P** in the Shortcut key text box, and release the **Shift** key

5. Click the **Store macro in** list box, select **Personal Macro Workbook**, press **Tab**, type **Trace precedents of a selection of cells** in the Description text box, and click **OK**

6. Click **Tools**, point to **Formula Auditing**, click **Trace Precedents**, and click the **Stop Recording** button on the Stop Recording toolbar.

7. Click **Tools**, point to **Formula Auditing**, and click **Remove All Arrows**

8. Press **Alt+F11**, click the Microsoft Visual Basic window **Maximize** button, drag down the **Project—VBAProject** scroll box in the Project Explorer window until you see the VBAProject (PERSONAL.XLS) object

9. Click the **+** symbol to the left of VBAProject (PERSONAL.XLS) to reveal Modules, click the **+** symbol to the left of Modules (if necessary) to reveal its modules, and double-click the **Module1** object under Modules in the Project Explorer window to display the macro code in the Code window. (If you do not see the PointOutPrecedents macro, then double-click the next module in the list, Module2. Repeat step 9 as needed until you see PointOutPrecedents in the Code window)

10. Replace the Selection.ShowPrecedents code statement with the following code, and type your own name in place of <your name here> in the comment (match the indenting, too):

    'Modified by <your name here>
      For Each FormulaCell in Selection
        FormulaCell.ShowPrecedents
      Next

11. Click **File** on the menu bar, click **Print**, and click **OK** to print your code

12. Press **Alt+Q** to save the revised macro and close the VB Editor

13. Select cell range **B16:D18** and then press **Ctrl+Shift+P** (hold down **Ctrl** and **Shift**, tap and release **P**, and release **Ctrl** and **Shift**). Excel shows the precedent cells

14. Add your name to the worksheet header and print the Phil 101 worksheet

15. Save the workbook, exit Excel, and click **NO** when asked if you want to save changes to the Personal Macro Workbook so you do not alter anything for the next user

1. Ticket Sales at Latron Theater

Latron Theater is a local playhouse whose proceeds provide scholarships for performing arts students. In addition to raising money through ticket sales, the theater has a fund-raising campaign in which donors become playhouse members based on their donation amount. The top three levels of membership are platinum, gold, and silver. As a token of appreciation for the support of members in these levels, the theater provides them with discounted tickets for each performance.

The newest production, *The Wrong Door*, is opening in two months and tickets will go on sale to the public this Saturday. Playhouse members have the ability to purchase tickets two weeks before the general public. Madison Lawson is the director of membership at the theater and responsible for member ticket sales. Madison uses a workbook, called Ticket Sales, to record information on member ticket purchases. It is organized by membership level and contains each member's last name, the evening for which they bought tickets, and the quantity of tickets purchased. Madison has asked you to insert macros and formulas into the workbook to help her record and monitor ticket sales.

Begin by opening **ex12TicketSales.xls** (see Figure 12.38), unprotect the worksheet, and save the workbook as **<yourname>TicketSales2.xls**. Madison has already created a documentation sheet and typed *Main Page* into its tab. In cell A9, she wants you to insert in bold type **Modified By**, followed by your name in cell C9, and in cell A11, **Modified On:**, followed by the current date in cell C11. Create macros that will quickly take

Madison from the main page to cell A1 of each of the membership level worksheets. Name the macros **View_Platinum**, **View_Gold**, and **View_Silver**. In the assigned buttons, type **Platinum**, **Gold**, and **Silver**, and make the text bold. Place the buttons side by side starting in A15. Test your macros to make sure they run as Madison requested. She is appreciative of how the macros will make the workbook more efficient and asks you to add an additional macro. She would like a button placed in cells F1:G1 of each membership level worksheet that will take her back to cell A1 of the Main Page. Name the macro **Return_Main** and type **Return to Main Page** in the buttons. Hide the gridlines in the Main Page.

Madison wants to be able to determine total tickets sold and their proceeds by membership level and the total proceeds from the members. In row 33 of each membership level worksheet, enter "**Total <level> Tickets Sold:**", and type Platinum, Gold, and Silver where appropriate. In row 35 of these worksheets, enter "**Total <level> Ticket Proceeds:**" and enter "**Total Membership Ticket Proceeds:**" in row 37. In cell **E33**, enter a formula that will calculate the sum of the total number of tickets sold per each membership level. In cell **E35**, create a formula that results in the total proceeds for that level, based on ticket price and number of tickets sold. Using the Options dialog box, remove all worksheet tabs. Finally, in cell **E37**, enter a formula that will calculate the total sum of membership ticket proceeds. Save your work, and print both the Main Page and your code procedures in Visual Basic Editor.

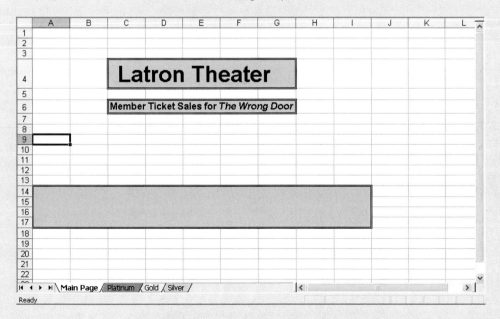

FIGURE 12.38

Latron Theater Main Page documentation worksheet

2. Automating an Employee Information Form

Bass Pro Fishing Outfitters, a large sporting goods store in Columbia, Missouri, conducts an annual review of each employee's performance and updates employee data using an Excel workbook. Corky Westfield, the human resources department manager, has developed a simple Excel workbook that meets his needs, but he'd like to automate it with buttons to open each of the workbook's worksheets. Corky wants you to create buttons and any VBA code needed to automate the workbook. In particular, he wants a button on the Cover Sheet that prints all three worksheets and buttons (and associated VBA code) on each of the two employee data worksheets that make the Cover Sheet active. He also asks you to remove the row and column headers and worksheet tabs from all three worksheets after you have tested the new macro instructions to open the worksheets.

Open **ex12EmployeeForm.xls** (see Figure 12.39) and save it as **<yourname>EmployeeForm2.xls**. Begin by recording a macro instruction named **PrintWorksheets** that prints all workbook worksheets. Create a button and attach the button to the PrintWorksheets macro. Label the button **Print Workbook** and place it over cell **C10**.

Record a macro to make the worksheet Employee Data 1 active and select the merged cells **C5:E5**. Name the macro **ED1Active**. Attach it to the Cover Sheet button labeled **Employee Data 1**. Record another macro (or copy and rename it in the VB editor) that makes the Employee Data 2 worksheet active and selects the merged cells **C5:E5** on that worksheet. Name the macro **ED2Active**. Attach it to the Cover Sheet button labeled **Employee Data 2**. Record a macro that makes the Cover Sheet worksheet active and selects cell **A1**. Name the macro **CoverActive**. Place a button on the Employee Data 1 worksheet and another button on the Employee Data 2 worksheet. Attach the CoverActive macro to both buttons. Shift-click each worksheet tab to group the worksheets, then click **Tools**, click **Options**, and click the **View** tab. Clear the **Row & column headers** check box and clear the **Sheet tabs** check box. Close the Options dialog box. Click the appropriate buttons to move to the Employee Data 1 worksheet. Fill out the white worksheet cells with data, move to the Employee Data 2 worksheet (go to the Cover Sheet and then to the Employee Data 2 worksheet), fill out white worksheet cells with data, and return to the Cover Sheet. Place your name in the header of all three worksheets, and click the **Print Workbook** button to print the three worksheets. Press **Alt+F11** to display the Visual Basic Editor and then print the Visual Basic code. Save your workbook.

FIGURE 12.39

Bass Pro Fishing Outfitters Cover Sheet worksheet

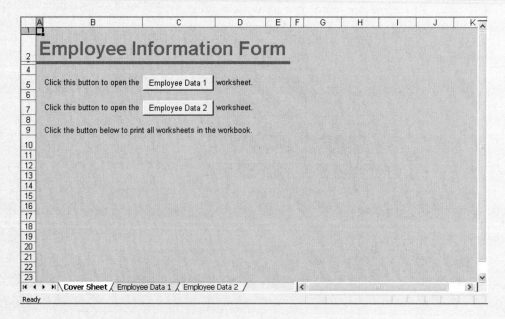

1. Viewing Audit Assignments at Dawson's Corporation

Dawson's Corporation is a specialty coffee company founded by Peter Dawson in 1974 in Oakland, California. Dawson's popularity grew quickly and Peter decided to both start a Web site and begin franchising the company throughout the United States. Within 10 years, Dawson's had grown to 119 locations with two corporate offices. A unique aspect of the company's Web site guarantees delivery of all orders within 24 hours. This is possible because the Web site routes each online order to the closest franchise location. That location then packages and delivers orders to each customer daily. It was crucial to Peter that each franchise truly represented Dawson's quality, so he designed the Quality Assurance Department to monitor each franchisee's location. Each of the corporate offices has such a department, with six analysts to supervise the quality and daily operations of the franchises.

The analysts are each assigned a new group of locations, called branches, each quarter to supervise. Peter requires that each branch be audited four times a year by a different analyst in order to give thorough audits. This requires the analysts to visit each of their assigned locations unannounced in order to see how the franchisees truly manage and run their locations and order fulfillment process. The new director of Quality Assurance, Julie Whitfield, feels that there needs to be stronger communication and support between the Oakland and Boston offices. Her first project was to prepare a new way to assign analysts their branches in an easy-to-understand accessible document. Since most of her communication with the analysts is through e-mail, she wants to make the audit assignments available on the company's network. Open **ex12AuditAssignments.xls**, which is Julie's workbook of audit assignments for next quarter. The worksheets are sorted alphabetically by analyst and include the branch number, franchisee name, state of the branch, and the office in which the analyst works.

Julie has given you the project of creating a Documentation sheet and macro buttons to help the analysts find their audit assignments for the quarter. Start by saving the workbook as **<yourname>AuditAssignments2.xls** and insert a Documentation sheet. In the Documentation sheet, enter the title **Dawson's Corporation**, and the subtitle **Audit Assignments for Third Quarter**. Beneath these, enter **Created for: Julie Whitfield**, **Created by:** followed with your name, and **Date:** followed with today's date. Next, you will create macros to take analysts to the audit assignments for their office.

Use the macro recorder to record the steps taken to move from the Documentation sheet to cell A1 of the Boston Assignments worksheet. Name the macro **Boston_Assignments**, and add the description **Displays the Boston office audit assignments worksheet**. Record the same steps for the Oakland Assignments, name the macro **Oakland_Assignments**, and add the description **Displays the Oakland office audit assignments**. Insert a button in cells D16:F17 for the Boston_Assignments macro. Type **View Boston Assignments** into the button. Insert another button into cells D20:F21 for Oakland_Assignments macro. Type the caption **View Oakland Assignments** for this button. Test your macros to ensure that they function correctly. Ensure that the buttons on the Documentation worksheet are visible on a printout of the Documentation worksheet.

Julie wants to use this workbook as her master copy for creating new workbooks. She needs you to create another macro, titled **New_Audit_Workbook**, which will open a new workbook with the same documentation information as her master workbook. Create a macro that copies the Documentation sheet titles, Created for:, Created by:, and Date:, then opens a new workbook, pastes the Documentation sheet information into the first worksheet, and types Documentation in the worksheet tab. Protect the Documentation worksheet. Save your work and print both the master Documentation sheet and the New_Audit_Workbook sub procedure in Visual Basic Editor.

2. Opening and Formatting Customer Data with a Macro

Fiddler Enterprises manufacturers guitars and sells them on the Internet. Whenever anyone visits its Web site, they have the opportunity to sign the guest book and indicate their product interests via a short questionnaire. All information collected from customers is kept private and used only by Fiddler Enterprises to enhance its customer service. Each week, Gary Wentworth downloads the Web customer survey information, which is in text form, and summarizes it in a nicely formatted workbook. The import and formatting process is repetitive and boring, so Gary wants you to create a macro instruction to import the text data, format the information, print the worksheet, and save the workbook.

Begin by opening **ex12Fiddler.xls**, and save it as **<yourname>Fiddler12.xls** (substituting your name for "<yourname>"). Create a macro, named **DataImport** to open the file **ex12FiddlerData.txt** using the Data, Import command: Turn on the macro recorder, click **Data**, click **Import**, navigate to the file **ex12FiddlerData.txt**, and record all the prompts. Indicate the following to the Wizard: data is delimited by tabs, do not import the column CustomerID, and store the data beginning in cell A1. Continue to record the following: Select the label row, apply boldface, and change the text color to red. Sort the data by the Product column (ascending) and then by the Model column (see Figure 12.40). Stop the recorder. Next, create a macro called **DataClear** to clear the query and all the data from the worksheet. Run the DataClear macro and then run the DataImport macro. Place your name in the worksheet header, print the worksheet, and print the two macros. Save the workbook.

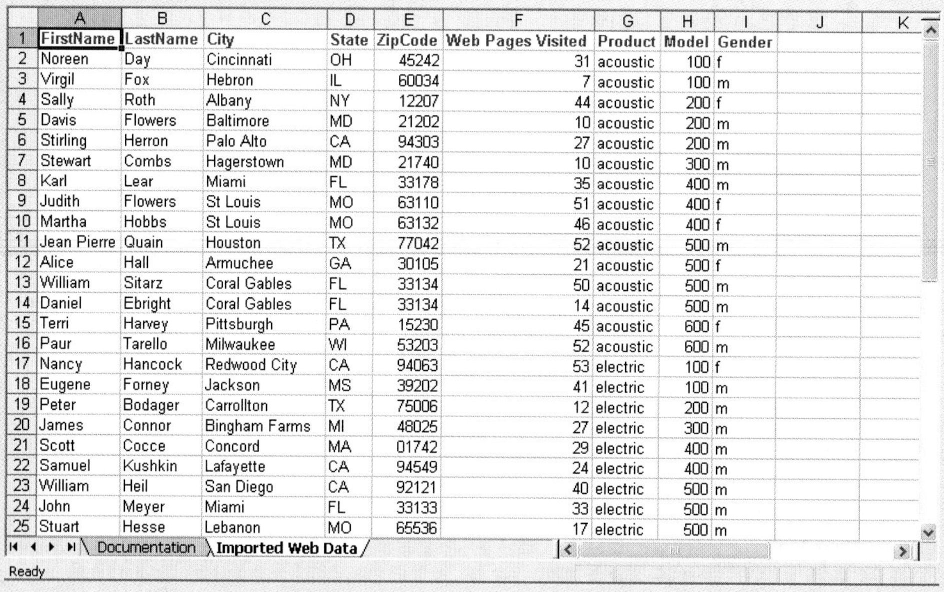

	A	B	C	D	E	F	G	H	I	J	K
1	**FirstName**	**LastName**	**City**	**State**	**ZipCode**	**Web Pages Visited**	**Product**	**Model**	**Gender**		
2	Noreen	Day	Cincinnati	OH	45242	31	acoustic	100	f		
3	Virgil	Fox	Hebron	IL	60034	7	acoustic	100	m		
4	Sally	Roth	Albany	NY	12207	44	acoustic	200	f		
5	Davis	Flowers	Baltimore	MD	21202	10	acoustic	200	m		
6	Stirling	Herron	Palo Alto	CA	94303	27	acoustic	200	m		
7	Stewart	Combs	Hagerstown	MD	21740	10	acoustic	300	m		
8	Karl	Lear	Miami	FL	33178	35	acoustic	400	m		
9	Judith	Flowers	St Louis	MO	63110	51	acoustic	400	f		
10	Martha	Hobbs	St Louis	MO	63132	46	acoustic	400	f		
11	Jean Pierre	Quain	Houston	TX	77042	52	acoustic	500	m		
12	Alice	Hall	Armuchee	GA	30105	21	acoustic	500	f		
13	William	Sitarz	Coral Gables	FL	33134	50	acoustic	500	m		
14	Daniel	Ebright	Coral Gables	FL	33134	14	acoustic	500	m		
15	Terri	Harvey	Pittsburgh	PA	15230	45	acoustic	600	f		
16	Paur	Tarello	Milwaukee	WI	53203	52	acoustic	600	m		
17	Nancy	Hancock	Redwood City	CA	94063	53	electric	100	f		
18	Eugene	Forney	Jackson	MS	39202	41	electric	100	m		
19	Peter	Bodager	Carrollton	TX	75006	12	electric	200	m		
20	James	Connor	Bingham Farms	MI	48025	27	electric	300	m		
21	Scott	Cocce	Concord	MA	01742	29	electric	400	m		
22	Samuel	Kushkin	Lafayette	CA	94549	24	electric	400	m		
23	William	Heil	San Diego	CA	92121	40	electric	500	m		
24	John	Meyer	Miami	FL	33133	33	electric	500	m		
25	Stuart	Hesse	Lebanon	MO	65536	17	electric	500	m		

FIGURE 12.40
Fiddler Enterprises worksheet

on the web

1. Following Stocks on the Internet

Brian Lucas has been handling his own investments for the past 12 years. After getting his graduate degree in finance, he started his career with an investment research firm. He has moved into another area of business since then, but still uses his investment skills learned years ago. Brian tends to be a conservative investor and mainly invests in value stocks. He carefully collects and analyzes data on companies' stock prices and fundamentals before determining if any are appropriate investments for him.

Brian hasn't had much time recently to research new investments. He has asked you to collect data from the Internet in order to help him. Open **ex12StockWatch.xls** and save it as **<yourname>StockWatch2.xls**. This is the workbook format Brian uses to record and update company information. Insert your name and today's date in the appropriate cells in the Documentation worksheet. The other worksheets in the workbook are labeled Stock 1, 2, and 3. Brian wants you to pick three companies that you feel will be successful for the long term. Go to a Web site such as www.msn.com to find the companies' ticker symbols and the information Brian has requested for each company. Enter the data you find into the corresponding cell in row D. The workbook already contains a macro that prompts Brian to enter which stock worksheet he would like to view. He wants you to add a message box that will tell him if he has entered an incorrect stock worksheet. Edit the Stock_Data macro to include the If-Then-Else control structure. Above the **Sheets(Sheetname).Select** line, enter **If Sheetname="STOCK 1" or Sheetname="STOCK 2" or Sheetname="STOCK 3" Then**. Under the line that selects cell D1, enter **Else**. In the next line, enter the message box function to display **"Please Select Stock 1, Stock 2, or Stock 3"** and title the box **Incorrect Stock Worksheet**. Be sure to end the If function (End/If) and test your macro. Save your work, and print both the workbook and the macro.

2. Web Banking, Inc.

You are to create a simple loan calculation workbook that customers can use without knowing anything about Excel. The workbook will contain a macro instruction you create that activates when a customer clicks a button. The macro prompts the customer for the four loan values through a series of dialog boxes that you create with the InputBox function. As the customer types each of the four values into the dialog boxes—purchase price, down payment, annual interest rate, and loan duration—they are placed into the appropriate worksheet cell. After a customer enters the last input value via the dialog box, Excel recalculates the worksheet and displays values for the loan amount, monthly payment, total interest, and total cost. First, search the Internet for today's prime interest rate. Add 1 percent to that value, and use that percentage when you test your macro at the end of this problem.

Begin by opening **ex12WebBanking.xls** and saving it as **<yourname>WebBanking12.xls**. Turn on the macro recorder, name the macro **LoanValues** (one word), make sure the Relative Reference button is not pressed in so that cell references are absolute in your recorded macro.

Record the following sequence: Click and drag the cell range **B4:B7**, and then press the **Delete** key to clear the range. Click cell **B4**, type **AA**, press **down arrow**, type **BB**, press **down arrow**, type **CC**, press **down arrow**, type **DD**, and then press **down arrow**. Stop the recorder.

Open the Visual Basic Editor, and edit the LoanValues macro. Replace "AA" (including the quotation marks) with **InputBox ("Price?", "Enter")**. Make three similar replacements as follows:

- Replace "BB" with **InputBox ("Down payment?", "Enter")**
- Replace "CC" with **InputBox ("Interest rate (0.065, for example)?", "Enter")**
- Replace "DD" with **InputBox ("Loan duration in years?", "Enter")**

Close the Visual Basic Editor, open the Forms toolbar, add a button, assign the button to the LoanValues macro instruction, and change the button's caption to **Input Values**. Change the button's property that makes it printable when the worksheet prints. Finally, write formulas in cells E4 through E7 for loan amount, monthly payment, total interest, and total cost (loan amount plus total interest). Save the workbook, then test the new macro by clicking the Input Values button, type in the values **50000**, **10000**, the current prime interest rate plus 1 percent for the interest rate, and **5** for the duration. Place your name in the worksheet header, print the worksheet, and print the LoanValues macro instruction code. Save your workbook again.

around the world

1. Bottling Options at Serechini Vineyards

Serechini Vineyards has been producing and selling red wine from southern Italy for six generations. Serechini's bottle supplier is closing its business and the owner has offered to sell the manufacturing plant to the vineyard. The plant will close in four months, and the owner needs an answer from Serechini by the end of the month. Pietro Serechini, the vineyard owner, has asked his accountant to determine whether this is a good investment for the vineyard. Pietro's main concern isn't the capital needed to buy or run the plant, but rather the cost profit per bottle.

Open **ex12SerechiniVineyards.xls**, which is the workbook Pietro's accountant has prepared detailing the revenue, costs, and profit per bottle for either producing its own bottles or outsourcing its manufacturing. Pietro wants to use the workbook to clearly show that the best alternative for the vineyard is to outsource from another bottle supplier.

Insert your name and today's date in the Documentation sheet and save the workbook as **<yourname>SerechiniVineyards2.xls**. Since Pietro and other managers will use the workbook, he wants you to place macros in the Documentation sheet that will open any of the worksheets. He wants the macro to display an input box that prompts users for the name of the worksheet they want to view. Record a macro named **View_Macro** that takes you from the Documentation sheet to the Italy sheet tab and selects cell A1. For the description, type **Displays chosen bottling alternative**. Through the Visual Basic Editor, edit the View_Macro procedure so that the macro contains an input box that prompts the user to **"Type Italy, Korea, Mexico, or Germany."** Title the input box **"Country of Alternative"** and use the variable **"Sheetname."** Place a button in cells D16:F18 of the Documentation sheet to run this macro and type **"View Bottling Alternative"** into the button.

In the Italy worksheet, create a macro that will return the user to cell A1 of the Documentation sheet. Name the macro **Return_Documentation** and for the description, type **"Returns user to Documentation Sheet."** Insert a button in cells E20:F22 for this macro and type **"Return to Documentation Sheet"** in the button. Copy and paste this button into each of the other alternative worksheets.

After reviewing the workbook, Pietro feels that to be effective, the percentage of profit per bottle should be added. In each of the alternatives worksheets, type **Profit per Bottle (%)** in cell A15. Through Visual Basic Editor, use the Insert Module command and the Insert Procedure command to create a function to determine this figure. Name the function **Profit** and use the parameters **Bottle_Price** and **Bottle_Cost**. (*Hint:* Profit = (Bottle Price-Bottle Cost)/Bottle Price). The syntax for the function should be as follows:

```
Function Function_Name (Parameters As
   Single) As Single
      Function_Name5Expression
   End Function
```

If you are having trouble, make sure that each argument and the entire function is declared **As Single**. Place this function in cell **H15** of each alternative worksheet and format the cell to display a percentage with two decimal points.

Remove all gridlines and column and row headers, save your work, and print the workbook and the Procedure code in Visual Basic Editor.

2. Solsona's Leather Goods

Alfonso Solsona is the owner of Solsona's Wholesale Leather. Headquartered on Rambla Catalunya in Barcelona, Spain, Solsona's sells a variety of very high quality leather coats to several major department stores located in Europe and the United States. Alfonso enjoys selling retail items to the people who happen to visit his store. He keeps an Excel workbook listing the sales for which he is responsible. Alfonso maintains the list in order by sale date, and the sale prices for each item in the list are in euros. He'd like you to write a function, called **USD**, that converts euros to U.S. dollars. (Assume a conversion rate of €1.00 equals $1.08.) The function has one argument, the cell containing the euro value. In addition, write a macro instruction, called **AddDoc**, to add a worksheet called "Documentation" to the workbook. The macro places the labels "Solsona's Leather Goods" in cell A1, "Developed by" in cell A3, and "Developed on:" in cell A5.

Begin by opening **ex12Solsona.xls** and save it as **<yourname>Solsona.xls**. Then, write the macro and the function. When you are done, print the function and print the macro. Place your name in both worksheet headers, and print the two worksheets.

Pro Golf Academy

Betty Carroll, Pro Golf Academy's manager, keeps a worksheet containing information about unpaid (outstanding) invoices. Located on the second worksheet, called *Unpaid Invoices,* the list contains the customer name, address, date that the invoice was mailed, and the invoice amount. Betty wants you to write a custom function called PastDue that will return one of three values, depending on the invoice mailing date. If the invoice date, in column G, is less than 30 days ago, the PastDue function returns 0 (zero) to the worksheet. If the invoice date is between 30 and 59 days ago, the function returns 30. If the invoice date is more than 59 days ago, then the PastDue function returns 60. PastDue has the form

```
=PastDue(invoice date, today's date)
```

Remember to type both arguments in the custom function prototype with "As Date" to properly identify the incoming argument data types. The entire function returns an integer, so type "As Integer" following the argument list in the prototype.

After you define the PastDue custom function, type today's date in cell G1 (or use the NOW() function). Write the PastDue expression in the cell range I3:I53 (see Figure 12.41). The function's first argument references the invoice date for the current customer, whereas the second argument references cell G1 containing today's date. Copy the expression from cell I3 to the remaining cells (I4:I53).

Record a macro to switch from the Unpaid Invoices worksheet to the Documentation worksheet, create a command button and place it on the Unpaid Invoices worksheet, and assign the Documentation worksheet activation macro to it. Similarly, create a macro to make the Unpaid Invoices worksheet active, place a command button on the Documentation worksheet, and assign to the button the macro you recorded to activate the Unpaid Invoices worksheet. (Unprotect the worksheet, place the button on it, and then protect the worksheet.) Set the properties of the two command buttons so that they will print along with the worksheet. Fill out the empty lines on the Documentation worksheet, place your name in the worksheet headers of both worksheets and the macro instruction worksheet, print the two completed worksheets, and print the PastDue custom function code.

	A	B	C	D	E	F	G	H	I	J
1	**Outstanding Invoices**					Today's date:	**6/14/2004**	Documentation		
2	Invoice No.	Name	Street	City	State	Zip	Invoice Date	Invoice Amount	Past Due (days)	
3	30132	Murray, T. Peter	550 Route 202-20	Fort Wayne	IN	46801	4/3/2004	$ 2,159.48	60	
4	30142	Kostantaras, Jar	90 Orville Drive	Nashville	TN	37214	4/4/2004	$ 332.25	60	
5	30148	Montrone, Frank	500 Washington	Buffalo Grove	IL	60089	4/5/2004	$ 558.06	60	
6	30149	Fox, Virgil B.	11100 Mead Roa	Racine	WI	53403	4/6/2004	$ 97.40	60	
7	30155	Crist, Dennis P.	120 Brighton Roa	Hermitage	PA	16148	4/7/2004	$ 2,314.04	60	
8	30159	Ivan, Rodney L.	30300 Telegraph	Omaha	NE	68124	4/8/2004	$ 1,076.81	60	
9	30164	Hill, Alex W.	8737 Wilshire Bo	Pottstown	PA	19464	4/9/2004	$ 2,247.18	60	
10	30170	Crosley, Lynn H	Amsouth-Sonat 1	South Milwaukee	WI	53172	4/10/2004	$ 30.47	60	
11	30183	Garcia, James D	300 Liberty Stree	Palo Alto	CA	94304	4/11/2004	$ 1,663.57	60	
12	30186	Graf, Robert R.	Northern Lights E	Owosso	MI	48867	4/12/2004	$ 555.35	60	
13	30190	Tobin, Clifford M	25701 Science P	Cleveland	OH	44114	4/13/2004	$ 1,268.63	60	
14	30221	Bianco, Andrew	303 Peachtree S	Rockford	IL	61104	4/14/2004	$ 2,189.20	60	
15	30231	Gray, Robert R.	C O Icon Health	Denver	CO	80222	4/15/2004	$ 347.25	60	
16	30258	Lebuhn, Eugene	20222 Plummer S	Seattle	WA	98104	4/16/2004	$ 562.00	30	
17	30325	Smith, Richard	14156 Magnolia E	Eden Prairie	MN	55344	4/17/2004	$ 511.50	30	
18	30327	Herd, Russell H.	19805 North Cree	North West Roanoke	VA	24017	4/18/2004	$ 865.69	30	
19	30353	Hesse, Stuart C	6700 Alexander E	Jacksonville	FL	32201	4/19/2004	$ 2,395.43	30	
20	30382	Brown, George S	300 Baker Avenu	Milwaukee	WI	53202	4/20/2004	$ 1,103.78	30	
21	30399	Cocce, Scott	Two North Nevad	Boston	MA	02110	4/21/2004	$ 1,235.09	30	
22	30429	McKenzie, Jame	421 East 30Th A	Cleveland Heights	OH	44118	4/22/2004	$ 2,355.46	30	
23	30449	Mattingly, Taka	255 Alhambra Cii	Asheville	NC	28813	4/23/2004	$ 1,499.99	30	

Documentation / **Unpaid Invoices** /

Ready

F I G U R E 12.41

Pro Golf Academy Unpaid Invoices worksheet

1. Macros

When you record a macro, you can choose to use absolute cell references or relative references—all by pushing a button on the Stop Recording macro toolbar. Explain and differentiate between when you want to record absolute or relative references. Does one way offer any advantages over the other?

2. Function or Sub Procedure?

Describe, with examples, the difference between a VBA function and a VBA sub procedure. How are they different? How are they the same? When would you use a function and when would you use a sub procedure?

reference 1

Excel *File Finder*

Location in Chapter	Data File to Use
CHAPTER 1	
Session 1.1	
Opening an existing Excel workbook	ex01Scrip.xls
Session 1.2	
Entering text labels	ex01Scrip.xls
Saving an altered workbook under a new filename	Scrip2.xls
Hands-on Projects	
Practice Exercise 1	ex01Income.xls
Practice Exercise 2	ex01Timecard.xls
Challenge Exercise 1	(new file)
Challenge Exercise 2	ex01Johnsons.xls
E-Business Exercise 1	(new file)
E-Business Exercise 2	ex01RedwoodRides.xls
On the Web Exercise 1	(create file from scratch)
On the Web Exercise 2	ex01Computer.xls
Around the World Exercise 1	ex01GNP.xls
Around the World Exercise 2	ex01SaltyWater.xls
Running Project	(new file)
CHAPTER 2	
Session 2.1	
Starting Microsoft Excel	(new file)
Saving your worksheet	Recycle.xls
Session 2.2	
Inserting rows into a worksheet	Recycle.xls
Hands-on Projects	
Practice Exercise 1	ex02Wages.xls
Practice Exercise 2	ex02Randys.xls

Location in Chapter	Data File to Use
Challenge Exercise 1	(new file)
Challenge Exercise 2	ex02Payroll.xls
E-Business Exercise 1	ex02EMerchant.xls
E-Business Exercise 2	ex02PlatosSanctuary.xls
On the Web Exercise 1	(new file)
Around the World Exercise 1	(new file)
Around the World Exercise 2	ex02Adventure.xls
Running Project	ex02ProGolf.xls
CHAPTER 3	
Session 3.1	
Opening the Exotic Fruit worksheet and saving it under a new name	ex03Fruit.xls
Formatting cells with Accounting format	ExoticFruit.xls
Saving your workbook under a new name	ExoticFruit2.xls
Session 3.2	
Increasing a row's height	ExoticFruit2.xls
Hands-on Projects	
Practice Exercise 1	ex03Bookstore.xls
Practice Exercise 2	(new file)
Challenge Exercise 1	ex03Schedule.xls
Challenge Exercise 2	ex03Payment.xls
E-Business Exercise 1	ex03Rowing.xls
E-Business Exercise 2	ex03Vroom.xls
On the Web Exercise 1	ex03Headphones.xls
On the Web Exercise 2	(new file)
Around the World Exercise 1	ex03Currency.xls
Around the World Exercise 2	ex03ComplexCell.xls
Running Project	ex03ProGolf.xls
CHAPTER 4	
Session 4.1	
Opening the Big Wave workbook and saving it under a new name	ex04BigWave.xls
Invoking the Chart Wizard to create a column chart	BigWave2.xls

Location in Chapter	Data File to Use
Session 4.2	
Selecting nonadjacent data ranges	BigWave3.xls
Saving a chart sheet as a Web page	BigWave.mht
Hands-on Projects	
Practice Exercise 1	ex04Olympics.xls
Practice Exercise 2	ex04Rainfall.xls
Challenge Exercise 1	ex04California.xls
Challenge Exercise 2	ex04RentalCar.xls
E-Business Exercise 1	ex04ExportCoffee.xls
E-Business Exercise 2	ex04HealthySkin.xls
On the Web Exercise 1	ex04Crop.xls
On the Web Exercise 2	ex04EnergyDrink.xls
Around the World Exercise 1	ex04HourlyLabor.xls
Around the World Exercise 2	ex04Unemployment.xls
Running Project	ex04ProGolf.xls
CHAPTER 5	
Session 5.1	
Opening the Employee worksheet and saving it under a new name	ex05Employee.xls
Freezing label rows and employee name columns	Employee1.xls
Session 5.2	
Filtering a list with the AutoFilter command	Employee2.xls
Session 5.2	
Creating the pivot table layout	Employee3.xls
Hands-on Projects	
Practice Exercise 1	ex05Fairmont.xls
Practice Exercise 2	ex05Grades.xls
Challenge Exercise 1	ex05Shores.xls
Challenge Exercise 2	ex05Doctors.xls
E-Business Exercise 1	ex05Service.xls
E-Business Exercise 2	ex05FuturesTrading.xls
On the Web Exercise 1	(new file)
On the Web Exercise 2	ex05Salaries.xls

EXCEL

Location in Chapter	Data File to Use
Around the World Exercise 1	ex05Tennis.xls
Around the World Exercise 2	ex05Varoom.xls
Running Project	ex05ProGolf.xls
CHAPTER 6	
Session 6.1	
Opening the Loan Analysis workbook and saving it under a new name	ex06CalsCars.xls
Entering input values in the Assumptions area	CalsCars1.xls
Session 6.2	
Writing the PMT function	CalsCars2.xls
Hands-on Projects	
Practice Exercise 1	ex06Savings.xls
Practice Exercise 2	ex06CarLoan.xls
Challenge Exercise 1	ex06Desserts.xls
Challenge Exercise 2	ex06Shipping.xls
E-Business Exercise 1	ex06Leitman.xls
E-Business Exercise 2	ex06Avocado.xls
On the Web Exercise 1	ex06Conservative.xls
On the Web Exercise 2	ex06Stocks.xls
Around the World Exercise 1	ex06AbroadCosts.xls
Around the World Exercise 2	ex06Marathon.xls
Running Project	ex06ProGolf.xls
CHAPTER 7	
Session 7.1	
Copying the Van Buren worksheet to the BECO master workbook	ex07Beco.xls, ex07VanBuren.xls
Copying the West Lafayette worksheet to the BECO master workbook	Bec02.xls, ex07WestLafayette.xls
Session 7.2	
Opening the Danielli workbook	ex07Danielli.xls
Opening the BECO workbook and entering a link formula	Danielli3.xls, Bec03.xls
Redirecting link references to a renamed supporting workbook	Bec03.xls, Acquisition.xls

Location in Chapter	Data File to Use
Hands-on Projects	
Practice Exercise 1	ex07ReedReps.xls
Practice Exercise 2	ex07DelzuraHawthorne.xls, ex07DelzuraPortland.xls, ex07DelzuraMain.xls
Challenge Exercise 1	ex07Kelleher.xls
Challenge Exercise 2	ex07Robot.xls, ex07RobotPets.xls
E-Business Exercise 1	ex07AIFlorida.xls, ex07AIGeorgia.xls, ex07AILouisiana.xls
On the Web Exercise 1	ex07LawSchools.xls
Around the World Exercise 1	ex07Wilton.xls
Around the World Exercise 2	ex07JumpStart.xls, ex07Tokyo.xls, ex07Beijing.xls
Running Project	ex07ProGolf.xls
CHAPTER 8	
Session 8.1	
Opening the Nivaca workbook and displaying the Formula Auditing toolbar	ex08Nivaca.xls
Tracing the precedent cells for a formula	\<yourname>Nivaca2.xls
Session 8.2	
Establishing a shared Nivaca workbook	\<yourname>Nivaca2.xls
Opening the shared and modified Nivaca workbook	ex08NivacaShared.xls
Reviewing others' comments	\<yourname>Nivaca3.xls
Session 8.3	
Opening the Nivaca workbook and saving it under a new name	\<yourname>Nivaca3.xls
Hiding select cells' formulas	\<yourname>Nivaca4.xls
Reviewing a noninteractive Web workbook page	NivacaSales.mht
Performing what-if analysis with an interactive Web workbook	NivacaSalesInteractive.mht
Hands-on Projects	
Practice Exercise 1	ex08ScripVantage.xls
Practice Exercise 2	ex08Grimwald.xls
Challenge Exercise 1	ex08PrinterTCO.xls
Challenge Exercise 2	ex08GradeCalc.xls
E-Business Exercise 1	ex08IncredibleCheesecake.xls
E-Business Exercise 2	ex08LathramInvoice.xls

EXCEL

Location in Chapter	Data File to Use
On the Web Exercise 1	ex08ExoticFruit.xls
On the Web Exercise 2	cx08Sunny.xls
Around the World Exercise 1	ex08AfricanCoffee.xls
Running Project	ex08ProGolf.xls
CHAPTER 9	
Session 9.1	
Opening the Artistic workbook, entering revenue values and formulas, and applying a default numeric format	ex09Artistic.xls
Performing what-if analysis of revenue	Artistic1.xls
Completing the two-variable data table	Artistic2.xls
Session 9.2	
Opening the Artistic Furniture Corporation scenario workbook	ex09ArtisticScenarios.xls
Defining names for selected input and result cells	Artistic3.xls
Hands-on Projects	
Practice Exercise 1	ex09Outdoor.xls
Practice Exercise 2	ex09PCCRC.xls
Challenge Exercise 1	ex09AbelMassey.xls
Challenge Exercise 2	ex09Loan.xls
E-Business Exercise 1	ex09GMercer.xls
E-Business Exercise 2	ex09WebVideo.xls
On the Web Exercise 1	ex09TravisStock.xls
On the Web Exercise 2	ex09UCexpenses.xls
Around the World Exercise 1	ex09Teak.xls
Around the World Exercise 2	ex09Katrina.xls
Running Project	ex09ProGolf.xls
CHAPTER 10	
Session 10.1	
Opening the ExerCycle workbook and modifying the worksheet tab	ex10ExerCycle.xls
Unlocking data input cells	ExerCycle2.xls
Session 10.2	
Opening the product mix workbook	ex10ExerCycleMix.xls

Location in Chapter	Data File to Use
Writing formulas for the recumbent exercise bicycle	ExerCycleMix2.xls
Hands-on Projects	
Practice Exercise 1	ex10OceanSpas.xls
Practice Exercise 2	ex10LoanGoal.xls
Challenge Exercise 1	ex10CreditUnion.xls
Challenge Exercise 2	ex10GreenCreek.xls
E-Business Exercise 1	ex10WebHosting.xls
E-Business Exercise 2	ex10Rugs.xls
On the Web Exercise 1	ex10DVD.xls
On the Web Exercise 2	ex10SlickSuits.xls
Around the World Exercise 1	ex10Shipping.xls
Around the World Exercise 2	ex10TradingEducation.xls
Running Project	ex10ProGolf.xls
CHAPTER 11	
Session 11.1	
Opening the fixed-length sales representatives text file	ex11SalesRep111.txt
Saving the imported employee text file as an Excel workbook	SalesReps2.xls
Importing comma-separated values into Excel	ex11SalesRep113.csv
Opening two other workbooks	SalesReps2.xls, ex11MBBW.xls, ex11SalesRep113.csv
Moving a worksheet to another workbook	ex11MBBW.xls, ex11SalesRep113.csv
Copying and pasting worksheet data	MissionBoats2.xls, ex11SalesRep113.csv
Sorting and formatting the Sales Rep worksheet	MissionBoats2.xls
Session 11.2	
Opening the Excel workbook and adding a new worksheet	MissionBoats2.xls
Creating a connection to a data source	MissionBoats3.xls, ex11MBBW.mdb
Saving the customer query	MissionBoats3.xls
Hands-on Projects	
Practice Exercise 1	ex11LincolnCollege.xls, ex11LincolnCollege.mdb
Practice Exercise 2	ex11StatePopulation.txt
Challenge Exercise 1	ex11OTWSales.xls, ex11MaripaOrders.txt
Challenge Exercise 2	ex11RugSpecialists.xls, ex11RugSpecialists.mdb

EXCEL

Location in Chapter	Data File to Use
E-Business Exercise 1	ex11KWeb.xls, ex11KWebMail.txt, ex11Kellson.mdb
E-Business Exercise 2	ex11Hydroponics.xls, ex11Hydroponics.mdb
On the Web Exercise 1	ex11Presidents.mdb
On the Web Exercise 2	ex11Racers.txt
Around the World Exercise 1	ex11EuropeanSales.txt
Around the World Exercise 2	ex11IrishGolf.xls, ex11IrishGolf.mdb
Running Project	ex11ProGolf.xls, ex11ProGolf.mdb
CHAPTER 12	
Session 12.1	
Opening the workbook and saving it under a new name	ex12ArtGlass.xls
Set up to begin recording the Bullseye Worksheet macro	Catalog2.xls
Session 12.2	
Opening the workbook	Catalog3.xls
Opening the Invoice workbook	ex12ArtGlassInvoice.xls
Writing a custom function to calculate a discount percentage	Invoice2.xls
Hands-on Projects	
Practice Exercise 1	ex12SalesQuota.xls
Practice Exercise 2	ex12Gradebook.xls
Challenge Exercise 1	ex12TicketSales.xls
Challenge Exercise 2	ex12EmployeeForm.xls
E-Business Exercise 1	ex12AuditAssignments.xls
E-Business Exercise 2	ex12Fiddler.xls, ex12FiddlerData.txt
On the Web Exercise 1	ex12StockWatch.xls
On the Web Exercise 2	ex12WebBanking.xls
Around the World Exercise 1	ex12SerechiniVineyards.xls
Around the World Exercise 2	ex12Solsona.xls
Running Project	ex12ProGolf.xls

reference 2

Excel *Microsoft Office Specialist Certification Guide*

Microsoft Office Specialist Objective	Task	Session Location	End-of-Chapter Location
CHAPTER 1	**Creating Worksheets for Decision Makers**		
XL03S-1-1	Enter and edit cell content	1.2	EX 1.36
XL03 S-1-2	Navigate to specific cell content	1.1	EX 1.36
XL03 S-1-3	Locate, select and insert supporting information	1.1	EX 1.36
XL03S-2-3	Insert and modify formulas	1.2	EX 1.36
XL03S-5-5	Preview data in other views	1.2	EX 1.36
XL03S-5-7	Set up pages for printing	1.2	EX 1.36
XL03S-5-8	Print data	1.2	EX 1.36
CHAPTER 2	**Planning and Creating a Workbook**		
XL03S-2-3	Insert and modify formulas	2.1	EX 2.36
XL03S-2-4	Use statistical, date and time, financial, and logical functions	2.1	EX 2.36
XL03S-3-3	Modify row and column formats	2.2	EX 2.36
XL03S-4-1	Insert, view, and edit comments	2.2	EX 2.36
XL03S-5-2	Insert, delete, and move cells	2.1	EX 2.36
XL03S-5-7	Set up pages for printing	2.2	EX 2.36
CHAPTER 3	**Formatting a worksheet**		
XL03S-3-1	Apply and modify cell formats	3.1	EX 3.41
XL03S-3-3	Modify row and column formats	3.1	EX 3.41
XL03S-5-7	Set up pages for printing	3.2	EX 3.41
XL03S-5-8	Print data	3.2	EX 3.41
CHAPTER 4	**Creating Charts**		
XL03S-2-3	Insert and modify formulas	4.1	EX 4.41
XL03 S-2-4	Use statistical, date and time, financial, and logical functions	4.1	EX 4.41

Microsoft Office Specialist Objective	Task	Session Location	End-of-Chapter Location
XL03S-2-5	Create, modify, and position diagrams and charts based on worksheet data	4.1	EX 4.41
XL03S-5-10	Save data in appropriate formats for different uses	4.2	EX 4.41
XL03E-2-4	Format charts and diagrams	4.2	EX 4.41
CHAPTER 5	Exploring Excel's List Features		
XL03S-1-2	Navigate to specific cell content	5.1	EX 5.52
XL03S-2-1	Filter lists using AutoFilter	5.1	EX 5.52
XL03S-2-2	Sort lists	5.1	EX 5.52
XL03S-5-6	Customize Window layout	5.1	EX 5.52
XL03E-1-1	Use subtotals	5.2	EX 5.52
XL03E-1-2	Define and apply advanced filters	5.2	EX 5.52
XL03E-1-3	Group and outline data	5.2	EX 5.52
XL03E-1-5	Create and modify list ranges	5.3	EX 5.52
XL03E-1-8	Create PivotTable and PivotChart reports	5.3	EX 5.52
XL03E-1-14	Define, modify, and use named ranges	5.3	EX 5.52
XL03E-2-2	Use conditional formatting	5.2	EX 5.52
CHAPTER 6	Employing Functions		
XL03S-2-3	Insert and modify formulas	6.1	EX 6.34
XL03S-2-4	Use statistical, date and time, financial, and logical functions	6.2	EX 6.34
XL03E-1-4	Use data validation	6.1	EX 6.34
XL03E-1-9	Use Lookup and Reference functions	6.1	EX 6.34
XL03E-1-14	Define, modify, and use named ranges	6.1	EX 6.34
CHAPTER 7	Developing Multiple Worksheet and Workbook Applications		
XL03S-3-4	Format worksheets	7.1	EX 7.39
XL03S-5-4	Organize worksheets	7.1	EX 7.39
XL03S-5-6	Customize Window layout	7.1	EX 7.39
XL03S-5-7	Set up pages for printing	7.1	EX 7.39
XL03E-1-14	Define, modify, and use named ranges	7.1	EX 7.39
XL03E-4-4	Create and edit templates	7.1	EX 7.39
XL03E-5-3	Modify Excel default settings	7.2	EX 7.39

Microsoft Office Specialist Objective	Task	Session Location	End-of-Chapter Location
CHAPTER 8	**Auditing, Sharing, Protecting, and Publishing Workbooks**		
XL03S-3-4	Format worksheets	8.1	EX 8.43
XL03S-4-1	Insert, view, and edit comments	8.2	EX 8.43
XL03S-5-3	Create and modify hyperlinks	8.2	EX 8.43
XL03E-1-11	Trace formula precedents, dependents, and errors	8.1	EX 8.43
XL03E-1-12	Locate invalid data and formulas	8.1	EX 8.43
XL03E-3-1	Protect cells, worksheets, and workbooks	8.3	EX 8.43
XL03E-3-2	Apply workbook security settings	8.3	EX 8.43
XL03E-3-3	Share workbooks	8.2	EX 8.43
XL03E-3-5	Track, accept, and reject changes to workbooks	8.2	EX 8.43
XL03E-4-3	Publish and edit Web worksheets and workbooks	8.3	EX 8.43
CHAPTER 9	**Using Data Tables and Scenarios**		
XL03S-1-3	Locate, select, and insert supporting information	9.1	EX 9.40
XL03S-1-4	Insert, position, and size graphics	9.1	EX 9.40
XL03E-1-6	Add, show, close, edit, merge, and summarize scenarios	9.2	EX 9.40
XL03E-1-7	Perform data analysis using automated tools	9.1	EX 9.40
CHAPTER 10	**Using the Solver**		
XL03S-1-4	Insert, position, and size graphics	10.1	EX 10.38
XL03E-1-7	Perform data analysis using automated tools	10.2	EX 10.38
CHAPTER 11	**Importing Data**		
XL03S-5-4	Organize worksheets	11.1	EX 11.38
XL03E-4-1	Import data to Excel	11.1	EX 11.38
CHAPTER 12	**Automating Applications with Visual Basic**		
XL03S-3-4	Format worksheets	12.1	EX 12.45
XL03E-5-4	Protect cells, worksheets, and workbooks	12.1	EX 12.45
XL03E-3-2	Apply workbook security settings	12.1	EX 12.45
XL03E-5-2	Create, edit, and run macros	12.1	EX 12.45

EXCEL

reference 3

Task	Page #	Preferred Method
Opening an Excel workbook	EX 1.10	• Click **File**, click **Open**, click workbook's name, click the **Open** button
Entering a formula	EX 1.16	• Select cell, type **=**, type formula, press **Enter**
Entering the SUM function	EX 1.19	• Select cell, type **=SUM(**, type cell range, type **)**, and press **Enter**
Editing a cell	EX 1.20	• Select cell, click formula bar, make changes, press **Enter**
Saving a workbook with a new name	EX 1.22	• Click **File**, click **Save As**, type filename, click **Save** button
Obtaining help	EX 1.23	• Click the **Microsoft Excel Help** command from the **Help** menu (or click the Microsoft Excel **Help** button on the Standard toolbar) • Click the **Answer Wizard** tab • In the What would you like to do text box, type an English-language question (replacing the words displayed and highlighted in blue) on the topic with which you need help and click the **Search** button
Clearing cells' contents	EX 1.25	• Click cell, press **Delete** keyboard key
Creating a header or footer	EX 1.28	• Click **View**, click **Header and Footer**, click **Custom Header** or **Custom Footer**, select section, type header/footer text, click the **OK** button
Printing a worksheet	EX 1.30	• Click **File**, click **Print**, click the **OK** button
Printing worksheet formulas	EX 1.33	• Click **Ctrl+`**, click **File**, click **Print**, and click **OK**
Closing a workbook	EX 1.34	• Click **File**, click **Close**, click **Yes** to save
Writing formulas	EX 2.8	• Select a cell, type **=**, type the formula, press **Enter**
Modifying an AutoSum cell range by pointing	EX 2.10	• Press an arrow key repeatedly to select leftmost or topmost cell in range, press and hold **Shift**, select cell range with arrow keys, release **Shift**, press **Enter**
Writing a function using Insert Function button	EX 2.15	• Select a cell, click the Insert Function button, click a function category, click a function name, click **OK**, complete the formula palette dialog box, click **OK**
Copying and pasting	EX 2.18	• Select source cell(s), click **Edit**, click **Copy**, select target cell(s), click **Edit**, click **Paste**
Copying cell contents using a cell's fill handle	EX 2.19	• Select source cell(s), drag the fill handle to the source cell(s) range, release the mouse button
Changing relative references to absolute or mixed references	EX 2.23	• Double-click the cell, move insertion point to the cell reference, press **F4** repeatedly as needed, press **Enter**

Task	Page #	Preferred Method
Moving cells' contents	EX 2.25	• Select the cell(s), move the mouse pointer to an edge of the selected range, click the edge of the selected cell or cell range, drag the outline to the destination location, release the mouse
Spell-checking a worksheet	EX 2.27	• Click cell **A1**, click the **Spelling** button, correct any mistakes, click **OK**
Inserting rows	EX 2.28	• Click a cell, click **Insert**, click **Rows**
Inserting columns	EX 2.28	• Click a cell, click **Insert**, click **Columns**
Inserting a comment	EX 2.34	• Click a cell, click **Insert**, click **Comment**, type a comment, and click another cell
Formatting numbers	EX 3.6	• Select cell(s) • Click **Format**, click **Cells**, click **Number** • Click format category and select options • Click **OK**
Copying a cell format to a cell or cell range	EX 3.9	• Select the cell whose format you want to copy • Click the **Format Painter** button • Click (click/drag) the target cell(s)
Modifying a column's width	EX 3.12	• Select the column heading(s) of all columns whose width you want to change • Click **Format**, point to **Column**, and click **Width** • Enter the new column width in the **Column Width** text box and click **OK**, or click **AutoFit Selection** to make the column(s) optimal width—as wide as the widest entry in the column
Wrapping long text within a cell	EX 3.15	• Select the cell or cell range to which you will apply a format • Click **Format**, click **Cells**, and click the **Alignment** tab • Click the **Wrap text** check box • Click **OK**
Applying fonts and font characteristics	EX 3.17	• Select the cell or cell range that you want to format • Click **Format**, click **Cells**, and click the **Font** tab • Select a typeface from the Font list box • Select a font style and a font size • Click **OK**
Clearing formats from a cell, cell selection, rows, or columns	EX 3.19	• Select the cell, cell range, rows, or columns • Click **Edit**, point to **Clear**, and click **Formats**
Modifying a row's height	EX 3.21	• Click the row heading • Click **Format**, point to **Row**, and click **Height** • Type the row height in the Row height text box • Click **OK**
Adding a border to a cell	EX 3.22	• Click the cell to which you want to add a border • Click the Formatting toolbar Borders list box arrow, and click the border you want
Activating or removing a toolbar	EX 3.24	• **Right-click** the menu bar • Click the name of the toolbar you want to activate or remove
Adding a text box to a worksheet	EX 3.25	• Activate the Drawing toolbar • Click the **Text Box** button • Click the worksheet in the location where you want the text box • Drag an outline away from the initial point until the text box outline is the right size and shape • Type the text you want to appear in the text box

Task	Page #	Preferred Method
Hiding rows or columns	EX 3.30	• Select the rows or columns • Click **Format**, point to **Row** (or **Column**), and click **Hide**
Applying color or patterns to worksheet cells	EX 3.31	• Select the cells to which you want to apply a color or pattern • Click **Format**, click **Cells**, and click the **Patterns** tab in the Format Cells dialog box • If you want to apply a pattern, click a pattern from the Pattern list box • If you want the pattern to appear in color, click the Pattern list box again and click a color from the Pattern palette • If you want to apply a colored background, click a color in the Cell shading Color palette in the Format Cells dialog box
Printing multiple worksheets	EX 3.39	• Ctrl-click the sheet tabs of each sheet you want to print • Click the **Print** button
Creating a chart	EX 4.11	• Select data cell range, click the **Chart Wizard** button • Respond to the series of Chart Wizard dialog box choices
Snapping an embedded chart into place	EX 4.15	• Select the chart • Press and hold the **Alt** key • Drag a chart left, right, up, or down until the chart edge snaps to a cell boundary • Release the mouse and Alt key
Adding a new data series to an embedded chart	EX 4.18	• Select the cell range of the data series you want to add • Move the mouse to any edge of the selected worksheet cell range • When the mouse pointer changes to an arrow, click and drag the range into the chart area and release the mouse
Deleting a data series from a chart	EX 4.19	• Select the data marker • Press **Delete**
Adding a data label to all data series in a chart	EX 4.22	• Select a data series • Click **Chart**, click **Chart Options**, click the **Data Labels** tab • Click the **Show value** option, click **OK**
Adding a data label to a data series	EX 4.23	• Select the data series • Click **Format**, click **Selected Data Series**, click the **Data Labels** tab • Click the **Show value** option, click **OK**
Adding a data label to a data marker	EX 4.23	• Select the data series, click the data marker in the series • Click **Format**, click **Selected Data Point**, click the **Data Labels** tab • Click the **Show value** option, click **OK**
Printing a worksheet and embedded chart	EX 4.28	• Click any worksheet cell • Click the **Print** button
Printing an embedded chart	EX 4.29	• Click the chart • Click the **Print** button
Selecting nonadjacent cell ranges	EX 4.31	• Select the first cell range • Press and hold the **Ctrl** key • Select additional cells or cell ranges • When finished selecting cells, release the **Ctrl** key
Deleting an embedded chart	EX 4.38	• Click the embedded chart • Press the **Delete** key
Deleting a chart sheet	EX 4.38	• Click the chart sheet tab • Click **Edit**, click **Delete Sheet**, click **OK**

EXCEL

Task	Page #	Preferred Method
Creating Web pages from an Excel chart	EX 4.38	• Click the chart or chart sheet tab • Click **File**, click **Save As** • Select a drive and folder • Click **Web Archive** in the Save as type list box • Click the **Selection: Chart** option • Optionally type a page title and click **OK** • Click **Save**
Freezing rows and columns	EX 5.5	• Select cell at upper-left corner • Click **Window**; click **Freeze Panes**
Adding a record to a list using a data form	EX 5.6	• Click list cell, click **Data**, click **Form** • Click **New**, type values in fields, press **Enter**, and click **Close**
Deleting a record from a list with	EX 5.9	• Click list cell, click **Data**, click **Form** • Click **Criteria** button, Click **Find Next** as needed, click **Delete**, and click **OK** **a data form**
Sorting a list on one column	EX 5.12	• Click cell in list • Click the **Sort Ascending** or **Sort Descending** button
Sorting a list on more than one field	EX 5.13	• Click list cell, click **Data**, click **Sort** • Specify Sort by and Ascending/Descending options • Repeat for up to two **Then by** fields • Click **OK**
Creating a custom sort order	EX 5.15	• Click **Tools**, click **Options**, click **Custom Lists** tab • Click **NEW LIST**, type each new member of the list in order • Click the **Add** button and click **OK**
Filtering a list with AutoFilter	EX 5.19	• Click list cell, click **Data** • Click **list arrow** on filtering column, click filter value from list
Clearing all AutoFilter filtering criteria	EX 5.21	• Click **Data**, point to **Filter** • Click **Show All** to remove all existing filters
Subtotaling a list's entries	EX 5.23	• Sort list by grouping column • Click a cell inside the list • Click **Data**, click **Subtotals** • Choose group column, choose aggregate function • Click **OK**
Displaying row or column headings on each page	EX 5.27	• Click **File**, click **Page Setup**, click the **Sheet** tab • Click **Collapse** dialog button on the **Specify Rows to repeat at top** or the **Specify Columns to repeat at left** • Specify row(s) or column(s) • Click **OK**
Applying a conditional format to cells	EX 5.30	• Click cell range to conditionally format • Click **Format**, Click **Conditional Formatting**, specify criteria • Click **Format** button on the Conditional Formatting dialog box and specify formatting options • Click **OK** • Click **OK**
Creating a pivot table with the PivotTable Wizard	EX 5.35	• Click **Data**, click the **PivotTable and PivotChart Report** • Specify the data's location • Select the **PivotTable** option and click the **Layout** button • Design pivot table layout by selecting row, column, data, and page fields and click **OK**

Task	Page #	Preferred Method
		• Designate location for pivot table as separate page or object on worksheet, click the **Finish** button
Selecting pivot table fields	EX 5.38	• Click and drag selected field(s) to summarize to Data Items area • Click and drag field buttons to Column, Row, and Page fields
Formatting pivot table fields	EX 5.40	• Select any cell in the pivot table data item area • Open the PivotTable toolbar, click **Field Settings**, and click the **Number** button • Select a format from the Category list and make associated format choices • Click **OK** to close the Format Cells dialog box and then click **OK** to close the PivotTable Field dialog box
Naming a cell or cell range	EX 6.12	• Select the cell or cell range you want to name • Click the **Name box** in the formula bar • Type the name and press **Enter**
Deleting a name	EX 6.14	• Click **Insert**, point to **Name**, and then click the **Define** button • Click the name in the *Names in workbook* list that you want to delete • Click the **Delete** button and then click the **OK** button
Using the VLOOKUP function	EX 6.19	• Create a lookup table and sort the table in ascending order by the leftmost column • Place in columns to the right of the search columns values you want to return as answers • Write a VLOOKUP function referencing a cell containing the lookup value, the lookup table, and the column containing the answer
Deleting a worksheet	EX 7.6	• Right-click the tab of the worksheet to delete • Click **Delete** on the shortcut menu
Saving a Workbook as a Template	EX 7.7	• Activate the workbook you want to save as a template, click **File** and then click **Save As** • Type the template name in the File name list box, click the **Save as type** list box, scroll the list box to locate and then click **Template (*.xlt)**, and click **Save** button
Copying worksheets from other workbooks	EX 7.8	• Open the master workbook—the workbook into which you want to copy worksheets from other workbooks • Open all other workbooks containing worksheets you want to copy to the master workbook • In any of the open Excel workbooks, click **Window**, click **Arrange**, click the **Tiled** option button, and click **OK** • Press and hold the **Ctrl** key, and then click and drag to the master workbook the tab of the worksheet you want to copy • Release the mouse when the down-pointing arrow is in the correct tab location in the master workbook, and then release the **Ctrl** key
Grouping contiguous worksheets	EX 7.13	• Click the worksheet tab of the first worksheet in the group • Use the tab scrolling buttons if necessary to bring the last worksheet tab of the proposed group into view • Hold down the **Shift** key and click the last worksheet tab in the group
Grouping noncontiguous worksheets	EX 7.13	• Click the worksheet tab of the first worksheet you want in the group • Press and hold the **Ctrl** key and then click each worksheet you want to include in the group • When you are done, release the **Ctrl** key
Ungrouping worksheets	EX 7.14	• Click the worksheet tab of any worksheet not in the worksheet group • If all worksheets in the workbook are grouped, right-click any worksheet tab and click **Ungroup Sheets** from the shortcut menu

EXCEL

Task	Page #	Preferred Method
Writing a formula containing a 3-D reference	EX 7.23	• After clicking the cell where you want the formula to appear, type =, type a function name, and type the left parenthesis. If no function is needed, then type = • Click the sheet tab of the worksheet containing the cell or cell range you want to reference • If a worksheet range is needed, then press and hold the **Shift** key and click the last worksheet tab in the range • Click the cell or cell range you want to reference • Complete the formula (type a concluding right parenthesis for a function, for instance) and then press **Enter**
Printing multiple worksheets	EX 7.27	• Group the worksheets you want to print by pressing **Ctrl** and then clicking the worksheet tabs or pressing **Shift** and clicking the first and last work-sheets in a contiguous group • Click **File**, click **Print**, ensure the **Active sheet(s)** option button is selected, and click **OK**
Deleting an Excel Template	EX 7.28	• Click **File** on the menu bar, click **New**, and click **On my computer** in the Templates panel of the task pane • Right-click the template which you want to delete, and click **Delete**, and click **OK** when asked if you want to send the template to the Recycle Bin
Building link references by pointing	EX 7.30	• Open the supporting workbook • Make active the workbook to contain the link reference and the cell to contain the link reference • Type the formula up to the point in which you reference the cell or cell range in another workbook • Click the Taskbar button corresponding to the supporting workbook to make it active • Click the worksheet tab containing the cell or cell range to reference • Click the cell or drag the cell range of the cell(s) you want to reference and press **Enter**
Opening a supporting workbook from a dependent workbook	EX 7.35	• Open the dependent workbook containing the link reference • Click **Edit** and then click **Links** • Click the name of the supporting workbook you want to open from the Links list • Click the **Open Source** button
Tracing precedent or dependent cells	EX 8.5	• Select the cell whose formula you want to trace • Click the **Trace Precedents (Trace Dependents)** button on the Formula Auditing toolbar to display tracer arrows pointing to the formula's precedent (dependent) cells
Tracing errors	EX 8.12	• Click the cell displaying an error value • Click the **Trace Error** button on the Formula Auditing toolbar • Follow any tracer arrows back to the error source
Finding subtle errors	EX 8.14	• Click the worksheet tab of the worksheet whose integrity you want to check • Click the **Error Checking** button on the Formula Auditing toolbar • Use the options available in the Error Checking dialog box to correct the errant formula or • Click the Next button to go to the next suspicious formula
Tracking worksheet changes	EX 8.20	• Click **Tools** • Point to **Track Changes** • Click **Highlight Changes** • Click the list arrow next to the When check box • Click one of the available time periods

Task	Page #	Preferred Method
		• Click the list arrow next to the Who list box • Click one of the available names whose changes you want to track • Click the **Where** reference box and indicate which part of the workbook you want to review changes • Click the **List changes on a new sheet** check box to collect • Display the changes on a separate worksheet • Click **OK** to finalize your choices
Accepting and rejecting suggested changes to cells	EX 8.22	• With a shared workbook open, click **Tools** • Point to **Track Changes** • Click **Accept or Reject Changes** • Click the list arrow next to the When check box • Click one of the available time periods • Click the list arrow next to the Who list box • Click one of the available names whose changes you want to accept or reject • Click the **Where** reference box and indicate which part of the workbook you want to review changes • Click **OK** to finalize your choices
Merging multiple versions of the same workbook	EX 8.24	• Open the workbook into which you want to merge changes • Click **Tools** on the menu bar and click **Compare and Merge Workbooks** • Press and hold the **Ctrl** key and click each workbook listed in the *Select Files to Merge Into Current Workbook* dialog box that you want to merge, and click **OK**
Hiding a worksheet	EX 8.26	• Click the worksheet tab of the worksheet you want to hide • Click **Format**, point to **Sheet** • Click **Hide**
Unhiding a worksheet	EX 8.27	• Click **Format**, point to **Sheet** • Click **Unhide** • In the Unhide dialog box, click the name of the worksheet you want to un-hide from the list • Click **OK**
Unlocking cells	EX 8.28	• Select the cell or cell range you want to be unlocked • Click **Format**, click **Cells**, • Click the **Protection** tab • Click the **Locked** check box to clear its checkmark • Click **OK**
Enabling worksheet protection	EX 8.29	• Select the worksheet on which you want to enable protection • Click **Tools**, point to **Protection** • Click **Protect Sheet**. Optionally enter (and remember) a password twice • Click **OK**
Protecting a workbook	EX 8.30	• Click **Tools**, point to **Protection** • Click **Protect Workbook** • Check or clear check boxes to set options as needed, type an optional password • Click **OK** • If you entered a password, then you are asked to retype it and then click **OK**
Publishing an Excel workbook as a noninteractive Web page	EX 8.33	• Click **File** • Click **Save as Web Page** • In the Save As dialog box, click **Entire Workbook** and clear the **Add interactivity** check box • Type a filename in the Filename list box • Optionally, click the **Change Title** button, type a new Web page title, and click **OK**, and click **Save**

EXCEL

Task	Page #	Preferred Method
Publishing an Excel workbook as an interactive Web page	EX 8.35	• Click **File** • Click **Save as Web Page** • In the Save As dialog box, click **Entire Workbook** and check the **Add interactivity** check box • Click the **Publish** button • Click the **Choose** list box and select the portions of the workbook you want to publish • Click the **Change** button to change the Web page title • Click the **Browse** button to specify a filename and folder location • Click the **AutoRepublish every time this workbook is saved** check box (placing a checkmark in it) • Click the **Open published web page in browser** check box (placing a check-mark in it) • Click the **Publish** button
Creating a one-variable data table	EX 9.15	• Decide if you want values for the input cell to appear in a row or down a column • If you arrange a data table in columns, then insert the input values in the first column beginning below the first row of the table and place a reference (a formula) to the result cell in the cell above and to the right of the column of input values • If you arrange a data table in rows, then insert the input values in the first row beginning in the second column of the data table and place a reference (a formula) to the result cell in the cell below the input row and to its left • Select the table, click **Data**, and then click **Table** • Enter the cell reference of the input cell in the Row input cell box if input values are in a row or enter the cell reference of the input cell in the Column input cell box if the input values are in a column in the data table • Click **OK**
Creating a two-variable data table	EX 9.19	• Type the formula or a reference to the input cell in the upper-left cell in the data table • Type the first variable values in the row to the right of the formula • Type the second variable values in the column below the formula • Select a cell range that encompasses the formula, row values, and column values • Click **Data** on the menu bar and then click **Table** • Type the address of the input cell that corresponds to the row values in the Row input cell text box • Type the address of the input cell that corresponds to the column values in the Column input cell text box • Click **OK**
Creating a scenario	EX 9.26	• Click **Tools** and click **Scenarios** to open the Scenario Manager • Click the **Add** button and type a scenario name • Specify the changing (input) cells in the scenario • Type commentary in the Comment text box and then click the **OK** button • Type the values for each changing cell, scrolling the list if necessary, and then click **OK** • Click **Close** to close the Scenario Manager
Viewing a scenario	EX 9.30	• Click **Tools** and click **Scenarios** to open the Scenario Manager • Select a scenario from the Scenarios list • Click the **Show** button
Editing a scenario	EX 9.32	• Click **Tools** and click **Scenarios** to open the Scenario Manager • Select a scenario from the Scenarios list • Click the **Edit** button • Make any changes in the Edit Scenario dialog box and click **OK**

Task	Page #	Preferred Method
		• Make any changes in the Scenario Values dialog box and click **OK**
Deleting a scenario	EX 9.33	• Click **Tools** and click **Scenarios** to open the Scenario Manager • Select a scenario from the Scenarios list • Click the **Delete** button
Producing a Scenario Summary report	EX 9.35	• Click **Tools** and click **Scenarios** to open the Scenario Manager • Click the **Summary** button • Click the **Scenario Summary** option button • Type the cell addresses in the *Result cells* box of all result cells you want to display in the report • Click **OK**
Producing a PivotTable report	EX 9.37	• Click **Tools** and click **Scenarios** to open the Scenario Manager • Click the **Summary** button • Click the **Scenario PivotTable** option button • Type the cell addresses in the Result cells box of all result cells you want to display in the report • Click **OK**
Using Goal Seek	EX 10.13	• Click **Tools** and then click **Goal Seek** • Click the **Set cell** box and type the cell address of the result cell • Click the **To value** box and type the result value you want • Click the **By changing** cell box and type the address of the changing cell • Click **OK** to solve the problem, and then click **OK** to close the Goal Seek Status dialog box
Using the Solver	EX 10.27	• Click **Tools** and then click **Solver** • In the *Set Target Cell* box, type the address of the cell containing the objective function • Click one of the **Equal To** option buttons and, if necessary, type a value in the *Value of* box • In the *By Changing Cells* box, type the cell addresses of all cells that Excel can change • Click the **Add** button to add constraints to the Subject to the Constraints box • Click the **Solve** button to create a solution • Click the **OK** button
Deleting a Solver constraint	EX 10.33	• Click **Tools** and then click **Solver** • Click the constraint you want to delete • Click the **Delete** button
Saving Solver parameters	EX 10.35	• Click **Tools** and then click **Solver** • Click **Options** and then click **Save Model** • Select an empty cell range and then click **OK** • Click **Cancel** and then click **Close**
Importing fixed-length data using the Text Import Wizard	EX 11.6	• Click **File** and then click **Open** • In the Files of type list box of the Open dialog box, select **Text Files** • Using the *Look in* list box, navigate to the folder containing the text file, click the filename in the list of files, and click the **Open** button • Click the **Fixed Width** option button in the Original data type panel • Click the **Start import at row** spin box to select the first row to import, and click the **Next** button • In step 2, click to the left of each field to add a break line, double-click a break line to remove it, or drag a break line to its correct position at the beginning of a column as needed. Then click the **Next** button to proceed • In step 3, for each column, click a **Column data format** option button to select a column format, or click the **Do not import column** option button to skip the column, and click the **Finish** button

EXCEL

Task	Page #	Preferred Method
Adding, moving, and deleting column breaks using the Text Import Wizard	EX 11.8	• Add a column break by clicking the position just above the ruler in the Data preview panel where you want the column break to appear • Move a column break by clicking it and then dragging it to its new position • Delete a column break by double-clicking it
Editing a query	EX 11.27	• Make sure that one of the cells containing imported database data is active • Click **Data**, point to **Import External Data**, and click **Edit Query** • Step through each of the Query Wizard's steps, make any necessary changes at each step, and then press **Next** to go to the next step • On the Query Wizard's final step, click the **Save Query** button to save your changes and then click the **Finish** button to refresh the imported data
Automatically refreshing data each time a workbook is opened	EX 11.28	• Ensure that the active worksheet cell is one of the imported data values • Click **Data**, click **Import External Data**, click **Data Range Properties** • Click the **Refresh data on file open** check box to place a checkmark in it • Click **OK**
Manually joining two tables in a query	EX 11.31	• Drag and drop the primary key from one table to the corresponding foreign key in the second table
Adding a column to a query	EX 11.31	• Double-click a column name to add it to the lower half of the query window or • Drag and drop the column name to the lower half of the query window
Removing a column from a query	EX 11.32	• Move the mouse pointer over the column name in the lower panel of the query • When the pointer changes to a down arrow, click to select the column • Press the **Delete** key
Adding criteria to a query using Microsoft Query	EX 11.33	• Click **Criteria** on the Microsoft Query menu bar and then click **Add Criteria** • Fill in the list and text boxes in the Add Criteria dialog box • Click the **Add** button to add the criteria to the query • Continue adding additional criteria, if needed • Click the **Close** button when the criteria are complete
Summing a value column in a query	EX 11.34	• Click any result in the column you want to sum • Click the **Cycle Through Totals** button
Recording a macro instruction	EX 12.8	• Click **Tools**, point to **Macro**, click **Record New Macro** • Type a macro name in the Macro name text box • Type a description in the Description text box • Click **OK** • Execute the tasks you want to record • Click the **Stop Recording** button
Assigning a macro to a button	EX 12.10	• Click **View**, point to **Toolbars**, click **Forms** • Click the **Button** tool in the Forms toolbar • Click a worksheet cell to place a button on the worksheet • Select the macro to assign to the button from the Macro name list • Click **OK** • Drag the mouse across the button's caption and type a descriptive name • Click any cell to deselect the button
Making buttons visible on a printout	EX 12.12	• Right-click the button you want to display on a printout • Click **Format Control** on the shortcut menu • Click the **Properties** tab • Click the **Print object** check box, and click **OK**
Selecting a button control without activating it	EX 12.16	• Press and hold the **Ctrl** key • Click the button on the worksheet • Release the **Ctrl** key

Task	Page #	Preferred Method
Unhiding a workbook	EX 12.20	• Click **Window** on the menu bar • Click **Unhide** • Click a workbook in the Unhide workbook list and then click **OK**
Hiding a workbook	EX 12.20	• Make active any worksheet of the workbook you want to hide • Click **Window** on the menu bar • Click **Hide**
Setting the macro security level	EX 12.21	• Click **Tools**, click **Options**, and click the **Security** tab • Click the **Macro Security** button • Click the security level option button of your choice • Click **OK** to close the Security dialog box, and click **OK** to close the Options dialog box
Opening the Visual Basic Editor	EX 12.24	• Click **Tools**, point to **Macro**, and click **Visual Basic Editor** or • Press **Alt+F11** or • Click **Tools**, point to **Macro**, and click **Macros** • Select the name of the macro you want to edit • Click the **Edit** button
Deleting a macro	EX 12.28	• Click **Tools**, point to **Macro**, and click **Macros** • Click the name of the macro in the Macro name list that you want to delete • Click the **Delete** button • Click **Yes** to confirm the deletion
Printing VBA Code	EX 12.44	• Click **Alt+F11** to open the Visual Basic Editor • Double-click the module in the Project Explorer containing the VBA code you want to print • Click **File** on the menu bar • Click the **Code** check box in the *Print What* panel • Click the **Current Project** option button in the Range panel to select all of the code in a project, or click the **Current Module** option button in the Range panel to select only the current module • Click **OK**

EXCEL

glossary

Absolute cell reference: A cell reference in which a dollar sign ($) precedes both the column and row portions of the cell reference.

Activating (toolbar): Making a toolbar appear on the desktop.

Active cell: The cell in which you are currently working.

Active sheets: Sheets that are selected.

Add-in: A specialized feature of Excel that not everyone uses on a regular basis.

Aggregate: Calculations that cumulate information about groups of data.

Alignment: The position of the data relative to the sides of a cell.

Amortization: The process of distributing periodic payments over the life of a loan.

Amortization schedule: Lists the monthly payment, the amount of the payment applied toward reducing the principal (loan amount), and the amount of the payment that pays the interest due each month.

Answer report: The most popular Solver report, which lists the target cell, the changing cells with their original and final values, constraints, and data about the constraints.

Argument: A symbolic name for a value, expression, or cell reference that is passed to the function for its use in calculating an answer.

Argument list, function: The data that a function requires to compute an answer in which commas separate individual list entries.

Argument list: The collection of cells, cell ranges, and values listed in the comma-separated list between a function's parentheses.

Arguments: A list of zero or more items enclosed in parentheses and following the function name.

Arguments, function: They specify the value that the function uses to compute an answer, and comprise the argument list that can be values, cell references, expressions, a function, or an arbitrarily complex combination of the preceding that results in a value.

Array formula: Special formula in a data table that is part of an interrelated group of formulas.

Ascending order: Arranges text values alphabetically from A to Z, arranges numbers from smallest to largest, and arranges dates from earliest to most recent.

Assumption cells: Cells upon which other formulas depend and whose values can be changed to observe their effect on a worksheet's entries.

Attached text: Chart objects such as X-axis title, Y-axis, title and tick marks.

AutoComplete: Excel offers to fill in the remainder of the cell with information that matches your partial entry from another cell in the same column.

Axis: Line that contains a measurement by which you compare plotted values.

Binding: A resource constraint that is a limiting factor.

Bottom margin: The area at the bottom of the page between the bottom-most portion of the print area and the bottom edge of the page.

Branching: A programming structure that evaluates a condition and then takes one of two actions based on the outcome of condition evaluation.

Break-even: Profit is zero.

Categories: Organizes values in a data series.

Category names: Correspond to worksheet text you use to label data.

Cell: The Excel worksheet element located at the intersection of a row and a column and identified by a cell reference.

Cell border: A format that applies lines of various types to one or more edges of cells (left, right, top, bottom) of the selected cell(s).

Cell contents: The text, formulas, or numbers you type into a cell.

Cell range: One or more cells that form a rectangular group.

Cell reference: A cell's identification consisting of its column letter(s) followed by its row number.

Changing cells: The cells defined in a scenario that contain values you want Excel to change.

Chart area: The area in which all chart elements reside.

Chart sheet: Chart on a separate sheet.

Chart title: Labels the entire chart.

Charts: Sometimes called graphs, they are a graphical representation of data.

Client: The program that receives the information copied from another program.

Column break: A line that appears in a text import step to indicate the beginning of a field.

Comma-separated values: Values separated from one another by commas.

Comments: Worksheet cell notes that are particularly helpful to indicate special instructions about the contents or formatting of individual cells.

Compound document: A document containing linked and embedded data drawn from several sources.

Conditional test: An equation that compares two values, functions, formulas, labels, or logical values.

Consolidate: Summarizing data from multiple worksheets.

Consolidation worksheet: *See* Summary worksheet.

Constrained optimization: A technique whereby you specify a set of constraints and an outcome or result that you want minimized or maximized.

Constraint: A limitation on the values that a cell can have.

Container or container program: *See* Client.

Contribution margin (CM): The amount remaining from revenue after deducting all variable costs.

Cost-Volume-Profit (CVP) analysis: Examines the relationship between a product's expenses (cost), the number of units of the product produced (volume), revenue, and profit.

CSV: *See* Comma-separated values.

Custom sorting series: An ordered list you create to instruct Excel in what order to sort rows containing the list items.

Data fields (pivot table): Numeric data that appears in the pivot table's central position and is summarized.

Data form: A dialog box displaying one row of a list in text boxes in which you can add, locate, modify, or delete records.

Data label: The value or name assigned to an individual data point.

Data marker: A graphic representation of the value of a data point in a chart.

Data points: The values that comprise a data series.

Data series: The set of values that you want to chart.

Data table: Summarized key input and output cell values of multiple what-if analyses in a single, rectangular cell range.

Data type: The type of information that is stored in a variable.

Date constant: A date such as 12/12/2003.

Database: A collection of information organized so that a computer program can select requested information from it quickly.

Database driver: Special software that translates Excel information requests into database commands.

Database management system: A program that takes in user requests and combs through a database to deliver requested information, update information, or delete information.

Database table: A two-dimensional arrangement of rows and columns and holds data.

DBMS: *See* database management system.

Delimiter: A character or group of characters that separates two pieces of data.

Dependent workbook: A workbook containing a link to a supporting worksheet.

Descending order: Arranges text values alphabetically from Z to A, arranges numbers from largest to smallest, and arranges dates from most recent to earliest.

Disintermediation: Eliminating the often expensive intermediary in a transaction.

Dock (toolbar): Toolbar adheres to one of the four edges of the window.

Drilling down: Entering data in the same cell of several workbooks simultaneously.

Drop shadow: The shadow that is cast by an object.

Dynamic link: *See* Link.

Editing: Modifying the contents of a cell.

Embedded chart: Chart on a worksheet near the data you are charting.

Embedding: Placing a copy of an object from one program within another program's file.

Equation-solving: Goal-seeking or back-solving method such as the method used by the Goal Seek command.

Error value: A special Excel constant that indicates something is wrong with the formula or one of its components.

Event procedure: A procedure that executes whenever a particular event occurs.

Exact match criteria: Criteria in which a row's field exactly matches a particular filter value.

External reference: *See* Link.

Field: An individual unit of data, either fixed length or separated from others by a delimiter. Each column of a list of related information describing some characteristic of the object, person, or place.

Filter: Selection criteria applied to a merge operation to restrict the source data records chosen to those that satisfy the criteria.

Filtering: A list displaying only records that match particular criteria and hiding the rows that do not.

Fixed cost: A cost that remains constant no matter how many or how few goods or services you manufacture and sell.

Fixed pitch (font): Every character is the same width.

Fixed-width: Data arranged into specific locations or starting positions.

Floating (toolbar): Toolbar that can appear anywhere on the work surface.

Font: The combination of typeface and qualities including character size, character pitch, and spacing.

Footer: Text that appears automatically at the bottom of each printed page in the footer margin.

Foreign key: A table column that identifies records in a different table.

Form: A dialog box that appears in response to a user-defined command key click or other event.

Format: Cosmetic changes to a worksheet that make the text and numbers appear different.

Formatting: The process of altering the appearance of data in one or more worksheet cells.

Formula: An expression that begins with an equals sign and consists of cell references, arithmetic operators, values, and

Excel built-in functions (see Chapter 6) that result in calculated value.

Formula bar: Appears below the menu bar and displays the active cell's contents.

Function: A built-in or prerecorded formula that provides a shortcut for complex calculations.

General (format): Formatting that aligns numbers on the right side of a cell, aligns text on the left side, indicates negative numbers with a minus sign on the left side of a number, and displays as many digits in a number as a cell's width allows.

Goal Seek: A worksheet command that works backward to compute an unknown value that produces the final, optimized result you desire.

Goal Seek objective: The end result you want to achieve using Goal Seek techniques.

Gridlines: Extensions of tick marks that help identify the value of the data markers.

Grouping: Joining two objects into one object.

Header: Text that appears automatically at the top of each printed page in the header margin.

Headings row: The list row containing the column headings appearing at the top of the list.

Hide (data): Reduce a row's height or column's width to zero.

Input cell: The key input variable that you want Excel to change in a one- or two-variable data table analysis.

Input values: The set of possible input values substituted into the input cell.

Iteration: *See* Repetition.

Join: An operation that matches records in two tables based on a field that each one has in common, such as a customer number or an inventory number.

Label text: Chart text such as tick mark labels, category axis labels, and data series names.

Landscape: Print orientation in which the width is greater than the length.

Left margin: Defines the size of the white space between a page's left edge and the leftmost edge of the print area.

Legend: Indicates which data marker represents each series when you chart multiple series.

Limit report: A Solver report that displays the range of values that the changing cells can assume, based on the constraints you have defined.

Linear programming problem: Such problems involve one or more unknowns and an equal number of equations.

Link or linking: To paste a copy of an object into a document in such a way that it retains its connection with the original object. Updates to the original object appear automatically in the documents in which they are pasted.

Link: Formulas that reference cells in other worksheets.

List definition table: A table with column names and their definitions.

List: A collection of data arranged in columns and rows in which each column displays one particular type of data.

Lookup function: Uses a search value to search a table—a range of cells—for a match or close match and then return a value from the table as a result.

Lookup table: The table that a lookup function searches.

Lookup value: The value being used to search a lookup table.

Looping: *See* Repetition.

Macro: *See* Macro instruction.

Macro instruction: A group of VBA statements that collectively performs a particular task or returns a result.

Main document: The document containing merge fields from which merged documents are created.

Mathematical operator: A symbol that represents an arithmetic operation.

Menu bar: Contains Excel menus.

Merge field: A special tag placed in a document into which an actual field value from a source data file is substituted.

Method: An action that takes place on behalf of the object to which it is attached.

Mixed cell reference: A cell reference in which either the column or the row is never adjusted if the formula containing it is copied to another location.

Model row: Contains distinct formulas that you can copy to other rows and not have to modify any copied cell formulas afterward.

Module: An Excel object where macros are saved.

Mouse pointer: Indicates the current position of the mouse.

Name box: Appears on the left of the formula bar and displays either the active cell's address or its assigned name.

Not binding: Solver constraints whose final value are less than the constraint values.

Object function: The cell containing a function whose value you want to optimize and whose value is affected by a change in the decision variables.

Object linking and embedding: A technology developed by Microsoft that enables you to create objects with one application and then link or embed them in a second application.

Paste: Placing information into one document that is copied from another document.

Path: The disk drive and folders that lead to a referenced workbook.

Personal Macro Workbook: A workbook that Excel always loads, and subsequently hides, whenever you launch Excel.

Pitch: The number of characters per horizontal inch.

Pivot table: An interactive table enabling you to quickly group and summarize large amounts of data.

Plot area: Rectangular area bounded by the X-axis on the left and the Y-axis on the bottom.

Point: The height of characters in a typeface; equal to $1/72$ of an inch.

Pointing: Using the mouse to select a cell range while writing a formula.

Portrait: Print orientation in which the length is greater than the width.

Positional arguments: Arguments whose position in the argument list is important and inflexible.

Precedence order: Determines the order in which to calculate each part of the formula—which mathematical operators to evaluate first, which to evaluate second, and so on.

Precedent cell: A cell upon which a formula depends.

Precedent value: The value on which a formula, or result, is directly or indirectly based.

Primary key: A table column whose values are unique for each record in a table.

Primary sort field: The first sort field of multiple sort fields required to reorder a list.

Principal: Amount of money borrowed.

Product mix: The quantity of each product to sell in order to generate the greatest profit.

Project: Contains forms, modules, and the Excel workbook objects.

Properties dialog box: Contains several text boxes that you can fill in with helpful information including the fields Title, Subject, Author, Manager, Company, Category, Keywords, and Comments.

Proportional (font): Each character's pitch varies by character.

Protect (worksheet): Excel disallows modifications to cells or new values in cells.

Prototype statement: The first line of the function definition.

Prototype: A proposed worksheet model.

Query: Combines related information from one or more database tables, based on your search and sort criteria, and returns a table as a result.

Range errors: Values that are either too large or too small (negative or too close to zero, for example) that do not make sense in the context of the application.

Range Finder: A feature that color-codes an outline surrounding each cell referenced by a formula.

Range name: A name that you assign to a cell or cell range that can replace a cell address or cell range in expressions or functions.

Rate: Percentage interest rate.

Record: A collection of related information about one object stored in a database table.

Record: Each row of a list containing the fields that collectively describe a single object, person, or place.

Reference: A link to an object identifying the filename and its location.

Refresh (pivot table): Make Excel recalculate the values in the pivot table based on the data list's current values.

Relational operator: Compares two parts of a formula.

Relational operator: Compares two values and the result in either true or false.

Relative cell reference: Cell references in formulas that change when Excel copies them to another location.

Repetition: A programming structure that repeats a series of steps until a special condition is recognized to halt the repetition.

Resource allocation problem: An optimization problem in which productive resources (people, raw materials, time, and so on) can be used in a variety of places or in different products, and in which those resources must be distributed in the best way possible.

Result cell: Holds the result that is affected by a change in the input cell.

Result values: The computed answer for each input value in a one-variable data table.

Revenue: Money or items of value a company receives during a given period.

Rich Text Format: A standard for specifying formatting documents in which the document contains text and special commands holding formatting information.

Right margin: Defines the white space between the print area's rightmost position and the right edge of a printed page.

Scenario: The combination of values assigned to one or more variable cells in a what-if analysis.

Scenario report: A report available in the scenario manager that summarizes the scenarios you have created.

Scenario management: The process of examining individual variables or changing cells and assigning a range of values to them.

Scenario summary: Outlines each scenario by displaying changing cells and result cells in a separate worksheet.

Search criteria: Values that the data form should match in specified data form fields.

Secondary sort field: The field used to break ties on a group of matching primary sort field values.

Selection: *See* Branching.

Selection criteria: Specifying values to limit the records retrieved from a table.

Selection handles: Small, white squares that appear around an object that is selected.

Sensitivity report: A Solver report that shows how sensitive the current solution is to changes in the adjustable cells.

Series in: Option that establishes the way the data series is represented—either by rows or by columns.

Server: The program from which you copy information pasted into another program.

Sheet tab scroll buttons: The buttons you click to scroll through an Excel workbook's sheet tabs.

Sheet tab: Contains the sheet's name.

Sizing handles: *See* Selection handles.

Slack: The quantity of a resource that has not been used or allocated.

Sort field: The field or fields you use to sort a list.

Sort key: *See* Sort field.

Source cell(s): The copied cell(s).

Source program: *See* Server.

Spreadsheet: A popular program used to analyze numeric information and help make meaningful business decisions based on the analysis.

SQL: An abbreviation for structured query language, it is a standard language for requesting information from a database.

Stacked bar chart: A subtype of the bar chart, combines the data markers in a data series together to form one bar, placing each marker at the end of the preceding one in the same data series.

Standard toolbar: Contains buttons that execute popular menu bar commands such as Print, Cut, and Insert Table.

Status bar: Bar appearing at the bottom of the display that shows general information about the worksheet and selected keyboard keys.

Summary worksheet: Contains a digest or synopsis of the information contained in the individual worksheets.

Supporting workbook: A workbook containing a worksheet to which a link formula refers.

Supporting worksheets: Worksheets that are referenced by other worksheets.

Syntax: Rules governing the way you write Excel functions.

Target cell(s): The cell or cells to which the contents are copied.

Task Pane: A dialog window that provides a convenient way to use commands, gather information, and modify Excel documents.

Term: Time period over which you make periodic payments.

Text (entry): Any combination of characters that you can type on the keyboard including symbols.

Text box: A rectangular-shaped drawing object that contains text.

Text data: Data that consists only of characters (letters, digits, and special characters) that you can type on a keyboard—devoid of any special formatting.

Text Import Wizard: A three-step process to help convert text-format data into Excel format.

Three-dimensional formulas: Formulas that reference other worksheets in the current workbook.

Tick marks: are small lines, similar to marks on a ruler, which are uniformly spaced along each axis and identify the position of category names or values.

Tie (sort): Exists when one or more records have the same value for a field.

Time value of money: $100 today is more valuable than $100 is next year.

Top margin: The area between the top of page and topmost edge of the print area.

Two-dimensional formulas: Formulas that reference cells on a single worksheet.

Two-variable data table: Computes the effects of two variables on a single formula.

UDF: *See* User-defined function.

Unattached text: Chart objects such as comments or text boxes.

Uniform Resource Locator: The global address of a document or other resource on the Web.

Unlocked: An attribute of a cell that leaves it unprotected.

URL: *See* Uniform Resource Locator.

User-defined function: A function you create.

Value (entry): Numbers that represent a quantity, date, or time.

Variable cost: A cost that varies directly with the number of units of a product a company produces.

Variables: Cells in which Excel substitutes different values.

VBA function: A procedure that returns a result just as do Excel's built-in functions such as SUM and PMT.

VBA procedure: *See* Macro instruction.

VBA subroutine: A VBA procedure that performs a particular task.

What-if analysis: Making changes to spreadsheets and reviewing their effect on other values.

Wild card character: A special character that stands for zero or more characters.

Workbook objects: A workbook's worksheets and chart sheets.

Workbook window: The document window open in Excel.

Workbook: A collection of one or more individual worksheets.

Worksheet: They resemble pages in a spiral-bound workbook like the ones you purchase and use to take class notes.

Wrap text: Formatting that continues long text on multiple lines within a cell.

X-axis title: Which briefly describes the X-axis categories.

X-axis: Contains markers denoting category values.

Y-axis title: Identifies the values being plotted on the Y-axis.

Y-axis: Contains the value of data being plotted.

index

EOB 2.9